ALSO BY SAMUEL FULLER

Cérébro-Choc (Brainquake)

Pecos Bill et le Kid Cavale (Pecos Bill and the Soho Kid)

Quint's World

The Big Red One

Dead Pigeon on Beethoven Street

144 Piccadilly

Crown of India

The Dark Page

Make Up and Kiss

Test Tube Baby

Burn, Baby, Burn

A Third Face

A THIRD FACE

My Tale of Writing, Fighting, and Filmmaking

SAMUEL FULLER

WITH Christa Lang Fuller AND
Jerome Henry Rudes

APPLAUSE
THEATRE & CINEMA BOOKS

A Third Face
My Tale of Writing, Fighting, and Filmmaking
by Samuel Fuller
with Christa Lang Fuller and Jerome Henry Rudes

Library of Congress Cataloging-in-Publication Data

Fuller, Samuel, 1912–1997
A third face : my tale of writing, fighting,
and filmmaking / Samuel Fuller with
Christa Lang Fuller and Jerome Henry Rudes.
p. cm.
Originally published:
New York : A.A. Knopf, 2002.
Includes bibliographical references and index.
ISBN 1-55783-627-2
1. Motion picture producers and directors—United
States—Biography. 2. Motion picture actors
and actresses—United States—Biography. 3.
Screenwriters—United States—Biography.
I. Fuller, Christa. II. Rudes, Jerome. III. Title.

PN1998.3.F85A3 2004
791.4302'33'092—dc22
2004001449

Front cover photograph by Phil Bath
Front cover design by Carol Devine Carson

Applause Theatre & Cinema Books
151 West 46th Street, 8th Floor
New York, NY 10036
Phone: (212) 575-9265
Fax: (646) 562-5852
Email: info@applausepub.com
Internet: www.applausepub.com

Sales & Distribution

NORTH AMERICA:
Hal Leonard Corp.
7777 West Bluemound Road
P. O. Box 13819
Milwaukee, WI 53213
Phone: (414) 774-3630
Fax: (414) 774-3259
Email: halinfo@halleonard.com
Internet: www.halleonard.com

OPEN MARKET:
Roundhouse Publishing Ltd.
Millstone, Limers Lane
Northam, North Devon
EX 39 2RG
Phone: 01237-474474
Fax: 01237-474774
Email: roundhouse.group@ukgateway.net

Contents

PART VI

Foreword

It's been said that if you don't like the Rolling Stones, then you just don't like rock and roll. By the same token, I think that if you don't like the films of Sam Fuller, then you just don't like cinema. Or at least you don't understand it. Sure, Sam's movies are blunt, pulpy, occasionally crude. But those aren't shortcomings. They're simply reflections of his temperament, his journalistic training, and his sense of urgency. His pictures are a perfect reflection of the man who made them. Every point is underlined, italicized, and boldfaced, not out of crudity but out of passion. And outrage—Fuller found a lot to be outraged about in this world. For the man who made *Forty Guns* or *Underworld U.S.A.* or *Pickup on South Street* or *Park Row*, there was no time for mincing words. There's a great deal of sophistication and subtlety in those movies, and it's all at the service of rendering emotion on-screen. When you respond to a Fuller film, what you're responding to is cinema at its essence. Motion as emotion. Fuller's pictures move convulsively, violently. Just like life when it's being lived with genuine passion.

I'll never forget the first time I met Sam. It was in LA in the early '70s, right after a screening of *Forty Guns* that I'd organized. When the picture was over, we started talking, and we couldn't stop. We talked for hours, but it seemed like a matter of minutes. When it was time to leave, we kept talking as we walked to our cars. When we got there, we were still talking. He would start telling a story, which would lead to another story, which would then lead to a whole other story—a quality that's reflected beautifully in this book by the way. We could have talked all night.

Fuller was one of the rare people who could both "talk" a great movie and make one, too. Many people can do either one or the other, but Sam could do both. I remember once when he and Christa came over to my house for dinner. Sam started talking about an idea that he'd had for a movie about nothing but objects, and drawing the emotion out of the objects. It was absolutely mesmerizing. If anyone could have made such a movie, it was Sam.

The first Sam Fuller movie I ever saw was his first, too. I was six years old, and I'd seen a preview for *I Shot Jesse James.* I wanted to see it just because of the title. When the day finally came, I remember sitting on the bus with my father on our way to the theater. I was so excited that I couldn't understand how everyone else around us could just go about their business—didn't they realize that *I Shot Jesse James* was playing? It's a feeling many of us have as children, and we're usually a little let down—the things you look forward to and fantasize about as a kid rarely equal the image you've built up in your head. But this was one time that the movie more than lived up to the image. *I Shot Jesse James* is a film about betrayal, and it goes right to the heart of it—the way it feels to betray and to be betrayed. I was really struck by the moment when Jesse is taking a bath and Ford aims a gun at his back: Will he shoot, or won't he? I've never forgotten this image, or many others from the movie. I've had them in my head since I was six years old. To this day, the film never fails to move me.

Sam's films had a force that blew all the clichés away from whatever issue they were dealing with. There are no cheap thrills in his work. He was always trying to fathom the unfathomable, whether it was a subject as broad as the inhumanity of war or the injustice of racism, or, on a more intimate level, the thirst for power or the infectiousness of paranoia. In Sam's movies, there's no difference between the personal and the political—both are part of the continuum of human experience. I think he was one of the bravest and most profoundly moral artists the movies have ever had. That's why his war films—*The Steel Helmet, Fixed Bayonets, China Gate, Merrill's Marauders,* and *The Big Red One*—are the truest, the least sentimental, and the toughest I've ever seen. I only hope that someday, *The Big Red One* is restored to its original form.

The kid finding his father's body in the alley and vowing vengeance as he makes a fist in *Underworld U.S.A.* The unbroken tracking shot that follows Gene Evans out into the street as he beats up his opponent in *Park Row.* The sad, lonely death of Thelma Ritter's stoolie in *Pickup on South Street.* These are moments of pure, raw emotion, unlike anything else in movies, created by a unique artist. I loved Sam Fuller as a filmmaker, and it's impossible for me to imagine my own work without his influence and example. I came to love him equally as a friend. This wonderful book, filled to the brim with his passion for life and for cinema, goes a long way toward keeping the memory of this precious man alive and well.

                                                    Martin Scorsese

Introduction

Sam and I started talking about doing his memoirs together several years before we actually went to work on them. He was reluctant because he felt he still had lots of good yarns in him about other characters. I convinced him that his greatest yarn might be his own life. He didn't like writing a tale with "I" as the central character. But forever young at heart and ready for any new challenge, he quickly adapted to this unique writing mode and relished the job.

Then in 1994, Sam got sick in Paris. We thought we might lose him, but he fought back. The following year, he was well enough to return to our home in Los Angeles. We were already at work on his life story, I typing and he guiding me as best he could. Many of the episodes in Sam's life I had heard recounted over our thirty-three years of living together.

My objective in taking on this challenge was to allow my husband the chance to tell his own version of a long, colorful, and complex life. So much has been written and said about Sam Fuller—the man and the artist—that was biased, exaggerated, simplistic, or just plain untrue. My husband fed the rumor mill, unwittingly or not, with his sometimes incendiary remarks. He was good at being controversial. He loved nothing better than provoking a good debate. "Culture, smulture!" he liked to say, playing down his own profound attachment to scholarship and enlightenment. Proud yet humble, complicated yet primitive, combatant yet peace-loving, Sam was full of contradictions. I am proud to have been the instrument for his own tale, a fascinating story about an admirable, ethical human being.

Our good friend Jerry Rudes has been an invaluable partner in this enterprise, organizing, checking, and editing the manuscript meticulously. Founder of the Avignon Film Festival in France and the Avignon/New York Film Festival in the States, Jerry was very close to Sam. They loved each other like father and son.

This entire project was one of love: Sam's love for the truth, for his country, for his family, for his colleagues, for the art of storytelling and moviemaking; and my love for this extraordinary man, whom I met in 1965 and didn't separate from until October 30, 1997, when he died in my arms.

For me, Sam is still very much alive. His spirit surrounds me. I feel his presence every day, smoking a good hand-wrapped cigar, laughing his inimical laugh, dreaming up stories, characters, and unusual camera angles, yet finally at peace after fighting so long and so hard for what he believed in.

I know Sam would approve of my dedicating this book to our new granddaughter, Samira. He didn't meet her on Earth, but he'll be following her proudly from his vantage point high up on the mountaintop where men who forged the twentieth century out of guts, hard work, and integrity now reside.

Here's a great man's great yarn, a love song to democracy, a hymn to independence, originality, and endurance.

Christa Lang Fuller
Los Angeles, 2002

*I was about seven years old when I donned
a navy uniform the first and last time.*

A Stroke of Good Fortune

Hammer!"

Hell if I know why that was the first goddamned word that came out of my mouth. Even more of a mystery is why I hadn't said anything until I was almost five years old. My brothers and sisters and, above all, my mother, Rebecca, were very worried about my abnormal silence. They suspected I was mentally retarded, or, worse, just plain stupid. It was a joyous occasion for my entire family when I finally uttered those first two pugnacious syllables.

In the eighty years since that summer of 1917, I've more than made up for my belated introduction to talking. I'm a storyteller. My tales were usually drawn from my own experiences. Other yarns were adapted from newspaper articles printed under big, bold headlines. Many stories I concocted from imaginary situations dreamed up over the cranky keyboard of an old typewriter as I smoked a good cigar. Even when I made up my characters, they were emotionally honest. Whether my yarn involved a whore, a general, an informer, or a cop, I tried to write them real, not heroic, nor patriotic, nor lovable, but real, meaning true to their background and longings.

To iron out the wrinkles, I used to tell my stories to just about anyone who'd listen, sometimes gabbing nonstop for hours. Storytelling made me forget about eating, pissing, sleeping—all body functions except smoking cigars. All that talk over the years must have raised my blood pressure and could be partially to blame for the stroke I suffered in 1994. We were still living in Paris then, having moved to a modest walk-up apartment in the Twelfth Arrondissement, a working-class quarter not far from Place de la Bastille. It was a beautiful autumn Sunday morning. Christa and I took a walk down rue de Reuilly to our favorite *boulangerie* to get a couple of those delicious croissants with almonds I loved. Then we strolled back arm in arm to our place at Number 61, past all the markets, bistros, and cafés.

We decided to have our breakfast at a little picnic table in the enclosed courtyard downstairs from our apartment, a picturesque place with cats lolling about, wet laundry fluttering in the wind, and friendly neighbors coming home with baskets of groceries. Christa made the café au lait and served it. Suddenly, I fainted dead away. The great French firemen, *les pompiers,* answered Christa's emergency call and rushed me to nearby St. Antoine Hospital.

I still can't remember very much about the next couple of months. Bless the French doctors and nurses who cared for me. They are wonderful men and women. We'd been paying social security taxes in France for over a decade, so my stays at St. Antoine and then at a rehabilitation center outside Paris were fully covered by the admirable French health care system.

How I survived the stroke I don't know. It just wasn't time to die yet. I'd had other close calls, like the wound in my chest from a stray bullet fired by a Nazi Luger during World War II. Five years before the stroke, I'd suffered an aneurysm in my main artery. Only a few months earlier, a doctor had discovered an abscess on one of my lungs and treated it. There I was in a Paris hospital, somehow still alive, but due to the stroke's brain jumbling, my tongue wouldn't form a single intelligible word. I was unable to speak, just like when I was a little boy back in Worcester, Massachusetts. I love the wonderful little ironies of life! As the French say, *plus ça change, plus c'est la même chose.* The more things change, the more they are the same.

I shared my hospital room with a very kind black man—he was from Senegal, I believe—who liked reading the Bible aloud. This man helped me with my food at mealtimes. He held my arm so I could walk to the bathroom. He passed me soap and warm water to wash myself. He was wonderful to me, and, holy cow, I don't even know his name! At the time, I couldn't even remember my own. But I will never forget him nor the compassion he showed his fellow patient. He began every sentence with *"mon ami"* in a deep rich voice. I've had many good friends in my long life. My nameless Senegalese roommate was one of the best.

Christa and my daughter, Samantha, were so distressed. They came to visit me every day at the hospital, shocked as much by my speechlessness as by my flaccid legs, now thin as matchsticks. They feared I wasn't going to make it. Even though I was quite a mess, I don't remember once thinking I was going to die. Nor did I ever tremble at the thought of what would happen to me if my time on Earth was actually up. Death is just the next part of our adventure. Subtly or overtly, our culture tries to manipulate us with anxiety about our own mortality. Death comes when it comes. Meanwhile, I'm eighty-five years old, feeling no qualms at all, just gratitude— thankful for having survived so many years already, thankful for having a loving wife and daughter, thankful for such a rewarding, creative life. Rather than making me fear death, my illness offered me a fresh vision of my good fortune.

After the stroke, my first thoughts were of my beloved mother, Rebecca, my brothers, Ray, Tom, and Ving, and my sisters, Evelyn, Tina, and Rose, all gone now. The rest of my life slowly began to reappear like images on photographic paper in a bath of development chemicals. My mental faculties came back, but my speech has remained impaired and the taut muscles that used to power my legs have become as fickle as a flophouse floozy. Nevertheless, I'm delighted to be alive. Having danced remarkably close to death's dark threshold, what a pleasure to smell the roses once more! Every day is like a gift from Heaven. That's what twenty-four hours really is, though we may not always realize it. There's nothing like a close brush with death to show you the truth about life.

To aid my recovery, we decided to move back to California after our self-imposed exile in France. In my mind, I'd never really gone away from America. No matter where I resided, my soul remained steadfastly American. We'd hung on to our little house up in the Hollywood Hills, hoping every year to come back. But film and writing projects kept happening in France and other parts of the world. More importantly, our daughter was being treated for Hodgkin's disease in Paris, so we needed to stay close to the Marie Curie Hospital and its competent doctors.

Affectionately, I referred to our home up in Laurel Canyon as "the Shack." I'd transformed its garage into a peaceful getaway lined with book-shelves, chock-full of books, press clippings, photographs, files, scripts, war mementos, and humidors. Other than some mouse-eaten scripts and a shattered globe broken by books toppled in the '94 earthquake, my office looked about the same as when I'd left it. It seemed I'd just gotten up from the cluttered rolltop desk and gone off for a coffee break that happened to last for thirteen years. Holy mackerel, it was so damn good to be back home! Our cherished dining-room table, which had once belonged to Samuel Langhorne Clemens, was steady as a rock, ready for long meals with family and friends. The spirit of Mark Twain was never far away.

Not only did the stroke make me realize the preciousness of every hour of every day, it also made me see that I've got one more great yarn to tell: my own. Hell if I'm going to sit around here with a goddamned somber face, grinning cynically, fretting about my demise. For Chrissakes, I feel like Irving Berlin, ready to sing until I'm a hundred and one! My life is a helluva tale. I've been too busy living it until now.

I'm going to tell it to you, dear reader, as if we were sitting around the Mark Twain table in our dining room, where so many stories and laughs have been shared. My wonderful Christa is helping me delve into these marvelous memories. We aren't overlooking demons that need to be exorcised or sugarcoating setbacks and frustrations. Our aim is to shape my eight and a half decades of experiences into a brisk and emphatically positive narrative.

All human beings are in the same mortal boat, each of us with our own baggage of defeats and victories. Why not carry our load with a smile, stubbornly optimistic, getting the most out of what remains of our lives? Why allow defeats to defeat us more than once?

The story of my life resembles that of Candide's, wandering around this Earth searching for truth, still laughing after so much adversity. Then again, maybe Don Quijote de la Mancha was my real role model. I've been inventing utopias and fighting for what I think is right for as long as I can remember. In the spirit of the great Miguel de Cervantes, I offer the following tale to you, whoever the hell you are and wherever on this great planet you live.

"If a man could mount to heaven and survey the mighty universe," wrote Cervantes, "his admiration of its beauties would be much diminished unless he had someone to share in his pleasure."

You, dear reader, are my someone.

Plunging in
Head First

I was born Samuel Michael Fuller on August 12, 1912, in Worcester, Massachusetts, the son of Rebecca Baum from Poland and Benjamin Rabinovitch from Russia. My parents had already changed their surname from Rabinovitch to the more American-sounding Fuller, probably inspired by a Doctor Benjamin Fuller who came over on the *Mayflower* in 1620, when doctors still thought bleeding their patients would cure them of their ills. There were plenty of other accomplished, more contemporary Fullers who could have motivated my parents.[1] But my mother had tremendous admiration for the courage of those 101 Pilgrims—the first Europeans to settle in America—who endured the hardships of bitter New England winters to found the Plymouth colony. Rebecca probably saw herself as a modern-day Pilgrim. She wanted her children to have a family name firmly embedded in the American dream. It was my mother who awakened in me a love for history.

The year I was born, lots of blood was being spilled in my father's old country under the oppressive rule of Czar Nicholas II. His son and heir to the Russian throne, Alexis, had been diagnosed as a hemophiliac. In their vain attempts to find a cure for the boy, Nicholas and his wife, Empress Alexandra, became prey to quacks and religious fanatics, notably the Siberian monk Grigory Yefimovich Rasputin. In 1912, China became a republic, the United States admitted New Mexico and Arizona to the Union, the *Titanic* sank, Robert Falcon Scott reached the South Pole, Ludwig Borchardt discovered Queen Nefertiti's painted limestone head, eternally gorgeous, in an Egyptian crypt, and Dr. Isaac K. Funk and Dr. Adam W. Wagnalls published the first *Funk & Wagnalls Standard Encyclopedia.*

I grew up believing that people make things move, like the word "movie." The world, like a moving picture, was moving forward. I wanted to advance too, as rapidly as my quick mind and fast legs would carry me.

I also grew up believing in truth—not just the word itself, but the deeper conviction that getting to the truth was a noble cause. My nature has always been to tell people the truth, even if they feel insulted. I care too much about people to bullshit them. If they're offended by the truth, why waste my time on them? When a young director comes to me for advice on a script, I don't pull any punches, especially if the thing's overwritten.

"Your script's got too much gibble-gabble," I say. "Show the action, for Chrissakes, don't describe it! It's a *motion* picture you're making, not a god-damned radio show. A *motion* picture with *emotion,* so let your characters speak from their hearts."

"But Sam, I'm worried about the budget," says the greenhorn.

"Don't ever worry about the goddamned money when you're writing a script. You can worry about the money later."

I come from a generation for whom telling the truth meant everything. I suppose I'm still pretty naïve about people being truthful. See, I still believe what James Cagney said in one of his movies: "You shake a man's hand and look him straight in the eyes and everything will be all right."

Recounting the story of one's own life means facing up to the truth. Why the hell even attempt it in the twilight of my years? See, I'd like to inspire others to be hopeful and daring, to follow their dreams, no matter the odds. Life is risky. It's like the film business, with its nectar and poison, its guile and greed, its commingling of idealism, betrayals, friendships, and hard work. Sometimes you have a smash hit; other times, a flop. There's no guarantee how you'll make out, yet in life and movies, pluck, perseverance, and a sense of humor will keep your head above water.

I trust my life story will be especially encouraging to young filmmakers trying to survive in the shark-infested waters of the movie business. Even sharks are more respectable than some of the hypocrites and parasites circling around moviemakers. It's an industry full of those who profess lofty ideals and artistic sensibilities even as they exploit and double-cross the real creators. Big budgets have fouled up this business. In America, the word "artist" is never attributed to a filmmaker unless his or her last picture sold a helluva lot of tickets at the box office. Then you become an "A" director, but the initial has nothing to do with "Art," only dollars.

It wasn't always this way. When I made *I Shot Jesse James* in 1949 for producer Robert Lippert, we closed the deal on a handshake because he liked my yarn. It was a business, damn straight, though big profits weren't the only motivation. My contract didn't even show up until six months later. When the movie unexpectedly made some dough for Lippert, I was happy for the guy. He shared the profits with me exactly as we'd agreed. His financial success made it possible to go on producing more movies with me and other directors.

With Alexandre Rockwell in Paris, 1991. I've always tried to befriend young directors, giving them encouragement in a damn tough business.

Joking around with Tim Robbins during the filming of The Typewriter, the Rifle & the Movie Camera, *Paris, 1994.*

Regardless of the obstacles, passionate, honorable artists will always be making good stories into good movies. Some of the younger ones, members of a new generation of writer-directors, have gotten close with me: Martin Scorsese, Jonathan Demme, Peter Bogdanovich, Curtis Hanson, Wim Wenders, Mika Kaurismäki, Alexandre Rockwell, Tim Robbins, Quentin Tarantino, Jim Jarmusch, and many more. Once, Jarmusch got a big laugh out of my advice to him about writing scripts, except I was dead serious: "If a story doesn't give you a hard-on in the first couple of scenes, throw it in the goddamned garbage." As corny as it sounds, I love all those young filmmakers like a benevolent papa and wish them continued success.

Even during the lean years, I've never stopped writing my own yarns. Working on all those stories got me excited viscerally, preventing me from ever becoming bitter or melancholic. Hell, I could live another hundred years and come up with plenty of original tales that, when turned into movies, would still grab audiences by the balls!

People are either amused or confused by the way I talk. Coming from Worcester gave me a nasal voice and a New England accent. My formative New York years changed everything. As a teenager, I started smoking cigars and had to learn to articulate words around the ever-present stogie in my mouth. In those days I puffed on "twofers," so called because you got two for a nickel. Veteran journalists like Gene Fowler, Damon Runyon, and Ring Lardner took a liking to me and slipped me a Havana from time to time. Without even knowing it, I also acquired their big-city, straight-shooting streetspeak. Naturally impatient, I found this quick-tongued vernacular a timesaver. Besides, it was the only way to make myself understood with the cops, firemen, pimps, whores, bartenders, bookies, and subway nickel changers I frequented on the tough streets of New York. Believe me, we weren't discussing Balzac.

Writing has always been my first calling. Since childhood, the power of the printed word has fascinated me. I am a great admirer of the foundations of our nation—the Declaration of Independence and the Constitution—because first and foremost, they're damn good writing. My ability to write punchy prose and my nose for news got me a job as a teenage newspaperman in the bustling, effervescent Manhattan of the twenties. After a stint as a freelance reporter, I went out to California to take a crack at writing yarns for the movies in the thirties. Inspired by the masters— Twain, Dostoyevsky, Dickens, Zola—I also tried my hand at fiction, knocking out about a dozen books over the years.

I got into journalism at a time when Americans learned about their country through newspapers, magazines, and books. The advent of television, with its immediacy and candor, has had an enormous influence on every facet of our society, an influence that I'm afraid hasn't been quite the boon to democracy that was predicted. Former Israeli prime minister Shimon Peres said that the good side of television is that it makes dictatorship impossible and the bad side is that it makes democracy unbearable. The real worth of all our newfangled, high-speed communication made possible by computers will be judged by one thing and one thing only: their contributions to democracy.

Before anything else, I am a democrat, firmly believing that democracy is the best system on this Earth for people to live under. I've fought for democracy and made movies exposing antidemocrats, whether they be false patriots, racists, mobsters, or fascists. One of my pictures, *Park Row,* is about the birth of modern American journalism at the end of the nineteenth century. A free press is an essential component of any democracy. It's protected by the First Amendment, but it lives and breathes because of hardworking reporters and editors at newspapers across this nation.

My long life has run parallel with most of the twentieth century, intersecting with some of its memorable characters and momentous upheavals. I've seen my fellow Americans at their best and at their worst. Their enthusiasm, gutsiness, ingeniousness, and sheer industry are truly remarkable. Yet into the fabric of my times have been woven devastating world wars, poverty and ignorance, social rifts based on race and wealth, psychopathic hate groups like the Ku Klux Klan, political witchhunters and religious fanatics. For me, the hatemongers and reactionaries are the most loathsome, thorns in the eye of a great democracy. Every generation will have their own. They must be fought and defeated.

I've never lost my ardor for history and its illuminations. Nor have I ever mislaid my optimism. Living on the edge of Hollywood for many years, physically and spiritually, I remain to this day an outsider. As for life, I've always plunged in head first without worrying about failure.

If there's one reason to recount my personal history, something inspirational that I'd like my life experiences to offer you, the reader, be you young or young at heart, then it would be to encourage you to persist with all your heart and energy in what you want to achieve—no matter how crazy your dreams seem to others. Believe me, you will prevail over all the naysayers and bastards who are telling you it just can't be done!

3

Mama's Boy

In Worcester, we lived in a small house on Mott Street, near Holy Cross Church. One of my earliest memories was of those church bells on Holy Cross. I was laid up in bed with a bad cold and a high fever. The bells started ringing like crazy. I heard loud voices in the street. Through my bedroom window, I could see it was snowing outside. I got up and opened the window to listen to the exuberant tolling. It was November 11. People down in the street were shouting that the "Great War" was over. I remember staring out at the snow, listening to the bells, watching the excited people scurrying by, wondering what was so great about a war anyway. My mother burst into the room, gave me a helluva spanking, and sent me straight back to bed.

Rebecca Fuller was a spitfire of a woman, afraid of nothing and no one, a remarkable human being. She loved to tell stories, listen to jokes, meet new people, and drink Irish whiskey. Coquettish up to the end of her days, she always wore a strand of pearls around her neck. She was my first and greatest booster. When I was about seven, she took me on an excursion to Plymouth. There was a sign at Plymouth Rock that explained that this was the "legendary" spot where the Pilgrims had landed, on November 21, 1620, from England. My mother pointed up the coast some distance from the sign to the north end of Cape Cod near Provincetown, where the Pilgrims had actually touched shore. I was appalled. Why did they have to lie? Why couldn't they have put the sign where the event really took place?

My mother explained that, as long as the date was commemorated, no one cared about the exact spot where the Pilgrims landed. But *I* cared, goddamnit. Our discussion that day at Plymouth Rock is vividly burned into my memory. Ever since I was a little boy, I've had a penchant for veracity, always looking for the real thing. This nose for facts remained with me all my life and served me well.

Hell, it still bothers me when they inaccurately label landmarks, arrang-

Polish by birth, Rebecca Fuller was determined to give her family a chance to share in all that America could offer.

ing historical markers for the convenience of tourists. When I visited Waterloo in Belgium, I realized that the fighting hadn't taken place anywhere near the official signposts, but in ditches out in the surrounding fields. Without those ditches to defend the massed armies of Great Britain, Prussia, Russia, and Austria, Napoleon would have probably won that battle on June 18, 1815. As it turned out, he was defeated and shipped off to exile on the island of Saint Helena. Those goddamned ditches were important to the course of European history. Why not show people where the battle really took place? Likewise, Cecil B. DeMille didn't direct his 1914 film *The Squaw Man,* starring Dustin Farnum, at the corner of Hollywood and Vine where there used to be a false plaque. DeMille made the picture in a nearby alley.

That day at Plymouth Rock was important because it showed my mother that I could think for myself, to the point of even disagreeing with her. She wisely encouraged me to articulate my own opinions. Ours wasn't a major argument, but it made for more interesting dialogue. Ever since, I've always liked to contradict others for the sake of thought-provoking conversation. Putting the shoe on the other foot, nothing is more boring than a person who agrees with everything I say. For Chrissakes, voice your own ideas instead of rubber-stamping mine!

I recall my father as a tall, handsome, taciturn man with black hair and blue eyes. Benjamin Fuller worked long hours in a factory that imported lumber from Canada, manufacturing all sorts of paper products, wallpaper, toilet paper, wrapping paper, newsprint. He only came home to eat and sleep. I always felt cheated that my father didn't have time for the stuff that fathers and sons do together. We never went fishing.

My father yearned to follow the dictates of strict Judaism, but my mother wouldn't have her children raised that way. She was vehemently opposed to the excesses of orthodoxy, no matter the religion. She thought it would be a disadvantage to us in America, where we were supposed to fit in, not stand out. Papa gave in and rarely took us to the local synagogue. None of the Fuller kids had any real religious training to speak of.

Benjamin died at fifty-one years of age, when I was eleven. I don't remember being devastated by his death. Nevertheless, his absence must have created an enormous vacuum of paternal support. Throughout my life, I'd search for father figures and, fortunately, find them, instinctively attracted to their experience, thriving on their wisdom.

From the time I was a little boy, I loved going to the Poli Theater in Worcester, the biggest movie house in town. I couldn't wait for Saturday morning to come around so I could stand in line outside the Poli with all the other kids, holding my nickel for a matinee ticket, rushing inside to get a seat to see those thrilling silent Westerns starring William S. Hart, Ken Maynard, Jack Hoxey, Buck Jones, and the great Tom Mix. They always threw in a serial with Pearl White, Eddie Polo, or Dick Talmadge, too. Each episode closed with the heroine in an agonizing situation—say, lying on the floor of a jungle, hands tied behind her back. A gigantic cobra would be slithering toward the terrified girl. The screen went black with the snake closing in on her. Those were the beginnings of pure Hollywood entertainment, a kind of fairy-tale approach to storytelling that gripped us in the same way that previous generations had been moved by the fables of Aesop, the Brothers Grimm, and Hans Christian Andersen. All I knew at the time was that, come hell or high water, I'd be back at the Poli for the following Saturday matinee.

I also remember seeing silent films from Germany and France at the Poli, my first contact with the two countries that would have such an enormous impact on my life. There was *The Man Who Laughs,* directed by Paul Leni, adapted from Victor Hugo's classic, starring the great Conrad Veidt. I can vaguely recall having watched silent French versions of *Falstaff,* adapted from Shakespeare's *Henry IV,* and *Volpone,* adapted from Ben Jonson's seventeenth-century play. I remember that the high drama mesmerized me.

The first book I remember reading was a pulp novel for kids that my mother gave me, entitled *John Halifax, Gentleman,* by Dinah Maria Mulock Craik (1826–87)—or "Miss Mulock," as she signed her book. Almost eighty years later, I still smile when I recall the first sentence of *John Halifax, Gentleman,* spoken by a man in a wheelchair as he runs into a bum and threatens the poor man with his cane, shouting, "Get out of my way, vagabond, out of the way of Phineas Fletcher!"[1]

What an opening line! Beginnings are always so important. So many works of fiction start off with boring, intellectual introductions or unneeded explanations. From early on, I loved action-packed openings. I still do, as long as the action tells us something essential about the characters' emotions.

Like my brother Ving, I had a knack for drawing when I was a kid. Ving was always more skilled but I loved creating my own silly cartoons. That's how I fell in love with newspapers. The local *Worcester Telegram* and the *Worcester Post* printed cartoons in every edition. The *Boston American* ran them in color in Sunday editions. I earned some extra pennies for my family by standing on a street corner in Worcester on Sunday mornings hawking those papers to passersby. Very often people would grab a paper and throw a quarter at me, telling me to keep the change. How I looked forward to those Sunday mornings on the street corner in Worcester! I'd take all the money home and give it to my mother. She was so proud of me.

Rebecca's unswerving love gave me great self-confidence as a little boy. She was my fervent supporter, even when my ambitions surpassed my abilities. Take baseball, for example. I yearned to get involved, but I was too small to play with the older boys in the big empty lot across the street from our house. So Mother would wait until the end of a baseball game and invite the players over to taste her blueberry pies. The pies had been tickling their noses all afternoon, baked with blueberries my brothers and I collected in pewter buckets in the woods around our Worcester. When the blueberry pies came out of the oven, the most delicious aroma would come wafting from our house. I can still smell those blueberry pies cooling off on our windowsill.

Thanks to Mother's pies, I became very popular with those baseball players. They promoted me from bystander to waterboy.

"Sammy! Water!" some guy would yell. I carried the brimming bucket over to the bench and the player drank gulps with a big wooden spoon. After the games, some of the guys walked me across the street, not to get me home safely, but for another slice of blueberry pie that my mother would happily serve them from her kitchen window.

That was how I got the chance to learn to play. I became pretty good in the infield and the outfield. I'm a southpaw, so they called me "Lefty." My hero was Carl Mays, whom I considered a greater player than Babe Ruth. I'd follow all the games in the local papers. At night, my dreams were filled with baseball, too. I'd hit the ball so hard that it blasted into the heavens and circled round the moon. I ran hard and tried to catch it but my little legs could never run fast enough in that ballpark in the sky.

Decades later, I needed a copy of my birth certificate, so I wrote to the authorities in Worcester. I guess they considered me somebody special because an article about me ran on the front page of the *Worcester Telegram,* the paper I sold on the street when I was a little boy. I was happy it was still being published. Along with a clipping of the article, the editor of the *Telegram* wrote me a note explaining that everything in town had changed.

In 1963 I went to Boston for the opening of *Shock Corridor.* It would have been easy to revisit my hometown in central Massachusetts. I was really tempted. But the little boy I'd been in Worcester had grown up fast. By then I was a hard-boiled middle-aged man who couldn't stand getting mired down in nostalgia. Burdened with memories of the intervening years, I never made that detour to Worcester. The kid in us embeds images from childhood in our mind's eye, beyond change. I wanted to remember the town as it was when our family moved away in 1923, never to return.

My father's death that year changed everything, including my destiny. With her seven now fatherless children, Rebecca decided to move us to New York City, where there were more opportunities to better ourselves. We boarded a train that momentous day with our bundles, suitcases, and trunks for the trip down to Manhattan. I waved good-bye to a couple of my baseball buddies as the train pulled out, bidding farewell to Worcester and my childhood.

4

Manhattan
Explorer

New York City in the early twenties seemed like a human beehive to my eleven-year-old eyes, with hustling, bustling people everywhere urging you forward, dozens of different languages spoken on crowded sidewalks packed with fruit and vegetable stands, vendors shouting, taxis, double-decker buses, trucks and horse-drawn carts jockeying for position on cobblestone streets, subways roaring underground, elevated trains overhead. My first explorations were exciting and anxiety-ridden, wandering around the different parts of the city as if I were Vasco da Gama discovering exotic lands. I got lost plenty until a cop explained to me that you couldn't ever get lost because the streets had numbers and the avenues ran north and south. New York made me dizzy with expectation.

We settled into an apartment my mother found for us in a modest neighborhood on the Upper West Side—172nd Street—not far from the Hudson. We all found jobs to pull our weight and support the family. Ving worked as an assistant designer for a newspaper. The girls cleaned houses and looked after children. Tom cashiered in a dry-goods store. My first job was as a bellboy in a modest hotel on weekends. The establishment wasn't very reputable, its clients traveling salesmen, sailors on leave, gamblers in town for some action, and ladies who rented rooms for a couple of hours with a gentleman friend. I spared my mother details about the goings-on at the hotel and its colorful clientele. The job was an eye-opener.

Before then, I'd never been aware of social classes. Suddenly they hit me smack in the face. We lived only a few blocks away from some elegant apartment buildings on the Hudson where doormen stood day and night in front of covered entrances helping well-dressed people glide in and out of their big cars. It struck me for the first time that theirs was a different universe from that of the people who rented cheap hotel rooms or that of my brothers and sisters scurrying to our jobs along with other working-class people.

*By age twelve, I was a newsboy
hawking papers on every
corner in Manhattan.*

If it rained on my way home from school, I tried to make some extra money by waiting outside the subway station near our apartment with a big umbrella, accompanying commuters to their front door. Hell, the umbrella was bigger than I was. The people gave me a few pennies or maybe even a nickel when we got there. When I came home, I proudly handed my mother all my earnings. Every cent helped us make ends meet.

In those days, kids of all ages sold newspapers on busy corners. I'd already had some experience in that business back in Worcester, so I asked a boy on the street where I could find out about becoming a vendor and getting one of those official wooden buttons that said "newsboy."

"Park Row," said the kid.

I'd never heard of the place, but it resounded in my head. The next afternoon after school I took the subway downtown. When I got off near Park Row, I looked up at the mighty Woolworth Building towering above me, a steeple of light, its zenith unattainable. Cass Gilbert's graceful sky-scraper, with its sheath of Gothic detail, was the most beautiful structure I'd ever laid eyes upon. I walked into a stationery store to get directions.

Seeing all the newspapers they sold in there, I asked the clerk, "How many different papers are printed every day in New York?"

"Eleven," said the clerk.

"Eleven," I repeated in awe.

"And a few editions of each," he added proudly.

I made it down to Park Row, the heart of the newspaper business in Manhattan, not far from the Brooklyn Bridge. I'd never seen so many newspapers piled up in one place at one time. Kids were everywhere, getting their allotments of evening newspapers to take out into the streets to sell. I felt right at home. A man signed me up and got me one of those wooden newsboy pins. For a penny a piece, I bought copies of five dailies with the change I had in my pocket. I got back on the subway and found a street corner near Grand Central. At two cents each, the newspapers sold out before I knew what had happened. From then on, as soon as school let out every afternoon, I'd hurry downtown to Park Row and get all the dailies I could carry in my shoulder pouch. Any street corner would be good enough for me to hawk my papers. When I sold out, I'd rush home to give the profits to my mother, have dinner, and collapse into the bed I shared with my brothers.

One day, a kid on Park Row suggested I try selling papers on the corner of Forty-second and Broadway, in the heart of Times Square. He said that I'd sell out my papers fast, and, holy smoke, was he right! I couldn't take in the money fast enough. People threw change at me so fast that I was stunned at first. I was even more stunned when, out of nowhere, somebody kicked me in the ass very hard.

"You little sonofabitch!" a man with a wooden leg screamed. "What the hell do you think you're doing? This is *my* territory!"

The one-legged man had a real newsstand on the corner with papers from all over the world. I told him I was just getting into the business. He didn't stay mad at me for long. His name was Hoppy Fowler, and he became my first Manhattan mentor.[1] Hoppy explained to me that he'd paid the city a helluva lot of money for a license to sell newspapers, and he wasn't about to permit free commerce on his corner. I'd see Hoppy a lot in the years to come. He'd tell me great stories about Times Square and all its diverse characters. It was Hoppy who advised me to try selling papers at the docks where people drove their cars onto the ferries for the commute to New Jersey. I did exactly what he told me. It worked great. Traffic jams were inevitable every evening, people waiting in their cars. I spent many months on those docks selling out every daily in my shoulder pouch.

I'd walk up and down between the lanes of idling cars, yelling, "Newspapers! Newspapers! I got all the papers!"

By the end of World War I, William Randolph Hearst's Journal, *with its banner headlines, was the keystone of a national press empire.*

That fall my mother put me in Public School Number 186. I was small but feisty. Selling newspapers on the streets of Manhattan teaches you how to fend for yourself. There were pencil sharpeners attached to the classroom windowsills. When I went over to sharpen my pencil one day, a tall black kid named Aloyicious Pope pushed me aside violently. His behavior made me so mad that I pushed him back as hard as I could. I didn't know he was the class bully. The little tyrant commanded me to meet him behind the playground after school. Without a split second's hesitation, I agreed.

The rest of the day I regretted my false heroism. I remember wondering to myself what my family would think if I died behind the playground. Why did I have to accept the big bully's challenge? I set my mind to figuring out how I could salvage the situation. First, there was the advantage of being shorter than Aloyicious, therefore more agile. Besides, I knew lots about the boxing champions of the day—Joe Louis, Lou Tendler, Jack Dempsey, and Kid Chocolate—by following Ring Lardner's stories on the sports pages. Lardner wrote plenty about guys getting hit in the solar plexus. I'd never really hit anyone, and I wasn't sure where the solar plexus was. But maybe I could save my ass with some sports savvy anyway.

More menacing than ever, Aloyicious Pope was waiting for me after school. I stared at him silently. Then I lowered my head and ran at him as fast as I could. I butted him right in the gut, knocking the wind out of him. He was stunned long enough for me to escape into the street. I ran home as fast as my legs could carry me. When I told my mother the story, she got very angry. She hated fighting and told me that a blow to someone's stomach was very dangerous. I had to invite Aloyicious home for a piece of her blueberry pie. She still made them, but now she bought the berries at a street market. The next day, I went right up to Aloyicious in the school hallway. He'd survived the blow to his solar plexus. We smiled at each other. He came home with me that day to savor my mother's delicious blueberry pie. We became good friends.

One unforgettable day down on Park Row, I was hanging around the loading dock at the *New York Evening Journal,* waiting for my papers. There was always a tremendous rumble coming from the building's basement, the ground shaking under your feet, as if a herd of stampeding elephants were coming down William Street. I asked a guy on the loading dock what caused those vibrations. The man laughed. He had only one good eye and was half deaf. I had no idea I was talking to the paper's press chief, Tom Foley, nor did I have any conception of what an important man he was at the *Journal.*

"Come on, kid," he said, holding out a powerful hand. "I'll show you."

I grabbed his hand and he picked me up like a feather, pulling me up onto the steel platform. He took me down to the press room to see where all the racket was coming from. The presses were immense, noisy machines in constant motion, spitting out piles of printed paper. Overseeing the enormous spinning rollers, slipping in and out between the churning gears, were a team of sweating print men. They wore ink-stained shorts and paper hats made out of newsprint. With my mouth agape, my eyes gazed farther down the assembly line at the finished newspapers flying out at the far end of the room, sorted and folded. Other workers bundled them up for distribution. I was completely smitten.

"You ain't seen nothin' yet, kid," said Foley. "Come on."

He led me to an elevator and told Bill, a man with a wet mustache, to take us to the sixth floor. I discovered that Bill's mustache was wet with tobacco juice, when he spit into a bucket in the corner. Bill pulled a thick cord and the elevator cranked and wheezed into motion. It stopped a foot shy of the sixth floor, so we had to hop out of the contraption.

As far as I could see was an armada of linotypes, big, noisy, smoking machines, each with an operator tapping on a keyboard, reaching up at regular intervals to pull a chain suspended overhead. The linotypes converted stories and headlines into lead type to make the engraved plates for the presses below. Foley explained that when the operators tugged the chains, big bars of lead descended into hot vats where the metal was melted, then remolded into individual characters. With a beautiful clanging and hissing, the linotypes spit out the hot lead type into neat metal columns.

All that feverish production was overwhelming to me, especially since I'd walked by the *Journal* building on William Street scores of times without ever imagining the intense activity inside. Holy smoke, it was paradise in there! Foley knew his history, too, explaining that on this very site was the old Rhinelander Sugar House, which the British had used as a prison during the Revolutionary War. He proudly told me that both the *Journal* and the *American*—the most powerful dailies in the country—were published right there, four editions every day, each edition selling one million, two hundred fifty thousand copies. That made five million newspapers spewing out every twenty-four hours. No wonder the goddamned sidewalks trembled! The owner of these newspapers, explained Foley, was William Randolph Hearst. The *Journal* was the flagship of Hearst's chain of more than thirty newspapers in cities across the United States.

Foley must have been infected by my boyish enthusiasm. "Now I'm going to show you the heart, the inner organ, of a newspaper," he said. "Without it, kid, there'd be no papers for you to sell."

We went up to the newsroom on the seventh floor. Scores of men and women were working at rows of desks in one large hall, typing, talking on telephones, perusing old newspapers, shouting quick questions at each other. There were pneumatic tubes everywhere and glass cylinders zipping back and forth. A constant *rat-tat-tat* came from the teletype machines spitting out wire stories from the press services. What really caught my eye was a group of teenage boys sitting on the edge of their chairs waiting to be called.

"Copy!" some reporter yelled out.

One of the boys immediately jumped up, rushed over, grabbed a sheet of paper from the reporter's outstretched hand, then darted away somewhere to deliver it. The boys were dashing all over the place, between the desks, out the doorway, then back again to their seats to await the next call.

"This is where the newspapers are written?" I asked.

"Yeah, right here," said Foley. "See that guy over there?" He pointed at a heavyset gentleman at a big desk. "That's the city editor. He's the number one guy in editorial. He's responsible for what gets in the paper. And what doesn't."

"What's their job?" I asked, pointing at the boys hustling everywhere.

"Copyboys," he said.

"I want to come and work here in this room," I announced to Foley without further ado. "Right here, as a copyboy. How can I get the job?"

"Slow down, kid," said Foley. "The managing editor is Joseph V. Mulcahy, and he does the hiring around here."

I was escorted to Mulcahy's glass-enclosed office. Mulcahy was a czar. He looked like he could breathe fire, his thick neck bulging from an unbuttoned shirt and loosened tie.

"I want to be a copyboy," I told Mulcahy.

"Is that right?" said Mulcahy.

"Yes, sir," I said. "I can do it."

"What's your name, my boy?"

"Sammy. Sammy Fuller."

"How old are you?"

"Almost thirteen."

"How much is 'almost'?"

"Maybe four or five months."

"No 'maybe's' for me, my boy," said Mulcahy. "You have to be exact around here."

"In six months, I'll be thirteen," I confessed.

"There are laws in this country about children working. You have to be at least *fourteen*. That's the law."

Dejection flooded across my face.

"Now look here, Sammy," continued Mulcahy, writing down a name and address on a piece of paper, "you go and see this man at his office near city hall. He gives out work permits over there. I'll give him a call on your behalf. But for Chrissakes, tell him you're fourteen. Once you've got the permit, we'll see about an opening on the paper."

Thanks to Mulcahy's backing and my lying about my age, I got the permit. After weeks and weeks of waiting, there was still no word. I'd almost given up hope. Then one day, Foley spotted me on Park Row picking up my allotment of newspapers to sell. He said Mulcahy wanted to talk to me in his office. I'd gotten the coveted job as a copyboy on the *Journal*. I proudly announced the big news to my mother that evening. "Mama, I'm going to work for Mister William Randolph Hearst!"

5

Run Sammy Run

Still shy of my thirteenth birthday, I'd shoehorned my way into the heart of the newspaper world. Out of school at 2:30 p.m., I was to report to the *Journal* by three o'clock, then work until the paper was put to bed. Sometimes I didn't finish until midnight. Many nights I ended up sleeping under a reporter's desk and showing up at school the next morning wearing the same clothes as the day before. My mother was very upset when this happened.

"Sammy, look at you!" she'd say, eyeing my soiled pants and dirty shirt when I finally got home. "Is this what you really want to do?"

"This is *all* I want to do, Mama!"

To this day, I don't give a good goddamn where I sleep or what I'm wearing as long as I'm involved with a project I love. Oh boy, how I loved working at the *Journal!* It was an incredible adventure for a kid like me, hungry to find out about the world. Sitting in a classroom at school, a book on my desk and the teacher droning on and on about a math formula on the blackboard, my eyes would be staring out the window, my mind still in the newsroom at the *Journal.* I couldn't wait to rush out of class and back to my job as copyboy.

On Park Row, surrounded by adults in the high-energy pursuit of news, I was growing up fast, mostly learning about the darker side of humanity. There was a mother lode of information to gather and organize every single day, but what really sold newspapers was violence, sex, and scandal. There were exceptions. Big trials, labor strife, filibusters, sunken treasure, daring exploits, and political upheaval might make front-page news. The death of a famous, powerful, or beloved person played well too.

Charles Dana, illustrious editor of the *New York Sun,* had set the standard for American reporters: "When a dog bites a man, that is not news, because it happens so often. But if a man bites a dog, that is news." Reporters were a special breed—part bloodhound, part charmer, part wordsmith—working feverishly to get their stories not only to scoop other papers but to best their fellow reporters as well. I was in awe of them.

Editors were different creatures altogether, omnipotent, wizened, steady. They were in charge of the entire look and tone of the paper. With a flick of their red pencils, they designated stories as front-page leads, slotting in big photos and screaming headlines. With another red mark, stories were relegated to page two, or even farther back to lesser consequence. The ghost of Horace Greeley, founder of the *New York Tribune,* must have been watching over editors. They had to make tough choices every day under impossible time restraints. As deadlines approached, you could cut the tension in the air with a knife.

"When *exactly* was the sonofabitch murdered?" an editor yelled at a reporter on the phone. "Two days ago? We need a witness. Find one! Yes, NOW! Any witness will do! Yeah, right away! We're going to press in one hour, goddamnit!"

At the bottom of the newspaper's hierarchy, copyboys came and went. I stuck. My age, enthusiasm, and quick legs made an impression. In no time, editors and reporters knew me and appreciated my speed and tenacity.

"Sammy, take this copy to the sports desk!"

"Sammy, run this up to the linotypes!"

"Sammy, get me the proofs from the press room!"

I was also the kid in charge of bringing up cases of bootleg beer stored down in the cellar. They served the stuff when athletes came by to visit the sports writers. There were the greatest baseball players in the world, guys like Tris Speaker, Roger Hornsby, and Babe Ruth, hanging out in our offices, chatting, cracking jokes, and sharing drinks with Ring Lardner, Damon Runyon, William Farnsworth, and Grantland Rice. I couldn't believe how lucky I was to be a small part of it.

During summer vacation, I was moved to the day shift. After months and months of jumping copy, beer, or anything else that required fast feet, I was assigned to the paper's morgue, down in the basement, where stories and photos were clipped and filed. I loved the treasure trove down there. Reporters needed facts for today's paper based on already-published articles. I'd dig for the information in the dusty files. In those days, memory was in a person's mind, not in his computer's electronic chip.

"Sammy," asked an editor, "when did Chapman rob that bank in Jersey City?"[1]

"July twenty-second."

"What time of the day?"

"Eleven forty-five in the morning. Just as the manager was going to lunch with his wife."

"Check it out and get me an illustration."

"Yes sir."

My all consuming ambition was to be a reporter—a *crime* reporter—with my own byline. You jumped copy or worked in the morgue until your name came up for any kind of promotion. They might even give you a crack at reporting if you were old enough. Just fourteen and the youngest copyboy on the paper, I felt there was an eternity of waiting before I'd ever get a chance to advance. The chasm between copyboy and reporter seemed wider than the Grand Canyon. But damned if I was going to wait! I was going to make reporter any way I had to. One day, maybe I'd become a fire-breathing city editor. For Chrissakes, why not even editor in chief of my own paper?

My immediate goal was to meet the *Journal*'s legendary editor in chief, Arthur Brisbane, in the flesh. Brisbane was like the pope. His Grand Eminence had never once set foot in the newsroom, though he cast a long shadow across every desk in the place. I'd heard a helluva lot of stories about Brisbane, how he'd built circulation, how he'd used the largest type in the business for banner headlines, how his column "Today" was the talk of the country, how he was the highest-paid newspaperman in the world. Brisbane's name was pronounced with the utmost respect everywhere on Park Row, yet I'd never so much as laid eyes on the great man. It seemed to me that nobody had ever seen Brisbane except the top editors.

Henry Hudson, one of the *Journal*'s veteran telegraphers, caught me one day hanging around the entrance to the men's room. I was hoping to get a glimpse of Brisbane when he came to take a piss. Old Hudson smiled and explained that the editor in chief had his own toilet. Did I really think the boss would use those rolls of newsprint for towels like us ordinary mortals? Brisbane even had his own private entrance to the *Journal* building.

Then one day I was in Mulcahy's office and heard him tell one of the oldest copyboys to report to Brisbane's office for a temporary jumping job. I followed the eighteen-year-old out and saw him go into the can to wash up and comb his hair. I saw my chance and took it. I ran down the hallway on the seventh floor through a gauntlet of forbidding wall signs: "Stop!" "Private Corridor!" "Don't Disturb!" "No Entry." I ran into the office marked "Editor in Chief" and found myself in an immense, quiet-as-a-tomb waiting room. Two secretaries were working at rolltop desks. There were stacks of newspapers and magazines everywhere. Stately bookcases stretched from floor to ceiling. The room and the secretaries seemed unchanged since Hearst had launched the paper a couple of decades earlier. One of the ladies eyed me silently.

Arthur Brisbane, demigod of Park Row and denizen of Hearst's front pages, would change my way of viewing the world.

"Mulcahy sent me," I said, lying through my teeth.

She picked up a telephone, said a few words into the receiver, then pointed to a carved mahogany door. I walked up to the sacred portal, opened it, and went in as if I were entering a temple. There he was sitting behind a big desk, the great Arthur Brisbane himself, the disciple of Joseph Pulitzer, the brains behind Hearst! He was tall and strong-looking, impeccably dressed, with an immense forehead. Though sixty-two years old that day, he moved like an athlete in his twenties. Brisbane was even more impressive than I'd imagined. Speechless, I stared at him as if he were a creature from another planet.

"Are you from editorial?" Brisbane said.

"Yes sir."

He tossed me a briefcase. "On the corner of Duane Street, parked on the left side of the police station, there's a Lincoln. The driver's name is George. He's wearing a red sweater. Take my briefcase to him and wait for me in the car."

"Yes sir." I paused momentarily, waiting for any additional instructions.

"What's your name?" asked Brisbane.

"Samuel Fuller," I said. "Everyone calls me Sammy."

"All right, Samuel. Get going."

I hurried out, ran down the hallway past the elevator, and flew down the stone staircase. There wasn't a soul on it, but many had rushed along those steps before me. We worked for a common purpose, that of publishing news day in and day out for a big city paper. The place smelled of history. I loved that aroma.

It would've been impossible to miss the big Lincoln on Duane. Brisbane came down a few minutes later and got in beside me in the backseat. The car pulled out, and we shot through the busy streets to his next appointment. He proofed some copy, signed it "AB," and told me to hustle it back to editorial. I slipped the pages inside my jacket, jumped out of the Lincoln at an intersection in midtown, hopped on a subway, then ran back to William Street and up to the seventh floor as fast as lightning.

As soon as Mulcahy found out about my stunt, he told me he was going to fire me. I'd pulled a fast one and deserved to be fired. I hadn't lied to Brisbane, but I hadn't told him the truth, either. Sure I was from editorial, except I wasn't next in line on the copyboys' roster. When Brisbane learned what had happened, he told Mulcahy he wanted to see me again.

I rushed down the corridor to Brisbane's office. The old secretaries waved me through. Brisbane stood up when I walked in. He was stern with me but admired my pluck. Then he said the magic words: "From now on, Samuel, you are going to be my personal copyboy," adding his signature line, "Don't let it go to your head."

Holy mackerel, I was cock of the walk! In the months to come, I'd see a lot of Brisbane's Lincoln. Outside some grand hotel, office building, or restaurant, I'd meet up with George and get in the backseat. Soon Brisbane would appear on his way out of a meeting or luncheon. On the wide, leather-covered seat was Brisbane's dictaphone, with a fresh wax cylinder on the drum. He'd push a button on the machine and the cylinder would begin to spin. Brisbane would put his mouth up to the device's microphone and dictate an editorial. When he'd finished it, he'd give me the cylinder and tell me to run it down to the *Journal*. He'd give me a silver dollar as I was getting out of the car.

"Take a cab, Samuel, not the subway. You may keep the change."

"Yes sir."

"Don't let it go to your head."

This was big league to me, and I'd make every second count. I was completely enamored with Brisbane. I had no idea how long I'd be his personal copyboy, but I was going to be the best one he ever had. As soon as the Lincoln pulled away, I hailed a taxi. Full of pride and purpose, I jumped inside and said one word: *"Journal!"*

That's all you needed to say to a New York cab driver in those days. Everybody knew the *Journal* was on Park Row. I rushed the wax cylinder to Brisbane's secretary, who slipped it into another dictaphone to transcribe his words on her typewriter. I rushed the text to the linotypes. I ran the proof down to editorial. Corrections were made. Then back to the press room for another proof and final corrections. That was "Today,"

Arthur Brisbane's famous editorial, a column that went out to every Hearst paper across the country.

As serious-minded as he was, Brisbane could be playful too. One day on the street outside the *Journal,* he bet me two bits he could beat me in a foot race to the Brooklyn Bridge. He'd even carry his briefcase to handicap himself. We ran up Park Row, the tall editor in chief and the little copyboy. Hell, that must have been quite a sight! I ran my legs off, but Brisbane beat me. I handed him a quarter, but he gave it back to me. Then he took me to Max's Busy Bee for hamburgers and milkshakes. Their hamburgers were swimming in gravy and cost four cents. Milkshakes were seven cents. With an egg, ten cents.

One day, Brisbane wrote down an address on Riverside Drive and handed it to me.

"This is where I'll be tonight," he said. "Bring me the proofs as soon as they're ready, Samuel."

"Yes sir."

With the "Today" proofs and a Winsor McCay cartoon in hand, I set off for Riverside Drive. The place turned out to be Hearst's Manhattan pied-à-terre, a magnificent apartment that looked out over the Hudson River. Brisbane met Hearst there regularly for strategy sessions. I'd deliver proofs or pick up dictaphone cylinders from a butler who answered the door up there.

On one of my visits to Hearst's Riverside apartment, the butler had orders to have me wait inside. I was told to stay in the living room with the magnificent divans and impressive shelves chock-full of books. I stood near the big glass window, enjoying the glorious view of the Jersey cliffs across the Hudson. Brisbane came out of an office with some executives. One of them was a tall, heavyset man with oblique eyebrows and very sad eyes. When he talked, he made birdlike noises. His voice sounded like a sharp little whistle. There was nothing pompous about him except for his very expensive-looking dark suit. That was my first encounter with William Randolph Hearst. You'd have never guessed that he was the most powerful newspaper publisher in the world. Not only was Hearst unassuming, but, as the other men continued their discussion, Hearst kept turning to Brisbane, asking, "What do you think, Arthur?"

Whatever Brisbane advised Hearst on the subject at hand was accepted as a final decision. The Hearst I saw was a far cry from the blustery, tyrannical character of Charles Foster Kane, whom Orson Welles created for *Citizen Kane,* based on Hearst's life. I loved the way Welles's movie underscored a major conflict in the newspaper world of my era, a conflict in which Arthur Brisbane had played a central role.

Hearst took over his father's *San Francisco Examiner* in 1887, then acquired the *New York Morning Journal* in 1895. In 1896, he launched the *Evening Journal* and built circulation with sensational reportage, color comics, and muckraking features, otherwise known as "yellow journalism." That led to a circulation war with Joseph Pulitzer's *New York World.* Fierce competition between the old and new schools of journalism was an essential subplot in *Citizen Kane.*

In reality, Brisbane tipped the balance in Hearst's favor. Brisbane had been managing editor at the *World,* an intellectually superior newspaper to the *Journal.* Hearst spent enormous amounts of money on making the *Journal* more graphic, more exciting, flashier than any paper in the world. He needed one more element: the greatest editor in chief in journalism. He convinced Brisbane to leave Pulitzer and come to work at the *Journal,* in 1897.

Brisbane gave Hearst journalistic credibility, paving the way for the *Journal* to get the crème de la crème of newspapermen. In the big party scene in *Citizen Kane,* celebrating the paper's mounting circulation, Kane announces the hiring of the best journalists money can buy from his chief competitor. That was pretty much what Hearst accomplished, once Brisbane came aboard. I just can't imagine Hearst doing a song and dance with a line of chorus girls, like Kane in the movie!

Brisbane had become unhappy at the *World,* very often in conflict with Pulitzer, who'd gone blind at the end of his career and lived on his yacht, *Liberty,* docked somewhere on the Riviera. Nevertheless Pulitzer was still the boss. He was idolized on Park Row, his integrity, legend. One felt safe reading the *World.* Every sentence in the paper was based on verified facts. Pulitzer had a lifelong aversion to any kind of sensationalism.

Like so many other immigrants to this country, Joseph Pulitzer came from Europe on a ship that was bound for Ellis Island in 1864. Having no papers, and afraid that he'd be sent back by immigration authorities, Pulitzer jumped ship in New York's harbor. He swam for miles until he was picked up by a military patrol boat. Not being able to speak one word of English, Pulitzer got his first job in this country cleaning donkey stalls for the First New York Cavalry during the American Civil War. From those humble beginnings, he rose to be the most respected newspaper publisher in the country. There's a helluva story somebody should make into a movie!

After seven years of working for Pulitzer, Brisbane was fed up. Hearst exploited the rift between the two journalistic giants. At the *Journal,* Brisbane would enjoy not only more freedom to express his opinions in front-page editorials but the biggest salary of any editor in the country as well.

Joseph Pulitzer, born in Makó, Hungary,
acquired the New York World *in 1883*
and made it a major paper, famous for its
strong pro-labor stance and crusades against
corruption.

In 1952, I got an opportunity to make a film about the origins of American journalism and the passion for a free press. *Park Row* was the only film I'd ever produce with my own dough. But I had to make it, if for no other reason than to pay homage to the memories of my youth on that street I loved. To this day, I feel a tremendous debt of gratitude to the dedicated journalists who created and sustained Park Row, who were so essential to my education, who engraved their virtues on my mind. See, *Citizen Kane* was about empire building, not journalism. I wanted to make a little black-and-white movie about the colorful lives of those early reporters and editors who were the backbone of New York newspapers.

The one thing about *Citizen Kane* that irked me was the way Welles handled Marion Davies, portrayed harshly as Susan Alexander in the movie. I'd seen Marion Davies on several occasions at Hearst's apartment. Contrary to Kane's empty-headed Susan, Marion was smart, charming, and funny. She was always very sweet to me. Hearst treated her deferentially at all times, and she seemed, even to my teenage eyes, very much in love with him. I remember going to see her movies at the Cosmopolitan, a theater on Fifty-seventh Street near Columbus Circle that Hearst had bought so that MGM would show films with Marion Davies.

Contrary to Hearst, who ran unsuccessfully for governor of New York and president, Brisbane had no political ambitions. Neither was he interested in becoming a tycoon. Working as an editor was his life. He came from an illustrious family. His father, Albert, had been one of the first socialists in the United States and had founded the Fabian Society together

The sober front page of the 1906 World that covered the sensational killing of Stanford White, architect of the Washington Arch, in Washington Square Park, and the first Madison Square Garden.

with George Bernard Shaw.[2] A respected adviser to leaders in many fields, Brisbane's views cut a wide swath in the twenties. While I rode around in the front seat of the big Lincoln, I'd turn and watch him discussing complex issues in the backseat with the likes of Bernard Baruch, Charles Schwab, and J. P. Morgan. My greatest pleasure was when I got to ride alone with Brisbane. Then I could bombard him with an avalanche of my adolescent questions. He was very patient with my rampant curiosity and always had a response, encouraging me to be inquisitive.

"Who invented the dictaphone?" I asked.

"Charles Sumner Tainter," said Brisbane.

"When?"

"1886."

"Who started the *New York Herald*?"

"James Gordon Bennett."

"When?

"1835. In his cellar. With $500 in capital. It was the first newspaper to use foreign correspondents, to illustrate articles, to print financial news from Wall Street."

Brisbane's encyclopedic mind always amazed me. He never patronized me, even for the most ridiculous question. His answers turned into fascinating stories. He explained so much to me about so many different subjects, from sports and how he'd covered the Boston Strong Boy–Charley Mitchell fight in England, to philosophy and Charles Fourier, the French utopian, who created a sensation with his Four Laws to attain universal harmony, touching on the socialists, and stories about his own father and Brook Farm.[3]

On one outing in Brisbane's big car, we started talking about the Civil War, one of my favorite subjects at school. Sitting next to me was a man born on December 12, 1864, the day of Stoneman's Raid, from Bean's Station, Tennessee, to Saltville, Virginia. Brisbane knew all about George Stoneman and told me more about the Civil War during that ride than I'd learned at school in months.[4] He dropped names of generals and politicians like old friends, and described battles like they'd happened yesterday. Brisbane had a gift for making you feel part of his colorful stories. I learned a helluva lot about storytelling from him. Most importantly, Brisbane gave me an enthusiasm to work hard at learning everything under the sun.

Another time in his office, Brisbane asked me my birthday. When I told him, he started reminiscing about August 1912, when he'd been covering Pancho Villa's war against the Díaz government in Mexico. When I was only four, Brisbane was in Columbus, New Mexico, reporting on Villa's raid there, in which sixteen Americans were killed. Describing Villa, Díaz, Madero, and Huerta from firsthand experience, he spun a thrilling tale that had me on the edge of my chair, eyes bulging out of their sockets.[5]

One Saturday night, I had to get Brisbane's okay on proofs for the Sunday edition. He was at Hearst's place on Riverside Drive, where a costumed ball was going on. Everyone was in disguise. The butler was dressed like Benjamin Franklin. He took me through the hallway to the kitchen. I got a gander of the goings-on. An orchestra was playing waltzes, and, dressed like counts, cowboys, and harlequins, some of the biggest celebrities of that period caroused in Hearst's noisy, smoke-filled living room.

Marion Davies with William Randolph Hearst at one of those costume parties they loved throwing. I saw them at their luxurious place on Riverside Drive.

Hearst's kitchen was like nothing I'd ever seen, a modern white-tiled room with little else but a stainless-steel table. The chef and his assistants were taking a break. Brisbane appeared, disguised as a chef himself, wearing a big white hat and apron. He looked damned funny, but I didn't dare laugh. He studied the proofs, initialed them "AB," then asked the real chef to prepare a chicken for me to take home. A button was pushed, and all the cooking utensils, even the goddamned stove, slid out of the wall. A tray full of roast chickens was taken from the oven.

Brisbane himself wrapped one of the birds in wax paper. Gravy was put in a glass jar and a separate bag.

"Here, Samuel," Brisbane said, handing me the two bags. "Now you won't get your clothes dirty. And don't talk about this to anybody at the office."

"Yes sir. And thank you!"

I rushed the proofs back to the *Journal* and brought the chicken and gravy home to my family. The next day, I couldn't resist mentioning to a certain reporter, Nick Kenny, that I was given a roast chicken from Hearst's fabulous personal kitchen by Brisbane himself. My bragging was stupid, a sassy teenage urge to rebel against Brisbane's orders.

"You're really in with the boss, Sammy," said Kenny. "You tell Brisbane that I'm a damned good newspaperman and I'll give you a dollar."

I took the buck. It was more dough for my family. A couple of days later, I found an opening with Brisbane to praise Kenny.

"How much did he give you to say that?" Brisbane said.

"One dollar," I said.

"Tell him it's not enough money." Brisbane grinned.

Nick Kenny was furious with me when I told him what had happened. The young reporter chased me around the editorial room, cursing and threatening to beat me to a pulp.

One of our most respected sports writers, Bill Farnsworth, used to corner me with questions about Brisbane, too. Did the boss ever make a crack about the sports pages, the cartoons, the columns? I shrugged.

"If you hear anything about our department, let me know," said Farnsworth, slipping me a couple of tickets to a big fight at Madison Square Garden.

By then, I was attending the large, modern George Washington High School on 192nd Street, the first racially mixed institution in the city. But my heart just wasn't in it. I was burning inside to be a crime reporter, only going through the motions of school to please my mother. One day, I pleaded with my illustrious boss to put me on the street and let me cover crime stories for the *Journal*.

"You're much too young, my boy," Brisbane said. "You have to be at least twenty-one for that kind of job. It would be irresponsible for me to let you hang around precinct stations or go to prisons to interview criminals. Samuel, crime reporting is tough work. You're far too young for it."

"But I've tagged along with reporters, been to murder scenes, to the morgue. I've watched how they talk to the police, to witnesses, how they get their stories. You know how fast I am, Mr. Brisbane. I can learn. I'm ready to start now. Please!"

There was no changing his mind. Still, I wasn't about to give up on my dream of becoming a crime reporter. Not even Arthur Brisbane could make me do that.

Then, on an outing to a speakeasy with *Journal* reporters, I met Emile Henri Gauvreau, editor in chief of the *New York Evening Graphic,* a daily that had been launched in 1924. Gauvreau was a short, spirited man, proud of his remarkable resemblance to Napoleon. He combed his hair in the same way as Bonaparte so the resemblance was even more pronounced. Gauvreau had come to New York from the *Hartford Courant.*

"I know all about you, Fuller," said Gauvreau. "You're Brisbane's copyboy. You make fourteen bucks a week. I also heard you've worked in the *Journal*'s morgue. Sammy, why don't you come to work for me at the *Graphic.* How'd you like to be chief of our morgue for eighteen a week?"

"I want to be a reporter, Mr. Gauvreau," I said. "A *crime* reporter."

"You're a little young for that, aren't you, Sammy? I could use a bright kid like you to build up our morgue."

"I'm only leaving Brisbane and the *Journal* if you let me be a real newspaperman. With a crime beat."

"Look, Sammy, it's 1928, goddamnit," said Gauvreau. "We've got to contend with Prohibition, anarchists, fascists, Al Capone, gangland killings, God knows what else, and you want to be a newspaperman. I can't let you do that, not at sixteen."

"Sixteen and a half!" I corrected him. Nevertheless, I saw I wasn't getting anywhere, so I proposed a deal. "If in six months, when I turn seventeen, Mr. Gauvreau, you let me be a reporter, I'll come to work in your morgue now."

"It's a deal," he said.

We shook hands on it.

It was hard to tell Arthur Brisbane that I was leaving him and the *Journal.* It was probably the hardest thing I ever had to do. We were in the backseat of his Lincoln when I explained the agreement I'd made with Gauvreau to work at the *Graphic.* Brisbane sat there silently. It was one of those moments that seemed to last forever. I had to bite my lip not to cry. Brisbane's face was grave. If he was upset, he didn't show it.

"Samuel, the *Graphic* won't last," he said. "What do you want to do in life, my boy?"

"I want to become editor in chief of a great newspaper, like the *Journal*!"

"Working for the *Graphic* will never get you hired as editor in chief anywhere."

"Maybe not, Mr. Brisbane," I said, "but I've got to grab this opportunity. I want to be a reporter, and the sooner the better."

"Then go be one, my boy," said Brisbane.

Having been Arthur Brisbane's personal copyboy for two and a half years would forever be part of my very fiber. Brisbane had become an essential father figure for me. Now I had to move on. I got out of his big car for the last time. We shook hands through the open window. He told me that I could call on him whenever I needed his assistance. I thanked him for the offer, though I never took him up on it.

Cut to twelve years later. Christmas morning, 1936. Hollywood, California. Corner of Hollywood and Vine. From that day's early edition, I learned that Arthur Brisbane had died. I stood there and cried unashamedly. The newsboy who'd sold me the paper asked me if I needed a doc. I told him I was sick with sadness and no doctor could help me.

"You go ahead and sell your papers," I said sorrowfully. "That's why they're printed."

Flash Like
a New Comet

The *New York Evening Graphic* was financed by Bernarr Macfadden, a crazy Irishman with a mane of long hair who'd made millions with a string of magazines exploiting physical fitness, true romance, violence, sex, or whatever else was the hot topic of the day. Macfadden was haunted by the specter of his parents' deaths from tuberculosis. He'd become a body-builder and general health nut, ate only raw vegetables, drank water and fruit juices, and took cold showers to jump-start his circulation. Here's how crazy Macfadden was about physical fitness: He'd regularly walk to the *Graphic* office from his home in Nyack, New York, an eight-hour stroll on hard pavement. And he did it barefoot!

Macfadden chose Emile Gauvreau to be his editor in chief because Gauvreau had already made a name for himself as a headline hound. When he was running the *Hartford Courant,* Gauvreau hid a murderer in his office who'd come to plead for mercy, then published a firsthand account of the crime. The scoop was nifty, but it got Gauvreau in hot water, indicted for complicity to a murder, a rap he eventually beat. Ben Hecht and Charles MacArthur turned the incident into the Broadway play *The Front Page.* The play became a movie in 1931, directed by Lewis Milestone, with Pat O'Brien playing the role of an editor who stashes a murderer in his rolltop desk to get a big story. Gauvreau's career was also the inspiration for Mervyn LeRoy's *Five Star Final,* starring Edward G. Robinson as the headline-hunting city editor.

Macfadden and Gauvreau had the unprecedented idea of taking out large ads in all the dailies to announce their exciting endeavor in enormous headlines:

A NEW EVENING NEWSPAPER FOR NEW YORK CITY.
A NEWSPAPER WITH A NEW IDEA.
NOT A PICTURE PAPER BUT A REAL NEWSPAPER
WITH ALL THE NEWS IN TABLOID FORM.

Bernarr Macfadden,
publisher of the New York
Evening Graphic, *circa*
1930, was in great shape for
his age and liked to
demonstrate it.

The publisher added a ballsy personal message that concluded with *"I intend to publish a newspaper that will flash across the horizon like a new comet."*

The first issue of the *Graphic* appeared on September 19, 1924. Across the front page was the headline "TWO FOIL DEATH CHAIR." The rest of the page was taken up by a huge picture of two men in prison uniforms, their arms wrapped around elderly women. The caption read: "Convicts Cling To Mothers As They Await Fate—Would Have Kicked Off With Grin." On page two was a story about one of the mothers with the banner headline "I CRIED FOR JOY AT NEWS FROM SING SING." Under a picture of a third convict was the caption: "I'm Guilty. Only God and I Can Understand." Decidedly, Macfadden and Gauvreau came from a different school of journalism than Joseph Pulitzer.

The *Graphic* carved out a unique niche for itself with its coverage of the

1926 death of Rudolph Valentino (born Rodolfo Guglielmi), the gifted silent-screen actor whose dark, intense eyes made millions of women swoon. It's difficult to understand today the fame and passion that Valentino acquired in a career that spanned just six years and produced only six films of any consequence.[1] His death at age thirty-one was a national tragedy. The front page of the *Graphic* that day was simple yet stunning: a full-face close-up of Valentino with just one word printed across the top in enormous type: DEAD!

By 1928, when I joined the *Graphic,* its reputation was well established. By covering crime and sensational happenings, Macfadden had found a way for the *Graphic* to survive in New York's very competitive daily-newspaper market. Gauvreau had invented the "composograph," a composite photo in which the heads of real people were superimposed on models posed in startling situations. Once they needed a kid's body for a young pilot who'd died in an airplane crash. Gauvreau asked me to pose, and of course I'd do anything he asked. Next day there was my body on the front page of the *Graphic* superimposed onto a head shot of the dead pilot, steering the doomed biplane with a scarf round my neck blowing in the fake wind. I was tickled pink to be part of the stunt. My mother was appalled with the sensationalism, irate that I'd participate in such trickery.

Hell, any break from the monotony of filing clippings in the *Graphic's* morgue was welcome. Before I could join the ranks of real reporters, as Gauvreau had promised, I had to sweat out my six months working in the archives. While the days and weeks dragged by, I'd use my spare time to draw characters in silly situations with one-liners inside bubbles coming out of their mouths. I'd sell my best cartoons to the *Graphic* for a buck, extra dough for my family. I even flirted with the idea of becoming a cartoonist. After all, my brother Ving, who was already drawing full time, encouraged me to hone my skills. Once, Ving introduced me to some of the greatest cartoonists of the day at a memorable dinner that he and his pals organized in the famous Chinatown eatery Lum Fong. They were great cartoonists—in a league of their own, each with nationally syndicated columns—and great guys. That night, we had a helluva good time together. However, drawing would never be more than an amusing pastime for me. What I wanted to be more than anything else was a reporter. My seventeenth birthday was approaching, and I was counting the hours and minutes until I could get out on the street and start writing articles under my own byline.

The big day finally arrived. True to his word, Gauvreau called me into his glass-enclosed office, pulled out his own press card, and crossed out his

EVENING GRAPHIC   THURSDAY, APRIL 25, 1929

NY TRYING TO FORGET FIGHT

"A Bengal Dish for Al"

Bride-to-Be Waits at Chu
As Gas Kills Fiance

Wedding

t "There Was I Waiting at the Church" is an old time vaudeville ditty, but to Miss Rosa Lapina, 21, of 201 Engert Ave., Brooklyn, it contains a world of sorrow.

For months she and her fiance, Joseph Bolessara, 26, of 197 Withers St., Brooklyn, had worked together prepraring their home and making ready for the wedding bells.

Jos. Bolessara,

All was ready for the wedding at 5 o'clock yesterday. Miss Lapina was at the church waiting.

Five o'clock came, but no Joseph. Six o'clock, still no Joseph at seven ____ in search of

One of those drawings I knocked off when I was on the staff of the Graphic

name. Then he wrote my name onto the card and handed it over. It wasn't much of a ceremony, yet I'll always remember that moment as one of the most glorious rites of my life. The name of Joseph P. Warren, police commissioner of the city of New York, was printed on the bottom of my press card. The smile on my face must have stretched from one ear to the other.

"Your salary," said Gauvreau, "is going to be thirty-eight fifty a week, plus a couple bucks for expenses, as long as you can justify them. You're going to meet a lot of shady characters from now on, Sammy, so you'd better be damn careful."

"When do I start, Mr. Gauvreau?" I asked.

"About five minutes ago," he said. "We've got a double suicide to cover."

A guy and his girlfriend had been found dead in a cheap hotel upstate. A note next to their bodies said that they'd wanted to die together. The town's sheriff was sticking to the double suicide theory. Gauvreau had received a tip that made him want to dig deeper. He was sending me up there to get the dope on a possible crime story as well as find some juicy information on the dead couple's past problems. Gauvreau probably had the big type already set for a screaming headline that said "DOUBLE SUICIDE, DOUBLE TROUBLE."

Since I was greener than a Martian, it was wisely decided to send an

Left: My big brother, Ving, at his drawing board. Unlike me, he was a talented, committed cartoonist.

Below: The big cartoonist dinner in Chinatown with (left to right) my brother Ving, Charlie McCadam of McClure Syndicate, Ham Fisher of Joe Palooka, *Ken Kling of* Joe and Asbestos, *restaurateur Lum Fong, Bud Fisher of* Mutt and Jeff, *Bill Gould of* Red Barry, *and me. Billy deBeck of* Barney Google *was next to the photographer, cracking jokes. My heart and mind was in reporting, not drawing.*

*Rhea Gore, mother of John Huston and
grandmother of Angelica, was a terrific
journalist and a helluva lady. She taught
me plenty about crime reporting.*

experienced reporter with me on the story. Rhea Gore got the assignment.
Rhea wasn't the only female reporter on the *Graphic*. Jean Campbell and
Lois Bull, terrific ladies and great writers, also worked on the paper. But
Rhea was a real gem, a tall and slender brunette, smart and sassy. Holy
cow, was I lucky to fall in with this fast-talking, savvy mentor!

All I knew about Rhea was that her marriage to actor Walter Huston
had produced a son, John, but had ended in divorce. Then she'd gotten
hitched to a guy named Stevens, president of the Chicago and Altoona
Railroads. Unfortunately, he'd died. She had more than enough money
and never needed to work again. But Rhea loved the newspaper business
and got back into reporting at the *Graphic*. "Gore" was the pen name she'd
chosen for her byline because she didn't want to ever be tagged as "the
wealthy widow," preferring to be judged on no other merits than her
work.

That was how I first met John Huston. Rhea got him hired as a *Graphic*
reporter, but John's heart was never really in journalism. In covering one of
his first murders, he described an innocent man as the murderer. All hell
broke loose, and John was fired on the spot. It turned out to be a big break,
because it liberated him to go out to Hollywood, where he met William
Wyler and cowrote *A House Divided* (1931). The rest is movie history.

To cover the double suicide story, Rhea and I headed upstate. We got
into this little town late at night. The taxi driver let us off at the cheap

hotel where the ill-fated couple had supposedly taken their lives. No one was around. We snooped around the joint until we found their room. The local sheriff had put an official seal on the door. That wasn't going to stop Rhea. There wasn't a seal on the window, so she opened it and we quietly slipped into the motel room. She figured the town didn't have a morgue. For chrissakes, right there on the floor waiting to be picked up by the county coroner were the corpses of the young man and the young woman laid out under sheets! We lifted the sheets. The two naked bodies took my breath away. The man's head was a bloody mess, but the woman looked unscathed except for her bruised neck.

"If this is a double suicide," said Rhea, after a careful look at the two bodies, "then I'm flying back to Manhattan tomorrow by flapping my arms."

She figured it as a murder, except the murderer had gotten away with his crime by putting a gun in his mouth and pulling the trigger. The only way to find out for sure, she explained, was to be invited to the autopsy. The next day, Rhea became the coroner's best buddy and wrangled her way into the county morgue, where they'd brought the corpses. Rhea's hunch turned out to be right on the money. The woman had died by strangulation, the man by a self-inflicted gunshot. They proved she'd fought like crazy, because they scraped little pieces of the boyfriend's flesh and hair from underneath her fingernails. Strands of her hair with their roots on his skin was clear evidence that they'd struggled. He killed her, then himself.

Step by step, Rhea led me through the investigation and the writing of our article. We interviewed the couple's parents and friends, who told us about their stormy relationship. It was a crash course in crime reporting. Rhea taught me that every detail, every strand of hair, was important. Gauvreau was delighted when we came back with a helluva story exposing the guy who'd killed his girlfriend and then shot himself to escape the law. Rhea Gore and I worked together on lots of stories at the *Graphic*. She was always full of enthusiasm and determination. I'll never forget her showing me the ropes when I was a cub reporter.

Many years later, John Huston and I were having drinks at some Hollywood watering hole. It must have been the fifties. Huston asked me the name of the sonofabitch editor who'd fired him from the *Graphic*.

"Gauvreau," I said.

"Gauvreau! God bless him!" cried John. "Let's drink to that wonderful man! Thank the Lord he had the good sense to can me!" A few drinks later, Huston teased me with his old refrain: "You know, Sam, you spent more time with my mother than I did."

As soon as I made reporter, my life changed. I'd come home late at night, if at all, sometimes not showing up until breakfast. After a bath and a quick bite, I was off to my classes at high school. Sure, my mother was plenty proud of her son's hard work and bylines. But she was terribly worried about her precious boy growing up too fast. By reading my articles, she correctly deduced that I was keeping strange company as well as strange hours. I explained to her it was all just part of the job. Covering crime obliged you to frequent some very disreputable places, rubbing shoulders with stoolies, bootleggers, prostitutes, and petty mobsters, the full gamut of characters from society's underbelly. I was most intrigued by the pickpockets, or "cannons," as they were called on the street, quick-handed grifters who lifted wallets and purses with remarkable skill, originality, and boldness. Needless to say, I kept the pungent details of all these rogues to myself, for the reality of my new life would have made Rebecca lose too much sleep.

A helluva lot of your time as a crime reporter is spent with cops, either at the crime scene or in the station houses. The police were essential sources of information, though sometimes unwilling to give reporters a lead on a breaking story. I used to walk from one precinct to another, slipping sticks of chewing gum to the desk sergeants in exchange for something newsworthy. After I started smoking cigars, I'd give out cigars. That worked better. Maybe I took up cigar smoking just so the police would think I was a grown-up. My teenage face never failed to betray me, sometimes causing chuckles when I hit the cops with hard questions. Everybody smoked cigars in those days. It was nothing stylish or extraordinary, just something men did. I got hooked on the pleasure. As you puff away—never inhaling, of course—the smoke warms your heart and your mind. In the last seven decades since my reporting days, I've rarely been without a cigar firmly planted between my lips. That chagrins some people, mostly the uninitiated. When they protest, I act deaf, smile, and take another puff.

See, the police didn't file charges against someone after a brilliant investigation. Unlike a Sherlock Holmes story or those page-turners by Raymond Chandler or Dashiell Hammett, solving crimes was never a very respectable enterprise. To incriminate suspects, the cops needed to be tipped off. The only way to get information was from an informer, somebody who sang on the guilty party. There were all kinds of pigeons. Some were professionals who regularly passed on information for cash or favors. Some were bystanders who witnessed the crime. Many were double-crossed women.

Let's say you rob a bank and shoot a teller in the melee, then hide out with your girlfriend. If you lie low with her and the money, nobody'll catch you. But being a dumb bastard, you decide to dump the girlfriend. You give her a wad of cash and tell her to get lost. The scorned lady goes away, but she's aching for a chance to get even with you. Six months later, when you're least expecting it, she calls the police and tells them to go to room 316 at the Olympia Hotel if they want to grab the guy who killed the teller in the First National Bank robbery. She hangs up, and it's the beginning of the end. Next thing you know, the police pick you up in the seedy hotel room, haul you back to the precinct, and book you for murder. When they strap you into the electric chair at Sing Sing and throw the switch, the jilted lady will be laughing.

Whenever I got a hot tip on a breaking item, I slammed a nickel into a pay phone and called my city editor, a guy named Shainmark. I'd give him a quick summary over the phone. He'd decide the importance of the story, maybe send a photographer to join me, and surely make me dig for more details. When I had all my facts straight, I'd get myself to the paper as quickly as humanly possible, either by subway, taxi, or on foot. Or all three. At the *Graphic,* I'd plop down at a typewriter and bang out an article for the morning edition, kicking it off with an eye-catching lead, giving the essence of the story in the first paragraph.

It was inevitable that my schooling would suffer, though I never expected to get booted out of Washington High. That's exactly what happened, but not because of bad grades or poor attendance, though neither were very brilliant. Hell, I was set up by Shainmark.

"Say, aren't you still going to George Washington, Sammy?" he asked me one day.

"Yeah," I said. "Mornings."

"You hear any rumors about parties up there, parties with teachers and students? Know anything about that?"

I shook my head.

Tedious, not titillating, was how I thought of high school. I had no time or interest in socializing with my classmates. Like a racehorse, I was out of class at the sound of the bell and back to work at the *Graphic.* When I was on a hot story, I skipped school altogether. The only reason I was still making a half-baked attempt to attend classes was to please my mother. Rebecca believed that without a high school diploma, I'd be seriously handicapped for the rest of my life.

"I got a tip that some teachers up there are throwing wild cocktail parties and inviting students," said Shainmark. "And there's some necking going on after class. Between teachers and students. Take a photographer with you to school tomorrow. Get him into the classrooms, show him the library, the gym, the football field. Help him take photos for a story we want to do about Washington High."

Pleased to do something at school that contributed to my job at the *Graphic,* I escorted the photographer, a guy named Frank Carson, into Washington High. Nothing out of the ordinary happened. At lunchtime, there *was* some necking going on behind the stadium, nothing to get excited about. There certainly didn't seem to be anything to hook an article on. But those were Prohibition days. Public morality was already whipped up to a feverish pitch. Back at the *Graphic,* Shainmark asked me to write down what I'd seen at school. A rewrite man took my first-hand account and added a lot of scandalous gossip about supposed goings-on at Washington High without asking my opinion or showing it to me for a final edit. The *Graphic* published it under the banner headline "HIGH SCHOOL ORGY." The article was signed "by Samuel Fuller for the *Graphic.*"

The next morning, all hell broke loose at Washington High. The principal called an assembly for the entire student body and gave us a fire-and-brimstone speech, calling the behavior described in the *Graphic* article reprehensible. He announced a series of strict new rules, so that there wouldn't be any more scandals at his school. Finally, to my complete surprise and embarrassment, he pointed me out in the back of the auditorium, saying how I'd betrayed my teachers and fellow students, the Judas Iscariot of George Washington High School. It was so goddamned unfair. There was no way to respond to his charge, but no denying that I'd participated in the muckraking story.

To my mother's great despair, I was suspended from high school that very day. She insisted on having the injustice repaired and my name cleared. I didn't have the heart to even try. Secretly, I was relieved I didn't have to show up for classes and go through the motions of being a student anymore. I never did get my high school diploma, nor any other diploma for that matter. Like all mothers, Rebecca had dreamed of me going to college and getting a higher education. Over the years, I've had to educate myself, gulping down all the classics I got my hands on, hungry for great writers like Flaubert, Faulkner, Dickens, Twain, Hugo, Dostoyevsky, and Balzac. By reading them, I was in touch with great minds without the fluff of a classroom. Gene Fowler, who was to have a big influence on me, wrote, "The best way to become a successful writer is to read good writing, remember it, and then forget where you remember it from."

To hell with college! How many mothers' sons learned nothing much higher on a college campus than betting on football games, drinking beer, and playing poker? Some very educated gangsters had attended college.

Still, my mother was disconsolate about the precipitous end of my formal schooling. For me, being a reporter was the greatest school of all.

That Shainmark—with Gauvreau's blessing—had manipulated me into getting that high school scandal piece published bothered the hell out of me. But I had no intention of jumping out of any window over the incident. I was just too busy covering all the other "leapers," as reporters called them.

We'd get an urgent call about some guy standing on the ledge of a skyscraper high above Manhattan, threatening to commit suicide. I'd get over there on the double with a photographer. The last thing you wanted was for a priest, a mother, or a wife to arrive before you, crawling out onto the ledge of the building screaming, "Please don't! Please don't!" The best way to save the leaper was to make him talk about himself and his problems. Besides, as he blabbered about his heartaches, you could jot down facts for your story. All the while, you had to watch his toes. That's how you could tell if the miserable bastard was really going to jump or not. As the toes went, so went the leaper. If the guy was inconsolable, he'd move his toes closer and closer to the edge of oblivion, determined to take the plunge. That's when you'd blurt out one last question for your article. The good photographers primed their cameras, ready to snap, for those photographers who knew about the toe business always got the best pictures of the guy leaping to his death.

God, I loved being a reporter! I was hungry to learn and picked it up quick. What I wanted more than anything was a lead that might produce the dream of every cub reporter: a scoop. Then it happened. One night in the early fall of 1929, I got a tip about a mysterious corpse at one of Manhattan's most exclusive funeral parlors. I was out the door and on my way over there before my informant, the maintenance man at the parlor, had hung up the phone. I'd befriended the guy on an earlier assignment when I wrote an article about New York mortuaries, mentioning this classy establishment. The owner threatened to call the police if I ever set foot inside his establishment again. He hadn't appreciated my piece, because it underscored how the rich got buried in opulence while the poor ended up in Potter's Field. This time, instead of walking in the front door, I used the service entrance in the alleyway.

The funeral parlor was partitioned into the "gold" and "red" rooms, both deathly quiet, swell places if you were a stiff. In the gold room, I saw a glorious coffin with six polished brass handles. Mountains of flowers had been placed around it on the rostrum. I lifted the massive cover of the coffin. Inside was the most beautiful corpse I'd ever laid eyes on, and, believe me, I'd seen plenty of them by then. I stopped breathing as I stared at

Jeanne Eagels, one of Broadway's most celebrated actresses. I could hardly believe it was her. Yet there she was, laid out in a stunning evening gown, her bleached-blond hair perfectly done up, as if she were going out on the town. She wasn't going anywhere. She was dead.

I was staggered. Jeanne Eagels had electrified Broadway with her performance in *Rain,* a play adapted from a Somerset Maugham story that opened in November 1922 and played for four years, nearly fifteen hundred performances. I'd taken my mother to see Eagels in another play Maugham wrote especially for her, *The Letter.* She was sensational. I adored Jeanne Eagels and knew she'd just finished doing the filmed version of *The Letter* for MGM. It would be her last performance. All that beauty and talent was now extinguished, nothing more than a cold corpse lying in that splendid goddamned coffin.

I heard voices in the funeral parlor. Before anybody saw me, I slipped outside into the alleyway. I ran to a pay phone and called Shainmark.

"Are you sure it's her?" said Shainmark incredulously. "In the casket?"

"Yeah," I said. "I'm absolutely sure."

"Wait for me in the alley. I'm going to check with the police, then I'm coming over there to see for myself. This is big."

Shainmark arrived fifteen minutes later. The police had told him they had no record of Eagels's death. We went into the funeral parlor through the front door. Someone was warming up the big organ. Near the entrance to the gold room we overheard the manager of the funeral parlor talking to somebody.

"We will take care of the corpse," said the man, as coldly as if he were talking about fixing a machine.

Quickly, I showed Shainmark the coffin and lifted the lid for him to look inside. He was as stunned as I was. The manager saw us and kicked us out. "There's got to be a death certificate," said Shainmark. "We need the cause of death. Get your ass over to the coroner's office."

I rushed down to the city morgue. The chief coroner said that it was Eagels in the coffin all right, but there wouldn't be an official announcement until the exact cause of death could be determined. Shainmark suspected that the authorities were buying time to conceal a drug overdose. In those days, alcohol abuse was commonly mentioned in the papers, but, because of all the moralistic reactionaries, the word "drugs" was taboo in the press. Even Gauvreau and Macfadden wouldn't touch the subject with a ten-foot pole. Nevertheless, we knew damn well that drug use—probably heroin—was common in the company that Jeanne Eagels was keeping. The cause of her death was eventually registered as "Intoxication of Alcohol, Deterioration of Organs." Somebody was trying to protect Eagels's

Jeanne Eagels in
The Letter *(1929).*
She was beautiful,
talented, and
destined for
greatness. Then a
drug overdose short-
circuited her life
and career.

reputation and doing a pretty good job. Later, the cause was changed to "self-administered sedative."

My front-page article on the mysterious death of Jeanne Eagels in the morning edition of October 4, 1929, scooped every other daily paper in New York. Under the *Graphic's* main headline, a smaller one said, "WE WILL TAKE CARE OF THE CORPSE." That mortician's words, so icy and unforgiving, still give me the shivers. After a big memorial service in New York, the glorious coffin was shipped back for burial to Kansas City, Eagels's hometown, a place she said she hated. I remember her philosophy: "Never deny. Never explain. Say nothing and become a legend." More than a legend for me, she was like a shooting star, ascending so magnificently, then falling precipitously into nothingness.

I wasn't the only one who'd never forget the beauty and talent of Jeanne Eagels. Several movies borrowed from her life and times, basing their stories on a talented young actress struggling against all obstacles, including herself, to achieve fame and glory. One of the wittiest was Gregory La Cava's *Stage Door* (1937), adapted from a play by Edna Ferber and

The year's 1930. I'm a cocky crime reporter at the Graphic *with a cluttered desk just around the corner from the men's room. The headshot is that of Jeanne Eagels, whose untimely death I covered.*

George S. Kaufman. It follows an up-and-coming actress from a wealthy family, played by Katharine Hepburn, who aspires to Eagels's brilliance. In 1957 George Sidney directed the biographical *Jeanne Eagels,* with Kim Novak playing the lead. But as beautiful as she was, Novak couldn't get close to Eagels's charisma. Joseph Mankiewicz told me once that the main character of *All About Eve,* Broadway actress Margo Channing, was inspired by Jeanne Eagels, though Bette Davis played the character caustically, more like Tallulah Bankhead.

Rain was made into a movie by Lewis Milestone in 1932, with Joan Crawford getting the role of Sadie Thompson—whom Jeanne had played so memorably on Broadway—a prostitute quarantined with other passengers on Pago Pago Island. While Sadie gets along with the American soldiers stationed there, the missionaries make her life miserable. The Reverend Davidson finally forces Sadie to repent, rapes her, and commits suicide. Only then is Sadie able to accept Sergeant O'Hara's genuine love. Crawford became a star after that movie, but for me, she couldn't ever equal the inimitable Eagels.

The tragedy of Jeanne Eagels would have a lifelong effect on me. She'd worked in the circus as a kid before moving into legitimate theater. I like to think she'd been a high-wire acrobat because she had an appetite for spectacular risks, both personal and professional. Her talent was like a shimmering diamond that transfixes your eyes on its brilliance. Her arrogance was legend, too. She changed the spelling of her name from "Eagles" to "Eagels" because "it looked better in lights." I was damned proud of my first scoop but, at the same time, deeply saddened by the terrible waste of the young actress, only thirty-five when she died. I'll always remember the angelic expression on Jeanne Eagels's face in that godforsaken coffin. Through her, I understood for the first time the quicksand nature of fame, a seductive mistress I'd never court.

World of
Nevertheless

My attitude about success was influenced by the brilliant and notorious Gene Fowler. "Success," he wrote, "is a whore. I can't afford her asking price." A gutsy, gorgeous human being who made you feel good just by being in his presence, Fowler had a vibrant, cavernous voice and an explosive laugh that resonated throughout any bar, boxing arena, or bordello he was in.

Gene Fowler had come to New York from Colorado in 1918 as a protégé of Damon Runyon after successful stints at the *Rocky Mountain News* and the *Denver Post,* where his brazen prose had set him apart.[1] He'd befriended one of America's greatest heroes, William F. Cody, known the world over as "Buffalo Bill." Cody was an aging demigod for whom Gene developed a fondness devoid of worship. Cody died in Denver in 1917. Fowler covered his passing this way:

> Indiscreet, prodigal, as temperamental as a diva, pompous yet somehow naïve, vain but generous, bigger than big today and littler than little tomorrow, Cody lived with the world at his feet and died with it on his shoulders. He was subject to suspicious whims and distorted perspectives, yet the sharpers who swindled him the oftenest he trusted the most.

Runyon encouraged Fowler to leave his native Rocky Mountains and try the big time in New York by inviting him to New York to visit the *Journal* and meet Hearst himself. When Hearst asked what Fowler would like as a starting salary, the audacious young journalist from out west answered $100 a week, a huge amount of money in those days. Hearst said that a fellow who placed such a high price on his talents might just have what it takes, so he hired Fowler to work at the *New York American* as a reporter, copyreader, and headline writer.

After conquering Park Row, Gene Fowler took his pungent prose and wry sense of humor out to Hollywood to make a pile of dough as a screenwriter.

"I expect great things from you, young man," said Hearst.

He got them. Only a few years later, Fowler would become the managing editor of the *American*. In his years on Park Row, Fowler became a legend, "easily the most colorful and adventurous newspaperman of our time," according to the prestigious Silurians Club, a select group of crusty newspapermen named after a paleontological age when some of its members started their careers.

Fowler went on to become a prolific author, producing four novels and a half-dozen biographies of his famous, rakish friends like John Barrymore

(*Good Night, Sweet Prince*), Mayor James "Jimmy" J. Walker of New York (*Beau James*), Jimmy Durante (*Schnozzola*), and that charming pair of bandits named Bonfils and Tammen (*Timber Line*), a speculator and a bartender who teamed up to make the *Denver Post* a financial and political powerhouse. During the thirties, Fowler moved out to Hollywood to become a screenwriter and script doctor.

When I first met him, Fowler was in his late thirties, one of the most well-known journalists on Park Row. There were plenty of prima donnas on the street, but Gene was sociable with everyone and generous with his time. I was sixteen, still a copyboy, and he took me under his wing. Hell if I know why. Maybe because he saw in me his own early passion for the newspaper business. He was a great mentor. Together we attended prize-fights, baseball games, benefits, political rallies, parades, and floating crap games. Gene knew everybody and everybody knew Gene, be they statesmen, cops, priests, heiresses, pimps, or bartenders. Especially bartenders.

Gene was a faithful patron of any saloon that sold alcoholic beverages. He took me to my first speakeasy. We were accompanied by three of the greatest writers and all-around good guys of that era, Ring Lardner, Damon Runyon, and Bill Farnsworth. The joint was in a basement somewhere near Times Square, and was owned by an entrepreneur named Lew Walters. Lew had a daughter named Barbara who became a journalist herself. The bouncer looked through a hole in the door, recognized Fowler, and let us in. I was bringing up the rear when I felt the bouncer's hairy paw on my shoulder stopping me dead in my tracks. The big palooka glanced at Gene with a raised eyebrow. Fowler swore that I was much older than I looked. The bouncer bought it. But the bartender didn't. I had to sip seltzer water through a straw while my elders knocked back whiskey. At least I could smoke cigars with them.

Walters's speakeasy was a fairly ritzy place. There were tall mirrors and paintings of nude women on the walls. There was a dance floor with a three-piece band and some beautiful hostesses whom you tipped generously if you wanted to be welcomed back a second time. A dollar changed hands, like Fowler said, in the blink of a pretty eyelash. It all seemed very exciting to my teenage eyes.

I'd frequent a fair number of speakeasies with Gene. There was Andy Horn's Bridge Café, Lipton's, Mike's, near the *American,* and Hesse's all-night saloon, down the street from the *World.* The layout was generally the same: a bar, spittoons, tables, and plenty of teacups to serve the booze. Glasses were taboo because they were incriminating if the police decided to raid the place, which they did frequently if bribes weren't paid on time. The gin was called "Prohibition Dew." A tough bouncer was a must for customers who got out of line, which meant drinking yourself senseless, failing to have the cash to pay the last round, or getting into a brawl with the other customers.

Brawling was a regular feature of bars before Prohibition. Speakeasies were milk dens in comparison, the discreet atmosphere more peace-loving. But booze and conflicts went hand in hand. Fowler never looked for a fight, but when the occasion presented itself, he threw himself into the mayhem with unmatched joy. I can personally attest to Fowler's strong, clean punches and quick feet. On a couple of our outings, he belted obnoxious guys to the floor with one nifty, surprise swing. Unfortunately, when the oaf got back on his feet, Fowler would end up sprawled on the floor. It was all over pretty quick because, in a flash, the bouncer would jump in and break the ruckus up. Fowler would slowly stand up, shake his big head, smile, and apply a handkerchief to the bleeding cuts as he asked for another drink.

There was one establishment—Perry's Pharmacy—I'll never forget, unorthodox in its normalcy. Perry's was a drugstore on the ground floor of the Pulitzer Building, near the entrance to the highly respected *World*. If you look closely at the set we built for *Park Row* in that long tracking shot at the beginning of the film, you'll see we included Perry's Pharmacy, because I wanted to honor the place that Fowler and his colleagues used to call the "Pot of Glue."

They'd meet up at Perry's at the end of a hard day of newspapering for a glass of "Brown Ruin," a special pick-me-up that chemist Tim O'Brien served in the back of the shop. Among the "fellows of good minds and limber elbows," as Fowler called them, I remember Nunally Johnson, who wrote the screenplay for *The Grapes of Wrath,* Walter Davenport, who became editor of *Collier's,* Charles Somerville, a protégé of the great O. Henry, and Ross Duff Whytock, an old-timer who'd scooped everybody for the *Evening World* with an article about Germany's submarine campaign in World War I. I thought I was the luckiest teenager in the world, hanging out in the Pot of Glue listening to those wizened reporters' tales as they knocked back glasses of Brown Ruin.

See, in my day Park Row was the undisputable center of the universe for journalists. Like Fowler, they'd come from all over the country to make a name for themselves. They worked hard, then retired to their favorite saloons to get drunk, exchange outrageous stories, and laugh about the whole goddamned grab bag of humanity that they had to cover. Thanks to Fowler, I not only rubbed shoulders with Runyon and Lardner, but also with social commentator Lucius Beebe, Kenneth C. Beaton, who had a popular column called "Ye Towne Gossip," humorist James Thurber, and

Although there were exceptions, the typical speakeasy eliminated frills and got straight to the business of tanking up the patrons with bootleg liquor.

Winsor McCay, the cartoonist who created the enormously successful comic strip *Little Nemo*. From editors to reporters, photographers, and cartoonists, right down to lowly copyboys, we all prided ourselves on having been part of Park Row's golden era in the twenties.

One night Fowler and some buddies from the *Herald Tribune* were carousing in a speakeasy in the West Forties affectionately called "The Artists and Writers Club," run by a guy named Jack Bleeck. Fowler, Beebe, an old-timer named Houghton, and I'm not sure how many others, were having a helluva good time when a panicked messenger ran into the joint with an urgent message from the *Tribune*'s angry publisher, Ogden Mills Reid.[2] Reid had discovered that there was no lead editorial for the morning edition. He was kicking the shit out of his desk in frustration. Houghton volunteered to rectify the oversight, even though his judgment may have been a little blurred by all the gin. He went back to the newsroom and laboriously typed out a page on his typewriter in about twenty minutes. Houghton handed the paper to a copyboy and returned to his chums at the speakeasy. Typesetters, makeup editors, printers, pressmen, hell, everyone at the *Tribune* was waiting for Houghton's seven column inches of prose to put the paper to bed. The copyboy rushed the proof copy to Mr. Reid. The furious publisher could hardly believe his eyes. The entire goddamned editorial was just one word, typed over and over and over again: "Nevertheless, Nevertheless, Nevertheless. . . ."

The crazy piece was never printed. Fowler wrote that Houghton's effort might have been the most apt description of that era: "It was the 'World of Nevertheless,' a rosy time, the complexion of which now has faded like a clown's face in the rain."[3]

Fortunately, Fowler was there for me when I made reporter. I desperately needed another father figure. Home had become hell. My mother and I were in constant conflict about my lifestyle and career choice. As if my abrupt dismissal from high school hadn't been enough for her, my coming home night after night looking less and less like a reporter and more and more like one of the criminals I'd been covering was a continual source of anxiety and disappointment for the poor woman. I'd been hanging around the morgue so much that my clothes stank of formaldehyde, the fragrance of death clinging to my threadbare suit. And to make matters worse, I was usually in need of a haircut.

"Why can't you get a job with a more respectable paper, with normal working hours?" my mother asked. "Why do you have to be out all night, chasing around after criminals, following the police, hanging around the morgue?"

"Because this is my work, Mother," I said curtly, unable to contain my fury.

"You're like a vulture!"

"I like being a vulture!" I said, slamming the door on my way out.

Rebecca didn't overlook the fact that I'd gotten a raise at the *Graphic* and brought home every penny I earned. To her, though, I was still wasting my life at a sordid job. To me, I was fortunate enough to spend my days and nights at the most scintillating profession on Earth and get paid for it, to boot. I figure that all mothers want their sons to succeed in a "respectable" profession, while the sons are trying to be true to their passion. Conflict is inevitable. In my case, Rebecca saw that I was far too infected with the writing bug to ever be cured. She had no choice but to leave me to my disreputable pursuits, hoping against all odds that I'd grow out of reporting. God bless my mother for loving me so much that she thought she could save me.

Fowler was a revelation for me, the real McCoy, an irreverent, hard-living, lusty newspaperman from the Nothing Sacred School of Reporting. He gave me so much, but one of his greatest gifts was introducing me to Jack Dempsey himself, heavyweight champion of the world. Holy cow, what a thrill to meet one of my childhood idols in person!

Dempsey and Fowler had been friends since their Denver days when Dempsey was starting out and Fowler picked up extra money by not only reporting on the fights but serving as the referee as well. I met the Manassa Mauler at Toots Shor's place one night, where Fowler and Farnsworth had organized a dinner for their boxing cronies, with plentiful T-bone steaks and an unending supply of Mr. Shor's private stock of ale. That night, Fowler recounted for us his elopement with Agnes, his fiancée, in a rushed service in Red Rocks Park, fifteen miles outside Denver. Dempsey had loaned the groom an expensive brown overcoat just for the ceremony.

"Dempsey didn't want to part with that coat," said Fowler. "I begged him to let me wear it so I'd remember my wedding day the rest of my life. And all I can remember is the goddamned coat!"

Gene was not only giving me firsthand lessons in his incorrigible zest for life, he was giving me valuable pointers on being a good reporter. "Writing is easy," he used to say. "All you do is stare at a blank sheet of paper until drops of blood form on your forehead." He'd read my articles published in the *Graphic* and give me potent criticism.

"You're on the right track now, my lad," Fowler said. "But when you cover a murder case, give your articles more spice. Spend some time alone with the criminal, get some personal stuff, a story from his childhood, anything that connects to the reader. No matter how violent the crime, the bastard has a pet canary or sends love poems to his mother. Some human-interest angle. Then follow the trial step by step, never letting up on the heart-tugging details. If the guy ends up frying in the chair at Sing Sing, then write it so strong that the reader can smell his flesh burning. Even if the criminal is a woman."

Fowler spoke from personal experience. He'd covered the sensational Ruth Snyder case, which had titillated America, knocking the Sacco-Vanzetti murder case off the front pages. The Snyder case had split America right down the middle into two camps, for or against the young woman they called the "Iron Widow," who'd killed her husband so she could be with her lover, Judd Gray. Ruth Snyder got the chair on January 12, 1928, the only woman ever to be electrocuted in New York State, providing Fowler with one of the biggest stories of his career.

I still have Gene Fowler's wonderful coverage of the Ruth Snyder trial and execution at Sing Sing. Ruth's life inspired James B. Cain's *The Postman Always Rings Twice* as well as a play and two movie versions adapted

Adulterer, husband killer, seductress, or victim, depending upon your outlook, Ruth Snyder was one of the biggest stories of the twenties.

from Cain's book. The case made a lasting impression on me. Over sixty years later I was going to direct an original movie called *The Chair vs. Ruth Snyder,* coproduced by Martin Scorsese and Jonathan Demme, before my stroke put me and the picture out of commission.

The first execution I witnessed at Ossining's famous prison is engraved forever on my brain. Only a handful of people were allowed into the observation room. Since I was pretty small, the prison warden, Louis Lawes, put me in the front row. The condemned man came in, having walked "the last mile," and sat down in the big wooden chair. Electric wires were attached to his head and to one of his legs. One guard made a brief, set speech, another threw the switch. Three powerful shocks hit the man's body like a runaway train. His body began to shake, his skin turned purple, then blue, and smoke started coming off his flesh. For Chrissakes, he actually started to burn right in front of our eyes! The odor of charred human flesh is something right out of hell. I shudder to remember it.

To watch such a gruesome spectacle turns all your insides upside down. When my mother found out I'd been an eyewitness to an execution, she really raised hell about my professional pursuits. She said that I was heading for something worse than Dante's *Inferno* and she had no intention of being my Beatrice. That first electrocution was followed by one after another until, after a half-dozen more of those revolting state-approved killings, I couldn't take it anymore. I begged Gauvreau to send somebody else to Sing Sing.

"You wanted to be a crime reporter, didn't you?" he said. "This is how society makes murderers pay for their crimes. You've got to cover them, Sammy."

"Give me anything else, even a hanging," I pleaded.

I watched too many people die in this macabre chair at Sing Sing. Hundreds of convicted murderers, including Ruth Snyder and Judd Gray, paid the supreme penalty to society here.

"Get a job in another state. Here, the bastards get the chair."

During my years at the *Graphic,* many fledgling writers worked at the paper. It was a talent incubator, giving cub reporters like me a fabulous opportunity to acquire valuable skills, experience, and moxie that would serve us well in years to come. Several *Graphic* alumni went on to outstanding careers.

Walter Winchell had his first column, called "Your Broadway and Mine," at the *Graphic,* honing the zesty language that, a few years down the line, would make Walter one of the most powerful syndicated columnists in the country. Ed Sullivan joined the *Graphic* staff as a junior sports reporter. Within a couple of seasons, Ed was sports editor, then developed a Broadway gossip column. From there, he got into radio, doing programs on personalities from the sports and theater worlds. By the fifties, Ed Sullivan had become a national television figure with enormous influence. Jerry Wald was seventeen when he convinced Gauvreau to let him write a radio column called "Not on the Air." Jerry went on to produce over fifty

Starting out on the staff of the Graphic
*like me, Ed Sullivan became a force to be
reckoned with on radio, then on television.*

movies, including three respected Joan Crawford vehicles, *Mildred Pierce*
(1945), *Humoresque* (1946), and *Possessed* (1947). For me, Wald's *Johnny
Belinda* (1948), with Jane Wyman, was one of his best. His mercurial career
was supposed to have been one of the inspirations for Budd Schulberg's
famous novel *What Makes Sammy Run*. Norman Krasna joined the
Graphic as a theater critic at age twenty. He'd write more than twenty-five
original screenplays, among them the Oscar-winning *Princess O'Rourke*
(1943), which he also directed.

All of us worked our asses off at the *Graphic* and learned a helluva lot. It
was a great time to be a reporter in New York. Notwithstanding my
mother's carping, I knew that the *Graphic,* for all the opportunities it had
provided me, was only a way station. Long before the paper went out of
business in 1932, I had a deep urge to go after stories with greater social and
political implications, travel to new places, meet different people. West of
the island of Manhattan, there was a big country out there I knew precious
little about. I was itching to discover it for myself.

8

Westward Ho

What reporter didn't get a hard-on from New York, with all its round-the-clock action, fast-paced banter, whiskey-drinking philosophers, glittering talent, and daily Greek tragedies played out on an ever-shifting stage of street corners, glowing skyscrapers, all-night bars, cheap tenements, Broadway theaters, and sports arenas? Manhattan was manna from heaven for a wordsmith. Hell, I loved the place. But now I needed to find out about the rest of the country.

I knew plenty about big-city crime and state executions, yet Philadelphia, Chicago, San Francisco—and everywhere in between—were just names on a map to me. I had to see them for myself. I figured I could hit the road and work my way across the country as a freelance reporter. One of my heroes, Mark Twain, had made it his business to know about the people and the places that made this country great by sailing the Mississippi. It was time for me to get a little firsthand American experience too.

The time and distance away from my mother would do us both some good. Rebecca and I were really getting on each other's nerves. Yet she was completely against my leaving town, worried about unforeseen calamities. I told her everything was going to be fine, promising to stay in touch and to send her money to help her through those tough times. As things turned out, I was able to sell not only freelance articles but also cartoons satirizing the political and social issues of the day. The cartoons went for twenty-five bucks a piece, a lot of dough in Depression times. I regularly wired money back home to Rebecca. Still, she couldn't fathom why her cherished son wanted to bum around the country with a typewriter. Hell, when you're eighteen years old, full of piss and vinegar, and you get a notion to do something, nobody can stop you—nobody—not even your own mother!

Before I left the *Graphic* in the spring of 1931, I had my first brush with

Hollywood. I'd covered a big murder case involving a wealthy business-man named Ridley and his male secretary who were both killed by the same bullet. My story about this unusual double-murder case had run under a big headline that said "WHO KILLED SANTA CLAUS?" See, Ridley was a miserly octogenarian and loved foreclosing mortgages on Christmas Day. I'd written several pieces about the developing investigation, but the murderer had never been found.

Some of the ink from my *Graphic* articles must have rubbed off on the busy fingers of a Hollywood studio story hound. A very classy letter showed up from an executive at Loews Incorporated, the company that owned MGM and a ton of movie theaters. The studio man offered me five grand to write a script based on the Ridley murder case. Five thousand bucks! It had to be a practical joke. I called the studio in Los Angeles and got this fellow on the phone.

"Is this on the level?" I asked.

"Yes, Mr. Fuller," he said. "We think this case would make a good movie."

"Yeah? Well, you know about everything I know. The story's there in my articles. It's public information now."

The studio man explained that they couldn't just lift the story from the newspaper, because of legal restrictions.

"Besides," he said, "we need to find out who was the murderer by the end of the picture."

"The murderer!" I laughed. "The entire New York City police department would like to know that too! They're offering twenty-five grand for any information that leads to his or her arrest."

"We could up the offer," said the studio man.

"You don't get it," I told him. "I'm not hitting you up for more dough. See, this crime may not be solved. Now or ever!"

"*You* don't understand, young man. We're a movie studio. We're just interested in a good story. Make up an ending."

"Make up an ending?"

I thought hard about the Hollywood offer, then turned it down. The money was sure tempting, not for me, but for my family. I just wasn't ready to make up endings for movies. I was a reporter trained to track down the truth. At the time, I wasn't interested in writing fiction. All I could think about was traveling across the country, banging out articles about the people and places I ran across. Real people and real places.

One heard plenty of talk about Park Row newspapermen, not to men-tion renowned novelists and playwrights, going out to Hollywood, bask-ing in the sun, and writing scripts in feathered opulence. Fowler was already out there, having accepted a writing gig on *State's Attorney* (1932), thanks to his buddy John Barrymore, who was starring in the picture. As Gene liked to say, "Let's take the big money and run."

A seed had been planted in my head. Why not give Hollywood a whirl someday, turning stories into movies that would be seen in hundreds of darkened theaters across the country? After all, the great Flaubert had lifted the basic tale of *Emma Bovary* out of a story in the newspapers and turned it into a magnificent novel, giving journalistic facts a psyche and a soul. What I really wanted to do was write a book like *Emma Bovary*, colorful, succinct, a page-turner full of blood and thunder that would grip readers, embroidering philosophy and morality into a heartrending story of love and betrayal. Hollywood could wait for a while.

Without too much fanfare and only a couple of all-night drink fests, I kissed my mother good-bye, said so long to my buddies on Park Row, and hitched a ride on a truck loaded with magazines heading for Pennsylvania. I'd start my American journey in Philadelphia, where our nation was born. I had to cross the Delaware River and see the Liberty Bell for myself. I visited Independence Hall, in Philly's historic district, as well as Carpenter's Hall, site of the First Continental Congress and Christ Church, where Benjamin Franklin is buried. It was really inspiring for me to see where the Declaration of Independence had been signed, in 1776, and where the U.S. Constitution had been drafted, in 1787.

The most exciting thing about Philly was walking in the footsteps of one helluva writer, Thomas Paine. On January 1, 1776, his magnificent *Common Sense* was published, a pamphlet spelling out how the American colonies received no advantage from their mother country, how common sense called for breaking loose from Great Britain. Paine shot straight from the hip, and people loved it. His pamphlet sold more than five hundred thousand copies. That meant that out of a population of about two and a half million, one out of every five colonists got one. Holy mackerel, can you imagine a best-seller today doing that kind of business? What's important is that one man's passionate, straightforward words got through to the people, convincing even the conservatives to declare independence from England half a year later and form a government of their own. Every generation needs to reread Paine's words. They helped create a nation:

> These are the times that try men's souls. The summer soldier and the sunshine patriot will, in this crisis, shrink from the service of their country; but he that stands it now, deserves the love and thanks of man and woman.

*One of the Hoovervilles
I visited in 1932 was south of
downtown Seattle, where the
residents elected their own
mayor and city council.*

From Philadelphia, I started zigzagging across the country by hitching rides on any truck or freight train that was going my way, my typewriter tied to my backpack with a cord. I ended up spending most of my time with people who had no real home. I wrote my first articles on the road about them.

See, outside most cities were "Hoovervilles," where families who'd lost everything had erected shacks made of cardboard, apple crates, scrap lumber, whatever the hell they could lay their hands on. These poor people had been thrown a nasty curveball by the Depression and gone down swinging. Now they were fighting to survive, a brassy, cantankerous lot who lived from hand to mouth. After arriving in some city, I'd get myself out to wherever the local Hooverville was pitched. I'd bring along something to eat, which I shared with the homeless around an open fire, talking to them about their lives, looking for an angle for a story. I'd sleep in a cardboard box or under a sheet of tin leaning against a tree, using my overcoat, my blanket, and my typewriter as a pillow. At the first light of dawn, I'd be typing a story about these forsaken folk, or drawing a cartoon about the lighter side of their gypsy-like existence.

Everywhere I traveled, the poor were trying to make the best of a nasty situation. Even those with homes and steady jobs lived in miserable conditions, almost impossible to understand with the level of affluence we have in America nowadays. This was the low ebb of the Depression, before anyone had heard of rural electrification, agricultural relief, or Social Security. Roosevelt was vigorously pushing through New Deal programs, but it would be years before the effects would take hold and improve conditions for the people I'd visited along my route. I wrote articles and drew cartoons about so many different Americans, coal miners in West Virginia, cowboys in Oklahoma, crab fishermen in Louisiana, cotton pickers in Georgia, milk farmers in Illinois, railroad workers in Florida. My stuff was published regularly in *American Weekly.* A decent check would be waiting for me at the local newspaper office in the next city along my itinerary, addressed to "Samuel Fuller, Freelance." Such was the trust that existed between editors and journeymen reporters in the newspaper business back then.

The closest I got to New York was a stopover in Rochester. I walked into the offices of the *Rochester Journal,* and the city editor handed me a check from the *American Weekly.* He bought one of my cartoons for his own paper. It was times like those that I could afford to check into a cheap hotel and smoke a cigar in a long, hot bath. I hung around Rochester for a few days, did a couple more stories for the paper, and was out of town on the next freight train.

I sent my mother postcards from all over the United States. I was having a terrific time. Sure, I didn't know where I'd be sleeping that night or with whom I'd be having my next meal. Nevertheless, seeing the Appalachians, the Great Lakes, the Mississippi River, the Florida Everglades; hearing the train wheels *clack, clack, clack*ing under my feet; breathing in the tingling air of the Rockies; watching the sunrise from a truck barreling through the wheat fields of Missouri; hitching a ride with a carload of cotton pickers rolling along Route 66; gazing at the glorious sunset across the big skies of West Texas, I was connected to my country like never before. Young people, if you want to understand America, get off your asses and go see it for yourselves! It's a big, breathtaking place!

One day I landed in a suburb of Chicago called Cicero. I was looking for a journalist pal of mine who was supposedly running a publication called *Chicago, America.* Maybe I could sell him some articles, or get some reporting work around the Windy City. I took a room in a cheap boarding house. Around the corner was a huge billiard hall whose owner befriended me. He let me set up my typewriter on an unused pool table in the back of the place under one of those low-hanging, stained-glass lamps. There was

There was no denying that
Al Capone, circa 1932, despite
his murderous profession, had
unmistakable charisma.

an awful racket in there, but I felt right at home because it sounded like a
city newsroom.

One night, I was smoking a cigar and banging away on my Royal when
all the noise in the billiard hall suddenly evaporated. I stopped typing and
looked up. A short, stocky, well-dressed man walked in like he owned the
place. Everybody froze and watched this little round guy and his entourage
of big toughs.

"Who the hell is that?" I asked the shoeshine kid in the corner.

The kid held his finger up to his lips.

"They call him Mister Brown around here," whispered the kid. "But
everyone knows he's really Capone."

"Al Capone?" I said as quietly as a mouse, excited and trembling inside.

Capone and his henchmen came over to play a game of pool at a billiard
table not far from where I was sitting. The noise in the place gradually
ratcheted back to normal, and I tried to resume writing. But it was hard to
concentrate. Then one of Capone's men walked over toward me. I stopped
breathing. The guy looked like a butcher in his best Sunday suit, his neck
bulging under his starched white collar and tie. The big lug put his massive
hand on the edge of the pool table, leaned over my shoulder, and stared at
the paper in my typewriter.

"Hey, kid," he said. "Mister Brown wantsa know what you're writin'."

I looked up and saw Al Capone peering at me with a little smile. He had thick eyebrows and a double chin. I could make out the famous scar on his cheek.

"I'm writing articles about the homeless," I said.

The guy went back over to Capone and whispered in his ear. Capone smiled at me, calling out in a high-pitched Italian accent, "Another Winchell!" His henchmen got a big laugh out of that line. "I'm homeless, too, kid," continued Capone. "Look me up and I'll give you an interview."

His goons started laughing again. I smiled and waved respectfully. I wished I were a million miles away from that pool hall in Cicero, Illinois. But I knew I had to sit tight. Capone and his men loosened their ties, shot some pool, and had plenty of laughs only a few feet in front of me that night. Prohibition was still on, but they were served mug after mug of cold beer as if the Volstead Act of 1919 didn't exist. If you hadn't known they were some of America's most dangerous gangsters, you'd have thought it was just a group of traveling salesmen having some hearty fun. I'd never forget that disturbing mix of charm and menace in America's greatest mobster.

The next time I saw Capone's mug, it was plastered all over the front page of a newspaper. He'd been convicted of income tax evasion and sentenced to eleven years in prison. Released in 1939, Capone spent the rest of his life an invalid, crippled by syphilis. I never looked him up to get that promised interview.

My travels took me across the country to the West Coast, ending up in San Francisco, a city I adored. There I found a temporary job as a crime reporter for the *Chronicle* under editor in chief George Cameron and stayed on for a while. I was in Frisco in 1934 when the General Strike was called. It grew out of a labor dispute on the docks that spread like wildfire. As the strike date approached, food supplies trickled into the city, then ceased being delivered altogether when trucks, trains, and ships stopped running. Hospitals closed their doors to the sick. Garbage piled up on street corners. Public transportation ground to a complete halt. Communication, whether by telephone, telegraph, or mail, was next to impossible. The putrid smell of decay wafted through the streets. For Chrissakes, it was like a war zone!

The city teetered on the edge of a violent confrontation between its hungry citizens and police. On the eve of the General Strike, it happened. A riot broke out in front of the Ferry Building, where hundreds of panicked people raided food stands and counters. The looting rapidly turned into general chaos. Wearing gas masks and armed with riot guns and tear gas, the police couldn't control the mobs. So they called in the army. I'll

On the eve of the General Strike, 1934, San Francisco police prepare for trouble. They wouldn't be able to contain the violence.

never forget that scene as the big green trucks rolled in, soldiers leaping out, firing their rifles in the air, then turning to shoot machine guns at some of the most virulent rioters, wounded men and women falling in the street, finally crushing the insurgence. Perched in the back of a jeep, calmly directing the madness, was General Douglas MacArthur himself. At the time, MacArthur was army chief of staff and only at the debut of his illustrious career. He would leave a bitter taste in people's mouths that day in San Francisco by attacking fellow Americans.

I wrote my mother from San Francisco on Sunday, July 15, 1934:

Darlink Mammy!
War is declared!
No kidding—there's actual warfare in this town now! *What scenes!* Hundreds of cops with machine guns riding up & down the streets in autos. Soldiers & sailors parading the streets
—windows smashed!—people starving! The main street—Market—is *deserted*! Can you imagine Times Square *deserted*?
Anyway, don't worry about me! I'm actually seeing Martial Law for the first time. I saw soldiers fire machine guns into 500 strikers!

I saw more cutthroats hanging in the alleys for holdups than I ever could hope to imagine.

Well, this store may have to close. I have a job on the local paper for $25 a week if I remain steady. Love to all—Gee, what a sight!

Sammy

A couple days after the riot, I was walking by Tiny's Waffle Shop, a San Francisco landmark. The city editor had sent me out on the street to get local-color stories about how the crisis was affecting Frisco residents. There was a long line of people waiting to get into the restaurant. I stood in line too, striking up a conversation with the friendly old lady behind me.

"Do you like pig knuckles?" she asked me confidentially.

"I'm so hungry," I said, "I guess I'd eat anything."

"Follow me, then," she said.

We walked over to the Francis Hotel, where the old lady lived in a tiny room that hardly had enough space for a bed. She was secretary to one of the organizers of the strike, Communist Party chief Earl Browder. She opened her closet. Where clothes should have been hanging up, she had suspended pig knuckles, dozens and dozens of them.

"How'd you get all these?" I asked.

"Before MacArthur and those army bastards opened fire on the people, I filled up two bags with pig knuckles and got the hell out of there."

"Did it feel like stealing?"

"Hell, no!" she said. "When you're hungry, you'll do anything. Anything!"

"Why were you waiting in line at the Waffle Shop?"

"Because I love waffles!" she laughed. "Can't get them at the hotel. I don't think I could eat another pig knuckle!"

Things got worse before they got better. No grocery store owner was safe because people were so hungry, they were on the verge of killing for food. Public order had totally broken down. As a reporter in New York, I'd seen a race riot in Harlem, with people looting stores for food. But that was nothing next to the panic and desperation of the 1934 General Strike in San Francisco. Hell, I saw corpses in the streets that weren't even picked up by the city morgue! My articles for the *Chronicle* described the hunger, violence, and anarchy I saw firsthand, mixing in some of the lighter aspects of the chaos, like the pig-knuckles. The *Chronicle* syndicated my stuff to other papers across the country. There were many angry reactions. People thought that scenes like those I'd described just couldn't take place in America. But they did.

It was the first time I realized how much human behavior was controlled by the belly, not the brain. I thought about *Les Miserables,* by Victor Hugo, and the deeper truth of Jean Valjean's plea for a little bit of bread. When people hear the growling of their empty stomachs in their own homes, it will soon turn into screams heard in their towns and cities and finally a roar throughout their country. At the root of social upheaval was poverty and hunger, breeding discontent and hatred.

Hatred was also born of fear. For a real eye-opener, there was nothing that could surpass the Ku Klux Klan meetings I covered in Little Rock, Arkansas. My editor at *American Weekly* had sent me to the cradle of the Klan to write a firsthand report about their strange rituals. I got to Little Rock and was tipped off where the Klan held their secret meetings. One night I found myself surrounded by thirty KKK members wearing white sheets and parading around a burning cross. It was an overwhelming spectacle that left me depressed and disillusioned that this could happen in America. My mother had raised me to respect people of all cultures, to honor the idea that America was great because of its melting pot of peoples. Those KKK psychopaths proselytizing about white supremacy, lynching, and violence deeply disturbed me, shaking up my youthful idealism that all Americans loved and respected real democratic values.

In my article about the KKK, I wrote about their hate-filled speeches, contrasting their rancorous words with the spectacle of a woman in a Klan costume nursing her newborn baby. The woman's face was hidden under that ridiculous pillowcase with holes cut out for her nose and eyes. She slowly opened the robe to put her breast into the mouth of the little baby, the Ku Klux Klan members screaming racial rubbish while the mother gave sweet sustenance to the infant. My editor at *American Weekly* cut the part about the woman nursing her baby because it sounded so far-fetched. When I saw the published version of my article, I was so upset that I called him to complain, making sure the operator reversed the charges.

"The way I wrote it was just the way it was!" I said.

"You should have taken photos of the woman with her baby," said the editor.

"I'm a newspaperman, goddamnit, not a photographer!"

My editor was right, though. A picture would have made my words believable. In fact, a photo of the Klan woman nursing a baby would have been more powerful than all my words. Then and there, I found a cheap camera in a pawnshop and began taking pictures to accompany my stories. I was beginning to realize that I could better convey emotions with words *and* images. And not just any image, but the precise image that captured a multitude of emotions in a frozen instant. Jean-Luc Godard's famous quip

514 LARKIN ST.
SAN FRANCISCO,
CALIF.

SAN FRANCISCO CALIF.
JUL 17
5:30 PM
1934

ADDRESS
YOUR MAIL
TO
STREET AND
NUMBER

U.S. POSTAGE

MRS. R. FULLER
436 FT. WASHINGTON AVE.
NEW YORK,
N. Y.

GUN

SAMMY FULLER

Tues. July 17, 1934

Darlink Mammy, Tina + Ray —

Well - this is the second
day of the General Strike.
Only about ½ doz. stores were
wrecked. Looks like serious
Trouble will begin tomorrow.
Whatever you read to N. Y.
papers — don't worry. I'm
okay. Theres a nest of
machine guns up here in

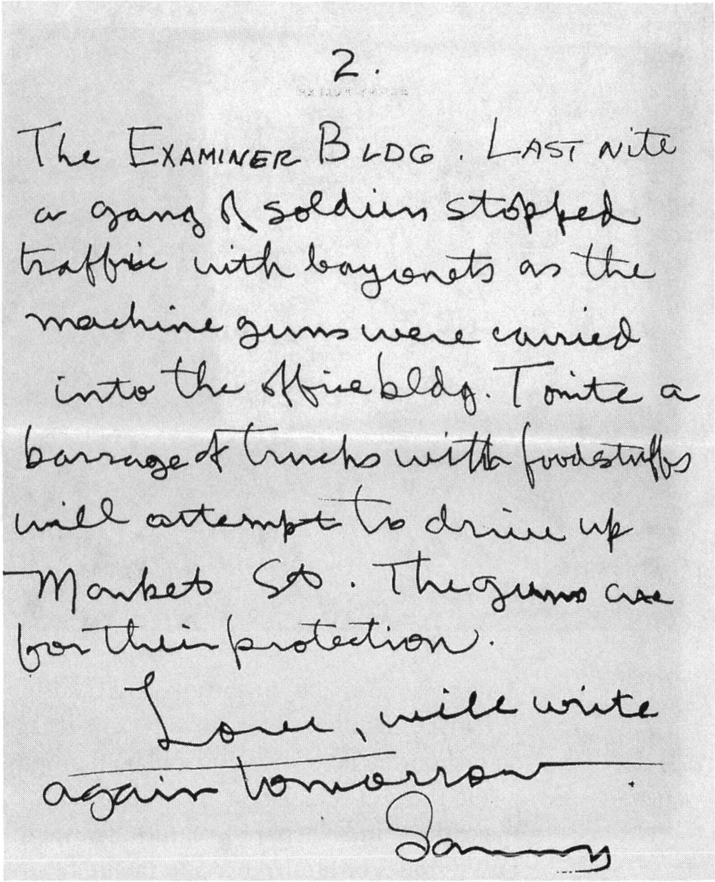

2.

The EXAMINER BLDG. LAST nite a gang of soldiers stopped traffic with bayonets as the machine guns were carried into the office bldg. Tonite a barrage of trucks with foodstuffs will attempt to drive up Market St. The guns are for their protection.

Love, will write again tomorrow

Sammy

A letter to my mother
from Frisco during
the General Strike.

hit the nail on the head: "Ce n'est pas juste une image, c'est une image juste" ("It's not just an image, it's a just image").

My travels finally landed me in San Diego. As usual, I took up quarters with the homeless at the edge of town. One day, the truckers called a strike protesting their wages and working conditions, stranding truckloads of fresh milk on the road. The homeless helped themselves to all the milk they wanted. We ended up filling barrels and taking milk baths like Marie-Antoinette. It was a unique moment of frivolity in a dark and disillusioned time.

I got a job at the *San Diego Sun* covering the waterfront and stayed there quite a while. I tried my hand at writing editorials, too, rousing people with my natural idealism. I loved spouting off my opinions in print.

If only I had had a photo like this one of a KKK rally, my article about their hate-filled meetings and racist babble would have been more convincing.

There was so much misfortune and hardship, it wasn't difficult at all for me to pick issues and start shooting fierce criticism and bold proposals at them. I was intent on using words to make the world a better place, turning over the heavy stones of intolerance and prejudice into the warm sunlight of truth. I suppose it was youthful fervor, but it's never gone away. I still believe we must fight intolerance in every way possible.

When I got the news that my twenty-seven-year-old brother Tom was very ill, I decided it was time to go back to New York. He'd contracted a rare kind of ulcer and died soon after I got back into town. It was a terrible blow to all of us, especially my mother. Rebecca was very brave, holding her head high and carrying on stoically, but inside she was heartbroken. We needed to mourn Tom's death together, as a family. I'd been on the road for a few years. Now I decided to stay home for a while, help out my mother, and re-plunge into the political and social turbulence of New York in the thirties.

9

Chaos and Bewilderment

I'd changed. America was no longer a mystery to me. I'd traveled to the four corners of this country, met its many peoples, and observed the ugly fault lines that were looming just beneath the surface of our nation.

New York had changed too. It was still a fabulously diverse city, capital of finance, disburser of information, platform of opinion, showcase of artists, leader of style, hotbed of crime. But the jazzy, frivolous breeze of the twenties had been knocked out of New York's sails, replaced by the harsh winds of the Great Depression blowing through its cavernous thoroughfares, its genteel parks, and its bustling boroughs, bearing the same disenchantment that I'd experienced elsewhere in the country.

The economic strife and social conflicts of the thirties swept not only across America but around the world, offering power-mad leaders the opportunity to serve up appealing yet virulent "isms" to people faced with hunger and hopelessness. I was about to run headfirst into the two ideologies—fascism and communism—that were to mark my life and times so deeply.

Although I was offered regular reporter jobs on big dailies, I'd gotten accustomed to working freelance during my travels. Thanks to my editor at the *American Weekly* and some friends on Park Row, I only took on special assignments for in-depth articles on subjects that intrigued me. What I really wanted to do was turn out a book. I'd started writing fiction while I was on the road. I was about twenty-two when I finished my first novel, called *Burn, Baby, Burn.*

The yarn kicks off with a pregnant woman condemned to die in the chair. I must have been so obsessed with the electric chair that I used it as a fictional hook, finding a release for some of my nightmarish memories of prisoners getting fried at Sing Sing. Is it moral to execute a condemned woman *and* her innocent, unborn child? My hero is a hotshot New York reporter, named Bradagher, who covers the story. The young wise guy

accepts an offer from a Hollywood bigwig to go out to the West Coast and
develop his articles about the case into a movie script. The brash, fast-
talking, whiskey-drinking Bradagher thinks he's got the world by the tail.
Then he falls for a gorgeous blonde who happens to be a reporter-turned-
screenwriter, too. She's developing a similar script for a rival studio.
Bradagher discovers he's in way over his head, and all his shrewdness
causes him to land flat on his face. Only by digging deep into his heart
does he find love and fulfillment in my closing chapter.

I got a big kick out of spinning that tale, weaving in tributes to Park
Row mentors like Gene Fowler, knocking out an unrepentant love story,
shifting scenes from Manhattan to Hollywood and the world of studio
screenwriting. The Hollywood stuff in *Burn, Baby, Burn* came from my
brief visit to see Fowler in la-la land during my hobo period. Gene had a
sumptuous setup out there, though he never took any of it very seriously.
He and his pals were cheerfully cynical about the fast bucks and shallow
nature of the movie business, calling Louis B. Mayer, chief of Metro-
Goldwyn-Mayer, "Louis B. Manure." Fowler let me camp out on the
couch in his luxurious Beverly Hills home and bought me some new
trousers. Most importantly, he introduced me to some of the renowned
writers who were doctoring scripts in those days. My most memorable
encounter was with Dorothy Parker, whose reputation as a caustic wise gal
didn't prepare me for her warmth and wit. Sitting around Gene's living
room one evening with some of his pals, knocking back one martini after
another, Parker recounted that some pompous studio executive was man-
gling one of her screenplays.

"Don't wave your finger at me," she'd advised him. "Remember when it
had a thimble on it."

Parker took a liking to me and told me to write her from the road and
tell her about my travels. She gave me her card and asked me for mine. I
didn't have one then or ever. I'll never forget how she scribbled my Manhattan address inside the hem of her dress. There never was any exchange
of correspondence. I lost her card, and she must have gotten the dress
cleaned.

My editor at *American Weekly* liked *Burn, Baby, Burn* enough to serial-
ize it. Then it was picked up by Phoenix Press, a small publishing house
that brought it out in 1935. Rebecca was so proud of her son, "the author."
I was thrilled to be a published novelist even if my book was what we
called "pulp fiction" in those days. It got one printing run, and I got a
check for a grand or two. That was that, no reprints or backlisting. I dedicated *Burn, Baby, Burn* to Perc Westmore, "the only man God can sue."
Out in California, I'd become pals with Westmore, one of the most impor-

tant makeup artists of the day. Perc had been very helpful by showing me around the studios, giving me an insider's look at Hollywood.

I began zigzagging between journalism and fiction, with the two usually overlapping. One of my freelance assignments was writing a piece on Dr. Alexis Carrel, the Frenchman who'd won a Nobel Prize in 1912 for the development of a technique for suturing blood vessels. At the time I met Carrel, he was working on an artificial heart pump. When I was walked into Carrel's office for my first interview, I was surprised to see none other than the tall, handsome Charles Lindbergh walking out. Lindbergh was, of course, a national hero since his historic flight across the Atlantic in 1927 in the *Spirit of St. Louis*. Carrel and Lindbergh, an engineer in his own right, were collaborating on the artificial heart and would coauthor *The Culture of Organs* (1938). That was the first of my three memorable encounters with Lindbergh in the thirties that would totally change my opinion of the man.

Meanwhile Dr. Carrel had pioneered research on artificial insemination, developing all the ideal conditions for conceiving an "ectogenetic baby" in the mother's uterus by laboratory means. My article painted a portrait of the brilliant doctor and discussed his groundbreaking studies. It also gave me an idea for my second novel.

Fascinated with the idea of a baby being cultured like a pearl, I came up with a tale about a mother who fervently desires her son to be perfect, only to see her beloved creation turn out terribly flawed. Entitled *Test Tube Baby*, my second novel was published in 1936 by another pulp fiction house, Godwin. My hero, Jimmy Garrison, is conceived scientifically, then brought up by his mother to be the ideal son. Things go awry when Jimmy falls in love with the wanton Peggy and commits a very imperfect murder. He is caught and brought to trial. The final melodramatic scene describes Jimmy's acquittal and his mother's remorse and apology.

No doubt about it, some of my anger against my own mother was allowed a healthy outlet in *Test Tube Baby*. With her abundant yet overbearing love, Rebecca was always urging me to better my station in life, driving me crazy with her good intentions. At the time, she was on a campaign to match me up with a certain young lady whose parents owned the Altman Department Stores, for no other reason than to see her dream for me—marrying a rich girl—fulfilled. Nothing could have been further from my ambition. Writing *Test Tube Baby* was therapeutic, because it allowed me to vent my frustration as well as to forgive my mother. The novel's troubling theme of human perfection resounded far deeper than one family's misguided idealism. I'd been closely following the political movements of the thirties, with both the left and the right trying to sell people on their flawed ideologies as the only way to a perfect society.

The rise of Nazism in Germany and its leader, Adolf Hitler (born Adolf Schicklgruber), was very troublesome. Hitler never tired of spouting that goddamned trash about an Aryan superrace, claimed that providence was on their side. No self-respecting Nazi would ever use the word "God," but that's what the sonsofbitches meant. It was the zenith of arrogance, twisting the perfection scheme that dated back to Aristotle into an incredibly perverse and destructive system. See, Aristotle taught his students, among them Alexander the Great, that all beings in the world aspire to be perfect because God is perfect. In old Greek, however, "perfection" means "arrogance." Aristotle's arrogance was a forerunner of the Nazi's superrace madness. The ancient philosopher condoned slavery and excluded women, children, non-Greeks, and manual workers from his perfection scheme. I've always been skeptical about any bastard, whether his name's Adolf or Aristotle, who claims that God is on his side, that certain races are superior to others, that people need to be subdued or brainwashed for the betterment of society. For Chrissakes, give people the truth! They can figure out what the hell they want to do all on their own.

By the early thirties, Mussolini had already imposed fascism in Italy. The Italians invaded Ethiopia in 1935. After attempting to resist the fascists, then pleading unsuccessfully for help from the League of Nations, Haile Selassie went into exile in England. I respected Selassie and rooted for that small, vibrant man whom they called the "Lion of the Desert," even if he sometimes seemed more concerned about his own power than his people's destiny.

The Spanish Civil War broke out in 1936. Franco and his band of generals seized control of the country and turned the Spanish armies against the elected Republican government. The Germans and Italians were sending troops and arms to Franco. He accepted their aid—as well as their fascist ideas—all too eagerly.

That's when I wrote a piece for *American Weekly* about the Lincoln Brigade, the regiment of American volunteers who were recruited to fight alongside the Republicans in Spain. I interviewed their leaders and talked to some of the men who were enlisting. Abraham Lincoln was one of my heroes. To use his name for a military squadron was magic for me. Lincoln was no innocent, but a shrewd politician and war strategist. The brigade's volunteers were working-class men, sensible and mature, not youngsters drafted into a war that they didn't understand. They thought they would make a difference by stopping the spread of fascism in Europe. Hell, I almost joined the Lincoln Brigade myself, writing a series of articles from the front lines in Spain. However, my first responsibility was to stay home and support my mother.

Even as events demanded that America play a leading role on the world's stage, the isolationist movement, led by conservatives like Senators Robert Taft and Arthur Vandenberg, became more powerful. The supposed free press in this country was leaning further and further right. Robert Rutherford McCormick, editor and publisher of the *Chicago Tribune,* made speeches asking Americans to overlook what was happening in Germany, Italy, Spain, and Ethiopia. More and more papers, including Hearst's, were veering further right in their coverage of the news. Something was very sick in our nation when big money and press barons hooked up to keep America aloof from the rest of the world. Holy shit, it was tantamount to giving fascists a green light!

To find out what was happening on the opposite side of the political spectrum, I visited the Park Row newsrooms of the *Daily Worker* and *People's World,* real papers back then, with linotypes, editing rooms, and a place on newsstands. I enjoyed their spirited slant on events, but I had enormous doubts about communism as an ideology, much less as a workable system. Thank God there was still a little room on that street to print diverse opinions! Many of America's finest writers and poets were published in the lefty papers.

Since 1918, communism had been called Bolshevism in the United States. The Soviet Union had only been officially recognized by President Roosevelt in 1934. I'd covered some communist meetings in Greenwich Village and sold some cartoons about Bolshevists, comically drawing them as men with beards and bombs. The communists I interviewed were intellectual dreamers and do-gooders, certainly not the dangerous revolutionaries that the conservative press invariably portrayed. I was lucky to be able to discuss communism with Maxwell Bodenheim, a fine poet and writer who was very close to John Reed, author of the best-seller *Ten Days That Shook the World* (1919), a firsthand account of the Russian Revolution. Bodenheim was a good friend of my mother's, and we both cherished him. A lovely, warm guy, Max often came to dinner at our apartment, and our animated discussions lasted late into the night. I was very pleased that Warren Beatty paid homage to Max in his film *Reds* (1981). I'll never forget how, back when I was still a copyboy at the *Journal,* Bodenheim had been invited to the newsroom to recite his poetry in front of scores of busy journalists. They were a noisy lot, but soon everyone fell absolutely silent, listening wordlessly to Bodenheim's remarkable voice. One of his best novels is *Blackguard* (1923). Max died in 1954. As a private tribute, I named the mad nuclear scientist in *Shock Corridor* Boden.

Some of our finest writers in the thirties were deeply influenced by Marx. I remember a photo of the prominent playwright Lillian Hellman

Our good friend Maxwell Bodenheim was a lovely human being, a distinguished poet and novelist, and an idealistic communist, in that order.

kissing Stalin on the cheek. I'd read Marx and found him tedious. My travels across America led me to believe that communism was a fantasy that would never supplant democracy among ordinary folk unless they were coerced. In succeeding years, it became clear to everyone that Stalin was a totalitarian who, like Hitler, resorted to shoving his "ism" down his own people's throats as well as those of his neighbors. The Hitler-Stalin Pact of 1939 proved conclusively just how much those two self-serving demagogues admired each other.

My second encounter with Charles Lindbergh was at the Teterboro Airport, in New Jersey, where he'd touched down in a small airplane on one of his goodwill tours. I was standing with a small group of newspapermen who were covering the event. Lindbergh had recently traveled through Europe, where he'd accepted a decoration from Hitler and praised the German air force. When Lindbergh asked for some help turning his plane around on the runway, not one reporter would give him a hand. I remember Lindbergh's face that day, stung by the resentment that his pro-German statements had provoked among the press. Sure, everybody felt sorry for him because of the great tragedy he and his wife had suffered in 1932, when their baby was kidnapped and killed. Yet Lindbergh had

The third and final time I ran into Charles Lindbergh in the thirties was an affront to American democracy.

become an embarrassment for America and democracy.

That sentiment was confirmed the last time I saw Lindbergh, at Madison Square Garden while covering an America First rally. When I got into the Garden and made my way to the press section, I could hardly believe that above our heads, where Jack Dempsey, Kid Chocolate, and Max Baer had had their slugfests, Nazi flags were unfurled. Throughout the crowd, people were waving small flags with swastikas. I was horrified, yet proud that I lived in a country where you could wave any goddamned flag you wanted.

Gerald L. K. Smith, founder of the America First movement and one-time lieutenant of Huey Long, keynoted that unforgettable evening with a reactionary speech, a clever concoction of patriotism, pacifism, and racism. One after another, the America First rabble-rousers rallied the crowd with their extremist, pro-Nazi speeches. I was shocked that they called themselves "patriots" even though the bastards were desecrating the very principles underlying our nation. For cryin' out loud, they were spouting this racist crap in the very arena where great athletes won or lost contests based on their abilities and determination, not on their politics or the color of their skin. These people may have had the right to fly their flags, but the swastikas floating above our heads were an insult to Americans everywhere.

In the middle of the mass hysteria, the great newspaperwoman Dorothy Thompson, wife of Sinclair Lewis, got up on the stage, walked to the podium, and demanded to speak. When she was refused, Thompson grabbed the microphone and shouted at the crowd, "What you stand for is the worst thing in the world . . . !"

Before she could get another word out, some strong-arms lifted Thompson up and forcibly escorted her off the stage. She struggled and even kicked one of the guys with her feet. Holy mackerel, what balls on that lady! The crowd booed, drowning out the wild cheers from us in the press section. I'll never forget the courage and single-mindedness that night of Dorothy Thompson trying to speak the truth.

I went to the Garden rally to see for myself why the America First movement was gaining support during such tough times. What I found out was that their simplistic, hate-filled message got through *because* times were tough. People were struggling to make ends meet, so their fears and baser instincts could be thumped like a drum, creating the specter of an intolerant people ready to neglect the basic rights provided for in the Constitution.

Charles Lindbergh was the featured speaker at the rally. He was wildly cheered by the swastika-waving crowds that night. His antiwar speech was laced with esteem for the German war machine. Something turned inside my stomach that a national figure would allow himself to be used as a vehicle for the disgusting Nazi propaganda.

As Clare Boothe Luce once said about the thirties, "Anyone who isn't thoroughly confused isn't thinking clearly." It was a time of chaos and bewilderment that helped me discover in myself a profound and unwavering commitment to democratic principles. I felt deeply that America needed to be a leader, not hide its head in the sand. Our nation should have been showing the way to democracy, helping to maintain world

Dorothy Thompson. We cheered like hell when she tried to call a spade a spade at the America First rally in Madison Square Garden.

peace and seeing that no one went hungry. It was utopian but feasible.

I love my country profoundly. But please, please, don't call me a patriot. The word has been used by so many hatemongers that I've grown to despise it. According to Mark Twain, "patriotism is the last resort of a scoundrel."

Smack dab in the middle of the period's upheavals, Hollywood came calling again. Big-shot Broadway producer Boris Petroff asked me to meet him for drinks at the Plaza Hotel because he'd read *Burn, Baby, Burn*. He'd produced Mae West's variety shows on the Great White Way. Petroff asked me to write a treatment for a lighthearted comedy, no matter how preposterous. I accepted the challenge and concocted a yarn about two prehistoric cities who declare war on each other. The cities square off because each wants the services of one of the great showmen of the day to create elaborate musical numbers with beautiful girls diving into swimming pools. My yarn started two million years ago, when our ancestors, the cavemen, were defending their families against saber-toothed tigers. I figured people would laugh about the chaos of our own times if they could see how little our society had evolved since prehistory. Petroff cut out all the political aspects of my story, kept only the most absurd stuff, and made *Hats Off* (1937), with John Payne, a big star in those days. I got my first writing credit on a movie, even though the finished film had just about nothing to do with my original story. Petroff fashioned a movie that made people for-get about their problems. I'd wanted to expose man's foolish belligerency.

Writing for the movies was a kick, a whole new world that seemed to have little to do with the truth as I understood it. The only truth that mat-tered in the movie business was selling a helluva lot of tickets to see your finished film. As a screenwriter, I was like one of those saber-toothed tigers in my story, burdened with the stripes of a reporter's instinct for facts, encumbered with the long teeth of social consciousness. If I really wanted to write scripts for a living, I needed to evolve into a more agile, stream-lined creature, wising up to the ways and means of making movies. What better way to find out if I could survive than to throw myself smack-dab into the middle of the Hollywood jungle?

10

Added Zeroes

My next book was called *Make Up and Kiss,* about the beauty-products industry and its enormous profits. It was another piece of pulp fiction, a tale about a young man who inherits a successful cosmetic firm only to uncover that the business is a high-stakes financial scam. There was the obligatory love story that allowed my hero to discover that the best beauty products are still water and soap.

After the publication of *Make Up and Kiss,* an important New York publisher called me into his office. I thought he was going to offer me a multibook contract. He did, but not for my novels. See, they had a best-selling author under contract who couldn't produce as many books as they could sell. So I was offered the job of ghostwriting books for him. I was happy to have the work. The publisher would give me a snappy title, a paragraph with the premise for the novel, the principal characters, and the required length. The rest was up to me. The books usually ran anywhere from fifty to seventy-five thousand words. Deadlines were tight, maybe three, sometimes four weeks to deliver the completed manuscript. The tales were usually murder stories, pretty easy for me to knock out. I really didn't give a damn about my writing being published under another author's byline. I was getting valuable experience and being paid for it. The money allowed me to move my mother into a more comfortable apartment. Who was the famous author I ghosted for? I'll never say. That was part of the deal.

Offers to write original stories for the movies also started to come my way. Hell, studio development executives were willing to pay a couple thousand bucks for a twenty-page treatment. With a few published books under my belt, not to mention the ghostwritten books that I could never take credit for, scriptwriting seemed the next logical step. I had plenty of yarns up my sleeve, so I decided to take a trip out to the West Coast and finally take a serious dip in Hollywood's seductive waters. I was being drawn out there like one of those Pullman cars I boarded with my trusty Royal at Grand Central Station, bound for California. I planned on staying a month. That month would last about three years.

A cross-country train trip back then took three nights and four days. It was hard to believe that only a couple years before, I'd made the trip in a cattle car on a freight train. Now I had my own compartment. I propped my typewriter up on the seat and typed away on the ghosted manuscript I needed to finish for an upcoming deadline. After a full day of writing, I walked to the dining car. In those days, they had steaks, linen tablecloths, heavy silverware, the works. After dinner, you could go out on the little deck at the back of the train and smoke a cigar. The great American countryside swept past you. Mountainous clouds overhead were turning orange then violet as the sun set behind the Rockies. When the tracks took a bend, you could catch a glimpse of the powerful locomotive at the head of the train, chugging relentlessly toward the Pacific, pulling me toward a new stage of my life.

A few days after my arrival, I had a little walk-up apartment in West Hollywood and an invitation to have lunch with Gene Fowler at RKO. It was great seeing Gene again. He was tanned and cheerful. Sitting in the studio canteen, we exchanged news of our journalistic pals back east. Fowler noticed me staring over his shoulder at Bette Davis, Victor McLaglen, Paul Muni, Louise Rainer, and Cary Grant. I couldn't believe all that talent was sitting there under one roof, almost like factory workers, having a quick bite to eat before resuming a normal workday on the assembly line.

Fowler didn't waste any time getting to the point. He motioned with his head at the actors and actresses, each of them stars.

"They need lines to say up there on the screen," he said. "That's why they pay guys like you and me, Sammy."

Gene took an envelope out of his breast pocket. Inside was a check. He unfolded the check and wiggled it under my nose.

"Watch the moving finger," he said.

Holding the check up directly in front of my eyes, he playfully hid the dollar amount under his thumb. Then he slowly slid his thumb to the right. Gradually, Fowler uncovered a "5," then a "0," then another "0," then, gleefully, another "0."

"That's spending money every week, my lad!"

I took a hard look at that check. I could hardly believe that five thousand bucks was nothing unusual for a week's worth of scriptwriting in Hollywood. Gene explained that it was no great shakes, that plenty of writers made more. Outside, the palm trees nodded invitingly, the sun was shining, the lawns were green and well tended. I envisioned my mother in white tennis shorts, tanned and enjoying herself. I saw myself driving a big convertible with Bette Davis in the front seat, discussing her next picture. Of course, I'd never actually written a screenplay, but with my enthusiasm and naïveté, there were no obstacles I couldn't overcome. Fowler reassured me that it was a cinch writing movies, as easy as "the twinkle in a starlet's eye." Why not give it a go?

That was a terrific time to be in Hollywood, the so-called Golden Age. Studios were enormous entertainment factories teeming with writers, actors, technicians, musicians, and editors, churning out movie after movie, their coffers overflowing with monies flowing back from the hundreds of movie houses they owned across America. They had another twenty years of good times before they'd be divested of their theater chains and contract players in the fifties, turning the gold to tinsel.

After lunch, Gene shoved a Montecristo No. 1 in my mouth and took me for a walk around the studio lot. He turned to me, as irreverent and playful as ever, and asked, "How'd you like to make a few hundred bucks right now?"

"How?" I said.

"By drawing a couple of cartoons."

"Okay."

He took me into one of the big soundstages at RKO, where they were shooting a picture with a script he'd doctored. It starred two well-known actors at that time, Eric Linden and Arlene Judge, to whom Fowler introduced me. The set designer needed some ink drawings for an insert in the next day's scene, something with a couple of arrows there, a pierced heart here, and a few drops of blood oozing from the heart. It took me about ten minutes to do them. The producer was pleased and told me to come by the production office the next day for my money. I'd earned my first Hollywood paycheck, and I hadn't been in town more than seventy-two hours.

Fowler showed me his office in the writers' wing. "You're going to do fine around here, Sammy," he told me, always my adviser. "We'll have a lot of laughs. But after you've made a little bundle, you've got to scram before you become like one of them." Gene pointed out the window at a couple of studio executives passing on the sidewalk.

As we chatted, the writer/producer Myles Connolly walked in. He was a wonderful man, and we hit it off immediately. Gene praised my writing skills, so Myles invited me over to Columbia to discuss a movie project. The very next day, Myles was showing me around the studio. He introduced me to a young director named Frank Capra. Born in Palermo, Sicily, Capra came out to Hollywood as a writer for Mack Sennett. He was warm and good-humored, with a winning smile and an unpretentious manner. When I met Frank, he'd already won an Oscar for best director, for *It Happened One Night,* in 1935. I'll never forget how encouraging he was to a novice screenwriter. Frank would always remain the same sweet gentleman.

Myles and I started throwing around ideas for his picture. It was supposed to be about a character based on Tom Mix, the cowboy star of silent films who'd made scores of Westerns. Then came the talkies, and Mix didn't make the transition successfully. Myles and I came up with a story about a silent cowboy star who doesn't want to play a gangster role in a talkie because he wants to be loyal to his fans. He doesn't want to disappoint the kids who are crazy about his Westerns. We called it *Once a Hero,* but after the movie went into production, they gave it the more commercial title of *It Happened in Hollywood.*

Harry Lachman, who'd been a successful painter in Paris, directed the picture. Lachman is forgotten today, but he made over thirty movies before he stopped directing in the early forties. Fay Wray played the female lead. This was after *King Kong* (1933) distinguished her from all the pretty blondes of the day as the one who could scream the best. The Tom Mix character, Tim Bart, was played by Richard Dix. *It Happened in Hollywood* was my first real credit on a picture.

Soon after that movie was released, a big executive at one of the studios called me into his office and offered to give me a job writing scripts adapted from famous books. It was very much like my gig ghostwriting novels. An established screenwriter would get credit for my work. The money was good, but I had to promise never to discuss my participation. I must have written a half-dozen scripts without my name appearing anywhere in those pictures' credits, some of them major productions.

That was my personal screenwriting school. I needed to get the hang of this unique craft. Being a ghost screenwriter was more amusing than being a ghost novelist. After all, my work ended up on the big screen. I didn't really care about the credits. Fowler and my other writer friends in Hollywood used to try to guess the name of the movie I'd worked on. It was one of their favorite games over martinis at Musso & Frank's. I puffed contentedly on my cigar and smiled like a Cheshire cat, never revealing whom I ghosted for. The steady pay would allow me to begin writing my own scripts.

I can talk about Otto Preminger, the last director for whom I wrote anonymously, because he mentions it in his autobiography. I enjoyed working with Otto, who looked like a mean old bulldog but was a complex, lovable guy. Preminger was especially criticized when Jean Seberg got

*Otto Preminger, with whom
my relationship was productive
but sometimes bumpy*

singed during the shooting of the final scene for *Saint Joan* (1957), but
Otto wasn't the only director who pushed actors hard for great performances.

Born in Vienna, Preminger got a law degree to please his parents. But
his heart was in the theater, working as an actor and director with the great
Max Reinhardt. To escape the Nazis, Otto emigrated to the States in 1935.
Before coming out to Hollywood, he directed the Broadway hits *Outward
Bound* (1938) and *Margin for Error* (1939). I used to go over to Otto's house
with my Royal and work alone with him on a script, never once meeting
the official studio screenwriters who'd been assigned to the project. Preminger paid me out of his own pocket so that there wouldn't be any record
of my participation on studio accounts.

Otto was then having a top-secret affair with one of the most beautiful
women in Hollywood, his Austrian compatriot Hedy Lamarr. As I was
leaving his place one day, Otto asked me to take a little box to Miss Lamarr
on the set of her new movie and instructed me to be extremely discreet. I
was on my way to the studio, so I said okay. But I was feeling a little roguish that day, probably miffed that Preminger was treating me like a messenger boy. I got the urge to play a practical joke on Otto the Great. So I
took a pair of scissors and carefully opened the box. Inside was a very
expensive diamond bracelet and a card that said: "I will love you forever,
your Otto."

I cut off the bottom of the card with some scissors and signed it "G." I figured there was a Gary, a George, or a Groucho in Hollywood who might have been just as happy to send Lamarr that strand of ice as a memento of his affection. Even now I chuckle when I imagine Hedy Lamarr opening the box and wondering who was the mysterious "G." Neither Lamarr nor Preminger ever made the slightest comment to me about the incident. Years later, when I was directing my own movies at Fox, I ran into Preminger and confessed to him that I'd tampered with his precious consignment for Hedy Lamarr. Otto laughed heartily. He and Lamarr had vowed to never show the faintest distress, thus having the last laugh on the rascal I'd been that day.

It may seem like I just slipped into screenwriting. Hell, it was damn hard work. As a novice in Hollywood, I took every assignment that came my way, no matter whether I was getting any credit or not. By doing it day in and day out, I learned the basics from the ground up. If you're any good at this racket, you have to know your story, the beginning, middle, and end, then allow your characters to act on their emotions. You set the scene, and the characters take over, moving the audience along with them. In journalism and fiction, you rely more on description to propel your story forward. Movies are about action, conflict, and sharp dialogue. I banged away at it until I felt comfortable with the form. Eventually, screenwriting would become second nature to me.

I learned that a screenplay must be a very personal vision of what a movie is going to look like. It's only a working model, not the movie itself; it's a means to an end, not a finished piece of art. Your characters respond to each situation according to their personal background and psychological makeup; otherwise their emotions look phony. A script isn't written in stone. You work like hell until you've got the best script you can write. It can always be improved. Still, don't let any sonofabitch weaken it by diluting what you know is genuine. All this is easy to say, but believe me, it took many years and a helluva lot of trial and error to learn how to create a movie from a blank piece of paper.

The first full-fledged script I wrote and sold under my own name was called *Gangs of New York* (1938). The story was about a government prosecutor working with the FBI who devises a plan to keep a Capone-like gangster in prison when the convict comes up for parole. They find an almost perfect double for the guy and put him in prison, too. They release the double and keep the real gangster locked up. The double makes himself credible. Even the gangster's dog thinks the imposter is his master. In the end, however, his mistress spoils the ruse, because no two men make love exactly alike.

In those days, we used to write scripts on legal-size paper, with the stage directions on the left and the dialogue on the right. Here's the opening scene from *Gangs of New York:*

FADE IN: NIGHT

Main and credit titles superimposed over establishing backgrounds of New York: its skyline, an effective angle of Brooklyn Bridge, silhouetted against the night sky, etc.

DISSOLVE TO:

1. EXT. NEW YORK STREET (NIGHT) LONG
A MATTE SHOT on almost deserted street in an unsavory section of Manhattan. The one illuminated store front bears flashing neon sign:

"MADDOCK'S—Pool and Billiards"
"The building is framed between elated pillars. The superstructure and tracks angle through the tops of our picture, and above them distant skyscrapers stand silhouetted against the night sky.

A single car—a large, dark sedan—stands in front of the pool room. From somewhere blares the tinny music of a mechanical piano. Otherwise the scene is quiet.

Then suddenly the air is rent with the rattle of machine-gun fire—three of four bursts in quick succession. Three men, coat collars up and hats pulled down to make them unrecognizable, dash from the pool room to the waiting car.

As the car speeds away, a figure staggers from the building, looks about confused, then suddenly collapses in a heap. Heads appear at tenement windows. A policeman races in past CAMERA and blows a police whistle in foreground. A crowd starts to collect.

The piano continues its tinny accompaniment.

DISSOLVE TO:

2. STOCK SHOT:
Of ambulance speeding through city streets.

3. INT. HOSPITAL ROOM: (NIGHT) MED.
A white gowned doctor is working over the figure of a man
in bed, feeling his pulse—watching his breathing, etc. A
nurse stands by. The man, a hard-looking individual, is
semi-conscious. A policeman and an orderly in b.g. Watching grimly are Detective Inspector Sullivan, huge, keen-eyed
and alert, and District Attorney Lucas, a forceful appearing
man in middle age.

As the doctor turns away, Sullivan addresses him:

>   SULLIVAN: (quietly)
>   *How about it, Doc. Can we talk to him now?*

>   DOCTOR:
>   *Yeah. I guess it won't make any difference. If he's
>   going to talk at all, he'd better do it now.*

Sullivan and the District Attorney move close to the bed.

4. INT. HOSPITAL ROOM: (NIGHT) CLOSE
At bedside. The patient is breathing hard.

>   SULLIVAN: (quietly)
>   *Who did it, Lefty?*

The man looks at him through glassy eyes.

>   DISTRICT ATTORNEY:
>   *You're through Lefty. You're going to die. Who
>   were they?*

>   LEFTY: (*laboriously*)
>   *What—what happened to Joe—and Louie—
>   and—*

SULLIVAN:
They got 'em all. Who did it?

LEFTY:
Rocky's boys. I—I—hope—they—rot! Rocky—
Thorpe's—boys!

4. CONTINUED:
Sullivan and the District Attorney look at each other.

CAMERA DOLLIES IN TO CLOSE SHOT OF D.A. AND
SULLIVAN.

DISTRICT ATTORNEY: (in undertone)
The guy's delirious. Rocky Thorpe's been out
of circulation for five years.

SULLIVAN: (musing)
I wonder.

Off scene, Lefty chokes, then goes quiet.

DOCTOR'S VOICE: (o.s.)
Wrap him up, Hank.

Sullivan and the D.A. look quickly toward the bed, o.s.

The picture ended up being directed by James Cruze, and starred
Charles Bickford and Ann Dvorak. No sooner was the picture in the can,
than I got a call from Sam Briskin, head of Columbia. Before I'd even settled my ass on the comfortable sofa in Briskin's big office, he asked me if I
could write an adventure movie for the studio. He may as well have been
asking me if I could bake a seven-layer cake.

"Of course!" I told him, without the faintest idea of what I was going to
say next.

"Great!" said Briskin. "Whaddaya got?"

"A damn good story," I said, staying light on my feet.

"So," he said, "spill it."

I took out a cigar and slowly prepared to light it, buying a few moments
to figure a way out of this mess. Briskin never took his beady eyes off me.
I lit the cigar, blew the smoke out of my mouth, and proudly announced,
"William Bligh meets Victor Hugo!"

"Who the hell are they?" snarled Briskin.

Bligh, I explained, was the betrayed captain played by Charles Laughton in *Mutiny on the Bounty,* one of the most acclaimed pictures of 1936, and Victor Hugo had written a tale about the French Foreign Legion that would be perfect for an adventure picture.

"Tell me more," demanded Briskin.

"It happens in a fort in the middle of the Sahara Desert," I explained. "The commander of the fort is the villain, so his men mutiny against him and throw him out into the desert with his officers. The Arabs are about to attack . . ."

"Yeah!" said Briskin, warming to the plot.

"The good guy, the leader of the mutiny, realizes that the Arabs are going to kill the evil commander and his men if they don't do something. So just as the Arabs attack, the mutineers rush out of the fort and beat back the Arabs, saving the evil commander and winning the battle for the legion. The commander awards the leader of the mutiny a medal for his courage. He kisses him on both cheeks because he saved his life. Then the sonofabitch condemns the hero to die because he started the mutiny in the first place!"

"That's terrific!" cried Briskin. "Let's do it!"

He sent me off to get right to work on the script and had a fat check sent over the next day. *Adventure in Sahara* (1938) ended up being directed by D. Ross Lederman. See, studio heads back then may have grown up selling furs instead of reading French literature, but they loved a good story. So thank you, Monsieur Hugo, for saving my ass with your wonderful novel *Ninety-Three.* The hell with those who were jealous of your talent, the revisionists of any generation who put down your work. You were a fabulous storyteller.

The most enriching experience of my debut years in Hollywood was meeting and befriending Herbert Brenon, a wonderful man and a great director. Brenon made his first picture, *The Clown's Triumph,* in 1912, the year I was born. He went on to direct about eighty feature films, including the original versions of *Peter Pan* (1924), *Beau Geste* (1926), and *The Great Gatsby* (1926). Brenon's last film was *False Rapture* (1941). I loved Herbert. He was another father figure for me, a wise guide who took a liking to me and showed me the ropes, introducing me to some of the great artists and craftsmen working within the studios at that time. Thanks to Herbert Brenon and his patronage, I met members of the "old school"—veteran directors like John Ford, Raoul Walsh, Howard Hawks, Leo McCarey, Tod Browning, Frank Borzage—the guys who created Hollywood out of a bunch of fruit orchards and dusty lots with a burning desire to tell great stories.

Herbert Brenon (in big sombrero) prepares to shoot a scene from Beau Geste *with (left to right) actors Ralph Forbes, Ronald Colman, and William Powell.*

All very different in their approach, each of these artists shared a true respect for their audiences. I'd remain close to Herbert and his wife, Helen, until his death, in 1958.

My next script was *Bowery Boy*, about a little newspaper vendor who suffers from a contagious disease and the young doctor who tries to contain it from spreading throughout New York. Although I dreamed up the story, my screenplay was rewritten by a team of studio rewrite specialists. Directed by William Morgan, *Bowery Boy* didn't go into production until 1941, delayed by all the goddamned rewriting. The experience gave me a taste of how the studios could dilute the originality of your screenplay. It wasn't a good taste, believe me.

I decided to go to work on another novel, this one more substantial than my first three. With a book, I could at least be assured that the finished work would be what I'd written. My yarn was a murder mystery that took place on my beloved Park Row. The murderer was a powerful city editor, the victim, his abandoned wife. The guy who fingers the murderer is a top crime reporter who follows the trail back to the boss who taught him everything he knows. I called it *The Dark Page*.

11

Forget About Greatness

While I was right in the middle of writing *The Dark Page,* an old friend from Park Row, Hank Wales, dropped in to see me. Twenty years my senior, Wales was a renowned journalist, having won a slew of prestigious newspapering prizes. During World War I, Hank had written a series of articles about a courageous soldier named Sergeant York which became the basis for the famous Gary Cooper movie of the same name, directed by Howard Hawks in 1941. Hank had also covered the execution of Mata Hari, the famous spy, and invented the word "tank" for those indomitable military vehicles. Wales was so well known inside press circles that Robert Benchley wrote a screenplay based on his career, called *Foreign Correspondent.* Alfred Hitchcock directed it in 1940, with Joel McCrea and Laraine Day.

"Let's you and I write a movie together!" said Hank. "Got any good stories?"

We both laughed. With all his amazing experiences, Hank Wales was asking me for a yarn. I was thrilled that such a remarkable guy wanted to collaborate with me. But I had a book to finish.

"Look, Hank," I said, "I'm writing the great American novel!"

"Everyone is writing the great American novel, Sammy. Forget about greatness. Let's have some fun."

It was not a lighthearted time. Events on the world stage were sobering. In the summer of 1940, Germany launched air raids on Britain. America watched and waited, because public opinion was against getting into the war. With his nation under siege, Churchill's magnificent "blood, toil, tears and sweat" speech had set hearts afire, establishing the tone for total war against the Nazi invaders:

> You ask, what is our aim? I can answer in one word: It is victory, victory at all costs, victory in spite of all the terror; victory, however

long and hard the road may be; for without victory, there is no survival.

Hank Wales and the Battle of Britain persuaded me to put aside *The Dark Page*. During the Nazi bombardment of London, amidst all the random destruction, we'd learned that the Associated Press offices were hit. I suggested to Hank that we pin our story around some newspapermen who have to hide out in the basement of a London hotel to survive the air attacks. With only a couple of typewriters and a telegraph, they keep sending out the news. The yarn was right up Hank's alley.

We went to work on the script on a Monday morning. Hank knew the streets of London by heart. As he paced back and forth feeding me local color, I pounded away on my Royal. By talking it out, we pieced together the action, plot twists, and dialogue. The first ninety-page draft was finished before breakfast on Saturday morning. After eggs, bacon, and hash browns, we found an agent, Charles Feldman, who happened to be in his office on the weekend. He sold our script to Twentieth Century Fox on the following Monday morning for fifty grand, which Hank and I split, minus Feldman's commission.

We called the movie *Confirm or Deny*. The only way for the trapped newspapermen in London to contact their New York office is by telegraph. Their frantic editor wants more information about the situation in England. From the other side of the Atlantic, it looks like Hitler will soon be attacking North America. While the bombs are falling on London, the New York office keeps sending urgent queries in Morse code, punctuating each question with the command: "Confirm or Deny."

Tension builds, causing the journalists to come to grips with their deepest beliefs and fears. It was a damn good yarn. Fox acquired it for Fritz Lang, who started the picture but quit after only a few days. Archie Mayo wound up finishing *Confirm or Deny* (1941) with Don Ameche, Joan Bennett, and Roddy McDowall.

Months after the movie was completed, I got a call from Fritz Lang, inviting me to lunch. That was the first time we actually met face-to-face. I loved Lang's films, above all *You Only Live Once* (1937), about an innocent man thrown into prison.

Lang wanted to explain to me why he'd left *Confirm or Deny* a few days after shooting had begun. He told me he loved our script but that the studio had insisted on rewriting it at the last minute and the revisions were disappointing. We agreed that the original script had more action, more emotion, and certainly more balls than the Archie Mayo movie that Fox eventually released.

The studio set up this publicity shot with Don Ameche (right), star of Confirm or Deny. *Guess which one of us was more camera-shy.*

That episode, along with many others during my early Hollywood years, made me more and more aware of the importance of the director. As a writer, my approach to a film had always been through the script. Increasingly, I appreciated the director's skills in setting up shots, getting actors to deliver lines, moving the camera. Each director had a signature way of telling a story. Why did certain movies make a lifelong impression? First, the story was great. But just as important was the way the director shot it. In the hands of talented directors, characters got under your skin, made you feel their pains and pleasures, talked to your soul. There were some terrific directors working in Hollywood in those days. A few of them changed forever the way I looked at movies.

I loved E. A. Dupont's *Variety* (1925) because he made me really conscious of style. It was a terrific tale about a former trapeze artist who gets released from prison after serving time for a murder. Dupont shot it like a poem. Another distinctively stylish movie was Mervyn LeRoy's *I Am a Fugitive from a Chain Gang* (1932), with the wonderful Paul Muni railroaded onto a brutal chain gang for a crime he didn't commit. LeRoy makes you feel the terrible injustice that his hero must confront. *Black*

Fury (1935), by Michael Curtiz, had a great deal of influence on me too. Paul Muni is again the lead, as Joe Radek, who must deal with all the lies and frustrations that take place during a mine strike. Having seen strikes during my hobo days, I felt the movie rang true.

William Wellman's superb *Ox-Bow Incident* (1943) also left a deep impression. Unlike most Westerns of the day, Wellman's showed honest, human reactions. A local farmer has been murdered and his cattle stolen. The townspeople, joined by some drifters led by Henry Fonda, form a posse to catch the perpetrators. In their rush to justice, they hang innocent men. Instead of false tears and remorse, the sonsofbitches drink to try to forget about their horrible act.

My favorite film of those formative years was *The Informer* (1935) by John Ford. It is truly a masterpiece. Of all the wonderful directors I met in Hollywood before World War II, I paid special attention to John Ford. John had a vision of each film he directed and the determination to get that vision up on the screen. John was very supportive of me in the early years when I needed it. He became a friend and a mentor. Ford invited me onto his sets, and, when I started directing, he'd drop in on mine. I cherished the times we were together.

Some critics, looking for a catchy tag line, have called me "the Jewish John Ford." It was a ridiculous thing to say, though I understand people needing reference points. But let's face it, next to the monumental Ford, I'd always be a neophyte. To understand the scope of John's career, you have to remember that he began as an actor way before the talkies, with a small role in *Birth of a Nation,* in 1915. Over the next sixty-odd years, John Ford would direct about 140 films. John was a giant, having done it all in Hollywood. I learned a helluva lot of stuff from Ford, but one of the most important lessons was modesty. Ford was the most self-effacing of guys. When asked what brought him to Hollywood, he replied, "The train."

Because he wanted complete artistic control, Ford started producing his own pictures. The desire to shape every aspect of his movies resulted in some of his finest work: *She Wore a Yellow Ribbon* (1949), *Rio Grande* (1950), *The Quiet Man* (1952), and *The Man Who Shot Liberty Valence* (1962). His mastery of the entire process was always an inspiration for me. I've never tried to imitate his work—nor anyone's, for that matter—but to be mentioned in the same breath as the great Ford will always be a profound compliment. I remained close to him until his death, in 1973. For me, John Ford was everything I loved and respected about Hollywood.

Two other accomplished directors, Howard Hawks and Raoul Walsh, also became friends of mine. Before he started directing, Hawks, nicknamed "the Gray Fox," had worked as an airplane pilot and race car driver.

Like Ford, Hawks wanted his independence, so he became his own producer on most of his films. I was impressed with Hawks's style, especially
the way he didn't hesitate to take on all genres, whether they be comedies,
whodunits, or Westerns. I loved *Scarface* (1932), *To Have and Have Not*
(1944), and *The Big Sleep* (1946). Yet Howard and I had very different personalities. He was a sophisticated social butterfly who loved parties. I was
more primitive, a loner who saw friends one at a time. Once Hawks asked
me, "Do you hunt?"

I shook my head.

"Don't you go fishing?" he asked.

"Nope."

"Well, what kind of sport do you practice?" demanded Hawks.

"I write."

"Now look, Sammy," explained Hawks avuncularly, "in this business,
there's a social code. You can't just sit at a desk all day and night, typing
away. You have to hunt or fish or play bridge, or something. You need to
go to parties, have drinks with people, be seen . . ."

"I don't like all that gibble-gabble," I said. "Socializing is a pain in the
ass. I enjoy being alone, making up characters and stories on my
Royal . . ."

"Come hunting with me," he said. "You'll enjoy it."

"Shooting some poor goddamned animal, Howard, whether it's a fox, a
rhino, or a rabbit, is unfair."

"Okay, Sammy, okay," said Hawks, catching my drift. "You're a writer,
not a hunter."

Regardless of our very different personalities, I was nuts about Howard
Hawks and the way he made films. I never did go hunting with him, but,
after the war, I gave him a double-barreled hunting rifle with an iron cross
that I'd brought back from Germany. On the gunstock was engraved "To
the glory of Hermann Göring." The Gray Fox loved it.

Like Ford, Raoul Walsh was a Hollywood pillar. He'd broken into the
business as an actor in silent films, playing the part of John Wilkes Booth
in *Birth of a Nation*. In a career that lasted fifty years, Walsh made over a
hundred movies, including the great *High Sierra* (1941). He loved directing
and sometimes took on projects just to keep working, without a gut conviction about the story. I loved Raoul's roguish sense of humor and self-
effacing manner, the kind of guy who works hard without taking himself
too seriously.

In the late seventies, I took Raoul to lunch at Musso & Frank's with
Christa. He must have been almost ninety years old by then. He still
looked great. Wearing a big cowboy hat, he could have starred in any-

body's Western. We had so much fun with Raoul. That would be the last time I'd see him.

I was making progress on *The Dark Page,* but whenever I needed some dough, the book had to be put aside. I'd write a script, sell it, then go back to work on the novel. *Power of the Press* was bought by Columbia, directed by Lew Landers, and finally released in 1943. It dealt with a Hearst-like newspaper publisher who dies, leaving his New York paper to an old friend, a respected newspaperman from the Midwest. *Gangs of the Waterfront* was a follow-up to *Gangs of New York.* Republic Pictures produced it, and George Blair directed. It wasn't released until 1945, a straightforward crime picture that I knocked out pretty quick.

My next script was called *Warden Goes to Jail.* John Huston had introduced me to his father, Walter. I was so impressed that I wanted to write a yarn that would be a vehicle for Walter. To research it, I needed to get some background material on Alcatraz, so I went to San Francisco for a couple weeks. My story was about a harsh prison director who kills a man over his wife and is incarcerated in the same prison where he was once warden. The prisoners don't exact revenge on him. They simply watch him go slowly insane, victim of his own prison rules. I loved writing the tale of a man who creates his own laws, then is killed by them. Paramount bought the script but never produced it.

I was learning that one of the most frustrating aspects of the Hollywood system was that, many times, hard-hitting stories like *Warden Goes to Jail* didn't make it to the screen. It made me so goddamned mad that I was seriously thinking about trying my own hand at directing. That way, my scripts would not just get made, but, once up on the screen, the movie would look the way I'd written it.

See, by 1941 I was doing pretty well in Hollywood, selling stories and scripts one after the other. I had some accomplished friends, and I was making pretty good dough. Yet I considered my stay in Hollywood as temporary. Deep down in my heart, I always dreamed of being an editor in chief. Even a small-town paper would do. It always seemed that I had one foot in and one foot out of the movie business. The way they rewrote my scripts made me increasingly dissatisfied with just being a screenwriter. I no longer could watch a film without questioning the director's judgment, figuring out how a particular shot could have been improved, wondering why the hell the director didn't yell "Cut!" sooner on a never-ending sequence.

Since the beginning of the movie business, there has always been a conflict between screenwriters and directors. The conflict continues to this day. There are screenwriters who are aggravated by how directors translate

THE WHITE HOUSE
WASHINGTON

TO MEMBERS OF THE UNITED STATES ARMY EXPEDITIONARY
FORCES:

You are a soldier of the United States Army.

You have embarked for distant places where
the war is being fought.

Upon the outcome depends the freedom of your
lives: the freedom of the lives of those you love—
your fellow-citizens—your people.

Never were the enemies of freedom more
tyrannical, more arrogant, more brutal.

Yours is a God-fearing, proud, courageous
people, which, throughout its history, has put its
freedom under God before all other purposes.

We who stay at home have our duties to
perform—duties owed in many parts to you. You will
be supported by the whole force and power of this
Nation. The victory you win will be a victory of all
the people—common to them all.

You bear with you the hope, the confidence,
the gratitude and the prayers of your family, your
fellow-citizens, and your President—

Franklin D Roosevelt

Every soldier got this letter from FDR.
That way, we knew our marching orders
came directly from the commander in chief.

their stories into movies. There are directors who can make a great film with only the wisp of a script. I've come to understand that it's impossible to say who's more important to the final product, the writer or the director. There's no solution to this natural antagonism in moviemaking, and there will never be one. My own approach to the problem was to become a writer/director.

But for the time being, there were more important conflicts to worry about. Hitler was master of continental Europe, having first occupied Czechoslovakia, then invaded Poland, swallowing up Denmark, Norway, and the Low Countries, then France. It was clear to everybody that the Nazis were criminals who had to be stopped.

Early Sunday morning, December 7, 1941, I was driving my car in Los Angeles, listening to the radio. That's how I heard the news about the attack on Pearl Harbor. My novel, the scripts I was doing in Hollywood, my plans to try directing—all of it—suddenly seemed unimportant. It was, as President Roosevelt told Congress, "a date which will live in infamy." America, the lumbering giant, was finally awakened to the danger of passivity. As soon as Congress had voted for war against Japan and Germany, I was very sure about what I had to do.

I went down to the U.S. Army draft office and got in line with all the young men waiting there. At twenty-nine years old, I was much older than the average guy who decided to enlist. Luckily, they needed plenty of soldiers, so there was no bias against "old" volunteers like me. There was a required interview with a recruiting officer. I requested a few weeks before being sent off to boot camp, in order to finish up a first draft of my novel. The officer gave me the extra time. Then he asked me why I wanted to go to war. Hell, I certainly wasn't enlisting with the idea of becoming a hero. I asked if I could level with him, and he said yes. So I told him that, sure, I was inspired by Roosevelt's call to arms against the aggressors; however, the prospects of military life—being in uniform, marching, carrying a rifle, fighting—didn't really give me a hard-on. What kept going through my brain was that I had a helluva opportunity to cover the biggest crime story of the century, and nothing was going to stop me from being an eyewitness.

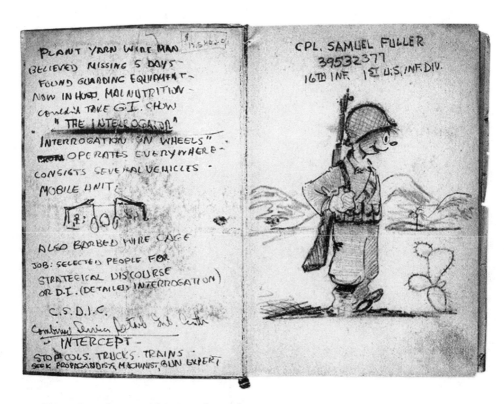

PART II

My war journals were quick jottings of story ideas
and combat incidents. This auto-portrait was done
in North Africa, a GI still wide-eyed and untested.
There was a lot more war to fight.

12

The Big Red One

I heard my mother shudder when I told her I was going to be a soldier. My country needed me for a little while, I reassured her, and everything was going to be all right. As deeply worried as she was, Rebecca kept her composure and did her best to back me up. I asked her to hold on to my most precious possession, the just-finished first draft of *The Dark Page*. As soon as I returned from the war, I'd find a publisher.

The army sent me to Fort MacArthur, near San Diego. Like every other draftee, I had to take a battery of standardized tests and answer a helluva lot of stupid questions. When I told them about my background in journalism, they sent me over to the Communications Department. An officer there offered me an assignment on the staff of the armed forces newspaper. I turned it down flat. I'd joined the army to be in the thick of the action, not behind some goddamned desk.

They marched all the draftees to a railroad station, each of us carrying two heavy canvas bags. A tall, broad-shouldered captain next to the tracks barked out our names one by one. I was sent into a line with maybe a thousand other men. Never had I seen so many men in one place at one time. A train was about to pull out of the station, packed to the gills with soldiers. Ignorant and impatient, I walked up to the captain.

"Where are those men on the train going?" I asked.

"Soldier, you'll call me 'Sir'!"

"Sir," I said, "where are those men going?"

"Infantry!" shouted the captain.

"I want to go with them," I said.

"Get your ass on the train!" he yelled, glad to be rid of me.

Relieved to be moving forward instead of standing in that endless line, I happily jumped aboard. The crowded train pulled out of the station. In my naïveté, how could I guess the horror that lay ahead for me and my fellow passengers? My precipitous leap onto the infantry train was one of the most decisive steps of my entire life. For Chrissakes, the infantry! Guys who joined the infantry, I discovered, came back from the war one of three ways: dead, wounded, or crazy. When you're a dogface, you're the lowest rung on the army's hierarchy. You're nothing more than an ant. Military attitudes about the infantry haven't changed much since Napoleonic times. Hell, you don't even have a name in the infantry, just a number.

They sent us to training camps in Georgia and Louisiana, two months in the first, three months in the second. Holy shit, you can't imagine how hard they trained us in those goddamned camps! I marched and marched and marched, until my rifle didn't feel like a rifle anymore but like a third arm. My forty-pound backpack became as light as a feather. We fired our rifles at targets until our shoulders were black-and-blue from the kick of the rifle butt. When you screwed up, a red flag was waved, signaling every-one that you'd missed the target. The red flag was called "Maggie's Draw-ers," named after some dame's underwear from the nineteenth century. The best shots were country boys from Tennessee, Arkansas, or Iowa.

Since we were all treated like shit, a healthy camaraderie developed among the recruits, an affinity that went beyond social and educational barriers. You name the ethnic background, we had it: Irish, Polish, Jewish, Italian, Latino, Armenian, Slav. Except black. At that time, blacks got sent to their own regiment. The guys grunting alongside me came from every walk of life, from cities, towns, and villages across America, most with rudimentary educations. We were all equal, militarily speaking, the lowest of the low. A real melting pot. When we weren't crawling on our bellies, marching, or shooting, we got bombarded with patriotic propaganda, slo-gans, music. Everywhere were those "We Want You!" posters, Uncle Sam's fierce eyes staring at us, reminding us that we were sweating our balls off for the home of the free and the brave.

In the second training camp, I ran into an officer named Kenneth Fox, who'd been editor in chief at the *Kansas City Star*. Fox couldn't believe that I'd enlisted in the infantry. He immediately took me over to see General Edwin S. Parker. Fox told the general that I was a helluva newspaper reporter and suggested that I be promoted to second lieutenant and trans-ferred to the war correspondents' detail. General Parker had no objection. But I did. I suppose it was my pride or my stupidity. Or both.

"I don't do publicity," I snarled.

"You're making a big mistake, Sammy," said Fox.

"Maybe," I said. "But I've got no one to blame but myself."

Resigned to my lowly rank, I went back to the barracks with the other recruits, proud of not having been tempted into some cushy office job. How many times would I think back to Kenneth Fox and General Parker, smiling to myself at what a dumb bastard I'd been not to have accepted their offer? Maybe a thousand!

The tough physical routine and the monotony of training were getting to me. The camps were morbid. Hell, I wanted some real soldiering. Tired and overwrought, I began to have nightmares. I regret not having written them down, because they were straight from some mysterious inner eye, perfect for a future novel or a movie script. I remember one about me being in a German village with Nazi signs posted in the place, people starving everywhere. That nightmare turned out to be disturbingly prophetic.

We thought we'd never get out of training. It was like being in a prison without bars. Seemingly chained to our sergeant, we marched our asses off all day long. When we got some leave, we went into the neighboring towns, which were almost as harsh and depressing as the camps.

"When are we going to do something?" I asked my sergeant.

"General Eisenhower has important plans for you," he told me.

"When, goddamnit?"

"Just wait."

"But when?"

"You'll see soon enough."

It was worse than waiting for Godot. Finally the big day came. We were put on a long train and shipped to Indiantown Gap, Pennsylvania. It was about midnight when we arrived there, the middle of nowhere, cold as hell, a moonless night. There were a million stars in the sky. A sergeant on the platform started yelling commands at us as we got off the train. He was wearing a dark steel helmet. Thanks to a solitary light in the train yard, I saw a red "1" reflected off the sergeant's helmet. Soon, we'd all be issued helmets like his, wearing them like another part of our skull, sleeping in them, fighting in them, dying in them.

"Listen up! I'm going to call out your names, followed by your assignments! First your regiment! Then your battalion! Then your company!"

I got assigned to the Twenty-sixth Regiment, Third Battalion, Company K. After he finished the entire roll call, the sergeant said, "You are now members of the First United States Infantry Division. Since 1775, it's been called 'the Big Red One'!"

At that point in our military training, it seemed like more indoctrination, so we didn't pay much attention. We didn't give a shit about 1775; we wanted to see some action in 1942. After more weeks of drills and training, we were moved to a base just outside New York in preparation for being shipped overseas. We had permission to make just one phone call. We couldn't talk about where we'd been. We had no idea where we were headed.

I called my mother. She wanted to come over to kiss me good-bye.

"We're not allowed to see anyone," I told her, trying to act tough.

"Where are you going, Sammy?" she asked.

"I'll let you know as soon as I get there." We caught up on family stuff. Then she told me she'd read *The Dark Page.*

"It's excellent, Sammy. Best thing you've ever written. I'm going to try to find a publisher for it."

"Okay, Mama. If you do, keep the money for yourself. Don't worry about me, for Chrissakes, just send some cigars once in a while!"

Then came the good-bye kisses. I tried to stay tough and not let the tears well up, but they did.

The next day we boarded the *Queen Mary* at Manhattan's Pier 90. The fifteen thousand men on board were crowded into every nook and cranny like sardines in a can. The luxury liner had been converted into a troop transport by taking out everything that wasn't welded to its hull, leaving its many decks bare. There were only a few square feet for every soldier to park his ass and equipment. We ate and slept in shifts. We wouldn't find out until we were in the middle of the Atlantic that we were heading for Scotland. Sailing for Europe! Hell, for many of the boys that was the first time they'd been away from home. At least whatever lay ahead was far away from those goddamned training camps.

We landed in Gurrock, near Glasgow, on August 7, 1942. It was colder than Kelsey's nuts. They moved us to southeastern England, near Salisbury, and put us through forced marches, drills, and assault maneuvers with real explosives and ammunition. We were ready for combat; or, at least, that's what we thought. By the end of October, the entire regiment boarded two British troopships, the *Warwick Castle* and the *Duchess of Bedford,* and set sail. We knew we were going on an amphibious operation but still had no indication of where the beachhead was. I felt lucky to be on the *Warwick.* The other ship was quickly renamed "the drunken Duchess" because its shallow draft caused it to roll miserably in the rough weather. We headed down the coast, rounded the Iberian Peninsula, past Gibraltar, and turned into the Mediterranean to join an armada of Allied ships sailing east. During the voyage, they briefed and rebriefed us on our mission: to land on the beaches of Arzew and Damesne, in Algeria, and move inland against Oran, twenty-five miles to the west. We were part of General Eisenhower's campaign to invade Africa, code-named "Torch." In addition to the military plans, they distributed pamphlets about the Arab culture, what to do, what not to do, admonishing us to be respectful of their conservative customs. It was pretty simplistic, but useful for doughboys from Alabama who couldn't tell an Arab from an Australian.

We were part of an armada of two thousand Allied vessels heading for the North African coast in November 1942 to take part in Operation Torch.

At 0100 on the night of November 8, my outfit boarded the landing craft that took us into Arzew beach. This would be the first Allied assault of the war, attempting to force the enemy off land it had usurped. The reputed balmy Mediterranean breeze was freezing cold that night. Still, when I took a deep whiff, I could smell the sand, the palm trees, the belly dancers, and the sheiks. Momentarily, my mind wandered to dashing legionnaires in Herbert Brenon's *Beau Geste* and exotic tales from Percival Christopher Wren's books. I'd soon be fighting alongside those hardened men from the Foreign Legion who'd left behind their prison records, unrequited love affairs, and broken families. As the boats approached the desolate beach, there were lights, as if we were expected. We were. Tons of leaflets in French and English about our arrival had been dropped by Allied planes.

"Put your rubbers on!" our sergeant yelled. "You're gonna get wet!"

We took out the standard-issue condoms and fitted them over our rifles to keep them dry. The doors of the landing craft were flung open. Waist-high in the water, we scrambled up the beach and hit the sand. Shots rang out. The French were firing at us. We fired back. It felt uncomfortable shooting at the French, even if they were with Vichy. There were strong

ties between France and the United States. For Chrissakes, American soldiers were killed at battlefields with names still fresh in our memories:
Soissons, Château-Thierry, Argonne. The French-American connection
went way back. How the hell would we have won our War for Independence without Lafayette? We'd been trained to shoot Nazis, and suddenly
we were forced to return fire at the French. Their shells were exploding
everywhere, and their machine guns were rattling at us from their positions in a seven-hundred-year-old Moorish fortress overlooking the beach.

I found myself eyeball to eyeball with my first vision of the horror of
war. One of our guys was hit by a mortar charge and blown apart, his head
severed from his body. It landed near me. I had a close-up view of his
shocked face, his bulging eyes filled with fear and surprise. I'd seen a lot of
corpses in city morgues, so I didn't turn away. I stared, almost hypnotized
by the soldier's head, forgetting where I was. The shell bursts snapped me
out of it. To this day, that first face of death is imprinted on my mind like
a leaf in a fossil, never to fade away.

Tossing smoke grenades to mask ourselves, our squad advanced, bullets
flying. Suddenly a French voice boomed out over a loudspeaker.

"Cessez le feu! Cessez le feu!"

After about thirty seconds of repeating the order to cease fire, the
French guns fell silent. Then a group of French soldiers emerged through
the smoke and advanced toward the beach carrying white flags. Colonel
Gibb, our battalion commander, seized his bullhorn and commanded us
to cease fire as well. The assault was over. But we remained in position.
Were they really surrendering, or was it a trap?

"Americans! Stop shooting!" yelled somebody with a heavy French
accent. "We will surrender!"

"Frenchmen," Colonel Gibb bellowed through his bullhorn, "we do
not accept your surrender!"

The white flags froze. We checked our weapons, waiting for the command to resume fire.

"You surrender only to the enemy!" continued Colonel Gibb. "We are
not your enemy! We are Americans, your allies! If you want to live, come
and fight on our side! Fight the real enemy! Fight Hitler! *Vive la France!*"

No one moved. Then the dam burst. With an enthusiastic roar, happy
French troops swarmed down toward the beach. Voices in French and
English were yelling and laughing. We stood up and rushed to meet them.
The French embraced us, many with tears in their eyes. They broke out
singing *La Marseillaise.* For cryin' out loud, we were having a beach party
with men who'd been trying to kill us only moments before!

See, the French didn't have any choice but to fight on our side. Rommel could have saved their asses, but his troops were in retreat, thanks to the British breakthrough at el-Alamein by General Bernard Montgomery's "Desert Rats." Montgomery had said, "Give me a fortnight and I can resist the German attack. Give me three weeks, and I can defeat the Boche. Give me a month, and I can chase him out of Africa." With our help, Montgomery would fulfill his promise. But it took him more time to do it than he reckoned, until May 1943.

Before our invasion, the Vichyists in North Africa could sit around over a glass of cognac discussing whether Pétain was a traitor or not. Now they had no choice but to fall in with us to free France. We found out later that Eisenhower had struck a deal with Admiral Darlan, Vichy's commander in chief. However, Darlan was assassinated, and General Charles de Gaulle would assume all authority for assembling the Free France troops.

We headed south through the Atlas Mountains, taking every city in our path. Sidi Bel Abbès. Ghardaïa. Ouargla. North Africa turned out to be not at all like the exotic place I'd imagined it. The climate ran to extremes, from sweltering heat to freezing cold. It hailed. It sleeted. It was cool in the morning, blistering in the afternoon, then bone-chilling at night. Every dogface was issued mosquito netting, overcoats, gloves, and several blankets. We needed all of it. I saw my first real legionnaire on our way into Sidi Bel Abbès, a tall, dark young man wearing a khaki uniform and carrying the longest rifle I'd ever laid eyes on. He was so ordinary, a far cry from the extras in *Beau Geste*. There wasn't a trace of anything remotely romantic in Algeria, just corruption, harsh tribal chieftains, thieving by the natives, unyielding customs.

What a thrill I got out of being in Sidi Bel Abbès, headquarters of the legion since 1831. The old telegrapher at the *New York Evening Journal*, Henry Hudson, used to tell me about the fortress at Sidi Bel Abbès and its role in the Dreyfus case. In 1893, Captain Alfred Dreyfus was charged and convicted of treason. He was accused of having written a list of secret French military documents to be delivered to the Germans. Colonel Picquart, then head of French military intelligence, defended Dreyfus, uncovering evidence that a French infantry officer, Major Esterhazy, had planted the evidence. Picquart was dismissed and confined for a time at the fortress at Sidi Bel Abbès. My sergeant didn't understand why I was so excited about going inside the fortress, but he gave me one hour to visit it. Holy mackerel, did I get a kick out of the commemorative plaque next to Picquart's cell with its brief legend about Dreyfus! It made me look upward and thank old Henry Hudson.

The Big Red One continued to move toward the Tunisian border, our three battalions spread out across the Ousseltia valley. On February 20,

We'd never forget the thrashing we took from General Erwin Rommel and his Afrika Korps at Kasserine.

1943, we took up positions in a place called Bou Chebka, in the vicinity of the Kasserine Pass. There, General Erwin Rommel's well-oiled killing machine, the Afrika Korps, counterattacked. Rommel's troops were faster and more experienced than us, and they had the Tenth SS Panzer tanks. They broke through and overran our outfit. We were like babes in the woods, trapped in the crossfire. There was nothing to do but die or retreat. So we retreated. There were so many American soldiers killed and wounded that day. The rest of our outfit ran for their lives, scared shitless, back into the Faïd Mountains. There we hunkered down and slept in total blackout.

Kasserine was the most disgraceful moment of the war. But plans were immediately made to reverse the setback. After replenishing our supplies, we counterattacked, backed up by the Twelfth Air Force squadron, which had been trimming down the German spearhead with strafing runs. The Germans suffered terrible losses in the ensuing battle, since we'd been able to move up our artillery. Kasserine Pass was retaken. The Sixtieth Infantry relieved us of holding the pass so that the Big Red One could regroup, bring in replacements, and prepare for the next attack on Gafsa. The First Division and the II Corps were now placed under the command of General George Patton. The British First Army and the French Nineteenth Corps joined us, backed up by Allied planes. A new offensive was launched in mid-March. One prong of the attack was against the Mareth

Line. My outfit's mission was to attack Rommel's flank as he retreated up the coast of Tunisia.

We'd become much tougher, thanks to the battle experience. Now we moved into positions confidently, fought like animals, and moved on to the next objective without a pause. First Gafsa, then El Guettar and el-Hamma fell, pushing back not only Rommel's Panzer Divisions but Italy's crack San Marcos Marines and the experienced Austrian Alpine troops. At night we'd dig into the sand for a few hours of shut-eye. I'd never seen anything like the magnificent night sky overhead, millions of stars shimmering like a painting by van Gogh. We lay down in ditches as deep as graves, the deeper the better. Falling bombs—if they didn't kill you when they exploded—would make you deaf forever. I'd already seen lots of guys killed, their guts spilled all over the desert. When I looked up at the stars, I saw those terrible images again and again, like a movie looped in a projector going round and round. I never thought about my own death. Nor did the fear of getting shot or blown up cross my mind. There was only one thing I was afraid of: stepping on a land mine and losing my cock in an explosion. The British, the French, and the Germans had planted so many mines along our route that our boys frequently stepped on the goddamned things, blowing off legs and genitals.

As if we didn't have enough things to think about at night, just as we closed our eyes to try to get some sleep the unmistakable voice of a woman floated to us from somewhere far-off in the desert.

"Hello, boys! Hey, Big Red One! Wake up, suckers! This is Axis Sally, ready to tuck you in for the night with the latest war news."

The eyes of every dogface opened wide.

"Don't look for the loudspeaker—other GIs have tried, and they're deader than door nails."

Axis Sally was one of the enemy's most vicious weapons, an American gal with a sexy voice that made every male reach for his crotch. We'd search futilely for the Nazi loudspeakers during the day. Somehow, they were back every night. So was Axis Sally.

"Just relax in your graves. Churchill is enjoying his cigar because the British army is fighting to the last American in North Africa."

We all had the same question. Was she blond, brunette, or redhead?

"Why are you fighting for the British? You fought against them, not Germany, during your revolution. In a few days, German soldiers will be washing down fish eggs with vodka in Moscow. In the Pacific the Japanese are slaughtering U.S. marines."

The meathead who wrote her copy should have been doing comic strips instead.

"Rommel's sixty-two-ton Tiger tanks are whipping the bejesus out of Mont-gomery's demoralized Eighth Army, and our well-fed, victorious Luftwaffe owns the skies over you suckers, so wise up and throw down your rifles. Don't be ashamed to cry uncle. Your own Uncle Sam doesn't give a damn about any of you dying. You're young. You've got a right to live. Hitler has nothing against Americans. His beef is with England. You boys should be on our side."

Finish your goddamned spiel and get to the music!

"And now for news from home! In the United States, instead of supporting you, those patriotic civilians are on strike at all major defense plants. You suck-ers are dying while back home they're demanding shorter hours. You poor slobs are being fed red, white, and blue trash by Eisenhower, who was never in com-bat, who hasn't the faintest idea of what it means to dodge bullets and bombs."

The song, goddamnit! The song!

"And on the North African front, more good news! I just got word that the Twenty-Sixth Regiment of the First Infantry was clobbered by our Panzers and practically wiped out."

We laughed like crazy. Axis Sally had greatly exaggerated reports of our demise. She tried so hard to demoralize us but instead ended up entertain-ing us.

"I am going to sing you suckers to sleep. Think of your wives and sisters and sweethearts getting fucked by draft dodgers, deserters, and those lucky, lucky 4-Fs. Good night, boys!"

A haunting harmonica accompanied Axis Sally as she sang "Lili Mar-leen" to us. She was full of bullshit, but, craving music, I loved to listen to her sing.

"This is Axis Sally, saying good night and sleep tight, because tomorrow you'll all be vulture food."

As we advanced toward Djebel Chemsi, all resistance evaporated. We were surprised by the German withdrawal, then learned that Gabès had been taken and the British Eighth Army was pursuing the enemy toward Sfax and Sousse. By day, we moved across the white-hot desert searching for any trace of the enemy. There was nothing for days on end. A small advanced patrol of our men was always sent ahead of our company, scout-ing for Germans and mines. A Bedouin tent appeared in the middle of nowhere. Shots rang out. Goats started bleating madly. My company ran for the tent and encircled it. Just as we got there, one of the advanced patrol soldiers emerged with an insane look on his sweaty face.

"No other Ay-rabs in there," said the dogface.

I followed the sergeant inside. Two Arab men and three Arab women were dead on the ground, their blood splattered all over the place. One of the women had been breastfeeding a baby.

Mildred Gillards, or "Axis Sally," as we knew her, was caught in Germany and flown back to the States to be arraigned for treason. I have no idea why a girl from Portland, Maine, would do those "go back to your wives and sweethearts" broadcasts on Nazi radio, but she was damned insidious.

The sergeant stared at the corpses. Everyone in our squad felt sick to their stomachs. The crazy dogface smiled proudly.

"Throw me your weapon!" the sergeant commanded.

The dogface reluctantly threw his rifle to the sergeant.

"Any of them open fire at you?" asked the sergeant.

"Didn't give 'em a chance."

"Did they pull a knife on you?"

"On *me*?" laughed the dogface, like a hyena. "You should've seen 'em flippin' like chickens."

"Killing them gave you a hard-on, didn't it?"

"You told me to wipe out the enemy, didn't you?"

"You call *this* the enemy?" said the sergeant, lifting up the bloody remains of the baby.

"Anybody ain't American's the enemy!" said the depraved dogface.

The sergeant laid the ten pounds of murdered humanity on the rug and swaddled it with a sheet. The sun was beating down. Flies were already swarming around the corpses. The sergeant washed the blood off his hands with water from his canteen. Then he aimed his own rifle at the wide-eyed dogface, clicked off the safety, and shot him twice through the heart. The insane soldier collapsed like a sack of potatoes. Horrified, we froze. The silence was broken by the sergeant clicking the safety on his rifle back on.

I will never forget the gruesome sight of all those bullet-ridden bodies as long as I live. Soldiers don't shoot civilians, let alone a woman nursing a baby, unless they're nuts. Yet, like everyone else, they lose their judgment and sometimes even go berserk. War itself is organized insanity. Both sides are trained to kill, and everyone is a potential enemy. We were given rules of conduct, but the rules were hypocritical as hell. When you see an enemy pissing, it's still your choice whether to shoot him or not. Civilized wars just don't exist.

Once in Tunisia, the First Division prepared for the final advance into Tunis the last week of April 1943. First, the hills on the road to Mateur had to be captured. The hills had no goddamned names on the maps HQ gave us, just numbers. The enemy was dug in, with those hills converted into grim bastions bristling with artillery, mortars, and machine-gun nests. The battles over the next days were furious. General McNair, chief of army ground forces, was even hit by German shrapnel. Our artillery hammered enemy positions mercilessly, hitting many of our own advancing troops in the process. Hill 523, Hill 609, Hill 575, one by one they were all taken.

Around the first of May, our final push began at 0300 on a moonless night. The Afrika Korps threw everything they had at us, yet their defenses were penetrated. Bizerte fell, and the way was clear for Montgomery and his Eighth Army to enter Tunis. The Germans and Italians were cornered with their backs to the sea, with nowhere to retreat. All along the coastline, ships, barges, anything navigable, fled Africa with enemy troops. Many were sunk by American planes. In one of the queer twists that happen in wartime, one of our planes strafed a German ship carrying American prisoners of war toward Sicily. Abandoned by its crew, the ship was taken over and brought back to shore under the command of none other than one of the Big Red One's battalion commanders, Colonel Denholm, who'd been captured in the bitter fighting on Hill 523.

The day it all ended—May 9, 1943—there was a strange lull in the combat at sunrise. Our orders had been to continue the advance. A school building up ahead was our next objective. Just as we were about to assault it, the front door opened, and out walked a British soldier with a black beret.

"It's over!" he yelled, waving to us. "Come have a drink!"

The British were already celebrating a great victory for their besieged nation. They hugged us and passed around bottles of whiskey. The Axis armies in Africa had surrendered, and the continent was recovered. Operation Torch marked a turning point in the war. The campaign was the first defeat for German and Italian armies—with over 250,000 enemy soldiers taken prisoner—giving us invaluable battlefield experience and renewed confidence. But the price of victory was heavy. The Allies lost over fifty thousand men.

"Up to that moment," wrote Eisenhower in his memoirs, "no government had ever attempted to carry out an overseas expedition involving a journey of thousands of miles from its bases and terminating in a major attack."

Rommel's defeat in North Africa was the beginning of his end. We would fight him again in 1944 during the Normandy invasion, but he was wounded there and sent home, where he was implicated in the failed assassination attempt against Hitler. Rommel was offered poison or a trial. He took the poison.

13

Husky

I began a journal in North Africa. If I survived, I was going to write about my war experiences someday. The journal wasn't much more than a small calendar book full of quickly scribbled notes, drawings, random thoughts, and ideas for characters and stories. I tried to make sense of our campaigns by getting the facts straight. I jotted down names of dogfaces. Many died before I could find out much about them.

As often as I could, I wrote my mother a letter on "V-mail" stationery, or on any piece of paper that was handy. Mostly I sent her cartoons and wrote quips about the lighter side of infantry life. I avoided talking about anything violent or sad. Telling her where we were or describing our actions too precisely was impossible, because all letters were examined for possible security breaches. My drawings were a way for both of us to keep our spirits up and to survive the nerve-racking reality of the war.

Survival was the one thought that held dominion over everything else in a doggie's universe. In that vein, we worried about simple but basic things: dry socks, edible chow, fresh water, the runs. I never saw anyone praying to God except in some Hollywood movies after the war was over, imagined by screenwriters who'd never been near a battlefield.

Almost forty years would elapse before I'd write a novel entitled *The Big Red One* and make a four-hour, twenty-minute movie out of it.[1] The book was like taking a hill. Once that battle was over, I had to move on toward the greater mission: a motion picture. I was driven to turn my wartime experiences into a movie in order to convey the physical and mental upheaval of men at war. That's how I ultimately came to grips with my experiences. Tactics, strategy, troop movements on maps were for military historians. My screenplay reduced the war to a small squad of First Division soldiers—a veteran sergeant and four young dogfaces—and their emotions in wartime. Each fictional character was an amalgam of real soldiers I'd known.

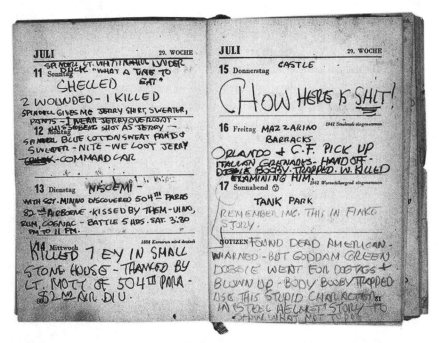

A page from my journal scribbled in Sicily in July 1943 during Operation Husky. Later in Steel Helmet, *I'd use the note "Found dead American—warned—but goddamn green doggie went for dogtags & blown up" for the scene about the booby-trapped corpse.*

See, there's no way you can portray war realistically, not in a movie nor in a book. You can only capture a very, very small aspect of it. If you really want to make readers understand a battle, a few pages of your book would be booby-trapped. For moviegoers to get the idea of real combat, you'd have to shoot at them every so often from either side of the screen. The casualties in the theater would be bad for business. Such reaching for reality in the name of art is against the law. Hell, the heavy human toll is just too much for anyone to comprehend fully. What I try to do is make audiences feel the emotional strife of total war.

During the North African campaign, I had to kill a man for the first time. The act begets the most basic revulsion. I couldn't believe it was me pulling the trigger. It left me feeling hollow inside. But a soldier must overcome that disgust if he is to survive. Afterward, when you kill, you're shooting the same man over and over again. Your will to survive surprises you, eventually kicking abstract thoughts like remorse or mercy out of your brain. The reality is, you're glad the other guy is dead and you're still alive. You become a killing machine.

To regroup before our next campaign, we were loaded into trucks and driven back along the coast road to Algeria. All the way, the convoy encountered continuous demonstrations of cheering civilians strewing flowers on the road and offering us wine. Battle-weary and ragged, we were much too tired to do anything more than smile and wave back at the crowds. For most of the next six weeks, we bivouacked about thirty miles from Algiers near a village called Staouli. The place was surrounded by dunes and magnificent hills. At dawn and dusk, the sun would hit the rocks and shimmer with millions of fragments of color. We lived in pup tents, ate hard-boiled eggs, drank Algerian wine, and tried to keep the mosquitoes from eating us alive at night by propping mesh nets over our heads with our rifles.

As soon as we regained our strength, there was a new round of training and exercises. There was also time to explore the Casbah in Algiers—nothing like the one in Julien Duvivier's *Pépé le Moko* (1937), where Jean Gabin, playing a Parisian gangster, hides out from the police and falls in love with a gorgeous tourist. The real Casbah destroyed, for once and for all, my exotic movie fantasies. The place was nothing more than a squalid quarter in a big, bustling city. Besides, the Algerians considered all soldiers, whether German, English, Canadian, or American, trespassers in their land. The French, however, were kind to us.

One day my sergeant and I went to a wine merchant at 14 rue de Janina to buy some good French wine. When we knocked at the door, a woman opened it and welcomed us inside. We'd gotten the address wrong, for this was a private home, not a wine store. We were embarrassed and tried to leave. The woman's husband made us sit down, introduced us to their little boy, and showed us pictures of their relatives back in France. They were decent, hardworking people. Since the war began, they'd had very little to eat. They opened a bottle of really good Bordeaux they'd put away for a special occasion and shared it with their "American liberators."

We thanked our hosts and left. Separating from my sergeant, I walked and walked, curious to see as much as I could of the Casbah. General George Patton's Seventh Army headquarters was in the Aletti Hotel. As I passed the Aletti, I saw trucks unloading crates of canned goods and vegetables. The driver saw my Big Red One patch and hollered at me. He belonged to the First Division, too.

"You know rue de Janina?" I asked the man.

"Sure," he said.

"A major in our regiment is staying at number 14," I lied. "The major would really appreciate some extra grub. Deliver a few crates, and I'll make sure he knows who took care of him."

I slapped the man on the shoulder and offered him one of the precious

No.

[CENSOR'S STAMP]

MRS. R. FULLER
#61D
330 W. 95 ST.
N.Y. N.Y.

Cpl Samuel Fuller 32583257
SIG US INF DU APO #1
(Sender's name)
(Sender's address)
POSTMASTER, N.Y. N.Y.
JUNE 6, 1943
(Date)

DARLINK FLOP -

ANOTHER BRIEFIE, ANOTHER DAY, AND
STILL AM COMING ALONG OKAY. AM WRITING
THIS ON A SULTRY SUNDAY IN A PUP TENT.
THE MOSQUITO BAR OVER ME KEEPS
SAGGING, SO AM KEEPING IT UP WITH
MY BAYONET AND GUN ROD. HAVE EATEN
ARABIAN (HARD-BOILED) EGGS. NOT BAD.
THE VINO ISN'T BAD. ARAB VINO IS TABU.
FRENCH VINO IS O.K. FRENCH WOMEN-TABU.
OH, WELL - UNTIL NEXT TIME, MOM,
                    LOVE,

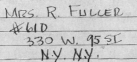

V···-MAIL

POST OFFICE DEPARTMENT PERMIT NO. 1

*A V-mail to Rebecca from Algeria. Letters
home had to be short, vague, and carefree.*

Optimo cigars that my mother had sent me. The driver delivered the crates, as requested. When I stopped in to see my French friends the following week, they were in seventh heaven. To show their appreciation, they gave me a white handkerchief with a little blue flower, as a souvenir. I carried that handkerchief with me throughout the war, my good-luck charm. Years later, I received a letter from my French friends from Algiers. They'd tracked me down through the War Department, inviting me to their son's engagement party in Paris. Their little boy had become an engineer. I couldn't go, but I was thrilled to hear from them, honored that they'd never forgotten our meeting in the Casbah.

One day a jeep with two soldiers from the Sixteenth Command Post drove up to our camp looking for me. The sergeant sitting next to the driver had written orders from Colonel George A. Taylor to bring me to his headquarters. What could the commander of the Sixteenth Regiment want with me, a recently promoted corporal in the Twenty-sixth? I got in the back of the jeep and drove with them to the Sixteenth's CP. Nobody spoke. The jeep stopped in front of a big tent. I walked in, clicked my heels, and saluted. It was the first time I'd needed to perform all that military crap since back at drill camp.

"Corporal Fuller, reporting as requested," I barked out.

"What kind of cigars do you smoke, Fuller?" asked Colonel Taylor.

"Optimos," I said. "Only thing I can get hold of over here."

"Everything else is in your file," said the colonel. "I've been reading about you. Impressive stuff. Reporter. Novelist. Movies."

"Yes sir."

"Now you're going to write for us."

"Write what, sir?"

"A full report after each battle. I want you to record exactly what you've seen in your own words. I want a detailed description of this regiment's actions, every combat, every movement, every victory, every error. Complete honesty."

"Why?" I asked.

"In all wars," said Taylor, hitting me between the eyes with his philosophy, "the only stories of individual battles that get written are those from the army's point of view. Military historians try to write history as if it belonged to the army. One regiment did this. Another did that. Always the same point of view. History, for me, is something that can save lives."

"I don't want that responsibility, Colonel," I said.

"Hell if I care what you want," he replied. "I'm giving you a great opportunity, Fuller. You'll get to observe the entire operation. No damned

Colonel George A. Taylor's earthiness, good humor, and steely determination come through in this drawing by William Fraccio. Taylor was an outstanding combat leader and a wonderful guy.

corporal has ever had the opportunity to see a combat plan, participate in it, then report on its execution."

"You asked for honesty, Colonel. I'm giving it to you straight. After a battle, all I want to do is laugh with the other guys, get a little drunk, and celebrate. If I'm still alive."

I felt free to refuse Colonel Taylor's offer, because I was about the low-est grade in the army. If they demoted me, there wasn't a long way to go before hitting bottom. I hadn't asked for the promotion to corporal at the conclusion of Torch, and I didn't give a shit if they took it away from me.

"Look, young man," said Taylor, "when I order a man to paint a fence white, white it will be! Understand? From now on, you're part of my regi-ment, the Sixteenth."

"But sir . . ." I began.

"But nothing!" said Taylor. "You were transferred to the Sixteenth the minute you got into the jeep that brought you here! Maybe you'll change your mind about writing for me. Meanwhile, I want you on hand at all times, Fuller."

We both smiled. That's how I got moved over to the Sixteenth for the rest of the war. Beneath all the officer veneer, Colonel Taylor had a heart of gold. I loved the guy. He became yet another father figure for me. I'd do anything for him, except write battle reports.

By June 1943, final preparations were being made for another invasion. We'd been put through more hard exercises to keep us in good shape. More importantly, we were battle-trained now, mentally ready to meet the Nazis head on, wherever the front would be. Tanks, jeeps, and trucks were painted to get them ready for another amphibious operation, then loaded onto waiting ships. The quays in the harbor at Algiers were crowded with more and more troop transports, destroyers, cruisers, and subchasers. Invasion rumors flew thick and fast. No one knew for sure where the beachhead was, nor did we have the faintest idea when we'd ship out. We were on tenterhooks. Even though we'd survived North Africa, a fatal bullet could be waiting for us in the next campaign.

As we were marching one day, a group of prisoners of war passed us going the opposite way. Among them was a dogface from our company. Turning my eyes away, I pretended not to recognize him. The American soldier had bandaged himself up and was standing in the line of Germans and Italians waiting to board a prisoner ship sailing for the States. Prisoners of war were sent to work on farms, the safest places to be for young Germans or Italians in 1943. The deserter's plan was to have a couple weeks lazing around the prison ship bound for New York, work on a farm, maybe get fingered and land in the hoosegow for a while. Whatever happened to him, he figured he'd be alive at the end of the war. The poor sonofabitch's timing was just a little off.

They identified the AWOL soldier during the Atlantic crossing, and MPs took him into custody as soon as the ship docked in Manhattan. Following Colonel Taylor's request to the War Department, the deserter was put on a transport plane and immediately sent back to Algiers, where he was urgently needed back on the front lines. He reappeared in our regiment the day before we shipped out. We teased the poor sonofabitch mercilessly.

"Tell us about New York!"

"Did you meet any pretty girls?"

"Any good whiskey?"

The deserter felt a little cocky about his caper. He was expecting much worse, but Colonel Taylor decided that his only punishment was to take the same risks as the rest of us. His face dropped when we told him that our next campaign was about to begin.

"When exactly?" he asked, his panicky eyes bulging.

"Don't know, but very soon."

"Where's the assault?" he asked, his voice trembling.

"No idea."

On July 3 and 4, the entire First Division was trucked in and loaded on the USS *Elizabeth Stanton* and the USS *Thurston*. The mighty fleet that had been assembling for weeks put out to sea on July 8. That's when we found out our target was Sicily. The code name for the operation would be "Husky." Booklets about Sicily were distributed to all dogfaces on board. Eager boys aching for action had replaced the soldiers killed or wounded in North Africa. I remember looking around at all the untried warriors and making a note in my journal, calling them "oatmeal invaders." One played the harmonica. Others sang. They had no reason to fear death by violence. They still didn't know what it was. Only a few months before, I myself had been an oatmeal invader.

The troop transports maneuvered into position off the southern coast of Sicily in very stormy weather the night of July 9. The ship was rolling violently in the heavy seas. The night was pitch-black, the Mediterranean, furious. The wind shrieked mercilessly. Waves crashed against the ship's bow like a relentless hammer out of a Greek myth. Suddenly navy destroyers opened fire, brightening the hostile horizon with crimson splotches. The sky vibrated with the roar of planes overhead. A searchlight from a destroyer right behind us blinded a plane. Anti-aircraft gunners on the ship opened fire. Holy shit, they were *our* planes, the Eighty-second Airborne, carrying the 504th Battalion of paratroopers! Over a loudspeaker, an officer screamed to cease fire. With a vicious wail and motors in flames, two C-47s plummeted into the sea right in front of our ship. Dead bodies tumbled from the sky. Some paratroopers barely escaped, by jumping out and hitting the silk. One of the jumpers, however, landed on the deck not far from me, his flesh still burning.

Wars are full of accidents. The sad fate of those Eighty-second Airborne paratroopers isn't mentioned very often in the history books. It made me sick to see it, even sicker to think of the families of those dead boys, confronted with the truth that they hadn't died by enemy fire but rather at the hands of their own countrymen.

Our big guns continued mercilessly, seeking out the enemy's coastal positions. We saw flashes on the horizon, shells bursting on the beach. The deafening crash of the artillery was like one long rolling peal of thunder, blending insanely with the quiet, calm command piped over the ship's sound system: "First wave to your stations."

Doggies ran to their boats, but because of the storm, we weren't able to board the landing craft until after midnight. Once lowered away, the cramped boats seemed like they would surely capsize before we ever reached the beach, tossing, bucking, and smashing against the side of the troopship. Vomit ambushed most of us. How could such small craft remain whole in that whirlpool of fury? Just as it seemed the invasion couldn't get any more nightmarish, someone screamed, "Incoming mail!"

We flattened ourselves down as much as possible. A shell from coastal artillery came crashing down on a landing ship tank—affectionately called a "long slow target"—making a direct hit on an ammunition truck on board the LST. The truck exploded, setting off chain reactions. It came a few days late, but we had the greatest July 4th fireworks show in history. Sheets of fire mushroomed upward, illuminating assault boats crammed with nauseous men armed with rifles, machine guns, and bazookas.

From ship to ship, silhouetted against the blazing horizon, scores of green lights blinked at red lights and yellow lights. One by one, the bucking boats pulled away from the troop transports and raced us to beachheads at Gela, a city founded by settlers from Rhodes and Crete in 688 B.C. Coastal searchlights streaked across the sky, hunting our ships. Our destroyers continued to rain hell on those beacons. Behind the beaches, our paratroopers were landing at their inland positions.

Safeties off, pieces ready, we crouched in the landing crafts, jammed one against the other, squinting at the quickly approaching sand dunes.

"Looks like Coney Island on a lousy night," said a lieutenant, binoculars glued to his eyes.

"She's gonna hit!" someone screamed.

We steeled ourselves for the jarring blow of the landing craft vehicle personnel, the LCVP (which we also referred to as a "Higgins boat"), against the sand. When it came to a sudden halt, we were thrown forward. LCVPs held thirty-two infantrymen and two marines. One marine was in charge, the other was an expert sniper. The ramp dropped. Machine-gun bullets cracked ahead of us in the dark. Many of the first men off the boat were almost always killed. We scrambled over their bodies and broke for shore without pausing. We were taught to never look at their faces. Never! The dead were dead. A split second wasted glancing at a corpse's haunting face and you'd wind up being a corpse too. We splashed forward into the water, dark, death-dealing figures, soaked waist-high, rifles held aloft, dashing through the surf.

"Somebody's pack!" a soldier yelled.

It was no pack. It was Sergeant Rideout, shot through the head.

"My toilet paper and tobacco are getting wet," griped another.

Our officers had welcomed the gale, saying it camouflaged the invasion.

Bullshit! The Italians were waiting for us. Those same officers had told us that Mussolini's men were laughable and their armies incompetent. More bullshit! At Gela, we were welcomed by highly trained professionals and fierce fighters. As our boats hit the beach, flares lit up the sky. A Breda heavy machine gun exploded through the slit in a concrete pillbox camouflaged high up on the beach. From dug-in positions, mortars, submachine guns, and rifles fired at our men as we plopped down on our bellies in the sand.

The North African landing had been kindergarten next to the invasion of Sicily. We were in Europe now. This was home turf to the Duce, backed by Hitler. There were three hundred thousand Italian and German soldiers occupying Sicily under Field Marshal Albert Kesselring. Each battle was going to be fought tooth and nail. For cryin' out loud, we were in their goddamned backyard!

I made it up the beach alive and shed my life jacket. There were bloody arms, legs, and heads strewn everywhere. That pillbox had to be knocked out. Our company commander sent a bazooka team over there. We covered them by unleashing a barrage of fire at the slit in the pillbox. A direct hit with a bazooka rocket blew the pillbox to smithereens, giving us momentary relief.

Up until then, Husky was the largest assault operation ever attempted by the Allies. The Third and Forty-fifth Divisions came ashore on either flank of the First. Up and down the beach, pillboxes were knocked out. Montgomery's Eighth Army touched down farther south, at Pachino. The timing of the invasion had to be precise. Wave after wave of men assaulted the beachheads. Nevertheless, we felt very alone out there. And goddamned wet. The big knot in the pit of my stomach was the same one that was churning in every other soldier's gut. We'd had battle experience, but the ferociousness of the fighting at Gela was beyond anything we'd ever seen before. We'd faced the enemy, but never this many. Our endurance had been tested, but never to this extent. The noise of all the machine guns, grenades, land mines, mortar explosions, and heavy artillery was maddening.

Gradually, we moved up the beach, knocking out their positions one after another. Demoralized, the Italians fell back. Dawn brought a lull. Thanks to the pinkish light, we could see the entire corpse-strewn beach. We had to keep moving up. Barbed wire barricades were cut through, and a railway embankment was scaled. We hustled through vegetable gardens and out into narrow streets, rooting out snipers as we advanced. We took a nearby airfield and blew up the Messerschmitts and Heinkels we caught on the landing strip. Patrols were formed. One of them rushed back to our

Early one morning during
a break in the action at
Gela, Sicily, I posed with
Sergeant Carpino.

base camp and reported that German tanks
and troops were moving back toward us. It was
the anticipated counterattack, like at Kasserine
Pass, led by the crack Hermann Göring Panzer
Division. German tanks got into position, expecting to hit us hard and
push our asses into the Mediterranean.

The battle was desperate, purely defensive, trying to hold our lines.
There could be no retreat, for that meant annihilation. Fighting with only
our rifles and a couple 57-mm antitank guns on hand, we tried to hold off
the advancing Panzers, knocking a few out of commission. But by 1100
hours, forty tanks had moved up, confronting us on the road to Niscemi,
the nearest village. A navy reconnaissance plane had radioed the Panzers'
position to the destroyer *Savannah,* which unleashed its heavy artillery.
The exploding shells were deafening but off target. The Panzers regrouped
and proceeded to smash through our positions, heading for the beach to
destroy supplies and cut us off from our support. Behind the tanks, over
fifty truckloads of Wehrmacht troops were unloaded to join the counteroffensive.

"Under no circumstances will anyone pull back," were Colonel Taylor's
orders.

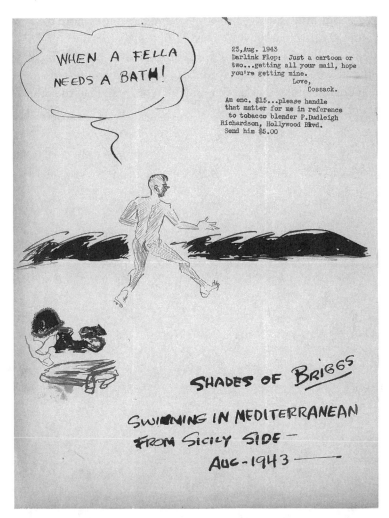

There would be many
more fierce battles to fight
in Sicily before we could go
skinny-dipping in August
1943, when I did this cartoon
for my mother.

For a while, it looked hopeless. Then, at
1930 hours, just in the nick of time, Cannon
Company landed and, under the command of
the amazingly accurate Captain O'Brien, our
big guns started getting in some licks. Within
minutes, Cannon Company had knocked out
fifteen tanks, methodically destroying the backbone of the attack. We
picked off soldiers jumping out of the flaming Panzers. The Nazi counterattack was stopped in its tracks, the Gela plain pock-marked with burning
tanks and dead Wehrmacht.

One of the many dogfaces killed during our victorious assault at Gela
was the deserter who'd been caught masquerading as a prisoner of war. We

often talked about him afterward. Had he waited a couple more days to make his getaway, maybe he'd have missed Husky altogether and survived. As it turned out, he was another corpse we leapt over on that Sicilian beach, losing his life like many other more courageous men. It didn't matter a good goddamn whether he'd been more or less scared than the others. He was just as dead as the heroes.

14

Just Stand There

Go like hell!"

Those were General George S. Patton's orders to the division commanders of the Seventh Army after our successful landing in Sicily. Patton was our commanding officer, but in name only. He was a brilliant tactician though he seemed more interested in headlines than in the men on his front lines. Once he was visiting a field hospital and saw a soldier with nothing apparently wrong with him, except the man was trembling and crying. Patton accused the dogface of cowardice and slapped him hard. As it turned out, the man had malaria. The incident was covered up, but eventually got back to the front lines. It was symbolic of why I didn't care for the flamboyant general.

Our fervent allegiance, on and off the battlefield, was to the First Division's commanding officer, General Terry de la Mesa Allen. A modest man, General Allen was loved by his soldiers because he really cared about them. What a helluva guy! He didn't give a damn about playing politics or being famous. Even when they tried to make a hero out of him—his photo would appear on the cover of *Time* and *Newsweek*—Terry said, "I'm no hero. Dead men made me a general." After the war, Terry Allen visited me in Hollywood and stayed at my home. John Ford called me up to ask if he could come over and meet the famous general. The three of us had a memorable dinner on my terrace next to the pool, smoking cigars and telling stories into the night.

According to General Allen, the primary attribute of the Big Red One, contributing more than any other factor to its combat success, was its sense of teamwork. That teamwork kicked in during the Sicilian campaign. We moved up the center of Sicily fast, taking every village we came upon. Niscemi, Barafranca, Enna, Villarosa, Alimena, Bonpietro, Petralia. It was exhausting work, with little time to sleep. Our nerves were frazzled, but we had to keep moving forward. Our sergeant wouldn't even let us piss

General George S. Patton in Sicily, with leather leggings and silver pistols. I didn't mind his outspokenness, uncompromising standards, and aggressive combat strategy. No doubt he played a key role in Allied victories. I just didn't like the man.

because it was too dangerous to stop. With his binoculars, he'd continually be checking for any sign of snipers up ahead. Without taking his eyes away from the glasses, he'd pause and say, "Anybody wanna piss, do it right now."

As we chased them north toward Messina, the Italians and Germans put up a dogged defense, setting up ambushes, minefields and SPs, self-propelled guns. Sicilian roads were narrow and primitive. To make the going even

FIFTEEN CENTS   AUGUST 9, 1943

TIME
THE WEEKLY NEWSMAGAZINE

MAJOR GENERAL TERRY ALLEN OF THE 1ST DIVISION
The Infantry, the Infantry, with the dirt behind their ears . . .
(World Battlefronts)

VOLUME XLII   NUMBER 6

A modest man, Terry Allen never was comfortable with the spotlight, though he got plenty of it.

rougher, the retreating enemy troops destroyed bridges. Our engineers would have to throw up trestles to bring up heavy equipment.

Somewhere in those Sicilian hills on the march inland, a dogface in our company stepped on a land mine. There was an explosion. We all hit the dirt, ready to return fire. When we realized it was a mine, everyone jumped up except for the dogface who'd been hit. His groin was splashed in blood. He was moaning.

"They forgot to undig that one," said the sergeant.

"Oh, no! No! No!" cried the doggie, clutching his crotch.

The possible loss of his cock had snapped his mind. He stared like a madman at the sky.

"Back off, everybody!" ordered the sergeant, as he looked around the ground on the hillside where the mine was planted. There might be others. Then he picked up something small and bloody.

"Found it," announced the sergeant casually. "One of your balls."

The dogface began to shake with terrible tremors. He looked at the sergeant with those crazed eyes.

"It's mine!" he said. "Give it back to me!"

The sergeant flung it over the side of the hill.

"You son of a bitch!" screamed the dogface.

"You think you're going to walk around with it wrapped up like a piece of dried sausage?" said the sergeant. "It's just one ball. God gave you two. You can still have kids."

"Are you sure!?"

"Feel."

The dogface groped his bloody crotch. Relief came over his face. He laughed hysterically. His eyes lost their mad glaze.

"I still got it!" he yelled. "I still got my cock!"

In one of those Sicilian villages, maybe Sperlinga, we were confronted by an enemy nest holed up in a monastery. We didn't know how many there were, how much ammunition they had, or if they were Germans, Italians, or both. I was part of the advance team sent in to check out the situation. They started firing at us as we zigzagged up to the monastery. There were a total of twenty-one SS, Wehrmacht, and Italians in the place. We caught them in a crossfire, killing about ten. The others surrendered quickly, aware that our invasion forces were about to sweep the area. Though they seemed to go on forever, skirmishes like that one lasted no more than five minutes. I was leading the line of prisoners back to our camp to be interrogated. My sergeant and a lieutenant brought up the rear. There was a gigantic German soldier marching right behind me, his big boots tramping on the back of mine. I stopped the entire procession and turned around to look up into that big Nazi's blue eyes.

"Listen, you sonofabitch!" I said. "Next time you step on my heels, I'll blow your goddamned head off! Understand?"

The big German didn't have the slightest reaction to my threat. No doubt my barking up into the big Nazi's blank face was more comical than menacing. The sergeant and lieutenant began laughing. We started off again, me taking bigger steps and the Nazi taking smaller ones. Our prisoners had no intention of escaping. Why die for the Führer or the Duce when you could be a prisoner of war?

All around us were vineyards, orchards, farms, the sweet smell of alfalfa, wheat, and jasmine in the air. We ate our fill of almonds, grapes, apricots, and figs. Sicily was a magnificently fertile island. "What a fool man is!" I kept thinking to myself, unable to reconcile the death and destruction with all that beauty and abundance.

Our prisoners were guys like us, except they were fighting on the other side. They thought they were doing the right thing, too. The difference was they weren't united. The SS were snobs who looked with contempt upon the Wehrmacht. None of the Germans would even sit next to the Italians, their Axis allies. What a sad joke their alliance was!

After Mussolini drafted all the fighting-age Sicilians, the island was left to the care of old men, women, and children.

Once we captured an enemy soldier, we routinely went through his backpack. Among one of the Germans' personal items, I found letters from his mother. She'd asked him to send her shoelaces from Italy. We turned over anything like that to guys from Intelligence. Even the slightest bit of information could be useful. If machines that manufactured shoelaces weren't operating in Germany, it meant that other machinery wasn't working, maybe even entire industrial sectors.

The Sperlinga combat, with three dogfaces taking twenty-one of the enemy, looked pretty good on paper. A quick ceremony was organized, and Colonel Taylor awarded me and the others the Purple Heart for the action. I was feeling rascally that day. While Taylor was pinning the goddamned medal on my dirty uniform, I told him, out of earshot of the outfit, "I don't want any medals, Colonel. We should give it to one of those Italians who was such a crack shot at Gela."

"They're dead. Shut up and take it," said Taylor, through smiling lips. "Or I'll pin it on your ass."

Psychology is an essential weapon in wartime. That's why we had trouble fighting against Italians. We didn't have the same venom for them as we did for Nazis. We hated Nazis. But in every outfit, there were Ameri-

cans of Italian descent. A few could even speak the language. We had one
dogface from San Francisco who was intent on locating his Sicilian grandmother in a village near Caltinessetta. And, for Chrissakes, he did!

The Sicilians usually welcomed us. After an assault, when all enemy
soldiers had been killed or driven away, the villagers—mostly women,
children, and old men—brought out wine, pasta, fruit, and flowers. All
the young men had been called up to fight for the fascists. Many were
never coming back. It was hard to feel contempt for civilians, even though
we knew that they'd been saluting Mussolini a few days before our invasion. Again, it was a question of survival.

One day, I was on another advance patrol when we passed a little farm
behind a stone wall. The entire family was outside the place, mama,
grandma, grandpa, and bambinos, chanting: "Mussolini, no good . . .
Mussolini, no good. . . ."

We were paranoid, suspicious of everyone and everything, so we
stopped to check out the farm, searching the house for weapons. There
was nothing irregular. However, when we went through the barn behind
the farmhouse, we found a young woman, about eighteen, hiding in one
of the donkey stalls. She was small and shapely, with a pretty face, dark
eyes, and black hair. She wore a salmon-pink blouse, a dusty skirt, and sandals. Her legs were unshaven. We dragged her outside kicking and screaming. One of our Italian-American dogfaces told her she had nothing to
fear. She started yelling profanities at him.

"What's her problem?" I asked.

The dogface explained that she wanted us to kill every fascist in Sicily
and burn Mussolini alive when we got to Rome.

"I think it's all bullshit," said our bilingual doggie.

The girl understood his drift and exploded with more epithets of hate.
Suddenly she stopped and opened her blouse. Instead of a bra, she had
soiled medical bandages covering her breasts.

"Was she hit in the chest?" asked the sergeant.

"No. She says a fascist raped her and bit off her nipples."

All of us froze, sickened at her plight.

"She's lying," said our translator.

"Why don't you buy her story?"

"I know these ass-kissers. When Mussolini was riding high, they were
crazy about the bastard. Now that they figure he's licked, everybody hates
him. We're supposed to believe that fascism never caught on in Sicily. The
hell it didn't! She's a liar."

He ripped off one of her bandages. The girl screamed. We stared at the
teeth marks on her mutilated breast. In place of a nipple, there was an ugly

black-and-blue wound. We paled and stepped back from her. Our sergeant gently took the girl back to her family and gave her fresh bandages and antiseptics. We stood speechless.

"Okay," growled the disbelieving, shocked soldier, "so I was wrong." Ashamed of himself, he walked up to the girl in front of her family. *"Signorina, per favore. Sono molto desolato, molto, molto."*

Messina had to be captured to stop the Germans from retreating to the Italian mainland. That port city, located on the northeast corner of Sicily, was also the golden fleece in a secret Anglo-American contest between Montgomery and Patton. Each wanted his army to take Messina first. We had no idea that we were players in this absurd game of death.

There were three ways into Messina: the first, along the northern coastal road from Palermo, a second, from Syracuse along the eastern coast of the island, and a third, inland by way of Randazzo on the slopes of Mount Etna. The Sixteenth drew the inland route, fighting alongside the Eighteenth, the Twenty-sixth, and the Thirty-ninth Infantry. First, we had to take Nicosia and Cerami, then finally Troina, a mountain village where the Nazis had held Montgomery's troops in check for a couple of weeks. We advanced through the Catanian plain, which we called "Panzerland" because it was so well suited to tank movements. As we marched through its pastures and wheatfields, a Nazi biplane with a black cross on its tail suddenly swooped down over our heads. It flew so close to the ground that we could clearly see the pilot's face.

A lieutenant who'd just joined our outfit, anxious to kill any German he laid eyes on, raised his rifle and aimed at the pilot as the biplane swooped down for another look at us. Our sergeant threw himself on the lieutenant to stop him from firing. The biplane made a couple more passes over us, then flew off. The lieutenant was mad as hell. Why the hell couldn't he shoot the sonofabitch Nazi? Because if he had, explained the sergeant to the greenhorn, our troops would have been blown to smithereens by enough heavy artillery to make it look like the Fourth of July and Bastille Day all in one. The biplane was looking for tanks and artillery, not foot soldiers. We couldn't shoot it down because the pilot was in constant contact with their command post, his radio emitting tracking signals. If the plane went down, enemy artillery would target the last coordinates they'd received and—*BA-BOOM*—we'd go up in fire and smoke.

The going was tough around Nicosia, where the rugged terrain and steep slopes made progress painfully slow. Mules were needed to haul supplies. A request for the animals brought this message: "Thirty burros can be picked up at the Gangi City Hall at 1500 hours." The animals were delivered to the regiment's CP but the war had to be momentarily forgotten when a group of impatient Sicilian farmers showed up to insist on immediate payment for their mules.

By the end of July, after twenty days of continuous movement, either attacking or dodging artillery, mortars, and rockets, our outfit craved a break in the action. But none was forthcoming. An assault on Cerami was planned for the next morning. We got word that the Thirty-ninth would lead the assault, giving the Sixteenth a much needed respite. We were delighted to be out of the picture for a few hours. However, Colonel Taylor sent out this warning to every one of his doggies: ". . . It would be folly to let a few victories lull us into a sense of security. As long as Sicily is not ours, we have cause for worry every instant."

The next morning, the electrifying news came through that Cerami had fallen without opposition. Whenever there'd been a tough battle, the Sixteenth was predestined to be on the front line. Now when there was no resistance, we were taking it easy. The true story of what happened in Cerami was one of the most amusing incidents of the campaign. One of our scouts, Private Wheeler of the Sixteenth's I Platoon, had been stuck near Cerami all night long, watching the village get blitzed by American artillery. Wheeler saw the Jerries evacuating, then got himself fixed up with chow from some locals. Before sunrise, he entered the town alone and was accosted by a solitary armed German who got left behind by the retreating First Panzer Grenadier Regiment. Wheeler disarmed the enemy soldier, and, with time on his hands, decided to take a shave. When the Thirty-ninth marched into town, they found that one of the Sixteenth's very own had taken it single-handedly and was having a shave in the middle of the main street.

There was nothing funny about the battle for Troina. It was the toughest of the entire Sicilian campaign. Its capture would open the road to Messina. Our attack began on August 1, 1943. The Nazis were dug in for a do-or-die stand in the hills and ravines outside Troina. There was fierce fighting for six long days and nights. As soon as we pushed the enemy back a little, they counterattacked. We lost many men, killed and wounded, but finally prevailed. At noon on August 6, Troina fell. The enemy had been defeated, but the lengthy battle had allowed thousands of German troops to escape to the mainland to fight another day, leaving the Italians holding the bag.

With the way now clear, our regiment moved back and allowed the Forty-seventh Infantry, Ninth Division, to pass through on their way to Messina, where Patton organized a victorious entrance thirty-seven days after the landing at Gela. Patton must have been satisfied with himself, because he'd won his goddamned race with Montgomery. We didn't give a damn about parades. After having taken eighteen towns and capturing six thousand prisoners, our outfit was exhausted. We were first moved to Randazzo, in the neighborhood of Mount Etna, which soared eleven thousand feet above us. We got our first complete night of sleep under the beautiful Sicilian night sky, the crimson light from Etna reflected in the clouds overhead, the red-hot lava lapping beneath its rim.

Then we were moved to a camp in Licata, not far from Gela, where the bloody battle with the Hermann Göring Panzers had taken place. There we got some R and R before the old grind of training resumed. Some of the NCOs thought providing us with prostitutes would be "regenerative." They rounded up some of the ugliest women in Sicily, who, for a special war-inflated fee in lira, were ready to take on anyone in a tent set up for the occasion behind our camp. Later, we'd visit Palermo, where the local pimps had gone to work. They'd stretch themselves out in a hammock with four or five girls hanging around, some of them sisters or cousins. Soldiers lined up like they were waiting for a bowl of grub in a chow line. It was horrible. Regenerative, my ass!

You'll rarely see women in my war films because I rarely saw women during the war. There were never any women around during the battles, except for the scared females scurrying from one building to the next to take cover during an assault. Women who suddenly appeared after a campaign—plying the world's oldest trade—were nothing to write home about. For cryin' out loud, after having seen bloody, mutilated bodies strewn everywhere, you were in no goddamned mood for sex. Everybody's nerves were shot, our brains fried with horrible images of devastation. Was it any surprise soldiers developed plenty of sexual problems that lived with them the rest of their days?

Thank God and the USO that we got to see those variety shows specially brought over from the States for us between campaigns. After Husky ended, I remember Al Jolson performing on a little makeshift stage in Sicily. Jolson was fabulous. He made us forget the war and feel like we were part of the human race again. It was heartwarming to see all our wounded soldiers in front of the stage, listening to Jolson crooning, "Mammy, how I love ya, how I love ya, my Dear ol' Mammy."

One of the soldiers near the stage had lost his right hand. Another soldier sitting next to him had lost his left. When Jolson finished his medley with "Alexander's Ragtime Band," these two delighted dogfaces jumped up and used their two good hands to clap as one. The sight made tears come to your eyes.

After Jolson, the actor Adolphe Menjou got up on the stage to give us a pep talk. A ham actor who'd never been on any front line was the last per-

In his sixties when he sang for us in Sicily in 1943, Al Jolson (born Asa Yoelson) was at the tail end of a glorious career that brought him from Saint Petersburg, Russia, to the pinnacle of Broadway success by way of vaudeville, then Hollywood stardom in the first talkie, The Jazz Singer *(1927).*

son we wanted to hear from after surviving all those vicious battles around Troina. "You have to destroy the Nazis," preached Menjou. "Don't ever give an inch to the fascists."

His silver-tongued speech was the most inappropriate bullshit I'd ever heard. Who the hell was that goddamned actor to get up and give us his stupid patriotic palaver? We were the ones doing the fighting. A drunken dog-face was so infuriated by Menjou's speech that he raised his rifle and aimed it at the phony sonofabitch while he was speaking. No one made a move to stop the soldier from pulling the trigger. It seemed the only way to shut

Menjou up. He left the stage to overwhelming boos and catcalls. Lucky for the thespian, our dogface never took off his safety.

The next time I ran into Adolphe Menjou, it was at a special screening of *Park Row* in 1952. Everyone in the world of publishing was there, William Randolph Hearst's son, representatives from over a hundred newspapers, plus special guests President Herbert Hoover and General Douglas MacArthur. I didn't know who let Menjou into my event, but there he was. The smug bastard would soon be giving a memorable performance before the House Committee on Un-American Activities, pointing an accusing finger at a number of Hollywood colleagues. That day he came over and sat on the other side of General MacArthur. Menjou started raving about what a beautiful film I'd made. I said nothing. Coming from him, the compliment meant less than nothing. Then Menjou leaned over toward me and asked if I'd been in the service.

"Hell, yes!" I said, feeling all the cockiness and satisfaction of having produced *Park Row* with my own dough. "North Africa. Sicily. France. Germany. Czechoslovakia."

"Army?" asked MacArthur.

"Yes sir."

"Which division?"

"First," I said proudly.

"Ah!" said the general. "Another one of Terry Allen's men!"

MacArthur started reminiscing about Terry de la Mesa Allen at West Point, where they were cadets together.

"I was in Sicily with our boys," said Menjou, butting in.

"I was one of the boys," I said with unmistakable contempt. "You almost got yourself shot that day, Mr. Menjou, but not by the enemy."

Menjou laughed, a slimy, yellow laugh, then shut up. He knew I knew that his presence in Sicily had been ridiculed and disprized by "our boys."

At that same USO show in Sicily, after Jolson and Menjou, the master of ceremonies introduced a British actress named Anna Lee. A young woman came up on the stage in a magnificent green gown. She was the most beautiful creature we'd seen in a long, long time.

"I can't sing," Anna Lee announced, embarrassed at her predicament. "I can't dance. I don't know what to do up here."

She was so sweet. All we wanted to do was feast our eyes on that heavenly creature.

"JUST STAND THERE!" we all shouted. "JUST STAND THERE!"

She did. There was a wonderful, indescribable moment of silence. Then we started cheering wildly for Anna Lee. After Torch, I came across a "stories-wanted" offer by the GI newspaper. I wrote a piece about Anna

Lee and how much her "performance" on the stage in Sicily meant to us. Years after the war ended, I was visiting John Ford on one of his sets, I think *Fort Apache*. Ford introduced me to one of the actresses who'd become a fixture in his movies, Anna Lee.

"I know you," I said. "From Sicily!"

We had a great reunion. Anna said she'd kept my article from the GI magazine as a precious souvenir of the war. I was very moved to meet up with her again. She'd been a big star in Great Britain before relocating to Hollywood in the late thirties with her husband, director Robert Stevenson. In 1958, I had the pleasure of working with Anna when I cast her as Mac, an alcoholic artist in *The Crimson Kimono*. She appeared in over seventy movies, including *What Ever Happened to Baby Jane?* (1962) and *The Sound of Music* (1965). In the seventies, Anna got married to Robert Nathan, a dear friend and great writer, author of *Portrait of Jenny* and *The Bishop's Wife,* and we were able to share some more good times. What a lovely spirit she was!

Our outfit boarded a British troopship, the HMS *Maloja,* one night in mid-October and shipped out of Sicily. No one would tell us where we were going. For days on end, the *Maloja* cruised back and forth in the Mediterranean, feinting a landing next to General Mark Clark's Fifth Army at Salerno as part of the invasion forces on the Italian mainland. Then we turned and sailed west, which meant they weren't sending us into Italy after all. We lingered at sea for a week near Algiers, then sailed east, back toward Italy, our hearts sinking. We really weren't going back into battle. At least not yet. The maneuvering was meant to mislead the enemy. Finally, the *Maloja* headed for the Atlantic, passing through the Strait of Gibraltar. Along with the open seas came the soaring hope that, after two successful amphibious campaigns, we were being sent back to the States. But Eisenhower had other designs for trained and experienced combat infantry like us.

Confusion buffeted every man on board when they made us take off all the Big Red One shoulder patches on our uniforms and remove the insignia from our helmets. All identification had to go. The ship was taking us back to Britain, where we were to spend many months in secret preparation for another amphibious assault, the biggest ever undertaken in history. We didn't know it yet, but we had an appointment on the beaches of Normandy on Tuesday, June 6, 1944.

15

Impossible to
Feel Blessed

You are in Liverpool," announced Major General Huebner, the new commander of the First Infantry Division.[1] We'd just debarked from the *Maloja* on the foggy night of November 5, 1943, jammed into a gigantic warehouse. Now we knew where we were. But why back to England?

"We will not participate in the invasion of Italy," announced Huebner.

We cheered the general like crazy.

"You were ordered to remove all insignia because we don't want the enemy to know we're here. We're a battle-hardened amphibious outfit, and they think we're still in the Mediterranean preparing to hit someplace in Italy. We want them to keep thinking that. The more false rumors, the better we like it. A year ago, we invaded North Africa, four months ago, Sicily. I am as sorry as any man here that our battle dead and wounded are no longer with us. But their job's going to be finished by you."

We looked at each other like prisoners waiting to hear our death sentences.

"You're going to train like you've never trained before. You won't like what I'm going to say—I don't like it either—but from this moment on, you are *not* the First Division, you never *heard* of the First Division, you haven't fought in North Africa or Sicily. As far as anyone, and that means *anyone*—military or civilian—is concerned, you men are all green troops just arrived from the States. If anyone asks, you tell them that you belong to the 315th Anti-Airforce Regiment. If they question you about how long you've been here, you answer three days. That's the only way we can keep Hitler guessing about what the First Division's going to do next."

A low grumbling swept across the warehouse.

"And remember this," added General Huebner. "I'll personally shoot any man who gives away our cover."

Our division was transported down to Dorset and bivouacked near a town called Bridgeport, not far from Exeter. For the next seven long months, they drilled the hell out of us. Training with our outfit were other U.S. divisions, as well as soldiers from France, Poland, and Hungary. We were allowed to go into Bridgeport once in a while. In a pub there, I heard a local woman tell one of our boys, "You Yanks have endless dollars and endless hard-ons. Bless you, dearie!"

It was impossible for me to feel blessed. Like many members of our outfit who'd survived the campaigns in North Africa and Sicily, I was in a foul mood when I got to England. My nerves were strained to the breaking point. I'd had my fill of combat. Now, there was more backbreaking training. Then, once a month, they loaded us on trucks and took us to a beach in Devon called Slapton Sands where we rehearsed amphibious maneuvers, with British soldiers on the cliffs playing the role of defending Germans. I was fed up with jumping off landing boats into the surf and crawling up beaches on my belly.

My bitterness would be replaced with pride. Battle-tested men were needed for their skills and more, as morale-raising symbols. We had plenty of replacements to fill up the Division, but one combat veteran was worth twenty greenhorns. My sergeant saw I was bitter. He told me I was an essential link in the next campaign. It was easy to say, but true. I bought the sergeant's read on my sour state of mind and accepted my predicament. Wherever the Big Red One was going to invade next, I had to be there. Most likely I'd die in combat. Okay. So why not call a ceasefire with my self-defeating scorn? What choice did I have? A Nazi bullet during the next campaign or an American bullet from a firing squad for desertion? With survival my only motivation, I began to enjoy mastering our practice sessions at Slapton Sands, conducting myself like the experienced soldier I was.

Real ammunition was used in the training sessions. That was another good reason to concentrate. Plenty of dogfaces were wounded or killed in training. I've always wondered about their families back home. How would they react if they found out that the "Killed in Action" telegram they received was only half true, that the bullet or shrapnel was "friendly fire"?

The pubs in town, with their warm beer, did not interest me. I had no patience for gibble-gabble or drinking myself into oblivion. I spent free time writing letters to my mother, which I usually began with "Darlink Flop," drawing cartoons all over the place to reassure Rebecca that I was in fine spirits. Guys in my outfit caught me drawing those cartoons, so they asked me to draw funny scenes on their V-mail, too. I wish I'd charged a nickel for every cartoon I scratched on dogface correspondence during the war. I'd have been the richest soldier in the infantry!

Throughout the war, my mother sent me care packages via APO with Optimos, Garcia y Suares, or maybe Pancho Arangos, king-size, which she'd get me at the Waldorf-Astoria Hotel. God bless that woman!

Rebecca's letters reached me regularly, usually accompanied by a box of Optimos. She wrote me in 1943 that she'd succeeded in selling *The Dark Page* to Sloan & Pearce without even a rewrite. They were going to publish it in hardback. I was thrilled, especially because Rebecca would have some dough to live on, thanks to the publisher's advance.

The local grocery store in Bridgeport, run by Mrs. Gibbs, was my favorite hangout on weekend leaves. I met some of the townspeople and found out how much they'd suffered since the beginning of the war. Mrs. Gibbs was very sweet to me. She cultivated roses, and, when I told her I was crazy about them, she showed me around her greenhouse. It smelled like a little piece of paradise. I couldn't discuss anything with Mrs. Gibbs about our military mission in England, but I could chat with her about movies.

"My cousin Alfred is in the movie business, too."

"Alfred?" I said. "Not Alfred Hitchcock?"

"Why yes," she said. "Do you know him?"

"Hell, yes!" I said surprised and delighted. "Just his work. I'd love to meet him. Maybe he'd like to direct one of my yarns."

"All right," said Mrs. Gibbs, always so kind and civilized. "I shall arrange it the next time you have a weekend furlough."

In May 1944, I finally got leave to go to London. I was to have tea with Cousin Alfred at the Claridge. I was also hoping to catch up with my old friend Hank Wales. Since I'd first gotten to England, I'd looked for signs of Hank in London, one of his stomping grounds. By calling an editor at the London office of the *Chicago Tribune,* I was able to locate Wales. He was waiting for me at Victoria Station the morning I came in from Devon. It was cold and rainy, classic English weather. I wore a plain army uniform, without any insignia. Hank showed me all over town. He took me to Fleet Street, the RAF Club, the Savoy. We walked along the Thames, through Hyde Park, on Grosvenor Road. For the first time, I saw locations we'd utilized for *Confirm or Deny.* I loved London and temporarily forgot about foxholes, mess lines, machine guns, and amphibious invasions.

With his broad experience as a war correspondent, Hank was an eminence grise for the Allies. They'd given him privileged access to sources in the U.S. high command. He took me to the George Club for lunch. Waiters were hurrying around tables filled with reporters, military brass, and government officials. They served every brand of whiskey ever made. As soon as we sat down at the polished wood table in the red leather booth, Hank peered at me hard and shook his head.

"You know, Sammy," he said quietly, "your life's at risk in the next Allied operation."

"Same as in the last," I said.

"What's your rank now, Sammy?"

"Corporal."

"That will work."

"Work what?"

"Look, Sammy, you don't have to explain anything to me about the First Division. You were on the front lines in Torch and Husky. All right. Now listen to me. You're a dead man if you continue with this soldiering game. You've got plenty of stories to write for years to come. That's enough! *Basta!* I'm going to get them to take you out of the infantry and put you in the news service department. You'll cover this damn war as a journalist from now on and save your own ass!"

"Holy shit, Hank! Hold on!" I said. "I could have done that from the very beginning. I was already offered that behind-the-lines crap. But when I'm at a typewriter, I like to write my own material."

"You don't understand, Sammy. All the glory, that heroic stuff, is over. Don't be a stubborn fool."

"My life was on the line in North Africa and Sicily."

"I know. I know. But this is different. This is big. Very big. Eisenhower has the leadership to open the new front everyone's been blabbing about. He's been at general headquarters for final planning sessions. Rumors are flying around but it's really going to happen, a gigantic operation like nothing anyone has ever imagined."

"They've got me crawling around beaches to get ready for it."

"Sammy, I'm asking you for the last time. Just say yes. If you think too much, you'll miss your only chance to survive this damn war. There are plenty of soldiers, but there are few correspondents with your talent. Most of the reporting doesn't have any punch. It's cold, impersonal, distant. You'd be great, Sammy. We need you!"

"Hank," I said, shaking my head, "you're awfully sweet to try. My answer is still no. I'm going to get the story—my story of the war—from the front lines."

Wales and I never said another word about it. He accompanied me over to the Claridge at tea time for the meeting with Alfred Hitchcock and waited for me outside. I don't think Hank wanted to explain to Hitch why he didn't care for *Foreign Correspondent* (1940)—remember, the film was supposed to have been based on Wales's career.

My encounter with Hitchcock was something out of the theater of the absurd, with a helluva lot of quid pro quos. I called his room from the lobby. He said he'd meet me in the bar. I sat down in one of those Queen Anne chairs and waited. Queen Anne must have had a very small ass, because when Hitchcock arrived, he could hardly squeeze into the damn thing.

"Let's go sit in the lobby," I said, seeing his discomfort. "These chairs are awful."

"Bless you, my lad," said Hitchcock.

We found a quiet corner with larger chairs. I launched into praise for his work. I especially loved *The 39 Steps* (1935) and *Secret Agent* (1936). I told him that I'd worked in Hollywood, mentioned some of my scripts, talked about *The Dark Page* getting published. We chatted a little about John Ford and Raoul Walsh, though Hitchcock didn't seem to have any interest in talking about movies.

"How long have you been in England?" he asked me.

"Three days."

"Which outfit are you with?"

"Anti-Air Force."

Hitchcock gave me a little skeptical smirk. "Where are you really based?" he asked.

I stopped cold and looked sternly at Hitchcock's pudgy face.

"I could be executed for answering that question," I said sarcastically. "And you could, too, just for asking it."

He turned as white as a ghost.

"No! No! You don't understand!"

"Yes, I do."

"Look, my lad," said Hitchcock. "I'm here making documentary films for England. We're fighting this war together."

"I can't talk about where I'm stationed."

"I had no right to ask you," said Hitchcock. "Forgive me. Can I invite you for supper?"

"Thank you, but I can't. I have to go soon. A friend is waiting for me."

I asked Hitchcock if I could eventually send him a script or an original story. Relieved that I was showing due respect and soliciting his expertise, Hitchcock gave me instructions about forwarding my stuff to his producer, David Selznick. He seemed pretty interested in a story I pitched him called *Command Post*. I stood to say good-bye, and he shook my hand cordially. That first encounter with Hitchcock, though full of wartime tension and miscues, was memorable. Unfortunately, we never worked together. Years later, whenever we ran into each other in Hollywood, Hitch and I always greeted each other warmly. We always laughed about our first meeting at the Claridge, where my mix of American bluntness and his proud British manners had blended like oil and water.

The other person I tried to look up during that trip to London was my brother Ray, who was an officer stationed somewhere in England. But even with Hank Wales's pull, I couldn't locate Ray. Everything was so goddamned top secret.

General Huebner assembled the entire outfit one night in late May. He congratulated us on our training and discretion. Not once had a careless slip of the tongue by any soldier revealed that the Big Red One was in England. The general told us we were ready for the biggest challenge of our military careers. Exactly where and when we'd go into action, however, wasn't mentioned.

"Soon you'll paint the Big Red One back on your helmets and put your patches back on your uniforms," said the general. "But tonight, there's a big dance in town. You are off duty. You cannot discuss the military situation, but you can have fun."

The men's cheers rose mightily as one. General Huebner waited for us to quiet down.

"Pay attention to one song tonight: 'I Can't Give You Anything but Love.' When you hear that tune, wherever you are or whatever you are doing, you will leave that instant and return to base camp."

My meeting with Alfred Hitchcock at the Claridge Hotel was a comedy of errors that we both remembered fondly.

Late that night, we were in a noisy pub in Bridgeport drinking everything in sight when that song came on the radio. It was the first time in seven months they'd played it. We looked at each other and instantly got the hell out of there. The place was teeming with dogfaces one moment and empty the next. When we got back to camp, they told us to start preparing our gear to move out. Still, we had no idea where we were going. They loaded us onto trucks in the middle of the night and took us to a marshaling area near Long Bredy, in Dorset.

Where or when Operation Overlord would take place was the best-kept secret of the war. There were six hundred miles of coast from Holland to Spain, and even high-ranking army officials didn't know the beachhead. Forget about war movies you've seen with handsome actors in uniforms discussing D day before the invasion. Bullshit! When we finally got down to final preparations, real places in Overlord were never mentioned, only code names that were attached to unspecified landing areas: Utah, Sword, Juno, Fox Green, Easy Red, Omaha.

The first time I heard the word "Omaha"—three syllables that would be part of my very being for the rest of my life—I was in a crowded tent erected on Dorset's muddy red earth while a captain showed us big mock-ups of an unnamed beachhead. Tiny white flags identified assault teams. The first village we were to liberate was called Colleville-sur-Mer. Then, and only then, did we know that the attack was aimed at the French coast.

We were invading Normandy for the same reason that William the Conqueror had done it nine hundred years before: it was the shortest distance across the Channel. This time, two million soldiers, five thousand ships, and two thousand airplanes had to cross that narrow waterway to breach Hitler's European citadel. Normandy was supposed to have fewer and less motivated Nazi troops. We'd find out the truth about that lie soon enough. Field Marshal von Rundstedt and our old foe General Rommel would make sure that every foot of those goddamned beaches would be bathed in Allied blood. The deception of an invasion at Calais, directly across from the cliffs of Dover, had been created with dummy troop and supply movements along with a diversionary bombing campaign. Thanks to that ruse, General von Rundstedt didn't pull out his Fifteenth Army and send them into Normandy until it was too late. Still, we'd have our hands full with the Nazis' Seventh Army and a dozen Panzer divisions.

Every dogface in our outfit studied the mockup of Colleville-sur-Mer round the clock until we knew the place so well it seemed we'd been born there. The left section of Omaha Beach was Easy Red, and the right, Fox Green. Omaha was two hundred yards from low water to high, loaded with barbed wire, tank traps, and mines. Then came the bluffs, a draw, a small stone house, a marsh, pillboxes atop the cliff, the village itself, a hill called Mount Cauvin. Next to the mockup were aerial photographs of where the beach was mined. American bombs were supposed to leave craters in the sand where we could take cover.

Over and over and over, our sergeant drilled assignments into our heads. Touch down at 0630 on Easy Red, exit the beach at E-1, pass the small stone house, work our way up the draw to the top of the cliff, bypass Colleville-sur-Mer, and, within an hour, take Mount Cauvin in order

I was part of the host detail for James Cagney when he visited our outfit in Long Bredy, probably because Colonel Taylor (kneeling next to me) thought I knew the actor from my days in Hollywood. I didn't.

to report on enemy tank movements from Bayeux. The Schnell battalions stationed in the town were supposed to be combat rejects, soft and fat after sitting on their asses for years fraternizing with the locals. Intelligence assured us that they'd cave in after navy artillery and air force bombing runs had softened them up.

"By the time your squad is halfway up Mount Cauvin," the captain told us, "those Schnell battalions will be dead or retreating. Intelligence says you don't have to sweat them."

"What if they're wrong?" somebody asked.

"We'll sue 'em!" cracked the sergeant.

Just before we were moved to Weymouth to board the ships that would spit us out on the beaches of Normandy, Eisenhower himself visited the First Division. Our helmets and uniforms again brandished the Big Red One. Eisenhower walked among us and spoke in that calm, reassuring voice. We listened to him and found strength in his words about sailing out on a great crusade. He spoke truly when he told us, "The eyes of the world are upon you." I'd find out later he was less than frank when he said, "You establish a beachhead, and we'll carry the ball from there."

H hour was approaching, so we were put in a marshaling area ringed by barbed wire and machine guns. I was doing last-minute checks on our outfit's rifles when a lieutenant came over to me.

"You got a brother?" he said.

"Yeah," I said, amazed he was bugging me with questions about my family on the brink of the biggest invasion in history. "I got more than one brother. So what?"

"One of them's here."

"You're nuts!"

I looked up, and there was my kid brother, Ray, trotting toward me in a dark green officer's uniform. His shoes were covered with mud, but he didn't give a damn. I jumped up and threw my arms around him.

"How in the hell did you get in here, Ray?"

"I have a map of the loading area," he said.

"A map?" I laughed. "We get dog tags, not maps! This place is off-limits to everyone!"

"I've got orders signed by Ike himself. I told your CO I had to see you before the big show."

"Colonel Taylor?"

"Yeah," said Ray. "We talked about you. He's the one who gave me the map. If I don't return it, they'll shoot me!"

"What are you, Eisenhower's personal assistant?"

"No," laughed Ray. "I'm with psychological warfare. But I pulled a few strings to drop in on you. Where are they sending you?"

"I can't talk about it, even with my own brother. I don't even care where it is. If they order us to go fight on the goddamned moon, then I'm there."

My brother couldn't understand my cynicism. Why should he? He hadn't been through two invasions or trained the last seven months for an operation that meant certain death for half of us. Ray was just wonderful to come see me before the invasion. He stayed a couple hours, until they took us away to the troopships. We talked about Mama and our futures. I

My brother Ray with my mother in March 1944 during his last regular leave. By June 1944, there was a good chance I'd never see them again.

was so thrilled to see my brother that I almost forgot where I was and what I was about to do. His appearance was proof there was still love in that war-torn world. The big knot in the pit of my stomach started churning, because I wasn't sure if I'd live to see Ray or the rest of my family again. Neither Ray's SHAEF (Supreme Headquarters Allied Expedition Forces) card nor Eisenhower's signature could get him anywhere near the loading ramps, even though he insisted on accompanying me. What he didn't know then was that he'd be kept under virtual house arrest for days to prevent any indiscretions about Overlord.

We boarded the troopships, First Battalion on the USS *Samuel Chase,* my outfit as part of the Second on the USS *Henrico,* and the Third, on the HMS *Empire Anvil.* As soon as we pushed off, they called us all down to a hall in the ship's belly. They'd set up that model of Omaha with the little flags. Easy Red. Fox Green. Colleville-sur-Mer. We knew it like we knew our cocks in the dark. Again, Colonel Taylor calmly ran through each facet of the assault. He called on various soldiers to explain their assignments in the invasion.

"You've been rehearsing hard for this operation," said Colonel Taylor. "You know your jobs by heart. When we hit that beach, there'll be eight hundred Nazis of the 726th—the Schnell Battalion—defending it. They have to be killed immediately. They aren't battle hardened. There has been no war in Normandy. They are an occupation army and have been living there for four years. Some have local girlfriends. They will die. Not you."

The colonel was all business, without a glimmer of his usual sly humor.

"The minute you get ashore, you will move toward the draw and get up that hill. It should take you about twenty-five minutes. From that hill above the beach, you'll see the road to Bayeux and their Panzers. You'll radio us down at the beach immediately about the tank movements. Any questions?"

There were none. Taylor looked hard at each one of us.

"Intelligence tells us that the people of Normandy have fraternized with the enemy. They did what anyone else would do to survive four years of occupation. Gifts, cakes, chocolates. They've probably accepted daily life with the Germans. Now *we* will be the *invaders.* What they call "libera-tion" is good for newspaper stories. We aren't liberating anything, we're turning things upside down. What you've got to tell yourselves is that Omaha is not just a beach. If you throw a light on it, that light will shine all the way into Germany. It's our doorway to the enemy. The Nazis have had it their way for a long time. You'll have to kill them like they've never been killed before."

Shut-eye was impossible due to the rough seas and the churning in my stomach. They got us up in the middle of the night. Overlord began to unfold according to a master timetable. Thousands of bombs from Ninth Air Force planes fell inland. Navy shells battered the coastline. The weather, which had been dicey on June 5, stabilized a little in the early hours of June 6. The sea was still damned choppy. We moved up on the decks. It was pitch-black. I saw flashes of our bombs and exploding shells

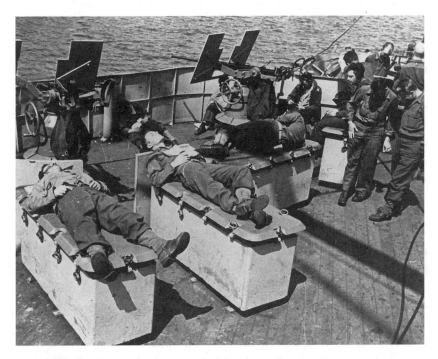

Above: Robert Capa took this shot of me (on the left can of ammunition, getting forty winks) on June 5 as the USS Henrico *got into position for our assault on Omaha.*

Below: Hungarian-born American photojournalist Robert Capa, on one of his innumerable journeys to where an armed conflict needed documenting.

in the distance. Around us were a multitude of massive silhouettes, the battleships *Arkansas, Texas,* and *Nevada,* assorted cruisers, destroyers, and rocket-launching craft, all getting in their licks. We hoped there'd be fewer Nazis defending Omaha after that shellacking.

How wrong could we be! Not only were our bombers and artillery off target, but one of the crack German combat units, the 352nd Field Division, moved back into our sector, thanks to a last-minute decision from General von Rundstedt to rehearse defense maneuvers alongside the 726th in case of an Allied invasion. Whether by impulse or instinct, knowledge or just blind luck, the best soldiers the Nazis had would be facing off with us during the invasion. Unbeknownst to us, enemy firepower at Omaha would be double what we'd been told in planning sessions.

We strapped on our life belts—"Mae Wests," as we called them—and put condoms on our rifles. Then we climbed down rope ladders into the LCVPs, the standard thirty-two men in each boat. A soupy fog blanketed everything. As the boat I was in pitched violently, I gripped the railing with one hand, and with the other, I kept guys from crushing me with their heavy equipment packs. Waves crashed over the boats, washing away the puke on the decks. I wondered if any of the history books would mention all the goddamned vomit that made our boots feel like ice skates.

The bombing faded away as Allied planes flew back across the Channel to their home bases. Our destroyers fell silent. Everything became ominously quiet. There were no "good lucks," no small talk, no prayers. All eyes peered into the fog toward the approaching beach somewhere in front of us. A wave of boats maneuvered away from the ship and moved toward Omaha every seven minutes. I was in the third wave. Our coxswain guaranteed us he'd get us to the right landing spot. How the hell could he guarantee anything? He was a twenty-two-year-old kid from Kansas who'd never seen Normandy in his entire life. He was piloting that goddamned boat on the same memorized map that they'd banged into our brains. The quiet was suddenly interrupted by an explosion forty feet off our starboard.

"What the hell was that?" shouted a lieutenant.

"A mine," said the coxswain. "The navy couldn't knock out all of them."

We were stunned. Mines this far from the beach? We thought we were still a couple miles out. Maybe we were there already. A second explosion blew up a mushroom of water portside.

"That's no fuckin' mine!" said our sergeant. "They're shelling us from the beach!"

We had fantasized that the first or second attack waves would be the most dangerous. We'd even joked about it. But the joke was on us. The first and second waves had hit the beach with at least an element of surprise on their side. By the time we were coming in, the Germans were alerted to the invasion and had time to adjust their artillery.

We began to see bloody bodies floating by us in the water. They were boys from the first two assault waves. A few were still alive, bobbing up and down in the swells, pleading for help as we passed. The coxswain was under strict orders not to stop for anything or anyone. We had to grit our teeth and look away, trying not to listen to the screaming men in the water begging us to pick them up. It was horrible, worse than Dante's *Inferno*.

Another shell screamed as it plunged from the sky toward us. We crashed helmets as we hit the deck. This time the explosion was just over our stern. The waves from the explosion almost capsized us.

Holy shit, our worst horror had become reality. Our bombs and artillery hadn't knocked out their positions. Like the first two invasion waves, we were rushing into a death trap.

The LCVP dropped its ramp. We plunged into the freezing, choppy water. We had to struggle to keep our heads above the surface. Bullets from Nazi machine guns splattered everywhere. A helluva lot of dogfaces were hit and killed before they got anywhere near the beach. "Rommel's asparagus," those mines attached to iron obstacles, were blowing up all over the place. I swallowed a ton of saltwater mixed with American blood. We struggled like crazy not to drown while making our way through those metal death traps and around all the floating bodies. Mortar shells started to fall like hail. It was two hundred yards from the landing craft to Omaha Beach, the longest distance I'd ever travel.

16

Send a Photo
to My Mother

Our well-laid plans to get off Omaha Beach in twenty-five minutes went straight to hell. We were trapped in that nightmare of mines, machine guns, and mortars for more than three goddamned hours. I remember it happening like an avalanche that grabs you and sweeps you up in its staggering violence, too stunning to understand its magnitude as you live through it, moment after endless moment.

Wave upon wave of our soldiers hit that beach. Nothing could stop the massive invasion. Machine guns rattled from up above, dropping dogfaces in the surf, turning the ocean red. Human screams were drowned out by the shrieking artillery shells that fell out of the foggy sky. Mines exploded underfoot. Smoldering bodies were everywhere. As thousands of dogfaces debarked, hundreds and hundreds dropped into the surf and across the sand. Heads, arms, fingers, testicles, and legs were scattered everywhere as we ran up the beach, trying to dodge the corpses. I saw a man's mouth—just a mouth, for Chrissakes!—floating in the water.

It didn't take long to figure out that the fingers on the triggers of those deadly Nazi guns didn't belong to combat novices. How could Intelligence have been so wrong about the presence of seasoned, battle-ready German troops above Omaha? As we scurried up to the only cover in sight, a sea wall that was nothing more than a low pile of shale, we expected to find craters from our own bombs. But there were none. Our bombs had hit too far inland and missed the beach completely. Through the smoke and fog, I spotted the stone house up above. I silently thanked our coxswain from Kansas for landing us close to where we were supposed to be. But there was nowhere to go. The narrow strip of American-held beach was soon choked with shoulder-to-shoulder survivors of the landing, some lying prone, their legs in the water, grateful to be out of the line of fire of Nazi machine guns. For Chrissakes, Easy Red on Omaha was the smallest beachhead of the greatest amphibious invasion in history! The only way to get off that goddamned beach was to cross a mine field and break through the barbed wire barrier that the Nazis had built 150 feet up ahead. Every time one of our bangalore teams tried to torpedo the barrier, they were devastated by cross fire and mortar shells.

English and Canadian outfits were landing on our left. The Twenty-fifth Infantry was landing on our right. Everyone was pinned down on the beach. What was left of our outfit was going to be wiped out unless we could break inland to the base of the bluff. Methodically covering each other with small arms fire, we established a human chain for the bangalore relay. The minutes went by torturously. Finally, Sergeant Philip Streczyck zigzagged through the mines and made it to the barrier, setting the charge that blew a breach in the wire. We yelled out a cry of relief. A lieutenant turned to me and screamed something. My ears were ringing so much, I barely heard him. He had to say it three times.

"Get back to Colonel Taylor. Tell him Exit E-1 is open!"

"Where's the CP?" I yelled.

"It's supposed to be on our left!" shouted the lieutenant. "Find the colonel, Fuller! Now!"

Without a moment's hesitation, I jumped up and ran back toward the landing craft, desperately searching for any sign of the colonel and what was left of our command post. Being vertical on Omaha was an invitation to death. God, how I ran! In all my years as a copyboy, my legs never moved that fast. The dead and the wounded lay everywhere, body parts strewn across the sand. Scurrying like a mad rabbit, I jumped over all the corpses. I stumbled once on somebody's leg and fell onto a dead dogface. Getting up, I careened into the surf, but floating bodies blocked me. Swerving from the water to the sand and back again, I ran until I thought my heart would burst.

I fell again, got up, and fell once more, this time landing on my face between a dead medic and a bandaged soldier, the one-eyed dogface staring at me as I gasped for air. The thought of just staying there and acting like a corpse crossed my mind. But I couldn't, for cryin' out loud, I had to find Colonel Taylor. Maybe he was already dead. Then I spotted a half-smoked cigar on the sand. I picked up the wet stogie and jammed it into my mouth. Hell, even in the eye of that tornado of bullets and explosions, there was no mistaking a Havana. Taylor smoked them. He had to be somewhere nearby. I lifted up my head and spotted him thirty feet up the beach, hugging another seawall with a captain. I scurried over to them and flopped down on my belly. Miraculously, there were no bulletholes in me.

"E-1's open!" I yelled.

"Who blew it?"

This shot was taken a few minutes after one of the first waves of the D-day assault made it to cover. Tired, hurt, but not beaten, Big Red One doggies try to assess the madness.

"Streczyck."

"All right," said the colonel, smiling at me. He reached into his bag and pulled out his private box of cigars and gave them to me.

"Enjoy 'em, Sammy. You earned them, running over here."

Then Taylor stood up. I couldn't believe it. He just stood up. Like me, everyone who saw him get to his feet thought he'd gone nuts.

"There are two kinds of men out here!" shouted the colonel to anyone listening. "The dead! And those who are about to die! So let's get the hell off this beach and at least die inland!"

He went from man to man, kicking and cursing every living dogface in his path, ordering them to get on their feet and get their asses into motion. He looked at me.

"We'll follow you, Fuller, back to the breach!"

"Yes sir!" I said, getting to my feet, knowing that I had to make that nightmare run through the dead and wounded all over again. This time, I was sure I'd catch a Nazi bullet. The sight of Colonel Taylor running up the beach inspired everyone who was still breathing to follow him. After fifty yards, Taylor no longer had to order men to their feet. Dazed dogfaces forced themselves to get up and move up the beach behind the colonel toward the only exit from that death trap. Many were hit and fell backward on the sand. One of the hail of bullets raining down on us caught Taylor in his arm.

"Flesh wound!" he told a medic as they bandaged him on the move. "Make it a temp!"

By then, a couple of our tanks had landed. One of them targeted the top of the bluff and, for the first time, started returning fire at the Schnell Battalions up above. Small teams were organized to lob hand grenades at enemy positions; then, in the resulting confusion, bazooka squads blasted the pillboxes overlooking the sector with split-second timing, giving us our first respite from Nazi machine guns. My company pushed through the open exit on tiptoe, staring at the ground anxiously. On Omaha, a lot of dogfaces had already stepped on land mines, disappearing in a cloud of smoke, sand, and fire. In single file, we got through the breach in the barbed wire and off that goddamned beach.

I was so exhausted, I collapsed at the base of the bluff for a momentary rest. I unwrapped one of the colonel's Havanas, bit off the tip, and lit it with my Zippo. How I'd survived Omaha without a bullet in my brain nor my guts spilled out on the sand wasn't, as my Silver Star citation would call it, "Gallantry in Action." Gallantry sounds dramatic and appealing. But the term should be used only for the way a guy cares for his lover. Omaha was more a game of Russian roulette that I somehow miraculously didn't lose.

Heroes? No such damned thing! You moved your ass one way, and you didn't get hit. You moved it another way, you were blown to bits. When the battle was under way, experience and intuition, not heroics, were useful. Luck had a helluva lot more to do with it. Lucky or not, you still might get hit. But if you were lucky, you got wounded in a way that allowed you to stay alive. Sure there were heroes, but not in the classic sense that many people imagine them. A soldier did something out of panic or hysteria, never considering the risks. He was too goddamned scared to understand the consequences. Or a guy deliberately risked his own life because he felt compelled to save other dogfaces. He didn't feel heroic in the heat of the moment. He followed his gut reaction. It was better not to reflect too much. The whole situation was so crazy, only a madman could find any rationale for being there.

When we'd first landed on Omaha, there was an ammunitions truck on the beach that had caught fire. It was on the verge of blowing to kingdom come. A soldier ran out of nowhere, jumped into the truck, and drove it madly toward the ocean, crushing corpses under the big tires. The truck exploded in the surf in a mountain of flames, killing its driver but saving other lives. He was crazy to have jumped into the driver's seat, though he probably didn't think he was going to die. What do we call that incomprehensible instinct to put our survival second to that of others? Heroism? Sure, *after* the act. During the act, you're just following your gut. Maddened by the chaos and cacophony, soldiers couldn't think straight. Due to the shock and stress of Omaha, I wouldn't even remember everything I did on that beach until sometime afterward. In the heat of the moment, nothing made much sense. Moments were hours. Minutes seemed like days. I was thirty-one years old when we landed. I'd aged years when we finally got off Omaha.

Later, I remembered a wounded dogface in the surf calling out my name. I'd run over to him and dragged him up on the beach. He was in excruciating pain, the saltwater burning his wounds. Other doggies yelled at me. I dragged somebody else out of the water toward a medic. A war historian wrote later that it was probably the only battle in history in which the wounded were brought *toward* the front line for first aid. Like us, medics were in the thick of the combat, risking their lives to work on the wounded. When I pulled guys out of the water, I don't remember thinking that I was risking my life. Who the hell considered risk? You tried helping someone the way you'd want him to help you. Hell, talk about risk, consider the medics who were getting shot at and didn't even have a gun to shoot back.

When I made movies about men at war years later, I'd try to show that survival, not heroics, was the basic motivation of soldiers on the field of battle. Heroes were anointed by brain-trust boys, generals, or newspaper editors behind desks far from the death and destruction. The last thing you ever thought about was winning a medal. Your biggest preoccupation was staying in one piece. When we did catch a bullet or shrapnel, and it didn't hit anything vital, it wasn't a big deal. At least, we acted like it wasn't. I got hit by a bullet in my chest as we fought our way toward Saint-Lô. Everyone got hurt one way or another. You pretended that your wound was nothing more than another little hole in your body. If you were as lucky as I was, the bullet missed vital organs and you survived. Wounds were as quotidian as drinking a cup of coffee or smoking a cigarette. We poked fun at anyone who made a fuss about a wound. That was one of the ways we made it through the craziness of war.

Above the Normandy beaches, we came face-to-face with the Nazi 352nd Infantry, and what was left of our outfit beat them back in fierce fighting. Of the 183 men who'd landed with my company, about a hundred were dead, wounded, or missing in action. Despite our ragged condition, we were ordered to push out for Colleville-sur-Mer in the early afternoon, moving along a road where enemy snipers and machine-gun nests hidden in farmhouses and trees had to be destroyed. We suffered more casualties as we reached the edge of town and ran headfirst into heavy enemy artillery fire. There, we had to dig in and hope that Cannon Company, plus our antitank platoon, would be able to land on the beach and make it through to help us. No such support materialized, because those outfits were decimated on Omaha. Then, to our surprise, U.S. naval artillery starting pounding the village in midafternoon, killing seven of our own men in the process.

One of the hundreds of amazing stories that came out of D day was that of two Big Red One privates, Joseph Parks and Peter Cavaliere, who were part of another company approaching Colleville from the other side. They found themselves cut off from their outfit when the German counterattack began in earnest. In no time, Parks and Cavaliere were confronted by two hundred enemy infantrymen moving forward, supported by a Mark IV tank. Parks and Cavaliere sniped at the assault wave for three hours, resisting every effort to dislodge them from behind a stone wall, which, as the hours passed, was almost totally destroyed. Believe it or not, the two dogfaces kept all those German troops at bay until reinforcements finally arrived.

The first Frenchman we found in Colleville was Monsieur Brobant, who led us to a building where he'd killed a couple of Nazis with a shovel. So much for the idea that all the local French were collaborating with occupation armies. That night, we liberated a bottle of Calvados from an empty bar after we secured the town, and we dug in north of Colleville. The brandy was passed around until the bottle was empty. Sleep was next to impossible, for our ships anchored off the coast pounded enemy strongholds with their heavy artillery throughout the night. At dawn, other sections of the Big Red One moved through our position to continue the main attack inland while we were given the mission of mopping up isolated enemy nests hidden in the *bocage,* those immense hedgerows that surrounded all the fields in Normandy.

With all the mountains of information they'd accumulated for Overlord, you'd think Intelligence would have told us about the strategic hell of battling the enemy in that hellacious tangle of hedgerows. They were dark, thick, impenetrable tangles of brambles, weeds, bushes, and trees rising up twenty feet high from ancient banks of packed earth. German snipers hid inside the hedgerows, intent on putting holes straight through our hearts. Not a word about the *bocage* was ever mentioned in our months of preparation. Maybe they figured that training us for the hedgerows would have given away Overlord's master plan.

It was slow, methodical, and dangerous fighting. We had to drive out the enemy cautiously. There were few dramatic charges like you see in Hollywood movies. Any patrol that tried something flashy or overt was devastated by cross fire from Nazi sharpshooters. You crept a few yards, waited, listened carefully, then crept a little more. You saw no one, yet bullets started flying everywhere. This may have been the road to Ger-

Me and an American tank somewhere in Normandy's bocage, *the French farmers' centuries-old defense against stiff ocean winds, shielding fields of grain, orchards of apples, and pastures of grazing cows*

many, but it had to be taken one hedgerow at a time. We didn't march across Normandy. We crawled.

Tanks got stuck and became easy targets. Our engineers wised up and eventually attached revolving iron blades to the front of our tanks—the very same "Rommel's asparagus" that had made Omaha a living hell—and tried crashing straight through the hedges. It was up to small squads of dogfaces to follow the tanks, eliminating all German resistance as we pushed forward. That was one of the most frustrating, dangerous battlefields we'd ever encounter. It made me think of Balzac's first big novel, *Les Chouans,* about the Breton peasants fighting in the French Revolution, sandbagging the Republicans in those very same hedgerows.

The situation shifted dramatically when American bombs started to fall. Eighth and Ninth Air Force heavy bombers broke the deadlock by leveling fields, farmhouses, and villages. It was the first time our planes worked so close to the front lines. Some bombs hit too close, inflicting heavy casualties on American troops. Among the victims was General Lesley J. McNair, chief of the U.S. Army ground forces. When the U.S. bombing subsided, German soldiers emerged from the hedgerows, shaking, vomiting, bleeding. They raised their hands above their heads, forming a grotesque serpent of confused men desperately searching for someone to surrender to. We moved toward the shuffling Germans and herded them together. No words were spoken. They offered no resistance, no tricks. The bombardment had destroyed their last hopes of standing fast against our invasion.

The bulk of enemy forces, about forty thousand troops, fell back behind the road from Coutances to Saint-Lô. Code-named "Cobra," an Allied operation was planned to break through their defenses, utilizing intense bombing, a breach led by tanks from the Third Armored Division, and, finally, an infantry assault by the Big Red One toward Coutances to isolate the German army. We'd have to face some of their best regiments, including several SS divisions, a half-dozen Panzer divisions pulled off the Russian front, and Göring's bombers and fighters. If Cobra failed, we'd be driven back into the English Channel, where there'd be no salvation. No doubt the German high command expected a repeat performance of the Kasserine Pass debacle. Operation Cobra was to begin sometime in July, though no one knew exactly when, for the surprise element of our advance was essential. As preparations for the next campaign proceeded, they gave our regiment a little time off. After so many casualties, there was no way we could carry on a sustained offensive.

The outfit was bivouacked in front of a château near Colombieres to allow time to recuperate and bring in replacements. Dogfaces hit baseballs and threw footballs around the beautiful grounds. Some shot baskets through a hoop made of de-barbed wire. Red Cross gals served us coffee and doughnuts. Letters were written home.

I strolled by a group of fresh replacements leaning against a stone wall and I spotted a young soldier reading an armed forces edition of some book. It was specially bound for GIs in the field. I looked closer. Holy cow, the title on the cover was *The Dark Page*! That was the first published copy of my novel I'd ever seen. I took a small bottle of booze out of my backpack. My mother had sent it to me in her last care package along with cigars and chocolate. I offered the young soldier a swig of whiskey. He felt pretty lucky.

"To your mother," I said. "And to mine."

"You guys sure know how to live," said the wetnose.

I shrugged. He would soon find out we knew more about dying than living. "How do you like the book?"

"The book?" he said. "It's pretty good."

"Pretty good? That's all?"

"Yeah. Why?"

"It's mine."

"No, it's not. It's mine. I bought it at the commissary in Saint-Lô!"

"I mean I wrote it, babyface."

"You *wrote* it?"

"Fuller," I said, pointing at my name on the cover. "That's me."

I plucked the book from the kid and called over some guys in my squad to show it to them. A couple of my pals were just as thrilled to see my byline as I was. I lay down in the sunlight on the château lawn and reread *The Dark Page*. It was good to feel the pages in my hands. The yarn took me back to working on Park Row and to Hollywood, far-off memories of life before Pearl Harbor. Hell, I didn't long for the good old days, nor did I have any interest in reliving the past. Nostalgia was a cop-out. I only yearned for one thing: to survive that goddamned war and keep on writing.

Another day during the lull in Normandy, I was taking a nap on the grass.

"Hey, Sammy," said a dogface, pulling me out of a deep sleep. "Remember that photographer who took a picture of you while you were snoring away on the troopship before D day?"

"Do I ever!" I said. "He went on patrol with us in Sicily. His name's Capa."

"Just went by with his cameras again."

"Sonofabitch!" I said. "Which way did he go?"

"Toward OC." That meant Officer's Country.

I jumped up and ran over to our command post. There was Robert Capa having a drink with my captain.

"Hey, Capa," I said. "Where's the photo you were supposed to send to my sweet little mother in New York?"

The photographer grinned and shook his head.

"Sammy Fuller! I'm going to send it to her," he said. "Promise."

With General Terry Allen's blessing, Capa had hooked up with our outfit during Husky to get some shots of dogfaces in action. While we attacked a Sicilian farmhouse, Capa had taken cover behind a big rock, snapping away as we zigzagged toward an enemy machine-gun nest. We

I got a kick out of seeing
The Dark Page *read by guys*
in my outfit, thanks to the
special armed forces edition
of my novel that surprisingly
showed up on the front lines.

caught some Wehrmacht and Italians in a cross fire and took them prisoner. Capa told our sergeant that the attack looked like choreography. He started asking for detailed explanations about our maneuvers, taking notes for captions to go with his photos. The sergeant didn't like Capa being there, because he thought the picture-taking would interfere with our concentration. I was brought over to help out because of my newspaper background.

Capa was delighted with all the details I gave him. I knew his work from the Spanish civil war, and I was glad to be of assistance.

"Where's your family, Fuller?" he'd asked me.

"My mother lives in New York."

"Give me her address. I'll send her your photo."

He took some shots of me chowing down on K-rations. It'd been an entire year since I'd met the famous *Life* photographer in Sicily. Capa and I had a good reunion in Normandy. The next time I'd run into Robert was in Hollywood years after the war. He was coming out of Howard Hawks's office as I was walking in for a meeting with the Gray Fox. Capa was so pleased to see me again that he invited me over for drinks at his place on Holloway Drive that very evening. His photos were everywhere.

This is the shot Robert Capa took of me during the Sicilian campaign, though I wouldn't see it until years later, when we ran into each other in Hollywood.

"So where's the photo for my mother?" I said.

We both laughed. One look around his apartment and I understood that the man was literally submerged in his work. At the time, he was doing a book entitled *Slightly Out of Focus.*

We talked about other battle zones Capa had covered. His war pictures had made him world-famous. On his wall was that unforgettable shot taken during the Spanish civil war of the Republican soldier hit by a bullet, falling backward, holding on to his rifle even as he dies. We went through some of the boxes of stills he'd taken during World War II, and that's how we found the photo of me sleeping aboard the *Henrico* just before D day. Capa gave it to me for Rebecca. Then we looked at those sensational photos he'd snapped on Omaha on June 6, 1944. There were only eight of them, all grainy and a little out of focus. Yet they vividly brought back that terrible day.

"I didn't see you on Omaha," I ribbed him. The only newspaperman that we heard about landing with us at Omaha was Beaver Thompson, from the *Chicago Tribune*. Thompson was nicknamed "the Beard" because he swore not to shave until Hitler was dead.

I asked Capa why there were only eight shots from D day. His face darkened. He told me that in all his battle experiences, he'd never seen anything as terrifying as Omaha. The exploding shells and bombs that morning were mind-boggling. With his telescopic lens, he'd focused on a German officer who was up on the bluff above the beach. The German stood with his hands on his hips, boldly barking out orders to soldiers behind him. The sight of that cocky Nazi officer, so sure of himself, was heart-stopping. Still, Capa snapped away, taking pictures of everything he could.

Even though he was accustomed to photographing men at war, Capa told me that D day had completely flustered him. He'd managed to get off Omaha with a boatload of wounded soldiers who were ferried out to the USS *Thurston*. He was lucky not to have caught a bullet as well. Still, he felt as if he were fleeing. When Capa got back to Portsmouth late on June 6, he took a train to London and turned in his film for development. A darkroom assistant was so eager to see the photos that they were dried too quickly, ruining the emulsions. Those eight shots were the only ones that survived.

"I was ashamed of myself at Omaha," said Capa.

"Why should you have felt ashamed?" I said. "We'd been training seven months for that morning. We'd rehearsed every goddamned thing. We were armed to the gills. You landed with only a camera and some lenses. That took real guts."

"I was scared out of my mind."

"Holy shit, so were we!" I told him, "Look, Robert, write exactly what you felt. Describe the fear. Every single soldier who survived D day will appreciate the honesty."

Capa was such a wonderful guy. Years later, my heart ached when I heard the news that he'd been killed while covering the war in Vietnam. I didn't know him that well, but I loved Robert Capa because he always tried to capture the truth with his images.

Delayed by rain, Cobra finally got under way on July 25, with saturation bombing from over twenty-five hundred American planes. Our regiment started moving toward Marigny on the twenty-seventh, encountering bitter resistance almost immediately. The Germans fought back with mortars and artillery and furious infantry fire. We suffered severe casualties but continued the advance, thanks to backup from the Ninth Air Force fighter

In the summer of 1944, all we could do was wave at the French gals as our outfit was trucked through the French countryside to catch the retreating enemy. bombers escorting us, strafing enemy armor as we went. As usual, friendly fire also killed some of our own. On August 1, long-inactive German planes struck back with a vengeance, killing and wounding many of our men. By mid-August, however, it was clear the enemy was confused and couldn't contain our assault any longer. We'd taken a German colonel prisoner behind our lines who didn't even know where his goddamned troops were. We were driving toward La Sauvager, northeast of La Ferte Mace, where the thick woods of the Andaine forest were full of enemy infantry and artillery.

To learn about the effects of our artillery fire and check enemy positions, volunteers from the Free French forces were used to filter through German lines and bring back information. Many of the Free French were only teenagers, allowed to move through battle lines as long as they had nothing on them that proved they'd had any contact with American troops. Their reports saved many dogface lives. One French youngster, however, forgot to spit out the chewing gum that a GI had given him and was shot on the spot by an SS officer.

By the end of August, we'd broken completely through the German right flank at Marigny. Enemy divisions were retreating faster than we could advance. So the Big Red One was loaded onto a long convoy of trucks and moved 150 miles toward Paris, rumbling along country roads. Not having to march for the first time since the war began, our outfit was in high spirits. Every time the convoy passed road signs that said "Paris," there were shouts and whistles. Paris! The very word aroused us, sending an electric jolt through every guy. In our minds, we'd soon be holding yearning demoiselles in our arms and dancing along the Seine. Hundreds of pricks got a little bit harder.

See, on the beach at Omaha, Paris had seemed light-years away. Now we were barreling toward it, chasing German troops fleeing to safer positions beyond the Belgian border. From the skies, the long line of U.S. trucks and tanks must have looked like a snake meandering across the French countryside. We stopped in the vicinity of Soissons, where our boys had fought a bitter victory in World War I, and camped at St. Pierre-Aigle, overlooking a church that had been our CP in 1918. That was the closest to Paris we'd get. The "snake" turned northeast at Laon with orders to bypass the capital in our race to catch up with the routed Nazis. We had no idea exactly when or where our path would converge with the enemy's. In any event, we'd have to wait to see the City of Light, because Germany had to be taken first and the Nazis put completely out of commission. Once the reality of our mission crystallized, all those erections wilted.

17

Detailed Description

Headquarters 16th Infantry, APO #1, U.S. Army.

Corporal Samuel M. Fuller, while serving with the Army of the United States, distinguished himself by gallantry in action.

The Sixteenth Infantry Regiment invaded the coast of France in the vicinity of Colleville-sur-Mer on 6 June 1944. The inland advance of our units was prevented by the minefields, wire, tank traps, while the massed men on the beach were raked by intense mortar, artillery, sniper and machine gun fire. The continued accurate enemy fire inflicted tremendous casualties on the thousands of men packed on the beach, rendering them a confused, leaderless mass.

Corporal Fuller, 16th Infantry, landed with one of the initial assault waves, and immediately began moving about the beach in an effort to aid the wounded and bring about some degree of control. Disregarding the intensity of the enemy fire, and the numerous mines and obstacles in the water, Corporal Fuller moved into the surf several times in order to drag wounded men to a point where they could be treated. When a breach was finally blown in the wire, the mission was given to Corporal Fuller of notifying the Regimental Commander of this. In order to reach the Regimental Commander, Corporal Fuller moved along one hundred yards of open beach, under constant heavy fire by the enemy. Persisting in his mission, Corporal Fuller reached his destination and delivered the vital message. Not content with just having delivered the message, Corporal Fuller once more crossed the fire swept beach and notified the Regimental S-2 that the message had been delivered, and preparations were made for the advance off of the beachhead.

Corporal Fuller displayed magnificent courage and outstanding devotion to duty, in saving the lives of wounded comrades, and then playing a vital part in the control and organization of the drive inland. The actions of Corporal Fuller are worthy of the highest praise and are a credit to the Service to which he belongs. Corporal Fuller was not wounded during this action.

John H. Lauten
Major, 1st U.S.
Infantry Division

18

Death Rained
Down

We finally caught up with the German army northwest of Maubeuge, France, on September 2, 1944. Their backs were up against the Belgian border, seeking refuge in the Laniere forest, whose thick woods concealed their numbers. Our battalion advanced cautiously through the forest until the retreating Germans' exact position was discovered. Then we began a ferocious attack, unleashing every weapon we had on hand—artillery, mortars, bazookas, machine guns, and flamethrowers—not knowing how many enemy soldiers we were actually fighting. They returned fire, and the battle raged all night long. At 0400 hours, a German officer showed up at the battalion command post asking for an armistice so that his wounded soldiers could be evacuated to Liège. The request was denied. His only alternative was unconditional surrender. The officer, who spoke English, eventually agreed to our terms, without the faintest idea that, in numbers, we were only a fraction of the strength of his force.

Starting at 0630 hours, groups of fifty Wehrmacht, accompanied by an officer, were to march into a designated prisoner area in a clearing. The first group appeared right on time. Shoulder weapons were thrown in a pile to the right, sidearms, in a pile to the left. By noon, about twenty-four hundred prisoners had come in from that forest. Ambulances and aid men were sent into the woods after another seven hundred wounded. Our over-whelmed medics detailed Nazi medics to help us out. Kitchen trucks were unloaded and turned into impromptu ambulances. Our prisoner-of-war cage, an open field surrounded by barbed wire, became so crowded that over a thousand prisoners had to be transferred to the Third Armored Division's big cage at Maubeuge. Hell, it was quite a sight, that enormous column of captured Germans moving out, led by just two American GIs, with one of our light tanks riding herd on the rear.

Advancing toward Mons, we moved cautiously into Belgium through the countryside on September 3. I really didn't know about the Belgian

We liberated these French peasants from a Nazi nest of snipers holed up at their farm in late August 1944 as we pursued the enemy hordes toward the Belgian border. After the snapshot, we moved out fast.

border crossing until that night, because there were no markers in the forest. When my sergeant confirmed it, I made a note about entering the new country in my journal. In Mons, we mopped up small enclaves of enemy troops and continued moving east. Somebody had permanently muzzled the sun in Belgium.

The cold, gray days had neither beginning nor end, forming a dispassionate backdrop to our short, furious forays through the rain and fog against Nazis left behind in order to slow our advance. The mud was their best ally. Our socks were permanently soaked.

One night, we camped in the countryside somewhere between Charleroi and Namur awaiting fresh supplies, especially gasoline, as our trucks and tanks were running low. As usual, it was raining cats and dogs. I was on patrol duty with a few other dogfaces, including our sergeant, keeping a lookout for rearguard actions. German troops were hunkered down all around us in the woods. Out of nowhere, a motorcycle with a sidecar came tearing down a dirt road and crashed into a ditch near us. We encircled the wrecked motorcycle, rifles aimed, ready to shoot. The driver had a bloody bandage around his chest and wore a white armband, meaning he was a member of the underground Belgian White Army. He'd probably gotten himself shot trying to blow up a Nazi munitions dump or sabotage a Wehrmacht troop convoy. The crash had killed him.

Inside the motorcycle's sidecar under a soaked blanket was a woman. She shrieked when we lifted her out. Her belly was big and round. She started to cry out desperate pleas. Our sergeant understood a little French.

"She's going to have a baby," he said.

"Jesus," murmured a stunned soldier.

We lifted the woman carefully into one of the abandoned Panzer tanks nearby. It was the only dry place around. Her belly was so big we almost couldn't get her through the hatch. The tank reeked of sweat, cheese, and brandy. We spread a blanket out on the steel floor, laid the suffering woman down gently, and crowded round her, staring helplessly at the painful contractions that racked her body. We knew a little about patching up wounds, but assisting a pregnant woman was completely foreign territory. First-aid training had simply omitted it.

One of our dogfaces, a country boy named Wilson, volunteered to help the woman have her baby. He'd seen how his parents had helped their cows birth calves back on the farm. With humans, Wilson figured hygiene was the first order of business. He called out for condoms to cover his fingers. We doused his hands in brandy, then fitted on the rubbers, one on his thumb, two for his other four fingers. He demanded a face mask, so we cut a piece of cheesecloth from the hunk of cheese hanging in the tank and tied it over his mouth. Machine-gun belts were looped overhead on fuel pipes, and the woman's feet were strapped into the makeshift stirrups, making sure the bullets in the belts were pointed away from her kicking legs. She groaned, grunted, and screamed. I suppose she was lashing out not only at us, but at the goddamned war and heaven itself for making her give birth in a stinking German tank with only a bunch of gawking American GIs to get her through it. She tried to hit all of us in our wide-eyed faces until we pinned her hands down.

Wilson put his hands on her big belly.

"Push, lady, push!" he said.

The enraged woman tried to kick Wilson in the mouth.

"How do you say 'push,' Sergeant?" asked Wilson.

"Poussez."

"Pussy! Pussy!" said Wilson.

"No, not pussy. Poo-*say*," instructed the sergeant.

"Poo-*say!*"

The woman began to push her abdominal muscles in rhythm with her contractions.

"Sonofabitch!" yelled Wilson. "It's working!"

We all started chanting "Poo-*say*, poo-*say*, poo-*say*."

A little bloody head appeared between the woman's thighs. Gently, Wilson pulled it out inch by inch. We watched the magnificent sight, our mouths agape.

"It's a boy," said Wilson. "What a pecker! Gimme some leggin' lace."

Somebody undid his bootlace, poured brandy on it and cut it with a trench knife. Wilson tied off the baby's umbilical cord. Then he slapped the infant on his bloody little ass. Not a sound came from its tiny pink mouth. Wilson slapped the little creature again.

"He's dead, goddamnit!" said Wilson, panicking.

"The hell he is!" said the sergeant, grabbing the baby away from him. He began slapping the baby's ass harder and harder. We held our breath. The mother's eyes filled with tears. Suddenly the baby let out a howl that resounded around the tank's cockpit, drowning out the thunder and pounding rain outside. The baby's cry made us all smile from ear to ear. I think it was the sweetest sound I'd heard in twenty months of military service. The woman took the baby into her arms, her face shining with relief. We laughed and celebrated with swigs from the brandy bottle. Wilson was elated with his maternity work. Even the battle-weary, sober-faced sergeant grinned with satisfaction.

On one of the supply trucks from France was a care package from my mother with a fresh supply of cigars, manna from heaven in that inhospitable place. Rebecca wrote me that *The Dark Page* had won some award as the "Best Psychological Novel" of 1943. She included an encouraging letter from my agent, Charlie Feldman, who was talking with Howard Hawks about buying the book's movie rights. Hawks wanted Humphrey

On the back of this drawing sent to my brother Ving from somewhere near Aachen, I wrote: "Dahlink Vingo, A doggie showed me a folded collection of Collier's Cartoons of the Month & smack in the center was your damned funny 4-box gag of the fortune teller who took her own (naval) advice. All the doggies got a big kick out of it!"

Bogart to star as the hotshot reporter and Edward G. Robinson to play the murderous newspaper editor in the film adaptation. Hollywood! Looking around our camp, I couldn't help smiling. It didn't seem possible that Hollywood could be on the same planet, much less in the same goddamned galaxy, as that rain-soaked Belgian forest. The news from the West Coast made me feel lucky. I'd been through three amphibious assaults and somehow survived. The war had to end someday. Maybe my luck would continue and I'd survive to write more books, especially one from the point of view of a lowly infantryman.

I tried to keep up my journal, scribbling dates, times, places, quick images, story ideas. It was far too hectic to jot down much else. Nevertheless, my brain was recording it, ready to pour out all those stories and impressions as soon as I could get my hands on a typewriter in a place where bullets weren't zipping around my head and shells weren't falling out of the foggy skies. I was already making plans to recount the gut-racking, nerve-mauling life of dogfaces at war in a motion picture.

In the town of Huy, we advanced on a slaughterhouse that thirty-odd SS were using as a hiding place. The abattoir was a big hangar filled with the sickening sight and smell of death. Moving past rows of loins and hams hanging from steel hooks, using live pigs as cover, we bellied forward. When the bullets began flying, the squealing of swine and the burst of machine guns was like music composed by a drunken organist. German and American blood mixed with that of the swine. When it was over, there was no time to reflect on the horrible scene. We had to move on rapidly, searching out the next pocket of Nazis trying to derail the American advance. The slaughterhouse firefight was just one of many rearguard actions we endured.

In a Belgian village south of Liège where most of the buildings had been damaged by repeated Allied bombings, more treacherous combat awaited us. Only a church in the center of the village was intact. There, a horse was hitched to a glass hearse. Some doggies from our company eased into the church to check out the funeral ceremony, while the rest of us stayed at the front door. Four women and two men, their heads bowed, stood around four infant coffins. A priest in a black cassock was saying mass. Suddenly, Nazis ambushed us from drainage ditches around the village square. They killed one of our new recruits as we dove into the church and took cover behind the pews. The priest pulled a Schmeisser from his black cassock and killed two more of our men. The mourners starting shooting at us, too. Grenades were thrown wildly. Bullets bounced around the church walls, breaking stained-glass windows. Smoke filled the place. Outside, the Nazis were cut down by machine guns fired by a group of Belgian Maquis who appeared out of nowhere. We finished off the fake mourners. The fight was over as quickly as it had begun.

The leader of the Belgian Maquis, a notary called Guinle, wore his white armband proudly. Thanks to him and the other members of the White Army, we'd escaped the ambush. He kicked the bullet-ridden bodies of the Rexists—Belgians for Hitler—to make sure they were dead. Then he put his boot on the neck of the priest and ripped off the black cassock, revealing an SS uniform underneath. The bullet-riddled coffins were empty. As we were thanking them, two of the Belgians started to argue vehemently. Threats were exchanged. Guinle had to keep them from striking each other.

"Sometimes," Guinle explained to us, "our differences endanger our country's actions. You see, Belgium is home to two peoples, the Dutch-speaking Flemish and the French-speaking Walloons."

It was the first but not the last time I'd hear the wonderful name "Walloon."

On the outskirts of Liège, enemy artillery fired on us from some old brick buildings attached to a watchtower. The complex turned out to be an insane asylum. Retreating SS troops had taken it and were using the mad people as hostages. One well-aimed American bomb would have blown the place off the map of Belgium, but targeting civilians, especially crazy ones, was out of the question for the Allied command.

The key to taking the asylum was a White Army agent posing as a mad-woman inside. She was a mythic figure in the Resistance. In the name of

Belgian sovereignty, she'd sabotaged German troop trains, masqueraded as a nun to halt a German convoy, and posed as a chambermaid in a fashionable hotel to slash the throat of a German general in his bathtub. She'd even shot her own husband when she discovered that the sonofabitch was secretly a member of the Rexists. This lady had balls. Her code name was Walloon.

A local priest got word to Walloon that we were planning an assault. At the appointed hour that night, we snuck up to the back of the asylum. Walloon had already slit the throat of the SS lookout. She threw down a rope. Silently, we climbed up on the roof, then followed Walloon down a spiral staircase and hid in the kitchen.

Acting like a nutty ballerina, Walloon danced round the SS soldiers in the dining room and got their full attention with her barely covered ass. We jumped them and cut them down with our bayonets. Just then, a Nazi officer walked in and started firing at us with his Schmeisser. Walloon hit the floor as we shot him. All hell broke loose. Meanwhile, the priest was letting the rest of our outfit into the asylum through a side door. The battle moved from the kitchen, through the wards, and down into the laundry room. Inmates dove onto the floor to stay out of the way of ricocheting bullets.

A madman named Rensonnet found the SS officer's Schmeisser, picked it up, and thought he could act as normal as the rest of us by pulling the trigger. It was a game for him. First he fired at pots, pans, and dishes, delighted with the racket. Then he starting shooting fellow inmates. One of our sharpshooters had to kill Rensonnet with a bullet through the heart. The crazy inmate was smiling when he died, happy that he could kill just as well as sane men.

When the fight was over, all the SS were dead. We'd lost five men. The asylum returned to its everyday lunacy. We stayed there that night, planning to push on at dawn. One of my buddies got an invitation from Walloon to pay a visit that night in her sack. The young soldier hesitated, because the lady was quite a few years older than him. He took me aside to ask what I thought about the liaison. For Chrissakes, I told him, who cares if the lady's face had a few wrinkles, her body was ready and willing. I told him to think about Benjamin Franklin.

"What the hell does Benjamin Franklin got to do with it?" he asked.

"Old Ben once wrote a letter to a young punk just like you," I said. "He recommended older gals. Said they were clean. Wouldn't get pregnant. Didn't have diseases. Said they'd teach you tricks you never heard of. Best of all, they're very appreciative."

"Yeah?"

"Yeah! And if you're worried about her face, old Ben had one last piece of advice: 'Cover her head with the American flag and shoot for Old Glory!' "

"But I like her face," said the soldier.

"Then stop acting like a schmuck and go to her," I said.

He did. In Walloon's arms, he was a man, not a soldier. Walloon, the legendary Resistance fighter, was a legendary lover. She inspired lusty passion. He gave her everything he had and then some. After all, it could have been his last lay. Tomorrow, maybe he'd stop a bullet. Tonight, he nestled his head against Walloon's warm breasts and remembered he was still alive.

At Liège, we found that the retreating Panzer divisions had blown up the bridge over the Meuse River. To hold their position on the opposite bank, the Germans had moved in an "88," their biggest artillery piece. We had to take it out so that engineers could build a pontoon bridge for our outfit to cross. I was picked to be on a five-man advance patrol that was sent far upstream in a rubber dinghy late one night.

Silently, we paddled across the river and ditched the boat on the other bank. Meanwhile, Battalion launched some dummy landing craft straight across from the enemy position. They headed out into the Meuse in full view of the Germans, guided by rudders that had been roped down, propelled by outboard motors whose throttles had been revved up and set with chewing gum. Stuffed potato sacks with steel helmets at the bow and stern looked exactly like dogfaces hunkered down in the dark boats. The Nazis began blasting away at the phony landing craft. Like cats, we moved through the brush toward the flank of the German artillery position. The decoys worked perfectly, giving us the split-second jump we needed.

First, we bayoneted the lookouts. Then, we tossed grenades at the artillery crew. Once we made sure they were all dead, we attached satchel charges to the big gun and piled on its own shells for the icing on the cake. The charge was set. We scurried away along the riverbank. The explosion and ensuing ball of fire that consumed the Nazis' 88 lit up the night, our own Fourth of July fireworks show, only a few months late.

The swift-moving tide of Allied might had, by this time, liberated most of France and a good part of Belgium. The Nazis had been driven back within the Reich, seeking the protection of their vast system of forts and pillboxes that extended from Holland down to Switzerland, the famed Siegfried Line. A helluva lot of journalists and generals had talked about the Siegfried Line without ever having seen it. By September 11, we were camped near Herve, Belgium, and I saw it for myself on a reconnaissance patrol that day. In a letter to my brother Ving, I described it:

> I'm on the Siegfried Line, Vingo, and I guess Wagner is turning over in his grave right now. Know what the line really is? It's a con-

tinuous series of emplacements extending along the West Wall of Germany, containing reinforced pillboxes for machine guns, anti-tank guns and open earthworks for heavier artillery. They become greater, denser in depth. The concrete installations are 20–30 ft. high, some ranging to 3 stories, with steel, then reinforced concrete. Walls and roofs, 3, 5 or 7 ft thick, in some cases more.

The Big Red One's job was to tear a hole in the Siegfried Line and push through to Aachen, the German border city that had become a symbol of resistance to the Allied invasion and therefore defended with fanatical fury. Like in Sicily, the desperate homeland equation had taken effect. The closer we got to the enemy's turf, the more zealously they fought the invaders.

As I jotted down in my journal later, the essential breakthrough happened at 0545 hours on September 12. In the endless rain, our outfit was moving cautiously through a foggy forest, every man's mouth shut tight, his ears and eyes wide open. We'd been sent out to destroy some of those monolithic pillboxes and attack a stubborn Wehrmacht position. In the dark, cold dawn, the fog got even heavier, closing in on us like a thick blanket. We couldn't see a damn thing, but we could hear German voices in the distance. Each dogface grabbed the shoulder of the man in front of him as we inched forward step by step. Radio silence had been imposed. Every cracking leaf, every creaking limb, every cawing bird made us hold our breath, clench our teeth, and grip our rifles with tense fingers. The unseen border was breached during that treacherous advance. We'd invaded Germany.

By blowing a few pillboxes and destroying some light artillery, we'd pierced the Siegfried Line. Just as quickly, we were forced to fall back when the enemy counterattacked. Their heavy artillery pounded our position with uncanny accuracy, causing many casualties, then their tanks and infantry swarmed in to push us back, turning the Big Red One from attackers into bitterly besieged defenders.

Enemy numbers dramatically increased. Instead of combats against fifty German soldiers, now there were hundreds of them to face. Mixed in with battle-hardened German soldiers were the young soldiers of the Volksgrenadier Divisions. For Chrissakes, some of them were only twelve years old, or younger! Captain O'Brien of Cannon Company sent this message back to HQ:

> This may sound funny, but it is serious. We just captured 4 children, the oldest one isn't over 7 years old. They were firing into one of my gun sections. One was using an M-1, loaded the wrong ammunition, and blew the end off the gun.

It was hard to feel sorry for the youngsters, because, like their elders, they were aiming between our eyes. Still, the presence of kids on the front lines was disturbing. They didn't even know why the hell they were there. Once captured, they were sent to POW camps, just like other prisoners. All they wanted to do was go home to their families. They would discover that their families, like the entire German nation, would pay dearly for Hitler's transgressions. American bombing squadrons were already bringing the whole world's wrath relentlessly down on the German Fatherland.

In battle after battle, the Siegfried Line started to crumble. Ridiculous rumors circulated that the enemy was demoralized and about to abandon. That kind of misinformation was dished out by army brass sitting on their asses back at HQ. It made men on the front feel pretty bitter. All our dead and wounded were proof enough that the Nazis showed no sign of surrender. Whenever they pulled back, they'd dig in, fight like mad to hold their ground, then come back at us with a vicious counterattack.

One of the exasperating and little-known facts of this period was that gasoline, spare parts, ammunition, food, and medicines for U.S. troops were running out quick. Hell, the beachhead that we'd first established on the sands of Normandy had rapidly telescoped to the pillboxes on the German border and was tricky to keep supplied adequately. What about Eisenhower's promise to the First Infantry Division back in England? We all joked about it. All we had to do was take Omaha, and somebody else would "carry the ball" from there. That goddamned beachhead extended from the English Channel and probably went right up to Hitler's front door. As battle-tested troops, we had to carry the ball.

To make our predicament even more maddening, the enemy had an almost impregnable position outside the nearby town of Verlautenheide, on Crucifix Hill, so called because of the huge cross that surmounted it. From there, a German observation post could see every American movement, at least during the day. That explained why their artillery poured down on us with such amazing precision. Holy shit, one dogface moving out of his foxhole would invite several rounds from Nazi guns as large as 88s!

In my movie *The Big Red One,* the sergeant and his squad are ambushed below a gigantic crucifix, where a furious battle has taken place. German soldiers, lying in wait for the American patrol, plant themselves among the corpses and charred tanks strewn across the plain. There's a helluva shot from the point of view of a German radioman who's climbed up the crucifix to coordinate the ambush. He hides behind the crossbeam, where a war-beaten figure of Christ—along with my camera—looks down on the battleground.

The scene was based on the terrible shellacking we took around Ver-

Eating slop was a dismal routine. When it was raining, we ate and drank rainwater. We tried having stimulating conversations to try to forget what we were ingesting, to take us back to the great past. What subjects did we discuss? The girl back home? Allied strategy? Liquor? Philosophy? Nope. Socks! Elevating, no?

lautenheide, thanks to that Nazi observation post on Crucifix Hill. For my film, however, I transported the cross to Soissons, because the place had a special significance to Big Red One veterans. As the graphic and emotional centerpiece of my yarn, the crucifix and its ravaged Christ fit. The image of a battle guided by a man behind a cross, high above the field of combat, would always be with me, triggering nightmarish truths about the bewildering and brutal nature of war itself. Nothing was sure. Nothing was sacred. Death rained down without notice or design, blindly killing everything in its path. A bullet, a bomb, or a shell from out of nowhere would tear your head off. Usually it had been fired by the enemy. Sometimes, somebody fighting on your own side had pulled the trigger.

For those lucky enough to survive it, war turned your deepest convictions upside down and inside out. Life was supposed to be precious. Every human being was supposed to be valuable. Yet all around you were the corpses of people killed in a conflict they hardly understood, lives wasted in intolerable ways and unthinkable proportions. What could those young men have accomplished, if only they'd survived? It was enough to drive you crazy. Many soldiers did go nuts. If you retained any sanity, you never thought about time the same way again. You were grateful for every moment of existence you were granted, and you didn't want to waste another split second on bullshit.

19

Eggs Off a
Woman's Belly

Pushing through the breach in the Siegfried Line, the stage was set for the final assault on Aachen, the first German city we'd attack. Aachen had enormous strategic and symbolic importance for the Nazis as the gateway to the Reich and the ancient citadel of Charlemagne. Thirty-two kaisers had been crowned in the Aachen Cathedral, and every single one of them was buried in its catacombs. Aachen was situated in a rich valley, surrounded by wood-covered ridges that bristled with enemy mortars, artillery, snipers, and machine guns. The plan was to surround the city in preparation for a coordinated invasion, so the nearby towns of Munsterbusch, Eilendorf, and Stolberg had to be taken. One by one, they fell, but in each one we ran into heavy resistance.

In Munsterbusch, every room in every building was contested. As we were cleaning up the town, a solitary sniper opened fire from the upstairs window of a large private home. I don't know what the hell I was thinking about at the time, but I didn't take cover fast enough. One of those Nazi bullets missed my ear by an inch. I think all the pounding day in and day out from enemy artillery shells was driving me batty, dulling my powers of concentration. One of our sharpshooters instantly fired and brought down the sniper on his first shot. We ran into the house and up the stairs, only to find a voluptuous young woman lying on the floor, buck naked, her hand still on her rifle. She was wet from the bath we'd interrupted. Blood was pouring out of the bullet hole in her chest, and scathing curses came from the delicate lips on her beautiful mouth. She died with hate in her eyes for the American invaders of the Fatherland.

"We should never have shot a girl. It's downright un-American," said a young soldier, his voice trembling.

"It's her or you," said our sergeant. "Take your pick." Then, turning to me, he barked: "You were daydreaming, Fuller. She almost got you."

I was furious with myself because I'd been so unprofessional. I was even madder at our sharpshooter. Why couldn't he have just wounded the sex goddess? That way, we could have interrogated her. I wanted to know why such a beautiful gal wanted to die for Hitler.

"You cost me a good character for my book," I said to the marksman. "But thanks for saving the author's ass."

There was no denying it, I'd let my guard down, like a wetnose. If I wanted to survive, it could never happen again. Luck was always welcome, but still an undependable ally on the battlefield. Observation, cunning, speed, discipline, and concentration were much better friends. Wetnoses proved me right. They'd been brought in by the hundreds to replace all the dogfaces killed or wounded in Belgium to get us up to full force before the Aachen campaign. On paper, the regiment had the required numbers. But those young soldiers were thrown onto the battlefield without enough combat experience. Some were fearful, freezing under enemy flare drops instead of taking cover from the bombs and shells that surely followed. Some were proud, forgetting caution in their show-off eagerness for a medal. Some were rebellious, hating discipline and orders. Some were cynical, not giving a damn. Some were unfocused, lacking the mental edge to avoid being killed. Some were still squeamish about killing the enemy. Who were the first soldiers to go down? Sadly but unsurprisingly, the wetnoses.

Stolberg was a typical infantry cleanup after being practically knocked level by our artillery. Nazi soldiers fought back from cellars, sewers, and tunnels, ambushing our men as we moved through the town's streets. We'd come to realize that no matter how much you bombed a German town, registered artillery on it, kept it raked with cross fire, lobbed mortars into it—whatever was the state of destruction of crumbling buildings and ripped-up roads—infantry had to be sent in to take out each Nazi defender. That meant you had to make sure you killed them. A wounded Nazi was like TNT, with so many underground places to hide in. If he could still move his trigger finger, a Nazi could score heavily for his side, shooting one, two, three of your guys in the blink of *ein auge*.

We still had to take Verlautenheide, the possession of which by the enemy had cost us so heavily. At 0400 on October 8, the Eighteenth Infantry pushed toward Crucifix Hill while the Sixteenth created a diversionary attack with mortars and artillery. By daylight, Crucifix Hill was finally occupied by the Big Red One.

The siege of Aachen would be long and brutal, unlike any battle we'd ever fought before. Before it began, General Huebner sent word to the German commanding officer, Colonel Wilck. If Aachen didn't capitulate, it would be reduced to rubble. Colonel Wilck rejected the ultimatum. His orders were straight from Hitler. Aachen would be defended to the last man. American shells and bombs started to hit the city, destroying half its buildings and badly damaging the rest. When the dust had settled, the historic cathedral and the ancient town hall were left standing, barely. Still, Colonel Wilck refused to surrender, instead launching counterattacks against our positions on the ridges to the south and east of the city. The final assault began when General Huebner gave the order to send the Big Red One into the heart of Aachen to root out and destroy every enemy soldier. None of the forty thousand civilians in the city were to be harmed, making our mission trickier than ever. Never before had we fought in a battlefield of avenues, streetcars, sidewalks, sewers, and rooftops with so many civilians present. We had to wipe out enemy sniper nests stashed in what was left of shops, offices, cafés, and hotels. It was confused slaughter on both sides. Unfamiliar with urban fighting, dogfaces shot other dogfaces. Many civilians were accidentally killed in the cross fire. The streets of Aachen ran red with blood.

When we took a building, we'd scurry up four or five flights of stairs to the rooftop to check it for snipers. Once it was secure, we'd shoot enemy on top of the next building, tossing grenades into the top-floor windows to cover our soldiers advancing in the street down below. On one rooftop, I confronted a German sniper who'd already unfurled a white cloth, as if to surrender. I motioned to him with my rifle to move forward. As he reached me, he pulled out a Luger and squeezed the trigger. It jammed. I lunged at him and swung the butt of my rifle at his head, knocking him over the edge of the roof. He fell five floors to his death.

Back in the street, we dashed past burning trucks and buses. At the town hall, we came face-to-face with a group of SS who'd taken cover behind some women and children. We stopped dead. The standoff lasted only half a minute, but it seemed endless. Suddenly, the SS started shooting at us. A couple of our soldiers were picked off. Still, not one American GI wanted to shoot German civilians to get at the real enemy. Only our sergeant knew that that was the only way out of the jam we were in. Before our horrified eyes, he fired rapidly, wounding two women and a child, killing five of the SS.

"Oh, my God!" cried a wetnose.

The SS were surprised, too. They shoved the civilians toward us and scattered. We screamed "DOWN!" at the women and children and shot every one of the bastards as they tried to escape.

That incident would inspire a scene many years later in *Forty Guns* (1957), when Barbara Stanwyck becomes a human shield for her nasty brother at the end of the picture. Instead of doing what everyone expects in that situation—holding his fire—my hero surprises everyone by wounding Stanwyck in the leg, then shooting the startled brother, who is suddenly vulnerable. Audiences always laugh nervously at that scene. It was an original way to handle a timeworn device. People are horrified by the violence to Stanwyck, but love the hero's line to her: "It's only a flesh wound."

Die-hard defenders were still hiding out in residential buildings and factories all over Aachen. The still-intact public library was bristling with them. Cannon Company blew out the front door, creating a gaping hole through which a light tank could have driven. We swept into the library building, tossing grenades, firing our rifles, stepping over gruesome corpses whose hands had been blown off by the direct shelling. From between the bookshelves, enemy soldiers fired at us. We pursued them down into the cellar, where we caught them in a cross fire among stacks of forgotten books. After it was over, I moved cautiously through the long rows of crowded bookshelves, searching for any last defenders. They'd all been killed. In the tomblike silence, I looked at all those books gathering dust. I prayed no book of mine would ever be used to stop a bullet.

Back in the city streets, we spotted some German soldiers slipping into one of Aachen's biggest cinemas. We ran in after them. The hall was pitch-black. Suddenly a blinding beam of light from the projection booth filled the screen. We bellied under the movie seats. German machine guns burst the glass window in the booth next to the whirring, white-hot projector, firing down at us. We all dashed out except for a soldier named Johnson, who stayed down during the flurry of bullets. A few of us ran around to the alley, scurried up the iron-wrought staircase, and got the snipers in the projection booth. Meanwhile Johnson was down in the theater, tossing grenades into the aisles and using up every bullet in his clip. The movie theater fell silent as a tomb.

We slipped back in there cautiously. Johnson had single-handedly massacred fourteen enemy soldiers. They were slumped over the remains of the red velvet seats, their blood oozing down the raked floorboards. Stunned, Johnson walked wordlessly up the center aisle, staring ahead as if in another world. We found him outside the theater hypnotized by a big movie poster. It was for a coming attraction, with a couple of cowboys in a violent fistfight while a beautiful gal looked on. As if nothing had happened, Johnson said, to no one in particular, "I love action movies!" We thought he'd lost his mind.

It had taken thirteen long days of intense fighting, street by bloody street, for us to take Aachen. The final blow came when our doggies loaded an abandoned trolley car with TNT and rolled it down the tracks on a

The main altar inside the historic Aachen Cathedral after the German surrender of the city.

steep street, crashing it into a couple of Nazi tanks positioned near their big ammunitions dump. The resulting explosion was enormous and sealed the city's fate. Already deprived of food and water, and now without ammunition, the city was defenseless. The enemy capitulated on October 21.

When the mortars and machine guns fell silent, civilians emerged cautiously from their underground shelters into the rubble-strewn streets. The last couple weeks must have been a living hell for them. Some wept with hysterical joy and thanked us for coming. Most were a filthy mess, hungry, dehydrated, suffering from shell shock. Dogfaces from my outfit found a strange-looking man wandering the streets and picked him up for questioning. The fellow wore a dirty robe and had that crazed look in his eyes that we recognized in people who'd been in close contact with total war. We rolled our eyeballs when the old guy said he was a bishop, even if he did have a certain dignity about him. Battalion HQ was radioed for advice. What should we do with the screwball who claimed to be a bishop? They told us to treat him like one, so we escorted him to the Aachen Cathedral, where he set to work cleaning up the mess of rubble and broken glass. He turned out to be Johanes van der Velden, bishop of Aachen.

A formal surrender ceremony took place a couple days later outside the cathedral. It was late afternoon. A few hundred German prisoners had been herded into the main square. Thousands of their fellow Nazis had died in the defense of the city. Over five hundred Big Red One soldiers from all three battalions surrounded them. We'd lost hundreds of our boys, dead and wounded. Civility in that situation was tough, but obligatory. General Huebner allowed Colonel Wilck to speak to his men over some crackly loudspeakers. His words were translated into English. Wilck explained why he hadn't fought to the last man. They were still German soldiers, and he reminded them to behave as such.

"I wish you the best of health and a fast return to the Fatherland," he concluded. "We need you to help rebuild Germany."

Wilck wanted to give his men a *Sieg Heil* and *Heil Hitler*. But Huebner wouldn't allow it.

"I can't lead you in a salute to our Führer," concluded Wilck. "However, we can still salute him in our minds."

Taking the microphone, General Huebner announced that we were being relieved by the 104th Infantry for some well-deserved rest in preparation for the next advance. That gave us something to cheer about. The general concluded by reassuring every man of Jewish faith in our outfit that, in response to a special request, they'd have the chance to participate in a makeshift service for Yom Kippur, the Jewish high holiday, which happened to fall that evening. With Bishop van der Velden's blessing, the Yom Kippur ceremony would take place inside the Aachen Cathedral. First, a replacement had to be found to sub for the Jewish chaplain, who was too busy burying all the dead. A doggie named Katz from the Bronx stepped forward and volunteered to lead the service.

"Every man of Jewish faith," announced General Huebner, "who wants to take part will immediately proceed with Private Katz into the cathedral."

The defeated Nazis watched us contemptuously. They were waiting to see how many Jews were wearing the Big Red One. Our sergeant, who was about as Jewish as a pork chop, turned and followed Private Katz inside the cathedral, as if to say, "Stick that up your *Mein Kampf,* all you Nazi mongrels fed on the bone of fear, hatred, and stupidity!" Every other dog-face in the square followed Katz and the sergeant into the cathedral, too. On that occasion, everybody was Jewish.

Our next objective was the Roer River crossing, east of Aachen. We moved into the Hürtgen forest near the town of Hamich. Besides the enemy's fierce resistance, the two biggest problems we had to confront were our ears and our feet.

See, the sound of artillery, both outgoing and incoming, was constant day and night—*Ack! Ack! Ack!*—replaced every hour or so with planes flying overhead. Maybe there were a hundred Allied bombers on their way to Germany, or maybe it was a single Jerry plane coming in at us. American arty would open up and—*Ack! Ack! Ack!*—you'd dive for your miserable life because some of that friendly fire might kill you. The Jerry plane would be driven off, and we'd sigh with relief. However, before we had a moment's calm, enemy artillery started up again—*Ack! Ack! Ack!* The interminable artillery was ear-shattering. First Battalion Commander Colonel Edmund F. Driscoll filed the following report at that time:

> The men here are going crazy. They are getting pounded day after day and attacking day after day. They are going wacky. It is real and not put on. I know the real thing. The Doc ought to make a report to Division. It isn't just one man, it's many of them.

As for our feet, the never-ending rain made life outdoors miserable, dramatically increasing the number of cases of trench foot. Want to know what trench foot was like? When you wash clothes by hand, you know how soft and wrinkled your hands become from the water and soap? Well, it was identical to that, only your feet slowly become paralyzed. I was lucky, I suppose, because I hadn't gotten it yet. It was only a matter of time.

No matter what we were going through in the Hürtgen forest, you had to realize that somewhere there were plenty of other doggies going through ten times worse. They too had to accept the fact that elsewhere, GIs were suffering even more than they. The only thing that kept us going was the realization that somewhere else, another dogface was worse off than you. Our psychology was vacuous, but it somehow worked in those trying days and nights.

The winter of 1944 kicked in early in Germany. It got much colder. Then the first snows fell. The ground turned white and the bitter cold kept it that way. We lost many, many men in the ferocious fighting in the snow-bound forest. Fresh replacements took their place. Blood from wetnoses turned the snow the same shade of red as that of battle-weary veterans.

Like enraged dogs, the Germans fought on. Their entrenchment, the encroaching winter, and the counterattacks threatened to paralyze our advance. Our worst nightmare was that of being frozen in, encircled, and cut down before realizing the victory that seemed closer than ever. Our hands and feet were blue with cold. Now frostbite became an ever-present danger. But we had to press on. To hesitate was certain defeat. Fear made us that much more determined.

One of the rare moments of joy we experienced was when mail from home somehow reached us, even in Hürtgen forest. After they passed out the precious envelopes and care packages, we read our letters while wrapped in blankets like mummies, one hand turning the pages, one hand on an ice-cold rifle. In Hürtgen, I received an allotment of cigars and chocolate from my mother, along with a letter in an abnormally thick envelope that, like an exploding shell, sent a shockwave through me in the snowy woods of Germany. Howard Hawks had ended up paying fifteen grand for the movie rights to *The Dark Page*. Charlie Feldman had brokered the deal and paid my mother the money, as I'd requested, so that she could make ends meet while I was away playing war games. Rebecca had included a wad of cash, one thousand bucks! One of my buddies asked what I was going to do with all that money, since it was completely useless for the time being. Out of the blue, I announced that I was going to throw a private party as soon as we got some R and R. At the time, I must have been feeling pretty high. Why not share my good fortune with the other guys? It could be the last party some of us would ever attend.

Word got around that I was planning a big shindig, and guys in every battalion wanted to come. I insisted that each guest had to dream up his own sex fantasy. My event was going to have lots of willing girls ready to help us realize our wildest dreams. Lack of originality was the only obstacle to an invitation. Sex, after all, was only a mental game for us, because the chow had been laced with so much saltpeter that we'd forgotten what a hard-on was. Just the prospect of a party generated a running banter of crazy, lusty speculation and macho gibble-gabble. The sergeant wanted a naked girl to put on a steel helmet and wear a cartridge belt and bandoliers. Another dogface wanted a woman to get on his back and ride him like a horse. Another fantasized about a gal's ass against a frosty window.

Several guests wouldn't make it to my party, killed in Hürtgen by snipers, artillery, or, believe it or not, wood splinters. When enemy shells came down in the forest, trees exploded and a deluge of sharp bits of wood

Women were on our minds, but never in our arms.

came raining down on us. During one such attack, Captain Thomas O'Brien, the wonderful guy who was so important to us on Omaha Beach, two-time winner of the Distinguished Service Cross, commander of Cannon Company, hit the ground and never moved again. A six-inch shard had been driven through his heart. O'Brien had played along with our shindig plans, fantasizing about breaking a half-dozen eggs on the hot belly of a gal at the party. He was going to eat them off her, one at a time.

My party would happen faster than anyone imagined. We got pulled off the front line for a week in mid-December and sent back to the Belgian village of Herve for some dearly needed recuperation time. I found a lusty little hotel in town run by Madame Marbaise. Madame was in her fifties, weighed about 250 pounds, and hated Nazis. She claimed that she always knew the Germans were going to lose the war, so she never despaired during the occupation. Projecting brighter days ahead, she'd stashed away an ample supply of liquor and wine in her secret stone cellar. Now that the

Germans had been pushed out of Belgium, Madame Marbaise's fortunes were already improving. GIs crowded the hotel bar, drinking anything that was wet, playing the piano, singing rounds of "Roll Out the Barrel," and renting rooms when they got lucky with local girls. The place was the perfect setup for my party. The kicker was that the village butcher was a drunk. With her limitless supply of booze, Madame Marbaise could get a limitless supply of steaks.

I met with Madame Marbaise late one night in her kitchen. With the help of my sergeant, who acted as interpreter, I explained to her that I was inviting my buddies to one night with all the booze, steaks, and women they wanted. Madame was dubious, to say the least. Did I even have a clue what such an affair would cost? It was out of the question. From the inside pocket of my GI overcoat, I pulled out the envelope with the thousand bucks and carefully laid out the greenbacks on the kitchen table like a cardshark at a carnival spreading a deck of cards for the suckers. All that moola, I explained, was for her, with the understanding that she'd provide us with whatever we wanted to eat and drink as well as some willing women to participate in special sexual antics. I'd sworn to myself back in Hürtgen that, in honor of O'Brien, some sonofabitch at my party was going to eat eggs off a woman's belly. It was done, just like every other sexual escapade that guys had dreamed up for their invitations. Several of my guests, like O'Brien, wouldn't make it to the fete.

Madame grinned her Cheshire cat smile.

"Vous êtes fou, fou, fou!" she said, scooping up the dough and placing it inside her brassiere for safekeeping.

"Yeah, we are," I replied. "But we're still alive."

20

A River of Tears

Rumors of the next German counterattack were flying, and this one was supposedly bigger than anything we'd seen previously. The enemy had been piling up an attacking force, getting ready for a massive attempt to smash through the Allied front. An ambitious operation, its goal was to recapture Paris, now hundreds of miles away. The offensive would become known, at various times, as "Breakthrough," "Battle of the Ardennes Salient," and, finally and forever, "Battle of the Bulge."

With very little rest, we were back in action by early December, as word had come down that the thinly held American line was being shattered by the new and powerful German thrust. Our outfit was moved to the town of Faymonville, Belgium. Our objective was to contain the strong enemy contingent that had moved back there, stopping them from overrunning any more Allied positions. News of the Nazi massacre of American POWs at Malmedy had reached us, along with other atrocity stories. Evidently, the Germans would stop at nothing to make this final effort succeed. Gas masks were passed out. Since the enemy had violated every other rule of warfare, it seemed probable that the bastards would end up using poison gas, too.

The most maddening trick that the Germans played on us was masquerading as war-weary dogfaces. Wehrmacht dressed as GIs, complete with American dog tags and legitimate-looking papers, infiltrated our lines, and threw us off-kilter at first. Fake doggies appeared out of nowhere, scouted our positions, then brought the death-dealing intelligence back to their artillery gunners. Some even opened fire on our soldiers before we caught on. Now, every GI who approached our position was suspect.

One day, a lone soldier with a Big Red One on his helmet showed up at our outpost. Our sergeant stopped him cold.

"How do I know you're a GI?" asked the sergeant.

"You crazy?" growled the doggie. "Here's my dog tag!"

"Proves nothing."

"Hell, I know everybody's touchy. Ask me anything you want."

"Take down your pants," the sergeant ordered.

"What? You guys queer or something?"

"Drop 'em. Or I'll put a bullet in your mouth."

The soldier dropped his pants. The sergeant took one look at the man's underwear and shot him in the chest. We were shocked until we found German dog tags inside the soldier's pack of American cigarettes.

"The Jerry's underwear gave him away," explained the sergeant. "They tuck their T-shirts inside. We don't."

In the freezing predawn fog of December 16, the German counteroffensive was launched. It was a massive thrust of enemy tanks and infantry troops that broke through our lines and headed for the Meuse. We were determined that this would not be another debacle like Kasserine. Our division was ordered to fall back and hold the southern flank of the thirty-five-mile-wide "Bulge." We fought like hell and held on, preventing the Germans from expanding the Bulge. We heard that in other parts of the salient, American infantrymen, armor, and airplanes were hacking their way through, trying to relieve besieged units within the Bulge's borders.

The brunt of the German thrust was against Saint-Vith and Bastogne, defended by our boys from the Twenty-eighth Infantry and the Ninth and Tenth Armored. That was a crucial junction in the Ardennes. Word had gotten back to us about the eighteen thousand Americans dug in over there, facing an onslaught of three German divisions, more than forty-five thousand men. Eisenhower had sent in the 101st Airborne to try to tilt the scales in our direction. After six days and nights of intense fighting, our guys were just about overwhelmed at Saint-Vith. On December 22, the Germans offered the "Battered Bastards of Bastogne" an honorable surrender. The regiment's CO, General Anthony C. McAuliffe, sent them back a one-word response: "Nuts."

We'd never forget the piss and vinegar of the Twenty-eighth Infantry. We'd never yield to the Germans, either. Our present assignment was to blunt the enemy's last great offensive operation, then break its back. The nasty winter weather made the job that much more difficult. With the wind whipping our bodies, the snow slashing our faces, we had to fight both the enemy and the increasingly blizzardlike conditions. Constant snowfall made every movement exhausting. I had it easy next to the doggies carrying heavy machine guns and mortars through the knee-deep drifts. All hands and feet turned numb with cold. Frostbite was eating at our toes and fingertips. If you didn't thaw them out once in a while,

In snowsuits, bedsheets, or any damned white coat, my outfit advances near Faymonville, January 1945. The snow and cold made the Battle of the Bulge a gruesome campaign. Living outside was a battle against frostbite.

gangrene would set in. Then there was only one solution. The rotten digit had to be cut off. But it might be too late. You could die from frostbite. Many of our boys did.

We spent New Year's, 1945, holding our position in Faymonville, waiting until conditions favored our next offensive campaign. On January 15, the long-awaited attack finally began. American artillery and bombs started and never let up. Again, our troops were hit by friendly fire. Seeing Americans killed by American shells drove me crazy. I wasn't the only dogface tempted to shoot at our own low-flying planes.

The horrible weather conditions worked to our advantage. The Germans couldn't see us moving up through the snow-blown landscape. We wrapped ourselves in snow capes, white blankets, and bedsheets, anything to blend into the all-white background. After Faymonville, town after town caved in as we reconquered Belgium and tried to breach the Siegfried

Line a second time. Schoppen was next. Amel, Mirfeld, Valender. Then we moved to a position overlooking the Roer River near the town of Klein-hau, almost demolished before we'd arrived.

Crossing the Roer was no piece of cake. Previous American units had thoroughly mined the area, and heavy rains aggravated our engineers' task of building a pontoon bridge. At any time, the Germans could blow dams upstream, which would turn our position into a watery wasteland. There were many delays, the last one being an enemy-aircraft strafing and bombing mission the night before the planned river crossing. The German planes caused casualties and knocked out one treadway bridge built for our advance. The problem was our antiaircraft guns had to hold their fire that night because the skies were full of RAF bombers and fighters. We finally crossed the Roer on some pontoon footbridges on February 25 and pushed eastward.

We began a nonstop marathon that was not to end until the Rhine had been reached. There were so many little towns we took, I lost track of their names. Krauzau. Vettweiss. Gladbach. Metternich. Rötgen. Rosberg, Merten, Trippelsdorf. We were in bad shape, but we pushed forward relentlessly, pursuing the retreating enemy, not giving them a chance to get set for a counterattack. Rest was snatched in periods of minutes, not hours. Fatigue and trench foot made every step of that operation tough as hell. We looked more haggard than the Nazis we captured.

Miraculously, our outfit was invited one cold and rainy night for a USO show that was in the area. It took place in one of those conquered German towns, Friesheim. Trucks slogged through the mud to bring us to the town's little theater. Soaked, exhausted dogfaces suddenly forgot all about weather and weariness, because the mistress of ceremonies that night was the one and only Marlene Dietrich, a woman who represented all women to us. She came onstage in the packed theater dressed in a flaming red gown that hugged her curvaceous body like a second skin. Not an inch of those famous legs could be seen, but we knew they were there. Dietrich told us that she was born a German but she was now an American. Having emigrated to the States after denouncing the Nazis, she'd taken U.S. citizenship in 1939. The only reason she'd come back to Germany was to give our morale a boost. Just seeing that gorgeous woman made us all feel better. We applauded her wildly.

Dietrich told us that she'd like us all to relax for the show by laying down our pieces. We loved it that she called our M1s "pieces," just as we referred to them. Rifles clattered as we lay them down. She smiled that indomitable smile and said she wanted to hear every single gun hit the floor. She knew it was hard to let go of your M1 and that many guys always held on to them, no matter where they were. They'd become another part of our bodies, a sort of third arm. Dietrich was masterfully charming as she waited patiently for the last piece to hit the floor. She didn't do much more than sing a couple of songs and introduce different USO acts that night. She didn't have to do anything. After all, she was Dietrich.

When the show was over, we cheered lustily, then filed outside to climb on the trucks waiting to take us back to the front. I jumped up on the runner and asked our truck driver how long it would take to load up and turn his vehicle around in the mud. He said about twenty minutes. I jumped down and ran around to the stage-door entrance. An MP stopped me. Backstage was off-limits. I told him I had to speak to Miss Dietrich about a "professional matter."

"Forget it," the MP snarled. "Get back to your outfit."

He wasn't getting rid of me so easy. I began to scream at the sonofabitch that this was professional. The MP relented, turned, and walked back to Dietrich's dressing room. Just like when I was a reporter getting to a reluctant source for a story, I followed close on his heels. The MP knocked on the bare dressing-room door, opened it enough to be heard, and started talking to Dietrich. I rushed over and stuck my head in the half-opened door.

"It'll only take a minute, Miss Dietrich," I said.

Surprised but cordial, she invited me into her cold, damp dressing room. She looked gorgeous, but she was shivering. The only light came from a bare lightbulb dangling from the high ceiling. I apologized about my appearance. I looked like hell. I was unshaven. My uniform was filthy. My boots were muddy. I must have stunk, too. But Dietrich didn't seem to mind at all. She'd probably seen worse on her tour of frontline troops.

"Miss Dietrich," I told her. "I'd like you to take a message for me back home."

"Impossible," she said. "Quite impossible."

She explained that she'd met many soldiers who wanted her to phone their mothers, their girlfriends. But she just couldn't do it, and she told everyone the same thing. It was really impossible.

I said I didn't want her to phone my mother. I wanted her to deliver a one-word message to Charlie Feldman in Hollywood.

"Charles K. Feldman?" she said, suddenly intrigued. "My agent? You know him?"

"Yes, Miss Dietrich," I said. "He's my agent, too."

She stopped dead and gazed at me.

"He's *your* agent, too?"

"Yeah, he is. He sold my book to Howard Hawks. A novel called *The*

During 1944 and 1945, Dietrich toured extensively behind Allied lines, giving hundreds of shows for GIs who loved her. It was cold, dangerous, and thankless work, but she seemed to relish every aspect of it.

Dark Page. The message for Charlie is easy, Miss Dietrich. One word. 'Cigars.' Just say 'Cigars' to Charlie when you get back to Hollywood. Okay?"

She laughed and poured us both a glass of good brandy.

"What's your name, soldier?"

"Fuller. Sammy Fuller."

She asked me to write it down. I refused.

"My name's not necessary," I told her. "Just say 'Cigars' to Charlie. He'll know who it is."

"Okay, soldier," she said, clinking glasses with me. "Is there anything else I can do for you?"

"Yeah, there is. My buddies will never believe I really talked to you."

I asked her to write some silly, personalized notes on scraps of paper, things such as "You can live with just one ball!" She laughed as she copied down my words. She signed each note "Marlene." We drank to Charlie Feldman, to the Big Red One, and to all the Allies.

Dietrich and I sipping brandy and laughing together in that cold dressing room over fifty years ago is a scene frozen in my mind forever. She told me to take the bottle of brandy with me. I kissed her and hurried out, reaching the troop truck just as it was getting set to leave.

My buddies asked me where I got the brandy.

"Dietrich," I said.

They laughed heartily. So did I. It was one of the few moments of pure laughter we'd had in a long time. My sergeant, who rarely even cracked a smile, chuckled, too. I gave the sergeant his note from Dietrich. The rain almost washed away her penciled words about hoping to wear nothing but a helmet and a bandolier for him someday.

The sergeant murmured something under his breath, then really smiled.

I passed out the other personal messages from Dietrich to my pals. In silent awe, the guys read the precious notes. Then they bombarded me with questions about the great lady. I smiled from ear to ear but said nothing, lighting the stub of a damp cigar. I looked back at Friesheim receding into the blackness, my contented smoke wafting out from the troop truck as it barreled through the German night. A box of good cigars arrived by APO from Charlie Feldman that spring. Dietrich had damn sure delivered my message.

In 1953, I'd run into Marlene Dietrich again under very different conditions. I was in the New York nightclub El Morocco for a party following the premiere of my movie *Pickup on South Street*. At my table was the wonderful actress Thelma Ritter, who'd given a terrific performance as Moe, the informer who only wants a decent funeral. She'd get nominated for an Academy Award for the role. At a table across the big room was the legendary producer Sam Spiegel. He waved at me. I went over to say hello. Sitting next to Spiegel was Dietrich. He introduced us. I told her we'd already met. She was very polite, but she shook her head, not remembering me or where we'd run into each other.

"Too bad," I said. "That's life."

I turned and started back to my table. All of a sudden, Marlene Dietrich was right behind me.

"Hey, soldier," she said, her eyes twinkling.

I turned and grinned at her. She put her arms around me. Tears were rolling down her cheeks. She'd heard so many stories about all the men killed in our outfit. Yet here I was, alive. She was genuinely pleased to see me again. We had a warm reunion. She'd given over five hundred shows for GIs during the war, but there was only one little corporal trying to squeeze some cigars out of Charlie Feldman back in Hollywood.

"The Big Red One!" she said, her voice cracking with emotion.

My outfit, the Sixteenth Infantry, led the First Division as we swept eastward from the Roer River in the First Army's drive to reach the Rhine. The speed of our advance saw us taking an unscheduled swing toward the southeast. Unexpectedly, Bonn now lay in our path. With the Twenty-sixth Infantry on our right and the Eighteenth on our left, we'd taken fourteen villages and towns among the low hills guarding Bonn to the west. By the evening of March 7, the Big Red One was within a mile of the city.

Our assault plan on Bonn, formulated by the new division commander, Major General Clift Andrus, would be daring and swift. He based the operation on an old Indian technique. We were to move against the enemy on a moonless night without firing a shot. The Germans knew we were coming, but not when and where. They were expecting a terrific pounding from artillery and bombers. Any objective the size of Bonn would normally get softened up beforehand. But our plan called for neither saturation bombing nor preparatory shelling. It depended on a completely audacious, maybe even impudent, dash into the city by a silent infantry column.

At 0330 hours on March 8, 1945, we moved out, marching as quietly as possible down the road in columns of twos behind four medium tanks, directly into the center of Bonn. Bringing up the rear were antitank and assault artillery. Because it was pitch-black that night, our tanks passed for Panzers. Before they knew what was happening to them, enemy sentries were disarmed and forced to marched along with us. As we passed the next Nazi position, our new POWs would respond warmly to greetings called out in our direction, their delivery considerably sweetened by the trench knives held against the bases of their spines. We were mistaken over and over for German troops retreating to safety across the Rhine. The city was swollen with enemy defenders, but not a round was fired.

Moving straight down Kölnstrasse, our platoon reached Rosental and turned left. We were in the heart of Bonn, and things were very quiet, too quiet. My company hit the Bonn post office, where over three hundred Germans were bunked down. Most of them threw up their hands rather than be killed.

When dawn came, the calm was finished, overwhelmed by some fast and furious fighting. The Germans realized we were in their midst and opened fire with SP guns and tanks. Our tanks retaliated.

We worked our way down toward the Rhine, using doorways, alleys, and windows for protection. At the Agricultural Institute of the University of Bonn, enemy positions in the classrooms stopped us in our tracks. A light-armored car slammed into a sandbag barricade just in front of us, its driver shot by one of our sharpshooters, its machine-gunners immediately surrendering. Our sergeant jumped into the driver's seat of the light-armored car and started its motor. Two other dogfaces manned the car's machine guns. The armored car drove up the steps of the Agricultural

Institute, smashed through the giant doors, and steered down the long, wide corridor, spraying bullets everywhere. Behind that cover, we charged into the university. When we walked out, we had 150 POWs in front of us.

The battle became even fiercer when German artillery, mortar, and rocket fire opened up on us from the other side of the Rhine, trying to protect the bridge that was so essential to their retreat. Other German elements south of the city and across the Bonn-Cologne autobahn had recovered from their surprise. Those of us on the assault team inside the city were cut off from the rest of the division until later that evening.

By nightfall, the roads into Bonn were opened by our forces and the enemy was in full retreat. The exclamation point on what was undoubtedly our best orchestrated action since D day was the Nazi explosion that night that blew up the bridge that connected Bonn to the rest of Germany. It was a tacit admission that the city was irretrievably lost. Scattered, last-ditch resistance remained to be cleaned up. Over fifteen hundred German soldiers were taken. The Sixteenth Infantry lost six men killed, fifty-one wounded, and three missing.

Our orders that night were to stay out of sight, find a safe building, and get some shut-eye until dawn. I loved how the street names in Bonn celebrated their great composers. Haydnstrasse. Brahmsstrasse. Bachstrasse. Late that night, Johnson and I forced open the backdoor on a building situated at 24–28 Beethovenstrasse. What a great name for a street! It was pitch-black in the place, so we crawled around on our hands and knees looking for a spot to lie down. I cracked my head on what felt like a big table. Then I realized it was a grand piano. We stretched out on the floor and fell asleep. In the first light of dawn, I woke up and saw the bottom of the piano over my head. Johnson was snoring away. In the half-light, I made out a music stand holding a large composition book. I moved closer. I looked at the notes scribbled all over the sheet music. Then I rose to my knees to inspect the title of the piece. "Heroica" was majestically written at the top of the page. It was clearly signed: "Ludwig van Beethoven."

My mouth was agape. For Chrissakes, the street name made sense! We'd stumbled into Beethoven's childhood home! I got to my feet and looked carefully at all the framed letters, paintings, and busts in the house. The place had been turned into a museum. Everything was intact. I wandered around the great Beethoven's home like a man dying of thirst, unexpectedly finding an oasis in the desert. I couldn't keep the news to myself for another moment. I had to wake up Johnson.

"What?" he asked, opening his eyes quickly.

I put my finger to my lips.

"What?" he said in a lower voice.

"Beethoven was born here," I whispered.

"What outfit?"

"*Beethoven,* goddamnit. You never heard of Beethoven?"

"Uh-uh," he said. "Was he an officer?"

"No! No! No!" I said. "You know the music: *Pum, pum, pum, paaahh-hhh.*"

"There's so many guys that come and go in our outfit, it's hard to remember their names."

"Goddamnit, he's a composer. Like Irving Berlin."

Johnson shook his head. He took one final guess. "Wasn't he one of the bigwigs who inspected the troops at Slapton Sands? You know, with Churchill? Before we invaded France?"

"For cryin' out loud, you've got to have heard of Beethoven!"

But he hadn't. Until then, I didn't believe that somebody in the United States of America could grow up, even on some godforsaken farm in Tennessee, without ever having heard of Beethoven, let alone his music. Despite my exasperation with Johnson, nothing could diminish my wonder and joy that, in the middle of a goddamned world war, I'd gotten to sleep in the childhood home of Ludwig van Beethoven, one of my heroes.

On March 10, with Bonn securely in American hands, we prepared to cross the Rhine on the Ludendorff Bridge at Remagen and enlarge the bridgehead that had been opened in a furious offensive on March 7 by other elements of the First Army while we were assaulting Bonn. The Germans tried to blow up that bridge as well. Under tremendous machine-gun fire, dogfaces dashed across the span and took it, discovering later that the only thing that prevented the Nazi demolition boys from destroying the bridge as they retreated was a stray bullet that severed the detonator.

Thousands of troops and tons of supplies began to move across the Ludendorff Bridge. We got our chance on March 17, and what a chance it was. Only a few hours after we'd crossed to the other side, the bridge collapsed, with four hundred soldiers still on it, killing and wounding many in the incident. We had to build a pontoon bridge across the Rhine so that Allied soldiers and materials could continue pouring into Germany.

Protected from enemy lookouts by smokescreens, we now moved northward to the front line, relieving elements of the 310th Infantry, Seventy-eighth Division. Ten relentless days of vicious, bitter combat awaited us toward the end of March in the so-called Ruhr Pocket, perhaps the most intense fighting on the entire western front. The Big Red One moved through a string of German towns—Weyerbusch, Laasphe, Winterberg, Büren, and Geseke—until the German hold was finally broken and the enemy driven north of the Sieg River. The strategy was to box in the retreating Nazis as the Ninth Army advanced to the north. It worked, at the cost of many American lives.

At the beginning of April 1945, my outfit was sent into the heavily forested Harz Mountains to spearhead the Allied attack to the east. Suddenly we were trekking up steep roads, delayed constantly by roadblocks and trees blown down by the retreating Germans. It was clear the enemy was in a state of confusion. Resistance was spotty. Among enemy infantry thrown up to fight us were youngsters and recently drafted civilians. Yet those days and nights were hell. The Nazis still had enough tanks and artillery, sharpshooters and land mines to wreak havoc on us. Besides, melting snow made road conditions terrible.

Despite the continued resistance to our advance, we sensed the war was winding down. Rumors were flying again, this time about the Germans surrendering at any moment. Our sergeant warned us to ignore all the hearsay. It was just bullshit until Nazi leaders and the Allied commanders officially inked an armistice. One bullet, either random or well aimed, could still rip off your head.

One last bullet almost did get me. It came from a German sharpshooter positioned strategically in an ancient castle overlooking a steep pass in the Harz Mountains. On our march toward Czechoslovakia, somewhere between Sieber and Sankt Andreasberg, we had to get through that pass. The medieval stone castle seemed to have grown organically out of the side of a cliff above a grotto. Water from a mountain stream rushed down the valley and roared below the castle.

I was talking to a dogface next to me named Switkolski about something stupid—maybe dry socks again—when a sniper's bullet zinged by my head and hit Switkolski in the chest, killing him instantly. Everybody dove behind trees and rocks for cover, firing back at the castle. The nest of snipers could have been located behind any one of a score of high windows. Led by our sergeant, a few of us quickly zigzagged up to the castle's massive front doors. One of them was ajar. Cautiously we moved up a stone stairway. It was dark in there. Far above us, we heard a shot from a Mauser. The bolt action was reloaded, then another shot was fired off quickly. The crack of the German gun echoed off the centuries-old stone walls. We listened motionlessly. No doubt about it, there was just one sharpshooter patiently picking off targets from his deadly vantage point above us. We had to put him out of commission.

We split up and quickly made it to the rooftop. We heard the sniper's running footsteps. There was silence. Bullets caromed off the stone walls, one grazing the sergeant's helmet. We finally trapped the Nazi sniper. One of our men jumped him as he was jamming another round into the

BUTCH'S BEER JOINT
GOERING BIERGARTEN

UNSER SIEG!

WAITRESS WANTED

CPL. SAMUEL FULLER
GERMANY

Mauser's chamber. Hell, he was just a kid, not more than ten years old!

The boy wore a *Hitlerjugend* armband with a swastika. His eyes were filled with murder. He screamed at us that he was a soldier and not afraid to die for Hitler and the Reich. The sergeant knocked him down with a slap. The boy jumped up and went for the sergeant, who cuffed him again, this time harder. His mouth bleeding, the boy got up again, ready to charge. The kid had guts.

"What do we do with the little sonofabitch?" asked a dogface.

"Shoot him," answered the sergeant.

"He's just a goddamn kid," I said.

"We're supposed to kill any bastard that kills us," said another doggie.

The boy had put a bullet in Switkolski and would have gladly shot me, too. But nobody wanted to shoot a child, even if he was a Nazi.

"Heil Hitler!" yelled the boy.

"That's enough of this crap," said the sergeant.

We shrugged. Nobody would pull a trigger. Disgusted, the sergeant lifted his rifle, took off the safety, and aimed it at the boy's chest. The boy stood as erect as he could, proud to be executed like a German soldier. The sergeant paused, then mumbled a curse to himself and put the rifle down. He grabbed the boy by the scruff of his uniform and pulled his pants down to his knees. The boy screamed like a pig on his way to slaughter and struggled furiously. The sergeant sat down and tore off the boy's underpants, exposing his bare ass. With the kid imprisoned across his lap, the sergeant began spanking that little ass with his big hand. The boy exploded in rage, demanding to be treated like a soldier. Ignoring his pleas, the sergeant whacked away at the kid's ass until his two little cheeks began to show welts. Suddenly the little sonofabitch began to cry.

"Papi! Papi! Papi!" he screamed, now nothing more than a child being spanked by his father for having been naughty. We stood there, mouths agape, observing the heart-wrenching scene. An end to the monumental struggle with the Nazis could not be far off. All that would be left of Hitler's thousand-year Reich was a river of children's tears.

21

Falkenau

By the end of April 1945, we'd advanced all the way into the Sudetenland region of Czechoslovakia. Six years earlier, on March 15, 1939, the Nazis had marched into the Sudetenland and dissolved Czechoslovakia, making it a German protectorate. The pretense was that the Czechs discriminated against people with a German background. In Sudetenland, Hitler had first shown his true colors as an empire-building, nation-crushing tyrant. Nobody discouraged Nazi aggression at the time. Now the war to stop Hitler had come full circle, back to its birthplace.

Our ultimate objective on this drive was Karlsbad, squeezing the Nazis between our advance and the Russians moving westward. Berlin fell. German armies in Denmark, Holland, and the North surrendered. Still the enemy held out in Czechoslovakia. If the Nazis wouldn't give up, we'd compel them to fight. On May 6, we were moving from the town of Eger toward Falkenau, a distance of about thirty kilometers, when enemy anti-tank guns knocked out four of our tanks. The regiment suffered fifty-one casualties before nightfall. The next morning, the assault was resumed. Our commanding officer, General Clift Andrus, sent an urgent order from HQ to "cease all forward movement." The minutes ground away while we waited to hear about the definitive German capitulation. Word finally came down a couple hours later that the Germans had signed a formal surrender and were attempting to communicate with their troops in Czechoslovakia and Austria to order them to stop fighting. The ceasefire of May 7 was universal.

We moved into Falkenau that night and were slapped hard in the face, first by hordes of Germans streaming into town from Karlsbad, fleeing the Russians in order to surrender to the Americans. There were thousands of soldiers, many accompanied by their wives and children. More than forty-five thousand POWs moved through Falkenau in the next three days, creating the monumental job of handling all those people. The most profound shock awaited us as we entered the front gate of the Falkenau concentration camp only a few thousand yards from the town, surrounded by barbed wire barriers. Between the camp's two main watchtowers, there was an ominous sign that said KONZENTRATIONSLAGER FALKENAU.

There were a few die-hard SS at the camp who didn't know the war was over. They fired at us, then tried to make a break for it in a command car. One of our doggies hit the car with a bazooka, ending their escape in a flaming mushroom of fire and smoke. We ran down the remaining Nazis and disarmed them. Then we discovered the horrible truth about the camp. In the barracks were men and women with hollow eyes, unable to move their emaciated bodies. They'd been tortured, beaten, and experimented upon. In another building were corpses thrown on top of each other like old newspapers. A few of them weren't corpses yet. Like zombies, they raised their bald heads and looked at us, eyes sunken in anguish, their mouths agape, a hand here and there reaching out, grasping for anything, begging us for assistance in helpless silence.

What had been happening in that concentration camp was beyond belief, beyond our darkest nightmares. We were overwhelmed to come face-to-face with all the carnage. I still tremble to remember those images of the living hunkered down with the dead. The stench of rotting bodies welled up in your face and made you want to stop breathing. In one building, we plopped down behind a white mound to take cover from any last Nazi defenders. It was only then that I realized that the mound was a heap of human teeth wrenched from the camp's victims. Farther over were heaps of toothbrushes, eyeglasses, and shaving brushes. Even more appalling was a smaller hill of artificial limbs. In a hut against one of the camp's walls was a pile of naked corpses stacked up like firewood.

One final vision of horror awaited us: the crematorium. When we burst into that building, smoke from the grenades we'd thrown through the windows filled the room. It was silent now. The row of steel doors to the ovens stretched in front of us. I stared at the ovens and then looked into the first one. When I saw the remains of the cremated bodies in there, I couldn't control my revulsion. I vomited. I wanted out of there at any cost, but I couldn't stop myself from looking into the second oven, then the third, mesmerized by the impossible. For Chrissakes, people had actually been cooked in those ovens! The incontrovertible proof lay right in front of my own eyes.

One of our soldiers, a doggie we affectionately called Weasel, checked inside the fourth oven. Staring back at Weasel were the frightened eyes of an SS who'd crawled in there backward to hide among the charred corpses. The Schmeisser in the Nazi's hands was useless, for he was frozen with fear.

From basic training throughout the war, Weasel always had a problem with killing. Pulling the trigger on his M1 was the hardest thing in the world. At that moment, however, he was so overcome with loathing that he fired point-blank between the eyes of the SS. Again and again, he pulled the trigger, emptying his clip. Then he jammed in another clip and emptied that one too. Wordlessly, we walked out of the crematorium as stiff as mummies, pressing handkerchiefs to our mouths and noses, trying to come to terms with the stench and revulsion.

The realization of what the SS had been doing to the inmates of the Falkenau camp was too much to bear. We found pictures of naked women chased by ferocious dogs running past grinning SS guards. They were perverse murderers, killing innocent civilians, a tragic mix of Jews, Czechs, Poles, Russians, Gypsies, and antifascist Germans.

The SS we'd rounded up at the camp immediately began denouncing each other. In defeat, the entire Nazi mentality—their grand philosophy of courage, loyalty, and Aryan superiority—turned to mush. I rarely saw soldiers behave that way. If only Hitler could have been there to watch his beloved SS turn on each other. Goebbels wouldn't shake hands with Jesse Owens at the 1936 Olympics because his superrace was superior. How I wished Goebbels could see his superrace in defeat, livid with fear, ready to sell out Hitler and each other. They were like vicious, cornered animals.

The medics arrived right away with food, medicine, and blood, trying to save as many lives as possible. We went back into the barracks full of undernourished inmates and separated the living from the dead. The survivors had macabre hands and bony arms with tattooed numbers, an Edgar Allan Poe tale come to life. We had to work with rags over our noses because the stench from the piles of corpses made you retch involuntarily. When we carried out a featherweight survivor, it was like cradling an infant. The forced labor and malnutrition would take a terrible toll. We were liberating them. But there was no way of saving them. Very few would survive. They were only free to die.

The town of Falkenau was a respectable community with upstanding townspeople living in clean homes with flower boxes on their windows. It didn't seem possible that just over the hill were hundreds of miserable people in subhuman conditions who had only two ways out. Quickly, in a gas chamber. Or slowly, by disease and starvation.

The commander of our battalion, Captain Kimble R. Richmond, took a squad into Falkenau and rounded up the mayor, the butcher, the baker, and other respected townspeople. He wanted to know how the hell they could go about their everyday lives while people were dying in the nearby camp. Every one of them swore that they didn't have any idea of what was

going on in the *Konzentrationslager.* Most said they were against Hitler.
Captain Richmond was disgusted. We'd learned to doubt the avowals from
civilians throughout our campaign. Every Arab in North Africa claimed he
was anti-Nazi. Every Frenchman swore allegiance to the Free French. Sicilians hated Mussolini. Belgians hated Hitler. We'd discover, as expected,
more and more Germans who'd never been members of the Nazi Party.

Captain Richmond ordered a delegation of
townspeople to appear at the gates of the camp
the next morning or face a firing squad. Richmond was going to make sure that these people
found out what had been happening only a few
steps from their front doors. That evening I was
called to the battalion CP. Richmond and I had
a good relationship ever since he'd been slightly
wounded by a Nazi bullet that had punctured
his steel helmet. When he came out of the
clinic, he was looking everywhere for his helmet. He considered it his good luck charm. I
was the one who'd been keeping it for him.

"Sonofabitch," said Captain Richmond,
smiling as I gave him the helmet with the bullet
hole, "if you want a helmet like this, Fuller,
you'll have to get shot at!"

*This is one frame from the
twenty minutes of 16-mm
film I shot at the Falkenau
concentration camp the day
that Captain Richmond
forced the townspeople to
give inmates a decent burial.
Here, some of the corpses
were laid out and wrapped
in sheets. Richmond gave a
harsh lesson in civility that
day. The suffering and
humiliation these people
had endured, however,
would always defy human
understanding.*

Richmond knew my mother had sent me a handheld Bell & Howell 16-mm movie camera. The captain wanted me to position myself the next day on a wall overlooking the concentration camp to film the gruesome spectacle. I was about to make my first movie.

I started shooting footage of Captain Richmond giving the upstanding citizens of Falkenau his orders. They were to prepare the camp's victims for a decent funeral, then take them to the burial site on a wagon. That way, they could never say again that they didn't know what was happening in their own backyard. I filmed a couple dozen corpses being taken out of that putrid hut against the camp's wall and laid out one by one, wrapped in white sheets on the ground, then piled on the wagon. When the wagon was full of corpses, the townspeople pushed it out of the camp to the specially prepared burial site. POWs, mostly teenage *Hitlerjugend,* helped place the shrouded corpses in a mass grave. One of our chaplains said a brief prayer. Earth was then shoveled into the mass grave. As paltry a consolation as it was, these Nazi victims were buried with dignity.

My twenty minutes of 16-mm film had recorded the sober reckoning of those civilians. The spectacle was heart-wrenching, leaving me numb. I'd recorded evidence of man's indescribable cruelty, a reality that the perpetrators might try to deny. However, a motion-picture camera doesn't lie. When I finally got home, in the fall of 1945, I put that footage away and never took it out again. It would be too painful to watch, bringing back all the horrors of the war years. Those twenty minutes were a testament to the victims at Falkenau and to all the millions of people who died in Nazi death camps.

On a final inspection of the camp's buildings, our sergeant heard a moan behind a pile of worn clothing. He whirled and almost shot the ghastly girl who slowly raised her head. Her black and sunken eyes were frightened. She seemed about eighteen because she was so fragile and gaunt. She could have been younger or older. The sergeant picked up the young girl in his arms and carried her to the SS commandant's ex-quarters.

Over the next days, as we bivouacked nearby and medical teams tried to save the camp's survivors, the sergeant nursed the young woman back from the threshold of death. He fed her C-rations, then convinced the regimental surgeon to dig up some milk, vegetables, and fruit for her. He even got her a steak. There was a music box in the SS command post. He gave it to her. The young woman was too weak to even speak. Gradually she began to take on a little color in her cheeks. She listened to the music box all day long and sometimes managed to smile. We'd never seen the sergeant so happy. He couldn't accept the fact that his young charge was too sick to survive. "I'm so tired of killing people," he said. "I'd like to keep one alive."

The girl died a few days later. The sergeant wouldn't allow any of us to help him bury her, refusing all assistance, even the chaplain's. He made a crude coffin himself. He dressed the dead girl in a pink dress and dark brown shoes that our company's mail clerk had somehow obtained for him. He carefully laid her out, placed the music box on her belly, and put her hands around it. She had a smile on her face. Then he closed the coffin. He dug a grave not far from the gates of the *Konzentrationslager* and put the girl's coffin in it. From a distance, we watched him filling the grave with shovel after painful shovel of earth. Once she was buried, the sergeant never mentioned the girl again. Neither did we. For all of us, however, she remained a symbol of those mournful times filled with incomprehensible suffering and loss.

The ending of all hostilities was a quiet shock. It was hard to accept that the war was really over. I couldn't believe that I didn't have to sleep with my hand on my rifle anymore, that every noise wasn't the start of an enemy attack, that I could light a cigar at night without worrying about a sniper putting a bullet through my brain. We'd be going home soon. Rejoining civilization was all we'd ever been talking about, joking about, dreaming about. But reentry was scary, too. How could we tell the world about what we'd experienced? About what we'd witnessed? How could we live with it ourselves?

22

Earthquake
of War

People associate me with my films about war. Sure, I made plenty of them, but I worked in other genres, too: Westerns, noirs, spy thrillers. It's easy to understand why war movies came naturally to me. I was one of a handful of Hollywood people who'd had battlefield experience. I used my firsthand knowledge to create films that, I hope, showed the truth about people at war. It would be hypocritical to deny that, as crazy, violent, and tragic as it is, war lends itself to filmmaking by stirring up the entire palette of our deepest feelings.

In a strange twist of fate, some people got the idea I was a warmonger, that my films promoted war. What bullshit! For Chrissakes, war is living hell. I hope no one ever has to have that goddamned experience again, either as a soldier or a noncombatant. Never! We must avoid war at all cost. Nowadays, even after all we know about the ravages of war, it continues to be very much a part of our world. As I near the end of my life, that is one of my only regrets.

The only war film I really wanted to make was *The Big Red One.* It wouldn't happen until 1980. Over the years, I could have made several more. Projects were offered to me that didn't ring true, so I turned them down. When I was under contract at Fox, I was asked by David Brown, a studio executive back then, to direct *The Young Lions,* based on the Irwin Shaw book. I loved David, who went on to become a successful independent producer, and I liked the story. But I turned the job down. They'd already cast Brando as a German officer. Brando is a genius of an actor, but his character irritated the hell out of me. How could a German officer in 1934 say he was sick of Hitler, that Hitler was wrongheaded? The son-ofabitch would've been thrown into a camp or shot on the spot for saying that stuff. Maybe toward the end of the war, when the Nazis were losing, there was talk like that. But not in 1934.

Another reason I didn't like the script for *The Young Lions* was the religious element they added, soldiers praying to God in between combat missions. It sounded good in Hollywood, but it just didn't happen. The truth is that in the middle of a war, you feel more like insulting the Almighty Creator than praying to Him. I suspect that He would respect the human race a little more if we reacted honestly, even bitterly, when confronted with such human misery and devastation.

Another time, Paramount offered me *Cross of Iron* to direct. They'd acquired the rights to Willy Heinrich's great book. In the script, they added a character named Schroeder, who, in the midst of all-out warfare, has great foresight about the future. Bullshit! There's something false about characters in a period piece who can predict future events. It always sounds phony. I said no thank you.

I was also asked to direct *Patton*. I'd been too close to events in his life to be objective. It would have been hard for me to make a film glorifying a man I didn't like or respect. I told them another director would be better suited for the job.

Following the German surrender on May 7, the silence that blanketed us was overpowering. We'd forgotten what stillness was like. With no thunderous bombs, no artillery shells blowing up, no mortars bursting, no V-1 missiles shrieking across the sky, no grenades exploding, no machine guns nor MIs nor Mausers firing, the quiet was incredible. The listless days following the ceasefire were disturbingly calm. We hardly spoke. Even the thousands of German soldiers who streamed into Falkenau to surrender to us were taciturn. They wordlessly laid their guns in a massive pile near our camp. If the Germans did talk to us, it was usually to criticize Hitler or deny any connection with the Nazi movement. We'd already heard that tune.

In my 1958 movie *Verboten!*, which deals with the problems of postwar Germany and U.S. occupation, I wrote in a scene that made fun of the sudden German aversion for Nazis.

"When they found Hitler's body in his bunker," recounts an officer in the American Military Government, "they discovered a piece of paper in his hand. When they opened the paper, the Führer had written: 'I was never a Nazi!' "

The war's end was no holiday for us. In addition to helping survivors and processing POWs, thousands of displaced persons needed assistance. Besides, a growing problem was sabotage by Hitler's "Werewolf" youths— whom I'd shown in *Verboten!*—disrupting food and medical supply lines. We were now part of the normalization process, trying to investigate and curtail the chaos.

Russian troops showed up a few days after the German surrender. They moved into our sector while occupation agreements were being worked out. There was a little bridge over a stream behind some barracks. We approached the bridge and found ourselves nose to nose with a group of Russian infantry. The atmosphere was convivial. Like us, they were dirty and unshaven. They had endured just as many—maybe even more—grisly hardships as we had. There were bear hugs and kisses. They gave us vodka. We gave them Mickey Mouse watches. For the next five days, we were all buddies. Then on the sixth day, the Russian infantry were replaced by clean-shaven, well-groomed soldiers in perfectly tailored uniforms, just arrived from Moscow. Those guys wouldn't talk to us. They wouldn't even smile when we waved. Something had changed irrevocably. It was the debut of the cold war.

I'll never forget the ice-cold faces on those Russian replacements. Together, our two countries had been fighting fascist armies at a terrible cost. Now, instead of continuing our cooperation, we were embarking on a period of alienation and confrontation. It was a ridiculous, disheartening turn of events. I've lived to see the murky shadows of the cold war subside. But for four decades, two nations who'd been Allies in the great crusade against the Nazis found it necessary to invent an icy contest to justify their own arms race. History is full of such ironies. That one was very painful for me to watch.

After Falkenau, the war was by no means over for every soldier in the First Division. We had a point system that designated who no longer had to fight. You needed something like 180 points to be given an honorable discharge. Married soldiers got a head start for home by getting twelve points just for having a wife. You got five points if you were wounded, five points for each battle action, and so on. I had more than enough points to stop fighting. But many GIs from our outfit, like thousands of soldiers recently arrived in the European theater, were transferred to the Pacific, where the war still raged. I ended up in Bad Kissingen, a town near Munich. From there, those of us who had enough points could hop on one of the military transports leaving for the States. Like me, a lot of soldiers dreamed of finally visiting Paris before going home. We'd have to make it back to the States the long way, by ship from Marseille.

It took three days to get to Paris. Just to reach the train station was a struggle. The truck that took us was blocked again and again by thousands of disheveled, exhausted German soldiers with backpacks, roaming the streets like lost cattle. The trains were a mess, and railway tracks were in bad shape, too. It was a very rocky trip. Everywhere were the scars of war, reminders of the grisly violence that had been wreaked on combatants and civilians alike. Many bridges had been destroyed, forcing the train to

"But I'm tellin' you, Yvette, this is
how to liberate."

*To see Paris before returning to
the States was every GI's dream.
French girls did things to our
libidos.*

zigzag across the countryside. One bridge collapsed right after our train passed over it. The
Allied invasion had left Germany in shambles.

We'd been given blankets in Germany in
case we didn't find a place to sleep in Paris. At
the Gare du Nord station, children followed on our heels as if we were
Pied Pipers. I gave my blanket to one of the kids, who probably sold it to
make some dough for his family.

To my war-weary eyes, Paris was an incredible sight in June 1945, better
than a hundred Mardi Gras in New Orleans and a thousand Carnivals in
Rio. Wherever we went, people kissed and hugged us. Music played in the
streets. Day and night, we were invited for drinks by total strangers, grateful to anyone wearing an American military uniform. I was anxious to
catch up with my kid brother, Ray. I found him at SHAEF headquarters in

My brother and I found this sweet, unknown French girl to pose with us. While Ray was with the French gal he would eventually marry, Pierrette, I was free to explore the City of Light on my own.

the Hotel Scribe, near the Place de l'Opéra. Ray was ecstatic to see me alive. He'd been worried sick about me surviving the war. He got me a small room at the Scribe. Holy mackerel, a hot shower and a bed with sheets!

Ray and I went down to the hotel's restaurant for a celebration meal that evening. They wouldn't seat us in the main dining room because it was reserved for officers only. My brother got so angry when they offered us a table in a back corner, but I laughed at the situation. After almost four years of infantry life, I was happy to sit anywhere. All that mattered to me after those weari-some years was that I was in Paris with my brother, safe and sound.

Then Ray's CO stopped by our table, a lieutenant general. When he saw the Big Red One on my uniform, he shook my hand warmly and asked why we were sitting in the back of the place. Ray explained the situ-ation, and the general immediately moved us to his table in the center of the room with a bunch of officers, including more generals. Everyone was respectful of the Big Red One number on my shoulder patch because of our outfit's record during the war.

That night, my brother and I went to a noisy club packed with soldiers. Liquor was flowing. Celebrating GIs danced with French girls and drank until they dropped. One soused man came over to our table. He was wear-ing a Big Red One, too. When he saw mine and found out that I was in the Sixteenth Infantry, he was ecstatic. He made a drunken speech, but I couldn't understand anything except that he'd been part of the Twenty-sixth. He said our outfit had saved his ass. Then he disappeared. A few minutes later, the soldier came back with a couple of red roses. He gave one to me, one to Ray. Then he grabbed me and kissed me on my goddamned mouth. Ray was so moved by the soldier's affection and respect that he kept that rose pressed between the pages of a book until the day he died.

Ray was perfectly fluent in French and knew a helluva lot about French literature. With my kid brother, I went to Paris bookshops and started buying novels by Hugo and Balzac and poetry by Baudelaire and Verlaine. Ray had a sweet French girlfriend in Paris named Pierrette, whom he ended up marrying. They showed me around the liberated city, which had been spared the war's devastation. Typical Parisian landmarks like the Eif-fel Tower, Notre-Dame, and Sacré Coeur, though beautiful to behold, didn't really excite me. What I loved seeing were all the statues by Rodin. Holy smoke, what a sculptor! To finally get the opportunity to see his work in person was a far bigger thrill for me than the Arc de Triomphe.

During my week or so in Paris, I left Ray and Pierrette alone to enjoy their romance and roamed the streets by myself. The great city was loaded with unassuming quaintness and mystery. Giants of history and art had walked these same sidewalks, lived and died in the shuttered houses behind those wrought-iron gates. I loved reading the historical plaques on the walls. They stirred my heart and imagination. Marie Curie worked here. Alexandre Dumas wrote there. Claude Debussy composed right here. Verlaine lived over there with Rimbaud.

I amused myself imagining movie scenes with those passionate charac-ters. Verlaine's wife and Rimbaud's mother would've been furious about the two men's love affair. Maybe the two women cooked up a scheme to

The Eiffel Tower was a must for every first-time visitor. It didn't thrill me, but there was no denying that the view from the top was magnificent. It was the only city I'd seen in the last three years that hadn't been scarred by the war.

break off the budding homosexual relationship. I could see the two women climbing the stairs to a doorway at the top. They're in front of the door. Behind it are the two poets, man and boy. Which woman is going to knock first? Neither woman wants to disturb what's going on behind that door. But they can't tolerate it, either. Someone must knock, but who? The scene ended with the two women standing there, neither daring to knock.

My visit to Paris, seeing my kid brother, was great, but I've always regretted one unfortunate aspect of it. By making the trip, I missed the interviews for the coveted assignments of guarding prisoners at the Nuremberg war trials that would begin that fall.

The train trip back to Munich in order to rejoin my division was not something I looked forward to. Ray had a pal in the air force, and thanks to him, I got a ride on a cargo plane heading over to Germany. Inside the aircraft, we sat on long metal benches facing each other, like on a New York subway.

The pilot saw my Big Red One and invited me up into the cockpit for a helluva view of the countryside below. Air force flyboys were always the brunt of our jokes whenever we'd run into them in Paris bars. For the first time, I realized how difficult it was to distinguish what the hell was going on down on the ground from up in the air. American bombs had been dropped accidentally on our GIs, and plenty of boys in my own outfit had been killed by them. I still had some "Made in USA" shrapnel in my back from friendly fire. On that flight, I suddenly understood the tough task our pilots had had during the war.

When we flew over Germany, the devastating destruction to their cities made me tremble. From my vantage point up in the sky, I was overcome with sadness about all the violence, the damage, the lost lives. I started to cry, the first tears in a long, long time. I got a grip on my emotions and wiped my eyes dry. When we landed in Munich, I thanked the pilot wholeheartedly for the ride. It had been illuminating.

One of the other passengers on the plane, a colonel, was also heading for the camp at Bad Kissingen, where our division was bivouacked. The colonel invited me into the mess hall for a meal with him. We arrived in a big hangar where officers and NCOs were waiting in lines with trays. German POWs were in charge of distributing meals. One of them who was serving chicken wore a small Nazi medal of honor.

"Twenty-first Panzer?" I said to the POW when the colonel wasn't looking.

"First Division?" he said.

We locked eyes for a complicitous moment. I turned so the colonel could see the enormous piece of chicken the German POW had served me. When I went for dessert, I came back with a gigantic piece of cake on my plate. The colonel burst out laughing.

"I better stick close to you, Corporal!"

To get to the First Division sector, I had to walk across the entire camp. The colonel accompanied me. There were thousands and thousands of prisoners living there, a massive flock of POWs like nothing I'd ever seen before. It was strange to be in uniform, engulfed by German soldiers, yet

"HEY, FRITZ, GOT A GOOD ADDRESS IN BERLIN?"

GIs had an awkward attitude about German soldiers, deadly enemies one day, defeated charges the next. And vice versa. I tried to poke fun at our bizarre relationship in this drawing to my brother Ving.

without a rifle in my hand. Parachutes were propped up everywhere in the fields for shelter. It was raining, and a strong wind blew across the area, flapping the parachute tents and rattling the tin plates that the POWs used at mealtimes. It was a surrealistic scene. Totally defeated, the Germans didn't look like they'd lost anything, much less a world war. Silently confident and contemptuous, they reminded me of big rats in some bizarre laboratory experiment.

Our division boarded a train that took us to the south of France. Because of bombed-out train tracks and stations, trucks had to drive us the final leg of the journey into Marseille. The locals weren't quite as happy to see us as the Parisians had been. People were still bitter about the massive Allied bombing mission in May 1944 on Marseille. It was intended to break the enemy's stranglehold on the southern flank, but the cost of victory was high. More than two thousand civilians had been killed and another three thousand wounded.

We were bivouacked just outside Marseille in an American camp called Delta Base, awaiting the arrival of a "Liberty Ship." Once her cargo was unloaded—wheat, cereal, coffee, cotton, and sugar for the undernourished French, after years of rationing—hundreds of discharged dogfaces could board the ship and sail back to the States.

During my days in Marseille, I saw many buildings still in ruins, some collapsed under the Allied bombs of '44, others burned and gutted by the Nazis in an infamous hunt for Jewish refugees in '43. The docks were damaged from bombings against the German submarine station there. I walked all over the city, visited the famous old port, went up the Canebière—the "Fifth Avenue of Marseille," as GIs called it—and climbed all the way up to the big white cathedral on the promontory overlooking the city, Notre Dame de la Garde. Messerschmitts had buzzed the cathedral and machine-gunned its marble walls just to terrorize people in the city below. The scars in the white marble from Nazi bullets were fresh.

From the cathedral I got a good view of the three austere, chalky white islands out in the bay. One of them, the island of If, rose like a jewel out of the Mediterranean. On its massive rocks stood the walled Château d'If, the garrison that had once served as an inescapable prison, immortalized in Dumas's *Count of Monte Cristo*. Seeing the Château d'If was worth my entire trip to Marseille.

I took time to hitchhike to Arles to see where Vincent van Gogh had lived and worked. When I saw the fields of sunflowers in Arles, big yellow petals all tilting up to worship the sun, I was thrilled. Van Gogh had captured them on canvas with his bold colors, and there they were, spread out between the tall cypresses, a symphony of gold and black. When I saw Provençal farmers working on their little plots of land, I was reminded of one of my favorite van Gogh paintings, *The Potato Eaters*. Van Gogh was a great inspiration for me, a guy for whom life was work and work was life. I wanted to be like him, except I didn't want to go nuts and cut off my ear.

One night while we were still waiting to board a ship for the States, the USO people set up a screen in Delta Base and showed us *The Thin Man*, starring William Powell and Myrna Loy. We were sitting on blankets on the ground looking up at Powell doing some comedy bit with his cute terrier. A door opened unexpectedly, then slammed right in Powell's face. A few hundred GIs sitting around me burst into loud laughter. Then suddenly, we heard a rumbling deep in the ground. It sounded like a thousand tanks heading right at us. The ground started trembling. For Chrissakes, it was an earthquake! It hit the camp like a herd of stampeding elephants. A few moments later, it was gone. The movie projector was knocked over, and the screen went dark. There were screams. Guys had fallen into a fissure that had opened in the ground. Jeeps were brought in to give us light so that we could pull up the wounded men. A couple of GIs died in the incident. It was one of the weirdest tragedies of the war. Soldiers who'd survived man-made combat were killed by a natural catastrophe only hours before going home.

It took a little while to get things back to normal after the quake. An officer with a brain the size of a pea announced on the loudspeaker system, "There are no more corpses. Thank you very much."

We sat there in a trance, not believing what'd just happened. No one made any stupid comments like "What a shame!" For the last four years we'd lived through much worse horrors. Still, we were numb from the deaths of GIs who'd died for nothing.

"Do you want to see the rest of the film?" asked an officer over the loudspeaker.

"SURE!" we yelled.

"From the beginning!" a GI screamed out.

"DAMN RIGHT!" we chimed in.

It was our way of expressing the inexpressible feelings of that awkward time. We really had forgotten the beginning of the film, just like we'd forgotten so much about our previous lives. Events had made us senseless. The earthquake of a world war had shaken up everything inside us.

PART III

*Studio portrait, circa 1959. In those
days, you had to dress to go to work.*

23

The Bubble Will Burst

Our troopship finally sailed from Marseille, docking in Boston in late September 1945. I took a train to New York to see my mother for the first time in almost four years. Though it was good beyond words to put my arms around her again, it became quickly evident that my homecoming was burdensome for me and everyone around me. I spent a helluva lot of time in bed but couldn't sleep for long stretches. Horrible nightmares kept rattling my head. Everyday sounds made me jump and shake uncontrollably. My family couldn't understand my constant grumpiness. No one who hadn't lived through the front lines of the war could. I was a textbook case of "war hysteria."

I couldn't stop thinking about all the men in my outfit who were dead or missing. To us, missing *was* dead. The army wrote to parents that their sons were "missing in action," but we all knew that was just good public relations. So many guys were blown apart on the battlefield, it was impossible to identify them. Squads collected whatever body parts they could find and threw them into a bag for burial. For the families, MIA meant there was still hope; however, their boys were hopelessly dead.

Faces of soldiers kept appearing in my dreams. For the last few years, I'd been fighting with them, eating with them, pissing with them, drying wet socks with them, eating horrible food with them, sleeping on hard ground with them. Most were gone forever. Their faces wouldn't go away. One guy I couldn't forget was Griff, who'd barely survived a land mine explosion. When I first got back to the States, I went down to Washington, D.C., and visited Griff at a veterans' hospital there. He was a basket case, no legs, no arms. Only mumbled words came out of his lips. Believe it or not, we had a wonderful reunion. Griff's eyes sparkled when he saw me. He laughed when I recalled some of the funny shit we'd gone through together in the war. I put my arm around his neck and kissed him, happy to find him alive. I couldn't keep the tears back. Griff didn't want me feeling sorry for him. He was a born optimist and refused to accept my pity. Or anyone's. I was trembling when I left the hospital that day.

Griff's invincible spirit would always be an inspiration. I will take his optimism with me to my grave. Life is too precious and far too short to get hooked on negativity. In my scripts and stories, you'll find a helluva lot of characters named Griff. It was my way of saying thanks for his will to survive.

In August 1945, President Truman had given orders to drop A-bombs on Hiroshima and Nagasaki. To my mother, that was barbaric. To me, it was logical. Sure, a nuclear bomb was a horrible act of violence, but wasn't prolonging the war a greater act of violence? The Japanese were intent on dragging out the conflict. We would've had to fight another six months, maybe a year or more. How many more American boys would have to be killed? Cruel as it was, the big bomb was the lesser of two evils.

My opinion shocked Rebecca. She called the A-bomb the lowest form of civilized cannibalism. She could hardly believe that a hundred thousand people had been killed in a matter of seconds. I called her a hypocrite. What difference did it make that a hundred thousand people were killed in six seconds or in six months? War wasn't a sport with a scoreboard and statistics.

"I'm horrified!" said Rebecca. "Just horrified by your attitude! What happened to you over there?"

"Plenty, believe me," I said. "But that's not important. For Chrissakes, I'm not *for* any bomb. I'm *against* losing one more American soldier."

The A-bomb was a horrible weapon. Like my mother, the press, the politicians, and a large portion of the public were dismayed by our dropping it. Hell, it was an emotional issue. But did they know anything about the horror of war? All they knew was what they read in their newspapers each morning over coffee and eggs. Total war is a terrible game of life and death. The sooner it's over, the better. War is not about emotions. It's about the absence of emotions. That void *is* the emotion of war. People who've never lived through it will never—never!—know what war's unfeelingness feels like, never know the cold taste of metal in your mouth just before the violence begins, the wet toes, the churning in your stomach that seems like it's going to burn a hole in your belly, the dull drumming in your brain, the ghoulish visions come to life. Hell, words just can't describe it.

Undoubtedly, the experience had left me as callous as a character out of a Camus novel, hardened in ways I still didn't understand, so much so that a big bomb that would put an end to the whole goddamned thing seemed okay to me.

I needed to somehow start earning a living again. *The Dark Page* had sold well, with four or five reprintings already, gotten great reviews and that award for "Best Psychological Novel." But you couldn't live on reviews and awards. The advance monies from the publisher and the film rights were gone.

I considered an offer to work with a New York psychiatrist who'd loved *The Dark Page* and wanted me to collaborate with him on a clinical study, but I turned him down. The job was just too cut-and-dry. Going out west and jumping back into the movie business was what I really wanted to do. New York was cold and crowded. The West Coast had all that space and good weather. I hesitated, though. It'd been a long time since I'd written a script, and I wasn't sure if I even remembered how.

Fortunately, an old reporter pal of mine named Jimmy O'Hanlon called to say he'd recommended me to a famous playwright living in Los Angeles. The playwright, who'll remain anonymous, was in a bind and needed assistance quick. He offered me money, a car, and an apartment in Santa Monica to ghostwrite a play. It would be about six weeks of work. But what did I know about playwriting?

"It doesn't matter," said the playwright, on the phone. "You've done screenplays. You know the technique. Three acts. Curtain. *Basta*."

My mother accompanied me to the train station. I promised her that I'd bring her out west and set her up in a sunny little house as soon as I made enough dough. Banging out story ideas on my Royal, I took the Silver Eagle back out to California. The playwright and I got right down to work. I gave him what he needed, plenty of good characters and tons of dialogue. We finished his play on time, and it was a big success. He was a damn good writer, but I knew the milieu of the piece better than he did. I promised to keep our collaboration a secret. I did, and I will.

Howard Hawks heard I was back in town and invited me over to his office. When I walked in, Howard greeted me warmly. He explained how he'd tried to make *The Dark Page* with Humphrey Bogart and Edward G. Robinson, but it just didn't happen. He ended up selling the movie rights to my book to Columbia for a neat profit, more than six times what he paid for it. Hell, that was his business, and he was good at it. What disappointed me was that Howard himself didn't direct the picture. As it turned out, the studio hired Phil Carlson and made the disappointing *Scandal Sheet* (1952) from my yarn. It was a lesson in losing artistic control of my work that I wouldn't ever forget.

As I was admiring Hawks's bookshelves, he pointed to a section with famous titles by Hemingway, Faulkner, and Fitzgerald.

"I own them," he said.

"I got 'em, too. So what? Buck and a half in paperback."

"No, Sammy, you don't get it. I *own* them."

One of the many best-sellers for which he'd purchased the movie rights was *The Sun Also Rises*. Hawks wanted me to take a crack at writing a script based on Hemingway's renowned novel.

"Like the book?" he asked me.

"Yes and no," I said. "It's a great love story. But you get to the end and find out the guy is missing one of his balls and you feel a little cheated, like you've been treated dishonestly."

Hawks wanted to know how I'd tell the story. Right from the start I'd take an honest approach, I told him. My opening would be a violent World War I battle. Cut to a hospital far from the battlefield. Our injured hero, Jake Barnes, is lying naked on the operating table. A nurse holds up a tin cup and the doctor drops the hero's testicle into it. The nurse takes her mask off. It's our heroine, Lady Brett Ashley. She knows what's up from the very beginning. Their love for each other would be heartfelt and honest.

"Are you crazy?" said Hawks. "You think Warner would buy that?"

"Why not?"

Hawks's face dropped.

"You can't show that on a screen, Sammy. At least not with Jack Warner's lion roaring on the credits."

"For thousands of years, Howard, we've had statues of naked men and women exhibited all over the world. Make it artistic. But show the truth. Otherwise you're shooting a goddamned fairy tale."

"You're great, Sammy," said Hawks. "But you're nuts." He quickly changed the subject to hunting, one of his favorite topics. Just like before the war, Howard asked me to go hunting on the weekend and shoot some poor animal. *That* was nuts. I refused.

One night there was a swank party over at Hawks's place. Howard insisted I come. It was a typical Hollywood get-together, plenty of booze and chow, starlets in long gowns, leading men in tuxes, a mogul or two, directors and producers exchanging gossip, columnists sniffing around for off-the-record material.

I met a dark-haired beauty named Martha Downes that night. She was from Kentucky and had come to town with aspirations of acting. She'd once been married. We had a couple of drinks and laughed a lot. Martha was saucy and spirited. I left Howard's early. I had too many scripts to write to waste my time at Hollywood shindigs. As I was walking out, Martha asked me for a lift home. I parked in front of her place, and we chatted for a while. My cigar didn't seem to bother her. Effortlessly, she

My first wife, Martha, and I at some gala premiere in the fifties. She had expensive tastes, so I needed to get my career in gear to support her in the style she expected.

reached over and put her hand on mine. I walked her to the front door and kissed her good night. Nothing else happened, but I was smitten.

Martha and I started seeing each other regularly. A few months later, I asked her to marry me. She said yes. We moved into a small house on Wonderland Park Avenue in Laurel Canyon next to Lena Horne. We were happy at first, so much in love that we overlooked each other's shortcomings. Deep down,

Martha never really accepted me, nor all the attention I gave my mother. A WASP from the Deep South, Martha was the polar opposite of Rebecca, which was probably why I was drawn to her in the first place.

My career wasn't nearly as hot as my private life. If it weren't for Jake Barnes's goddamned testicle, maybe I'd have gotten a shot at adapting some of Hawks's literary treasures. It wasn't the first time, nor would it be the last, that my straightforward vision of things put me out of step with Hollywood decisionmakers.

Charlie Feldman took me to lunch at the Brown Derby.

"Sammy, I've got you a sweetheart deal with Jack Warner."

"Writing what?" I asked.

"Anything you like," Feldman said. "An original story with your kind of characters. They'll buy the script you turn in. And if they don't shoot the picture, you keep the money anyway."

I chuckled.

"What's so funny?" asked Feldman.

"Nothing," I said, thinking of the sweet irony that I'd ended up working for Warner anyway.

The first script I wrote for the studio was a police exposé called *Murder—How to Get Away with It.* Yarns about cops always make good movies because there's plenty of conflict and action. This one was about a case of corruption that's traced to a couple of important New York judges. One was a woman. The police commissioner is implicated and commits suicide. The story was loosely based on a real scandal that newspapers across the country had covered.

Whether it was topical or not, my script wasn't at all what the studio was looking for. They wanted a classical detective yarn, with the hero solving the murder by the end of the movie. My story line strayed too far from the typical formula. Even worse, I had a police commissioner and judges implicated in the murder. Jack Warner hated it. He probably considered it unpatriotic. His studio wasn't about to make that kind of a picture, but they paid me for the script. That permitted me to bring my mother out to California and rent her a little house with a white picket fence in the San Fernando Valley.

RKO had also read my script for *Murder* and loved it, though they didn't want to make it either. Still, the guys at RKO were more democratic in their approach. Over there, several executives decided on the fate of each script. They asked me to come up with another story. So I wrote a yarn called *Uncle Sam.* It was about the hypocrisy of the new anti-immigration act, shutting the gates of the U.S. to minorities, with a son-ofabitch reactionary character based on the real Senator McCarran. My finished script scared the RKO boys. The story was too violent and the characters—even if names were changed—were too unsympathetic. RKO was afraid of protests from right-wingers like the Daughters of the American Revolution, so the movie went unproduced. But they paid me for the script, which allowed me to get some nice furniture for Rebecca's place.

"Sammy," said Charlie Feldman, "you're working again, making good money. But you don't get credit for scripts they don't shoot. Why don't you try to write something a little more commercial? I know you can do it. MGM is looking for a good murder yarn."

"Okay," I said. "But it won't be my fault if those guys don't have the balls to make it!"

I wrote a third script, called *Crime Pays,* about a big bank holdup with a twist. A police detective who was a war veteran is investigating the heist. He sees how the bank was hit with grenades, how the robbers were positioned. It reminds him of how he and his infantry squad had assaulted a Nazi pillbox on Omaha Beach. The detective tracks down the only three GIs still alive who were under his command on June 6, 1944. He knows they were hoods before the war and figures out that they've gone back to a life of crime after their discharge. One by one, he finds them and kills them. The detective ends up with a couple million dollars. He settles down on Rara Tonga, an island I invented west of Tahiti, surrounded by gorgeous native girls. He's the happiest and most satisfied of ex-cops. His last line in the movie is, "Who says crime doesn't pay?"

After I turned my script into MGM, Louis B. Mayer himself wanted to see me. When I walked into his big office, he was smoking a cigar. He offered me one, a damn good one. Mayer struck me as a very sensitive and intelligent man. He came from a working-class background like myself.

"I love your way of telling a story, Sammy," said Mayer. "But we want sympathetic characters in our movies. We're careful not to irritate the public. We don't want our stories antagonizing government, mothers, children, or animals. You see, Sammy, we have a dog here named Lassie who's making a mint."

"What's the problem with *Crime Pays*?" I asked.

"First, you can't show a lawman killing the bad guys, then keeping the stolen money for himself. Second, you can't show men coming back from the war and turning to crime. That means that the army fabricates criminals."

"I'll add a scene showing how those guys were criminals *before* the war."

"That's worse, Sammy. That means we sent criminals over to fight the Nazis and the Japs. I don't want that stuff in an MGM film. No criminals in the United States Army."

For Mr. Mayer, the worst thing was that my hero keeps the money and lives happily ever after.

"He's got to return the money to the bank," said Mayer. "Then he gets a medal."

"Only a fool would return the money," I insisted.

Is it any wonder that my third script was rejected? I couldn't blame Mayer for not producing my yarn. He and the other Hollywood moguls were sons of immigrants. They were grateful to this country for getting the opportunity to become rich and famous. Mayer wanted to reach as many people as possible with each movie. He felt that if he liked and understood a film, it would sell tickets. He was a master of not stepping on toes. Hell, I was the son of immigrants, too, and I wanted to reach a mass audience as well. But I'd do it with truthful stories, without the sugar coating.

Studio executives haven't changed much. Nor has the system. They think they know what audiences want. They have a flair for mass-appeal movies. Writers who have the same kind of tastes as the studio boys do better than those trying to create something original and hard-hitting. Kipling wrote adventure stories. He didn't have the same difficulties getting established as Kafka or Baudelaire. A writer with a unique, personal vision will almost automatically turn away from popular tastes. I'd written three scripts since my return to the West Coast. Each one had been bought but remained unproduced. I wasn't discouraged. I'd done good work and earned a helluva lot of dough. Life was good, and to top it off, my mother was enjoying sunny California. Except she had one big worry.

"I'm afraid if they ever make one of your scripts into a movie, Sammy," said Rebecca, "the bubble will burst."

"Let it burst, Mama."

Believe it or not, the same Louis B. Mayer who thought *Crime Pays* was too harsh for MGM offered me a seven-year writing contract. I passed. Sure, I wanted to make steady money. But I couldn't see myself being one of the studio's paid chattel, having my yarns diluted or shelved at their whim. For cryin' out loud, I wanted to see my stories up on the god-damned screen the way I'd originally envisioned them!

My next yarn was called *The Lovers*. Feldman sold it to Columbia. It was about a female ex-con named Jenny Marsh and her parole officer, named Griff Marant. The great Douglas Sirk directed that script in 1949. Apparently they didn't like my title, so the studio renamed it *Shockproof*. One of my postwar scripts had finally been made into a movie, so I didn't give a damn what they called it.

My next project was supposed to be with Fritz Lang. We'd always wanted to work together again since the prewar days of *Confirm or Deny*.

I always considered myself lucky to have spent time with some of the greatest directors, among them Fritz Lang. Here, Lang (on the platform at right) directs a scene from his masterpiece Metropolis, *circa 1926, at UDF studios in Germany.*

When we crossed paths again, we started talking about psychotics. He'd read *The Dark Page.* Both of us were interested in why ordinary people go nuts in extraordinary situations. Lang had a special fascination with people with mental illness. His first wife had committed suicide. His second wife and writing partner, Thea von Harbou, had become a Nazi sympathizer and betrayed him.

I'd seen plenty of guys going berserk during the war. One GI named Brown lost his mind in the cacophony of an enemy bomb attack. On top of the explosions, our artillery was firing back at the enemy. Brown ran insanely toward our big guns.

"Stop this noise!" he screamed. "I want you to stop this noise!"

The officer in charge pushed him away.

"I'm asking you politely!" Brown continued. "Stop it now! My ears are hurting! STOP IT!"

"Put him down," the officer ordered, meaning someone was supposed to shoot Brown in the leg. No one would obey the order, not to one of our own. So the officer shot Brown himself, wounding the crazed dogface before he got himself killed.

Another time, in the Harz Mountains in Czechoslovakia, we'd taken cover in a cave. One of our men just wouldn't come out the next morning. He wanted us to leave him alone in that cave. He stared at us with his pathetic, crazed eyes, but he wouldn't budge. We had to carry him outside. It was tough just to get him to stand up on his own two feet.

Behind each battlefield, medics would set up a big tent for the wounded. On one side were soldiers who'd been hit, blood all over the place. On the other side were soldiers lying in silent shock without any apparent wounds. We didn't pay much attention to them. We were too busy carrying in the bloody GIs for emergency treatment. The sad truth was that the soldiers in shock were deeply wounded, too, whether we knew it or not.

Going back to my childhood, I remember a kid named Zookie who hawked newspapers near the Brooklyn Bridge. One day, he killed his mother. What would drive a son to kill the woman he most adored in the world? What caused the tension inside that boy to build and build until he exploded in violence? What writers do is recreate the inner tension that leads to abnormal behavior. It is our responsibility to portray a character's breaking point, his or her emotional threshold. Cold, clinical explanations of criminal conduct are for scientists. Robert Louis Stevenson's *Dr. Jekyll and Mr. Hyde* is breathtaking because it shows a man driven into the depths of his ugliest self.

I pitched Fritz Lang a yarn about a mental hospital that I called *Straitjacket*. It opens in the asylum's corridor with men and women chained to a bench. Inmates have to shit and piss right there because nobody's attending to them. The camera dollies down the hallway shooting close-ups of their anguished faces. I'd heard about asylums abusing patients, making money off their relatives, and I wanted to expose those kinds of institutions. My subplot followed the relatives who, outside the asylum in "normal" society, acted just as crazy as the patients inside.

From my newspaper days, I knew the milieu. Once, I'd witnessed first-hand an unforgettable scene in New York's Bellevue Hospital, when a tough cop demanded to interrogate a patient. They let the confident cop into a room full of nutcases. Somehow, the big iron door automatically clicked shut. Suddenly, the cop's face changed. He started to perspire.

"I'll get someone right away," I said from outside the door.

"Don't talk so loud!" whispered the panicked officer, terrified to be stuck with all those loonies.

The tension of that incident gave me an idea for a scene in *Straitjacket* in which my lead, an investigative reporter, gets accidentally locked inside a ward with a bunch of sex-crazed female patients, who attack him. Fritz loved my script. However, he wanted me to change the main character to a woman so that Joan Bennett could play the role. Fritz had a production deal with Universal in association with Joan and her husband, Walter Wanger. Bennett was a great actress, but I was worried that a woman in the lead would transform the whole tone of the story. For Chrissakes, a woman being attacked in the asylum by crazed men just wouldn't work. A violent fight scene ended my yarn. I just couldn't see a woman playing that role.

Straitjacket never got made. The story would become, about fifteen years later, my own film *Shock Corridor.* However, to have spent time with a master like Fritz Lang was a privilege in itself. His career would span forty years, from his first film, *The Golden Lake,* in 1919, to his last, *Diabolical Dr. Mabuse,* in 1960. Hollywood, where Lang moved in the thirties, didn't care if Fritz was a world-class artist. I did. His *Metropolis* (1927) is still one of the greatest films ever made. Whenever I saw Lang over the years, we talked about him directing one of my yarns. It would never be. I loved the man and his acidic sense of humor, remaining close to him until he died, in 1976. Toward the end of his life, Fritz turned a little bitter about not having a family and children. When Christa came out to California with me, people thought she was Fritz's niece, since Christa's family name was Lang as well. In their sweet complicity, Christa and Fritz allowed the confusion. It tickled both of them.

By the end of the forties, I'd decided that I could direct my yarns as well as anybody else. Maybe even better. Sure, I was still happy working behind a typewriter. But now I started looking for an opportunity to direct a picture of my own, using a motion-picture camera to tell my tale. All I needed was a producer who'd put his faith in me. Just when I needed him, Robert L. Lippert showed up in my life.

24

The First Adult Western

Because of Robert L. Lippert, I got my first opportunity to direct a picture in 1948. Lippert was an independent producer who'd pioneered drive-in theaters in 1945, starting in Fresno, California. Eventually he controlled over a hundred movie houses. He got into producing pictures in 1946, turning out over 245 features in the next twenty years, first under Lippert Productions, then as an executive producer at Twentieth Century Fox. In 1965, Lippert built the first multiple theater, or multiplex, in Alameda, California, with the idea of showing several films at once in the same building, giving more movie choices to patrons. Lippert tracked me down through a secretary in the New York office of Duell, Sloan & Pearce, publishers of *The Dark Page*.

"I'm interested in backing you so that you can turn one of your stories into a movie," Lippert said when we met. "What've you got?"

"I want to do a film about an assassin," I told him between puffs on my cigar. "Cassius!"

"Who's that?" he asked.

"He's the man who had the idea to murder Caesar. Brutus did it. But Cassius plotted it. I want to hook the audience on the question of who's the guilty one. Is it the guy who plans the assassination? Or the one who does it?"

"Caesar?" said Lippert. "You want to make a film about naked guys hanging around Roman baths wearing bedsheets?"

"Exactly."

"Weren't those guys . . . ," he said bashfully, "you know, *funny*?" Lippert was too uptight to even pronounce the word "homosexual."

I was laughing inside, but I played it dumb.

"What do you mean, Bob?"

"Look, Sammy, I don't want to make a picture about guys in bedsheets."

My first producer, Robert L. Lippert (1909–76), made his entry into the movie business when he was fourteen, playing the pump organ to accompany silent pictures. When talkies were introduced in 1929, Lippert rented some portable sound equipment and went on tour showing the new sensation throughout the western United States. Lippert was a dynamic guy with a pioneering spirit and, most important, integrity.

"It's a murder movie, goddamnit!"

Lippert shook his head. He produced small films, so period pieces seemed expensive to make.

"I want to do a little film with a good story, Sammy," said Lippert, "where we can have some fun and both make a profit."

"Okay," I said. "I've got another assassin yarn. It's even more exciting. It's about Bob Ford, a great character. Nobody ever made a movie about him."

"Who did he murder?"

"Jesse James."

"Jesse James!" said Lippert. "Now we've got a movie!"

I didn't want to undermine Lippert's belief that Jesse James was a red-blooded hero. The real Jesse James was bisexual, masquerading as a girl to hold up trains that were carrying medical supplies. The guy was a low-down thief, a pervert, and a sonofabitch. But you couldn't show that stuff on a screen back then, demystifying one of the great American icons. I had a knack of talking a movie to death by insisting on reality. The whole truth didn't help get films made. This time, I'd be smart and keep my mouth shut.

"So your movie's about Ford, the assassin?" asked Lippert. "Can't we show Jesse, too?"

"Sure," I said.

Lippert was thinking about all those people in his movie theaters eating popcorn and ice cream and watching macho John Wayne Westerns. He expected my picture to fill the seats the same way. He agreed to let me write and direct the movie. The pay was low, but that was all right by me because if there were any profits, I'd share in them. We shook hands on it. That was all that was needed. Lippert was a smart, honest businessman and always respected a handshake deal. Immediately I went to work on the script for *I Shot Jesse James,* a yarn about a guy who kills the man he loves. Making just another Western wasn't going to give me a hard-on. Holdups, revolvers, leather gloves, and galloping horses didn't do anything for me. The real aggression and violence in the film would be happening inside the head of a psychotic, delusional killer.

Lippert insisted on my using horses in the opening scene of the picture. I went along with him on that one. After all, he was gambling about a hundred grand on my movie. He was sure that you couldn't market a Western without men on horseback. So I wrote in a scene with Jesse and his gang riding out of town after a bank holdup. It didn't hurt the story. Maybe it even helped. Lippert wanted to protect his investment, and I respected his faith in me.

Ford's story wasn't a morality tale. Sure, he shoots his best friend in the back and he's going to get punished for it. What excited me about the yarn were the echoes of the Cain and Abel fable in Genesis, the first murder. The "brother" killer is condemned to relive his crime over and over, never escaping the shame and outrage of it. I wanted to show Ford realizing that he's sick, then follow him as he sinks deeper into his sickness.

When my film opens, Ford looks like just another tough, half-witted outlaw member of the James gang as they hold up a bank in Topeka. But the robbery is foiled when a teller sets off the alarm with his foot. During the getaway, Ford gets shot and drops the loot, yet Jesse overlooks the incident. Right away, I establish the special fondness between Jesse and Bob after the botched heist. Jesse brings Ford back to his place in Missouri, where he lives under a fake name with his wife and children. As he recovers from his gun wound, Ford stays on with Jesse and his family for six months. He runs into his old girlfriend, Cynthia, an actress in a traveling show. Cynthia won't have anything to do with Ford until he leaves the James gang and becomes a farmer. But Ford is stuck. He's a wanted criminal and faces twenty years in jail, minimum. He has one way out, that of betraying Jesse James by killing him. Murder becomes Ford's escape.

Ford has his first chance when Jesse is taking a bath, but he can't bring himself to shooting his friend in the back. Instead, he picks up a brush and scrubs Jesse's exposed shoulders. Something is warped about these two guys' relationship. And betrayal is in the air. Another time, Ford wants to plug Jesse on the porch of his home, but misses his opportunity again. On his third try, Ford ends up shooting Jesse in his own living room. Despite the vile deed, Ford is given amnesty by the governor, earning a little reward money in the deal. Jesse's dead, so Ford is a free man. Cynthia accepts him. Now he has to live with the terrible guilt of what he did. He's like a caged animal. Wherever he goes, people revile him as a Judas. Insolent and unrepentant, Ford tries to make money by reenacting the murder for audiences seeking cheap thrills. But his theatrics only sink him deeper into his own guilt, driving him crazy.

To show Ford's self-hatred, I put in a scene in a saloon with a minstrel singing a ballad about Jesse James:

> *Cause it was Robert Ford,*
> *That dirty little coward*
> *Wonder how he feels?*
> *He ate of Jesse's bread, and slept in Jesse's bed.*
> *Then he laid poor Jesse dead in his grave!*

"I am Bob Ford," blurts out my antihero.

The minstrel stops abruptly, scared for his life.

"Go on! Sing!" Ford orders him. "I want to hear it!"

How long can Ford survive with his own guilt? How much more scorn can he endure? How far will his craziness take him? The core of the movie is the descent into his own private hell. My ending reinforces the dark idea that people kill what they love the most. Ford gets shot by the marshal and lies dying in Cynthia's arms. He's almost relieved to be put out of his misery.

"I am sorry for what I did to Jes'. . . . I loved him," Ford whispers to her.

The punishment for betrayal is terrible, but there's also forgiveness for even the most wicked acts. Lippert never objected to a man declaring his love for another man. I don't think he noticed the subtle suggestion of a homosexual bond between Ford and James. Critics did, calling *I Shot Jesse James* "the first adult Western."

I cast John Ireland as Bob Ford because I loved his intense performance in Howard Hawks's *Red River* (1948). Lippert wanted a name actor in the picture, so I hired Preston Foster as John Kelley, the marshal. Foster had been in one of my favorite films of all time, John Ford's *The Informer*

(1935), in which he played the head of the Irish Republican Army. The tall, handsome Reed Hadley played Jesse James, with his deep baritone voice. Barbara Britton got the role of Ford's gal, Cynthia Waters.

A wonderful craftsman, Ernest Miller, came on as my cameraman. Lippert rented a frontier street at Republic Studios for ten days to shoot the entire movie. I'd storyboarded the scenes and rehearsed the actors. On our first day of shooting, we were going to film the movie's final scene. I was very nervous. Even though I'd been on many movie sets, I'd paid little attention to how the camera and lights were set up. I told Ernest and the lighting people about the dark mood I wanted. See, Ford marches down the street toward the marshal, whose back is turned, just like Jesse's was. Now all I had to say was "Action." Instead, I fired one of the prop department's Colt 45s into the air. Everybody jumped, but they sure understood I wanted to get the scene going. At the end of the scene, I yelled "Forget it" instead of "Cut." Holy cow, now I was a movie director!

The time constraints and small budget made *I Shot Jesse James* one of the toughest films I ever did, but I loved every minute of it. The scenes with little or no action were the most difficult. I used close-ups to reveal as much as possible about my characters' emotions. Everything was done on the cheap. When we ran out of money at the end, we had to film the opening credits on posters tacked to a wall.

The film premiered in Los Angeles. I was a bundle of nerves that night. After all, I'd taken a big risk on my very first film. I'd made a Western without it being a Western. I'd jumbled genres, which could have led to confusion, maybe even disaster. The audience seemed to enjoy it. But the critics could still massacre me the next morning. After the screening, I went out drinking with my friend, the German director E. A. Dupont. There was a lot of vodka consumed into the early hours of the morning as we waited for the dailies to hit the newsstands. Dupont loved my movie and predicted it would get rave reviews. He was my buddy and European, so he could be wrong. I drank until I couldn't feel my anxiety anymore. We got the papers before dawn. The critics loved it.

Lippert had a small distribution company that booked his films into his own movie houses as well as into little theaters across the entire country. Lippert's network was especially strong in the South and the Midwest, the so-called Bible Belt, cradle of American bigotry. After a film played on that circuit for a while, it was destined to be forgotten. But I got lucky.

Out of the blue, the manager of the Palace Theater in New York City decided to book *I Shot Jesse James* after the film's regular run in the Bible Belt. Word of mouth among movie bookers had it that the film was a hot ticket. The Palace, at Forty-seventh Street and Broadway, was one of the

With Preston Foster (left) and John Ireland (right) on the set of I Shot Jesse James. *The ham I'm holding was given to us by some Big Red One pals for Thanksgiving 1948, when we were in production.*

greatest movie houses in the country. Before it became a two thousand-seat movie house, the Palace was a legitimate theater with big-time headliners like Eddie Cantor, Al Jolson, and Fanny Brice. When it was transformed for the movies, the Palace played big Hollywood productions with major stars. The fate of my film, and maybe other low-budget features, changed overnight. *I Shot Jesse James* opened at the Palace in early 1950. A little movie did great business in a big theater in New York City. The door was suddenly open for independent pictures to get a release in major movie houses in big cities across the country.

I had no idea that audiences from other countries would love the film, too. It got picked up, subtitled, and played around the world. A French critic wrote that the close-ups in my movie had "an oppressive intensity the cinema has not experienced since Dreyer's *Joan of Arc.*" The critic's name was Jean-Luc Godard.

I Shot Jesse James was a big boost to my confidence. Lippert had trusted me, giving me the independence to do the film my own way, and I hadn't let him down. The film's critical and box-office success was thrilling, espe-

The original release poster from
I Shot Jesse James

cially after having had my three previous
scripts turned down. There were scores of
phone calls from producers with all kinds of
offers. But I was going to stick with Lippert because he'd believed in me.
Now he wanted to produce my second picture. For that, I settled on a yarn
about one of the greatest con men of the nineteenth century.

25

Earning Some Clout

I'd come across the story of *The Baron of Arizona* during my hobo days in the thirties. I was sitting in a bar in New Mexico one day drinking whiskey with another newspaperman when the man pointed out the window at a government building across the street.

"See that place?" he said. "That's where Reavis worked."

"Who's Reavis?" I asked.

"James Addison Reavis. Fooled the U.S. government into thinking he owned all of Arizona."

I was intrigued. After doing some research, I'd written an article for the *American Weekly* about Reavis, a bizarre character from nineteenth-century frontier days who'd falsified official documents about territorial grants, creating one of the greatest land scams of all time. The federal government was forced to attack Reavis's claims to Arizona and parts of New Mexico. If Reavis had prevailed, he'd have been the legitimate owner of an enormous piece of the United States, including all its resources.

Bob Lippert was ready to produce another film with me directing, and he liked my pitch about Reavis. He asked that I put a tagline on the movie's writing credits that said "from an article first published in the *American Weekly*." I agreed to this little conceit. At the time, the majors were adapting classics into movies. David Selznick was producing Dostoyevsky's *The Idiot* at MGM and Paramount was making Dickens's *Oliver Twist*. Like the big Hollywood studios, Lippert wanted to produce an adaptation too.

I had to get into Reavis's head to write that script. Reavis was a flamboyant and ingenious gambler, so I wanted to use as much of his real-life personality as possible. From there, I concocted a yarn that was more interesting than Reavis's actual story. I imagined his fraud being meticulously planned and carried out over many years. I also invented a love story between the swindler and a little Mexican girl whom Reavis trains to become his baroness. Lippert was concerned about the implications of a little girl living with a grown man. The censors might make us cut it. I promised I'd soft-pedal the situation. Until Sofia becomes a grown woman, I always have a governess or Pepito, the girl's guardian, in her scenes with Reavis. When Sofia is no longer a minor, Reavis proposes marriage. Now a respectable young woman, Sofia falls in love with the swindler, no matter that he's more than twice her age.

The real Reavis was caught and convicted because of the ink on the documents he forged. I definitely wanted to use that historical aspect. I was fascinated that ink was able to condemn a man. Since my days as a copyboy, the gooey black substance that the presses used to make type appear on blank paper had always tickled my imagination. I remember the printmen on Park Row screaming out as the presses rolled, "We need ink! More ink!" In my research, I discovered that Spanish monks had used bark from oak trees growing at the monasteries to fabricate their own ink. Over the years, the ink faded in a special way. Reavis's crime was exposed because one of his forgeries was written with modern ink. His writing was perfect, but the ink wouldn't lie.

For the role of Reavis, I needed an actor who'd pass as an erudite fraud. My first choice was Fredric March. I met with March to explain the story. He was enthusiastic about the part. However, he was one of the top actors of that period and Lippert couldn't pay his asking price. I kept looking. On a trip back to New York, I saw a tall actor in a Broadway play with the dignified appearance of an Old World gentleman. He had an impressive voice and all the gestures and movements of a bygone era, just the guy I needed. I went backstage to his dressing room and introduced myself. He'd never heard of me. That was all right, as I'd never heard of him either. We smoked cigars. I told him about the Reavis character, and he loved it. Then and there, I offered him the part in my movie. We shook hands on it. The actor towering over me was Vincent Price.

Central to the movie is the struggle betwen Reavis and John Griff, the forgery expert who demasks the fraud. Reed Hadley, who had played Jesse James in my last picture, got the role. Reavis and Griff are archenemies, yet there is also a bond of mutual admiration between them.

In my yarn, Reavis builds his swindle around the fact that the United States promised to honor Spanish land grants from the eighteenth century. Reavis invents a phony eighteenth-century grant from the king of Spain to a certain Miguel de Peralta. He then finds Sofia and convinces the orphan's guardian that the girl is the rightful heir to the Peralta grant, and therefore the baroness of Arizona.

To make the scam credible, Reavis must falsify records in the archives of

On the set of Baron of Arizona, *with Vincent Price as James Addison Reavis and Gene Roth as Father Guardian*

an isolated Spanish monastery. He spends years doing this to perfection. Then he returns to the States and marries the grown-up Sofia.

Staking his claim, Reavis pretends to be the baron of Arizona, setting off a panic among the local settlers that reaches all the way to Washington.

I wrote Reavis as an arrogant sonofabitch, always maintaining his aloof composure, treating everyone, except Sofia, like shit. No one can dissuade him from taking possession of the lands "rightfully" left to his wife by the fake Peralta grant. The government tries to get Reavis to drop his claim with a multimillion-dollar bribe, but Reavis even refuses that. The townspeople hate him because he threatens to evict them. Later, they try unsuccessfully to lynch him. Even with a noose being tightened around his neck, Reavis still manages to belittle them, screaming, "You're hypocrites!"

Griff suspects the truth about Reavis and relentlessly closes in on him with evidence of the forgeries. In one of the film's final scenes, Reavis knows he's about to be found out. Cornered and humbled, the phony bastard must confess the truth to Sofia. Her love is his only real treasure.

REAVIS
You still want me?

SOFIA
I'll want you until the day I die. It is not
death, it's dying that alarms me. It is not your
crime, it's your weakness that alarms me.

REAVIS
Arizona! It seems so small. You suddenly seem
so great. I know what I was looking for. A
woman who would love me for what I am. No
man can live without that. No man can ask for
more.

Six years later, Reavis is released from prison. He's broken and lost.
Sofia, wise and masterful, is waiting for him at the prison gates in a horse-
drawn carriage. Their relationship has come full circle. I wanted an upbeat
ending to the picture, even though I knew that it wasn't historically fac-
tual. The real Reavis lived out his final years in a shack, penniless and
abandoned. In the movie business, a good ending must sometimes hold
sway over the truth.

I was lucky to have James Wong Howe, one of the greatest cameramen
in Hollywood, working with me on *The Baron from Arizona*. I'd met and
befriended Howe in the late thirties, thanks to Herbert Brenon. Howe was
a great guy and a great artist. When word got out that *The Baron of Arizona* was going into production, James came knocking timidly at my
office.

"Sammy, I want to shoot your picture," he said.

"You must be crazy, James!" I said. "The whole movie costs less than
your salary!"

"I don't care about the money. There are more important things in life."

Howe kept his word and shot the film for a fraction of his normal fee.
He gave the film the dark, Gothic look I wanted. For the monastery
scenes, our location was in a nearby canyon where they used to film a ton
of Westerns. Howe captured the austerity of the place beautifully. When
Price, as Reavis, jumps into a wagon and flees the monastery, Howe made
the ensuing crash and the tumble down the hillside look exciting and real.
In the lynch scene in Phoenix, I told Howe that I wanted the mob to look
like a Ku Klux Klan rally gone mad. He shot the crowds scurrying around
with burning torches. Juxtaposed with those shots are close-ups of the
main characters' faces, making you feel the mob's hatred and terror.

The cameraman's job was complicated because I insisted on using direct
sound. Dialogue on the set is much more real than what you can repro-

In Baron, *Reavis arrives to stake his claim to Arizona. The townspeople watch, but later their fear and hatred will push them to try lynching the phony bastard.*

duce later in a studio. While the actor is walking and talking, his or her words seem more natural. I liked to get the whole shot, dialogue and all, without having to go back on a soundstage and fool around with the actors' voices later.

I never interfere with my cameraman on the set. I simply tell him how I envisioned the scene in my head when I wrote it, without going into much detail.

"You see the eyes of that woman?" I'll say. "That's all I want to see on the screen."

The cameraman is master of his own kingdom. I feel the same about the rest of my crew: sound technicians, makeup people, hairdressers, costume designers. We'd discuss the kind of picture I wanted to make. Then I'd give them ample freedom to get the job done. They always did, no matter the budget or time constraints. I was always lucky with my production crews. Preparation, resourcefulness, and perseverance were the keys to staying lucky. *The Baron from Arizona* wasn't a big success. At least it was fun to make. More importantly, I was becoming more confident as a director and earning some clout in the movie business. After *Baron,* James Wong Howe wanted to do another film with me. James was determined to find the money to produce it, with me writing and directing it. I'd pitched him a story idea called *Sampan* that he loved. The whole movie takes place in China on the Yangtze River among the boat people, showing their way of life on the water. It was a great idea, but we never got to do it.

Newspaper headlines pointed me toward my next yarn. In 1950, the controversial war in Korea was raging. It seemed a natural for me to come up with a tale set in that ongoing conflict, utilizing my own firsthand experiences from World War II. Whatever the confrontation and wherever it's happening, the underlying story is one of destruction and hatred. I wanted an opportunity to show audiences that war was more complex than the front-page newspaper articles. You never saw the genuine hardship of soldiers, not ours nor the enemy's, in movies. The confusion and brutality of war, not phony heroism, needed to be depicted. The people who chanted "We are right, and they are wrong" needed to be debunked.

The Steel Helmet was written quickly, like a reporter on a scoop, the story "torn from the headlines," as they used to say. I concocted a squad of GIs in Korea cut off behind enemy lines. They're of different races and backgrounds. Together, they must assault a Buddhist temple, now an enemy observation post, as part of a big offensive operation. The first image on the screen is a dogface's helmet with a bullet hole in it. The helmet rises slowly to reveal the gritty, cigar-chomping face of Sergeant Zack, a World War II veteran. The bullet hole makes that steel helmet "lucky." It becomes an essential symbol of survival throughout the movie.

When I pitched *The Steel Helmet* to Bob Lippert, I told him the last image wouldn't be a typical "The End" but would say "There Is No End to This Story." Bob asked me why. It was my way of saying that, until we end the violence, this was just one episode in a continuum of horrible war tales. Violence begets violence. I sensed that if we started to fight in any corner of the world, it would be a repetitious cycle. Lippert gave me a green light, thank God, for if I were to make it my way, *The Steel Helmet* had to be done independently.

One of the major studios heard about the picture and offered to produce it, with John Wayne playing Zack. That would have taken all the reality out of the film. This wasn't a gung-ho war movie. I was determined to make it look real, my soldiers human and deeply flawed. War brings out the best and worst in you. With Wayne, I'd end up with a simplistic morality tale.

Again we had a strict budget and a tight ten-day schedule, but this time I'd get a bigger piece of the profits. As we approached our start date, we started rehearsals even though I was still missing the actor who could play my hard-boiled sergeant. Only a few days before the shoot was to begin, I was sitting in the production office when an agent walked in with a guy named Gene Evans. Evans was a tall, broad-shouldered actor who'd never had a major role in a movie. I liked this big, slow-talking fellow immediately.

"You in the war?" I asked him.

"Yes, Mr. Fuller," said Gene. "Three and a half years."

"Infantry?"

"Engineers."

"Too bad."

"Well," he said, smiling modestly, "we cleaned up a lot of stuff for the infantry."

I had an M1 on my desk. Without any warning, I threw it at Gene's chest. He grabbed it in midair.

"Rack it back," I said.

Without even thinking, Gene's hands worked the bolt, his fingers moving effortlessly.

"Follow me," I told Gene, taking him upstairs to introduce him to Lippert. "I found my Zack," I said as we walked in.

Lippert asked Gene a few questions. Then we sent the actor out to read the script. As

Just before shooting The Steel Helmet, *Gene Evans (here with Richard Loo as Sergeant Tanaka) showed up at our production office. I didn't give a damn about his being an unknown. He was perfect for the part of the sergeant. Hell, he* was *Zack.*

soon as Gene was gone, Lippert said, "Sammy, this guy's an unknown."

"Yeah, but I want him. He's exactly what I'm looking for."

Gene reappeared in my office a couple of hours later.

"Mr. Fuller," he said. "Sergeant Zack only has four or five pages of lines in a ninety-page script, yet he's on camera most of the time. There's got to be other stuff to say, right?"

"No, my boy," I said. "The other stuff's called acting."

"Well, I'm not crazy about a couple of my lines that I have . . ."

"Now listen, Gene," I cut him off. "I write the words. You get up there and say them. Everything will be fine once you understand that. We start in three days."

Lippert let me hire Evans. But a couple days into rehearsal, Lippert's associate producer, William Berke, tried to sandbag my star. Without telling me, Berke called Gene into his office and told him they were paying him off and letting him go because a more famous actor was coming in to replace him. Understandably, Gene was crestfallen. When I saw him later on set, I asked him what was the matter. When he told me, I was furious.

"You stay right here," I said. "You're Zack, or there won't be any goddamned movie!"

I went up to Lippert's office and demanded to know what the hell was going on. Rumors were flying that actor Larry Parks was going to have to appear in Washington at the McCarthy hearings. The bastards would threaten to blacklist him. Then Parks's name would be on the front page of every paper in the country. The guy was probably going to be unemployable, and most likely desperate to work. Lippert's partner had the brainstorm of contacting Parks about playing my sergeant. Parks would work on the cheap and be worth a fortune in free publicity when the shit hit the fan.

I really blew my stack. Hell, I knew Larry Parks very well and felt bad about what those reactionary McCarthy bastards would eventually do to him. Larry was an idealist and a wonderful human being. He'd appeared in one of the first pictures I wrote before I left for the war, *Power of the Press*. It was a shame the way those sonsofbitches would torture him in Washington. But I'd already cast Gene Evans for the role, and that was that. I stormed out of the production office without closing the door.

"Let's get the hell out of here!" I yelled at Gene. "This place is history!"

We got in my car and sped away. Gene was living in some fleabag hotel. I drove over there and told him to get his stuff, that from then on he was staying at my place. He said he owed them about $200. I gave him the dough, he got his suitcase, and we went home. The phone started ringing off the hook. I told Lippert that I wasn't coming back until I got his promise that there'd be no more tampering with my cast. We patched things up that night. The next morning we were back on set. I had a big sign hung on the stage door: NO ASSOCIATE PRODUCERS, CO-PRODUCERS, EXECUTIVE PRODUCERS OR ANY PRODUCERS ADMITTED HEREIN.

Exteriors for *The Steel Helmet* were shot in Griffith Park. My cameraman, Ernest Miller, made it look wild and rugged. In the movie's first scene, Zack's life is saved by Short Round, a Korean war orphan. Short Round's faith and devotion to Zack are crucial to the story. I established the sergeant's rambunctious, unlovable character right away in his first exchange with the boy.

> SERGEANT ZACK
> Quit following me.

> SHORT ROUND
> *Cachi cachida.* That means we must travel together.

> SERGEANT ZACK
> You go cachi cachi by yourself.

> SHORT ROUND
> But your heart is in my hands.

> SERGEANT ZACK
> My what is where?

> SHORT ROUND
> Buddha say when you save a friend his heart is in your hands.

> SERGEANT ZACK
> Look, you've done your good deed for the day. Now blow! I don't like kids around me.

> SHORT ROUND
> But I good scout.

> SERGEANT ZACK
> Don't need one.

To Mr. Fuller
a fine man to act
with and if it wasn't
for your confidence
I won't of have seen
such a part
*   Thanks a lot*
*   William Chun*
*   "Short Round"*

William Chun in
costume check for his
role as Short Round.
He was a good kid.

SHORT ROUND
I know where river is.

SERGEANT ZACK
So do I.

SHORT ROUND
But you said . . .

> SERGEANT ZACK
> Beat it!

Zack relents and lets the boy stick with him. They meet up with a lack-luster bunch of dogfaces on patrol. Instead of a happy-go-lucky, melting-pot squad, these soldiers are angry and frightened. They capture a wounded North Korean officer, and Corporal Thompson, the black medic, patches him up. As a black man, Thompson has suffered at home. Now the North Korean forces him to consider his predicament:

> POW
> I just don't understand you. You can't eat with them, unless there's a war. Isn't it so?
>
> CORPORAL THOMPSON (*Dressing* POW's wound)
> That's right.
>
> POW
> You pay for a ticket. But you even have to sit in the back of a public bus. Isn't that so?
>
> CORPORAL THOMPSON
> That's right. A hundred years ago, I couldn't even ride a bus. At least now I can sit in the back. Maybe in fifty years, sit in the middle. Someday, even up front. There are some things you just can't rush, buster.
>
> POW
> You're a stupid man.
>
> CORPORAL THOMPSON
> You're the stupid joe. Why don't you get wise, buster?

(*POW spits. Thompson gets even by ripping some tape away from POW's wound*)

> You're ruining my dressing.

That kind of dialogue was a slap in people's face. Yet why back away from confronting racism in America? After all, it wasn't just blacks who suffered injustices. I wanted to show that other minorities were abused, too. Long before the Nisei internments of Japanese Americans was general knowledge, I had my characters in *The Steel Helmet* talking about it.

The picture tries to convey the violence through the eyes of a soldier on the front line, not from the safe vantage point of the generals' map room. In my climactic scene, Zack rises silently in a fog of smoke and confusion after the enemy attack, stunned beyond words. We shot the scene to look like an excruciating nightmare, harking back to the horrible images I'd never forget from Omaha Beach.

All hell broke loose as soon as *The Steel Helmet* was released. Despite, or maybe because of, the controversy, the film did great business. One reporter, Victor Reisel, called me pro-communist and anti-American. One of the country's most reactionary newspapermen, Westford Pedravy, wrote that I was secretly financed by the Reds and should be investigated by the Pentagon. My mother telephoned to congratulate me about all the great publicity for the picture.

"Hello, comrade!" laughed Rebecca.

With my military record, how could those conservative bastards attack my integrity? For Chrissakes, I'd fought a war for freedom of expression and real democracy. Nevertheless, I heard that J. Edgar Hoover and the FBI started an investigation. Just as irrationally, the lefties loved my movie for their own agenda. The *Daily Worker* wrote, "This shows what beasts American soldiers are." The reviewer called me a "reactionary" for making a "beast" the hero of the movie. Hedda Hopper, grand dame of patriots and conservatives, put in her two cents: "I can't see anything in *The Steel Helmet* that the Commies can use to their benefit, except smearing the picture, by implication, with their support. It's strongly anti-red."

I didn't give a good goddamn whether lefties or righties liked the picture. I didn't make *The Steel Helmet* to please any constituency. At its origin, a work of art is apolitical. Popular taste and history can transform it. So what if Hoover and McCarthy didn't like my film? Our country was supposed to be founded upon free speech, not only allowing for controversy, but fostering it. My goal was to show the organized insanity of war. The movie had touched some raw nerves. That wasn't my purpose but, hell, it was a free country, wasn't it?

What really made reactionaries go nuts was my scene in which Zack gets so mad that he kills the POW with a machine gun in cold blood. The Pentagon asked me to come to Washington to be questioned about the movie. So I went. It turned out to be more like an inquisition. About

On location in Griffith Park for The Steel Helmet, *shooting with direct sound and natural light. The tight budget and ten-day schedule made us get it right the first time and move on to the next scene.*

twenty officers sat around a big conference table. There was a screen and a projector. They'd just watched *The Steel Helmet* before I walked in.

"Your film looks like communist indoctrination, Fuller," said one general.

"You're joking!" I said.

"Hardly," said another general. "The black medic. His name is Thompson, isn't it?"

"Yes, Thompson," I said.

"Why did you call him Thompson?" asked a colonel.

"I don't know," I answered. "I've always liked the name because of my friend, Turkey Thompson, the heavyweight fighter. It's a good, strong name for the character. I liked it."

"It sounded good for the character?" said another general. "Thompson," explained the colonel, "is a code name for clandestine communist workers in the United States."

My mouth dropped open. I didn't know a damn thing about code names for communists.

"It's pure coincidence," I said.

"Pure coincidence, Fuller?" said another officer.

"You know Turkey Thompson?" I said.

They all nodded, recognizing Turkey's name, for he was a helluva boxer in those days.

"Call my house," I said. "Turkey is staying there while I'm away. He's looking after things for me. Ask him about me using his name for a character in *The Steel Helmet*."

The colonel shifted gears.

"You show the squad hiding out in a Buddhist temple, Fuller. I've been to Korea. There are no Buddhist temples there."

I pulled out of my file a map of Korea that I'd gotten from the Korean consulate when I was writing the script.

"Look!" I said, pointing at the map. "Here's the site of an ancient Buddhist temple."

"Fuller, what we're most concerned about is your showing an American soldier shooting a prisoner of war. Why did you do it?"

"Because it happens!" I said. "I fought a war. Things like that happen! And you know it!"

I asked to make a phone call. They brought in a telephone, and I got Colonel Taylor, my old company commander and now a brigadier general, on the line.

"Did a prisoner of war ever get shot?" I asked him.

"Of course they did," said General Taylor.

I thanked him and hung up. We all knew the Geneva Convention rules. But war's irrational. Order breaks down. A guy who's been trying to kill you sticks his hands in the air and says that now he's your prisoner. Sometimes it doesn't fly, because he just shot your buddy. You kill him. It's shameful. It's against the convention. But it happens, damn it. I was only reporting it with a camera.

"I answered every one of your goddamned questions!" I said to them as I got up to go. "If you have any more, you call me *Mister* Fuller! I'm a civilian now! And happy to be one!"

Soldiers were trained to fight the fascists during the war. Now the bigoted winds of McCarthyism were blowing across democratic America, spreading the seeds of another kind of fascism. The only way to fight those people here at home was to expose their stupid, reactionary ideas. I was proud to poke holes in their fundamentalist bullshit.

Maybe *The Steel Helmet* cast a stone at the facade of intolerance and simple-mindedness. Maybe it didn't. In any case, the picture was an unexpected box-office smash. Unbelievably, my share of the profits was a couple million bucks after taxes. That gave me a little financial independence. One of the first things I did with my dough was buy that house in the San

Outside a New York movie theater that was playing The Steel Helmet. *The line of patrons was mostly men, many veterans, no doubt, who were hooked on the distributor's tag line: "The roughest, toughest bunch of guys who ever called themselves U.S. Infantry!"*

Fernando Valley that I'd been renting for my mother.

Now the offers came streaming in from the majors. I met with all the studio heads, Louis B. Mayer, Jack Warner, Harry Cohn. They were interested in me for no other reason than the big profits they dreamed about making on small-budget pictures. The last man I saw was the head of Twentieth Century Fox, Darryl Francis Zanuck. He was a writer by background. As a young man, Zanuck had turned out scores of stories and scripts for studio pictures, usually under the pseudonym of Melville Crossman or Gregory Rogers. He was the uncredited writer of *Little Caesar* (1930), one of the classic gangster pictures of all time. The Rin Tin Tin pictures were Zanuck's, too. When I first met him, Darryl was already a mogul, the only mogul who didn't talk about money.

"What story do you want to make next, Sammy?" he asked me. Holy smoke, that was the question I was waiting to hear! More than any other studio head, Darryl loved stories. That made me love the guy from the first moment I met him. He'd get excited hearing about the yarn for your next picture. His big office had animal heads all over the place, moose, lions, bears, a whole goddamned menagerie gazing down upon you. Darryl would act out scenes with me. He'd even get on the floor when there was a body in the script. If he said "Okay, let's do it," your movie was in production. My deal with Darryl was for six pictures. Half a year I'd work for Fox, the other half I could do anything I wanted. A new period of creativity and accomplishment was dawning. I knew I'd have to fight to keep making hard-hitting movies on my own terms, rejecting all the labels people wanted to stick on me, except the only one that really mattered: "Writer-Director."

Pursuit of Happiness

The *Steel Helmet* paid off big. Those were the days when an independent producer guaranteed you a piece of the action and you actually got it. When I worked for Zanuck, each picture at Fox generated paychecks for screenwriting and directing. All the dough never meant very much to me. Certainly, I never lusted after the loot. All I ever wanted was to write my stories and direct them. Money meant freedom to do just that. I didn't need much to make me happy other than my Royal, plenty of ribbons, cigars, and vodka. For someone like me, coming from a modest background, having money in the bank felt good, especially with a wife with sophisticated tastes.

I bought a beautiful house on twenty acres of land in Coldwater Canyon, above Beverly Hills, for Martha and myself. Designed by Julia Morgan, architect of William Randolph Hearst's castle at San Simeon, the house had been originally built for one of Hearst's sons. There were a helluva lot of bathrooms in the place. Each one had a unique design of hand-painted tiles. I hired a lovely Chinese couple to cook and clean for us and a full-time gardener for the grounds. It was a swell lifestyle and, for a while, glossed over our incompatibility.

It came time to do my first picture for Zanuck. We were sitting in his big office, smoking cigars. The stuffed animals were looking down on us as we tried to figure out what my movie was going to be about. Darryl was still raving about *The Steel Helmet*.

"What a movie!" he said. "No star. Not even a girl in the cast. Those gritty shots, so real, almost surrealistic. Sammy, your picture is being screened at all the studios. They'll copy it one way or another."

"Let 'em try," I said.

"So, what's next?" asked Darryl.

"A story about Russia," I said, taking a puff on my cigar. "A story that's never been made."

Darryl Zanuck presenting me with a commemorative admiral's cap on the set of Hell and High Water. *Zanuck was one of the greatest movie producers of Hollywood, with groundbreaking films like* Public Enemy *(1931),* The Grapes of Wrath *(1940),* Gentleman's Agreement *(1947), and* The Iron Curtain *(1948) among his many, many credits. I loved the guy.*

Zanuck chuckled. "There isn't any story that's never been made, Sammy," he said.

"Oh yeah?" I said. "Wanna bet on it?"

"Okay," said Zanuck without hesitation. "How much?"

"One hundred cigars," I said. "I'll win the bet with just two words!"

"Then let's bet two hundred cigars on it," said Zanuck.

Darryl was pretty sure of himself. Why shouldn't he be? He was one of the most prolific producers in town.

"All right," I said, feeling pretty cocky. "If I win, I want my brand of cigars, not those horrible cigars you smoke, without nicotine."

"Okay, Sammy," he laughed. "Shoot."

"*Red Square,*" I said, taking a contented mouthful of smoke.

The film, I explained, would be a slice of life about an ordinary Russian, a guard at Lenin's tomb. I'd imagined a love story between the guard and his girlfriend, with all the necessary emotional conflict. I'd show American audiences how Russians really lived in those days. They must have had the same concerns as Americans about job pay, raises, medical insurance, pensions. How did their apartments look? How did their trains run? What made them laugh? What made them cry? I'd go to Moscow with a small crew, hole up in a hotel, and write my script over there as we shot background footage. Since my story was apolitical, I didn't see anything that the Russians would object to.

"Impossible!" Darryl said, waving his hands in the air. "In these times, shoot a film in Russia? Or any Eastern Bloc country? Why, the Pentagon wouldn't allow it."

"With your clout in Washington?"

"Sammy, don't be so naïve. There's a war going on, a *cold* war. Fox produced Fred Zinneman's film with Monty Clift, *The Search,* and the whole thing had to be shot here on the back lot, not in Germany."[1]

Nevertheless, I won our bet and got my cigars. Never before had any American movie been made like *Red Square.* There still hasn't been one like it. I was disappointed we couldn't do it, but I immediately pitched Darryl another original story.

"What about a movie about the birth of a newspaper?"

"Bad timing," said Zanuck. "Your buddy Richard Brooks is about to make *Deadline—USA* for us."

Brooks and I had both come out of the newspaper business. He'd been writing scripts since the forties, notably *Key Largo* (1948), John Huston's Bogart-Bacall vehicle. Richard got his first shot at directing with *Crisis* (1950). The two of us raised hell wherever we went in Hollywood, enfants terribles before anybody ever heard of the "New Wave." To set the record straight about the rumor going round that we wanted to start a revolution, we took out a full page ad in *Variety* that said: "We love everybody. Sincerely, Richard Brooks and Samuel Fuller."

Lightheartedness was welcome in Hollywood in those days. The artistic climate was appalling. Studios were factories, grinding out "safe" movies like bland sausages, anxious to please right-wing review boards scrutinizing all material for suspicious ideas. In 1950, Congress had passed the McCarran Internal Security Act, which established a permanent subversive activities control board. President Truman vetoed the bill on the grounds that it disregarded "ideals which are the fundamental basis of our free society." Unfortunately, Congress overrode Truman's veto. The McCarran Act led straight to Hollywood's front door, because the infamous Senator Joseph Raymond McCarthy of Wisconsin exploited it to "uncover" communist influence in the arts.

Brooks and I tried poking holes in the black clouds of doubt and anxiety. Richard once came on the set of *I Shot Jesse James* and filmed some "home" movies. Later he threw a party for me at his place and screened his

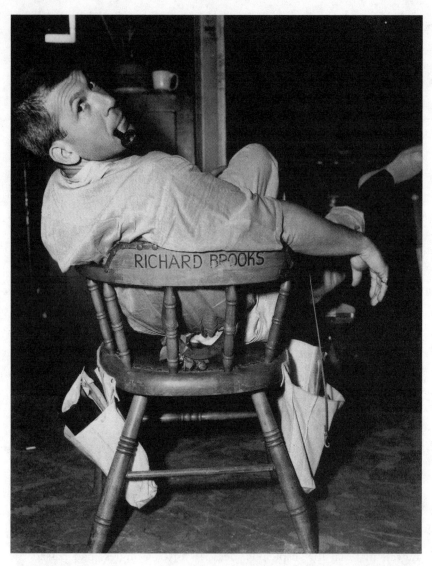

Richard Brooks was a close friend, a helluva guy, intelligent, witty, and decent. In Hollywood, Richard and I were known as rebels. The truth was we just wanted to make movies our way.

footage for all the guests. We were watching a scene of Jesse talking to Robert Ford, and out of nowhere flashed a couple of seconds of a girl's bare ass. It was hilarious. People giggled, completely thrown off balance.

In between the practical jokes, we had our serious moments. Richard helped me throw a party at my big place in 1952 for presidential candidate Adlai Stevenson. Everybody who was anybody in Hollywood, no matter their politics, came to my shindig. Stevenson's speech that night was powerful, yet soft-spoken and idealistic. His book, *A*

Call to Greatness, was one of the most inspiring of the fifties. I thought Stevenson would have made a helluva president.

What title was more appropriate than *Park Row* for my movie about the spirit and passion of my early days as a reporter? The film would be set on that great street that I first discovered as a newsboy in the twenties. My characters were scrappy reporters and crusading editors fighting for the truth as they scrambled to publish the first popular newspapers. The yarn would remind people of the very foundations of our country, those of tolerance and freedom of speech, that McCarthy and his supporters were assaulting. Richard Brooks's *Deadline—USA* dealt with the newspaper business too, but it was contemporary, the story centered on a tough editor in chief named Hutcheson, played by Bogart, trying to save his paper with a last-ditch crusade.

"I've read Richard's script," I said to Zanuck. "It's about the death of a modern-day newspaper. Mine is set in the nineteenth century, when Pulitzer was establishing the standards for all newspapers."

Zanuck listened to me thoughtfully. But he wasn't budging on *Park Row.* For him, the timing was wrong.

"Here's what we do now, Sam. A small group of soldiers in Korea. One set . . ."

"Holy shit, Darryl!" I said. "Korea? I did that already. I don't want to think about Korea again."

"Yes, you do," said Zanuck. "Look, Sammy, the only guy who can make another movie as good as *Steel Helmet* is you. The other studios will turn out cheap imitations with no style. Your ego won't allow you to copy yourself."

I thought fast. Why talk myself out of directing a picture? I was married now and had a helluva lot more expenses.

"Okay," I said, "but I want to shoot the entire picture on one goddamned hill covered in snow."

Zanuck picked up his phone and called in the studio's set designers. The department head was Lyle Wheeler, who'd won, among many other awards, an Oscar, for *Gone with the Wind.* I sketched out the set I had in mind: an icy hill, a snow-banked trail, a cave on the side of a cliff.

"No problem," said Wheeler.

My ultimate concern about the new picture was that we were just making an overhaul of *The Steel Helmet.*

"Look, Sammy," said Zanuck, trying to reassure me, "we made a movie at Fox with Henry Fonda and Maureen O'Hara called *The Immortal Sergeant* in '42. John Stahl directed it, based on a John Brophy novel. Did you see it?"

"Yeah."

"Like it?"

"Yeah."

"Well, we own the rights. So we'll just say that your movie is based on Brophy's book."

"My story will be an original," I insisted. "Almost nothing will be lifted from that goddamned book."

"Who cares?" said Zanuck. "Only a few people in the industry will even notice, and they'll think we've been reworking the story over here. The point is that before anyone can copy *Steel Helmet,* you'll have another picture under your belt."

What dawned on me was the realization that I was now a small player in a very big game. Studios were in fierce competition with each other. In addition to his savviness about stories, Zanuck was a tough businessman. The studio bosses reminded me of newspaper publishers constantly trying to scoop one another.

I set to work writing a script for Darryl called *Fixed Bayonets.* It was about a small squad of soldiers sent to stall an enemy advance while their division pulls back from a snowy mountain region in North Korea. Of course, my yarn included stuff I'd lived through on the front lines, such as the risk of frostbite in freezing weather, an officer's misgivings about having to order his men into danger, and a soldier's fear about pulling the trigger.

"You take care of her," says one of my characters, looking at his M1, "and she'll take care of you." I'd heard my sergeant say that again and again.

I threw in a crack about the controversy surrounding the Korean conflict.

"They told me this was going to be a police action," a soldier says to his buddy.

"So why didn't they send the cops?" the GI shoots back.

Somebody at Fox wanted to take out that exchange, afraid of possible repercussions from the McCarthy clowns. Zanuck came to my defense. My script would remain exactly as I wrote it. Darryl always stood up for the writer, because he'd been one himself.

People continued trying to pigeonhole me as a lefty or a righty, and my work as being liberal or conservative, projecting their own notions on me. I wouldn't let them affect my deeply held belief system. Peace and ethics were my beacons. I wanted to transcend the narrow political terms and emblems that imprison a creative person. McCarthyism had spawned a horrible climate of fear and suspicion. The blacklists, coercion, witch-hunts, accusations, and self-imposed censorship were inadmissible in our democracy. It was execrable how artists felt compelled to label themselves as "left" or "right." I was deeply hurt by what was happening in America so soon after putting my life on the line to fight the fascists in Europe. All the venom and general hysteria at home seemed like just more fascism.

One of the most reactionary columnists of the period was George Sokolsky. I'd met Sokolsky several times, and we'd talked politics. Those were heated discussions, because I always tried to poke holes in his idiotic ideas about what was politically correct or incorrect. He'd listen to me because he considered me a war hero and above suspicion of being a lefty. I told Sokolsky to his face that he was full of bullshit.

Once at a brunch at Richard Brooks's house, I ran into Edward G. Robinson. I loved Robinson as an actor and had always wanted to work with him. He'd recently been crucified in one of Sokolsky's columns as having flirted with communism, a charge that at the time was tantamount to saying the actor had strangled his mother. Robinson confessed to us that he thought his career was over. For cryin' out loud, one of our greatest actors was being put out of action by a gossip-mongering newspaperman! I phoned around until I found Sokolsky. He was in some meeting at the Ambassador Hotel. He took my call. I didn't go into what I thought of his shitty journalistic standards, publishing destructive hearsay without ever having talked with Robinson himself. I told the sonofabitch that he had to meet Robinson, write a new column, and apologize for the false charges. Sokolsky hesitated. I threatened that I was going to get some of my Big Red One pals together from the war and pay the bastard a visit to discuss politics. I told him to stay on the line and got Robinson to pick up the phone. Right then and there, Sokolsky and Robinson made an appointment for a face-to-face interview. Subsequently, an apology appeared.

Another time, I was at a well-known Hollywood hangout having a drink with Dalton Trumbo. A reactionary sonofabitch named MacColly stood near us. He'd asked me, after my reception for Stevenson, if he could use my house for some kind of right-wing political meeting. I refused. MacColly started insulting Dalton at the bar, goading him into a fight. Despite my war experience, I don't consider myself a violent person. But don't push me, goddamnit! This creep MacColly really got me angry. Like in a saloon scene from a Wayne Western, I picked up a whiskey bottle from the bar and waved it in front of the sonofabitch's face. Maybe the little coward's aggression toward Trumbo was meant for me. I told MacColly that I was going to shove the bottle down his throat if he didn't shut up. He shut up.

The fact remained that many intellectuals like my friend Trumbo were

attracted to communism. I couldn't understand why. Hell, communism
was nothing new. Our very own Pilgrims who'd arrived on the Mayflower
in 1620 agreed on a "communistic" compact, that the same amount of
farmland would be given to all members of the community. They were
soon embroiled in disputes. Selfishness and greed pushed them to want
more terrain. Filching it from their neighbors was the next natural step.
Fighting broke out. Marxist theories were similarly utopian.

Stalin's working model was totally abusive, though few realized it yet. I
found out about what was going on in Russia thanks to an old newspaper
pal, Walter Duranty, who'd been a correspondent in Moscow for twenty-
five years. Walter had sent me his fascinating 1937 book called *One Life,
One Kopeck,* describing in detail a harsh system gone haywire, the wide-
spread repression of the people, the churches that had been transformed
into prisons, the lands that were confiscated by the government, the forced
labor, the killings. The title of Duranty's book was a rough translation of a
Russian proverb that literally meant life isn't worth a shit.

What good was a movement that espoused great ideals while abusing
the human rights of its own people? Hitler and Mussolini had tried to pull
off that trick. Now Stalin and his regime were taking the same murderous
approach. I lived to see the day when everyone finally recognized the terrible truth about Stalin.

Hollywood was a microcosm where the turbulence of those times surfaced frequently. I vividly remember the now-famous meeting of the
Director's Guild of America when Cecil B. DeMille was trying to unseat
Joe Mankiewicz as president. In those years, the president of the DGA was
an important spokesman for all filmmakers in Hollywood. The vote was a
clarion call to take a stand in that tense period of reprisal and repression.
Two Hollywood goliaths faced off for the post. DeMille was one of the pil-
lars of the industry, having made movies for over forty years, ever since *The
Squaw Man,* in 1914, one of the first films ever shot in Hollywood.
Mankiewicz was an éminence grise, having written and directed a score of
intelligent pictures since the late twenties, among them the formidable *All
About Eve* (1950).

The DGA election was a rambunctious gathering of independent-
thinking people. Directors got up and made fiery speeches in favor of
Mankiewicz, considered a lefty, and DeMille, as conservative as they came.
Insults and barbed quips were yelled across the room. Then, John Ford
rose to his feet like a towering volcano about to erupt. Everybody shut up.
All eyes turned toward the big man with the black eye patch.

"My name is Jack Ford, and I make Westerns," he began. "We owe
Cecil a lot."

It was a fact, said Ford, that DeMille had been the one who'd first made the public aware of the importance of the director in moviemaking. Before Cecil, people only talked about pictures in terms of their stars. A wave of panic washed across the "liberal" directors who backed Mankiewicz for the president's job. What was Ford up to? How could he support DeMille? Jack was standing only a few feet away from Cecil, determined to speak his mind face-to-face.

"But I don't like Cecil's politics," Ford concluded. "So I'm voting for Joe. The rest of you can do what the hell you want."

Rouben Mamoulian, director of *Dr. Jekyll and Mr. Hyde,* gave one of the many moving speeches that day. "You were all born in the United States," he said. "But I *chose* to live in this country. This country didn't choose me. Now that I live and work here, I want Joe Mankiewicz to be president of our guild."

For ethical reasons, not political ones, I voted for Mankiewicz and against DeMille that day. DeMille called himself a patriot, then insisted that all directors sign a moronic loyalty oath. What bullshit! It was contrary to our country's foundations. DeMille was an elitist. For Chrissakes, there is *nothing* elitist about our very own Declaration of Independence:

> We hold these truths to be self-evident: that all men are created equal; that they are endowed by their creator with inherent and inalienable rights; that among these are life, liberty, and the pursuit of happiness.

Production of *Fixed Bayonets* got under way in the summer of 1951. We shot the movie in twenty days, twice as much time as I'd ever had on a movie set. For my lead, Corporal Denno, an officer who panics in the heat of battle and loses control, I cast Richard Basehart. He wasn't a big star, but just who I wanted. He'd go on to play opposite Guilietta Masina in Fellini's masterpiece *La Strada* (1954). Basehart's character was unheard of in war movies, but I knew officers goofed up because I'd seen it first-hand. Corporal Denno is ambivalent about why he's even in the army. I had a GI asking Corporal Denno about his reasons for being a soldier. "That's something I've been trying to figure out for a long, long time," he replies.

Even though he wouldn't tamper with my script, Zanuck thought lines like that one would get me into hot water with the Pentagon again. I firmly believed that the only way to honor GIs at war was by showing the truth. There's nothing romantic about the infantry. If you survive, you'll be proud of having been a foot soldier until the day you die. As it turned out, the army would request permission to show *Fixed Bayonets* to soldiers in their own training schools.

The popular misconception was that professional soldiers signed up for idealistic motives. The truth was that most men joined the army because they needed a roof over their heads or they craved a medal to impress the girls they wanted to marry or they had no career designs other than letting Uncle Sam decide for them. The military has always been a catchall. In Stendhal's *The Red and the Black* (1830), there were only two honorable choices for young men of that era, the black—the priesthood—or the red—the military.

Since Gene Evans had brought me luck with *The Steel Helmet*, I wrote the part of Sergeant Rock for him in *Fixed Bayonets* and made sure that he was paid well for it. Gene's best scene was the one with bullets ricocheting all around a cave where his squad is hunkered down. When a soldier fires at you in the field, you know more or less where the bullet is going. But if the enemy shoots at you in a cave, no one knows where the bullet is going to end up. What you think is a well-protected

On Lyle Wheeler's great set for Fixed Bayonets, *my dogfaces get their marching orders. One of those boys was a young actor named James Dean, in his first movie role. My heart goes out to any infantryman in any army in the world. Wars are started by politicians, orchestrated by generals, but fought by soldiers on the ground.*

position becomes a death trap. I wanted the movie's cave to feel like an agonizing prison, dangerous inside and out. Its usefulness against the enemy and the cold is short lived. The soldiers must move on. By doing so, they risk death.

One of the truths about human existence is the struggle to be free of boundaries, real or emotional. Almost all my movies touch on that idea in one way or another. We emerge from a mother's womb and end up in a box at death. In my later movies, there'd be social prisons to escape from, like O'Meara's defeated Confederacy, in *Run of the Arrow* (1957), or Kelly's big-city prostitution, in *The Naked Kiss* (1964). In *White Dog* (1982), a dog tries to escape from the prison of its conditioning. I like turning the tables, too. In *Shock Corridor* (1963), Johnny Barrett volunteers to be locked up in an insane asylum to crack a murder, then can't ever escape.

To convey the isolation in *Fixed Bayonets,* a soldier yells out, "Who goes there?," and all he hears is his own voice echoing over and over. The actor we cast for that part was a young, sensitive kid in his first movie, James Dean. Dean had just come out to Hollywood to find work after having studied at the Actor's Studio. I liked his face and gave him a crack. I hoped it would bring him luck.

The primary motive for all action in *Fixed Bayonets,* as in all my war movies, is survival, not heroism. I wanted to underscore the futility of battle and the tragic human waste. In one scene, I have the sergeant goad a soldier into firing his M1 by saying: "Shoot, for Chrissakes! I'm not asking you to kill eight. But at least one or two." A bullet cost five cents in those days. Every dogface had eight bullets in his rifle's magazine. The sergeant is just doing his job, asking to get something for the army's investment, which means a nickel a life, eight lives for forty cents. I was goading audiences to understand war's senseless cheapening of human life.

There were two big openings for my first studio film. One was in New York, at the Rivoli, and one was in Hollywood, at Grauman's Chinese. Charles Einfield, head of worldwide publicity at Fox back then, sent me to New York for the East Coast premiere, part of some military benefit. When I got off the plane, I had one of the happiest surprises of my entire life. A dozen reporters I'd worked with in the old days on Park Row showed up at the airport to greet me. I was overwhelmed by their warm welcome. After the screening of *Fixed Bayonets,* we had a raucous dinner at Toots Shor's place, like in the old days, with an abundance of steaks and vodka. I don't know how I got back to my hotel that night.

Fixed Bayonets did solid box office for Fox. Zanuck was proud of the movie. He told me that the studio was investing the film's profits in a new invention by Frenchman Henri Chrétien, the "anamorphic" lens, key to

*The New York opening
of* Fixed Bayonets *had a
marching band and
a helluva lot of army brass,
plus a large contingent of
my pals from the old days
as a reporter. I had a great
time that night.*

the new process of CinemaScope. Darryl wanted me to shoot my next movie in the new format.

I had other ideas for my next project. I longed to make *Park Row*, finally shooting a movie about the men and women who worked on that wonderful street. All my love and respect for newspapers would go into it. The real hero would be our nation's freedom of the press. I was willing to take a big gamble for my love song to American journalism. And to get *Park Row* produced, I'd have to.

A Little
Black-and-White
Picture

One day, Zanuck joined me in a screening room at Fox to watch rushes from *Fixed Bayonets*. I was carrying my 9-mm Luger, a war souvenir, which I fired to cue actors and crew. When the lights came up, Darryl questioned me about the ricochet scene in *Fixed Bayonets*. Did bullets really bounce around a cave like that, shrieking like a banshee? I looked around the screening room's cement walls, then pulled my Luger out of its holster.

"A hundred cigars says it's exactly that way."

"You're on," said Zanuck, looking at the pistol. "It's loaded?"

I took some real bullets out of a leather pouch on my belt and replaced the blanks in the Luger's clip.

"Now it is," I said as I handed the Luger to Darryl.

"All right," he said, chuckling. "Let's see."

He fired a couple of rounds with the Luger. The bullets went zinging around the cement walls. *Bang! Bing! Bang!* The echo was deafening. The shots continued to resound for a long moment. We both started laughing uncontrollably. Lucky neither of us was hit!

It was a perfect moment to bring up *Park Row* again with Darryl. My script for the movie was done, written with the hope that Fox would finance the project. I'd never stopped thinking or talking about the famous street in lower Manhattan between the Bowery and Brooklyn Bridge where American journalism was born. Zanuck shared my enthusiasm for the story but wanted major changes, beginning with the title.

"We made a film here with Tyrone Power in 1938 called *In Old Chicago*," he explained to me. "Very successful. Sam, forget your title. Nobody's ever heard of Park Row. We'll call the picture *In Old New York*."

"Impossible," I said. "It's got to be *Park Row*, goddamnit!"

"What actor do you want to play your editor?"

"Gene Evans."

"Evans? What? For the lead? Never."

"He promised me he'd lose thirty pounds."

"Look, Sam, your script is terrific," said Zanuck, shaking his head as he puffed on his nicotine-free cigar. "But your hero is in love with a linotype machine. The audience won't get it. We need stars. We need color. We need CinemaScope. Here's what we do. We cast Greg Peck as your crusading editor. Then we get Susan Hayward as the love interest. Or maybe Ava Gardner. Dan Dailey can play the guy who jumps off the Brooklyn Bridge. Mitzi Gaynor can be the barmaid. We write some songs and make it as a musical!"

"A musical?" I cried. "For Chrissakes, Darryl, you want to make *Park Row* into a musical? It's a little black-and-white picture, a period piece. It has to look real. It has to be intimate and powerful."

"With unknown actors in a black-and-white picture, your period piece is a loser, Sam," said Zanuck reluctantly.

Something in me snapped. I loved the actors Darryl had offered me, but I couldn't see *Park Row* as a big musical comedy in color and Cinema-Scope. No way. For the first time, I craved complete artistic control over a movie to get my own vision up on the big screen. I wouldn't compromise on this project, because it was just too important to me. Goddamnit, Park Row *was* me!

I wasn't angry with Zanuck. He was a studio boss with his own priorities. Yet, he was always a straight shooter, unflinchingly supportive of me, fair even when we disagreed. Over the years, I did plenty of pictures with him. We had a great working relationship. Besides, I'd turn down plenty of big pictures Darryl offered me to direct. First, there was *The Desert Rats* (1953), with James Mason and Richard Burton. Darryl thought that I'd be interested in Rommel as a character after my combat experience against the real Rommel in North Africa. I wasn't. Robert Wise ended up directing the movie. I also turned down his offer to direct *The Longest Day* (1962). A reputation for making war movies made Darryl think of me. My own vision of war and the world made me say no. I couldn't see myself mixed up with those overblown, glaringly inaccurate Hollywood productions.

I decided that the only way to make *Park Row* was to put up my own dough and produce it myself. Two hundred grand, to be exact. To hell with Zanuck and Fox! Fuck the entire studio system! My film was going to be a personal gift to American journalism. I knew exactly how I wanted *Park Row* to look, right from the first frame. Thousands of names of real newspapers scroll down the screen, then in bold letters we read:

THESE ARE THE NAMES
OF 1,772 DAILY NEWSPAPERS
IN THE UNITED STATES.

More names of newspapers scroll, then:

ONE OF THEM
IS THE PAPER
YOU READ

More names of newspapers scroll, then:

ALL OF THEM
ARE THE STARS
OF THIS STORY

More names of newspapers scroll, then:

DEDICATED TO
AMERICAN
JOURNALISM

As promised, Gene Evans, slimmed down for the role of Phineas Mitchell, became my lead. After *The Steel Helmet,* I felt completely confident about Gene. He had real sincerity in his mannerisms. He could explode at any time, violence simmering just beneath his skin. Unlike a war movie or a Western, *Park Row* was about the violence of competing ideas. Mitchell must fight for what he believes in with words rather than guns. Words are more powerful weapons. Fists might come in handy, however.

Like other famous Manhattan streets—Maiden Lane, for jewelers, South Street, for fishermen—Park Row was not a place for the fainthearted. The men and women who worked there had principles and were ready to fight for them. Joseph Pulitzer, whom I'd learned about firsthand from my old boss, Arthur Brisbane, was a peace-loving person. But once, a man called Pulitzer a liar in a bar on Park Row. The man went so far as to slap Pulitzer across the face. Pulitzer walked out of the bar, came back in a few minutes with a pistol, and shot the man in the leg. Though the wound didn't kill the guy, Pulitzer went to jail for the incident. However, no one ever questioned his integrity again.

Park Row opens with a boom shot of a bronze statue in a turn-of-the-century cobblestone street:

NARRATOR (*Camera moves in on statue*)
This is Johannes Gutenberg, who invented
moveable type 500 years ago and printed the

On the set of Park Row.
*Benjamin Franklin
was one of my heroes,
so I made his statue a
centerpiece of the set.*

first Bible. Recognized as the father of modern
printing, Gutenberg stands on Park Row, the
most famous newspaper street in the world,
where giants of journalism mix blood and ink
to make history across the front pages of
America. Our story takes place in New York in
the lusty days of the "Golden Eighties" when
Park Row was the birthplace and graveyard of
great headlines.

(Camera moves along street to another statue.)

> The street of America's first world-famous
> journalist, a printer's devil who helped draft
> the Declaration of Independence and was one
> of its signers: Benjamin Franklin.

The camera picks up on Phineas Mitchell and follows him down three
blocks of Park Row, past wagons, drugstores, and tobacco shops, in front
of the offices of the *New York Times,* the *Herald,* the *Evening Post,* and the
World. It was one long, complicated shot without a single cut. I needed it
to immediately establish the excitement and diversity of that street. There
was no zoom available so my cameraman, Jack Russell, had to be pushed
backward on his dolly.[1] The first time we ran through the shot, Jack fell off
his perch. He finally managed to get the opening sequence just as I'd envisioned it. I was writing with a camera now, painting a character and his
environment on film. Most of my budget went into constructing the four-
story set of that street and its buildings. The designers thought I was nuts,
because no one built sets four stories high. Yet that street was my movie,
and everything about it had to be authentic.

Mitchell walks into a saloon on Park Row, and a foamy beer slides
across the bar directly into his hands. He's not really interested in getting
drunk. He's a reporter with a nose for the news and a respect for the truth,
dreaming of starting his own newspaper.

> PHINEAS
> Know what I'd do if I had a paper? The first
> thing I'd do is christen it. I'd call it *The Globe.*
> I'd make it the best newspaper on Park Row,
> that's what I'd do. I'd give away free ice and
> coal and summer excursions. Christmas din-
> ners for the poor. That would make 'em
> happy, and make news. News makes readers,
> readers makes circulation, and circulation
> makes advertising. And advertising means
> that I'd print my newspaper without the sup-
> port of any political machine. That's what I'd
> do if I had a newspaper.

Mitchell launches the *Globe* with the assistance of veteran journalist
Josiah Davenport, played by Herbert Heyes. The old-timer takes his
young editor aside as the first number of the *Globe* comes off the press:

BENJAMIN
FRANKLIN
1706-1790
PRINTER PATRIOT
PHILOSOPHER
STATESMAN
PRESENTED BY
ALBERT D'GROOT
TO THE
AND PRINTERS
OF THE
F NEW YORK
NVEILED
UARY 17. 1872

My lead, Phineas Mitchell, is ready to fight to defend his ideas and his reputation.

JOSIAH

I've seen a lot of Volume Ones. Number Ones. This is beautiful make-up! Greeley started with forty dollars credit. Bennett started in his cellar. You're in good company.

PHINEAS

How come you never got to be an editor?

JOSIAH

Edinburgh, about twenty years before I was born, stood up in Parliament and said there were three estates of the realm: the Peers, the Bishops, and the Commoners. Then he looked in the reporter's gallery and said: "Yonder there sits a Fourth Estate, more important by far than they are." Somebody's got to go out and get the news. People like me get it. People like you see that it gets to the readers. Some men are born editors. Some are born re-porters. But a fighting editor is a voice this

The first issue of the Globe *(above)* comes off the press with
the inside story about Steve Brodie's leap from the Brooklyn
Bridge, celebrated *(below)* by a parade down Park Row.

world needs! A man with ideals! And the joy
of working for an ideal is the joy of the living!
I know.

Once launched, Mitchell must struggle to make the *Globe* an enduring
success. He attracts stiff competition from the *Star,* the big paper he used
to work for, and its newspaper heiress owner, Charity Hackett. Charity has
the means to demolish Mitchell with her money and power but lacks original ideas. Mitchell has ideas but no money. He has to fight her with words
alone. Despite the fact Mitchell fancies Charity, they struggle against one
another, then, as opposites sometimes do, fall in love. The *Globe* survives
and even manages to help finance a pedestal for the soon-to-arrive Statue
of Liberty.

To play the complex character of Charity, I hired Mary Welch, a gifted
actress whom I'd seen in Eugene O'Neill's *Moon for the Misbegotten.* I was
very taken with Welch's performance in the play, so I went backstage to
meet her. She was a beautiful, self-possessed woman with an inner strength
that shone through her personality. After trying to derail Phineas and his
newspaper, Charity ends up helping the competitor she wants in the
sack.

My yarn had to be much more than a period romance. It had to drama-
tize the importance of ethics in the press. A powerful, free press was a necessary element in a democracy. When the press became corrupt, it was
harmful. Newspapers were only as good as the men and women running
them. They could lie by skimming the complexities of crucial topics and
avoiding controversy.

My movie paid special tribute to Ottmar Mergenthaler and his linotype
machine, too. With the invention of the printing press, Gutenberg opened
the door to publishing books for the general public, allowing everyone to
develop their knowledge of the world, until then reserved only for the
elite.[2] Hundreds of years later, Mergenthaler was responsible for another
milestone by vastly improving the speed and accuracy of typesetting for
newspapers. Getting the news promptly, not only from their own country
but from around the world, meant people were better able to understand
their times, their society, their leaders. Without Gutenberg and Mergenthaler, we'd still be living like cavemen.

Sid Grauman loved *Park Row* and offered to premier it at his Chinese
Theater on Hollywood Boulevard. We set up a big printing press outside
the theater, ran off one-sheets about the picture, passing them out to the
waiting crowds. The ink was still fresh, so people's hands got stained black,
like printer's devils. The critics gave us great reviews. Zanuck loved the

Discussing a scene with my two leads, Gene Evans and Mary Welch. Tragically, Mary would die in childbirth the year after Park Row *was finished.*

finished film, but his prediction that *Park Row* wouldn't do much business came true. I'd made a deal with United Artists to distribute the picture, but it never clicked with audiences. All the money I'd sunk into the production was a wash. Nevertheless, I was thrilled to have made it my way.

One of the most memorable screenings of *Park Row* was a special premiere in New York at the Waldorf-Astoria Hotel for a convention of the Newspaper Publishers and Editors Association of America. Representatives of seventeen hundred dailies from across the country were there. Among the guests were General MacArthur, President Hoover, and William Randolph Hearst Jr. That enthusiastic audience stood and applauded the picture like no other. Many cried. They really understood the spirit of the movie and the importance of journalistic freedom.

Years later, I was asked to be president of a film festival jury in Strasbourg, France. The festival was dedicated to the relationship between the cinema and the press. Newspaper writers and editors from Europe and the States were there. They screened *Park Row*. In the lobby of our hotel, the editor of a big French magazine stopped me to say the film had moved him very deeply. Phineas Mitchell's struggle, his emotions, his guts, every scene in the picture, meant something special to this man. He was sincere, almost breaking down into tears right there in the lobby. I was surprised and moved that a picture I'd made three decades before could hit this guy so hard. Hell, I hope my films will be able to continue to touch people that way for as long as there are movies!

Park Row was a turning point for me. I was more confident than ever after having made that picture, ready to broach any material, even the most controversial. I was better able to write with my camera, inventing techniques to capture the atmosphere I wanted on film. For example, in the movie's climactic riot scene, we strapped a camera to the back of an operator and had him run down the street, bobbing and weaving, to get the visceral effect of mass violence. The heavy camera attached to the man's body was a forerunner to today's light, efficient Steadicam.

One scene from *Park Row* will remain engraved on my mind forever. Before Josiah Davenport passes away, he writes his own obituary notice for the paper. Mitchell reads it to his staff:

MITCHELL
Josiah Davenport, seventy-five, journalist, died today at peace with Park Row. His search for a man to carry on the fight of Horace Greeley was successful. His last words were written to this man:

"Phineas Mitchell, *The Globe:*

"In most countries, there is no freedom of the press. In the United States, there is. This freedom was born in 1734 in the libel trial of John Peter Zenger, printer and publisher of the *New York Weekly Journal.* He was acquitted by jury.

"When anyone threatens your freedom to print the truth, think of Zenger, Franklin, Bennett and Greeley. Think of them. Fight for what they fought for and died for. Don't let anyone ever tell you what to print. Don't take advantage of your free press. Use it judiciously for your profession and your country. The press is good or evil, according to the character of those who direct it. And *The Globe* is a good newspaper.

*At a New York convention of newspapermen from
across the country, I screened* Park Row *and met
former president Hoover (second from left). Among
other guests sitting at the president's table that day was
General MacArthur (seated fourth from left).*

*Despite a big opening at
Grauman's Chinese Theater and
encouraging reviews,* Park Row
failed at the box office.

"I've put off dying waiting for a new voice that needs to be heard. You are that new voice, Mr. Mitchell. Now that I have found a man worthy enough to die for, I'm ready to die. The old press is silent. If there's a place where newspapermen go when the last edition is put to bed, I want to be there to hear the roar of *The Globe,* the thunder of her type. I want to be there still covering a story on the cuff of the last of the survivors who saw American journalism born on Park Row.

"Thirty."[3]

28

Don't Wave the Flag at Me

I hate violence. That has never prevented me from using it in my films. It's part of human nature. People have been writing about violence since the Bible. Holy smoke, *that's* one helluva violent book, a running account of wars, feuds, corruption, and vengeance! Jump ahead a couple thousand years and take a look at Shakespeare's work. His plays are full of raw, uncamouflaged bloodletting. Children are thrown over castle walls, fathers and mothers murdered, throats slit, tongues cut out, heads severed. Certainly, all that violence is deplorable, but alas, it's part of our brutal heritage.

Our world is still a very new one. We can only trace it back a few thousand years. Maybe in another couple thousand years, violence won't exist in any form. I hope so. Future audiences might watch our movies and wonder how we could have been so barbaric, just like when we watch gladiator movies and shake our heads at those ancient Romans organizing gruesome spectacles with man-eating lions in packed coliseums. For cryin' out loud, that was *their* show business.

Like the air we breathe, violence is always there, all around us. Animals kill when they're hungry. Man kills for power. And man's lust for absolute power fosters totalitarian governments, the most destructive of all goddamned regimes. Violence breeds violence. Even a nonviolent person, when attacked, will kill if he or she has to defend a loved one. Inexplicably, some people have a ticking time bomb in their brains. Sex, religion, politics, or a dripping faucet can make them go berserk. No one knows when they'll blow. A good story probes why and how they resort to violence, then follows them to some kind of resolution.

If you're trying to be honest, how can you make a gangster movie or a Western without showing their savage tools of trade? How can you tell a story about war without showing the bloody absurdity of warfare? How can you depict gangsters, cowboys, or soldiers motivated by anything other than their will to survive? You can't, unless you're John Wayne.

Don't get me wrong, I loved Wayne personally. But he became a star because audiences were sold fantasy, which, unfortunately, sells better than fact. Entertaining as they are, those heroes that Wayne played just didn't exist in reality. See, one thing I hate in Wayne's war movies is when some officer invariably says, "These men have given their lives for their country."

What bullshit! They didn't *give* their lives. Their lives were *taken away*. They were *robbed*. When we signed up for military service, if somebody had told us from the get-go that we had to give our lives, nobody would've enlisted. We all thought we'd make it back to our wives and mothers. Sure, there are madmen who know in advance they're going to die, guys like kamikaze pilots, terrorists, or mad bombers. They are usually part of a lethal fringe that borders on hysteria.

I hope one day, maybe in the year 2293, a film student will be analyzing one of my films on a desktop gizmo. He'll ask his professor what's that funny "thing" the soldier is holding. "Well, my boy," the professor will answer, "that was a weapon, in those days. They called it a 'rifle.' You only see them in museums nowadays. We no longer need weapons."

With *Park Row* under my belt, Zanuck gave me a script called *Blaze of Glory*, written by Dwight Taylor. Darryl thought this yarn should be my next Fox movie. I liked the idea. A woman lawyer falls in love with a criminal she's defending in a murder trial. I knew from my newspaper days that courtroom cases take a long time to play out. So I told Darryl that I'd like to do a story about an outlaw and his gal, but that I wanted to go down a few rungs lower on the ladder of criminality. Why not make the lead a small-time thief, a pickpocket, for example, a wily guy who lives in the shadow world of petty criminality? Zanuck had his doubts, but he let me go to work on an original script, fleshing out the main characters and redoing the story my own way.

Skip McCoy is the pickpocket, known as a "cannon," on the street, with a record of three convictions. Completely antisocial, he's an outsider who doesn't give a damn about the rest of the world. The only use he has for a newspaper is to conceal his nimble fingers when he's grifting a purse. This time, the purse belongs to Candy, a good-looking, streetwise dame with a checkered past. My cop's called Tiger, the captain of the anti-pickpocket brigade who's trying to put Skip away for life. Moe is an old lady who makes a living by selling information, a stoolie whose one goal is to save up enough money for a decent cemetery plot. That way, she'll escape the most hated fate of poor people. "If I was to be buried in Potter's Field, it'd just about kill me," says Moe.

All over the world, you'll find small-time crooks like Skip, Candy, and

Richard Widmark was perfect for the role of Skip in Pickup, *an antihero you root for even though he doesn't do a damn thing to deserve it, except beat the crap out of my heavy in the climactic subway scene.*

Moe living on the underbelly of society, struggling to survive with their scams, abiding by their own unwritten code of ethics. I'd seen plenty of these people firsthand when I was a crime reporter. They are individualists, trusting no one, beyond politics, changes in governments, intellectual labels, and fashion.

My yarn opens in the New York subway at rush hour. There isn't a single word of dialogue in the scene. People are packed together on the crowded train like sardines. Candy is being trailed by two FBI agents when Skip masterfully edges closer and closer to her and slowly opens her pocketbook, drawing out her purse with his agile fingers. Like a neurosurgeon, his hands are his future. Skip doesn't know that there's a piece of microfilm in Candy's grifted purse. It contains a new patent for a chemical formula. Joey, her ex-boyfriend and a sonofabitch, is selling the hot item to some communist spy ring. Candy's making the delivery until Skip filches the microfilm without knowing its value. Joey and the spies will go to any length to recover it.

Thanks to Moe's tip, the cops haul Skip in for questioning. An FBI agent tries to make Skip cooperate, but he's contemptuous of all authority. Naturally, he's only thinking about saving his own skin. Skip's too marginal and irreverent to fall for their patriotic appeals.

FBI AGENT
That film you stole had government information on it. Classified. We'd been following this
girl for months. And just as we were about to
grab a top Red Agent receiving the film from
her, you broke up the ball game. Now can't
you see how important this is? We just want
your cooperation and the charges against you
will be dropped. Isn't that right, Captain?

TIGER
You know, I'd like to make this rap stick. But
what he's got to do is more important.

SKIP
Well, you guys are talking in the wrong corner. I'm just a guy keepin' my hands in my
own pockets.

FBI AGENT
If you refuse to cooperate, you'll be as guilty as
the traitors that gave Stalin the A-Bomb![1]

SKIP
Are you waving the flag at me?

TIGER
I know something that you should get. . . .

SKIP
And I know you picked me up three times,
got me convicted three times. And made me a
3-time loser. And I know you took an oath to
put me away for life. Well, you're tryin' awful
hard with all this patriotic eyewash. But get
this. I didn't grift that film and you can't prove
I did. And if I said I did, you'd slap that fourth
rap across my teeth no matter what promises
you made.

FBI AGENT
You know what "treason" means?

SKIP
Who cares?

TIGER
Answer the man!

SKIP
Is there a law now that I got to listen to lectures?

That night, Candy comes looking for the microfilm at Skip's shack on the waterfront. In the dark, he takes a swing at the intruder's jaw, and cold-cocks her. They end up in each other's arms, kissing passionately. It's a mercenary kiss. Candy and Skip both want something from each other. It isn't sex. Neither of them yet knows the microfilm's importance. Candy's naïve about politics, but she's streetwise. She knows Skip's not a nice guy. She'll never see him feeding birds in the park. He's too busy scheming his next scam. Yet she's attracted to his no-bullshit style.

Skip quickly figures out how he can get a bundle for the precious microfilm, setting himself up for the rest of his life. And he isn't going to let Candy botch up the deal. No woman is worth that. He wants nothing to do with women. Home? Family? Love? Useless middle-class pipe dreams to Skip. Candy irritates the hell out of him, interfering with his work. Everything changes when Candy gets beaten up trying to save Skip's life. Why would anyone risk her neck for him? It makes no sense in Skip's primitive world, where sacrifice is laughable. Nevertheless, the seeds of love have been planted.

All the newspapers at that time in the United States were talking about Klaus Fuchs, the spy who operated from England, selling secrets on microfilm to the Soviet Union. There was general paranoia in our country about communists. Richard Nixon had just been chosen as the Republican vice presidential candidate, having made a name with his phony Alger Hiss exposé.

But alluding to those cases, I wanted to take a poke at the idiocy of the cold war climate of the fifties. Sure, there were communists who believed fervently in Marx and Lenin. But there were also crumbs like Joey who'd go to work for any "ism" if there was a payoff. People living on the edge of society don't give a damn about politics. I wanted my film to be told through the eyes of the powerless. Cold war paranoia? Hell, these crooks were more interested in just getting by.

One of my first casting choices was the great Thelma Ritter as Moe, the stoolie. She is at the bottom of the criminal food chain but understands

Captain Tiger, played by Murvyn Vye, extracts information from Moe, the stoolie, played by Thelma Ritter.

the difference between her and Joey's kind of crooks. One night, Moe comes back to her dingy rooming house after a hard day peddling ties and information. She puts a French record on her Victrola. Joey comes out of the shadows with a pistol, putting his dirty shoes up on her clean bed. He's in a rush to get the microfilm back.

MOE
. . . *You* haven't got a lot of time? Listen, Mister, when I come in here tonight, you seen an old clock runnin' down. I'm tired. I'm through. It happens to everybody, sometime. It'll happen to you too someday. With me, it's . . . a little bit of everything . . . backaches, headaches. I can't sleep nights. It's so hard to get up in the morning and . . . and get dressed . . . walk the streets. Climb the stairs. I go right on doin' it. Well, what am I gonna do? Knock it? I have to go out and make a livin' so I can die. But even a fancy funeral ain't worth waitin' for if I have to do business

with crumbs like you! And I know what you're
after.

JOEY
What do you know?

MOE
I know you Commies are lookin' for some
film that don't belong to you.

JOEY
You just talked yourself into an early grave.
What else do you know?

MOE
What do I know about Commies? Nothing. I
know one thing: I just don't like them.

(*Hearing JOEY cocking his pistol*)
So I don't get to have the fancy funeral after
all? Anyway, I tried. Look, Mister, I'm so tired,
you'll be doing me a big favor if you blow my
head off.

My camera panned to the Victrola. As the French ballad plays on, the
scene closes with a violent pistol shot. That ballad was a popular French
tune entitled "Mam'zelle." I went to see Al "Pappy" Newman, the legendary music composer at Fox, to see how we could get those rights from
France. Newman burst out laughing.

"That song's not French!" said Newman. "Edmund Goulding wrote the
song himself for *The Razor's Edge*. We already own it."

Goulding, a veteran director, stopped by my office one day during preproduction, happy that I wanted to use his little song for my picture. A
lovely man, Goulding was in the twilight of his career, having made pictures since the twenties with every major Hollywood star, notably Greta
Garbo in *Grand Hotel* (1932), Paul Muni in *We Are Not Alone* (1939), and
Bette Davis in *The Great Lie* (1941). Goulding told me his secret ambition
had always been to be a songwriter, so he was delighted for me to use his
tune.

I was going to call my film *Pick-Pocket*, and this was years before Robert
Bresson would make his film with that title, in 1959. As we started prepro-

duction, Zanuck called me in for a meeting with some top executives at
Fox. They loved the project, but not the title. It was too "European,"
whatever the hell that meant. I argued without prevailing. They asked me
to come up with another title. I had *Cannon* in mind, but that would've
conveyed the idea of a war movie. New York's South Street had a special
memory for me from my newsboy days, so I came up with *Pickup on South
Street.*

For my research, I went back to New York and paid a visit to Detective
Dan Campion of the NYPD. He gave me plenty of background material
to make *Pickup* look realistic. Campion knew every cannon in the city.
They knew him, too. One look at Campion's face on a subway and any
self-respecting pickpocket who wanted to stay out of prison abandoned his
prey instantly. The captain gave the cannons some rope to exercise their
craft, though you never saw that kind of thing in a movie. When Campion
came down on a pickpocket, he came down hard. He'd been suspended
without salary for six months for manhandling a suspect. I based Tiger on
Campion, making my cop one tough sonofabitch, too.

The movie's decor came from sketches I drew for Lyle Wheeler. The
look of *Pickup on South Street* was primordial. How could you tell a story
about petty thieves, informers, and spy rings without a realistic portrayal
of their dilapidated, predatory world? The murky bars. The flophouses.
The out-of-the-way streets. The tattoo parlors. The subway stations.

In the fifties, filmmakers like Roberto Rossellini, Vittorio De Sica, and
Luchino Visconti had established a gritty visual style with *Rome, Open City*
(1946), *The Bicycle Thief* (1948), and *Bellissima* (1951). They shot their films
on city streets, capturing everyday life in postwar Italy. I envied their
"neorealistic" approach, because I was stuck on the back lot at Twentieth
Century Fox with make-believe streets. I needed the noise, the traffic, the
towering buildings, the elevators, the alleys, the things that make a big city
feel like a big city.

Lyle Wheeler could work wonders on a Hollywood soundstage. I asked
him to make *Pickup* look as natural as possible. What great work Wheeler
did for that picture! For example, he made Skip's shack on the waterfront
look just right. I remembered those rickety wooden things built on pilings
over the water, connected to the shore by wooden bridges oscillating above
the river. Two-bit criminals lived down there. They put their beer into
wooden crates and, with a rope and pulley, lowered their drinks down into
the river to keep them cool. My pickpocket lives in one of those shacks
and chills his beer in the river too. Except Skip arranges his booty in cello-
phane paper and hides it in the false bottom of his refrigerator crate,
knowing exactly what he's going to do with every hot item he's filched.

Preproduction on Pickup on South Street *meant making the sets look believable. Skip's waterfront shack by Lyle Wheeler was essential.*

Being on Lyle's sets for *Pickup* was like being transported back to the beguiling Manhattan of my journalism days on the *Graphic*.

The sets for the movie were coming together faster than the cast. The only actor I ever had in mind to play my lead was Richard Widmark, who was under contract at Fox then. A born individualist, Widmark had a strange face, with that twisted, arrogant smile, that didn't fit into anybody's scheme of Hollywood handsomeness. He walked and talked like nobody else, yet there was nothing ostentatious about him, the kind of man who wouldn't call too much attention to himself on a crowded subway. Widmark was perfect for Skip.

Plenty of actresses approached me about playing Candy. Shelley Winters wanted to do it, but she wasn't right for the part. Ava Gardner was after me to read for it. She was too luscious a beauty to be credible. The character's not sexy enough to be a hooker, not smart enough to be a housewife. Betty Grable wanted the role as long as she got a dance number. For Chrissakes, a dance number! Even if she was one of the highest-paid stars in Hollywood at that time, Grable wasn't at all right. I needed my Candy to be an average-looking woman, not a glamour-puss. Grable started lobbying Zanuck for the role. We were approaching the production start date, and I still didn't have the right actress for the part.

We turned our attention to other characters. I'd seen Richard Kiley on a TV drama and picked him to be Joey, the communist agent. Kiley played my heavy with just the right amount of paranoid fury. It was hard to believe that in real life, Richard was a devout Catholic, a loving family guy with lots of children. Kiley would later become famous playing that marvelous dreamer, my kindred spirit, Don Quijote in *Man of La Mancha*. As Moe, Thelma Ritter would give one helluva performance, for which she'd receive an Oscar nomination. For Tiger, I brought the solid Murvyn Vye out from New York.

One day, I was rehearsing Widmark and Vye in my office at Fox along with Billy Gordon, our casting director. A good-looking gal appeared at the doorway, a scarf over her hair, wearing sunglasses, a big sweater, and no makeup. We all looked up. For a split second, you couldn't tell who it was.

"Can I just sit here and watch you work, Sammy?" said Marilyn Monroe, with that breathless voice of hers. "I'll be as quiet as a mouse."

I motioned her in with a wave of my cigar. I'd crossed paths with Monroe at the studio, and we'd become pals. Who could forget those sparkling eyes and that radiant skin of hers? Monroe sat down in a corner and watched us rehearse, never uttering a sound. After the session was over, Marilyn asked me if she could read for the part of Candy. I gave her a script and showed her the scene I wanted her to do. There was something childlike about her that you wanted to protect, an innocence that was sincere and untainted. After she read for a while, I knew she wasn't at all what I had in mind for the part. Marilyn didn't speak, she purred. I told her straight that if she walked along my decrepit waterfront, her overwhelming sensuality would obscure my yarn. She was so disappointed. I put my arm around her and said we'd look for another picture to do together.

When Billy Gordon first proposed Jean Peters for my female lead, I didn't even want to have her read for the part. I'd seen her in an uninspired sword-and-dagger picture directed by Henry King, *Captain from Castille* (1947). Then one day I was having lunch with Henry and actress Jeanne Crain at the studio commissary. Jean Peters came by our table, and I was introduced to her. Jean had just finished her biggest role yet, playing Marlon Brando's wife in Elia Kazan's *Viva Zapata!* (1952). She had a lilting voice. As she walked away from us, I looked at Peters's pert figure and her legs and thought to myself that she had Candy's bowed legs, the kind of gams you get from streetwalking. Peters came to read for me on a Friday afternoon. The sets were all built. We were going to shoot a week from that coming Monday.

"So," said Jean, smiling. "I guess I'm the bottom of the barrel."

"Not at all," I said. "I just didn't like those phony gypsies in *Captain from Castille.*"

"Blame your pal Henry King, not me," she said. "I'm just an actress. Besides, that was my first movie."

I loved her spunkiness. We chatted for a long time about a wide range of subjects, from literature to politics. I found myself talking with a very intelligent woman, a fine human being. Jean read a scene. I realized she was perfect for the part and told her she was going to be Candy. Jean asked only that she be accorded the same rehearsal time as Widmark and Ritter. She knew that she had to hold her own with two experienced actors. So in the final hectic week of preproduction, I came in at dawn and worked with her every morning from six to ten a.m.

A big car would slowly drive onto the Fox lot and deliver Jean to my bungalow-type office right on time every morning. While we rehearsed the scenes, Jean's driver sat behind the wheel of the car reading newspapers. He always wore sunglasses. I couldn't make out his face, but I knew the big guy wasn't just reading. He was constantly keeping an eye on Jean, too. When we finished the session, Jean went outside and got into the front seat of the waiting car and they drove away. On the second day of rehearsal, it became pretty obvious that the driver was her boyfriend. I asked Jean if she wanted her fellow to come inside and wait for her on the couch in the outer office where he'd be more comfortable.

"No, no, it's fine this way," she said, grinning at me.

Widmark came by the last couple of mornings and ran through the love scenes with Jean. There she was in Richard's arms, rehearsing hot embraces and smoldering lines. Jean's boyfriend observed their make-believe passion from the driver's seat of the big car parked outside. It was a little uncomfortable at first, then we forgot about the situation. One of my secretaries clued me in. Jean's driver who never budged from the parked car was Howard Hughes. Hell, one of the richest and most powerful men in the

Candy (Jean Peters) is grilled by Captain Tiger (Murvyn Vye) and an FBI agent, trying to manipulate her into cooperating with them. She won't.

world was chauffeuring Jean to my morning rehearsals and keeping a watchful eye on the proceedings. At the time, their romance was top secret. Hughes ended up marrying Peters, the woman he was so zealously chaperoning.

During those last rehearsals, and only a couple of days before the picture was to begin shooting, I got an urgent call from Zanuck's secretary to get over to Darryl's office on the double. I rushed out. When I got there, Darryl might as well have hit me in the face with a baseball bat. Betty Grable was insisting that she be in my picture, even if she didn't get to dance. To make matters worse, Grable had an option in her contract with

Fox that stipulated she had to be indemnified if she were turned down for any role she wanted. To refuse her would cost the studio three hundred grand.

I told Zanuck I wouldn't do the film without Jean Peters. But I was stuck. If I walked, I knew that there were other directors who'd be happy to direct the picture with Grable. Forlornly, I went back to my office. I said nothing about the situation. Rehearsals continued. The scenes flowed so naturally with Peters. I had the whole film in my head visually with her as Candy. I put the situation with Grable out of my head until a little before six that afternoon. The phone rang. It sounded like a death knell.

"You're shooting on Monday," Zanuck said. "With Peters."

My heart pumped with joy. I don't know how Zanuck arranged it with Grable, but, once again, he'd stood by me. I never mentioned the Grable incident to Jean. She was a pleasure to work with, exquisite and dedicated, a true professional.

When we were already into production, Jean asked me one day, "What made you change your mind about me, Sammy?"

"The truth?" I said.

"The truth."

"Your legs, kid. They're very sexy. They're also a little arched. I'm not saying a tank could drive through them. But maybe a small jeep."

Peters laughed warmly. She was a good sport, easy to work with, fun to be around. To shoot those legs the way I wanted, I placed a camera below the rickety bridge to Skip's shack. Jean walked across it with a little sashay, her hips swinging, the bridge swinging, the whole set swinging. My cameraman, Joe MacDonald, innovated to get that shot just the way I wanted. To make other scenes look real, MacDonald took a helluva lot of risks for me. He shot sequences in one single camera movement, not knowing what the hell we had in the can until we'd looked at the dailies. It was the first time in his career that MacDonald had worked like that and he loved it.

At first, Richard Widmark was cantankerous and insular, sometimes thoroughly uncooperative. As a star at Fox, he had an attitude. I didn't give a damn about his status. The only thing that mattered to me was the work. It was inevitable that we would knock heads. The first week of production, we set up the scene when the cops bring Skip into Tiger's office for questioning. I told Widmark I wanted him to zigzag through the police desks, pausing here and there to comment on a guy's tie, filch a piece of candy, then stroll casually into Tiger's office. Widmark looked at me with that superior grin of his.

"Why wouldn't I just breeze straight into the captain's office?" said Widmark.

I looked into his face silently, took a puff on my cigar, and shrugged. I turned to the assistant director and said, "Strike the set! Let's move straight into the captain's office!"

We started setting up the following scene. Widmark was caught off guard with my instantaneous acceptance of his refusal to follow direction. He turned to the script supervisor and asked why in the hell would his character zigzag through the police desks. She explained to him that the pickpocket had been hauled into police headquarters so many times before that it was like a second home. Skip would have known all those guys. The zigzagging would have shown his familiarity with the place and the people.

"You know, Sam," Richard said as I was preparing the next scene, "that zigzagging stuff sounds pretty good."

"Too late," I said. "The set's struck. We're in here now. Let's move on."

He stood there wordlessly, the smirk wiped off his face. During the rest of the shoot, I rarely had any more trouble with Widmark following my directions.

We finished the picture on schedule. When it was released, it got the full rainbow of reviews. Critics judged *Pickup* according to the ax they had to grind. Liberals welcomed the movie as outspoken about cold war nonsense. Conservatives condemned it as pro-communist. A screening was set up for J. Edgar Hoover in Washington. He really hated it. Zanuck told me Hoover called the studio to raise hell about my hero being "anti-American." The pickpocket's political apathy infuriated Hoover. However, Skip's a guy who doesn't give a shit about the cold war. He isn't letting anything get between him and a big score. The character is true to himself. I didn't give a damn whether Hoover approved or not. I figured that, after *Steel Helmet,* the FBI had been keeping a file on me anyway. *Pickup* would give them some more material to chew on.

One of the movie's themes is about rushing to judgment. Skip doesn't condemn Moe when she sells information on him to the police. She's got to earn a buck. Moe reserves judgment on Candy, despite her questionable past. Candy doesn't look down on Skip for picking pockets to make a living. Nobody in this milieu is quick to judge others, because everyone is struggling to survive.

The picture was invited to the 1953 Venice Film Festival. There, the French critic Georges Sadoul, a Stalinist, crucified *Pickup* as anticommunist propaganda. Other lefty critics were outraged by *Pickup* too. There was a resurgent communist party in France with powerful press ties. The

A ceremony at the Italian consulate to present the Bronze Lion that Pickup *won at the 1953 Venice Film Festival. Thelma Ritter, my Moe, was with me on this proud occasion.*

French distributor of the film would be so intimidated by all the hulabaloo that, before the film opened in Paris, he retitled my movie as *Le Port de la Drogue—Port of Drugs—* changing the French-dubbed version so that, instead of microfilm destined for the communists, the pickpocket intercepts a drug shipment. The French not only tampered with my title but with the movie's basic story. I was furious. France! Where I thought the artist's work was revered, no matter his or her politics. What bullshit! I had no intention of making a political statement in *Pickup,* none whatsoever. My yarn is a noir thriller about marginal people, nothing more, nothing less.

I didn't make it to Venice because I was working on *Hell and High Water* that summer. Early one morning, I was preparing for a scene on one of Fox's big sound studios when Tyrone Power came up to me on the set with the morning edition of the *Los Angeles Times.*

"You're on the front page, Sammy," said Power. "Congratulations."

"What for?" I asked.

"*Pickup* won a prize in Venice."

I grabbed the paper out of Tyrone's hands and read the article about receiving the festival's Bronze Lion. I didn't give a damn about awards. But it thrilled me to learn that the president of the Venice jury that year had been Luchino Visconti. I wouldn't find out for many years that Visconti had actually opposed my winning the prize because of his own communist convictions. He was overruled by the other jury members, who thought *Pickup* was just a damn good movie.

29

Wide-Screen
Sub Picture

Easily, my least favorite picture is *Hell and High Water*, though it wasn't a stinker. It's just that the movie didn't come from one of my own stories or original scripts. See, after *Pickup* was released, plenty of scripts came my way, but nothing I could get my teeth into. One day, Darryl Zanuck called me into his office and handed me *Hell and High Water*, by Jesse Lasky Jr. and Beirne Lay, based on an article by David Hempstead. Beirne was a friend of mine, an army pilot in the war. He'd already written *Toward the Unknown* (1956) for Mervyn LeRoy and *Twelve O'Clock High* (1950) for Henry King. Zanuck asked me to give the project serious consideration.

Most of the action in the yarn took place on a submarine. A private peace organization wants to discover if the communists are developing an A-bomb somewhere in the Arctic Circle. The picture's cliché-ridden premise was what I liked the least. They hire a veteran U-boat skipper to make a secret voyage to the North Pole in a reconditioned sub. A couple of nuclear scientists are brought along to uncover the truth.

Zanuck said it would be a personal favor if I directed that picture. He didn't say why and didn't need to. Zanuck had always championed me. He didn't always agree with me but he'd tell me face-to-face, no matter. Once he'd okayed a project, Zanuck was there for me, always fighting for my vision. Hell, Zanuck even stood up to J. Edgar Hoover for me.

The FBI chief was very disturbed about *Pickup on South Street* and wanted to see Zanuck and me about it. A lunch meeting was set up at Romanoff's. Hoover was sitting alone at a table in the back. His squad of bodyguards in black suits were at the next table. They never took their eyes off Darryl and me as we sat down across from Hoover and one of his top Los Angeles lieutenants. The FBI chief told me he didn't care for *The Steel Helmet* or *Fixed Bayonets*, but that *Pickup on South Street* had gone too far. First of all, he didn't like the hero doing business with both communists and Americans.

"How could an American think only about money at a time like this in our history?" Hoover asked.

"He doesn't give a damn about history," I explained. "He's an outlaw. The guy's only motivation is to score."

What Hoover hated the most was the scene when the FBI agent asks the pickpocket to cooperate.

" 'Are you waving the flag at me?' " said Hoover, reading from some notes. "What kind of a thing is that for an American to say?"

"That's his character," I replied. If it were another character, I explained, he might say, "By God, I'll do anything for my country!" Hoover was like some of the biased critics I've run into over the years. They look at everything exclusively from their own perspective. If a movie is in line with their position, it's good. If it's out of line, it's bad. Hell, a writer has to write from the character's viewpoint. I explained to Hoover that if I write believable dialogue for an unpatriotic character, it doesn't make me un-American. It's not *me* talking, it's my character.

Hoover was also shocked at the way the G-man in the movie, working with a New York cop, bribes a stool pigeon to get information.

"The Department of Justice would never do that," he said.

"Mr. Hoover, I was a reporter in the precincts myself," I said. "I've seen cops haggling with the Feds about fink money. I've even seen the Feds give cash to the cops for stoolies."

The power that Hoover wielded back then was incredible. The truth about the formidable FBI chief wouldn't be known until many years later. There he was, questioning my integrity and honesty while he was blackmailing people to keep himself in power.

Zanuck never flinched in his support for my work. Hoover asked that the offending scenes in *Pickup* be cut or reshot. Politely, Zanuck refused. "Mr. Hoover, you don't know movies," he said. He might as well have been telling the director to go fuck himself.

So I agreed to make *Hell and High Water* for Fox. I insisted, however, on rewriting the script to suit my style, and Zanuck gave me the green light. The picture was supposed to be an adventure movie, but it was just too predictable. For me, an adventure movie is about my hero searching for something. Say he's looking for a certain lion. He goes to Africa to find the beast. He starts searching at point A. But for some unexpected reason, he gets lost at point C. That's when the goddamned adventure really begins.

I reworked *Hell and High Water* into a stylized, cartoonish tale, like Spielberg would achieve later on with *Raiders of the Lost Ark*. Zanuck approved my version of the script, as did Lasky and Lay, the original screenwriters. Above all, Darryl wanted me to shoot the movie in CinemaScope. Fox had bought the rights to the new process from a French company in 1952. All the studios were rushing wide-screen movies into production to compete with the burgeoning television networks. Thanks to Henri-Jacques Chrétien's anamorphic lens, the normal 1.85 ratio of a movie image was lengthened to 2.35, meaning that the picture up on the screen was about 25 percent wider.

The first three films released in CinemaScope in 1953 had been box-office hits: Henry Koster's *The Robe,* Jean Negulesco's *How to Marry a Millionaire,* and Robert D. Webb's *Beneath the 12-Mile Reef.* Audiences wanted more. To play the films, theaters had to outfit their projectors with new lenses and install new screens. The studios wanted the theaters to commit to the improvements, but theater owners resisted the investment, complaining that the first releases in CinemaScope didn't have enough action.

Like other directors, I was initially suspicious of CinemaScope. Fritz Lang complained that the wide-screen format was "good only for snakes and funerals." Henry Koster had invited me onto the set of *The Robe,* where I saw how gigantic everything was. Camera movements were minimal, because the new lens captured so much of the panorama. Characters kept walking around the set without the camera having to pan. Director Jean Negulesco told me CinemaScope had changed the way he directed, and not for the better. It was like working in a theater, the camera as stationary as the audience. I listened to him respectfully. Jean was an old pro, having made thirty-five pictures by then, including *Humoresque* (1946) and *Johnny Belinda* (1948). But when I saw the finished version of his *How to Marry a Millionaire,* I realized that Negulesco made CinemaScope serve the story, and not the opposite. The panoramas of New York were great, not to mention those of Monroe, Grable, and Bacall.

Negulesco's *Millionaire* gave me an idea. I'd make the new technology work for me too. I met with Monsieur Chrétien, who was in California. We got along great. Chrétien gave me one of his special anamorphic lenses for my old 16-mm camera. I shot some footage in CinemaScope myself, practicing with the enlarged field of view. Fox executives were anxious to see if a CinemaScope movie could be made without gigantic sets and thousands of extras. They had a helluva lot of money invested in that contraption. I told Zanuck I was going to have a lot of camera movement.

"Do whatever you want with the damn camera," Darryl told me. "Just make people forget it's CinemaScope."

So I had the camera moving all the time on *Hell and High Water.* I panned it. I put it on boom. I did dolly shots inside the submarine. I even staged the final fight scene like a ballet, with the goddamned camera swinging all over the place.

As for cast, I hired Richard Widmark again as my lead, playing the sub commander Adam Jones. For the part of my nuclear scientist, I chose Victor Francen, a Belgian actor under contract over at Warner Brothers, where they had him playing Nazis in war movies. Victor had a dry sense of humor that I loved, and we became good friends. I wrote special dialogue for Victor so that he could use his sarcasm freely in his scenes with the submarine crew.

During rehearsals one day, Victor brought a French movie magazine to the set. It was called *Cahiers du Cinema* (*Cinema Notebooks*). It had a distinctive yellow cover and was edited by a man named André Bazin. The magazine's contributors were young men named Jean-Luc Godard, François Truffaut, and Luc Moullet. I'd never heard of the magazine or its writers. The publication was refreshing, with passionate, in-depth articles about techniques and themes in contemporary movies. Victor translated a few passages from *Cahiers* that praised me and my work. I was surprised and thrilled. That was the beginning of a long love affair. I was a fan of the magazine for many years. *Cahiers* was a fervent supporter of my work. Luc Moullet later wrote an article comparing me to Christopher Marlowe. Marlowe, for Chrissakes! I could hardly shave after that came out, having to look at myself in the mirror, the ghost of Doctor Faustus over my shoulder.

For the role of the professor's multilingual assistant in *Hell and High Water*, the studio's casting department wanted me to try out a young actress who'd recently arrived from Europe. Her stage name was Bella Darvi (born Bayla Wegier). Bella was smart and beautiful. All I knew about her then was that she was Polish and had been in a concentration camp during the war. Zanuck had taken me aside once to explain that the girl was his protégée. The name "Darvi" was conceived as a combination of Darryl's name and his wife's, Virginia. Zanuck was steering the girl's career, but I didn't guarantee him the girl would get the part. I insisted on doing a screen test with Bella, shooting her in one of the opening scenes that introduces her scientific training and language skills. She'd play the role if I liked her acting. I did. When I hired her, I didn't know anything about her personal life. I found out later that Zanuck and Bella were having an affair. I cast Bella because she was the right person for the role. She was convincing in the part and professional on set. We all had a good time working with her.

Later, when it became public knowledge that she was Zanuck's mistress, Bella became a scapegoat for anybody who didn't like Darryl. Ugly rumors started flying. See, I don't really care about people's personal lives. That's their business, as long as they conduct themselves as professionals. I

YOU SEE IT WITHOUT GLASSES IN... **CinemaScope**

20th Century-Fox presents

RICHARD **WIDMARK**

BELLA **DARVI**

with

VICTOR **FRANCEN**

CAMERON **MITCHELL**

GENE **EVANS**

DAVID **WAYNE**

Stephen Bekassy · Richard Loo

in

HELL AND HIGH WATER

PRODUCED BY RAYMOND A. KLUNE · DIRECTED BY SAMUEL FULLER · JESSE L. LASKY, JR. AND SAMUEL FULLER SCREEN PLAY BY TECHNICOLOR DELUXE Based on a Story by DAVID HEMPSTEAD

Copyright 1954 20th Century-Fox Film Corp.   COUNTRY OF ORIGIN U. S. A.   3   Property of National Screen Service Corp. Licensed for display only in connection with the exhibition of this picture at your theatre. Must be returned immediately thereafter.   54-37

The official poster from the release of my wide-screen sub film featured (from left to right) Gene Evans, Richard Widmark, Victor Francen, and Bella Darvi.

couldn't give a damn who they *are* or *aren't* sleeping with. Besides, most rumors are bullshit. I avoid listening to that crap unless it's so funny and unusual that I can use it in a script. As for gossip, it's horrible, and so are the people who spread it. I've been the target of gossip, lies, and innuendos for as long as I've been in the movie business. It's no big deal. My advice to young directors? Laugh and forget it.

To prepare myself for shooting *Hell and High Water,* I went to see Frank McCarthy, an old friend of mine who'd been an aide-de-camp to General George Marshall and had become a consultant at Fox. Frank arranged for me to spend a couple of days on a navy submarine stationed off San Clemente Island. The captain allowed me to time every maneuver they performed, from taking the sub down to the bottom to bringing it up again. I bombarded the captain with questions about the sailors' lives underwater. If the information wasn't classified, he was always cooperative.

One day, I asked the captain if someone's hand had ever gotten caught in the hatch when the sub was about to dive. One of the sailors within earshot laughed and held up his left hand, which had only two fingers on it, explaining that his other fingers had been lost in exactly such an accident. I used that in the movie. Victor Francen's Professor Montel gets his

finger caught in the sub's hatch, and it has to be sliced off with a knife by
the sub commander.

Fox's special-effects man, Ray Kellogg, devised miniature submarines
for me and helped me shoot the movie's underwater scenes in an enormous water basin on Fox's back lot. Ray became a good friend. He'd been
in the marines during the war and had worked on a bunch of John Ford's
movies. I discovered that a sub could move like a murderer lying in wait
for his prey, so I decided to film the U-boats in underwater battle like two
men in hand-to-hand combat, locked in mortal confrontation. Intent on
killing each other, they hide, hold their breath, then pounce when the
other is least expecting it. I also wanted to give the audience the visceral
emotion of being cooped up underwater. I'd spent no more than fifteen
hours under the Pacific on that U-boat, yet it was like being buried alive.
Weeks on end would drive you completely nuts. Men in those conditions
could easily become maniac murderers.

The final evening I was on the navy sub, the captain presented me with
a beautiful souvenir diploma signed by the whole crew. We were submerged during the ceremony, sailing back to port. Without warning, the
lights on the sub went red. The captain explained that red lights were standard operating procedure for getting the crew's eyes accustomed to the
darkness when they surfaced at night. That gave me the idea to put a scene
in *Hell and High Water* that would be shot entirely with red lights.

My cameraman, Joe MacDonald, told me it would be impossible to
have all the lights go red during the sequence without cutting away to
another shot. There wasn't any room on the crowded set for another set of
lamps.

"Then make room, Joe," I said.

"Impossible, Sam."

"Look, Joe," I said, thinking as I puffed on my cigar for a moment.
"Nobody in the audience has ever been in a sub. Nobody knows what the
hell the interior of a sub looks like. Just put the lamps in the shot. They'll
think that they're part of the sub's equipment."

That's exactly what he did. You can see the red lights when the camera
dollies around the sub's cramped compartment. No one really cared except
Joe.

Hell and High Water begins with a nuclear bomb going off, then the
credits roll. The idea of displaying the credits next to the mushroom cloud
was my way of saying that this bomb may seem like an ally today but
could become your worst enemy tomorrow. The bomb footage was real,
acquired from military archives. The government made us erase certain
colors from the sequence "that could reveal nuclear secrets." We acqui-
esced, but I didn't understand what the hell they were talking about.

The movie did good box office at home and abroad. They had big premieres in Los Angeles, New York, and London. George Jessel emceed the one in New York, and Noël Coward did the one in London. Believe it or not, the picture was a big hit in Germany. Here was a military adventure without a word about Nazis. For a country trying to come to grips with the aftermath of a world war, *Hell and High Water* was like a breath of fresh air.

Lefty European critics wrote that the picture was anticommunist propaganda. For Chrissakes, it was an adventure yarn. Besides, I don't make propaganda films. When I write a book or a script or make a movie, I'm only interested in one thing: a good story. If the story has conflict, there's action. If there's action, there's emotion. That's what I call a movie. See, 95 percent of all movies are made because people have to earn a living. That's okay. Only 5 percent are made because one passionate man or woman had an idea and nothing could stop him or her from getting it up on the screen. Sure, I've done a few bread-and-butter movies. But far and away, my pictures are "must makes." I'd come up with a story and I needed to tell it.

Zanuck and his studio executives were happy with my quirky little adventure picture. *Hell and High Water* made plenty of dough for Fox. As soon as I'd finished it, I packed my bags, said good-bye, and headed for London to write and direct a film with Trevor Howard at the invitation of the Woolf brothers, the producers behind John Huston's *The African Queen* (1951). How could I possibly know then that I'd actually end up in Japan shooting a totally different yarn with the veteran Robert Ryan and an up-and-comer named Robert Stack? But that's another chapter.

Fast forward twenty-five years. Cut to 1979 and the Hollywood studio where I was doing a walk-on for Steven Spielberg in his adventure picture *1941*. After lunch, Steven asked me to accompany him to the parking lot to see his car. I told him I didn't want to see his goddamned car, but Spielberg insisted. We got out there, and he explained that he always carried one of his favorite films around with him in his trunk. He opened the trunk. Believe it or not, he had a print of *Hell and High Water* in there.

Cherry Blossoms
and Whirligigs

My wife, Martha, and I took up residence in a posh apartment on Belgrave Square in London in the fall of 1954. My deal with Zanuck gave me six months off to do any picture I wanted. In those days, if you worked fast that was enough time to write, cast, and shoot a movie. I worked fast.

John and Jimmy Woolf were based in England. Thanks to John Huston, I'd met the Woolf brothers while they were on the West Coast and had hit it off with them. We ended up making a handshake deal to do a picture together. They put me up only a stone's throw from Hyde Park Corner. While I was walking around Kensington Gardens and St. James's Park, I'd figured out a way to rework my yarn about a bank heist committed by some ex-GIs. I'd set the story in England, with Trevor Howard and Celia Johnson as the leads. It would be my way of tipping my hat to David Lean's *Brief Encounter*. But the Woolf brothers and I didn't see things the same way. They wanted bigger stars. They also wanted me to eliminate scenes that they considered too violent, scenes that I knew were essential for my story. Things were not going well.

John and Jimmy Woolf were honorable, and they knew how to do things in style. As much as we tried, however, our project together didn't get off the ground. They'd go on to make *Room at the Top* (1959), *Of Human Bondage* (1964), *Oliver!* (1968), and *The Day of the Jackal* (1973). They were good men and good producers.

Zanuck called me from Hollywood to see how things were going in London. I had to admit I was unhappy about the turn of events.

"Sam, I want you to come home and direct *Soldier of Fortune*."

I knew the novel by Ernest Gann, a story about a mercenary hired to search for a woman's husband imprisoned by the Chinese.

"Come on, Darryl, that story's been done a million times," I said. "You know I like to do new yarns. Originals."

"But you'll get to work with Gable, Sam."

"Gable or not," I said, "that's not my cup of tea. People have seen it before."

"What about *The Left Hand of God*?" suggested Zanuck. "We own the book. We can get Bogart to star."

I'd read William E. Barrett's novel. I liked his heavy, a guy who disguises himself as a priest to escape the cops. I'd top that, showing the criminal climbing up the church's hierarchy until he finally becomes pope. The higher the sonofabitch's station, the more crimes he commits. Zanuck chuckled on the other end of the line.

"You'll get us all excommunicated, Sam! We're going to give it a military twist."

Edward Dmytryk ended up directing both those pictures for Fox. Even with Gable and Bogart, they were forgettable.

"What about Japan?" asked Zanuck. "Would you like to shoot a picture there?"

"Holy mackerel, Darryl, now you're talking!"

Zanuck knew me damn well. I'd been fascinated with the Orient all my life, read a great deal about it, and would jump at the chance to work there.

"No major studio has ever made a movie in Japan," Darryl told me. "Especially since the war."

"Let's go!" I yelled happily into the phone.

Zanuck wanted me to use Harry Kleiner's script from *Street with No Name* (1948) as source material. He had it couriered to me in London. I took Kleiner's structure—that of a police agent going undercover to infiltrate a gang of criminals—and wrote my own screenplay. I called it *House of Bamboo,* incorporating into the yarn some features from my story about ex-GIs planning crimes like military operations. I moved the entire she-bang to Tokyo, added stuff about Japanese contemporary life, threw in some sexual exploitation and interracial romance, and then, for some unexpected pizzazz, wrote a violent love scene between two hardened criminals. The core of the movie was about betrayal.

I put the final touches on the script and delivered it to Zanuck. Led by tough gang leader Sandy Dawson, a ruthless mob of ex-servicemen is holding up ammunition trains in Japan. Dawson's prepared to kill anyone to maintain his power, even Griff, one of his closest accomplices. Down-and-out ex-serviceman Eddie Spannier arrives from the States and hooks up with the gang. His real name's Kenner, and he's a plant working for the cops. He falls for Mariko, a Japanese gal who's Griff's widow. Mariko and Eddie join forces to bring down Sandy and his gang.

Zanuck loved it, even the homoerotic scene with the two gangsters, which at the time was very daring. See, the Sandy Dawson character is pivotal to my yarn. When he feels his power as the "Ichiban," the number one man, dwindling, he blows his top. He ends up murdering Griff, his closest accomplice (played in the movie by Cameron Mitchell), whom he thinks betrayed him. Dawson really loves Griff but shoots him anyway. He plugs him while he's taking a bath. The bullets go clean through the tub and Griff's body, puncturing six neat holes through which hot water spurts out. Dawson takes Griff's limp head in his hands and talks to him as he gently caresses his hair. There's a terrifying sincerity in his manner, an utter negation of reality. The unpredictable machinations of his twisted brain are now fully exposed:

> SANDY (*with compassion*)
> I wish I hadn't been right. But I was, Griff.
> Like always. But I didn't figure you'd run to
> the police. I didn't know you were that far
> gone. But I understand what made you do it,
> Griff. Believe me I do. A man with your ambition, with a crazy idea in his head I was trying
> to shove him out. . . .

(*gently*)

> You see it now, don't you, Griff? Why I had to
> pull you out of the line? I couldn't jeopardize
> the whole outfit. You had it, Griff. . . .

(*patting the dead man's head*)
> But it's all right now, Griff. All right.

Two gangsters, one alive and one dead. Sandy is gentle for the first time, almost sensual. Except the object of his affection is his dead victim, showing just how insane the sonofabitch has really become!

In the fifties, homosexuality was taboo. No studio would go anywhere near it. Zanuck allowed me to use that scene because it was dressed up like a gangster vendetta. Darryl was a coolheaded studio boss with one eye always on the box office. He knew gangster movies sold tickets. Remember that when he was at Warner Brothers, Zanuck worked with Hal Wallis on masterpieces like *Little Caesar* (1931) and *I Am a Fugitive from a Chain Gang* (1932), both smash hits.

When I grew up, people knew very little about homosexuality. There was a book on the subject that I remember reading in the thirties entitled *The Well of Loneliness,* by Radclyffe Hall. It was a big success. Of course,

Getting ready to shoot a scene from House of Bamboo *with (from left to right) Cameron Mitchell, Robert Stack, and Robert Ryan, 1955*

people thought there was something illicit about reading it. Radclyffe Hall was a lesbian and wrote well. Her book made people jealous, because, like alcoholic beverages, it became popular even though it was banned. The silliest damn thing was that even discussing the subject of homosexuality was frowned upon. Since the world began, it's existed. Even when you do talk about it, you can't stereotype people or generalize their relationships, each one being special. Hell, I hate stereotypes and categories, whether it's about homosexuality, heterosexuality, race, nationality. What good do stereotypes do us, except to turn us into simple-minded bigots or fundamentalist zealots?

For *House of Bamboo,* I knew I wanted tall actors to play the gangsters because their height would immediately distinguish them from the Japanese actors who were, for the most part, small in stature. When I explained this to my producer, Buddy Adler, he thought of Robert Ryan for Sandy. Buddy called him from my office, and, after only a brief explanation of the role, Ryan accepted. Robert became a true friend. He was well read and balanced, a kindhearted man with grand democratic ideals.

For the role of Eddie, we considered Gary Cooper. I knew Gary well. He'd wanted to buy the remake rights to *I Shot Jesse James,* so we'd met several times to discuss that project. Cooper and I had a lot of warmth for each other. He called to say he'd love to play the part of the infiltrator in *Bamboo.* But I had to turn him down. See, Zanuck wanted the picture shot in CinemaScope. We could get some great panoramas in Japan. My plan was also to film in the streets of Tokyo for local color. Had I cast Cooper, an international star, he'd have been recognized wherever he went. I needed an unknown actor for Eddie.

Robert Stack was tall and handsome, and nobody knew who the hell he was back then. Stack was recommended to me by writer-director Budd Boetticher, for whom Stack had played the lead in *Bullfighter and the Lady* (1951). Budd, an ex-bullfighter himself, was a great guy and a good friend. I used to go over to Budd's office and pace around his desk, reading him some scene I'd just knocked out. I must have waved my cigar around like a paintbrush, because Budd always complained that I'd burn holes in his fancy jackets. It was Boetticher who told me that Stack was a helluva good actor, professional and energetic.

Nothing in Stack's training could have prepared him for *House of Bamboo.* In one early scene, I hid our cameras on a tough Tokyo street where gangs, winos, and derelicts lived. I costumed Bob in an old raincoat, and told him not to shave so that he'd fit right in. He was supposed to rummage through the garbage cans, then run down the street when we cued him. The cameras started rolling. Bob did exactly what I asked him to. Suddenly, my Japanese production assistant screamed something in Japanese and started pointing at Bob. People came running. Bob didn't understand Japanese, but when he saw the mob rushing toward him, he took off and ran like hell. I'd told the assistant to yell out: "Thief! Thief! Get him!" People didn't know that it was a movie, so they chased after Bob. It looked damn natural. That was the idea.

What I hadn't figured on was the mob assaulting Bob. Fortunately, a Japanese cop was nearby and put an end to it, telling the people that caught Stack that he wasn't really a thief, that we were making a movie. Unfortunately, it all happened too fast for my camera crew and we never got the scene on film. Bob resented me for that incident for many years, but eventually got over it. It helped that I introduced him to Rosemary, his beautiful wife. They have one of the most enduring Hollywood marriages of anybody I know.

Another tough scene for Bob was when his character was supposed to be romantic with his Japanese lover, Mariko, in a park full of cherry trees. It was February and freezing. Bob had on slacks and a thin shirt. The entire crew were bundled in quilted jackets. There was an assistant art director up in the trees gluing on paper cherry blossoms because the real ones weren't out yet. Everything was finally ready.

"Bob," I shouted. "Goddamnit, warm up to her!"

"How?" cried Stack. "I'm freezin' my ass over here!"

I wanted to find a special Japanese actress for my female lead. Billy Gordon screened a slew of Japanese films for me. One actress with wonderful high cheekbones caught my eye. Her name in the credits was "Yoshika." Billy tracked her down to New York City, where she was living with her sculptor husband. Her name was Shirley Yamaguchi.[1] Incredibly, she was a socialite in America and an accomplished actress in Japan. Billy had Shirley do a screen test, and everybody loved her. She got the role of Mariko.

Working in Japan was a dream come true. When I was growing up, my mother had a few good Asian friends who frequently came to visit us in Washington Heights. I was mesmerized by the strange perfumes and spices of the Far East that turned up in my own home.

When I was still a copyboy, I ran across a writer named Robinson from *National Geographic* who told me enchanting stories about Asia, its people, and its geographical wonders. I vowed to myself that someday I'd get over there. As a young man, I found out that Americans had a helluva lot of preconceived notions about Asians. We first encountered them in America when they came here as immigrant laborers. I've always wanted to make a movie about that period, when the "coolies" laid train tracks across the American continent, mistreated by barbarian railroad contractors.

Like most of the Far East, Japan remained a mysterious place until well into the nineteenth century. Commodore Perry and Townsend Harris, the first U.S. consul general to Japan, didn't make their historic voyage to establish trade relations until 1854. Japan was veiled in its own opaque curtain of isolation, rigidly enforcing its *sakoku* policy that barred all foreigners.

A hundred years after Perry, I finally got to Japan. I was delighted to plunge headfirst into their culture. What better way to do that than by going to local movie theaters to watch their films? The Japanese made magnificent pictures and used color so wonderfully. Mizoguchi, Gosho, Naruse, Murata, Imai, Yamamoto, Kurosawa, Ozu. What directors! What technique! What balls they had! I remember being particularly impressed by the power and beauty of the movies made by Teinosuke Kinugasa. There was a Kinugasa movie playing at that time called *The Gate of Hell* (1953), and I loved it.

Japanese audiences were such serious moviegoers. They'd line up early

With Shirley Yamaguchi, setting up a tricky scene at the waterfront markets in Tokyo

in the morning for a show. They were so connected to the stories and the characters up on the screen. Through their films, I discovered some of their folklore. I learned that the Japanese had their own type of cloak-and-dagger yarns, Western tales, and gangster stories. They even had their own Gary Cooper. For every one of our myths about cowboys riding off into the sunset or knights jousting for a maiden's honor, the Japanese had something comparable. Their movies had everything: neorealism, fantasy, subtlety, epic narrative, lyricism, violence. Unfortunately, their pictures didn't often make it to the States, except for the notable exception of Kurosawa's masterpiece, *The Seven Samurai* (1954). Even then, they chopped Kurosawa's movie down to only one-third of its original length. It was still a magnificent work.

I wanted to capture a certain mood in *House of Bamboo* that I hadn't seen in either Japanese or American films: the clash between our culture and theirs. At that time, Japan was very anti-American, not only because of the scars of war, but also because of the growing influence of the Japanese communists. I got a taste of their antipathy at a press conference that was organized before we started shooting the picture. Journalists were testy, their questions combative.

"You want to use one of our trains for your film," said a newspaperman who worked for the biggest communist paper. "What is going to happen to the poor people who take that train every day to go to work?"

I told him that Twentieth Century Fox would pay to have those people picked up and taken to work in comfortable buses.

Another newspaperman asked me if my film was political.

"Of course," I said. "The villain in my story wants to have more money. Exactly like you would like to have more money. The difference is that in my movie the man kills for it. You won't do that because you don't want to wind up in jail."

That caused some chuckles, but there was no denying the tension, just beneath the surface, simply because I was an American shooting a Western film in their country. Sometimes the tension erupted. On one of the first days of shooting, Robert Ryan had a straightforward scene in which he was supposed to drive up a busy city street and hop out of his car. When our production crew arrived that morning, a truck with red flags and loudspeakers was already parked there, playing loud music. The protesters chanted anti-American slogans, trying to ruin the scene as best they could. I approached the situation with a sense of humor, because they were doing their job and I was doing mine. I told Joe MacDonald, our cameraman, to set up as if nothing were wrong. Then he was to pan the camera around to the demonstrators and film them demonstrating. We'd use their rally as background footage somewhere in the movie. As soon as Joe panned the camera to the protesters, they got scared and beat it.

Well into production, I still hadn't decided where to shoot the chase scene I'd written for *House of Bamboo*. Shirley Yamaguchi and I took a walk one day along a busy Tokyo street. A child's ball landed near us. I looked up at a big department store, maybe twenty stories high. Shirley explained there was a playground on top of it. We went up there. On the roof terrace of the store, there was a free nursery where parents left their children while shopping. There were great views of the entire city. On a corner of the rooftop sat a steel contraption, a gyrating carousel that rotated at a dizzying angle.

This was it, the perfect location for my ending. We asked permission to use the space, but the store manager refused. The owner, Mr. Nikkatsu, wouldn't allow us to disrupt his nursery, not even for one minute. We offered more money. No way. The manager said it wasn't a question of

*The revolving contraption high
above the city where we shot my
finale for* House of Bamboo

money. After all, Mr. Nikkatsu was a prominent businessman, owner of stores, hotels, and
even a movie studio. I asked for a meeting and
went to see Mr. Nikkatsu, who was an elderly gentleman. I told him I
didn't want to deprive children of their playground either. I needed them
to be in my picture, playing in the background to make the scene look
realistic. Mr. Nikkatsu and I hit it off. I filled him in on my yarn. Not only
did he agree to let me use his rooftop playground, but he also asked to play
an extra, a doting grandfather, in the scene. That way, he could oversee the
situation.

The day of the shoot, Mr. Nikkatsu watched over our preparations like
a bird of prey. We put three cameras on the rooftop. One of them was in

that whirligig hanging over the edge of the building. I wanted Ryan and Stack to have their final confrontation on that crazy contraption. The scene was tricky to pull off. The gunfire didn't scare the children at all. It was part of a game and they loved playing. Mr. Nikkatsu got caught up in the action too, moving around like a spring chicken. The old fellow had such a great time that he waived all rental fees for the use of his rooftop.

House of Bamboo was a financial and critical success for Fox. What made me proudest was that it broke race barriers implicit in American movies at that time. In the fifties, a white man still didn't fall in love with an Asian woman in Hollywood. In those rare films with interracial couples, the ending was usually tragic. I wasn't going to yield to that hypocrisy. My lovers got a happy ending. Besides, I insisted on casting a native for my lead, not an American actress made up to look Asian, like Lillian Gish in D. W. Griffith's *Broken Blossoms* (1919). Ridiculous as it may seem today, it was revolutionary to use ethnic actors at that time. I wouldn't have done it any other way. Two years after *House of Bamboo*, Robert Rossen's *Island in the Sun* (1957) told a love story with Joan Fontaine and Harry Belafonte. Hot love scenes? Passionate kisses? They don't even touch hands. Hell, some love story! In my picture, Eddie and Mariko are plainly hot for each other, and they don't end up regretting it, like the star-crossed lovers in Puccini's *Madame Butterfly*.

A couple of years after I finished *House of Bamboo*, director Joshua Logan came to see me before he left for Japan to scout locations for *Sayonara* (1957), adapted from Puccini's opera. Joshua congratulated me on the success of *House of Bamboo*. I shared all my research with him, saving him a helluva lot of time preparing his film. It was a professional courtesy common among directors back then. I sensed Logan was worried about *Sayonara*, also an interracial love story, except with a tragic ending, like the opera. Josh told me he'd considered making the picture's ending more upbeat. The white man, played by Marlon Brando, would show up just in time to prevent the suicide of his Japanese lover, played by Miiko Taka. Brisk competition among the studios pushed creative people to consider changing a story line, even that of a classic tragedy, to make a box-office hit. Thankfully, Logan ended up sticking to the original.

Making a movie in Japan is a grand experience. I consider my life richer for having done it. The light there is unique and wonderful. Colors come out looking postcard crisp. Even their blacks and whites are different, sharper and purer. Mount Fujiyama is velvety black, and its summit snow white. It's a remarkable sight that I'll keep in the back of my mind for the rest of my days.

Mato Grosso

With eight pictures under my belt, now established as a writer-director in Hollywood, I should have been sleeping peacefully under those silk sheets in my big house in Beverly Hills. Nothing could have been further from the truth. I tossed and turned all night long, racked by horrific nightmares. Terrible visions from the war buried in my brain rose up as soon as I dozed off. Heaps of dead bodies. A gaunt hand stretching skyward for help. Bombs exploding. Soldiers ripped apart.

Music was my immediate remedy. I got up, went downstairs, and immersed myself in Beethoven, Bach, or Mozart. They soothed my spirit. I figured that the only way to free myself of my war memories was to make a film about them. The entire yarn was already in my head. I'd been carrying it around with me like a piece of heavy luggage. It would capture the reality of combat without any Hollywood crap—no heroes, just soldiers trying to survive. My take was deeply personal, yet the violence and insanity was universal. I began writing scenes and dialogue. A script would come together over many years and many rewrites. Maybe after I made that movie, I'd sleep better. In my wildest dreams, I never thought that it would take another twenty-five years before I got my chance to direct *The Big Red One*.

In those days, Zanuck organized weekend get-togethers at his place in Palm Springs. Martha and I went a few times. My wife enjoyed socializing with the studio executives and movie stars who came out there, so I put up with those affairs. The cigars and the vodka were okay, but I had better at home, and, besides, I could have been at my Royal writing scripts. Still, I ran into some interesting characters. I was fond of Darryl's wife, Virginia, a fine lady. Hedda Hopper, the Hollywood columnist, seemed to always be invited. I got along well with Hedda. She even asked me to do a movie about her life, but that was just cocktail gibble-gabble.

Howard Hughes showed up once. We talked for a while. He knew all about me from Jean Peters. Hughes was a strange guy, but we got along all right. He called me a couple times afterward to make a movie with him. Like so many projects, it just never materialized.

One weekend, Zanuck took me into the private study off the terrace of his Palm Springs place. He'd just gotten back from some big-game hunting on a ranch in the wild central region of Brazil called Mato Grosso. He gave me a book to read entitled *Tigrero,* by Sacha Siemel. The studio had acquired the rights. Zanuck explained that when a wild cat preys on live-stock down there, the ranch owners hire a *tigrero* to track down and kill the culprit, usually a jaguar, though the predator could be one of a variety of cats. The best *tigrero* Zanuck heard about was an old Indian from the jungle who never used a gun or a rifle, only a spear, to hunt the cats. We talked about concocting a picture that would take place in the Mato Grosso. I read the book. There was some good background material. The best thing about it was the title.

Before I wrote a script, I told Zanuck I needed to see the Mato Grosso for myself. Darryl agreed. My appetite for making movies in faraway places had already been whetted by *House of Bamboo.* Maybe the Brazilian jungle would take my mind off those painful war memories. I packed up my typewriter and my 16-mm movie camera, said good-bye to my wife and my mother, and hopped on a plane down to Rio.

People I met in Rio said I was crazy to go into the Mato Grosso. Indian tribes in the interior were still renowned for cutting off and shrinking their enemies' heads. In a bar in Rio, I heard about an old Shavante Indian whose picture was on all the front pages of the Brazilian newspapers. His piercing eyes seemed to be staring at me. The man had gotten separated from his tribe by a big flood. He was found far from his tribal land, refus-ing all nourishment until he died like a starving animal. Now I really wanted to explore the jungle and see those Indians for myself.

From Rio, I flew down to São Paulo. There I hooked up with my guide, who knew a few of the many native dialects. I thought I also needed some strong arms, just in case. A couple of ex-members of the Brazilian air force I met in a bar seemed to fit the bill. I offered to take them on as scouts. They thought I was some kind of Hemingway character on a big-game hunt. I told them I was scouting locations for a movie, not hunting wild animals. Instead of money, they wanted to be paid in jaguar skins. I told them to go to hell.

Fox had chartered a private plane to take me inland. It was a two-seater, the kind of aircraft that sprayed pesticides on crops and landed supplies at remote airstrips. Zanuck had the plane stocked with plenty of vodka and cigars. First, we flew to Rebeirão Prêto, then changed to an even smaller

I thought I might be able to use these two Brazilians on my trip into the Mato Grosso, in 1956. I was wrong, so I gave them a couple of good cigars and sent them packing.

plane for the flight to Goiãnia. We finally landed in the heart of the Mato Grosso, in a little place called Tesouro. The pilot said he'd be back in a few weeks to pick us up.

The jungle was a wild and uncompromising place. We traveled by horseback and canoe. The first Indians we found were the Jívaros. They weren't at all happy to see us, so we moved on. I started shooting footage of the terrain with my camera. On the banks of the Araguaia River, we came across members of the Karajá tribe. They immediately invited us to visit their isolated village. On the other side of the Araguaia, which the Karajá called the "River of the Dead," lived the Shavante tribe. I remembered the newspaper story of the Shavante who starved himself rather than be separated from his tribe. Here I was, a stone's throw from the homeland he died for.

Being small in stature, I didn't pose any threat to the Karajá. Right away, I hit it off with their chiefs, who invited me and my guide to stay with them for as long as I wished. The Karajá had three chiefs. One was a hunter, one, a priest, and one, a warrior. The warrior chief had the least influence, because the tribe never fought any wars. What I discovered in that remote corner of Mato Grosso was a society far more peaceful and caring than ours. Little by little, I began to feel like the savage and see the Karajá as the civilized ones.

The Karajá were descended from the Incas, and their language sounded

Back in the fifties, the only way through the Mato Grosso was on horseback, with mules to carry supplies.

like Japanese. My interpreter couldn't figure it out. But language was never a problem. The Karajá spoke with their eyes, and I understood them. Physically, they were a beautiful people, with dark skin, high cheekbones, and ebony hair. Spiritually, they were beautiful too, joyful, hospitable, generous human beings. They didn't have laws, judges, or police, nor did they need any. There was no crime, jealousy, or greed.

From dawn to dusk, they were constantly busy, taking care of their children, repairing their huts, fishing in the Araguaia. The abundance of fish guaranteed plenty of food for everyone. Money was useless. When they needed rice and medicines, they traded fish for supplies from the whites downstream. Their huts were simple and well kept. Mangoes were growing all over the place. Kids were sucking on them like lollipops from morning to night.

The Karajá had their gods for the rain, sun, and trees. Certain fish and birds were sacred. Before each hunting or fishing expedition, the Karajá prayed with their chiefs. The tropical climate imposed a natural limit on how much food they brought back to the village, because leftovers would spoil. They knew exactly what they needed to survive and never abused the jungle's abundance. The men inserted little sticks under their lower lips to emphasize their masculinity, and also painted their bodies with black and white circles.

Though they didn't have any musical instruments, the Karajá loved to dance and sing. Their fertility dance was a special appeal to the God of fruitfulness for his good will. The women put beautiful flowers behind their ears and started moving their feet to the beat, rubbing their bellies. The rest of the tribe chanted and clapped their hands. The men wrapped their heads in twigs and circled round the women.

Karajá couples were monogamous, though they walked around naked except for a loincloth tied to their waists. I wore a pair of shorts all the time and got very tanned, except for my ass. When I was washing myself in the river, the whiteness back there surprised everybody. They'd take berries they used for tattoos and rub them on me, trying to "cure" my pale skin.

Among the Karajá customs I got on film, one of the most dramatic was a boy's puberty rites. Every thirteen-year-old boy had to submit to it in order to become a man. First, they pierced his penis with a wooden needle. The boy couldn't move a muscle during the ritual. Then they took a piranha tooth and scratched the boy's legs until blood appeared. Still, he couldn't move. If he did, they stopped the ceremony and started the ritual all over again. Teenage girls had their own rites of womanhood, too. It took place inside a hut, away from the men. I didn't even consider asking to film it, because I already felt like an intruder. At night, if I had to take a pee, the whole village woke up to make sure I wasn't attacked by a wild animal when I walked out of the hut. They were very tolerant with me. I managed to receive the ultimate gesture of acceptance by being invited to sleep in the chief priest's tent. He was a revered man, blind and gentle. It was one of the greatest honors I'd ever receive.

During my stay with the Karajá, I wrote a treatment for *Tigrero*. My story started in a prison in Rio. A woman helps her husband escape by killing a prison guard. Then she hires a *tigrero* to take them across the Mato Grosso. The *tigrero* lives in an isolated world, but one rich in colors, sights, and sounds. He finds poetry in the trees, in the calls of exotic birds, in the animal tracks on the jungle floor. He gets the couple across a mighty river to an island that is shrinking in the aftermath of the great rains. As the waters rise, the woman suddenly slips and falls in. Her husband can try to save her from drowning, but he just looks on while saving his own skin.

The Karajá allowed me to film many of their rituals, like their fertility dance.

The woman survives, but her great love for her husband is transformed into hatred. My yarn was not about cowardice or selfishness. The idea was that you can't hate someone for saving himself. The husband in my yarn loves his wife but loves himself a little more.

It was time to go home. I'd been living with the Karajá for several weeks. I left reluctantly, half-tempted to postpone my return, but I had a wife and a mother to take care of and a script to write. It was damned hard to leave a place where I'd experienced so much peace and happiness. I knew I wanted to return and shoot my movie in the jungles of the Mato Grosso. I thanked the Karajá from the bottom of my heart and promised I'd be back.

Zanuck loved my yarn and the home movies I'd shot during my stay in Brazil. He could see for himself that my vivid descriptions were taken from reality, and he shared my enthusiasm for making the picture on location in the jungle. He lined up John Wayne to play the *tigrero,* Ava Gardner as the wife, and Tyrone Power as her husband.

I'd imagined a great opening for the picture and shot some of it with my 16-mm camera and anamorphic lens. An alligator attacks a bird in the Araguaia. A second alligator shows up, bigger than the first, and snatches the booty. They fight over the prey, twisting and thrashing in the water. The big alligator kills the small one, turning the water red. A school of piranha shows up, attacking the victorious alligator. Finally a condor swoops down and flies off with the prey. There was the goddamned cycle of life: survival. At the end of the sequence, one gigantic word would come up on the screen: TIGRERO. It was going to be a pisscutter of a movie!

Everything for the production was on track until the insurance companies raised a red flag. It was risky for big stars to shoot a film in the wilds of Brazil, so premiums were sky high: $6 million for Wayne, $6 million for Gardner, and $3 million for Power. Darryl got very angry. He showed the insurance executives my location footage around the Karajá's village. Clearly, the whole area was safe. There'd be more danger shooting the film on Fox's back lot. But those insurance guys in the gray suits and bow ties wouldn't budge. After all, the Brazilian jungle was full of savages and man-eating animals. The studio decided to shelve the project. Unproduced films are as much a part of this business as those that get produced.

I was terribly disappointed about the fate of *Tigrero*. Yet I came to see that the time I'd spent with the Karajá had given me a new vision of life, renewing my faith in the entire human race. Against the backdrop of their untamed land and the cruelties of Mother Nature, the Karajá had created a society full of kindness and happiness. Laughter was an essential element of their culture. Most of the time, I didn't know what they were laughing about. Their laughter was contagious, so I laughed with them. An important piece of my wounded soul had been healed during my time in the Mato Grosso. I relearned the difference between joy and pleasure. Pleasure was transient. Writing, listening to music, sharing, and real friendship gave me joy.

Immersing myself in writing and research, I quickly completed another script, called *Run of the Arrow*. I stopped going to Zanuck's shindigs, preferring to hang out with more nourishing people, like my musician friends Max Steiner, Victor Young, and Harry and Gretchen Sukman, or my writer friends, like Richard Brooks and Dalton Trumbo. I cherished those people because they knew the value of life, friendship, and integrity. Their enormous creativity fueled me, and their affection helped me cope with my violent war memories. The Karajá had shown me that life was a delicate balance between violence and nonviolence.

I've never met a gentler group of people. The most boisterous I ever saw them was when they were playfully wrestling with each other. They were always careful not to hurt anyone or anything. However, if a member of another tribe invaded their territory and took away one of their children, they'd hunt down the trespasser and kill him. Their children were their future, so the thief was victimizing the entire tribe. It happened once while I was there. They cut off the head of the child stealer and brought it back to the village. They hung the head outside the parents' hut and made a fire underneath it with special wood and herbs to shrink it. The process lasted several days and nights. They believed the thief was not all evil. What little good was in the bastard would pass on to the bereaved parents, thus creating some retribution for the lost child.

Where's Your Pride, Ma?

The new head of RKO, William Dozier, approached me at a dinner party following some Hollywood premiere. He introduced himself, saying he was a fan of my work, especially *Park Row.* I told him the picture hadn't been a commercial success, but he didn't care because the critics loved it. Dozier said he wanted to be associated with directors who were artists. Bill was well read, honest, and straightforward, with a great sense of humor. He'd been married to Joan Fontaine for a few years, but when we met, he had gotten remarried to Ann Rutherford, a gracious woman who'd played Scarlett O'Hara's little sister in *Gone with the Wind* (1939). Martha and I shared some great evenings with Bill and Ann, listening to Ann's hilarious stories about working with Mickey Rooney in the "Andy Hardy" movies. Bill ended up a television producer and a very wealthy man, thanks to his fathering the *Batman* series on TV with Adam West in 1966.

Dozier understood I was under contract at Fox but could do my own projects as well. He invited me to meet his boss, Tom O'Neill, president of the General Tires Company, which owned RKO. Businessman and movie lover, O'Neill asked me if I had a picture I wanted to produce with them. I told Dozier and O'Neill about my unforgettable experiences with the Karajá. Propelled by my frustration about the nixing of the *Tigrero* project, I'd written an Indian yarn called *Run of the Arrow,* set in the far West. I'd done a lot of research on American Indians, going through stacks of materials I requested from Washington about each of the tribes.

I pitched them my story. O'Meara, an embittered Confederate soldier, shoots the last bullet in the Civil War, wounding a Union officer named Driscoll. But O'Meara can't accept surrender to the North. He heads out west, teaming up with an Indian scout, Walking Coyote. The two of them are captured by the Sioux. O'Meara is forced to make the "run of the arrow," a tribal ritual and grueling test of endurance. His life is saved by Yellow Moccasin, the squaw he ends up marrying. The Sioux are now his

With Rod Steiger on Run of the Arrow, *in 1957. I'm trying to show Rod how I want him to play the opening scene when he fires the Civil War's final bullet. He was going to do it his way, no matter what.*

people, but the real test of allegiance is for O'Meara to kill an American. The Sioux attack an American fort, under the command of the same Driscoll from the Civil War. O'Meara shoots Driscoll, but saves the soldier from slow torture at the hands of the Sioux. In his heart of hearts, O'Meara is still an American.

The boys at RKO loved my yarn and gave me a green light to produce the picture the way I wanted. Indians would be depicted as a community of people with their own rules and rituals, not—as in most studio movies—like a pack of marauding killers. My deal stipulated that RKO and I had to agree on the principal cast. Dozier wanted Gary Cooper to play O'Meara. I'd have loved to work with Gary, one of the most handsome and popular leading men in Hollywood. Except he wasn't right for the part.

"I need the opposite of Cooper," I explained. "The character's hateful, a misfit. I want this newcomer, Steiger. He's got a sour face and a fat ass. He'll look awkward, especially when he climbs up on a horse. See, my yarn's about a sore loser, not a gallant hero."

"Sam, this Steiger fellow has never had a lead in a picture," said Dozier. "A lead with a fat ass and a sour face? Who's going to want to see a picture starring that guy?"

I spewed off a short list of leads played by character actors. Of course the best example was Charles Laughton as Quasimodo in William Dieterle's 1939 classic, *The Hunchback of Notre Dame*.

"Look, Bill, as much as I am dying to work with Coop, if he plays O'Meara, my story's unbelievable. I don't know this Steiger personally, but I saw him in Elia Kazan's *On the Waterfront*. He's got a face right out of a Matthew Brady photograph. I want Steiger."

Dozier continued to push for Gary Cooper. I finally convinced him to hire Steiger. This was a decade before Steiger's great performances in Sidney Lumet's *The Pawnbroker* (1965) and Norman Jewison's *In the Heat of the Night* (1967). It was the first time Steiger got top billing and the money that went with it. I think he earned more on that picture than I did. After all, I was only the writer, director, and coproducer.

Steiger couldn't have cared less that I'd fought for him to be my lead. From day one when he arrived on our set in St. George, Utah, he manifested his I'm-going-to-do-things-my-way-and-you-can-all-go-to-hell-if-you-don't-like-it attitude. I felt confident Steiger could play O'Meara the way I wrote the character and make his inner turmoil believable. That was key to making the entire story credible. So for the good of the picture, I had to find a way to work with this erratic, brooding actor. Sometimes that required direct confrontation. Other times, I let him have his way. The problem was Steiger had talent but he tended to overact.

O'Meara was of Irish stock. He needed to have a southern accent tinged with bitterness. With my coaching, Steiger worked on a believable Irish brogue, laced with a deep southern drawl. To get the character's gloomy contempt, Steiger decided on his own to mumble his lines. It was a trick he must have picked up with Marlon Brando and his other pals at the Actor's Studio in New York. Rod kept demanding reshoots to get his lines just right. I never like to do more than a couple of takes, but I let Steiger have his way, even if it was terribly boring for everyone except him. A

Up on the crane, Joe Biroc, preparing a shot of the Sioux on horseback. A consummate cameraman, Joe was open to my crazy ideas about unusual angles.

helluva lot of his lines were muttered. I'd make sure that stuff would end up on the cutting-room floor.

When it came time to shoot Steiger's "run of the arrow" scene, he was sick. He insisted that I postpone the scene so he could do it himself. We were on a tight schedule. I said no and went ahead with a stunt man, mounting a camera on a truck and focusing on the stunt man's feet as he raced across the prairie. Steiger was pissed off. He decided to be even more mule-headed, if that were possible.

There's a scene in the movie when the cavalry and the Sioux meet on horseback. It was a long dolly shot that we set up early in the morning. I told Steiger how I wanted him to play the scene. He listened to me, then went ahead and did it his own way. It was all wrong. I knew what he was trying to pull, and, goddamnit, he wasn't going to have it his way that time.

"Rod, let's do it again! Whether you like it or not," I yelled down to him from the crane, "you're going to do it *my* way!"

We shot the scene over and over. Steiger refused to follow my direction. By noon, cast and crew were losing their patience with this war of wills between the director and his lead actor.

"Listen, Rod," I called out. "You're going to do it my way or we'll stay here till the goddamn moon comes up!"

Stubborn and enraged, Rod started screaming all kinds of insults up at me.

"Okay, lunch!" I yelled.

By the time we came back from lunch, Rod had figured out that he couldn't win. He finally did the scene my way. There were other incidents like that, but, thank god, I've forgotten them. Despite the clashes, I still have a lot of admiration for Steiger. He did some terrific work in that picture. The scene when O'Meara and his mother are talking on a bridge at the end of the Civil War always brings tears to my eyes.[1] O'Meara is deeply angry about losing the war. Steiger's face is seething with frustration. You can see in his eyes the terrible damage the Yankees have inflicted on him, his family, and the South.

"Where's your pride, Ma?" Steiger mutters. "Where's your pride?"

When O'Meara confesses that "the savages have more pride than we do," he's setting up his pivotal decision to leave home rather than accept the Yankees' sovereignty. All Southerners felt what he's feeling after their loss. To this day, Southerners never refer to the "Civil War," but opt for the more equitable "War Between the States."

Another scene where Rod excelled as O'Meara is when, on his way home after the war, he sits listening to a man who's singing a soft, slow Confederate ballad. We'd researched that song and made sure it was authentic. At first it sounds like just a nice tune. Gradually, the lyrics make you realize the deep hatred that burned in the hearts of Southerners. You can see it on Steiger's face. He was able to reflect their reality.

I insisted on putting that resentment in a historical context by announcing at the beginning of the movie:

THE DEFEAT OF THE SOUTH WAS NOT THE END OF THE WAR,
IT WAS THE BIRTH OF THE UNITED STATES.

Setting up for the "run of the arrow" scene, a genuine Sioux test of endurance

Up in Utah, I had few diversions except visiting my old friend Raoul Walsh, who was up there at the same time shooting *The King and Four Queens* with Clark Gable and Eleanor Parker. Our locations were only a couple miles apart. Hell, isolated out there in that barren place, it was like working ass to ass. After sundown, Raoul would come over to see me in my trailer. He was always fun to be with. Over cigars and drinks, Walsh told me he loved his actors but hated the script he was shooting. When I told him my story, he liked it better than his own.

"Why don't we swap?" he suggested one evening.

"Swap?" I said.

"Sure, Sammy!" Raoul laughed, winking at me with his one good eye. "You do my picture and I'll do yours!"

I laughed with him, but explained how much this picture meant to me after the demise of my *Tigrero* project. Every time he'd come over to our set, Raoul would continue to rib me, saying with a twinkle in that good eye, "Just let me do a few scenes, Sammy!"

Walsh wasn't the only director who wanted to take a crack at *Run of the Arrow.* Back in preproduction, I'd gotten a call from Mervyn LeRoy, one of Hollywood's preeminent moviemakers, who'd heard about the project.

Surely one of the great ones, Mervyn was having a difficult period in the fifties. He offered me a helluva lot of money up front to let him direct the movie. I had to say no thanks.

Over and above my Indian obsession, I had another objective in doing *Run of the Arrow.* I wanted to create the rare Western that linked powerful images with emotional turmoil. The bright, clear Utah landscapes are constantly contrasted with O'Meara's dark, brooding nature. Full of hate and confusion, O'Meara is trying to make hard choices between his own self-interest and larger responsibilities to his family, his people, his nation. Every facet of my yarn is full of contrasts, but nowhere more obvious than in the confrontation between races.

First, it's whites against blacks. An early scene in the movie has a Yankee soldier and a Southerner talking. The Yankee, superbly played by Brian Keith, asks the Southerner about the KKK people who dress up in white robes and attack blacks.

"Free, white, and Christian," says the Yankee sarcastically, "putting pillowcases over their heads and lynching black people!"

The Southerner replies that he doesn't know what he's talking about.

"Yes," says the Yankee, "it's always the other guy."

Then, it's reds against whites. When O'Meara meets up with the Sioux, a lot of racial bells start ringing, usually in unexpected ways. First, they almost kill him with their run of the arrow, one of many genuine Sioux rituals that intrigued me in my research. O'Meara is easily caught in that deadly pursuit, but Yellow Moccasin saves his life out of compassion, even though whites are considered invaders to the Sioux. I threw a wrench into the typical movie plot by having O'Meara marry the squaw. He goes through with it to save his ass. Later, he learns to love her. His new life with the Sioux is about as far from his beloved Dixie as you can get, physically and spiritually.

In my research, I'd studied the Oglalas, the Iroquois, and the Seminoles, who migrated, along with the Sioux, from the North, sometimes from as far away as Canada. I also read a great deal about the Cherokees, the Cheyenne, the Shawnee, and the Apaches. I found mention of plenty of mixed marriages in frontier days. Indian women who married white men fared better. In most cases, white women who married Indian men were ostracized by their own people and barely tolerated by the tribes.

The heart of my movie is about O'Meara's personal reconciliation. It's a painful journey, smoothed a little by the loving squaw, played by Sarita Montiel. Sarita was the Brigitte Bardot of Spain back then, married to my dear friend, the director Anthony Mann. Red skin or not, Yellow Moccasin is the best thing that ever happened to O'Meara. I wanted to show that different races can get along if there's real tolerance. In one of the early drafts of my script, I was trying to show the couple's intimacy while revealing O'Meara's ironic self-deprecation. I had O'Meara asking Yellow Moccasin, "Did you marry me to change your luck?"

When I grew up, there was an old saying that when you slept with a woman or a man of a different race, you were trying to change your luck. It was too long to explain and could have been misconstrued, so I cut the line out of the final draft.

Mixing whites and Indians in movies was hardly original. Ford often had Indians capturing white women as slaves. Hawks had a white man marrying an Indian woman in one of his pictures. It was Cecil B. DeMille who made the first picture about a relationship between a white man and an Indian woman, *The Squaw Man*. He did that story three times, in 1914, in 1918, and again in 1931. In the first version, he used a real Indian, Red Wing, to play the role of his heroine, Naturich. In the second version, he used a white actress, Ann Little. And in the third version, he gave the part to Lupe Velez, a Mexican.

I wanted to cast as many real Indians as I could get. We hired all the Sioux we could find in Utah. I also made a scouting trip through the Dakotas, locating more Sioux, real descendants of Sitting Bull and Red Cloud. I ended up with a few white actors playing Indian roles. The great Jay C. Flippen played Walking Coyote. A handsome Mexican American named Frank de Kova played Red Cloud. A stunt man named H. M. Wynant was Crazy Wolf. I cast newcomer Charles Bronson as the Sioux chief, Blue Buffalo, who incarnated everything I cherished about American Indians from my boyhood readings of James Fenimore Cooper.[2] Bronson (born Buchinsky) was at the very beginning of his career, twenty years before those *Death Wish* films. He looked magnificent as an Indian, with that strong, muscular body, hard face, and stony smile.

The Indian boy, Billy Miller, was half Cherokee and half Apache. I made him mute like I was until the age of five. I remember Billy fondly, as I do all the youngsters I used in my other films. They were scripted into adult tales brimming with problems and struggles. That came from my own youth, a very small person thrown into a world full of adult predicaments. I respect children in all my movies. Like me, they have to figure out things fast. Father figures help them grow up. Whatever they see, hear, or feel will help them forge the future, *our* future.

Once back from Utah, I needed a good editor to work with me on the movie. Out of the blue, Gene Fowler, my old friend and mentor, dropped in at our RKO production office to visit me. I was thrilled to see the Grand Old Man again. It'd been a long time. His roguish sense of humor was as

Sam Fuller's Tutor,
Prof. Fowler. (See other
note)

On the back of this photo with
his handwritten dedication
"Sam Fuller's tutor, Prof.
Fowler," Gene Fowler wrote:
"Honorary Doctor of Social
Security and President
Emeritus of the Free Loading
Sons of America, I am shown
here accepting new awards
bestowed on me for my
invention of the streamlined
celluloid cuff. The Oscars were
donated by a pawnbroker who
is retiring from business."

fresh as when I'd first met him in the twenties. Gene was accompanied by his son, Gene Jr., who'd worked as an editor with Fritz Lang. I asked the young Fowler if he'd like to cut my new picture. He said okay, so I hired him on the spot. My life was full of happy coincidences. Fowler Senior had edited my writing, and now Fowler Junior was editing my movie. I couldn't have been in better hands.

While Gene Jr. and I were cutting *Run of the Arrow,* Steiger's mumbling was just one of the many problems we had to solve. Sarita Montiel was gorgeous to look at, but her accent was incomprehensible on the sound mix. We needed somebody to rerecord Sarita's lines in a hurry. My wonderful secretary and assistant, Anita Uphoff, who was with me for almost twenty years, brought in a gal she knew named Angie Dickinson. Angie was holding down a day job at RKO, waiting for a break as an actress. Angie had a great voice, not to mention those gorgeous legs. I told Angie to come over to the editing room when she got off work. She ended up redubbing every word of Montiel's dialogue. When she finished the job, I promised Angie

I'd repay her effort by finding a part for her in an upcoming film. As it worked out, Angie Dickinson played the lead in my next movie, *China Gate* (1957), her first starring role and the start of a big career.

My friend Victor Young was working on the score for *Run of the Arrow* when he passed away. That was a very sad day for me. What a wonderful man he was! I was asked to write Victor's obituary, and I agreed as long as it was incognito. Victor had had a fabulous career that began back in the thirties, with over 170 films scored and Oscar nominations all over the place. He finally won an Oscar at the end of his life for "Written on the Wind," for which Sammy Cahn did the lyrics.[3] Victor was doing some of his greatest work when I knew him: *The Quiet Man* (1952), *Shane* (1953), *Johnny Guitar* (1954), *Three Coins in the Fountain* (1954). Victor knew how to enjoy life and make others enjoy theirs. I'd miss him terribly. Our mutual pal Max Steiner finished the score for my film as a token of friendship to Victor. Max made sure all monies were paid to Victor's estate. The loving credit in the film reads:

"MUSIC BY VICTOR YOUNG,
EXTENDED BY HIS OLD FRIEND, MAX STEINER"

When *Run of the Arrow* was released, one of its first public screenings took place in Washington, D.C. I was invited to Capitol Hill to show the picture to a committee of U.S. senators who were making budget recommendations for the Indian reservations. A number of tribal representatives were in the audience. They came up to me afterward and congratulated me warmly. For them, my picture was authentic and forceful. For me, it was one of the proudest moments of my career.

Fast forward about three decades to about 1990. Christa and I walked over to a movie house on the Champs Elysées to see a new American film that had just opened in France called *Dances with Wolves*. When the film was over, we strolled back to our apartment, also in the Eighth Arrondissement. I took Christa's arm with one hand and smoked my cigar with the other. It was a lovely evening for a walk, but my wife was very upset. According to her, the basic plot of Kevin Costner's movie had been lifted from *Run of the Arrow*. She saw lots of details they'd "borrowed" from me, like a close-up I'd gotten of a horse that had "U.S. Cavalry" branded on one of its legs. Christa was furious. According to her, *Dances with Wolves* was an expensive, uncredited imitation of my 1957 movie.

"It's plagiarism!" she said.

I heard her out, puffing my Camacho as we walked along those lovely Paris avenues.

"Not plagiarism," I said, mimicking Jean-Luc Godard when I told him face-to-face he'd stolen ideas from me. *"Hommage!"*

I laughed. Christa wasn't satisfied.

"So what do you think?" she asked.

"About what?"

"Stealing!"

"Nonsense!" I said. "Remember my finish in *Run of the Arrow*?"

"Your finish?"

"Yeah, the big titles across the screen: THE ENDING CAN ONLY BE WRITTEN BY YOU! It's an invitation to go on with the story."

"So?" said Christa.

"So, they went on with the story!"

Christa joined me in my laughter. It was the best response to all plagiarists.

PART IV

With the great Jay C. Flippen (1899–1971)
on the set of Run of the Arrow

33

Grab 'Em. Slap 'Em. Shak' 'Em Up.

Young writers and directors, seize your audience by the balls as soon as the credits hit the screen and hang on to them! Smack people right in the face with the passion of your story! Make the public love your characters or hate them, but, for Godsakes, never—never!—leave them indifferent!

My next project at Fox was called *China Gate* (1957). There were enough hot topics in this adventure love story to push everybody's buttons. Communism and colonialism. Racism and tolerance. Black markets and capitalism. Abandonment and fidelity.

The yarn was set in Indochina in 1954, before it became Vietnam. Ruled by the French as one of their colonies, the country is under siege by the communist-supported revolutionaries, led by Ho Chi Minh. Russia and China are pumping in supplies and ammunition. Angie Dickinson plays Lea, nicknamed "Lucky Legs," a half-caste who resorts to smuggling to feed her five-year-old son. Since she's part Chinese and knows her way through the jungle, she accepts the assignment of leading a bomb squad of French legionnaires behind enemy lines to destroy the communists' main ammunitions dump. The French, however, must first promise Lea that they'll arrange for her boy's evacuation to America.

The squad is lead by Brock, played by Gene Barry. Brock is an American Korean War veteran who married Lea but abandoned her when his son was born with Chinese features. Brock is a sonofabitch racist who gets some straight-shooting advice about Lea from the one-legged village priest, played by the veteran French actor Marcel Dalio:

FATHER PAUL
. . . I know this woman. I know what she went
through to feed your child.

(standing, leaning on a crutch)

LOVE AND WAR IN FRENCH INDO-CHINA!

SAMUEL FULLER'S

china gate

CINEMASCOPE®

GENE BARRY · ANGIE DICKINSON · NAT "KING" COLE   WRITTEN, PRODUCED AND DIRECTED BY
(AS BROCK)   (AS LUCKY LEGS)   (HIS FIRST DRAMATIC ROLE)   SAMUEL FULLER

For China Gate, *I pinned my entire yarn on a little boy's future.*

The Communists sawed off my leg and knifed a sign in my side that said "Capitalist Spy." Lea found me on the outskirts of the village. She cut off the gangrenous flesh and carried me to the hospital. Help you? Stay out of her life!

To accomplish their difficult mission, Lea and Brock have to deal with mines, snipers, and touchy dynamite. Worse, they must overcome their mutual antagonism.

> BROCK
> I'm learning a lesson in hate, just watching you.
>
> LEA
> I'm too tired to hate anymore. It was all my fault, not yours. I'm really to blame. You knew all about me, but I didn't know all about you. Sure, you had traveled all over the world, but you hadn't learned anything. Not where it

counts. I should have investigated your heart
and your brain. I should have seen you weren't
adjusted yet. That you couldn't face facts that
involved people. Oh, you're tough. You handle explosives. But you're not tough enough
to handle life, Brock! That's where I made a
mistake.

BROCK
Everybody makes mistakes.

Brock is forced to face up to his narrow-mindedness. Lea is tempted by
the ambitious Major Cham, played by Lee Van Cleef, who offers her and
her son a new life in Moscow. The sabotage mission on the ammo dump is
a success, but Lea gets killed. In the end, Brock takes his son by the hand
and leads him out of the war zone toward America.

Zanuck loved the script. My yarn didn't make any judgment about who
was right or wrong in the Indochina conflict. Lea is looking out for herself
so that she can get a better life for her son. She has no cultural or political
bias. Her only motivation for going on the mission is to get an American
visa for her boy. America is the Promised Land.

One day, Zanuck came by our production office and asked me about
the big posters of Ho Chi Minh I'd put up on the wall to get everybody in
the mood of Indochina. It was the first time the name of the Vietnamese
leader would be heard in an American movie. Zanuck wasn't impressed
that Minh spoke seven languages. But when I told him that Minh had
once been an assistant pastry chef in a London hotel, Darryl got excited.

"A pastry chef, goddamnit!" said Zanuck. "Went on to become his
country's leader! There's a great story!"

Even though he was the head of a major studio, Zanuck was a writer at
heart and always defended the writer's viewpoint. In the fifties, movies that
even whispered the word "communism" had to portray it as evil. I wanted
China Gate to be different, to show "isms" reduced to gut decisions of survival. My story was based on research I'd done on the French Foreign
Legion fighting in Indochina. The French connection enticed Darryl into
green-lighting the picture, because Darryl loved everything French. He
was proud of having received a *Légion d'honneur* in Paris. I didn't give a
damn that my characters were fighting for the French. The Indochina conflict was based on nothing but goddamned economics. My legionnaires
are from different countries, each with his own personal reason for being a
paid soldier in Southeast Asia. It certainly wasn't about French patriotism.

Zanuck approved of my choice of Angie Dickinson for the lead, even though she was an unknown. She had a strong presence in the tests we did with her. With her high cheekbones and slanted eyes, Angie passed for a Eurasian. And those legs of hers stretched all the way across a Cinema-Scope screen. The crew loved her. Warmhearted and caring, Angie was everybody's pal. Angie and I became pals, too. I sang her praises to everyone in Hollywood. Howard Hawks hired her for *Rio Bravo* (1959), opposite John Wayne. She was on her way to a big career. My close friend Richard Brooks and Angie became a couple. I shot some home movies of the two lovers cavorting in my pool. Unfortunately, their affair wouldn't last, and Brooks ended up marrying Jean Simmons.

The late fifties was a prolific yet painful time for me. I was working like crazy, cranking out scripts, getting them produced one way or another, making dough, and spending it on an expensive lifestyle. When my friends needed help, I didn't think twice about slipping them a few grand to help them out. But then my two remaining brothers died one after the other, Ving of an ulcer, and Ray of leukemia. At the tail end of the decade, my mother passed away. Martha had told me she couldn't have children, so I put the idea out of my mind. But did I? I thought of my scripts as my children, puttering over them like an anxious father. Not having a kid of my own must have weighed on me. Buried with other frustrations, it probably doomed my marriage to Martha. In one of the crucial scenes in *China Gate,* I wrote a speech for Goldie, letting my anxiety rise to the surface.

> GOLDIE
> I always wanted a kid, Brock. My wife was told we couldn't have one. We put in papers to adopt one when my wife got sick. Eaten up inside, not being able to have one. Just eaten up. I watched her go down to 75 pounds. She died feeling sorry for me. That's how much she knew I wanted a kid. When I learned you walked on yours . . . Let me tell you something, Brock. I've belted through two wars and I'm coming out of this one. You know why? Cause I've got a reason. I'll get my release when they know why I want out. I'll tell you one thing. Lucky Legs is going through hell for your son. And if something happens to her on this job, he'll still get to the

States, even if I have to crawl all the way with
him on my back.

(*reflecting*)

I've always wanted a son, Brock. Especially a
five-year-old one.

I'll take my share of responsibility for my marriage problems. Hell, I
wasn't an easy guy to live with. One time we were having dinner at La Rue,
a swank Hollywood place, when Charlie Chaplin came over to our table.
He'd been staring from across the room at Martha the entire evening.
Martha was a very beautiful woman, with high cheekbones, black hair,
green eyes, and a great figure. Chaplin asked her to come by his offices and
do a test for a role in his new film, *Monsieur Verdoux,* to play one of his
wives. Paulette Goddard would eventually get the part.

"I'm a big admirer of yours, Mr. Chaplin," I blurted out. "But
Martha's my wife and if she does a test for you, I'm going to have her face
changed!"

Chaplin's mouth dropped open. I don't think he knew I was joking. He
turned around and walked straight back to his table without another
word. He kept looking over at our table, then sent us a bottle of champagne. There was no denying it, my remark was out of line, much too
aggressive for the situation. I don't know why I reacted that way. I regretted it right away. What could have been going on in my mind to make me
react so jealously? It was unlike me to enslave a woman. Maybe I was feeling possessive because, with the deaths of my brothers, and without any
children of our own, Martha was all I had. She was very unhappy about
my behavior. Who wouldn't be? She was living with an intense, nervous,
sometimes belligerent guy.

When I think of *China Gate,* I always think of the Goldie character. I'd
given Goldie a soldiering background very much like my own. Zanuck
liked the role, too, and asked me about who I had in mind to play the part.
I said I wanted a man's man yet a guy with a warm, tender-looking face. I
picked up an album on top of a pile next to Darryl's record player. If my
soldier were black, he'd look just like the guy on the album cover, Nat
King Cole.

"Sammy, Cole's a big star," laughed Zanuck. "We paid him seventy-five
grand just to sing a title song. He's the most popular singer in the country.
Do you have any idea how much he'd ask for appearing in your picture?"

I shook my head. Immersed in my scripts, I was often naïve about
financial considerations and popular trends. The cigar in my mouth

Going through a scene with Nat King Cole, playing Goldie, his first dramatic part in a Hollywood movie. Nat was one of the biggest singing stars of that era and a delight to work with.

An evening out with Nat and Maria Cole after we finished China Gate

almost dropped out when Darryl said, "Cole probably makes in a couple weeks the entire budget for your film."

Still, I was infatuated with that face on the album cover, so I persisted. A dinner was arranged so that I could meet Nat and his exquisite wife, Maria. They were both moved by my story for *China Gate*. I told Nat point-blank that I didn't write the part for a black actor. I needed Goldie to be the diametric opposite to Brock, the bigot who rejects his own child because of the little boy's slanted eyes. Nat agreed to do the picture right away and asked for a minimum fee for his appearance.

Cole wasn't supposed to sing on screen or off. But Victor Young had written a title tune for the picture before his untimely death. When I played Victor's music for Nat, he said he'd love to sing it to Lea's little boy on camera. I wasn't crazy about the idea at first. But after Harold Adamson wrote some lyrics and I heard Nat's velvet voice croon the song, I couldn't resist.

> *China Gate,*
> *China Gate.*
> *Many dreams and many hearts,*
> *You separate.*
>
> *Like two arms,*
> *Open wide,*
> *Some you welcome in,*
> *And some must stay outside.*
>
> *Bowl of rice,*
> *Bitter tea,*
> *Is this all the good earth*
> *has to offer me?*
>
> *Will I find*
> *peace of mind?*
> *Does my true love wait*
> *behind the China Gate?*

We followed Nat with a camera on a boom crane high above the set as he walked and sang through the bombed-out village. I wanted his voice to seem like a nightingale flying safely above all the destruction. Believe it or not, I suggested that Nat try singing the song poorly. After all, his character is a soldier of fortune who probably sings off-key in the shower.

Setting the tone for my motley band of soldiers of fortune, the guys that Brock must lead deep into communist territory to destroy the crucial ammo dump behind the China Gate. *Nat King Cole is at the far end, next to our script girl.*

"Sammy, I can't sing badly!" Nat said. "What would my fans say? And what would people in the profession think if I sang off-key?"

He was right, of course. After we'd finished the picture, Nat invited Martha and me over to his place for dinner. Nat had some enormous catalogues of recordings next to his piano. I started thumbing through the big book to get to the Cs, for "Cole."

"Sammy, the *whole* catalogue is of my songs," he laughed. "What's your favorite tune?"

" 'I'm Forever Blowing Bubbles,' " I replied without hesitation.

"Okay," he said. "Let's record it together."

Nat had a little recording studio at his house. We went in there and sang the song together. What fun that was! "I'm forever blowing bubbles, pretty bubbles in the air. . . ."

Nat King Cole brought out the loving child in everybody. I certainly fell in love with the guy. Nat's gone now, but I'm still in love with him. People are never gone as long as they are loved.

With its highly stylized characters, *China Gate* may seem like a cartoon today. However, the picture didn't shy away from the conflict of ideologies that were struggling for future power. Nor did it waver in condemning racism. My tale is full of human foible and confusion. I deliberately wanted that confusion. I was still thinking of Clare Boothe Luce's remark that "anyone who isn't thoroughly confused, isn't thinking clearly." I wanted the picture to make a plea for understanding and tolerance, the keys to coexistence between couples, between peoples, between nations.

I pray that democracy is not like the bubbles that Nat and I blew in the air in the fifties, dreams that fade and die. It's up to the people of this tiny planet Earth to think in more humane, more global terms if our children are to have a future with no more goddamned wars.

Just before *China Gate* was to be released, I got a call from the French consul general in Los Angeles, Romain Gary, inviting me to lunch. I knew Gary as the author of *Company of Men*. He'd seen a rough cut of my movie. He told me the prologue was too harsh toward his country and asked me to change it. His mission was to make sure France was portrayed fairly in Hollywood. I told Romain that he had a job to do, and so did I. France had been colonizing countries for hundreds of years because it was good business. What I didn't like about all those colonial powers, whether they were French, British, Spanish, or Dutch—I didn't give a damn who—was the way they disguised their exploitation of their colonies by hanging a pretty veil over the whole affair. They were just "helping the people." Bullshit! My movie's prologue was accurate and would stand.

I asked Romain a blunt question. What if my movie had said the same things about another country, say Italy or Spain? Would he have objected? No, he replied, he wouldn't give a damn about me knocking the Italians or the Spanish. I loved his honesty. We talked about *Company of Men*. He joked that only two people had read the book, him and me. Then he asked if I wanted to do a movie based on the yarn. I declined. The story had already been told in De Sica's *Bicycle Thief*. Instead of Italian boys shining shoes in destitute postwar streets, Romain's Parisian boys scour the garbage for used condoms and resell them.

By a curious turn of events, I'd eventually make *White Dog*, another one of Romain's stories, into a movie. But that would be fifteen years later. When I met him, Romain Gary seemed to be on top of the world. He had a prestigious post with the French government, a beautiful wife—actress Jean Seberg—and a respected literary career. For Chrissakes, who could imagine that his life would turn out the way it did? He was obliged to write his novels under a pseudonym, Emil Ajar. Seberg committed suicide in the eighties, and Romain would take his own life a couple years later. From his standpoint, his life must have been terribly dark. Appearances, especially in Hollywood, can be so deceiving.

Regardless of my good rapport with Romain Gary, he obviously put a bug in the ear of somebody at the foreign ministry in Paris. A chancellery officer must have submitted a top-secret report taking my film to task for showing the French in an unfavorable light. Hell, I was merely a reporter, showing what the French had done in Indochina. I didn't write their history, *they did*. *China Gate* was a success for Fox all over the world, except for France, where it was never released.

34

Stuffed with
Phalluses

Juvenile delinquency was a hot subject in the fifties. Nicholas Ray's *Rebel Without a Cause* (1955) was a damned good picture, probably the decade's most important one about rebellious youth. I'd dabbled with the theme in *Run of the Arrow.* I wanted to show that juvenile rebellion existed even among Indians. Jay C. Flippen's Walking Coyote tells Rod Steiger's O'Meara that the young braves "... drink, they loot, they rape, and they have no respect for their elders."

My next films would delve deeper into the problems of misguided youth. In *Forty Guns* (1957), the heavy is the heroine's punk brother, a rotten, trigger-happy teenager. In *Verboten!* (1959), a violent gang corrupts an impressionable adolescent. In *Underworld, U.S.A.* (1960), a boy nourished on hate avenges his father's murder.

Each society has its own way of taming young people so they won't destroy themselves and can mature into useful citizens. By focusing on bad boys, I wanted to thank my mentors for helping me stay on the high road. I was lucky. At critical moments in my life, role models like Arthur Brisbane, Gene Fowler, Terry Allen, George Taylor, Herbert Brenon, and John Ford took me under their wings and kept me from derailing, showing me how to be a *mensch.*

Economic conditions in my youth had a lot to do with my attitude today. I feel sorry for today's affluent kids who don't have to strive for anything. When I was growing up, my family had very modest resources. My mother needed my financial help. There was no hardworking daddy or rich uncle to keep food on our table. I couldn't afford to be a rebel. There's nothing like work to make teenage bums into responsible adults.

In *Forty Guns,* the juvenile delinquent theme is a subplot intended to enhance the dominant nature of my lead, Jessica Drummond. The first time we see Jessica, she's dressed in black, riding her white stallion across Cochise County followed by forty men on forty horses. It's the 1880s, and

Stanwyck had what I wanted for the part of Jessica Drummond in Forty Guns. *Besides, she was ready to do whatever you needed, even if it meant falling off her horse and being dragged along the ground.*

this powerful gal owns those guys just like she owns most everything else in two-bit Tombstone, Arizona. Her one weak spot is for her punk brother, Brock, who shoots up the town just for fun. Brock gets arrested by a stranger, Griff Bonnell, who's on his way to California with his two brothers, Wes and Chico. Thanks to his big sister's influence, the good-for-nothing Brock is released from jail.

Griff is a retired gunman, having forsworn

his previous life as a marshal, a "legal killer." He and Jessica are drawn to one another, their passion finally exploding during a violent storm. Sheriff Ned Logan, who's not only on Jessica's payroll but also in her bed at night, is afraid Griff will expose the town's corruption. Jessica has no more use for Logan. She writes him a check and gets rid of him. Men do that all the time to women, but when Jessica does it, Logan's male pride is so wounded that he hangs himself.

Griff's brother Wes, marrying a local gal, is murdered by Brock at his own wedding. That bullet changes everyone's destiny. It pushes Griff over the edge. He hasn't touched a gun in a decade. He's reconditioned himself to shun the destructive power of guns. He taught Wes never to use a gun except for self-defense. Now he must exact justice for Wes's killing.

See, one goddamned bullet has always been decisive, from Sarajevo to Dallas. There are no more alibis with a bullet. Conventions, treaties, all good efforts, all bullshit! Phony! What really determines the beginning and the end of every conflict since the invention of gunpowder is the trajectory of one bullet.

Griff arrests Brock for his brother's murder and throws him back in jail, causing an angry rift with Jessica. When Jessica goes to visit her brother, Brock grabs her and uses her as a human shield to make a break for it. The final confrontation in *Forty Guns* has Brock taunting Griff, holding Jessica as protection, screaming, "Let's see you shoot her!" Brock knows Griff loves his sister and surely won't shoot a woman. He's wrong. Griff plugs Jessica in the leg and, as she slides to the ground, empties his pistol into the bastard brother. Brock sinks to his knees, screaming, "I'm killed, Mr. Bonnell, I'm killed!" Griff strides past Jessica, muttering to a bystander, "Get a doctor. She'll live."

Griff doesn't kill Brock out of vengeance. He's eliminating a cancer that's terrorizing the community. But he's disgusted with himself. By resorting to guns, Griff sees the last ten years vanish in a flash, as he becomes the killer he'd renounced.

My original script had Griff killing *both* Jessica and her brother, stepping over their corpses in a daze, throwing his gun down—this time for good—and walking up the dusty street without a pause. Nothing and no one exists for Griff anymore.

The End.

That version ran into trouble at the studio. Zanuck loved it, but his marketing people said they couldn't sell a Western where the hero kills the heroine. I told them that that was my story. The moment my hero picks up a gun again, he's honest, he knows he's going to kill. And he hates the killer in himself.

Fox's marketing people insisted that movie bookers and theater owners would never play a film like that. I was in a strange creative dead end. For Chrissakes, my gunman had to think about box-office receipts before he decided to pull the trigger! Zanuck asked me to come up with something different, so I changed the ending to suit the studio people. Griff only wounds Jessica, making sure that her life isn't in danger. We tacked on a closing scene with Griff riding a wagon out of town. Now fully recovered, no longer wearing black leather but a frilly white dress, Jessica runs after him.

I wanted *Forty Guns* to be a different kind of Western, as good as the trail-blazing movies that had inspired me: King Vidor's *Duel in the Sun* (1946), Anthony Mann's *The Furies* (1950), and Nicholas Ray's *Johnny Guitar* (1954).

My story hinged on America's pervasive fascination with guns. Hell if I know why people think guns are sexy. I cooked up a helluva lot of sexual metaphors playing with the idea. A couple flirts as assorted weapons in a gun-shop window shadow their faces. Wes looks at his future bride down the barrel of a rifle. A woman is "built like a 40-40." Jessica describes a man as "everything with two feet and a gun." When Griff starts flirting with Jessica, the sexual tension goes through the roof. Facing Griff across the dining table, Jessica asks him if she can feel his gun. He replies, "Uh-uh, it might go off in your face." Hell, the movie's stuffed with phalluses!

Guns in movies are fantasy objects. In real life, there are just too many guns and too many violent people who have access to them. The argument that our Constitution gives everyone the right to carry guns is stupid. It was written in 1789, when we were afraid that the British might return and we'd have to fight again for our independence. The situation is crazy today, and something clear-cut must be done to keep the tools of violence away from destructive people, especially youngsters. We must teach our children tolerance and forgiveness, not how to resort to guns. If films like *Forty Guns* serve any greater purpose at all—and who the hell can say if they do!—it's to show how inhumane and fruitless violence is.

A wonderful cast came together, with Barbara Stanwyck playing Jessica, Barry Sullivan as Griff, Dean Jagger as Sheriff Logan, John Ericson as Brock, and Gene Barry as Wes. Not long before we were to begin production of *Forty Guns,* I was working late at my office when Marilyn Monroe dropped in to say hello. She was wearing one of her big woolen sweaters and carrying a fat Dostoyevsky novel. She'd heard that Stanwyck was playing my heroine. Monroe asked me why I didn't let her read for the role. I told her that it would have been a comedy if she did the picture.

"But why?" asked Marilyn.

Griff (Barry Sullivan) pays a call on Jessica (Barbara Stanwyck) at dinnertime with her "guns." Fox's great set designer, Lyle Wheeler, retooled Tara, the famous plantation from Gone with the Wind, *to become the Drummonds' extraordinary ranch house.*

I summarized my story, cutting to the chase. My forty guns were forty pricks. My powerful heroine had her way in the sack with all forty, then cast them aside for the forty-first "gun," Griff. Monroe's wholesomeness wouldn't have been believable, her innocence out of place, and, finally, just funny. Marilyn listened and nodded thoughtfully. There was nothing phony about her. I told her I'd love to work with her and promised I'd keep looking for a part for her.

Monroe was a wonderful person. I'd always hold her in esteem because she was gracious enough to accept a blind date with my brother Ving. In the early fifties, Ving came out to the West Coast for a visit and asked me to fix him up for a night on the town. Marilyn happily agreed to my request. When Marilyn Monroe showed up,

In this early scene from Forty Guns, *we dollied the camera up the entire length of Fox's frontier street on specially laid tracks. It was the longest dolly shot in the history of the studio.*

Ving's mouth dropped open. Marilyn and Ving had a good time, dining and dancing at some swank place. My brother treated her with respect. She spent a pleasant evening with a normal guy without once talking about show business. She told me she was happy when she could be just a normal gal.

We had a very short shooting schedule on *Forty Guns,* so there wasn't much time for retakes. My cameraman, Joe Biroc, moved quickly from one setup to the next. We made most of the picture on Fox's back lot in the studio's Western town, a set that had already served as backdrop for hundreds of frontier movies. To convey the power and dominion of the Drummond clan in Tombstone, I wanted to shoot a scene from one end of Main Street to the other in one take. It was complicated, because the camera had to move all the way up the entire length of the set. We'd tried using the big Chapman crane, but the road was too rough, and the camera bounced all over the place.

So I had about fifty men come in and lay track all the way down the street—over a thousand feet of it—to have a smooth run for our dolly. We rehearsed a little, then we shot the scene, actors coming and going, greeting each other, the camera constantly moving up the street following a man on his way to the post office to send a telegram. At the corner, he walks past forty men sitting on forty horses, waiting for their boss. Jessica shows up, jumps up on her white stallion, and rides off, her forty horsemen galloping away behind her.

We got it in one take. I wanted the whole thing to look unstaged, dust and all. Joe Biroc had never shot a scene like that one, and he joked that he never wanted to do anything like it again. When those forty-one horses flew by him and the camera, only a couple of feet from his head, he said he was too scared to bat an eyelash.

For the long outdoor shots, we went up into one of those arid California valleys with unbroken vistas. Stanwyck insisted on doing all her own horseback scenes out there, even the stunt shots. The most dangerous one was when Jessica has to fall off her saddle in a violent dust storm and be dragged along the ground by her horse, one foot in the stirrup.

When Gene Fowler Jr., my editor on the picture, heard that Stanwyck was going to do the falling-off-the-horse scene, he confronted me in the cutting room.

"You're out of your mind, Sammy!" he said.

"Why?"

"What if something happens? The horse could step on her face. The picture isn't nearly finished. You've still got a lot of days to go with her. She's a big star."

"Well, nothing's going to happen. Barbara said she wanted to do it, and that's that," I said, ending the discussion.

Not only did Stanwyck do the stunt, she did it over and over. Because of technical problems, we had to reshoot the damned scene three times. You couldn't believe the dust storm we concocted. It was ferocious. We brought in an extra wind machine and threw in bags of stuff called Fuller's Earth, a brand of cement. I liked the wild effect it created. But the crap didn't feel too good in your mouth and your eyes, especially when they whipped it up to about eighty miles an hour. Barbara was a little bruised at the end of that day, but she never murmured a word of complaint. What a trooper!

They showed *Forty Guns* at the Locarno Film Festival in Switzerland a few years ago as part of a tribute. There were two thousand spectators in the Piazza Grande. On the big screen, you could see the tiny veins in the necks of those galloping horses. That's how close Joe Biroc's camera was in that dolly shot. To see the film projected on that size screen was really exciting. For the festivalgoers, they subtitled the picture in French and Italian. Whatever language they spoke, everybody understood Jessica's passionate, forceful character. Several women came running up to me afterward and said *Forty Guns* was "the most feminist movie" they'd ever seen.

In a lot of pictures, you saw the heavy grab the leading lady and make the hero drop his gun. I wanted to do this scene in a way the audience wasn't expecting, so Griff first wounds Jessica, then takes out the sonofabitch brother, Brock.

I think the poet Petrarch claimed that a woman had to have some masculine qualities to seduce a man. Griff falls for Jessica because she's one powerful lady. *Forty Guns* is not only about strength. It's about modesty, too. Jessica rides in on a horse followed by forty men, but, at the end, she's on foot, running after the guy she loves. Her power is just as great, but it's been altered by love, forgiveness, and humility. Griff killed her brother, wounding her in the process, but she forgives him.

"You have to be big to forgive," says Griff.

Of all the articles and reviews that have been written over the years about *Forty Guns,* the one I most appreciated was a French writer's fascination with the way my gunman walks toward his adversary. I was intent on

Stanwyck was a helluva gal.

getting that right, that rhythmical, stalking gait as he relentlessly closes in on his victim. The Indians perfected that stride. It required patience and timing. You can see Griff using his entire body to do "the walk."

For the showdown, I had Joe Biroc set up his camera behind Griff as his remaining brother, Chico, carefully moves into place at a window to cover him. When Griff captures the eye of his adversary, he's out of danger. The guy's as good as dead because he's in a death trap. See, real gunmen in the Old West never walked down the middle of some dusty frontier street like you see in the movies. They moved in stealthily, like a mongoose closes in on a cobra. They always—always!—had an accomplice hidden somewhere behind a window or a door aiming at the victim's back. It was usually that guy who did the killing. Professional gunmen wanted to live a long life and put their victims away quick. That way they could collect the bounties—their paychecks—at the end of every month. Go out west and look at the tombstones of marshals, sheriffs, and other paid killers, as I have. Compare the dates after "b." and "d." Those guys died late in life, probably asleep in their beds, not in a heroic gunfight with a badman.

With *Forty Guns,* I'd really hit my stride. I considered it one of my best efforts so far. Sure, there were some compromises—like the ending—but it came pretty close to my original vision. At the time, very few people were given the opportunity to write, produce, and direct their own movies. In France in the sixties, they'd call it *cinéma d'auteur*. Maybe after the New Wave boys had blazed a trail, filmmakers expected independence. But in America in the fifties, it was very tough to maintain that kind of autonomy unless you financed your own pictures. It would get even tougher in the decades to come. One of my inspirations was Joseph Mankiewicz, the great writer-producer-director. Joe encouraged me to never stop fighting for my personal vision in Hollywood. He'd fought some hard battles himself in the forty years he'd been in the business. Joe was suspicious of any project that needed five screenwriters. He would puff on his pipe, shake his head and say, "Sam, too many cooks spoil the brew."

For my next picture, I felt like a chef making a hardy soup—blending together postwar Germany, Beethoven, Wagner, unrepentant Nazis, and the Nuremberg war trials into a forceful yarn I'd call *Verboten!*, German for "forbidden."

35

I Used My Own
Voice

Long before I went to war against Germany, I was fascinated with German culture. As a young man, I was deeply moved by Goethe's *Faust.* I still have a cherished edition of Heinrich Heine's *Germany, A Winter's Tale.* When I listened to Beethoven, I got a million images in my head, a million ideas for stories. Other composers didn't have that cosmic effect on me. It was like one mountain calling to another, one ocean inviting another to join it. Beethoven made the blood rush through my veins. In his sweeping symphonies, I heard echoes of real people I'd known and voices of imaginary characters.

Beethoven was even in my dreams. At night, he showed up to reassure me, as if we were of one family. He came to me in nightmares, too, with harsh words. Shaking his big mane of hair, he'd say, "Go and write your stories, Fuller, but please, *please,* don't touch my music." I remembered lying in the desert in Tunisia during the war dreaming I could hear Beethoven. Then Axis Sally started singing "Lili Marleen" on Nazi loud-speakers. "Lili Marleen" was a gorgeous song, but it was used as propa-ganda, promoting fascist lies and doom. Beethoven wrote life-giving music, opening doors, not locking them.

In the late thirties, I wanted to do a movie based on the life of Herman Ullstein, the German press magnate who'd opposed Hitler and was destroyed by the Nazis. I talked to the actor Albert Basserman about play-ing Ullstein. War seemed imminent, and no studio was in the mood to make a movie about a German who was anti-Hitler. For Hollywood, every German was a Nazi.

Thanks to my war experiences, I'd learned firsthand that every German was *not* a Nazi. Still, the studios shied away from any picture dealing with contemporary Germany. Americans had been overwhelmed with images of the Holocaust, proof of Hitler's monstrous Final Solution. The public couldn't empathize with German civilians who'd been caught up in the

Nazi madness. If they didn't wear swastikas, went popular opinion, then they all looked the other way during Hitler's reign.

I showed William Dozier at RKO my script for *Verboten!*, set in post-War Germany. Dozier thought it was a good story, honest but risky. If I could shoot the picture fast on a tight budget, he'd green-light it. Bill was worried about my scene at the Nuremberg trials where I have my characters in the back of the courtroom watching the proceedings.

"How are you going to make it look authentic?" asked Dozier.

"I'm going to use war footage and actual film taken at the trials," I told him.

"How can you get that material, Sam?"

"The war stuff, from military friends in Washington. The Nuremberg stuff, from Ray Kellogg, my special-effects man. Ray was a cameraman at Nuremberg. He gave me twenty reels of 16-mm, black-and-white footage he shot at the proceedings."

I have few regrets about my life, but one of them concerns the Nuremberg trials. Behind each Nazi prisoner at Nuremberg was a guard. Those guards were soldiers from my outfit, the Big Red One. The military was screening candidates for that assignment when I went off to Paris to visit my brother Ray. I'd already promised him that I'd meet him in Paris, and there was no way in hell I'd let him down. But what a missed opportunity. I could've watched the Nuremberg trials in person.

As soon as RKO okayed *Verboten!*, we cast and shot it quickly, maybe ten days, maximum. My yarn begins as the U.S. Army is rolling over the last traces of German resistance. Sergeant Brent, part of a patrol flushing out snipers from a bombed-out town called Rothbach, is wounded in the ass. When he wakes up, a picture of Hitler is staring down at him. A German woman, Helga, has dragged him to safety in a bombed-out ruin that used to be her home. Her mother is bedridden. Helga patches Brent's wound and hides him from the retreating Nazis. He finds out she's got a bitter teenage brother, Franz, whose arm was mangled by an American bomb. Brent's suspicious of Helga's real motives:

> HELGA
> My family lived on lies since 1933.
>
> BRENT
> What's that got to do with this?
>
> HELGA
> That was the year Germany was murdered by Der Fuehrer.

> BRENT
> But you all strung along with him while he was winning, didn't you?
>
> HELGA
> We believed him, until it was too late to learn he was only interested in Adolf Hitler.
>
> BRENT
> Then why didn't you Germans open your big mouths when he began throwing people into gas chambers?
>
> HELGA
> We are all guilty for not opening our "big mouths"!

As Brent recovers, he falls in love with Helga and arranges to stay on in Germany after the war so he can marry her. Working as a civilian liaison, Brent keeps Helga supplied with food, goods, and silk stockings during the harsh postwar period. But in the occupied zone, *Frauleins* are *verboten*. Brent's superior officer tries to discourage him from his romance with a German woman, assuring him that, whether Germans deny it or not, "they've had a fascist education." Meanwhile, young Franz falls under the influence of Bruno, an unregenerate Nazi and leader of the Werewolves, a secret, Himmler-inspired militia that aids escaped war criminals and wreaks havoc on occupying Allied forces. Bruno manages to get a day job at the U.S. Army HQ, allowing him to plan his attacks from within.

An American Forces radio network announcement sets the stage for the upcoming war trials:

> RADIO ANNOUNCER
> Before the international military trial at Nuremberg, United States Chief Prosecutor Robert H. Jackson told the court that he not only is appearing as counsel for the Allied Powers but for the entire civilized world. He said, "The real complaining party at your bar is civilization."

Bruno and his Werewolves pursue their campaign of sabotage and violence against the Americans, provoking food riots and anti-American

In Verboten! *Brent (James Best) tries to talk common sense to demonstrators (above) in the Occupied Zone but a riot breaks out (below) as soon as his speech is over.*

demonstrations. Brent himself is roughed up by demonstrators, getting suspended after the melee. That causes a big row at home with Helga, who is now pregnant. She confesses she married Brent for the food and supplies he could provide, but that she really loves him now. He feels double-crossed, and walks out.

Young Franz witnesses the murder of one of the Werewolves' gang members who challenges Bruno's power lust. Helga tries to tell her brother the truth about the Werewolves, but Franz refuses to listen to her. So she makes him sit through a session at the Nuremberg trials. Among the defendants are Göring, Hess, von Ribbentrop, von Papen, Bormann, Speer, Frick, Seyss-Inquart, and Keitel. Footage screened as evidence against the war criminals—horrifying scenes of Nazi cruelty and destruction—open the adolescent's eyes to the Werewolves' real motives.

"I didn't know!" mutters the stunned Franz. "I didn't know!"

Franz's painful awakening pushes him to recognize the truth about Bruno and his gang of young fascists. The teenager helps American authorities bring a quick and violent halt to the Werewolves' activities.

My yarn was ripped from the headlines of that time. In the postwar period, the threat of a renaissance of the Nazi movement was very real. Young Hitlerian extremists had formed secret gangs. Nazism was outlawed, so the gangs went underground. They were controlled by veterans who refused to acknowledge defeat. Eventually, their movement made its way across Europe and to the United States. These lunatic sonsofbitches exist even today in America. There they are, decades later, with their fascist ideas and secret camps, their guerrilla training and their swastikas. It's absolute insanity, yet it's real.

I wanted my movie to go beyond the isolated problem with the Werewolves to the universal struggle of poor people in war-torn countries everywhere, trying to survive without a future, susceptible to extremists who promise them food and hope. In times like those, a despot can easily come to power. To prepare my movie, I'd read *Little Man, What Now?*, by Hans Fallada. According to Fallada, if there hadn't been a depression after the kaisers, there wouldn't have been a Hitler. Appealing to people's bellies, Hitler promised the Germans a better life, if only they gave him total power.

Music was one of the keys for me to convey the chaotic emotions of the period. The opening of the picture has four soldiers flushing out Nazi snipers to the music of Beethoven's Ninth. No dialogue, just noble, grandiose music and ballsy, man-to-man combat. Later Brent, played by James Best, proposes marriage to Helga, played by Susan Cummings. Here again the music is Beethoven. She accepts. No sooner has the exuberant

Brent gone off to his new civilian job than Bruno, the Nazi war veteran, shows up. His entrance is accompanied by a heavy Wagnerian overture, like the first act of a tragic opera. Bruno has an emotional claim on the woman, too. The contrasting music underscores the audience's doubt about Helga. Is she or isn't she a Nazi in her heart of hearts?

The first time we see Bruno, he's carrying a heavy backpack. The defeated soldier symbolizes all that's left of German youth after the Third Reich. I saw a helluva lot of young men like Bruno at the end of the war. Thousands of them were walking like robots along bombed-out roads, their faces empty, their eyes deadened. Shell-shocked and war-weary, they carried on their shoulders, along with all their worldly possessions, the crushing weight of defeat. It was a sad sight that made the futility of war stunningly clear.

Bruno was played by newcomer Tom Pittman. He had an unaffected quality I liked and a calmness that only good actors have, even if they are boiling with emotion inside. Gary Cooper was one of those natural ones. Awkward, timid, and embarrassed on the screen, Gary always appeared not to be acting at all. A casting director at Warner Brothers looked at some of my rushes with Pittman and thought the young actor had the intensity to be a star. The studio offered Tom a seven-year contract, the kickoff for a big career.

After we'd wrapped *Verboten!*, Tom said he was taking a little vacation and drove away in his sports car. The following week my office tried contacting him. We still needed him to come by the studio and loop some dialogue. We couldn't reach him. No one had seen him for days. Tom's worried father contacted me. I called a pal who was a journalist to see if he'd heard anything. Finally we called the sheriff's office. The manhunt ended when they found Tom's corpse in his smashed-up sports car at the bottom of one of those curvy, dangerous roads up in the Los Angeles canyons. We all felt terrible about Tom Pittman's tragic and untimely death.

Among the actresses who'd read for the part of Helga was Anne Bancroft. She was under contract at Fox at the time. I adored Bancroft. She told me that she was always getting cast as the girlfriend to leading actresses, never as the lead herself. She wasn't happy about her Hollywood career and was toying with the idea of going back to the New York stage. Bancroft had a strong presence, but she just didn't correspond physically to the girl I had in mind. I would have loved to work with her on another project, but it never happened. I wished I'd written a part that suited her as well as the famous role of *The Graduate*'s Mrs. Robinson.

To arrange and direct the musical score for *Verboten!*, I turned to my

Susan Cummings hadn't been in town too long when she came in to test for Helga in Verboten! *The studio people said she looked too European, but, damnit, that was exactly what I wanted, so I hired her. She was a sweet person and did a fine job.*

friend Harry Sukman. There was a musician's strike going on, so Harry decided to record the Beethoven and Wagner pieces in Germany. Harry told me that when he lifted his baton the first day in that Munich studio, he was sweating. Being American and Jewish and leading a German orchestra on German soil made Harry tremble.

The movie's musical credits cite Sukman, Beethoven, and Wagner. I wanted to stick with a classical score, but an RKO executive convinced Sukman to write a pop song for the soundtrack, too. Pop singer Paul Anka showed up at my office one day to sing the tune for me. Mack David's lyrics began, "Our love is *Verboten!,* they tell us we are worlds apart. . . ." The studio thought a pop tune like that would make the picture more commercial. Paul was a sweet kid and had a great voice. But I didn't want to use that goddamned tune. I eventually relented and let them put the song over the picture's opening credits.

See, music is an essential part of every picture I make, maybe as important as the story. Before photographs and movies, people were listening to music and getting strong emotional messages. When I write, I visualize what I want to happen on the screen and imagine the accompanying music. I can actually "see" the action and dialogue better by adding music early on in the script. The music even gives me story ideas. I always provide composers precise instructions about the kind of music I'm looking for. Then I leave them totally free to come up with a soundtrack that best corresponds to each section of the picture.

There was tremendous competition among the Hollywood movie composers of the day, talented guys like Sukman, Dimitri Tiomkin, Victor Young, and Alfred Newman, but there was also great camaraderie and respect. When you picked one of those great composers to do your score, the others wished him well and meant it. I didn't always work with experienced musicians or classical themes. One day in the early fifties, a tall, handsome man walked into my office at Fox with a slight limp and introduced himself as Paul Dunlap. He said he was a composer. I'd never heard of him.

"I wrote something for you," he said. "If you like it, I'll write any kind of music you want."

I liked Dunlap's work and felt he deserved a chance. He ended up doing the musical scores for *The Baron of Arizona, The Steel Helmet, Park Row, Shock Corridor,* and *The Naked Kiss.*

Columbia picked up *Verboten!* for distribution and did pretty well with the picture at the box office. Critics were divided. As usual, those who had an ax to grind wrote bad reviews. Believe it or not, one reviewer said my movie had "intended to minimize the Nazi movement." Holy shit, what an utterly preposterous idea, especially after I spent almost four years in the infantry dodging Nazi bullets! Commentary like that smelled of bad faith, plain stupidity, or both. It was a fact that a helluva lot of Germans were anti-Hitler. Hell, people didn't realize that a hefty slice of the twelve million prisoners in the camps were non-Jewish Germans, locked up for not supporting the Nazi regime.

French critics were crazy about the movie. A young critic named François Truffaut wrote a deliriously enthusiastic review for *Cahiers du Cinéma.* Jean-Luc Godard said *Verboten!* made him want to stop writing about films and start making them.

While we were cutting *Verboten!,* I realized that the movie's Nuremberg trial scene was the most crucial, the emotional centerpiece of the picture. I'd written sober words to accompany the ghastly montage of war scenes and concentration-camp footage, borrowing heavily from Supreme Court Justice Charles H. Jackson's actual opening statement at Nuremberg:

> NARRATOR
> . . . A most intense drive was directed by
> Hitler and his Nazis against German Protes-
> tants, Lutherans, Catholics. Pastor Niemeier

was sent to a concentration camp. Bishop Gräber was beaten up. Hitler inspired vandalism against church property. Nazi teaching was inconsistent with the Christian faith. It was the Nazi plan to suppress the Christian church completely after the War.

But with the War, the number of victims swelled to include citizens of all the nations in Europe. Included among the executed and burned were citizens from Holland, France, Belgium, Poland, Hungary, Czechoslovakia, Greece and other countries.

But perhaps the greatest crime against humanity the Nazis committed was against the Jews, whom they used as the scapegoat to camouflage their plan to make Hitler God and to make *Mein Kampf* the Bible.

Goebbels was Hitler's co-pilot. Goebbels catered to children with campaign cries that went to the heart of the Nazi movement. Hate was the Nazi religion. Hate was their battle cry. Hate was their God.

Children of tender years were invariably exterminated since they were unable to work. The Nazis endeavored to fool them into thinking they were going through a de-lousing process.

A thousand years will pass and this guilt of the Hitler gang will still not be erased. It took from three to fifteen minutes to kill the people in the gas chamber, depending on the climatic conditions. The Nazis knew when the people were dead because the screaming stopped. After the bodies were removed, special Hitler commandos took off the rings and extracted the gold from the teeth of the corpses. Much of this loot was then transferred to secret vaults of the Reichsbank at Frankfurt-am-Mein.

This was genocide, the premeditated destruction of entire peoples. Genocide, the direct result of the Nazi's claim that they have the right to destroy Hitler's opposition.

Tomorrow the world, dead or alive.

We were in a hurry when it came time to record that narration, and I couldn't find an actor to do it the way I wanted. It had to be delivered like a reporter, serene and emotionless. I'd been an eyewitness to that great agony, so I used my own voice. It was tough to do, believe me. With *Verboten!*, I wanted to tell people the harsh truth and never let them forget what really happened during the Holocaust.

36

Los Angeles,
Mon Amour

Throughout the fifties, I got offers to direct big movies adapted from best-selling books with major stars attached. One after another, I turned them down for a variety of personal and professional reasons. In general, making less expensive movies meant maintaining my independence, avoiding the studios' tampering with my scripts, imposing their casting and editing choices. Maybe it was a fatal career flaw, but small-budget independence was more appealing to me than all the thunder of major productions.

Following Harry Cohn's death, Sam Briskin became head of Columbia. Briskin invited me over to his office to pitch him another movie, no doubt when the studio accountants told him *Verboten!* was selling tickets. I told him about a murder yarn that had been bouncing around my head for years. I called it *The Crimson Kimono.* Two cops in charge of a murder investigation fall for the same gal. One of the detectives is white and the other is a Nisei, a Japanese American. The two men have been inseparable since their tour of duty in Korea. The girl goes for the Nisei cop, not the white one.

"Well, Sam, can't you make the white guy a sonofabitch?" asked Briskin, a little worried. "We've got to market your movie all across the country, including the Midwest and the Bible Belt."

"The girl chooses the Japanese guy because he's the man for her," I said. "Not because the white guy's a sonofabitch. The whole idea of my picture is that both men are good cops and good citizens. The girl just happens to fall in love with the Nisei. They've got chemistry."

"That's gonna be hard for average American audiences to swallow, Sam. We've got to sell 'em tickets. Look, can't you make the white guy a *little* bit of a sonofabitch?"

"No, I can't! A girl can't be a *little* pregnant! She is or she isn't. My white cop is a regular guy."

For Chrissakes, we were supposed to be living in a "modern" age. As a boy, I remember how I wanted Lillian Gish's heroine to end up with the sweet Chinese guy in D. W. Griffith's *Broken Blossoms*. Back then, I suppose it couldn't be. Thank God, times had changed. My heroine could choose the Asian guy over the white guy without the white guy being a villain.

It took some talking, but I was able to convince Briskin to do the picture my way. I got a green light to go into production with the script almost exactly as I'd written it. We shot in Los Angeles's Little Tokyo district in the winter of '59. Nobody'd ever made a movie there before. I loved the Japanese look of that location, smack in the middle of LA's urban sprawl.

The movie opens with a stranger armed with a .32-caliber Smith & Wesson confronting a platinum-blond stripper in her dressing room at a seedy LA burlesque house. With hardly any clothes on, Sugar Torch runs out the stage door and gets shot dead in the middle of a busy thoroughfare. Detectives Charlie Bancroft and Joe Kojaku are put on the case. They're roommates and close friends. The investigation leads them to Christine Down, a beautiful artist who once painted a portrait of the victim as a geisha girl in a red kimono.

Charlie, the white cop, falls for Christine first. But she prefers Joe, the Nisei. He suppresses his warm feelings for the girl because he doesn't want to betray his best friend. Furthermore, Joe is neurotic about his racial background, believing that his growing love for Christine has brought out long-buried racist hatred in his buddy. The situation explodes at a kendo sword-fight exhibition, where the two friends go at each other violently, almost getting Charlie seriously injured.

With Christine's help, Sugar's killer is tracked down. It turns out to be a woman who mistakenly believed her boyfriend was seeing the stripper on the sly. Joe sees a parallel between the killer's crazed behavior and his own mistaken reaction about Charlie. The two buddies are able to finally talk openly about their shortsightedness. However, their love for Christine has permanently damaged their friendship. The picture closes at the Nisei Festival in Little Tokyo as Joe and Christine embrace in the middle of a group of Ondo dancers.

Though it looked like a pretty conventional cops-and-criminals movie, *The Crimson Kimono* was almost operatic in its tone. I was trying to make an unconventionally triangular love story, laced with reverse racism, a kind of narrow-mindedness that's just as deplorable as outright bigotry. I wanted to show that whites aren't the only ones susceptible to racist thoughts. Joe is a racist because he transfers his fears to his friend. I wrote a confrontation scene for the two buddies that comes right after their dangerous kendo sword fight. Charlie can't understand Joe's anger. This exchange gives him a clue to Joe's problem:

> CHARLIE
> You mean you want to marry her?
>
> JOE
> You wouldn't have said it that way if I were white!
>
> CHARLIE
> What the hell are you talking about?
>
> JOE
> Look at you! It's all over your face!
>
> CHARLIE
> Have you gone crazy?
>
> JOE
> What burns you is that you lost her to me!
>
> CHARLIE
> Is that what you think?
>
> JOE
> It's not what I think! It's what I know. It makes you sick to your stomach! Look at your face!

Joe's wrong—as wrong as Othello in his unjustified accusations of Desdemona. Charlie confronts him honestly. Joe is blind to the truth. He's going away.

> CHARLIE
> Will it do any good if I talk?
>
> JOE
> Nope.
>
> CHARLIE
> Even if you went off half-cocked?

JOE
I'm not scouting for an apology.

CHARLIE
Apologize for what? I apologize when I'm wrong—not when you put words in my mouth!

JOE
You're wasting your time.

CHARLIE
Joe, you threw me off guard when you told me about Chris. Maybe there *was* a look on my face. A look of hate—normal, healthy, jealous *hate*! Look at me, Joe! You know me better than anybody else. I'm even carrying a pint of your blood inside me, remember?

JOE
Never missed it.

CHARLIE
Glad it's not a piece of your brain muscle! When are you turning your badge in?

JOE
Soon as the chief gets to his office.

CHARLIE
The case isn't closed yet.

JOE
Mine is.

They run down Sugar's murderer, a gal named Roma, who confesses with her dying breath that she was mistaken, and that she killed because she was jealous of her boyfriend without having proof he was cheating. Suddenly Joe understands his own misplaced aggression and poor judgment.

"Love is like a battlefield. Somebody has to get a bloody nose," con-

With James Shigeta and Victoria Shaw, my lovers in The Crimson Kimono, *breaking worn-out Hollywood racial stereotypes that a white woman and a Japanese-American couldn't get together*

cludes Mac, my cigar-smoking female muralist on Skid Row. The part was played by the lovely Anna Lee, costumed to conceal her beauty and femininity.

Hell, history is full of little misunderstandings and imaginary demons, little bumps in the road that overturn the entire apple cart of human relationships. A bloody nose on Cleopatra could alter the course of history.

James Shigeta got the role of Joe. Shigeta had been a singer in Honolulu before getting a role in the smash Broadway musical *The Flower Drum Song.* Glenn Corbett got the part of Charlie, the white cop. For Christine, the woman they both fall in love with, I picked Victoria Shaw, an Australian actress I'd seen in George Sidney's film *The Eddy Duchin Story* (1956), in which Victoria played alongside Tyrone Power and Kim Novak. When I walked out of that formulaic movie, I thought more about Victoria's character, a sweet girl who takes care of children, than about the sexy one that Kim Novak played. I wanted a normal-looking yet classy actress to play the role of the white artist who falls for the Nisei. Victoria Shaw was poised and steady at all times, with Romy Schneider–like beauty. She was a far cry from the flaming-hot blondes who were so popular back then.

My opening shot was from a helicopter flying over Los Angeles at night. We had trouble getting permission to fly as low as I wanted, but we pulled it off. Another rough scene to shoot was when the stripper flees the burlesque house and gets shot on a downtown street. I had problems finding a stunt woman who'd actually run around the street half naked in heavy traffic. We finally found a large blond lady to do it. The passing cars weren't aware that we were using the street as a movie set. While we were shooting, the real cops showed up. Somebody had reported a woman running around in her underwear. They also reported a corpse, which is what she became at the end of the scene. By then, we had the scene in the can. When I looked at the rushes with Sam Briskin, we realized that nobody—not even a passing sailor or a homeless drunk—was paying any attention to the big, scantily clad gal running along that downtown street. Nobody gave a damn. "What the hell's wrong with this country?" asked Briskin.

To recreate the kendo sword fight and make all the action scenes look realistic, I hired a martial arts expert, George Okamura, to oversee the stunts. Okamura was a heavyset man who appears with Joe and Charlie in a fight scene in a pool hall. Okamura insisted that my actors actually hit him in that scene. They were reluctant, but when the cameras rolled, they really banged away. Okamura was right. The fight looked genuine. Hell, it was.

I wanted to get the kendo scene right because that sword fight sends an emotional message about Joe that's essential to my yarn. When Joe blows his stack and tries to beat up Charlie during the exhibition, he transgresses the protocol of a discipline whose basic rules have been developed over the last two thousand years of Japanese culture. He strikes out at his best friend and at the basic mores of his people. A person that far overboard is in terrible pain. Joe goes off the deep end and may never regain his balance. I wanted to show that the violence was directed as much at himself as at his buddy.

Upsetting the apple cart is fair game if you're striving to develop a character or underscore an emotion. In *Run of the Arrow* and *Forty Guns,* I'd broken plenty of rules to make characters more credible. And I'd do it again, as long as it gave my stories a fresh twist and allowed my characters to stay true to themselves.

We finished *The Crimson Kimono* on schedule and under budget. When Columbia released the movie, I was disappointed by the way they marketed it. They went against my express wishes and slanted the campaign with banner catch phrases such as "L.A. BY NIGHT" and "WHY DOES

SHE CHOOSE A JAPANESE LOVER?" To me, the Los Angeles setting was of minor importance. My story could have taken place in Tallahassee in broad daylight. I was trying to develop original characters in an unusual story line. That's why I'd cast the picture with unknowns. Stars would have been less credible. I complained bitterly about how they'd cheapened the movie. I was told that, now that the film was finished, I should leave the marketing to them. The film was released as just another Hollywood "B" exploitation picture.

It didn't have to be that way. I still have two 1960 reviews—printed side by side in the same issue of an English newspaper—of Alain Resnais's *Hiroshima, Mon Amour,* and of *The Crimson Kimono.* The headline over both articles said "Los Angeles, Mon Amour." By sheer coincidence, both movies had been released about the same time. Both stories dealt with white women falling in love with Japanese men. Both reviews were extremely favorable, delving into similarities and contrasts between the two works. The writer treated both films with respect and intelligence, understanding all the themes I was hitting upon. He said very nice things about my film because he got it. When you are the sole author of the story as well as the director, you only have yourself to blame if your movie is misunderstood. On the other hand, when your film breaks through and speaks to people, maybe just one person next door or across an ocean, you feel deeply satisfied.

I didn't give a damn if *The Crimson Kimono* looked like one of my "minor" works. I was proud of the picture. Was I completely satisfied with it? Not really. One story, one script, one book, one film never really gives me complete satisfaction. Nor should it. All creative people must learn how to deal with the imperfect and the incomplete. There is no end in art. Every accomplishment is the dawn of the next challenge. The kismet of artists is to accept partial fulfillment. As I look back now, I know that I've only achieved a small slice of what I wanted to do. Not one of my films is all I'd hoped it would be. Still, the smile on my face is just as broad and grateful.

Breathing Revenge

My mother died in the spring of 1959, at the age of eighty-five. All my life, Rebecca Fuller had been my greatest supporter. There's nothing to say when a man loses his mother. It's just a terrible emptiness. My marriage to Martha wasn't going well, and my mother's death sealed its fate. I wanted to move out of the big Hearst mansion with the servants to return to living more simply, to work on my stories in peace and pull myself back together. I decided to leave Martha the house and everything in it except for my Royal typewriter and the Mark Twain table that I'd bought from Twain's daughter, Clara.

Martha filed divorce papers against me for "mental cruelty." I okayed the whole thing. What difference what they called it? The relationship was finished. My lawyer said that I was completely nuts to leave her the house. He threatened to never talk to me again unless I asked for a fifty-fifty split. Nevertheless, I insisted on Martha keeping everything. I knew I could start again and wanted to make sure she was taken care of. I had no heart for a messy divorce settlement.

Through me, Martha met her next husband, Ray Harvey. Ray had been a highly decorated army officer during the war. He'd relocated to Hollywood and was then working for the studios as a "technical adviser." As a guarantee of authenticity, I'd hired Ray on *Fixed Bayonets* and *Verboten!* He'd been over to our house on many occasions. The three of us used to have good times together.

In the summer of 1959, I was finally on the brink of a multimillion-dollar deal with Warner Brothers to write, direct, and produce *The Big Red One*. The picture would follow a gritty sergeant and his squad of dogfaces during the First Division's campaigns in North Africa, Sicily, and Europe. I'd amassed a thousand pages of action and dialogue and storyboarded most of the film in my head.

Jack Warner loved my yarn and lined up John Wayne to play the part of the sergeant. I wasn't crazy about the idea of Wayne doing the role, but I put my reservations aside for the time being. Warner coughed up the dough for a scouting trip for me to revisit all of the Big Red One's important battlefields. I decided to take Martha with me. It was our farewell voyage together. I also took Ray Harvey along with us. While I shot photos of locations, Ray drew up plans for the production's technical details, as he was going to be our liaison with the U.S. Army on the film.

It was during that trip to Europe and North Africa that Martha and Ray started to have serious feelings for each other. I wasn't going to stand in their way. When we came home, I moved into a modest place down in Hollywood, allowing Martha and Ray to take up life together. We all remained friends, which seemed bizarre to outsiders. People thought of me as an incorrigible eccentric for having changed lifestyles so drastically. I didn't give a damn what anybody thought, for I was too busy with preparations for the most important movie I'd ever make.

Richard Brooks and Dalton Trumbo advised me against doing *The Big Red One* with John Wayne. Their contention was that Wayne would succeed in shrinking my story from a dark struggle for survival and sanity into a patriotic adventure movie. I thought a lot about it and decided they were right. I couldn't risk having to compromise on that movie. When I told Jack Warner that I wanted someone else besides Wayne, the deal fizzled.

My mother's death, the divorce, and the suspension of *The Big Red One* all weighed heavily upon me. I became a solitary figure, not even socializing with my cherished writer friends or musician buddies. All I wanted was to be left alone so that I could absorb all the pain in my own way. Thankfully, there wasn't much time to mope, because I was working on dozens of ideas for movies. With the business being as crazy as it was, my next project came from Columbia, the studio that I'd had words with about the release of *The Crimson Kimono*. Despite my problems with them, they offered me another film with producer Ray Stark.

Ray wanted me to write and direct a movie based on a magazine article that he'd bought the rights to. The article, written by Boston newspaperman Joseph Dineen, talked about gangsters operating not only in Chicago and New York but also in other cities across the country, like Boston. Boston even had its equivalent of mob boss Al Capone. Stark loved the title of the aricle, "Underworld, U.S.A." And so did I.

The first gangster movie I ever saw was Josef von Sternberg's *Underworld* (1927), with Clive Brook and George G. Bancroft. Ben Hecht won an Academy Award for that screenplay. The film defined the genre by its story and lighting, long before the elements became clichés. I wanted to go beyond classical gangster movies like *Public Enemy* (1931) and *Scarface*

(1932) to talk about alienation and corruption, inspired more by Greek drama. I was also influenced by an excellent book entitled *Here Is to Crime,* by Riley Cooper, a newspaperman whose extensive research proved that crime in the United States really did pay. My take on *Underworld, U.S.A.,* was to focus on a criminal who's a loner, a man whose entire motive for breathing is revenge. A loner cannot, by definition, be a "gangster." He or she never feels comfortable being a member of any group.

My relations with the studio boys started off on the wrong foot, right from the moment I let them read my first scene, a hell-raising opening that began with a close-up of a beautiful young woman's back, the camera rising on a crane to reveal more and more attractive women, scantily clad and positioned to form a map of the United States. Then one of the women begins a stirring speech about the new "Union of Prostitutes" that she explains is necessary for the advancement of their careers. Cab fares and laundry bills would be tax-deductible. Pimps would be outlawed. Prostitution is a job like any other, she says, and they want official recognition. Prostitution would always be part of the national economy, so why not unionize, set their own minimum wages, and get social security and retirement benefits, just like any other worker, male or female. As the woman concludes her glorious speech, the fat title comes up across the screen: UNDERWORLD, U.S.A.

The camera follows the rabble-rousing prostitute into a changing room. While she's getting dressed, the muzzle of a gun slips into her mouth and fires, exploding her head. The movie's titles and credits continue to roll. The other prostitutes run for their lives. One of them hooks up with my loner lead, implicating people very high on the social ladder in prostitution, rackets, and drug pushing.

Sam Briskin and other Columbia executives found my opening scene downright shocking. Hell, I was showing how crime had become part of the very fabric of our nation. How else could I present it if not in a shocking, almost lewd way? I'd done the research to prove that no region of our country was untouched. For cryin' out loud, crime *was* shocking! There I was face-to-face with Hollywood tastemakers, America's puritanical attitude from the fifties still deeply embedded in their brains. Briskin told me that my whole opening sequence had to go. It was too carnal, too brutal, to fly. Why not replace it with a voice-over narrative? I snapped back at him that if I couldn't show my ideas visually, why not make a radio show instead of a movie?

"Sam, your prostitute scene is too much," said Briskin.

"Okay," I said, not disturbed at all about refocusing my yarn. "Let's concentrate on my loner. The seed of a lifelong vendetta has been planted in his head long before, like Dumas and *The Count of Monte Cristo.* Maybe when he was just a kid."

"Yeah," said Briskin, "the public loves revenge."

"How about this: a little sonofabitch raised in the world of crime sees his father being murdered by gangsters. His father's only legacy to the kid is an obsession to take revenge on the murderers. The boy grows up and gets into crime, too. He concocts a scheme to use the United States government's own people to eliminate the men he wants dead."

"How's that?" asked Briskin, looking worried again.

"You know, federal prosecutors."

"You can't touch them, Sammy."

"Why not? I've already been in contact with the Department of Justice. Their people provided me with information. I've also spoken to Charles Anslinger."[1]

Briskin said it wasn't believable for my main character to be dealing directly with federal officials. I told him that it happens all the time. The idea was to show a criminal mind at work. My loner is slow at certain things that so-called "normal" people do rapidly, but he's ten miles ahead of the game for everything that concerns his obsession with vengeance. Cold-bloodedly, he will use everyone he can, even the girl who's in love with him. Why not the Feds, too? If the audience understood that kind of obsession, they'd understand my lead character and the climate of my film.

"Do you have to mention the word 'commission'?"

"Okay," I said. "I'll call them the 'federal crime committee.' There's eight to ten highly intelligent lawyers working in an office, accumulating evidence on all sorts of criminal activities. But they're not as devious as my lead. When it comes to outsmarting people to get what he wants, he's as smart as Machiavelli's prince. He has only one thing in mind: getting even with the bastards who killed his father."

After a couple more rewrites, Briskin gave us the green light. The aspect of my yarn that finally convinced him was the idea of a son avenging the death of his father. In my final draft, we meet Tolly Devlin as a boy in the first scene of *Underworld, U.S.A.* He's already a street thief. Tolly and his surrogate mother, Sandy, see a man being beaten to death in a dark alley. It's Tolly's father, a small-time crook. Although he can finger one of the killers, a gangster named Farrar, the boy refuses to cooperate with the district attorney, Driscoll. Just a kid, Tolly already knows he wants to seek vengeance on his own terms.

Twenty years of crime later, Tolly, now played by Cliff Robertson, catches up with Farrar on his deathbed in a prison infirmary. Tolly tricks the dying old man into naming the other three killers, taunting him with forgiveness. The three killers, Smith, Gunther, and Gela, are part of a huge crime syndicate. Methodically, Tolly goes after them, one by one.

First, he rescues Cuddles, a syndicate moll, and convinces her to rat on Smith for another murder she saw him commit. Then Tolly gets a job inside the syndicate, cutting a deal with Driscoll, now the crusading crime commissioner, to frame Gunther as a traitor. Gunther gets killed by one of the syndicate's own assassins in a rigged car explosion. Then, Tolly ingratiates himself to the boss of all the syndicate bosses, Connors. Connors has Gela eliminated because Tolly sets him up, too.

Meanwhile, Cuddles falls for Tolly, who at first belittles her for wanting a family, then finally decides she should be the mother of his children. Tolly's decision to go straight doesn't mean he'll cooperate any further with the crime commissioner. He refuses to bring down Connors, the big boss. Tolly's only motive has been personal revenge against his father's murderers. But when Connors puts a contract on Cuddles, Tolly hunts him down in his swimming pool headquarters and brutally kills him. Wounded in the melee by a syndicate henchman, Tolly stumbles through the streets, crumbling in the same dark alley where he saw his own father die. My final shot closes in tight on Tolly's clenched fist, dying proof of a life filled with hate and frustration.

Tolly is hostile, rebellious, and self-centered, altogether not very likable. Motivated by self-interest and survival, Tolly is very much in the same mold as Skip McCoy in *Pickup*. When I write a character like that, I never think about whether the public will find him likable. Some people will. Others will shake their heads in disapproval. All I try to do is be truthful. I'd met plenty of these crooks on my beat as a crime reporter back in New York. That was exactly the way they were. A petty criminal in Manhattan, a wino in Clichy, a prostitute in Frisco, a guy on the needle in London, they exist and they have a story. It's not a nice story, either. They are, like Milton wrote, "swallow'd up and lost in the wide womb of uncreated night."[2]

I'm not dealing here with beneficent kings, ravishing princesses, or charming princes who are born with castles, jewels, and juicy legacies. Ever since my characters were born, their lives have been harsh and unfair. They're going to have to learn how to fight to survive. They are anarchists, turned against a system that they feel has betrayed them. That's why they end up taking the law into their own hands. Tolly goes one step farther, exploiting the hateful system to get his enemies eliminated.

My lead's anarchistic attitude owes a debt to Jean Genet, the mid-twentieth-century French novelist and dramatist whose writings were deeply rebellious against society and its conventions. Genet's books and

THE FACTS... THE FACES... THE FILM
THAT CRACKS AMERICA'S ORGANIZED
CRIME SYNDICATE WIDE OPEN!

LABOR
RACKETS

VICE

GAMBLING

NARCOTICS

COLUMBIA
PICTURES
presents

UNDERWORLD, U.S.A.

starring
CLIFF ROBERTSON · DOLORES DORN · BEATRICE KAY · Written, Directed and Produced by SAMUEL FULLER
and featuring PAUL DUBOV · ROBERT EMHARDT · LARRY GATES · RICHARD RUST · A GLOBE ENTERPRISES PRODUCTION

Copyright © 1960 by Columbia Pictures Corporation. All Rights Reserved.   PRINTED IN U.S.A.

I got information from the Department of Justice about the profits that were generated by organized-crime activities, and it was astonishing how successful they were. The studio made me take out those figures. They were afraid everyone would go out and try to join the rackets.

plays are full of society's outcasts, confronted by omnipresent crime, sex, and death. His plays are laced with cruelty. For Genet, moral concepts are absurd. I'd read a helluva lot of Genet's stuff and felt a kinship with his harsh universe.

I also loved Jean-Paul Sartre's biography of this controversial man, *Saint Genet, Actor and Martyr* (1952). Genet was the illegitimate child of a prostitute, and was caught stealing at the age of ten. By early adolescence, he was serving a series of sentences for theft and homosexual prostitution that spanned nearly thirty years. In 1947, following his tenth conviction for theft, Genet was sentenced to life imprisonment. While in prison, he had started writing and getting published. His growing literary reputation induced a group of leading French authors to petition a pardon for him. The president of France granted it in 1948.

See, in my yarns, I never judge my characters. The pope preaches peace. The gangster preaches death. Their ways and means, their sermons, make sense to them. But a writer doesn't favor any character. He observes. He recounts. He depicts. It's the audience's job to react. My head mobster coldly explains to Tolly how the mob always stays one step ahead of law enforcement.

For the finale of Underworld, U.S.A., Tolly (Cliff Robertson) extracts his ultimate revenge on the underworld big boss, Connors (Robert Emhardt).

CONNORS (*smiling*)
There'll always be people like Driscoll. There'll always be people like us. But as long as we don't have any records on paper, as long as we run National Projects with legitimate business operations and pay our taxes on legitimate income and donate to charities and run church bazaars, we'll win the war. We always have.

It's up to the audience to judge this guy, not the writer. One spectator thinks, "Hell, what a smart bastard!" Another thinks, "My God, he's like all clever leaders!" Still another thinks, "What a horrible man, a cold-blooded killer!"

The killers and mobsters I ran across when I was working as a reporter wanted just one thing: to survive. Capital punishment for those criminals is all about revenge, a powerful emotion in all of us, very human, very tough to transcend. Still, I think we have to avoid succumbing to revenge. Capital punishment has never dissuaded anybody from murder. I'm against it, only because it's so inhumane. It makes us, indirectly, into killers, too.

Hell, I understand the good arguments for capital punishment, since the murderers and rapists aren't humane either. They are released from prison and sometimes commit similar crimes. Our first reaction to a vicious crime is to say, an eye for an eye, a tooth for a tooth. What about all the innocent people who've been executed in retribution for a crime they were falsely accused of? The greatness of the American system is that the Fifth Amendment provides protection against the human compulsion for quick revenge, with "due process of law."

In *Underworld, U.S.A.,* I wanted to show how gangsters are no longer thugs but respectable, tax-paying executives. Hardworking government people are trying to eradicate crime by lawful means in the movie. My crime commissioner gives a talk to his staff of young lawyers, laying out the difficult terrain ahead.

> DRISCOLL
> Organized crime is much more intellectual than it was years ago and much more difficult to prosecute so we lawyers have been appointed to find a way to prosecute it. . . . Our job's to cut red tape and come up with a lethal and legal battle plan for prosecuting the syndicates.

To get the dark, austere look I needed for the picture, I hired Hal Mohr as my cameraman. Hal had shot about eighty movies in his long career as cameraman, going all the way back to the twenties, including *The Jazz Singer* (1927), *Shanghai Lady* (1929), *Captain Blood* (1935), and *The Wild One* (1954). I asked my friend Harry Sukman to compose the soundtrack. Once again Harry came up with just the right mix of tension, melodrama, and violence.

Casting the actor to play Tolly was my most important choice. I had a number of up-and-coming stars read for the part. Cliff Robertson stood out. Cliff and I hit it off right away because he'd been a reporter before turning to acting. He'd never had a starring role, but he convinced me he could be Tolly. Downplaying his handsome leading-man looks, Cliff gave Tolly a smooth exterior, piloted inside by a dark and tortured soul. Cliff went on to have a helluva career. He played a wide range of roles, even portraying John F. Kennedy in *PT 109* (1963), and he won an Oscar for his performance in *Charly* (1968). But I'd venture to say Cliff never had another part that was quite as haunting as my Tolly.

Of all the many reviews and analyses of *Underworld, U.S.A.,* that have appeared over the years, one remains with me. It got back to me through the Hollywood grapevine, a remark from a real gangster apparently made to his colleagues about Tolly's all-consuming obsession to avenge his father's death.

"If only *my* son," said the mob boss, "would have that kind of affection for me!"

38

The Smell
of Truth

In the spring of 1961, I found myself in the Philippines, doing a war movie about the 5307th Composite Unit, instead of in Europe doing one about my own First Division. We'd climbed up to a high point overlooking a gorgeous landscape next to the ocean. The location for one of our battle scenes was down below in the countryside outside Manila. I thought about a line from a poem by Rimbaud, the French poet with whom I'd always been fascinated: "The sky above my head, so calm, so blue." Japan's invasion of the Philippines in 1941 had been terrible. When MacArthur and Nimitz retook the island in 1944, all hell rained down again on the Filipinos. Underneath that grand, placid sky, mankind continually devastated the planet with malevolent wars.

Milton Sperling, a producer at Warner Brothers, had asked me if I'd write and direct a movie based on Charlton Ogburn's book *The Marauders*. The book was about a famous campaign in the Pacific theater, the true story of a three-thousand-man infantry unit under the command of Brigadier General Frank Dow Merrill that fought behind Japanese lines in Burma in 1944. The only World War II yarn I really wanted to direct was about the Big Red One. I was turned off by the idea of using someone else's book to show combat life that I hadn't actually lived through. Jack Warner called me in to discuss the project.

"Sam," Warner said, "what's the military expression for a rehearsal, when you prepare your outfit for a big battle?"

"Dry run," I said.

"Dry run," repeated Warner.

There were other studio executives in the room. They nodded and repeated "dry run." It reminded me of a military debriefing, with Warner as the four-star general and the studio execs as his battalion commanders. Warner gave me a complicitous look to make me understand that my *Big Red One* project could still happen at his studio. Maybe by doing this picture I'd be getting myself in position to make *The Big Red One*.

Warner promised I could write a script in my own style for *Merrill's Marauders* and make my own casting choices. It was the opportunity I'd been looking for to finally work with Gary Cooper, who was perfect for my lead. Coop thought he might be too old for the part when we discussed the picture. I told him that when I was writing the script, I saw only him as my Merrill. The real-life general was a tough father figure with a commanding presence and an iron will. He'd advance with his troops until he dropped. Then he'd get up and still keep going. As demanding as he was on himself, Merrill showed great empathy for his soldiers. Embodied by Cooper, the character would be a tribute to my own commander, Terry Allen, who was always there for his men.

The structure of the script had to be different from anything I'd written before. There was little dialogue. I tried combining lots of quick shots to capture the raging storm of combat. Here's an example:

> ENEMY
> as white smoke pops, making it impossible for them to know where the hell the Marauders are.
>
> KOLOWICZ
> waves cease fire. His riflemen hold their fire, giving:
>
> DOSKIS AND MEN
> the chance to advance closer to the enemy and lob in more frag grenades.
>
> ENEMY
> grenaded. Black smoke bursts in midst of blinding white smoke.
>
> STOCK AND TAGGY
> firing as they advance from the flank.
>
> HANK AND MEN
> leapfrogging Dopskis' group with more smoke grenades hurled at:
>
> ENEMY
> White smoke pops in midst of black smoke.

KOLOWICZ AND RIFLEMEN
firing as they advance.

STOCK AND TAGGY
angling toward enemy, firing as they advance. They are now joining up with others. PRIVATE O'BRIEN is hit. He falls.

STOCK
Medic! Medic! O'Brien!

The studio hired Colonel Samuel Wilson as a technical adviser on the project. Wilson and I struck up a warm friendship. He'd fought alongside the real General Merrill in Burma and survived their historic victory at Myitkyina. Wilson and I spent many evenings together drinking vodka and talking about the infantry in the Pacific and European theaters. Hell, foot soldiers always had it tough. Twenty percent of all soldiers were in the infantry, yet they suffered 75 percent of the casualties. Wilson described the nightmare of fighting in those jungles without any air force or artillery backup. My movie had to convey the nerve-racking, gut-wrenching madness of the Burma battles.

While we were in preproduction, Gary Cooper got sick. We learned it was cancer and that he didn't have too long. I had a tough time getting Gary out of my mind for the lead in *Merrill's Marauders*. As Coop's health declined, I knew he wouldn't be able to do it. In my search for a replacement, I found Jeff Chandler.

Born Ira Gossell, in Brooklyn, Jeff was an officer in World War II. After his discharge from the service, he worked in radio before signing with Universal. His premature gray hair and dark features got him cast as Cochise in *Broken Arrow* (1950), for which he was nominated for an Oscar. They continued to assign Jeff roles in Westerns and period pictures. I thought he could do better. He proved it with his heartfelt performance as Merrill in my movie.

There we were in the middle of the Pacific shooting *Merrill's Marauders*. We'd flown our cast and crew over to Manila and set up our general headquarters at Clark Air Base. Their enlisted men would serve as our extras. Before long, the officers insisted on being in the movie, too. I always would appreciate their hospitality.

Between takes, Jeff used to throw a football around with other actors and some of the air force officers. Chandler was a good athlete, good enough to be offered a job in professional football when he was younger.

Clowning around with Jeff Chandler and some of the crew on Merrill's Marauders. *I thought the picture was going to be the start of a new phase of Jeff's career. Instead, it was his last movie.*

However, he had a bad back, having injured it on a movie set years before, and he had suffered from it ever since. Our seven-week shoot was strenuous, but Chandler never complained about his back, or anything else. He was a real trooper. During one of the scenes we shot in a hot, humid jungle, however, Jeff fainted. An army helicopter flew him back to Clark. He was fine after a day off and finished the film without any further health problems. However, when he returned to California after shooting with us in the Philippines, Chandler decided to have surgery on his back. Inexplicably, he died in the hospital, apparently from blood poisoning. His death, at age forty-two, was deemed malpractice and resulted in a large lawsuit and settlement for his children. I was sick when I heard the news, just sick.

In my movie, Merrill has a heart condition, like the real general. Just as dangerous is his emotional condition, the inner overload that can sometimes kill you faster than a bullet. It sounds crazy, but a lot of soldiers die in battles of heart failure, without a scratch. I wanted this war movie to be truthful about it. The regimental surgeon, Doc, is the only one who knows about the general's coronary problem.

> DOC
> . . . You're kidding yourself, General. You've got no decision to make. These men are at the end of their rope. And so are you.
>
> MERRILL
> When you're at the end of your rope, all you have to do is make one foot move after the other. Just take the next step. That's all there is to it.

Just before the final push against the enemy, Merrill has a heart attack, falls to his knees, and pitches facedown on the ground. His surrogate son, Stock, rallies the soldiers to move on. My original ending had the Americans successfully attacking their objective, the enemy's air strip, as Merrill looks up at the watchful gaze of Doc:

> DOC
> Those are our planes, Frank. Your men are taking the strip.
>
> MERRILL
> Who led them?
>
> DOC
> Stock.

(Merrill smiles)

> I don't know how they did it. They fought when they had typhus. They fought when they had malaria. They fought when they were starving. They fought when they were wounded. They fought on their knees. What kind of men are these? *What* are they? *Who* are they?

(Merrill tries to say something but he can't. Doc lowers his head to Merrill's lips to hear.)

> MERRILL *(whispering)*
> They're Infantry.

To my surprise and anger, the studio decided to cut my final scene in the editing room. Right after Merrill's collapse, they spliced in footage of a victory parade of soldiers marching down Fifth Avenue. Jack Warner and his executives wanted an overt patriotic ending, and they decided to end the picture with that propaganda-like crap and a pompous narrator bragging about the American victory at Myitkyina. I went toe to toe against the studio on that one, but I lost.

We had another big clash about a violent scene I'd shot in the Philippines in a concrete maze—immense supports for fuel tanks—a confusing battleground where soldiers can and do fire at their own comrades in the panic of the combat. I did this whole sequence in one single take, panning the camera across the battle, instead of cutting to close-ups to show who was shooting whom. They told me it looked too artistic. For Chrissakes, I'd been in the infantry, I knew combat was chaos and pandemonium, I knew Americans sometimes shot Americans in the heat of a battle. They hired a second-unit director to reshoot the scene. The reshoots looked ridiculously theatrical. Only one brief sequence of the second-unit stuff ended up in the final cut of the movie. And anyway, what's so wrong with looking "artistic," goddamnit?

One of the scenes I'm most proud of in *Merrill's Marauders* is when Sergeant Kolowicz, played by Claude Akins, stumbles upon a village and is served a bowl of rice by an old woman. There's not one word of dialogue. The haggard, unshaven soldier is stunned by the tenderness of the old woman and the curious children who watch him eat the rice. Kolowicz breaks down into tears. Every time I see that poignant scene, I start crying as well.

The movie is an honest tribute to Merrill and his soldiers, *sans* phony patriotism. Exhausted or wounded, they try to stay alive as they accomplish the mission at hand. For cryin' out loud, the work of GIs at war is nerve-racking and frustrating, *not* glorious!

When George Patton's son came to see me later about doing a film about his father, he told me he loved *Merrill's Marauders,* but that, in Pentagonese, "it had no recruitment flavor." That's why he wanted me to direct *Patton.*

"I know you disliked my father," he said good-humoredly, "but at least you'll make a hard-hitting movie!"

One of the wonderful memories from our stay in the Philippines was meeting the leading member of the country's Liberal Party, Benigno Aquino, and his wife, Corazon. He asked me to call him "Ninoy," his nickname. When President Ferdinand Marcos declared martial law in 1972, Ninoy was imprisoned. Later, he was allowed to move his family to the U.S., where he underwent heart surgery and then served as a research fellow at Harvard. In 1983 he flew back to Manila to work in the legislative election and was assassinated as he deplaned. Corazon Aquino went on to run against Marcos and get elected. Long live peace, ethics, and the will of the people! To hell with dictators!

Merrill's Marauders got good reviews. Critics for *Time* and *Newsweek* remarked that the film had a documentary flavor, giving a realistic depiction of war's simplicity and death. The only thing they said was "Hollywood" in the film was the ending. Ironically, the opposite was true. The ending that Jack Warner's boys tacked on was real documentary footage of a military parade. In the context, it seemed phony. My film was fiction. But it smelled of truth.

39

Tempted by Television

Merrill's Marauders turned out to be a financial and critical success. Yet I had two big regrets about the picture. Gary Cooper's illness and death denied me the chance to cast him in a role that would have provided him one last triumph. I'd never get that chance, and it made me sad. Jeff Chandler's premature death immediately after the shoot, due to his back operation, was also very disturbing.

Jack Warner was so pleased with the box-office results on *Merrill's Marauders* that he offered me a bonus. He'd pay for any car I wanted to buy. Though I considered several makes, I ended up picking a Cadillac. It was pricey, but Warner could afford it. The picture made an $18 million profit, a helluva take back then.

I never gave a damn about fancy cars, or any of the other frills in Hollywood. By the early sixties, my lifestyle had never been more modest and solitary. Living alone, I wrote day and night, knocking out yarns one after another. It was my salvation. Offers came and went but still no studio or producer was ready to green-light *The Big Red One.*

Little Rebecca Baum from Poland was constantly in my thoughts. I remembered my late mother's sense of humor, her feistiness, and her mettle, raising seven children all by herself. I could see her in my mind's eye, wearing her polka-dot dress and her pearl necklace, a warm smile on her face, ever ready to tell a funny story to cheer me up. She was vital until the very end. At the age of eighty-five she'd been repainting her house the day before she died. She went to sleep and never woke up.

Nobody ever really gets over the death of a parent. At first, you resent a mother or a father for not being immortal. Time soothes the pain and brings perspective. You remember beloved qualities, not human imperfections. Even today, three decades after her death, my mother's spirit remains with me. Loving one's parents is a lifelong undertaking. There is no greater satisfaction than showing respect and gratitude for parents.

After they pass on, your affection and dedication remain intact. As long as you are thinking of parents with love, they aren't dead. They're right there in your heart and mind.

People in Hollywood had nicknamed me "Slam-Bam" Sam. Surrounded by the town's honey-tongued characters, I guess I seemed pretty brusque. Deep down, I was full of love and gratitude. Hell, injustice made me damned angry. When I felt frustrated—which is how Hollywood made you feel most of the time—I could be harsh. One thing was for sure, I was always up front with people. I've never talked behind anyone's back. Good or bad, I'll tell you straight to your face what I think about you.

A man who always liked my candor was my screenwriter pal, Charles Marquis Warren. Warren was also a director, having made movies out of his own scripts, like *Hellgate* (1952), *Arrowhead* (1953), and *Flight to Tangier* (1953). He'd gotten into television by producing the series *Gunsmoke* (1955–56), one of the biggest successes in early TV history. He'd also launched the hit TV series *Rawhide* (1959–61). Charles came over to visit me one day in late 1961.

"Sam, I want you to write and direct the pilot for a new TV show I'm going to do based on *The Virginian*. You know the novel by Owen Wister?" said Charles.

"I loved that book when I was a kid!"

In the twenties and thirties, all boys my age read *The Virginian*. Wister published the book at the turn of the century, the first Western in American literature. His romantic approach to frontier life encompassed all the clichés that became emblematic in Hollywood's early movies.

"Forget the original," said Charles. "Universal is putting up the dough for the series. They bought the title and are letting me do whatever I want. The show needs your own special vision. You'll be doing me a great favor, and you'll get a crack at TV. Believe me, it's well-paid work."

"Okay, Charles. What kind of characters do you have in mind?" I asked.

I was talking like a chef who is willing to adjust his recipe to hit the client's taste buds right on the head. Didn't Bertolt Brecht say that art was a culinary experience?

"I want a judge who incarnates the law," said Warren.

"Who do you have in mind to play him?"

"Lee J. Cobb."

"Great!"

I was a happy chef. Cobb was like a good soup bone for my stew. I needed some tasty meat, so I told Charles that I wanted to use Lee Marvin

My tastes were simple. I was happiest smoking a good cigar and writing yarns on my old Royal, circa 1962.

as a cattle rustler, the villain. Lee was my kind of actor, a real tough-looking, tough-talking sonofabitch.

"Okay, Sam," said Warren, "we'll get Cobb and Marvin. Now write me a script for the first show in the series."

I dreamed up a European-style crime, the kidnapping and ransoming of a king. Frontier judges were like kings in the Old West. They held sway over vast domains and thousands of cattle. My villain, a cattler rustler, concocts a scheme to kidnap a powerful judge. The judge turns out to be a thief too, exploiting the law for his own benefit. The rustler is caught and brought to trial. Only the rustler knows that the judge is just as much a criminal as he is. Since the judge has the law on his side, he condemns the rustler and ends up looking like a saint.

I was pleased and surprised that the studio execs at Universal okayed my unorthodox yarn. The minute the trade papers announced I was writing and directing an episode of *The Virginian,* the editor in chief of the *Saturday Evening Post* wanted to do a story. It was a big deal that a movie director was making a two-hour program for television with major actors. Back then, it was unthinkable for filmmakers to work in both mediums. The *Post* reporter showed up on the set and stayed throughout the shoot.

I was disappointed with TV production people from Day One. They spent money on unimportant things, then they were cheap with essential elements. We were always haggling over important details. I'd done big pictures in ten days because I was working with experienced, capable movie people. We used plenty of tricks that saved money, but not at the expense of what the audience gets to see up on the screen. The climate on a TV set irritated me. Besides, the production results didn't justify all the money they were spending.

Charles Warren seemed pleased with the episode I directed for him. It was entitled "It Tolls for Thee." The *Post* piece was published soon after the show was broadcast. The writer pinned his article on the day-to-day struggles of a moviemaker in TV land. The execs at Universal weren't at all happy about the unfavorable behind-the-scenes account. Still, the studio offered me ten more episodes on *The Virginian.* I turned them down. I'd had it with television, explaining to Charles Warren that I couldn't take any more sausage-factory storytelling, that I needed the biosphere of a movie production to breathe creatively. Charles laughed at my reaction. Deep down in his heart of hearts, he understood, because he preferred doing movies too. But he was a better businessman than I was and foresaw the huge profits that television would make for its producers.

More offers for television series came in. The only one I seriously considered was from Jackie Cooper, the Hollywood icon turned TV producer. Cooper had been around for decades, ever since becoming a child star as the lead in *The Bowery* (1933). Jackie wanted me to take on a project about an American Indian detective in New York entitled *Hawk,* starring an up-and-coming actor named Burt Reynolds. With my New York background and experience as a crime reporter, Cooper thought I'd be perfect for the job. He offered me total freedom to write the scripts. The pay was hefty. I sensed that TV would devour me, drying up my creative juices. I passed on Jackie Cooper's series and turned my attention back to getting a feature film into production.

I thought I was finished with television. Yet Charles Warren would entice me to get involved in yet another TV series a few years later. Charles was doing a show called *Iron Horse* in 1966. I needed the loot, so I accepted Warren's offer to write and direct five episodes on the show. The only one I remember—probably because I came up with the original story and wrote a terrific billiard scene for that episode—was called "The Man for New Chicago." It starred Dale Robertson.

What I discovered from my foray into TV was how much I loved filmmaking. I was used to seeing my characters on a big screen. I wasn't even that impressed with the immediacy of monitoring actors on video. I prefer the surprise of seeing performances at the end of the day's work, in the rushes.

The worlds of moviemaking and TV production are no longer as remote as they were in those days. There've been so many improvements to movie cameras since then. The Steadicam, which allows for smooth traveling shots, is one of the most marvelous. Technology will continue to improve, with 35-mm cameras getting lighter and more mobile. The goal is to make the storytelling process less cumbersome, so the director, his cast, and his crew can concentrate on the emotions of the characters. In my day, the camera, lights, and sound were obstacles that had to be overcome. I hope making movies for future filmmakers will be as simple as typing was for writers like me. A young director with a good script won't need a ton of money to put his movie into production. We'll have all kinds of movies being made, quicker and cheaper, maybe even some good ones.

Television has seen vast changes, too, with a helluva lot of advancements in cameras, broadcasting, and video projection. Good directors don't hesitate to work in both feature films and television nowadays. I think all that versatility is great. And I love all the new technologies as long as they are utilized to bring people together, not alienate them. Rabelais once said that science without a conscience spoils the soul. Moviemaking without a gripping story and believable characters spoils the film.

A script that I'd been polishing for many years was finally ready to go into production. I'd written a version of the yarn fifteen years earlier for Fritz Lang to direct, called *Straitjacket* back then. All the time I was dabbling with television, I yearned to get back into moviemaking with a picture that embraced the craziness of the early sixties. That movie would be *Shock Corridor*.

Love Your
Country Despite
the Ulcers

In *Straitjacket*, the yarn that I'd written for Fritz Lang in the late forties, there was a journalist trying to solve a murder that was committed inside an insane asylum. The point of that script was to expose the pitiful living conditions in mental institutions. I showed Fritz photos I'd obtained from newspaper files of mentally ill patients vegetating in American asylums. Sick people were denied basic human dignity, treated almost like animals. It was happening in asylums all over the world. I carried the story inside me like brain baggage throughout the fifties, rewriting it as *The Long Corridor.* The title was based on my idea for the interminable hallway that would be the principal set for the picture. No doubt, my story had been shaped and sharpened by the legacy of the cold war years.

From abroad, playwrights Eugène Ionesco, Jean Genet, and Samuel Beckett had used the "theater of the absurd" as one of the only sane modes to approach the madness of the era. At home, racism and intolerance were still prevalent in the world's greatest democracy. Jim Crow had been outlawed by the 1954 Supreme Court decision in *Brown v. Board of Education,* but President Eisenhower had to dispatch troops to accompany black children into a "white" high school in Little Rock, Arkansas. The horrible McCarthy period had left ideological scars, the witch-hunting so unworthy of a democracy.

My title became *Shock Corridor.* It had the subtlety of a sledgehammer. I was dealing with insanity, racism, patriotism, nuclear warfare, and sexual perversion. How could I have been light with those topics? I purposefully wanted to provoke the audience. The situations I'd portray *were* shocking and scary. This was going to be a crazy film, ranging from the absurd to the unbearable and tragic. My madhouse was a metaphor for America. Like an X ray that fathoms a patient's tumors, *Shock Corridor* would probe our nation's sickness. Without an honest diagnosis of the problems, how could we ever hope to heal them?

On the surface, *Shock Corridor* was a murder mystery. Newspaper reporter Johnny Barrett wants a big scoop, so he manages to pass himself off as a sex pervert, with the reluctant help of his stripper girlfriend, Cathy. She pretends to be his sister and files a formal complaint against him for sexual harassment. All this so Johnny can get himself committed to an asylum where an inmate was stabbed to death by a still-unidentified murderer. Without arousing suspicions, Johnny hopes to solve the murder by getting close to three patients who witnessed the killing. His articles will be published under big headlines.

The premise was not as far-fetched as it seemed. I remembered bizarre assignments that newspapermen accepted just to get their scoops. There was a reporter who spent the entire night in a funeral home in order to catch a suspected necrophiliac in the act. There was actually a woman reporter who wrote a famous exposé of the asylum on Wards Island by pretending to be nuts.

To get this unusual picture going, I needed a producer like Robert Lippert from the old days, a guy who'd give me the dough and have the good sense to let me make the movie my own way. Bill Shiffrin said he knew the perfect guy to help me. Shiffrin was an old-time agent with clients like Bette Davis and George Sanders. He had taken on Robert Stack since *House of Bamboo* and orchestrated the deal that made Stack the lead in the popular series *The Untouchables.* Bill used to come around my place to propose TV projects. I turned them all down. We gibble-gabbled about movies in general. Shiffrin had an incredible sense of movie history, rare in Hollywood. Unfortunately, Bill couldn't hold his vodka. He'd get foulmouthed, putting down producers, directors, or writers, assigning them to his own personal blacklist. The next day, he'd be on the phone getting the same people deals. Beneath his brash veneer, Shiffrin was an idealist with a heart of gold.

Bill brokered a two-picture deal for me with real-estate tycoon Samuel Firks. Firks said he'd operate tight budgets just like Lippert, paying me a fee and a share of the profits. I'd have complete artistic control of the production, including final cut. Maybe I should've checked out Firks beforehand, but the deal smelled okay, and I was anxious to get back into movie production. After my early experiences, I trusted producers implicitly. Unfortunately, Firks was no Lippert.

Shock Corridor opens with this legend: "Whom God Wishes to Destroy He First Makes Mad. Euripides, 425 B.C."

Then the screen goes black. In the center of the screen, a dot of light appears. We hear a man's voice:

*Johnny (Peter Breck) reassures his gal, Cathy (Constance Towers),
that his stay in the insane asylum will get him a big scoop as a
journalist. His city editor, Swanee (William Zuckert, far right),
and his shrink, Dr. Fong (Philip Ahn, far left), are not so sure. In
this scene, notice the one source of light, which cameraman Stanley
Cortez used so effectively throughout the movie.*

*Mad women attack
Johnny when he walks
into the wrong ward.
Later we added Peter
Breck's panicked
voiceover: "Nymphos!"*

JOHNNY'S VOICE
My name is Johnny Barrett. I'm a reporter on
the *Daily Globe*. This is my story . . . as far as
it went.

The dot slowly grows until we see a bleak corridor that runs off into
infinity. The mental patients call it "the Street." Down the full length off
the hallway is a ceiling light. Ghoulish music composed by Paul Dunlap
comes up. We're in a modern version of Dante's *Inferno,* which my main
character will voluntarily enter, and from which he will never return.

The bleak central corridor of the asylum was essential to get right. At
first I'd considered using the hallway of a real mental hospital in order to
convey the place's invasive claustrophobia. I was able to hire the art director Eugene Lourie and explained to him exactly what I had in mind.[1] We
didn't have much money for sets, but Lourie didn't mind. Eugene convinced me that we needed to devise a special set to allow plenty of space
for cameras and crew to move freely yet still be able to drive home the
idea of total confinement. He built an ingenious corridor of walls and
mirrors. At the far end of the set, he painted a hallway that never ended.
We hired dwarfs, dressed them as mental patients, and had them drift
around down there. The corridor created the perfect illusion of infinity in
a finite space. I was grateful to have the experienced and visionary Lourie
on my team.

The three mad witnesses Johnny must befriend in the asylum to crack
the case allowed me to develop a loose three-act structure. Their sicknesses
gave me metaphors to spotlight some of the biggest issues in American
society. Stuart, a southern redneck, is a Korean War veteran who collabo-
rated with communists, then repudiated his brainwashing. He now
believes he's a Confederate general. Trent is a black man who blew a fuse
from the pressure of being a guinea pig for segregation at a racist southern
university. His lunacy drives him to believe he is a vicious KKK bigot.
Boden is one of the genius scientists who helped develop the A-bomb.
Unleashing nuclear devastation has driven him into the mindset of a six-
year-old.

Barrett's investigation is torturous. He is constantly under assault from
the asylum's aggressive lunatics. His rotund roommate, Pagliacci, a fanatic
opera lover, uses an imaginary dagger to act out the climactic stabbing
from Leoncavallo's opera by the same name.

To gain Stuart's trust, Johnny plays bizarre Confederate battle games
with him. During a dance-therapy class, Johnny gets them to play *Dixie*
for Stuart. But when Johnny goes into an adjoining room for some water,

he finds himself encircled by a group of women patients, all aggressive nymphomaniacs. The crazed women attack him mercilessly.

Bitten, battered, and bruised, Johnny is at wit's end about how to get Stuart to talk sanely. For no reason, Stuart suddenly obliges him.

> STUART
> I know why I went over to the Commies. Ever since I was a kid, my folks fed me bigotry for breakfast and ignorance for supper. Not once did they ever make me feel proud of where I was born. See, that was the cancer they put in me. No knowledge of my country . . . no pride . . . just a hymn of hate. I'd have defected to any enemy. See, it was easy because my brains was cabbage. They taught me everything from cabbages to commissars. And they gave me a woman. And she called me mister. And she made me feel important!

Before Stuart sinks back into schizophrenic incoherence, Johnny finds out an essential clue. The man who killed Sloan in the kitchen was wearing white pants. James Best, the lead in *Verboten!,* plays Stuart. He's outrageous, yet strangely believable. His scene with Johnny always touches me with its crazy truth about the results of breathing hate into children.

Cathy comes to visit Johnny. She's shocked at the way he looks, the way he talks. He's obsessed with his mission. All he cares about is getting to the other two witnesses so he can write his big story and win a Pulitzer Prize. He tells Cathy to tell his editor that he's close to cracking the case.

Then, Johnny meets up with Trent, the second witness, who's marching down "the Street" carrying a placard that says:

INTEGRATION AND DEMOCRACY DON'T MIX
GO HOME, NIGGER

Trent, a black man, has been driven insane by tremendous self-hatred. He's ended up thinking that he's a white member of the Ku Klux Klan. He filches pillowcases, makes holes in them for his eyes, and covers his head, in a sick parody of a KKK member. To ingratiate himself with Trent, Johnny encourages him to spout his hysterical hate talk. Suddenly, Trent launches into one of his maniacal, sickening monologues.

> TRENT
> If Christ walked the streets of my home town
> he'd be horrified. You've never seen so many
> black people cluttering up the cafés and
> schools and buses and washrooms. I'm for
> pure Americanism. White supremacy!
>
> (*jumping on bench, screaming*)
> Listen to me, Americans! America for Ameri-
> cans! We've got to throw rocks and hurl
> bombs—black bombs for black foreigners. So
> they like hot music, do they? Well, we'll give
> them a crescendo they'll never forget. Burn
> that Freedom Bus. Burn those Freedom Rid-
> ers. Burn any man who serves them at a lunch
> counter. Burn every dirty nigger-loving pock-
> etbook integrationist!

Trent's chilling sermon starts a race riot in the corridor, with Johnny being swept up in it. The attendants overpower the two men, put them in straitjackets, and tie them down in adjoining beds.

We set up the light in the next scene so that Trent and Johnny, one black and one white, are lying side by side, almost touching, yet incapacitated by their straitjackets and unable to move. The shadowy glass wall between them is an unbridgable chasm. Trent has a nightmare. I used my footage from the Karajá Indians in Brazil to make Trent's delirium that much more surreal. After the nightmare, Trent has an unexpected moment of lucidity. He tells Johnny that the killer was an attendant, but stops short of saying his name. More importantly, Trent tells Johnny he feels like a failure being a guinea pig in segregation. He's let people down.

> TRENT
> You know, I was brought up to have pride in
> my country. Call it *esprit de corps*. It's inside
> me. I love it. It's a blessing to love my coun-
> try—even when it gives me ulcers.

Trent is speaking for me and intelligent, sensitive people all over the world who feel the same about their countries, too. Despite some wrong-headed politicians, misguided wars, and small-minded laws, I love my country. Nothing and nobody can take that deep love away from me. But, goddamnit, this nation gives me ulcers sometimes!

I cast an unknown actor named Hari Rhodes as Trent. I thought Hari should have won an award for his performance. When his character stands up on the bench in the corridor and shouts his inflammatory harangue, audiences feel uncomfortably mesmerized. Hari shows how hate is both repellent and infectious, how cruelty and intolerance can drive people insane. Hari wound up making a good living doing television, notably *Daktari,* a sweet show about animals in Africa for children.

Cathy comes to the asylum for another visit to see Johnny. She sees he's changed. It is beginning to dawn on her that his obsession to score a Pulitzer was probably an early sign of delirium. In terror, Cathy discovers that Johnny is coming unhinged. When she kisses him, he wipes off her kiss violently, screaming, "Don't ever kiss me like that!"

Cathy's startled. She realizes that her Johnny is already over the edge. Holy cow, audiences everywhere were stunned by that kiss! In a movie filled with emotional jolts, I was surprised to find out that the kiss was one of the most shocking things for audiences wherever it played.

My statuesque stripper, Cathy, needed beauty, sex appeal, and intelligence. I picked Constance Towers because she had all three, in spades. John Ford had introduced me to Constance. She'd appeared in Ford's *Horse Soldiers* (1959) and *Sergeant Rutledge* (1960). A trooper all the way, Constance became a good friend. Cathy is sucked into Johnny's crazy scheme because it means a better future for her, too. His perverse kiss proves to her that nobody can live in a psychiatric ward without being affected. Maybe Johnny was crazy right from the start. Cathy is scared and confused, allowing the asylum permission to subject Johnny to electric-shock treatment. She thinks it's his only chance. It will be his doom.

To convey how appalling electric-shock treatment is for a patient, we put together a montage, superimposing it across Johnny's convulsive body, along with shrieking sounds. The scene still makes me shiver, dredging up memories of electric-chair executions at Sing Sing that I had to witness as a crime reporter.

Holding on to his own sanity by a slender thread, Johnny reaches the third murder witness, Boden, who went nuts working on atomic fission. The nuclear physicist with the mentality of a child is played by Gene Evans. If there had been a Fuller stock company of actors, Gene would be one of the founding members, having already done *Steel Helmet, Park Row,* and *Hell and High Water* with me. Johnny panders to Boden by playing hide-and-seek. The scientist's window of sanity opens long enough to explain why he's there.

At the conclusion of Shock Corridor, *inmates are condemned to spending their lives on "the street," the bleak hallway of the asylum. From far left (seated): Pagliacci (Larry Tucker), Johnny (Peter Breck), Boden (Gene Evans), Trent (Hari Rhodes), a real mental patient, and Stuart (James Best)*

BODEN

. . . Today, with all the talk of the panic button, we're right on the brink of disaster. Today everybody is giving the human race two weeks to get out. Now I cannot live with a two-week notice. So I quit living.

Cathy has another visit with Johnny. Suddenly, he's upbeat and seemingly normal, on the verge of getting his story. She's happy for him, but confused. He seems sane. But is he? Johnny's craziness comes and goes in cycles.

Johnny finally gets the killer's name out of Boden. It was Wilkes, one of the attendants. Just as Johnny breathes a sigh of satisfaction, he looks at the portrait in Boden's sketchbook. The audience never sees that drawing, only Johnny's ferocious reaction to how Boden has portrayed him. He becomes a wild man, viciously attacking Boden, and ends up in a straitjacket again. Johnny's sanity is disintegrating. He knows who the murderer is, but he can't say his name. He starts accusing everybody, even Cathy, then breaks into demented laughter. He's over the edge.

Final confirmation of Johnny's delirium comes in "the Street" as he sits on a bench next to Pagliacci. Johnny hears an approaching thunderstorm. He holds out his hand and "sees" raindrops hitting his palm. He looks up and down the corridor. No one else feels the weather change. The storm hits with fierce lightning and thunder. Suddenly Johnny is all alone in the storm, rain falling like cats and dogs, the corridor flooded. He panics, bangs on locked doors, and hysterically calls for help. There is nobody. The lightning strikes him in his chest, and he collapses. Faces of other patients flash in front of him. He screams like a banshee. That brings him back to reality on the bench with Pagliacci, where everything is exactly the same.

> PAGLIACCI (*amused at the scream*)
> That was such a sour note, Johnny. You are way off-key.

With the wisp of lucidity he still has, Johnny remembers that the murderer is Wilkes. He finds Wilkes in the hydrotherapy ward and lunges at him, hoping to beat the truth out of him. They have a tremendous brawl that takes them into the kitchen, pots and pans flying everywhere. Finally Johnny straddles Wilkes and grabs him by his ears, forcing a confession out of him.

Johnny somehow files his story. But they won't let him out of the asylum to pick up his Pulitzer. He's no longer able to live in the real world. Weeks later, Cathy is still trying to save him. But it's too late. He no longer knows her. My last sequence is of a new mental patient being ushered into the asylum, passing the crazed inmates—Stuart, Trent, Boden, Pagliacci, and Johnny—who are all beyond the pale.

We shot *Shock Corridor* in about ten days. Once, John Ford stopped in for a surprise visit. It was a tremendous morale booster.

"Sammy, why're you shooting on this two-bit set?" he asked.

"No major would touch my yarn, Jack," I said. "It's warped. It's about America."

"You're going to stir things up again, like *Steel Helmet*."

"Maybe. I've just got to do this movie."

I strolled with Ford down the long, white corridor, both of us puffing cigars. Something jarred his memory.

"Here was the church," he said, pointing. "There was my set for the prostitute. Way over there was the IRA interrogation."

Was it possible that he'd shot one of his greatest movies, *The Informer,* on the same miserable soundstage? Yes, he explained, back in 1935 RKO

It was a grand day when John Ford (left) dropped in on the set of Shock Corridor. *Only then did I learn that he'd filmed* The Informer, *one of my favorite movies, on the same soundstage.*

was upset about his plans for a picture based on Liam O'Flaherty's proletarian novel about the Irish Republican Party rising against the British. They gave him an embarrassingly small budget, forcing him to rent that very space to shoot the picture. I was stupefied that the great John Ford had been treated disparagingly. He read my face.

"Me too," he said. "I had to make that movie."

My cameraman on *Shock Corridor* was the great Stanley Cortez. I was a big fan of Stanley's work on, among so many pictures, *The Magnificent Ambersons* (1942) and *The Night of the Hunter* (1955). He was an outstanding craftsman. Stanley had a reputation of being slow on a set. He had no time to be slow with me. He worked as fast as I did and got exactly the absurd look I wanted for the picture. I wrote with Stanley's camera, showing characters' emotions and mental states by utilizing close-ups, dolly shots, swivel shots. He filmed the picture in black-and-white. From the first scene in the psychiatrist's office, I told Cortez I wanted just one source of light. From then on, we lit every scene that way. It gave the picture a stark, taut look, allowing us to get the insane grimaces and gestures with straightforward simplicity.

The handsome Peter Breck did a fine job as Johnny. Up until then, he was mostly known for his TV work, especially as Doc Holliday in the popular series *Maverick.* He was normal-looking, making his descent into madness that much more shocking. The role was physically demanding. The nympho attack scene was tough because the girls really threw themselves on him with all of their weight. In the thunderstorm scene, there wasn't any place for all that water to drain off. The set wasn't designed for it, but I wanted a ton of water coming down that hallway. We shot that scene last because I knew the set would be destroyed by the flood. Peter had no idea we were going to use that much water. Slipping and falling all over the goddamned place, he really panicked. The fear helped him create one of his most realistic performances.

For Pagliacci, I couldn't find any actor I really liked. One night, I dropped in at a nightclub on Sunset Boulevard to take a look at a young woman in a show whom Barry Sullivan, from *Forty Guns,* had asked me to see. There was a two-man comedy act at the place that night, a fat guy, Larry Tucker, and a small, thin one named Paul Mazursky. They were terrific. I hired Larry on the spot to play my obese, opera-singing Pagliacci. Larry's wife used to come to the set along with their new baby. During one of the crazy scenes, the baby started crying. My soundman told me that we had to reshoot that scene because he could hear the baby's cries on the soundtrack. I told him the more screaming, the better. Larry's yelling kid added to the chaotic atmosphere of the asylum.

Tucker and Mazursky went on to write screenplays together. Paul directed two of them before they split: *Bob & Carol & Ted & Alice* (1969) and *Alex in Wonderland* (1970). I lost track of Larry over the years. But Paul and his sweet wife, Betsy, met up again with Christa and me at the Avignon Film Festival. Paul has had a marvelous career as a director, with outstanding films like *Next Stop, Greenwich Village* (1976), *Tempest* (1982), and *Enemies: A Love Story* (1989). Still the funny man, Paul cracked that he was hurt that I'd hired Larry for *Shock Corridor* and not him. He asked me why.

"Paul," I said. "You were too goddamned skinny."

Shock Corridor did great business. Critics called it the most daring film of the year. It has gone on to play all over the world, becoming a cult classic and, I hope, an inspiration for young directors to go beyond conventions to achieve their own vision. *Shock Corridor* has been honored in many ways over the years. I'm most proud of the 1968 Prize of Human Values, awarded by the Catholic church in Valladolid, Spain. Nowadays, when people talk about my "tabloid-philosopher" style, they are probably thinking of *Shock Corridor.* Recently, the film was named by the Library of Congress as one of their official two hundred "American Classics." A

The RKO Palace Theatre, in New York City, during the first run of Shock Corridor. *The marketing boys had a field day with clever hooks like "Shocking world of psychos and the sex-crazed exposed."*

French critic wrote that *Shock Corridor* looked as if it took place in a spaceship. I hope one day people will watch my film as nothing more than science fiction. Until then, it stands as a mirror of the madness and destructiveness in our society.

For all the film's remarkable staying power over the last thirty years, *Shock Corridor* was a financial debacle for me. Firks turned out to be a totally unethical producer. I still had another picture to do with him, so I didn't complain when not one royalty statement ever showed up in my mailbox. Needless to say, the promised share of the profits never materialized either. It was only after I finished my next film, *Naked Kiss,* that the situation with him became glaringly clear. I asked to see Firks's books. The sonofabitch was insulting and rude to me. I'd never been treated that way. It would leave a sour taste in my mouth.

Ironically, there's always a silver lining. Firks, who turned out to be financially unreliable, never tried to change a single frame of film. *Shock Corridor* is exactly the way I conceived, shot, and edited it.

41

Want to Be
a Lindy?

I'd met my first prostitute when I was a seventeen-year-old crime reporter for the *New York Graphic*. A veteran newspaperman walked me into a brothel at the corner of Ninety-seventh Street and Broadway, giving me a tip about saving nickels on phone calls. Instead of using the pay phone at the neighborhood drugstore to call my city editor, why not ask "the girls" if I could use theirs? Madame thought I was cute and let me make my call. From then on, I used to drop by the house of ill repute when I was on the Upper West Side and needed to phone in a story. It was a fascinating environment to my young eyes. At the beginning, there was little contact between me and the employees. I was pretty nervous about being in a place like that. I'd heard so many terrible things about prostitutes. Sergeant Peacock down at the precinct tried to scare me about the "ladies of the night" with some bullshit about your balls dropping off if you hung around them. Society and the media made the very word "prostitute" engender fear and distaste.

My mother had also filled me with a load of crap about prostitutes. Did she have a conniption when I told her I used the brothel as my office when I was uptown! Rebecca launched into a righteous speech about immorality and hygiene. Syphilis was a big problem in those days, blinding, even killing, people who caught it. I reassured my mother that I'd never had any sexual contact with the girls. But for Chrissakes, I told her, nothing prevented me from talking with them. Little by little, I got to know the girls as people. They treated me like a kid brother, though they weren't that much older. Any sensual urges I might have had were quashed by the girls' businesslike approach to their job. I was never tempted to sleep with a prostitute because I knew them too well. They told me all about their lives, and I grew to respect them.

In the morning, they sat meditating like nuns in a convent, wearing nothing but negligees and pajamas to entice the early-bird customers. If I showed up, they would give me some money and ask me to go out and bring them back coffee and donuts. I did these little chores gladly. Once I brought some hot coffee to a girl named Helen. Before Helen could drink it, Madame called her upstairs for a gentleman who'd just walked in. Helen asked me to hold on to her coffee until she came back.

"It'll be cold," I said.

"Uh-uh," said Helen, glancing at the guy. "I know my clients. Believe me, it'll be warm."

The girls had their own code of ethics, their own dreams. A lot of them wanted to have children and a family. That was their ticket out of that dead-end life, back to normalcy. Very few made it happen. Most languished in that netherworld where Madame provided for everything in exchange for sixty-five cents of every dollar the girls took in. From my perch in Madame's office, I overheard their conversations about laundry bills, cab fares, and backaches. When Helen once complained about the exorbitant commission extracted from her pay, Madame looked at her with a harsh glint in her eyes and asked her, "Do you want to be a Lindy?"

The not-so-subtle threat to be out on the street, all on her own, was a reference to Lindbergh's solo flight across the Atlantic. The life of an "independent" was much harsher, for the girl had to be much more wily to survive, preoccupied with her physical safety to boot.

They had a terrible complex about their work. When they went out, the girls imagined everyone knew, with just one glance, what they did for a living, as if the word "prostitute" were branded on their foreheads. Secretly, they clutched onto romantic visions, hoping a well-to-do client would invite them to a swank restaurant or club. That rarely happened. The smart ones put aside as much money as possible, then resettled in a place where no one knew them.

There were two separate doors to the brothel, an entrance on one side of the building and an exit on the other, so clients wouldn't run into each other. Appointments were mandatory. Madame had it all organized and coordinated down to the minute. Part of her success was due, no doubt, to some local politicians who were regulars at the brothel. From Madame's little office, I could see the living room if I leaned over and glanced through the doorway. There on the couch one day was a prominent city councilman. I'd been at a press conference at city hall when that same councilman had made a big speech condemning prostitution in Manhattan. The goddamned hypocrite had vowed to abolish it.

One of my pals, Dotty, managed to move out of the brothel into a luxurious apartment on Manhattan's Upper East Side. My city editor sent me to interview Dotty about a crime story I was on. She was almost a prisoner in that swell place, kept on a tight leash by the well-to-do man who'd rescued her. She answered my questions, but she made me promise not to use her name in the story. It would be bad for her new life. I promised and kept my word. Dotty had a gorgeous smile.

Cut to thirty years later. I was meeting one of my lawyers for lunch at the Beverly Hilton Hotel. I arrived early, walked up to the bar, and ordered a Bloody Mary. Somebody tapped me on my shoulder. I turned around. An elegant woman stood there smiling at me.

"I remember you," she said. "Do you remember me?"

I looked at her lovely face and couldn't place it. I shook my head.

"Corner of Ninety-seventh Street and Broadway," she said.

I suddenly remembered. Dotty, the girl who got out.

"I told my husband that you had ethics," she said.

Her dapper elderly husband walked over with their daughter, already a young woman. The husband was a well-known lawyer for the mob. The daughter looked exactly like her mother had when I'd met her in the early thirties. We gibble-gabbled, and I was careful not to say the wrong thing. We said good-bye, and she gave me that beautiful, mysterious smile before I turned and walked away.

Those recollections jarred me into writing *The Naked Kiss,* a yarn about a prostitute who decides to start anew in a small town where nobody knows her. She thinks she can escape the double-dealing and deceit of the big city. However, she'll have to struggle against just as much ill will and hypocrisy in the sticks. My story would delve into the small-mindedness that thoughtlessly points its finger at sinners, fostering intolerance and hate.

I wanted to grab the audience like a screaming headline, and quickly establish the character of my lead, Kelly, in the first scene. Critics have called this sequence my "signature" scene. That's bullshit, because every scene in every movie I ever made bears my imprint. Here is the opening from *The Naked Kiss* from the final version of the script, which we shot almost exactly as written:

INT. FARLUNDE'S APARTMENT—NIGHT

   1. A WOMAN
   is attacking a drunk with her handbag. The woman is
   KELLY, exquisitely filling a fitted sheath dress with spaghetti
   straps, revealing an eye-shattering figure. Her chic hat is on
   a lovely coiffure; her features are extraordinarily flawless.

*In my opening for
Naked Kiss,* Kelly
(Constance Towers) beats
the crap out of her pimp.
*My cameraman, Stanley
Cortez, started the
prologue from a low
angle, with lots of grays
and shadows. Then he
got the struggle between
Kelly and her pimp by
sticking the camera in
Connie's face.*

PULL BACK with FARLUNDE, the drunk, as she advances, smashing him with blows. Even as she hammers the helpless drunk, she is an artist's unblemished masterpiece of consummate grace, regally groomed. Trying to ward off her blows, trying to remain on his feet, Farlunde reels and staggers into his bar, sending glasses, bottles crashing to the floor. On wall a picture gallery of women watches Kelly and drunk in noisy battle. Props crash. Chairs are overturned. He loses his balance, crawls across room. She batters him with handbag.

> FARLUNDE
> Please Kelly! I'm drunk!

Her handbag smashes his mouth. Lips bleeding. Cheeks cut. He protects his head, leaps to his feet, loses his balance, swings, knocks her hat off, grabs at her gown, pulls it off. She is in a bra and half-slip, black satin with lace. He grabs at her hair, pulls. *Her wig comes off. She is bald.* His hand finds her mouth, pulls. She bites. He shrieks, retreats in pain, reels drunkenly against writing desk, sends lamp and desk props crashing to floor. Lamp bulb on floor continues to burn. Farlunde falls, his head striking a table leg. He is out. Only sound: her hard breathing. She stares. Dead? She checks him. Relief. Alive! She grabs a bottle of siphon water, sits on his stomach, squirts water in his face. He chokes, coughs, comes to. His eyes bulge. Panic. She finds his wallet, takes out his fat bankroll. He grabs for his money. She slaps his face. He whimpers. He is too drunk to fight her off. She swiftly counts bankroll.

> KELLY
> Eight hundred dollars.

(*peeling off each bill deliberately*)
> Ten. Twenty.

(*slaps his face*)

> You parasite! Thirty. Forty. I'm taking only what I earned. Fifty. Sixty. Seventy. Seventy-five.

(*slaps his face*)

> I'm not rolling you, you drunken leech. I'm
> only taking the seventy-five dollars that's com-
> ing to me!

She flings rest of money in his face, stuffs the $75 into her
handbag, gets into her dress, swiftly repairs her shoulder
strap, gathers up her wig and hat, goes to wall mirror, stares
at her weird reflection.

2. CLOSEUP KELLY

staring into camera lens (which now has become the mirror)
as anguish sweeps her smeared features. She is a shorn
image. Carefully she fits the wig on her head as THE
NAKED KISS crashes over her face with MAIN MUSIC
THEME. As she repairs her face, CAST AND CREDIT
TITLES appear over it. The finishing touch is her hat. She
steps back to appraise herself. Once again she is the extraordinarily beautiful woman. She starts out, remembers something, goes to the picture gallery, rips off her photo, tears it
up, throws pieces at the drunk, proudly exits. MOVE IN to
Farlunde on the floor, drunkenly counting his money,
whimpering. HOLD on CLOSE SHOT of desk calendar on
the floor. It is: "JULY 4, 1961."

FADE OUT

I was lucky enough to have Stanley Cortez again as my cameraman on
Naked Kiss. For the opening, Stanley attached a camera to an assistant's
back. There were no Steadicams back then, and believe me, those cameras
were heavy. Another guy had to kneel behind the cameraman and hold
him by the waist so he wouldn't fall over backward. I told Constance Towers, who played Kelly, to smash the camera's lens with her bag as if she were
hitting the pimp's face. In the editing room, we cut back and forth
between her and the pimp getting the hell beaten out of him, then added
a jazzy soundtrack.

That sequence was the last thing we shot, because I wanted Constance
to shave her head. She did it without a qualm. In France after the Liberation, I remembered how they'd shaved the hair off women who'd been
sleeping with German soldiers. Kelly's pimp pulls this horrible trick on her

as punishment for her revolt against his authority. Right after the fight, Kelly puts on her wig and arranges her makeup. The audience knows right away that there's an unbridgable breach between Kelly's harsh life and middle-class respectability. A final close-up in the opening is of a calendar on the floor of the pimp's place. It's Independence Day for America *and* Kelly. She walks.

When I was a crime reporter, I covered suicides. A helluva lot of them left behind suicide notes for their loved ones. Typically they wrote things like "God forgive me" or "I can't go on." I'd never forgotten one note written with an eyebrow pencil on a paper bag by a prostitute: "Today is my independence day. I am going to celebrate it now."

Film directors all over the world have told me how much they have been influenced by the opening sequence in *Naked Kiss*. I'm always pleased to hear that. At the time, however, I was only thinking about portraying my character honestly. Extending the language of film sometimes starts with just trying to show one true thing.

Naked Kiss skips forward two years. Kelly resurfaces in a typical American town called Grantville. They have a little movie house there that's playing—what else?—*Shock Corridor*. As soon as Kelly steps off the bus, Griff, the local cop, is on to her. He picks her up and takes her back to his apartment, where he pays twenty dollars for a taste of Kelly's "Angel Foam Champagne," her traveling prostitution gimmick. They spend the night together.

Like Kelly, Griff's a complex character the audience can't easily figure out. There's no phony romance between him and Kelly, just a professional liaison. Kelly wants to have a cop on her side. Griff's a loner, ambivalent about his small-town police work, yet pleased to be the big fish in a little pond. He's paid to keep the peace and maintain the town's facade of civility. That means blinking at the prostitutes across the river at the local brothel run by his pal Candy. Griff would love to be a big-city cop, but he can't hack it. When the sophisticated Kelly shows up, she sets him on his ear, exposing Grantville's phoniness and Griff's hypocrisy. See, he wants Kelly out of his territory, but not so far away that he can't partake in her charms from time to time.

Kelly wakes up the next morning in Griff's bed and looks at herself in the mirror. As if for the first time, she peers at her face and hardly recognizes the person she's become. Then and there, she decides to stop turning tricks. Kelly rents a room in Miss Josephine's house and finds a job as a nurse's aide at the local hospital for crippled children. She turns out to be a big success with the kids, earning respect and appreciation from her colleagues. I put in a musical number with all the children in the hospital singing sweetly to Kelly:

I didn't give a damn if people thought it was corny for a reformed prostitute to end up in a children's hospital. I wanted to show a "tainted" woman succeeding in the pure world of children. Kelly's warmth and sincerity attract the attention of the town's popular philanthropist, Grant, a man with a terrible secret.

Mommy, dear, tell me please,
Is the world really round?
Tell me where
Is the bluebird
Of happiness found . . .

Kelly befriends Buff, a beautiful young nurse, lending her one of her elegant gowns for a night on the town. Buff comes back with twenty-five dollars she's "earned." Kelly suspiciously asks about the cash. Buff confesses that Candy gave it to her as an advance against future earnings at her brothel across the river. Kelly explodes, first slapping Buff silly, then sitting down beside the girl and telling her about her own hard lessons in the flesh trade. I wrote the following monologue for Kelly so she could talk about her life and the lives of all prostitutes.

> KELLY
> . . . You'll be every man's wife-in-law and no man's wife. . . . Why, your world will become so warped, you'll hate all men and you'll hate

yourself because you'll become a social problem, a medical problem, a mental problem
and a despicable failure as a woman.

Kelly goes out to Candy's brothel and smashes the madam in the face
with her purse, forcing the twenty-five dollars into her mouth and warning her to keep away from Buff. Kelly has balls and a sense of justice. It's
her beauty and romanticism that get the immediate attention of Grant,
the town's handsome and well-respected philanthropist. In Grant's mansion, he connects with Kelly as Beethoven's "Moonlight Sonata" is playing
in the background. In a romantic reverie, they watch home movies taken
from a gondola drifting through the canals of Venice and recite Lord
Byron's poetry.[1] Kelly is lifted into another world, a world of imagination
and wonder. Seducing her with his idyllic nonsense, Grant is totally insin-
cere, a pretentious bastard covering up his perverse character with a veneer
of charm and generosity.

Grant kisses Kelly. She pulls away and looks at him strangely. There's
something uncomfortable about Grant's kiss, though Kelly can't say what
it is yet. Later she comes to understand that it's a "naked kiss," the kiss of a
sexual pervert. Kelly is upfront and confesses to Grant that she was a
hooker. Regardless, he pledges his love and asks her to marry him. The
very day she comes to his house to show him her new wedding dress, Kelly
finds out the truth about Grant. He's a pedophile. She catches him in the
act of molesting a little girl named Bunny. The child runs away. He
explains to Kelly his take on their upcoming marriage.

> GRANT
> Now you know why I could never marry a
> normal woman. . . . That's why I love you . . .
> *you* understand my sickness. You've been con-
> ditioned to people like me. . . . You live in my
> world . . . and it will be an exciting world.
>
> (*dropping to his knees*)
>
> My darling, our marriage will be a paradise
> because we're both abnormal.

Shocked and disgusted that he would use her to cover up his perversion,
Kelly crushes Grant's skull with a telephone receiver. Her anger against the
child molester is overwhelming, as if she's striking out against all the men
who've abused her. Grant's dead, and she's thrown in jail for murder, her

past splashed across the headlines. Everyone in the town turns against her. They'd like to burn her at the stake like a witch. After all, she's killed their patron saint, the richest man in town. The only thing lower than a prostitute to those churchgoing, law-abiding citizens is a pedophile. Bunny, Grant's child victim, is finally identified and coaxed into telling about her "games" with Grant. All charges against Kelly are dropped.

The entire town shows up the day Kelly is released from jail. They stand in silence. She is suddenly a hero for attacking the child molester. Kelly looks at the crowd coldly, then walks off wordlessly to catch a bus out of Grantville, pausing only to glance at an infant in a baby carriage. She doesn't give a damn about anyone or anything. Her dreams are broken. Their reactionary little town can never be home for her.

The End.

The Naked Kiss did great box office when it was released. Thirty years later, it continues to play at art cinemas and on cable television channels all over the world. Of course, I'd never see a nickel of those promised residuals. Inexplicably, I'd become a "Lindy" in the world of filmmaking, an independent making movies whenever and wherever I could find a producer. If the producer was dishonest, I was screwed. There was little defense against the crooks except to keep writing original yarns and hope my next producer would honor his side of the deal.

I was almost fifty-two years old when I finished *The Naked Kiss,* proud of what I'd already accomplished, bursting with energy and original stories, full of anxiety about the new period in my life that was dawning, that of an independent moviemaker. It was going to be a wild ride. I fastened my seat belt and held on tight, ready and willing for whatever the rollercoaster of life would bring me.

PART V

*Going over the D-day invasion scene with Lee
Marvin before we shot it for* The Big Red One

42

Two to Tango

I was afflicted early on by an irresistible longing to rove. Even today, no matter how luxurious or cozy the roof over my head, I'd leave it behind in a flash for the chance to travel to some exotic locale. Especially to make a movie. Hell, I guess I'm really a goddamned tramp at heart.

When I was a kid, I got hold of a helluva autobiography, first published in 1910, called *Life and Adventures of A-No. 1, America's Most Celebrated Tramp,* and devoured it. At eleven years old, A-No.1 was a bright boy who spoke several languages, did well at school, and was doted on by his well-to-do parents in San Francisco. Then one day, consumed by wanderlust, jolted by a hundred-franc note that arrived from an uncle in Paris which could only be spent in France, the kid set out on his own, hitching rides on trucks, boxcars, and freighters, roving all over the world. The kid got his nickname from a fellow hobo, a grown man who'd been riding the rails all his life. That bum's words were burned into my memory: "If you have to be anything in life, even if a tramp, try to be 'A-No.1' all the time and in everything you undertake, wherever you are."

A-No.1's tales have stayed with me since my childhood. I think it was those stories that inspired me to hitch around the country on my own in the thirties, filing colorful articles from the road, fulfilling my own need to ramble, discovering what America was really like. World War II was another chance to act out the strange malady that makes you itchy to abandon home and loved ones to see the world. My infantry years opened my eyes to life and customs in Europe and North Africa, teaching me more about mankind in four years than some people learn in a lifetime. The fifties saw me settle in Hollywood, yet I jumped at every opportunity to shoot movies in far-away locations, be it Japan, South America, England, or the Philippines.

Wherever you go in the world, hard-hitting pictures are never easy to get off the ground. It was especially so in the early sixties. Hollywood was

In his preface to this unforgettable autobiography, the author wrote: "This book is filled with funny adventures, as well as sad features, and I beg my readers to remember that a person cannot be a tramp and an angel at the same time."

still very conservative. I'd really been bucking rough seas by making *Shock Corridor* and *The Naked Kiss.* The only way I could get them done was independently, outside the studios. Let's face it, there were few studio heads around with the balls and intelligence of a Zanuck.[1]

By the mid-sixties, America's mood had changed drastically. The horrible assassination of President John Fitzgerald Kennedy was just the beginning of the turbulence. Martin Luther King and Robert Kennedy were gunned down. Urban ghettos erupted. War in Vietnam wrenched American society apart. Youthful idealism and vigor were struggling against narrow-mindedness and intolerance. The counterculture rejected bourgeois goals and conventions. Our society was in upheaval. For cryin' out loud, it seemed like a perfect time for me and my ballsy yarns!

Of course, life doesn't ever work out the way you think it will. Rather than prolific, the sixties turned out to be tough-going. The seventies and eighties didn't get any easier. I resorted to my tramping ways, going wherever in the world a producer would back one of my projects. Even then, I didn't make half the movies I wanted to. Don't get me wrong, not a single moment do I regret. Even when things looked really bleak, I remained optimistic, excited by the yarns I was working on. One of the tricks I've learned is to tap constantly into my creative juices, no matter whether there's a producer to finance a movie or not. When you're least suspecting it, one'll show up. You damn well better be ready to pull a script you really love out of your desk drawer!

I don't know what the hell it was—you name it, too controversial, too direct, too raw—but after *The Naked Kiss,* moguls, producers, and starlets weren't knocking on my door anymore. To survive in the movie business, I considered whatever propositions showed up, even the half-baked ones.

Along came a young man named David Stone with an intriguing idea about a modern adaptation of Aristophanes' *Lysistrata,* to be shot in Paris.[2] David assured me that his partner, Mark Goodman, had the financing for the picture all set up through his millionaire father. They wanted me to write and direct it. Only half believing the project would materialize, I said I'd do it. Then a decent check showed up with a contract. Attached was an airline ticket to France. Packing up my cigars and my Royal, I was on my way.

It was late September 1965 when I arrived in Paris. David and Mark had rented me a furnished apartment in Montmartre on a narrow dead-end street called Impasse Trainee. The boys also provided me with a car, though I rarely needed it. My driver parked the limo downstairs, next to a wax museum off Place du Tertre, then drank coffee, smoked cigarettes, and waited. It was nice to know the car was there if I needed to go somewhere. But I didn't. At the conclusion of a long day of writing, I sent the chauffeur home.

Autumn in Paris is a wonderful time. From my apartment's window, I had a great view of Tertre, and beyond, the steep rooftops and thin chimneys jutting into the gray skies above the city. I settled into daily life in Montmartre. The only breaks I took from banging out my script were for long walks at dawn to buy my baguette, grabbing a café au lait and reading the *Herald Tribune* at a corner bistro that came straight out of a Toulouse-Lautrec painting. The leaves were turning golden. They drifted down into the gutters on either side of the cobblestone streets, swept away by the never-ending stream of water from some faraway hydrant.

I was having a ball with *Lysistrata.* Right off the bat, I told the boys my script wasn't going to be anything like the original as written by Goodman and Noel Burch. The story I concocted was semi–science fiction—very contemporary stuff at the time—about a secret international society of gorgeous women who use sex, science, and violence to maintain peace around

In my Montmartre apartment in the fall of 1965. Paris was a helluva place to write and fall in love.

the world. I called the yarn *Flowers of Evil*, borrowing from one of Baudelaire's famous lines: "I have found it amusing to extract beauty from evil."

One evening, I had my driver drop me off at the bottom of the Champs Elysées. I lit up a cigar and strolled up the broad, tree-lined avenue. From a distance, I saw the big words SHOCK CORRIDOR on the marquee of the MacMahon Theater. My picture had opened in France and was doing great business. I was curious to see how it played to a French audience. When I reached the movie house, I saw the jostling lines of film fans waiting outside for the next screening. I stood there puffing on my cigar, enjoying the scene. After they let the crowd in, I went up to the box office to buy a ticket for myself, but there were no more. The lady in the glass booth was sweet, but the screening was sold out. I tried to explain to her that I just wanted to stand in the back and watch my own film for a few minutes. The answer was still no, some crap about security. I made a big stink. The theater manager came over. I pointed at the words "Directed by Samuel Fuller" on the poster, then showed him my passport. He finally let me in.

That French crowd was really hooked on my yarn. They were a rowdy bunch, here and there laughing, yelling, and whistling at scenes, but mostly wordless and engrossed. Maybe they loved it. Maybe they hated it. What was important for me was that *Shock Corridor* was getting a gut reaction. What can be better than having your picture shown to a packed audience, their faces arched upward toward the screen, everyone into a story that you've created from scratch? It was one of those moments when all the struggles and bullshit of moviemaking seemed worthwhile.

As I continued my stroll along the Champs Elysées, a young man came up to me and introduced himself as a writer for *Cahiers du Cinéma*, I think, Luc Moullet. I was happy to meet him because he worked for a helluva movie magazine. He invited me for a drink in the bar at Fouquet's. Moullet pulled out a recent issue of *Cahiers* with an article by Jean-Luc Godard calling *Shock Corridor* a "masterpiece of barbarian cinema." I didn't know what the hell that meant, but I was happy if it helped sell tickets. By then Godard had successfully made the transition from critic to New Wave director, with *Breathless* (*À bout de Souffle*, 1961) and *Contempt* (*Le Mepris*, 1963). Godard was still contributing reviews. Moullet wanted to set up a dinner so Jean-Luc and I could meet.

About a week later, I showed up at Brasserie Lipp, just across from the Café Flor on St. Germain des Près. Bazin and Godard were already sitting at a table by the window. With his thick black glasses, long curly hair, black beret, and Gaullois hanging off his bottom lip, Jean-Luc looked like Central Casting's choice for the role of "young French intellectual eccentric." Being eccentric was the only thing Godard and I had in common. Otherwise, we were really opposites, me coming out of a working-class background, Godard from an upper-class Swiss family whose money allowed him the luxury of bucking the French establishment. I was prone to excess, while Jean-Luc was a minimalist. I liked the guy, but certainly not because he told me how much my films had influenced him. I laughed at that influence crap. Let's face it, Godard had stolen a bunch of my ideas from *Pickup on South Street* and *Underworld, U.S.A.* for his early pictures. I didn't mind, but why not call it what it was.

Jean-Luc was going to shoot a new film, called *Pierrot le fou,* with Jean-Paul Belmondo and wanted me to appear in a scene. I suppose it was his way of saying thanks. I said I'd do it. Without the faintest idea what I was supposed to say, I showed up at a studio on the outskirts of Paris the day of the shoot. Godard stood me up against a wall in some fancy cocktail party set full of half-naked women and intellectuals, and put a glass of vodka in one hand and a good cigar in the other. He let me wear my sunglasses because of the bright lights. The Belmondo character strolled in and was introduced to me, "the American film director." Belmondo turned and asked me, "What is cinema?" We never rehearsed the damn scene. I wasn't sure what Jean-Luc wanted, so I took a puff on my cigar and played myself, blurting out a line in my tough-guy vernacular, which a bilingual lady repeated in French as I spoke.

*Jean-Luc Godard directs
me for my walk-on
in* Pierrot le fou.

"Film is like a battleground," I said. "Love.
Hate. Action. Violence. In one word, emotion."
One take, and that was that. Godard loved it.
Believe me, I'd be rich if I had a nickel for every film magazine and festival
program around the world who printed that goddamned line!

A memorable evening that fall was organized in my honor at the Palais
de Chaillot by Henri Langlois, founder of the French Cinémathèque. Langlois was a big man who, behind his lumbering frame, dissimulated an
incredible zeal for movies and moviemakers. The foremost archivist of all
time, Langlois was personally responsible for saving thousands of films.
Through year-round Cinémathèque screenings, Langlois popularized classic movies and lost masterpieces. Every director in the world owes Langlois
a debt of gratitude. My way of paying tribute to the great motion-picture
collector was to name one of my characters Langlois in *Quint's World,* a
novel that was first published in Paris under the title *La Grande Mêlée* in
1985.

That fall night back in 1965, Langlois screened a couple of my pictures.
There were many admirers hanging around at the reception afterward. I
slipped outside, lit up a cigar, and had a smoke by myself in the lovely gardens of the stately Chaillot Palace, built for the Paris World's Fair of 1901.
Just across the esplanade was the Eiffel Tower. A small, unpretentious man
came over to me and introduced himself. He was François Truffaut. I told

him I'd loved his picture *The Four Hundred Blows* (1959). It was great because the story was told through the eyes of a troubled boy. He said he identified with the children in my movies, characters like Tolly, in *Underworld, U.S.A.,* and Short Round, in *The Steel Helmet,* kids struggling with adult problems.

Like me, François had had a tough childhood. I liked this shy man, his warmth and thoughtfulness coming through immediately. He was a person of few words who chose them carefully. A friendship was forged then and there. Over the next two decades—through letters, books, and phone calls—Truffaut and I'd stay in touch. He came to see me whenever he was in Los Angeles. Once we met up at a reception at Universal for Alfred Hitchcock. Besides being a helluva director, François was a lovely person. I'll never forget the telegram he sent my daughter, Samantha, the day she was born: "I love you already. Your friend, François."

Before I left the festivities at the Cinémathèque that night, a gorgeous gal walked up to me and introduced herself as "Miss South America." Her name was Maria-Rosa Rodriguez. She came from Ecuador and was working as a model and actress in Paris. We chatted a moment, then I said good night and got the hell out of there. Thinking that it's good for their careers, actresses always strike up conversations with directors. It's no big deal. How could I have known then how important the encounter with Maria-Rosa would turn out to be?

One afternoon a few days later, I was typing away in my place in Montmartre. Through the windows of my apartment, I could see the top of the Sacré Coeur cathedral, with its steeples, like sugar-iced tits, and its flocks of filthy pigeons, the rats of the air. I went to the window and relit my cigar, taking in the view. In the street below, there was a beautiful young woman posing for photographers in front of the wax museum. From a distance, she looked just like Sophia Loren. Suddenly, she spotted me and waved up at my window.

"Hiya, Sam!" she yelled in her sexy Latino accent. "Don't you remember me? The Cinémathèque? Why don't you come down?"

It was Miss South America again. I went downstairs. Once the photo shoot was over, Maria-Rosa and I went into one of the nearby cafés and had a drink. She was not only gorgeous but very sweet. The next natural step was to invite her to dinner that night. She accepted. I hadn't had any female company since I'd been in Paris. I was old enough to be her father, so it would just be for fun. We made a date to meet in a bistro called La Cloche d'Or, the Golden Bell.

Later, I found out that Maria-Rosa went home and immediately called up one of her best friends, a German actress who was also just getting

Tall, smart, and gorgeous, Christa Lang happened into my life in 1965. She'd be my gal for the next thirty years. She was good with pistols, too, here playing a tough extortionist babe in Dead Pigeon on Beethoven Street, *in 1971.*

started in the business. The two young women shared cheap pasta dinners and exchanged precious gossip about upcoming films. The German actress spoke excellent English, French, and Spanish. She could translate my impossible American accent. I got a call that afternoon asking if I would mind if Maria-Rosa brought along her young actress friend. Having a chaperone sounded quaint, so I said okay. Hell, it was good for my libido to have a date with two young actresses. Maria-Rosa's friend turned out to be the woman who'd become my wife, companion, and partner for the rest of my days, Christa Lang.

Destiny had concocted a far-fetched plan for the two of us to cross paths in Paris. Christa grew up in a working-class family in Germany but always dreamed of seeing the world. She was an excellent French student. When she was offered a position in France as an au pair with a well-to-do family, she grabbed it. It was her ticket out of boring middle-class sobriety. She quickly tired of baby-sitting and got herself to Paris to take up acting. By the time we met, Christa was starting to get small but credible roles, having been cast in films by Pierre Chenal (*The Murderer Knows the Score,* 1963), Roger Vadim (*La Ronde,* 1964), Claude Chabrol (*The Tiger Likes Fresh Blood,* 1964), and Jean-Luc Godard (*Alphaville,* 1965).

Christa had just arrived back in the capital after shooting with Chabrol in Spain. That very day, she was on the Champs Elysées and got into the line of people waiting outside the MacMahon to see *Shock Corridor.* Her friends had told her the movie was a "must-see." Later, she would say my picture was like someone slapping her in the face.

To Christa's delight, Maria-Rosa was having dinner that very evening with the director of *Shock Corridor.* Could Christa come along with them? You bet she could. She got all dolled up for the occasion. When Christa walked into the La Cloche d'Or with Maria-Rosa, I only had eyes for her, a blond bombshell with powdered cheeks and red lips just aching to be kissed.

I started telling Christa all about my *Flowers of Evil* yarn, scene by scene. She said it reminded her of Ring Lardner's writing. Holy smoke, this young woman was not only gorgeous, but she knew a helluva lot about American literature. I told her how important a person Lardner had been in my life, how I used to hang around the great man as a young copy-boy. One story led to another, and another. Christa and I talked the night away. She made a valiant effort to translate my nonstop storytelling into Spanish so Maria-Rosa could keep up with us. I almost forgot Miss South America was at the table! As we were leaving the restaurant, I promised Christa that I'd get her a copy of Lardner's complete stories from Brentano's, the English-language bookshop near the Paris Opéra. I asked her if she would like to have dinner again sometime, just the two of us. She said yes. Both our hearts were bubbling.

It was ten days before I called Christa again. Later, she told me those ten days were interminable for her. I kept postponing our next meeting because I was frightened by my sudden, strong feelings for this young woman. I'd vowed to myself to stay single. After the failure of my first marriage, I figured I just wasn't cut out for married life. Resigned to being a permanent bachelor, I was suddenly confronted by this smart, sassy German beauty who was thirty-two years my junior. Our age difference tortured me. Starting a relationship with Christa was a big responsibility. Tossing around in my bed at night, I kept asking myself what the hell a beautiful young woman like her would want with me. I wasn't making big money anymore. I couldn't help her in her career. Every bone in my body disavowed the possibility of Christa and me ever having a life together. Our connection was too goddamned spontaneous and irrational. But boy oh boy, was I smitten!

Listening more to my heart than my brain, and with the pretext that I wanted to give her the book of Ring Lardner's stories, I finally called Christa. We met at a subway stop in Pigalle and walked up the hill to the Montmartre plateau above. She wanted me to try out one of her favorite restaurants, whose specialty was snails from Burgundy. I recoiled when she suggested I have a dozen of those slimy creatures. I'd never eaten snails before. But after I tried one of hers, dripping in butter and garlic, I ordered a dozen of my own. We ate and drank and talked and laughed away the night. Afterward, we walked arm in arm through Montmartre, stopping at the foot of Sacré Coeur to kiss. We ended up at my apartment, where Christa spent the night. It was marvelous.

For the next few months, my bachelor pad became our love nest. During the day, I worked on my *Flowers of Evil* script. In the evening, I met Christa. She really knew her way around Paris. I was getting invited to all kinds of openings, parties, and cultural events. Christa was constantly at my side. She enjoyed the socializing. All the attention being showered on me was flattering at first. But it began to wear thin. The French were crazy about my movies. I came to understand that their infatuation was more to do with the fact that my films were American than that they were written and directed by me. It made me realize how much I missed America. As great as France was, I was far away from home, geographically and spiritually.

David Stone and Mark Goodman loved the first draft of *Flowers of Evil.* I'd come up with a helluva ending for the picture that would take place in outer space. My leading lady is abandoned, revolving endlessly through the infinite cosmos as the screen fades to black. I turned the script over to them and waited to hear about when we would begin production. The answer was never. The project collapsed because the elder Goodman had no intention of financing the picture. The old man didn't want to see his son getting involved in the movie business. I certainly could see his point, but there I was in Paris with a worthless movie deal.

At first, I blew my top. I could've even sued the two would-be producers. But I felt that the boys had been sincere about wanting to make the movie with me, and they were so disappointed about the turn of events. It would've been perverse to take them to court. I don't like legal wrangles with people. Besides, to kick a guy when he's down is just not ethical.

Even if I was upset about the unraveling of the *Flowers of Evil* project, I had to admit that the end result was surprisingly wonderful. By coming to Paris, I'd met a woman I loved and who loved me. Christa and I were already talking about getting married. Except for her, there was no reason for me to be in France anymore. I kept postponing my departure even though we knew it would be best for me to go home and find some real work. Christa would join me in the States as soon as possible. Our separation was going to be difficult, but I needed to get my life in order back in California to make room for a new partner.

Before I packed my suitcase for the trip home, we took some last nostalgic walks together along the Seine, through the Orangerie, around Montmartre. Who knew when or if I'd ever be back? When I said goodbye and kissed Christa, I promised her I'd write every day and bring her over as soon as I'd squirreled away some dough. I left Paris in January 1966.

When I got back to Hollywood, reality came hurtling down upon me. My career as a director seemed totally derailed. I certainly wasn't going to make any more movies with my last producer, Firks, or his distributor, Allied Artists. I was still angry at the way I'd been treated on *Shock Corridor* and *Naked Kiss*. I realized how spoiled I'd been by producers like Lippert, Zanuck, Dozier, and Warner. Those guys loved good stories. They fulfilled their financial obligations. They had class. They were mensches.

Back home, there were few credible offers coming my way, except for Charles Warren's *Iron Horse* TV series. I decided to go back to writing fiction again. First, I did a novelization of *The Naked Kiss,* which turned my tight one-hundred-page script into two hundred pages of free-ranging prose with plenty of back stories about my central characters, Kelly, Griff, and Grant. I also put the finishing touches on *Crown of India,* a globe-trotting adventure story about some jewels stolen en route from India to New York's '64 World's Fair. It was published in 1966.

My first wife, Martha, was still friendly with me. Because of our divorce, she'd done well for herself financially, buying two houses, one next to Elizabeth Taylor's on Schuyler Drive and one for investment purposes on Cherokee Lane. She offered to let me stay in the place on Cherokee, probably because she felt guilty about having all that money and me just scraping by. That's the way I'd set it up after I walked away from our marriage, so I had no hard feelings.

Once I'd moved into her place on Cherokee, Martha started coming round a little too often. She even joked that our divorce had been a mistake and that we should get back together. I wasn't laughing. Not only was Martha now remarried to the dependable Colonel Ray Harvey, but I was in love with Christa. I suspected Martha secretly wanted both Ray's steady companionship and my energetic creativity. No way. I may have loved François Truffaut's films, but I wasn't made for triangular affairs straight out of his *Jules and Jim* (1961).

When the opportunity presented itself, I told Martha that I was with Christa and that she was coming to join me as soon as possible. Martha was stunned. Then I dropped the other shoe. My new love was thirty-two years younger than me. Martha was really burned up that I'd taken up with a "European gold digger." I laughed, because there was no gold to dig. I was living from hand to mouth. Martha had an ax to grind, but the grinding landed on deaf ears.

I counted the days, weeks, and eleven long months until Christa's arrival, writing her a love letter or a postcard every day. On the big day— November 19, 1966—I drove my gleaming "Jack Warner" Cadillac to the Los Angeles airport to pick her up. It was terrific to be together again, this time for good. Like children, we relished every aspect of life, loving each other from moment to moment.

All my friends wanted to meet Christa. Stanley Cortez, my cameraman on *Shock Corridor,* Ray Kellogg, the special effects man, Harry Sukman, the composer, and his wife, Gretchen, Peter Bogdanovich and his wife, Polly Platt, all dropped by the house on Cherokee to wish us well. Peter and Polly, who were closer to Christa's age, became our constant companions. The four of us would go for Sunday brunch at Nate 'n' Al's Delicatessen and have a lot of laughs.

One of my old friends, John Ford, startled Christa when he called that summer. It was June 6. Ford telephoned me every D day. Since I wasn't in, Christa introduced herself and asked if she could take a message: "Jack Ford here. Tell Sammy to fuck the Big Red One." Then he hung up. I explained to her it was a running gag between Ford, a navy man, and me that had been going on for years. At first, Ford's particular sense of humor baffled Christa, but they later became buddies.

With Christa at my side, I'd been given a new lease on life, a fresh reason to rededicate myself to moviemaking. Although we didn't make it official until the following summer—July 25, 1967, to be exact—we lived like man and wife from the day Christa came to the States. Our wedding ceremony in Santa Monica was presided over by Judge Eddy Brand, who'd also officiate at the marriage of Henry Miller and his wife, Hoki, a few years later. We told no one we were getting hitched, preferring to keep it intimate. It was so intimate that I had to grab a couple of cops in the hallway of the courthouse to be our witnesses. Afterward, Christa and I had some Chinese chow and a romantic walk on Malibu beach.

Looking back at my three decades with Christa, I confess I was a tough guy to be married to. Somehow, we made it work, realizing right away that it takes two to tango. I made her laugh a lot with my yarns and optimism. I worked hard to support her dreams of a family and a higher education. Christa has been my loyal, shrewd, realistic Sancho Panza, without whose understanding and loving support my mad quest to make hard-hitting movies would have long ago come crashing down in a self-inflicted heap of frustration, vodka, empty bank accounts, and unproduced stories.

43

Sharks

Five long years had gone by without a movie offer coming to fruition. Sure, there was plenty of high-paying TV work around, but in those days, you had to choose as a director between making feature films and television. Hungry to direct a picture, I agreed to take on a project in Mexico based on an obscure novel called *Twist of the Knife* by Victor Canning. Before the book ever showed up came a check, a contract, plane tickets to Mexico, and a treatment about an out-of-work gun runner in Sudan who hooks up with a mysterious couple searching for sunken treasure in the Red Sea. The book never arrived. It was the debut of one of the strangest goddamned pictures I'd ever be involved with.

I let myself be convinced by a couple of American wheeler-dealers, Skip Steloff and Mark Cooper, along with their Mexican playboy partner, Jose Luis "Pepe" Calderon, to get involved in that project. See, they assured me that they wanted a "Fuller" picture based on this sunken treasure tale. I should have had my head examined before getting mixed up with those guys or their production company. But the fact that good movie offers were no longer coming my way was making me stir-crazy, so I bit the bullet and threw myself into this caper. I convinced myself that, at the very least, Christa would get to see Mexico. Just like every descent into hell, it started off gloriously. They put us up in a luxury hotel called Las Brisas, in Acapulco. I went to work on the script, turning their thread of a plot into an action movie, weaving in a slew of double and triple crosses with some cagey characters called Doc and Mallare, some underwater scenes, and some shark attacks. Don't forget this was five years before Spielberg's *Jaws* (1975). I called the movie *Caine*, after my lead character. Only Caine and the female lead, Anna, are alive at the end, when they exchange caustic good-byes, thinking the other's screwed.

We moved to Calderon's private mansion outside Acapulco, with servants running all over the place, and I finished *Caine* there on schedule. A stomach virus turned tropical paradise into living death, making us so miserable we thought we were going to die. An American doctor was called in, but his medicine made us even sicker. A Mexican doctor finally cured our malaise. Once recovered, I owed it to Christa to take her out to some Acapulco nightspots. At one of them, we became friendly with the talented Cuban singer Celia Cruz. Celia gave us some of her records. Back home, Christa would play Cruz's sensual, rhythmic numbers for me when I was working on my next script, about the Spanish-American War, *The Charge at San Juan Hill.*

Considering the banality of the original treatment, my *Caine* script turned out pretty good. How I was ever going to get it made into a motion picture was still a mystery. Sloppy and disorganized, the Mexican production company didn't have a clue about making movies. I figured I'd be innovative. Hadn't Orson Welles shot *Touch of Evil* under very tough conditions too? With *Caine,* I'd stay on my toes, inventing tricks as I went along. I actually believed I could turn out a jewel of a movie. Of course, I was bullshitting myself.

We moved to Mexico City for preproduction. The producers had hired Burt Reynolds as the male lead. Reynolds was a television actor still a couple of years away from his breakthrough film, *Deliverance* (1972). For Doc, we cast Arthur Kennedy, who came down from New York, straight from his Tony-winning performance in Arthur Miller's *Death of a Salesman.* And for Mallare, I persuaded my old friend from *Forty Guns,* Barry Sullivan, to join us on this Mexican escapade.

For Anna, our female lead, we sought out the lusty Mexican star Silvia Pinal. She'd been outstanding in Luis Buñuel's *Viridiana* (1961). A dinner was arranged with Silvia and Mexican rock star Enrique Guzman, the third of her four husbands. Pinal was so good-humored and gorgeous, I hired her on the spot. She turned out to be one of the lovely surprises of that shoot, a real pro. Christa and I became very close with her, even spending a couple of weekends at her place in Cuernavaca.

In Mexico City, Luis Buñuel heard I was in town and invited Christa and me to dinner at his place. There, we met his French wife, Jeanne. We had a fabulous evening with Luis, a kindred spirit, every bit as much of a maverick as I. I'd first met Buñuel in Hollywood before the war when he was making ends meet by dubbing films for Warner Brothers. *The Naked Kiss* and Buñuel's *Belle de Jour* (1967) both dealt with the double life of prostitutes, exposing perversity without being perverse. Both poked fun at the small-minded mores of the righteous middle class. Luis told me how much he'd loved *The Naked Kiss,* but that he hadn't seen it before he made *Belle de Jour.* So much for critics who thought my film inspired his.

With Luis Buñuel in Mexico City in 1970. The father of cinematic surrealism, Luis was given a strict Jesuit education, sowing the seeds of his obsession with religion and subversive behavior. His last picture was That Obscure Object of Desire, *in 1977. In his autobiography, Luis said he'd be happy to burn all the prints of all his films—a surreal gesture if ever there was one. He was a true original.*

The fact remains that we were both interested in probing beneath society's saccharine superficialities.

At dinner that night, Buñuel said he'd love to see my last film, *Shock Corridor*. Another guest at the table was Alberto Isaac, head of the Mexican Cinematheque. Isaac knew where to get his hands on a Spanish-subtitled print of my picture, so a screening was set up that week. Christa accompanied Buñuel, telling me afterward that she was in heaven that day, sitting next to Buñuel, one of her favorite directors, savoring his reaction to her husband's film. Mumbling compliments in Spanish after key scenes, Buñuel kept squeezing Christa's arm to show her his approval. It was his way of applauding.

Caine was to be shot on location in Manzanillo. Calling the town primitive would be diplomatic. Hell, the plane carrying our crew and equipment over there was the first commercial flight to land at the new Manzanillo airport, nothing more than a goddamned pasture with grazing cows. My producers had been grazing, too. Nothing was organized. Nevertheless, I concentrated on shooting the best movie I could with the resources at hand. The next six crazy weeks were as challenging as flying an airplane while you're building it. Thank God I had veteran cameraman Raúl Martínez Solares with me down there. With thirty years of experience, "Papa" Solares had not only a great eye but an endearing character. He called me *hijo mio,* and we worked great together.

The production got off on the wrong foot right from the start. After we'd finished rehearsing one evening, Burt Reynolds almost walked off the picture. It was something I said to him at a restaurant on the beach while we were having a cold beer. Burt was whining about his wife, Judy Carne, leaving him for another guy. I told him that he'd get over it, making a wisecrack about the girl wanting a smarter, more talented guy. Reynolds stood up with tears in his eyes, said he was quitting, and stomped outside and walked off into the Mexican sunset. Hell, I was just kidding, trying to de-dramatize Burt's blues and get him to focus on the movie. I wasn't about to traipse after Reynolds. Christa did. She apologized for my insensitivity and consoled Burt with some sweet talk. For Chrissakes, I was making a picture in a primitive place with incompetent guys who called themselves producers, and now I had a tantrum-throwing, ham actor to boot!

Fortunately, Burt's fragility disappeared on set. He was a hard worker. It was one of his first movie roles, and he obviously wanted out of television for good. My opening sequence was shot in one take. I put Reynolds in a truck careening wildly down an abandoned road. The truck exploded. He managed to jump to the ground, reappearing through a cloud of smoke and fire. As he sauntered straight toward the camera, the movie title, CAINE, would come up on the screen. Burt did the scene without a stunt man. He was damn good.

My story was as dry as its Middle Eastern setting. There were no fairy-tale romances, no happy ends. Anna and Caine don't have the slightest feelings of tenderness for each other. By reversing the predictable, I'd show the absurdity of romanticism. Thanks to the camera work of Papa Solares, all the beautiful elements in the sublime countryside of Mexico became visually hostile. I wanted things to even sound hostile. Every time Caine tosses a cigarette into the water, it makes a hissing sound, and a shark comes to the surface and gobbles it up—*whooooshhh!*—and then the surface of the ocean becomes as still as death again.

My finish was as troubling as that environment. Anna thinks she's pulled a fast one on Caine by grabbing the loot and making a getaway. Caine chuckles because he knows her boat is booby-trapped. The camera holds tight on one last cigarette he tosses into the water, the final shot of

Burt Reynolds in Shark.
*He did a good job in a
bad film.*

the movie. A shark snatches it. *Whoooshhh!*
The audience would understand that the
double-crossing Anna was doomed.

I made up the cigarette schtick, just like every other shot in *Caine,* as I
went along from one setup to the next. I wanted the picture to say something about greed. The loot everyone lusted after didn't mean a goddamned thing. In my own way, I wanted to pay tribute to Erich von
Stroheim's *Greed* (1925). In that film's unforgettable climax, shot in Death
Valley, von Stroheim's lead is trapped in the desert. The man ends up
paying a king's ransom for nothing more than a goddamned glass of
water. And to think that Louis B. Mayer cut about eight hours of footage
out of von Stroheim's masterpiece for the studio's two-hour version. I
pray *Greed* is put back together someday, the way von Stroheim originally
envisioned it.

We returned to Mexico City for another month of editing. I was able to
spend more time with Buñuel as well as get acquainted with the talented
Arturo Ripstein. I also ran into my old pal Budd Boetticher, who was
working on his masterpiece about bullfighting, *Arruza* (1971). That picture
was as important to Budd as *The Big Red One* was to me. *Arruza* is as
much a memorial to the great matador as it is a testament to Budd's unwavering fascination with the art of life and death in the bullring.

Christa and I stayed in a plush hotel on Calle Hamburgo. On weekends, we went over to Cuernavaca, the locale for Malcolm Lowry's masterful *Under the Volcano,* one of my favorite novels. I remembered Lowry's description of dead dogs in the streets. Sure enough, there were dead dogs all over the place, struck down by dehydration. Experiencing Mexico firsthand made Lowry's surreal book seem so much more real to me.

I delivered my cut of *Caine* on time to the producers, a good little adventure movie with reasonable commercial potential. Christa and I packed up our things and went home. A few months later, the producers invited me to a private screening room back in Los Angeles to see the fully finished picture. I brought along Peter Bogdanovich, who was at that time a critic for *Esquire.* What a horrible shock I had! They'd completely recut my movie, retitling it *Man-Eater,* refashioning almost every scene to suit their tastes, which were lousy. My opening sequence was now cut into three parts. It no longer looked like Caine was narrowly escaping death. What the hell kind of adventure movie doesn't kick off with risk and suspense? Over and over, the producers had butchered scenes, destroying all trace of timing and subtlety. I was flabbergasted with their reediting.

When the lights came up, I hit the ceiling. I told the bastards straight out that that wasn't my picture, that they had tampered with my work without asking me and, more importantly, without a clear idea of what the hell they were doing. I've rarely felt so disrespected. If Peter hadn't restrained me, I would've strangled the sonsofbitches. Instead, I walked out and immediately requested that the Guild remove my name from the movie. I'd have nothing more to do with it. The picture was eventually retitled again, as *Shark,* and had some kind of theatrical release and TV syndication, making a good return for the producers. Of course, I'd never see a penny of the residuals they'd promised to pay me. I never want to think about sharks again, neither the ones swimming in the ocean nor those wearing expensive silk suits who produced that Mexican fiasco.

44

Lean Times

My ex-wife's house on Cherokee Lane was no longer the place to be living with my new wife. Martha kept showing up at odd times with the pretext of wanting to work in the garden. It was bizarre. I scraped together some dough and bought a little place with a pool up in the Hollywood Hills on Woodrow Wilson Drive. In those days, your status in Hollywood dropped the farther you moved away from Beverly Hills, so we were really in the boondocks. I didn't give a shit about status. What was important to me was that we now had our own little home. Affectionately, I've always called it "the Shack." I converted the garage into an office where I set up an old rolltop desk right out of *The Front Page.* Surrounded by my books and scripts, file cabinets, and war mementos, I banged out my yarns. It was a damned good place to work.

Not far down the street lived John Cassavetes and Gena Rowlands. David Hockney moved into the neighborhood a few years later. More and more creative people bought houses up in Laurel Canyon and fixed them up. Nowadays our neighbors are a mixed crew that includes the head of a big German movie studio and Quentin Tarantino. Modest by any standards, the Shack is packed with marvelous memories. Our daughter, Samantha, spent some of her childhood here. Over the years, so many good friends came by to spend time with us. During all our sojourns around the world, the Shack was always there, beckoning us to come home.

I paid for the place by writing scripts, not directing movies. Sam Arkoff gave me a fat check for a black exploitation yarn, then never made the picture. Bobby Cohn, the nephew of the late mogul Harry Cohn, optioned my Civil War yarn called *The Toy Soldiers,* but never made that movie either. Believe me, it was quite a struggle to keep up the mortgage and pay for my cigars.

Sure, offers came my way. In 1969, producer Frank McCarthy asked me to direct a biopic about General George S. Patton. I turned it down, just like I'd passed on the request by Patton's own son in the fifties. Hollywood people thought I was a meathead for turning down a big-budget studio picture. Franklin J. Schaffner ended up directing *Patton* (1970), a damn good movie with an outstanding performance by George C. Scott. Not for one instant have I regretted not making it. After my war experiences, I didn't have the necessary detachment to do a picture celebrating the man.

In 1968, I got an enticing offer to write and direct a movie in Spain for Emiliano Piedra, who'd made a helluva lot of dough distributing *Shock Corridor*. Piedra was one of the backers of Orson Welles's *Chimes at Midnight* (1965). Reputable and serious-minded, Emiliano would go on to produce some of Carlos Saura's best pictures. I pitched him a story that I'd been incubating, called *The Eccentrics*. A famous woman writer, a combination of Virginia Woolf and George Bernard Shaw, cracks up, isolating herself on a houseboat with a band of hippie admirers. They soothe her ego with their devotion but end up destroying her. With its tense emotional scenes and stream-of-consciousness nightmares, the yarn had a ton of potential. It would be a helluva lot more personal movie for me to make than *Patton*.

One day Peter Bogdanovich came by the Shack with Danny Selznick, associate producer of Peter's first film, *Targets*. Danny's father was David O. Selznick, of *Gone with the Wind* fame, and his mother was Irene Mayer, Louis B.'s daughter. When I told the boys my story, Danny thought the role of my eccentric woman writer was perfect for his stepmother, Jennifer Jones. Danny's dad had divorced his mother in the late forties and married Jones (born Phyllis Isley). Jones had won an Oscar for her role in *The Song of Bernadette* (1943), but I think she did even better work in King Vidor's *Duel in the Sun* (1946). She was looking for a comeback vehicle, so Danny set up a dinner at the Selznick villa, a swank place, to say the least. Jennifer loved the part. Over the course of more meetings, I tailored the script for her like a seamstress fitting a wedding dress to a bride.

For my male lead, I contacted the French actor Maurice Ronet, whom Christa had worked with on a Claude Chabrol movie. I knew Ronet from his terrific performance in Louis Malle's *Le Feu Follet* (1963). Emiliano Piedra also wanted me to use Charlie Chaplin's daughter, Geraldine, as one of the young hippies in the movie. Geraldine was already living in Spain, mother to two children with Carlos Saura.

Christa and I left for Spain in May 1968 to work on the script and scout locations. Emiliano and his partner, Octavio Lieman, put us up in the posh Torre de Madrid Hotel. We had a chauffeur-driven car day and night. I reworked the story, injecting more local color based on our day trips to Aranjuez and Toledo. As soon as I had a finalized script, I sent it to

Jennifer Jones back in California, along with photos of a houseboat we'd found where Jennifer's character was supposed to be living. Jones was enthusiastic. Then the shit hit the fan. No sooner had we set a start date than a feud broke out between the two production partners. Both Emiliano and Octavio came to me for my blessing to buy the other one out. I was in a real bind, especially so close to the shoot date. I decided that the only ethical thing to do was to stick with Emiliano. I'd started the picture with him and would finish it with him, one way or the other. Emiliano was a real professional, the rare combination of shrewd businessman and movie lover.

The production was back on track. Then, one week before Jennifer Jones was supposed to arrive in Spain, we got the horrible news that she'd tried to commit suicide. She wouldn't be able to come at all. As it turned out, she'd never make another movie. The disturbing irony was that my script opened with the Jennifer Jones character contemplating suicide, having reached painful middle age, surrounded by admirers, fearing that she had nothing to say anymore through her art. Jennifer recovered, but *The Eccentrics* didn't. Desperately, we tried to pick up the pieces. Janet Leigh wanted to play the lead in the movie. So did Jeanne Moreau. But everything was canceled when Emiliano threw in the towel. Sure, we'd been living in splendor for five months in Spain, but now it was time to go home with another fiasco to swallow.

At least the Shack was still in good shape. Our young friend Curtis Hanson had been looking after everything for us. The only way I knew how to recover from the setback was to plunge into another yarn. I wrote a script for a children's movie called *Pecos Bill and the Kid from Soho.* It was lighthearted and mischievous. Pecos Bill is an adult who never really grew up. He tells tall tales about the West to a little English kid with a Cockney accent. The two of them take imaginary trips. Christa got it optioned to Sid and Marty Krofft, who owned a toy factory and produced the TV show *H.R. Pufnstuf.* We made some dough, but the option expired and they never made the picture.

I locked myself away in my study and kept on writing, not knowing when my next movie would get off the ground. I wrote a comedy called *The Lusty Days,* bringing a little laughter back into our lives. It's still one of my favorite scripts, a swashbuckling Civil War movie without a battle or a death, told like a forgotten chapter of American history.

See, a politico is hired by President Abraham Lincoln to comb the battlefields convincing soldiers to vote for "Honest Abe" in his campaign to get reelected. The politico must use any means at hand to influence the voters. He teams up with a beautiful French dancer, who shakes and shimmies her ass to get the soldiers' support. The dancer's generous derriere does more to get votes than any politician's campaign speech. Because she thinks she's getting rich, the French girl puts up with the scam. But one day she spies soldiers wiping their asses with Confederate money. That's the currency she's accepted as payment for her services. She blows her top and turns the cheating politico over to the enemy. He gets chucked into prison. Since my story was all tongue in cheek, the politico and the dancer end up together at the end of the picture.

I had a ball portraying President Lincoln as more shrewd than idealistic, and Jefferson Davis, the Confederate leader, as a stubborn, bumbling adversary. Martin Poll, producer of *The Lion in Winter* (1968), loved *The Lusty Days*. His offer to option it was ridiculously low, but since Marty not only appreciated the yarn but was such an intelligent producer, I accepted it. After all, Marty was going through a divorce and couldn't come up with a lot of dough until a studio signed on the project. We met with Henry Fonda, who was ready to play the roles of both Lincoln and Davis. Even with Fonda on board, Marty couldn't get a green light. The rights for *The Lusty Days* eventually reverted back to me. It was filed away on a shelf in my study, where it lies today with a helluva lot of other unproduced scripts.

Christa got a call from a well-known German critic who was in Hollywood with a film crew to shoot interviews of famous American directors. The critic and his crew came up to the Shack to interview me. They stayed on to share a meal with us. The wine, the German jokes, and the laughter were flowing. I called up John Ford and Howard Hawks to set up interviews for the German critic. The guy was so grateful that he asked me if I wanted to make a picture in Cologne, where he had good contacts in the film industry. Nobody was banging down my door, so I said, what the hell, I'd consider any proposal. Shooting a film in Germany sounded like fun. Besides, it would give Christa the opportunity to spend time with her family in Essen, only a short distance by car from Cologne. Soon after, a German producer named Joachim von Mengershausen contacted me. We negotiated a deal by which I'd shoot a movie for the big state-controlled TV production company. My film would be broadcast in Germany, but I'd retain all American rights.

When I first started out as a director, I never bothered with ownership issues. All I wanted to do was finish one picture and go on to the next. But after my problems with producers, I'd been dreaming of the chance to own the rights to one of my movies. So I jumped at the opportunity. Christa and I packed our suitcases and were off to Germany to make a cartoon caper movie called *Dead Pigeon on Beethoven Street*.

45

Off the Radar Screen

As soon as we'd arrived in Cologne, Joachim von Mengershausen screened a few films for me that were written and directed for *Tatort*, one of the country's most popular TV shows. My movie would be the first broadcast on that show. The program's "realism" was admired in Germany in the late sixties. Some of the stories were quite good, but others were goddamned dull. Hell, I wanted *Dead Pigeon on Beethoven Street* to be funny and self-mocking, bringing a breath of fresh air to their stale realism. A highly cultured man, Joachim laughed when I growled about the dreariness of the *Tatort* series. I think he hated producing the show; he was in it purely for the dough. Von Mengershausen and I enjoyed each other and had a good time working together. I couldn't pronounce the man's name correctly, so I called him "JM."

"Sam," JM told me, "you make the film you want to make, as long as you respect our budget. I only have two specific requests."

"Shoot," I said.

"First, we want Christa to play a part in the film."

"I'm writing the female lead especially for her."

"Second, you have to find a role for Eric Caspar, the actor with whom we have a contract for the series."

"Fine. He'll be my heavy, Charlie Umlaut."

For the rest of the cast, I had a free hand. To play Mensur, the head of the syndicate, I cast Anton Diffring, a celebrated German character actor who'd made a career of portraying Nazis. Glenn Corbett, whose first picture was *The Crimson Kimono*, would play Sandy, my American detective. Glenn had appeared alongside the likes of James Stewart (*The Mountain Road*, in 1960, and *Shenandoah*, in 1965) and John Wayne (*Chisum*, in 1970, and *Big Jake*, in 1971) since last we worked together.

My yarn was a tongue-in-cheek adventure inspired by the headline-making Profumo affair in England. That scandal was big news in those

In Dead Pigeon, *an American detective is gunned down on Beethovenstrasse while hot on the track of a syndicate blackmailing diplomats.*

days, filling the papers with real-life tales of blackmailed politicians and high-class call girls. In *Dead Pigeon,* an international syndicate is blackmailing diplomats. One of their victims is a liberal U.S. senator who is butting heads with the Republicans for the presidency. An American private eye is hot on the track of the damaging photo of the senator and a luscious blonde with a strawberry birthmark on her left thigh. The detective is gunned down in Beethoven Street. His partner, Sandy, comes to Germany to pick up the trail of the blackmailers through their beautiful bait, Christa, the girl with the birthmark. He drugs and frames her to get himself into the syndicate. Then they start working as a team for the extortionists. Christa poses with the drugged V.I.P. while Sandy takes the photos.

Sandy and Christa fall in love. She promises to help him get the negative of that compromising shot of the senator. In her attempt, it appears that she gets herself killed by Mensur. Sandy and Mensur have a bizarre duel with antique swords and spears. Mensur dies. Christa reappears with a gun. She's not only very much alive but she wants all the negatives so she can control the syndicate herself. My finale is a shocker. Christa and Sandy genuinely love each other, but they love the buck even more. She wounds him in a street chase. Just as she's about to finish him off, he shoots her under the *Beethovenstrasse* sign.

The German producers put us up in a grand hotel in Cologne, while I was working on the script. I'd get up at the crack of dawn and walk around the city, observing the hustle and bustle in the streets. Whenever I'm in another country, I love my morning walks. It brings me up close to real life and working people, the glue of a nation, before I head back to the solitary endeavor of inventing dialogue and images.

At first, it was strange for me to be back in Germany, the country that, thirty years before, had been our total enemy, where my life was at risk every moment of every day, where visions of destruction and death had been hammered into my mind. I couldn't help reseeing those bleak scenes looping in my brain. I'd look at the beautiful banks of the Rhine and listen to the soothing sound of a foghorn on some faraway riverboat, the present mercifully pulling me back from the past.

I wanted *Dead Pigeon* to be full of high jinks and hilarity. People expected me to be doing war movies or action pictures. I'd always dreamed of doing a comedy, a film of pure entertainment. Here was my chance.

Just before the shoot began, I got a call from Rainer Werner Fassbinder, one of Germany's up-and-coming directors. He'd go on to make forty films in his short life, including the excellent *Marriage of Maria Braun* (1979). Fassbinder said that he loved my movies and wanted to meet me. A screening was set up so that I could see one of his films, a Western. It was a terrible movie, and I told him so in a teasing way. He took it warmly. He asked me if there was a role for him in my new film. I seriously considered hiring him, except the only role he could play was that of the heavy. The German bosses would never have accepted substituting Fassbinder for their contract actor. Besides, Fassbinder would corroborate their suspicions that my picture was completely frivolous and eccentric.

I regret not casting Fassbinder. The man was a visionary with real flair and honesty. In his plays and movies, Fassbinder portrayed postwar Germany trying to shake off its Nazi past while striving for material success. Rainer made Germans look at themselves. If they didn't like what they saw, they blamed the messenger. I felt a comradeship with the man. I remember Rainer telling me about the bad rap he'd got for writing a play about an unscrupulous real-estate broker and unrehabilitated Nazi, based on firsthand knowledge from his own father's slumlording days. The play's lead made a crack about Jews. Because of what his character said, critics pegged Fassbinder as an anti-Semite for years.

Nothing could have been more incorrect. Fassbinder just believed in showing people the truth. I agreed with him that it was stupid to hold young Germans responsible for their elders' mistakes. I cherish the several times Rainer and I got together during that stay. As a going-away present, he gave me a book of poems by Heinrich Heine. I was very moved by his gesture and thought we'd begun a long-term friendship. Fassbinder's premature death, in 1982, at the age of thirty-eight, cut short a prodigious career, though leaving behind a body of work that another director, if he were damn lucky, might produce in a life twice as long.

No matter where I went in the world, there were always talented young directors who sought me out and befriended me as a mentor. Like Fassbinder, they were experimenting with fresh ways of telling stories on film, breaking new ground, making thought-provoking films on every continent. We talked and talked about movies, past and future. It wasn't much, but I always tried to be encouraging. No matter what setbacks I've had in my career, I'm damn proud to have been thought of as a "director's director."

The *Dead Pigeon* shoot went great. Cologne is very Latin, its cathedral an essential landmark. The French poet and novelist Apollinaire loved the town and praised it in his poetry because his German mistress came from there. During Carnival, the people of Cologne, normally a dignified lot, dress up in costumes, put on masks, and go haywire. They have a song they sing that instructs revelers to have fun and adventures but cautions, "Please, please, don't ask for my name."

For the movie's opening credits, it seemed like a good idea to have the whole cast and crew dress up in wild Carnival costumes so the audience would know we weren't taking ourselves too seriously.

One of the recurring gags in the film was to underscore Sandy's naïveté. The Yankee gumshoe is thrilled to be on a big case in Europe. He doesn't anticipate any danger whatsoever, so he never carries a weapon. In real life, detectives are pretty boring people. They take few risks, live a long life, and rarely do anything more adventurous than sit in a car with their thermos full of coffee, eating donuts and spying on cheating wives and husbands. I asked Glenn Corbett to play the nutty detective straight-faced. He did, except once. I had him duck into a movie house where they were screening a Western with John Wayne. Glenn couldn't control his laughter when he saw his pal Wayne speaking perfect German up on the screen. The laughter was so spontaneous, we left the sequence in.

My cameraman on *Dead Pigeon* was the accomplished Jerzy Lipman, the Polish cinematographer who'd shot Roman Polanski's brilliant *Knife in the Water* (1962). Jerzy accepted without a murmur every camera setup I suggested. It made me suspicious. I like to challenge people and for them to challenge me. When there is a difference of opinion or approach, any enterprise is more creative. I asked Jerzy why he was being such a yes-man. He joked that Polanski had ordered him to "say yes to everything Fuller wanted." Jerzy honestly liked my crazy camera angles and unconventional shots. To get some of those sequences, I asked Jerzy to use my trusty old 16-mm Bell & Howell. We had a lot of fun together.

My German crew was shocked when I requested that they stop referring to me as "Herr Direktor" or "Mister Fuller" and just call me "Sam." They were uneasy about using my first name. It was a sign of disrespect in Germany. That was just one of the many cultural differences. Their society seemed charmingly Old World but took authority too seriously. My demeanor and hands-on approach was entirely New World to them, a little brusque and sometimes too candid. I felt like a Connecticut Yankee in King Arthur's court.

We went to Bonn to shoot a scene in the Beethoven Museum. I hadn't been in Bonn since the Big Red One had taken the city and that unforgettable night when I'd slept under Beethoven's piano. The museum director appeared at the entrance and said that having our film crew inside the building was out of the question. The floors were too fragile. I asked if I could take a walk through the museum with Herr Direktor. Holding the man by his arm, I strolled into the place. After a few puffs on my cigar, I asked him how they'd moved the piano on such a fragile floor. The director was caught off guard, curious how I knew about the original position of Beethoven's piano. I also told him there used to be a portrait of an Indian chief above the piano. The young Beethoven was crazy about American Indians.

Now I had Herr Direktor's attention, so I went into my story of that March night in 1945 after the invasion of Bonn when I accidentally broke into Beethoven's home and slept there with another dogface. Before we knew it, a bottle of schnapps appeared, and we were knocking back shots with Herr Direktor as I rolled out one story after another about the Big Red One. I told him that when all hostilities were over, our outfit came back through Bonn for a twenty-four-hour rest period. Every dirty, tired doggie got a little soap and a change of clothes from a supply depot located on Beethovenstrasse. That street was heaven for us. Herr Direktor had tears in his eyes. Permission for us to shoot in Beethoven Museum was granted.

When *Dead Pigeon* was broadcast on German television, audience ratings were high. They seemed to like my disregard for the typical style of *Tatort* productions. German TV magazines voted Christa the most popular actress of the year for her performance. The producers sold the movie all over the world, making a good return on their investment. The English were most receptive to the picture's wacky humor.

"A box office bonanza with the impact of a sledgehammer," wrote Ken Welachin, of the National Film Theatre in London. "*Dead Pigeon* assaults today's diplomatic blackmail with sharp humor. Fuller has made the timeliest film of the year."

"Long live Fuller's *Dead Pigeon*!" wrote *Time Out–London*. "Hammered out word for word on the screen, any distributor would have to be deaf, dumb and blind to pass it up—a juicy, spoofy, action-packed morsel."

The French made me laugh. The Cannes Film Festival invited *Dead Pigeon* to screen in one of its several sections. An intellectual magazine awarded the movie its top critics prize. However, the rest of the French press dismissed it as "anarchistic." For Chrissakes, people have always been trying to pin political labels on me. First, I was supposedly a right-winger, then, a left-winger. Now I was off the radar screen. I hate all those labels and the lazy goddamned writers who try to stick them on you. Critics and commentators are constantly projecting their own fantasies on every artist who does something original. All artists are anarchists, okay? We want to shake up the audience, to question what's acceptable, to set off earthquakes in the brain. Otherwise, why not look for a secure, regular-paying job as a teller in a bank?

Ownership of the American rights to *Dead Pigeon* turned out to be just about worthless to me. A distributor who'd made some dough on the cult movie *Mondo Cane* (1962) released my movie in theaters around the States with pretty good reviews. Box-office results were nil.

My taste for making movies in Europe had been whetted. The studio system in Hollywood had shifted into a phase I no longer understood nor wanted to. Directors with a distinctive vision like me seemed less welcome than ever before. Hell, *Dead Pigeon* wasn't my most accomplished movie, but it was an accomplishment for me to have made it in Europe instead of in my own country. While we were still in Germany, a deal was struck to make another picture, this one in Spain, from a cherished script that I'd been polishing for years. I called it *Riata*.

46

Turmoil
and Waste

Riata is probably one of the best scripts I ever wrote.[1] It hit on all the themes I loved telling stories about. Father-son relationships. Outlaws and lawmen. Revenge and forgiveness. Fidelity and betrayal. Violence and peace. Love and rancor. Sacrifice and satisfaction.

Riata is an implacable Texas lawman who is tracking a barbaric killer halfway across Mexico to avenge his son's death. He faces incredible hardships. Before he can catch Brubeck, the bastard who killed his beloved boy, Riata must confront Paco, a Mexican magistrate who's chasing the same killer, and Pompy, the smart French temptress who's Brubeck's lover.

My opening was guaranteed to grab any audience by the balls. During a violent bank robbery in 1868, as Riata corners Brubeck in a schoolhouse, the outlaw kills a child and throws the body out the window. The little boy turns out to be Riata's son.

I'd been working on the *Riata* script since the mid-sixties, when Christa first came to live with me in California. Maybe that's why I was so attached to the project. Sharing my life with this smart, beautiful gal made me bubble with ideas. She was someone I could tell my stories to and get some valuable feedback. She especially loved this yarn.

Christa had immersed herself in French literature classes at UCLA. At dinner, our discussions were stimulating, though sometimes they'd heat up past the boiling point. We passionately disagreed on plenty of stuff. Hell, with the age difference and our Old World–New World cultural cleavage, it's a goddamned miracle we agreed on *anything*. Besides, being in the States was a cultural shock for Christa. It took time for her to get accustomed to the strange new reality of southern California. She made friends with my pals easily, then enlarged her circle, and was appreciated for her warmth and intelligence.

Once, at a Beverly Hills reception, we ran into Jacques Demy and his wife, Agnès Varda, both talented directors from France. Agnès had begun as a still photographer, then started making movies about women, such as her well-regarded *Cleo from 5 to 7* (1962). Demy, like me, came from a working-class background. French people loved his musicals *Umbrellas of Cherbourg* (1964) and *Young Girls of Rochefort* (1967). Jacques and Agnès were sweet, unpretentious people. Christa got close to them and their ten-year-old daughter, Rosalie. One day while Christa was visiting Agnès and Jacques at their place, she met the rock star Jim Morrison. Morrison got all excited when he heard whom Christa was married to. He swore he was a fan of my movies and pleaded with her to introduce him to me. Christa didn't promise the kid anything. She was already functioning in the role that she would assume for the rest of our marriage, that of polite guardian against time-wasting admirers. I'd never even heard of this kid Morrison, or of his group, the Doors. I didn't give a damn about meeting a rock star, or anybody else for that matter, because I was so engrossed in writing *Riata*.

Nevertheless, Christa persuaded me that this young man was a serious artist and that we should accept his invitation to have dinner at some Italian place on Sunset Boulevard. The evening was strange but memorable. Morrison, a charismatic kid, gabbed on and on about his desire to be a filmmaker. About twenty-three years old at the time, Jim was already a veteran in the music business. Drugs were obviously part of his daily existence. Morrison was so high that night, on God only knows what, that he tried to do a handstand in front of our table, right there in the middle of the crowded restaurant.

I liked this crazy, gifted young man, and sensed that he was desperately looking for a father figure. I invited him up to the Shack. He came by often, and I put aside *Riata* to spend time with him. He was on his best behavior with me, telling me how he wanted to get out of the nutty world of music and into film. It was hard to believe that this kid's concerts were wild events, with Jim unzipping his fly, exposing himself, and taunting the audience with lines like "I want to kill your fathers and fuck your mothers!" Jim told me about growing up in the South, and about his disapproving father, a military man. I found it hard to believe I was a role model for him, but Morrison swore that I was. He'd made some experimental films and begged me to look at them. He set up a screening at UCLA, and I sat through them. They weren't much to see but showed promise, and I encouraged him to stick with it.

Morrison's desire to reinvent himself was something I could empathize with. To keep working in the arts, you had to do it. He was learning, as I was, that notoriety was a double-edged sword. The more famous you became, the harder it was to stay fresh and creative. I was in my forties when fame caught up with me, mature enough to handle it. Still in his

Jim Morrison. How could I say or do anything that would affect the trajectory of this rocket of a man hell-bent on crashing?

twenties, Jim was the object of enormous worldwide renown. Nobody that age can handle that much adulation. It made him a desperate human being, looking for an exit from the self-destructive castle of his own reputation.

I felt powerless to be of much help except to listen to him when he dropped by to see me. Morrison was extremely lucid, with flashes of real brilliance, especially when we talked about films and poetry. Like every intensely creative person, he had a touch of madness. Drugs and drink were leading Jim toward his own annihilation. Once Jim came up to the Shack with a book of his poems as a present for me. With great solemnity, he signed it, "To Samuel Fuller, Morrison." It was entitled *The New Creatures*. Another time he gave me the manuscript of a novel he called *Look Where We Worship*—more stormy, inspired writing.

I let Jim read one of my drafts of *Riata.* Through mountain ranges and immense canyons, sandstorms and desert mirages, the outlaw Brubeck races down through Mexico, with Riata and Paco hot on his trail. Trained by Chiricahua Indians, Riata is as good as they get at following the tracks of a man on the run. Along the way, he battles bandidos, Indians, and the double-crossing Pompy. Paco gets shot. Before he dies, he makes Riata promise he'll bring Brubeck in alive. He does, winning hard-won revenge for his son and making peace with himself.

Morrison loved my yarn. One day, he was over at the Shack and picked up a recent issue of *Life* magazine that was lying around, with Mick Jagger on the cover. I cracked a joke that Jagger looked just like my script's kid killer, Brubeck. Christa said I should approach Jagger about playing my heavy. Morrison grabbed that opportunity to ask me to cast him as the lead in the movie. I told him straightforwardly that he was too baby-faced for the part of Riata. He was crushed, not like an actor who doesn't get a role, but like a kid being reprimanded by his papa. Morrison felt that I'd rebuffed him. He walked out with his tail between his legs.

I never saw him again. I'd given him my word that when he wrote a screenplay for his first feature, I'd be there for him, giving him guidance with scenes and characters. But he never reappeared at the Shack. I felt terrible that I couldn't help this tormented young man who had just too many demons to exorcise. He ended up exiling himself to Paris, where he overdosed in his bathtub in July 1971. Christa ran into Morrison in La Coupole in Montparnasse that summer, just a few days before he died. She was with her sister, Renate. Both women were shocked to see that the once-handsome young rock star was now so fat and distorted, his skin pale and sickly. His self-abuse was an altogether awful sight and a painful tragedy.

We were still in Germany finishing *Dead Pigeon* when my agent at the time, Mike Medavoy, called to say MGM wanted to do *Riata*. They put a producer in charge of the project whose first name was Barry and whose last name I've forgotten on purpose. He was another double-crossing wheeler-dealer. I blame myself for getting mixed up with this guy, because I'd been warned about him by Alex Jacobs, an old friend who'd written the script for John Boorman's *Point Blank* (1967). I was hungry to get *Riata* into production, so I looked the other way. When the deal at MGM fell through and Warner Brothers picked up the rights, this Barry character begged me to let him stay with the picture because he had a wife and two kids to support. I relented to his pleas, a misjudgment that would cost me dearly.

Warner agreed to finance my film in Almería, the barren southern region of Spain. A cast was put together rapidly, with Richard Harris starring as Riata and Alfonso Arau as Paco. Richard was a big draw after *A Man Called Horse* (1970). Alfonso was just starting out, long before he turned to directing, with his impressive *Like Water for Chocolate* (1992). The studio considered my suggestion of Mick Jagger as Brubeck, but instead went with the up-and-coming actor Bo Hopkins, who'd appeared in *The Wild Bunch* (1969). Bo wasn't the vicious, playful-looking clown I'd originally envisioned, but a more rugged killer with an infantile look, à la James Dean. I rewrote the part for him.

Christa and I went directly to Spain from Germany to get the production under way. Meanwhile, Barry what's-his-name went to Paris to find a French actress to play Pompy. I told him I wanted someone to play against type, like Juliet Berto, the intelligent-looking young actress who'd been in Godard's *La Chinoise* (1967). The beautiful Berto was smart enough to become a director herself, with the formidable *Neige* (1981), a tale about cocaine addiction.

We'd already begun shooting in Almería when Barry showed up with some unknown French gal whose only qualifications as an actress were her oversized breasts and her willingness to sleep with whomever would help her "career." Thank God her name has also escaped me. We first met this lady in the hotel bar after a hard day's shoot. One look at the "actress" that Barry had brought us and I knew we were in trouble. We were sitting there with some of the sweaty, dusty crew having a cold beer. The French lady showed up wearing a fur coat in the middle of summer in southern Spain, no doubt imagining in the peanut she had for a brain that she looked like a vamp, instead of simply stupid. We asked her if she wanted a beer. No, she said, she only drank champagne. The mostly British crew could hardly contain their giggling at this ridiculous creature.

I was between a rock and a hard place, having to integrate into my movie an actress who couldn't act. We shot a few scenes with her. It was horrible. She was painfully inappropriate. Richard Harris complained that she couldn't act her way out of a paper bag. Mike Medavoy called, and I told him about my predicament. He advised me to keep going and just get the picture finished. I figured I'd cut the French floozy's role down to a minimum in the editing room. Her involvement, however, triggered a violent reaction from studio executives back in Hollywood. After the boys at Warner Brothers saw some of the latest rushes, they decided to shut the movie down.

I was devastated. I'd already shot some terrific stuff and thought the picture was going to be one of my best. Mike Medavoy explained to me that it was more complicated than just the disastrous French actress. The studio was seriously in the red. Other movies in production at that time were way over budget, most notably *The Mackintosh Man* (1973), by John Huston, starring Paul Newman and Dominique Sanda. It was a professional judgment, just cost-cutting, Medavoy said, and I shouldn't take it personally.

I took it *very* personally. The collapse of *Riata* was a wound that would never completely heal. Richard Harris was sweet to try to find other financing, but to no avail. The upshot was that Warner Brothers sold all my footage to an Egyptian producer named Fouad Said. Said finished the movie in Mexico with another director, releasing it as *The Deadly Trackers* (1973). They completely lobotomized my story yet left my name on that piece of garbage as a cowriter. Christa and I packed up and came home by way of London.

The collapse of *Riata* was like *coitus interruptus.* The studio put us up at the elegant Dorchester. Even though I was down in the dumps, we decided to dress up and celebrate the debacle by having a big dinner at one of London's best restaurants. The opulence couldn't make the pain go away. I tried to be stoic with Christa at dinner, but little by little, I got rotten drunk to forget my woes. My head actually fell on the table. Christa had to go through the pockets of my jacket to find the dough to pay the bill. Then she carried me out to a cab and back to the hotel. It was a horrible experience for her. I apologized the next day and promised it would never happen again.

As soon as we got back to Hollywood, studio executives John Calley and Frank Welles invited me in for a meeting. They assured me again that the cancellation of *Riata* was an economic decision. Everyone knows, however, that nothing in show business is simply business. Overnight, it seemed, my career had hit rock bottom. It was terrible for Christa. She suffered bouts of anxiety, combined with vertigo and dizziness, a kind of nervous breakdown, worried about my future, *our* future.

Then there was the onus of the Manson murders. Christa had known Roman Polanski in Paris. He'd arrived in Hollywood to do *Rosemary's Baby* in 1968. Roman and his wife, Sharon Tate, had come over to the Shack for drinks and meals a few times. We'd had a lot of laughs with them. I loved Roman's horror spoof, *The Fearless Vampire Killers* (1967), in which he'd cast Sharon as the female lead.[2] Sharon came from a family of military men. One of her favorite uncles, a Colonel Tate, had appeared in *Merrill's Marauders* while he was stationed in the Philippines. He always talked fondly of the experience, even though I'd made him limp throughout the movie. That uncle had kindled the movie bug in Sharon. Roman and Sharon had recently moved into a new place up on Cielo Drive.

One day in August 1969, Sharon dropped by the Shack in her red sports car. In the final month of her pregnancy with their first child, she was on her way to see a girlfriend who lived near us in Laurel Canyon. Sharon wanted us to come up to her place for a party the next evening. We didn't go. Christa had her parents in town. She took them to Disneyland that day. I was writing all day and much too tired to go out. Had we shown up, we would've been slaughtered like the others. The tragedy of Sharon's death, the devastation of Roman's family, and our near brush with murder weighed heavily on Christa for years.

To make matters worse, Polly Platt and Peter Bogdanovich, two of our best friends, were divorcing just as Polly was pregnant with their second child. Christa felt somehow implicated in the failure of their marriage. See, when Peter was looking for an actress to play Jacy in *The Last Picture Show* (1971), he stumbled on Cybill Shepherd's photos in a fashion magazine and thought she looked interesting. Christa remembered that French director Roger Vadim had already done a screen test with Cybill, and she volunteered to get a copy of the test for Peter. She called Vadim and the reel arrived a week later, with scenes of Cybill cavorting at a beach. Christa and I went to the screening to watch Vadim's footage. The test looked like a seduction number by an old expert and made us all laugh. After all, Vadim had had an incredible string of gorgeous mates, like Brigitte Bardot, Catherine Deneuve, and Jane Fonda, to name a few. Bogdanovich loved the way Cybill moved in Vadim's little film and eventually cast her as his lead. Peter's romance with Shepherd grew from their working together. Christa really had nothing to do with it, but she was deeply hurt by Peter's split with her pal, Polly.

With so many disappointments and cruelties in Hollywood, Christa immersed herself in her university studies. She dreamed of getting a doctorate, then teaching, writing, making a real contribution. I thought it was great that she was studying for a degree. At the University of California, she'd gotten involved in politics and the women's movement, befriending the antiwar, black power professor Angela Davis. Back in those days in Hollywood, when a woman opened her mouth to voice an opinion, they called her nasty names. I always liked smart women who could speak their minds. Christa started going to meetings at Benjamin Spock's and hung out with Davis and Jane Fonda at Dalton Trumbo's place. Jane was then living with the actor Donald Sutherland and getting vocal in her protest against the Vietnam War.

I'd finished my own Vietnam protest, a terrific yarn called *The Rifle.* First, I'd written it as a novel. Then I'd adapted the book into a film script. The story was centered on an old M1 rifle, a World War II relic, which passes through the lives of my main characters, a legendary colonel with a death wish, a fourteen-year-old Viet Cong murderer, an insane French nun, and a crazed soldier who steals blood from the wounded. The movie would show the war from the perspective of the "little people" who are most affected by the violence. My dream was to shoot the picture from the viewpoint of the rifle, in continuous ten-minute takes.

I'd been trying to get *The Rifle* into production for years. Even if my reputation hadn't been tarnished by the *Shark* and *Riata* debacles, no Hollywood producer would go near a movie about the Vietnam War, unless you count John Wayne's *Green Berets* (1968). Wayne wanted to bolster the American war effort by stirring up patriotic sentiment back home, so he bankrolled that blundering movie himself. Americans lost the real-life war because we didn't comprehend Vietnam, its people, or their goals. We pursued our own aims, regardless of realities. So did John Wayne. *The Rifle* would eventually take its place on my shelf of unproduced projects.

One of Christa's pals from that period was Henry Miller. Although Miller was best known for *Tropic of Cancer* and *Tropic of Capricorn*, I thought *The Colossus of Maroussi*, published in 1941, was his finest writing. Christa met Miller through her friend, the actress Gia Scala, who'd played in *The Guns of Navarone* (1961). Gia was living up the street from us and brought Henry over for lunch one day. I loved Henry's spirit, exemplified by his famous line: "Don't look for miracles. YOU are the miracle." Henry and Christa wrote to each other often when we were in Europe on *Dead Pigeon* and *Riata*. That was how we learned that Gia had been institutionalized and finally committed suicide with an overdose. Holy shit, it was another waste of a beautiful life!

Christa was so concerned about all the madness in Hollywood that she discussed doing a book with Miller about people who'd been undone by a life in the arts. She found a line from the French poet René Char, which Miller loved. As I look back, I see it could have been a motto for that difficult period of my life: "Lucidity is the wound closest to the sun."

47

Making It All
Worthwhile

You've got to be philosophic about hard times. People think Hollywood is a heartless and destructive place. I don't believe that crap. Sure, it's a stressful trade, because a lot of talented people are striving for access to limited resources. You just can't let the stress get to you. The studio boys could take a movie away from me, but they couldn't take away my optimism. I was chock-full of ideas, determined to do whatever was needed to support my young wife. Blaming the motion-picture business was useless.

My writing took many forms, be it a treatment, script, novel, or play. Some of my projects developed over many years, as I slogged away at rewrite after rewrite. By the seventies, *The Big Red One* was over a thousand pages of narrative and dialogue. I'd been working on *Balzac* for a long time, too. Whether or not you'd ever heard of Honoré de Balzac or his grand designs for *The Human Comedy*, you'd get a kick out of my movie about the great writer. My ball-grabbing opening had young Balzac and his mother in a runaway stagecoach, hurtling along a treacherous road next to a cliff, the future novelist struggling with the reins of the startled horses and finally saving the day. Hell, *Balzac* was going to be a sexy adventure picture with plenty of action!

Other projects of mine, like *The Charge at San Juan Hill*, were light-hearted and quick-paced. That yarn came to me by way of an auspicious encounter back in the fifties with a veteran of the Spanish-American War. The man had been the trumpeter who blew the charge in Cuba in July 1898 as a member of Teddy Roosevelt's "Rough Riders." My story of that battle would make a pisscutter of a movie, more exciting than anything Hearst's yellow press had reported at the time.

And talk about whimsical circumstances inspiring a yarn, what about my novel *144 Piccadilly?* I'd been invited to Scotland in 1969 by Murray Grigor, head of the Edinburgh Film Festival, for a retrospective of all my films. I came down to London afterward, where the National Film Theater was organizing a similar tribute. Unable to sleep in the Dorchester, I took a long walk late that night along the Strand, strolling through favorite places like Covent Garden, Belgrave and Grosvenor Squares, along Baker and Regent Streets, past Piccadilly Circus. Before dawn, I saw a group of flamboyantly dressed youngsters breaking into a four-story Georgian mansion in Mayfair. They were "liberating" an unoccupied house in order to make it their home. Squatting was trendy in London in those days for activist hippies, striking a blow, albeit a peaceful one, against the establishment.

With my newspaperman's nose, I approached the kids, starting up a conversation. I was obviously sympathetic to their outrageous behavior, so they showed me the fourteenth-century "Forcible Entry Act" in a British law book. It was "an offense to dispossess unlawful occupiers with a strong hand or with a multitude of people." The disheveled squatters invited me to stay on. If I hadn't had prior commitments, a wife, and a flight back to the States the next day, I would have. The English papers and TV news portrayed the kids' benign act like a declaration of war. The situation turned violent when some gang of skinheads tried to move into the mansion, too. The British police felt compelled to use force to reestablish order. The squatters got beaten up for doing something original, and I was damn mad about it.

Inspired by that encounter, I knocked out a fast-paced novel about the counterculture, portraying these revolutionary young people as healthy and admirable. An American film director very much like me participates in an illegal entry in London, then tries to bridge the generational gap by becoming the group's mascot and witness. The fictional "me" does what I was tempted to do but couldn't, abandoning his hotel suite for a mattress on the floor with the flower children. *144 Piccadilly* depicts the idealists in a favorable light despite their self-absorption and elixirs. My fictional incarnation roars around London on the backseat of a Hell's Angels motorcycle, falls into the enthusiastic arms of a beautiful squatter, and comes head to head with violent skinheads. I even fantasized about "me" getting high on drugs, something I've never done in real life.

144 Piccadilly was published by Richard Baron, a progressive, eccentric American publisher who brought out, among other titles, Thomas Berger's *Little Big Man*. The reviews were good, the first time I can remember anyone using my name as an adjective, calling the novel "Fullerian," whatever the hell that meant. Critics make me chuckle. I take them with a grain of salt. Every artist has a defense system with critics, but the simplest and most efficient is this: When the critic is complimentary, he or she is brilliant, and when they knock the hell out of your work, he or she is shortsighted and foolish. This simple survival mechanism works for me.

Curiously, Richard Baron never really promoted *144 Piccadilly.* When I inquired about it, I was told the publisher had disappeared, rumored to have sailed off on a yacht, never to be heard from again.

To keep our own ship afloat financially, I accepted acting gigs whenever I could fit them into my schedule. Christa encouraged me to get in front of the camera to keep me "in circulation." Since my walk-on in Godard's *Pierrot le fou,* there had been several offers, but nothing very intriguing until Dennis Hopper called one day after his box-office hit *Easy Rider* (1969). Universal was backing his next picture, *The Last Movie* (1971), to be shot in Peru, and Dennis wanted me to play the part of a macho film director, a tongue-in-cheek parody of myself. It sounded like fun, and there was some dough in it. Besides, I'd never been to Peru.

They flew me down to Lima and then drove me out to the set—a dense piece of untamed countryside—in a jolting Jeep. Everyone was stoned on the local marijuana. Fortunately, I had just enough cigars to get me through the three-week shot. One of Dennis's pals who was also down there was Michelle Phillips, of the singing group the Mamas and the Papas. She was a sweet young lady and ravishingly beautiful. Michelle and I used to hang out together and had a lot of laughs.

To get from one location to the next, there was a lot of walking to do. Dennis, Michelle, and the rest of their young friends were huffing and puffing after a steep climb up one of those Peruvian hills. They were all amazed that an old fart like me, pushing sixty, could traipse around without even breaking a sweat. I attributed it to smoking cigars, which, unlike their cigarettes and joints, didn't affect the lungs. See, you don't ever inhale a cigar.

The Last Movie was about a film production in Peru's backcountry. In the story, they're shooting a Western while the natives observe the moviemaking process in wonder. The indigenous Indians of the area have never even seen a movie, much less a movie shoot. Much to the Indians' surprise, actors stand up after fake violence. Things start to go very wrong when an actor is really killed in a stunt. The script was a sort of a Pirandello approach to the clash between two cultures, between instinct and reason.[1] Dennis wanted to show how our sophisticated culture could backfire. The natives, long exploited by whites, try to emulate their masters' behavior, only to find out that it can be deadly.

Back in California, Hopper invited me to see the first cut of the picture. I thought he had let the film get away from the simplicity of the script's central clash of cultures. Dennis was undecided about his ending. Hell,

Down in Peru with Dennis Hopper on the set of The Last Movie. *It was a kick.*

you've got to know your ending before you start shooting a single frame of film. Otherwise, your picture is like a goddamned train without a final destination.

A few years ago, Christa and I saw *The Last Movie* again, at a Paris art cinema. I thought the picture held up pretty well, though I still looked ridiculous in that Confederate officer's getup. My trip to Peru to be in Dennis's movie was like working in Hollywood in the thirties, like being in an old Tom Mix picture. I'd always treasure the experience.

Another young director I liked working with was Wim Wenders. I'd met this talented filmmaker in the early seventies and quickly developed a great friendship with him. Wim and I used to talk about everything under the sun, especially the yarns we wanted to shoot. One of Wim's long-cherished stories was entitled *The American Friend.*[2] I made a crack about hoping nobody would get assassinated because of it. His title reminded me of *Our American Cousin.*[3] Wim asked me if I'd play the role of his mobster when he got the movie financed. I gave him my word I'd do it. *The American Friend* didn't go into production for another five years. By 1977, I was in Tunisia scouting locations for *The Big Red One.* Wim found me in Tunis and told me he was going to shoot the movie right away, so I hopped on a plane for Hamburg to join the rest of the cast.

The sonofabitch character I play in *The American Friend* is a porn-film producer. He's going to get knocked off when the lead shoves him off a moving train. I told Wim I was no athlete, but I could do that fall without

Wim Wenders and I had a silent bond, difficult to explain, between a guy who's as taciturn as him and as loquacious as me.

a stunt man. After all, in my infantry years, I'd learned how to hit the ground. I suggested he attach a camera to me, in the same way I shot the opening of *Naked Kiss,* capturing the last things the character sees as he falls to his death. Wim loved my idea, but he just wasn't sadistic enough to let me risk my neck on a stunt like that.

Nicholas Ray and Jean Eustache also had parts in *The American Friend.* It was Wim's way of showing his admiration of older directors who were mentors for him. I was pleased to renew old ties with Nick Ray, whom I'd known well in the fifties. Back then, Nick was more handsome than any leading actor in Hollywood. He was doing wonderful work like *Johnny Guitar* (1954) and *Bigger Than Life* (1956). Nick got tired of Hollywood life, starting to direct in Europe with *Bitter Victory* (1957). Nick's eye patch made me miss John Ford, my own mentor, who'd passed away in 1973.

By the time we met up again in Hamburg, Nick had come down with the lung cancer that would kill him, in 1979. All the time that had passed since our Hollywood days and all the different roads we'd traveled couldn't diminish the genuine fondness we had for each other. That was why I decided to look Nick up in a New York hospital when I was in town, passing through on my way home from Europe. Wenders had been documenting Nick's struggle with cancer, in *Lightning Over Water* (1980). I asked Nick how he was feeling.

"Fine," he said, almost coughing out his brains.

In 1976, with Nicholas Ray, a helluva director, a lion of a man

Jean Renoir, the French director, had died a couple of days before. Nick asked me if I was going to Renoir's funeral when I got back to LA. I assured him that I would. I'd known the great man and considered *La Grande Illusion* (1937), starring Jean Gabin, Marcel Dalio, and Erich von Stroheim, one of the masterpieces of all time. Having Marcel Dalio play in *China Gate,* I felt I'd somehow been able to touch a facet of Renoir's universe. I told Nick about an evening I'd spent with Renoir and his Brazilian wife, Dido. Their home, whose location was a closely guarded secret, had priceless paintings by Jean's father, Pierre August Renoir. Nick wanted to write a eulogy for Renoir's funeral. He asked me to deliver it by hand. I gave him a piece of paper and a pen.

"Go ahead and write it, Nick," I said.

Nick closed his eyes in meditation, then opened them and started scribbling words. I watched in silence, remembering how I'd written my mother's obituary before she passed away and showed it to her. I wanted her okay. Rebecca was a little surprised but pleased with my words about her, always taking my eccentricity in her stride. I think people should read their own obituaries while they still can. It's a healthy exercise in living one's life to the fullest.

Nick gave the piece of paper back to me and closed his eyes. The effort had exhausted him. I read the paragraph he'd written about Renoir and his legacy. I don't remember the exact words. I wish to hell I'd kept a copy somewhere. It was pure poetry, condensed and heartfelt. Few healthy people could have written those lines, much less one who was in such a weakened condition. I carefully folded the paper, put it in my pocket, and said good-bye. It would be the last time I ever saw Nick.

Just before Renoir's funeral, I gave Nick's beautiful message to an officer of the Director's Guild. Among the many tributes of loving admiration, Nicholas Ray's was read aloud at the service. Most of the time, you're so busy plying the movie trade that you forget why the hell you ever got involved in this racket in the first place. Nick's words made us all remember the passion that's the bedrock of great moviemaking.

The Unmaking of
a Klansman

In 1973, my friend and sometime agent Bill Shiffrin set up a meeting for me with a smart and convivial television documentary maker named Bill Alexander, a guy who had more big gold chains than I'd ever seen around one man's neck. Alexander had optioned William Bradford Huie's book about the KKK, *The Klansman,* with Paramount backing the project. We made a deal for me to write an adaptation and direct the movie.

Working hard and fast, I knocked out a fierce script. Holy smoke, I put everything I had into that one! Using Huie's book as a starting point, I dreamed up an angry yarn, completely changing the finale. In the book, the KKK leader miraculously recognizes the horrible crap his organization represents and he gets killed by his own Klan members for his change of heart. It seemed to me too classical to be believable. An audience would never buy it. So I invented a smart, beautiful, committed female character, patterned on Angela Davis. She goes to the South to get black people out to vote. The Klan leader's son falls in love with her and joins in the struggle against the KKK hatemongers, seeding doubt in one of his father's top lieutenants. The end of my yarn had the Klan leader giving a rabble-rousing speech to thousands of men and women dressed in white sheets. They march up a hill carrying torches. Three crosses have been set up. On the first cross, they crucify the KKK lieutenant; on the second, the black woman; and on the third, the leader's own son.

"They're better off this way," says the Klan leader in my closing shot, as the sonofabitch picks up a burning torch and sets fire to the crosses himself.

That was honest. For Chrissakes, those KKK bastards have been spewing racial hatred and white supremacy for a hundred years without a chink in their hard-line thinking. Why would a Hollywood movie portray them any other way?

Bill Alexander and Bill Shiffrin were crazy about my script. We started casting. Lee Marvin accepted the role of the Klan leader. My neighbor and friend John Cassavetes said it was one of the best scripts he'd ever read and that he'd love to be part of it. I chose Cassavetes to play the Klan lieutenant. Then out of the blue, Paramount changed course. The studio had a prior commitment with their Italian partners, who, in turn, had a deal with the English director Terence Young.[1] Incredibly, Young was brought in to direct *The Klansman* as a payback for some prior deal. Overnight, I was dropped from the picture. To make matters worse, they hired an old studio hand, who rewrote my screenplay into a styleless melodrama. The studio justified the revision on the grounds that they needed to tone down the violence. Tone down the violence? How can anyone make an honest movie about the KKK *without* violence? The bastards have been burning churches and lynching people since before the Civil War.

The rewritten script had an FBI agent infiltrating the KKK, with Lee Marvin's role changed into a southern sheriff. Richard Burton was cast as a local landowner, and O. J. Simpson, the ex–football star, was given a part for good public relations. A white woman is raped, and white townspeople try to lynch a black man as the innocent victim. What a tired goddamned plot device!

The reworked story made no sense as social commentary and was repugnant as entertainment. They'd turned my original work into a disastrous piece of bullshit and launched the production. Against my objections, they left my name on it. I challenge anyone to read my original script and then compare it to the finished version of *The Klansman*. It's like night and day.

Lee Marvin was as furious as I was. However, he was under contract and had to do the movie. I understood his predicament.

"The limey doesn't know what he's doing," Lee told me in a phone call from the set, referring to Terence Young. "And he doesn't care either."

As first-time producers, Bill Alexander and Bill Shiffrin were powerless against the studio's demands. They felt terrible about the situation and invited me up to the set, somewhere on location in northern California. It was crawling with press because Richard Burton was getting frequent visits from Elizabeth Taylor. I declined to go anywhere near the place, feeling double-crossed by this new episode of commerce triumphing over art. I told myself that at least I'd made some dough on the deal, trying not to acknowledge the deep hurt of having another original script taken out of my hands and bastardized. For Chrissakes, I could've made that script into a terrific picture!

Foolishly or not, I held a grudge against Terence Young for a helluva long time. Years later, I ran into him in France, when we were both members of the jury at the Cognac Festival. I brought up *The Klansman.* Terence swore he'd never meant to squeeze me out of the picture. He'd never even read my original script and couldn't have cared less about America's social problems. His manager had pushed him to accept the job purely for the paycheck. Terence had big expenses to keep up on his estate on the Côte d'Azur and an expensive French girlfriend. He knew he'd made a lousy picture. How could I begrudge such an honest guy who freely admitted his greed? To this day, I've never had the courage to sit through *The Klansman.* Lee Marvin invited Christa to the premiere. She couldn't believe how they'd totally distorted every scene that I'd written. When the lights came up, Lee said nothing about how bad the picture was, or about his own disappointment. He just gently touched Christa's big belly, for she was already pregnant. "Let's think about future projects," he said.

One day, I ran into Lee Marvin at Wittner's, my favorite cigar store, right across from Farmer's Market on Fairfax. For as long as I could remember, Hans Wittner had been selling cigars to me and many of my Hollywood colleagues, including Ernst Lubitsch and Alfred Hitchcock.

"Sammy," said Lee, as we leaned on a glass countertop and lit up a couple of my favorite Camachos, "when are we doing *The Big Red One?*"

Marvin knew about the precious movie that I'd been working on all those years. I'd kept him in the loop.

"You'll be my sergeant!" I said, making a promise I'd never break.

There were just two projects I wanted to focus on now: the baby that Christa was about to have and *The Big Red One,* the movie that I had to find a way to give birth to. To hone my story, I set to work on a novelization of the material. Bantam brought out *The Big Red One* as a paperback before the movie happened. The book stood on its own through three printings. But I still wasn't getting any closer to finding a producer. My old friend, Peter Bogdanovich, decided to get involved. He'd formed a production company with Francis Ford Coppola and William Friedkin.

One day Peter came up to the Shack to announce that he'd convinced his partners to back *The Big Red One* if I could make the picture for a million dollars. I told Peter that I appreciated the offer, but it couldn't be done for that small a budget. He promised to keep trying to convince a studio to kick in more. Peter was now living with Cybill Shepherd in Bel Air. He'd alienated a lot of people, but it was mostly jealousy. With me, Peter was generous and caring. I'll always be grateful for his efforts on behalf of *The Big Red One.*

Christa's pregnancy went to term without a glitch. On January 28, 1975,

our beautiful daughter, Samantha, was born. It was one of the most glorious days of my life. At the age of sixty-three, I'd become a father for the
first time. I'd never felt more ambitious or energetic. Nothing and no one
could ever get me down again. After all, I wanted my little girl to be proud
of her daddy.

49

Let Them Judge
for Themselves

At Peter Bogdanovich's urging, Paramount offered me a deal to do *The Big Red One*. Frank Yablans, the studio's chief, understood that I didn't want to make just another war film. I told him how I'd turned down *The Longest Day* and *Patton* to do a movie without any grand combat or glorious heroes. My story followed four young GIs and their sergeant into infantry battles, first in North Africa and Sicily, then at Omaha Beach on D day, through the snowy forests of Belgium and the cities of Germany, finally discovering the terrible truth about the Nazi camps in Czechoslovakia.

See, I'd stored up all the nuts and bolts of foot soldiering—the condoms over the M1s, the wet socks, the land mines, the ricocheting bullets, the grenades, the K-rations—but I had no intention of making a documentary. No audience would stomach the reality of war. It was too gruesome. I had to use images straight out of my imagination—like the shell-shocked black stallion galloping wildly in my prologue—to convey the horror of war and the harsh life of the men who had to fight it.

Every frame of my picture would be based on firsthand knowledge. A wristwatch on a severed arm floating in a sea of blood was a sight from Omaha Beach that had stayed with me my entire life. For the movie, I'd tone down the terror by focusing on the hands of a wristwatch as the lapping waves get redder and redder, blood from all the dying soldiers offscreen. Beyond the realism, my four infantry soldiers and their sergeant had an allegorical dimension. They were symbols of survival. Their relentless advance was a strange death dance, absurd and incomprehensible, like war itself. With the conclusion of hostilities comes the recognition that the healing must begin. I wanted *The Big Red One* to end on hope.

Writing that script affected me viscerally. During the final months of revision, Christa told me I'd have terrible nightmares, screaming out unintelligible phrases in the middle of the night. My subconscious was teeming with all that war stuff, and the movie finally allowed painful memories a spout to pour out.

Before we could get the movie into production, Frank Yablans left the studio, and the new boss at Paramount let the option expire. We were back to square one again as all the movie's rights reverted to me. Bogdanovich was just as upset as I was. He brought his friend and lawyer Jack Schwartz-mann over to discuss what could be done.[1] Jack had become a top execu-tive at Lorimar, a new independent movie outfit headed by Merv Adelson and Lee Rich, guys who'd made a lot of dough with the TV show *The Wal-tons*. We struck a deal with Lorimar to produce *The Big Red One* with a tight budget and deferred payments to all participants. I'd get a slice of profits as writer-director. Bogdanovich was my personal choice as pro-ducer on the project, but the Lorimar people were dissuaded by Peter's recent box-office setbacks. Instead, they hired Gene Corman, brother of independent producer Roger Corman. Gene turned out to be an excellent team member, calm and even-tempered, making smart decisions through-out the difficult shoot.

Gene wanted me to cast Steve McQueen as the sergeant. Steve was interested, and I would've loved to work with him on a movie. He did a helluva job in Don Siegel's *Hell Is for Heroes* (1962). The truth was that I couldn't imagine anyone except Lee Marvin as my lead. Lee's wonderful horse face combined with his low-key style made him born for the part. I sent over the completed script to Lee's place by messenger. He called me the very next morning.

"Sammy," he barked when I picked up the phone, "this is your sergeant speaking!"

It was Christa's idea to cast Mark Hamill as Griff. Mark had just appeared in the enormous box-office hit *Star Wars* (1977) and would help the picture find a younger audience. I was doubtful Mark would accept a supporting role under an old-timer like Lee Marvin, but he did, appar-ently on the strong urging of George Lucas. The role of Zab, the dogface who's loosely based on me, went to Bobby Carradine. At one point, Cor-man and I discussed casting the twenty-eight-year-old writer-director Martin Scorsese as the Italian soldier Vinci, but the part finally went to Bobby Di Cicco. Kelly Ward, who'd had a role in *Grease* (1978), got the role of Johnson.

Where do you shoot a film about a world war thirty-five years after the fighting is over? Our top three contenders were Yugoslavia, Tunisia, and Israel. Gene brought back a good scouting report from Yugoslavia. They had everything we needed, but their bureaucrats hiked prices sky-high because we were an American production. I took a scouting trip to

The sergeant (Lee Marvin) with his four dogfaces (left to right), Griff (Mark Hamill), Zab (Bobby Carradine), Vinci (Bobby Di Cicco), and Johnson (Kelly Ward), on the beach at Normandy (Israel)

Tunisia, where producer Tarak Ben Ammar invited me to look over all their wonderful beaches, ruins, woods, and deserts. Tunisia had it all. Besides, Tarak came from a very influential family, so we were promised government cooperation. Still, costs were too high.

Meanwhile, a series of interminable budget meetings were taking place at Lorimar, itemizing the cost of each scene in my shooting script. They came up with a total of twelve million dollars. That was whittled down to ten. The cost cutting continued until we had less than four million to do the entire movie. I had to pare down scene after scene without truncating the rhythm or the truth of the movie. We decided to shoot in Israel, where we'd get the most bang for our buck. The only problem was that they had no forests in Israel.

Before I gave Corman the green light, I flew to Israel and immediately went over to the beach. Alone, I walked along the Mediterranean thinking about our nighttime invasion at Staoueli, Algeria, trying to relive that first amphibious campaign. Yes, the Israeli beach would do. But to recreate Omaha Beach at Normandy, we needed a large stretch of sand, plus a high plateau looking down upon it. Gene suggested we build a riser out of rocks and scaffolding to replicate Omaha's topography. When I saw the design by our art director, Peter Jamison, I was sold.

One of our Israeli crew members heard I was looking for a wooded area. He took me to see a sanctuary outside Tel Aviv that had a patch of beautiful trees. The trees had inscriptions on them, having been planted thirty years before by member states of the United Nations, when President Truman recognized the state of Israel, in 1948. It was an unforgettable place but much too small to use as a location. We'd end up shooting the Belgian and Hürtgen battle scenes in the forests of Ireland.

My biggest location headache was the Falkenau concentration camp scene. After much searching, we located an abandoned armory in the heart of Jerusalem called Camp Schneller. The Israeli army had used the place to store ammunition during the Six-Day War. It was just what we needed. The problem was the armory was just across from a Hasidic religious school. Corman tried to discourage me from planning the scene there, figuring that we'd never get permission from the military authorities.

Camp Schneller's commanding officer was General Shilo. The general and I shared a passion for cartoons. With the aid of a drawing pad, I showed the general what we wanted to do in the armory. Then I gave him the drawing pad as a souvenir. I promised to shoot as quickly as possible and then remove the portraits of Hitler and the swastikas before the Hasidic Jews found out about it. Formal permission was granted.

To populate the movie's concentration camp, I picked the skinniest, boniest extras I could find, framing their dark eyes as they stared blankly into space. The camp and its prisoners needed to look like they came out of Picasso's "blue period." In the camp scene, Griff comes upon the startling evidence of Hitler's Final Solution, finally confronting a young SS soldier hiding among the ashes and bones inside an oven. The actor we hired to play the SS soldier was a young Israeli attending a religious school. The kid confessed that he didn't know that the camps were as horrible as the set we'd recreated. Taking him aside during a break, I explained how the real camp we liberated at Falkenau was much, much worse. I told him about the smell of death that permeated the place, about the emaciated corpses. He was stunned. What the hell were they teaching those kids at school? Certainly not reality.

The camp scene was emotionally draining for everyone on set. Griff loses his control and brutally kills the SS trooper. Many crew members ended up in tears. Mark Hamill played it beautifully, a sweet young man out of place as a warrior, turned suddenly vicious when face-to-face with the evil he's been battling.

One of Gene Corman's principal worries was Lee Marvin's reputation as a hard drinker. Lee did get drunk a couple of times, but, for cryin' out loud, he was carrying the entire picture on his shoulders! Lee's infrequent binges never interfered with our tough shooting schedule. It was a dream come true to make a movie with an actor like Lee Marvin. We didn't have much to say to each other before we'd shoot a scene. He'd always get himself in character. Many times, a glance, a nod, or a grin would be all the direction I'd give him. I've rarely been as locked in on the same wavelength with an actor.

The entire cast worked hard to hit each emotional nail on the head. The frills of larger budget productions were completely absent from *The Big Red One*. My crew needed to be innovative in every scene, relying many times on close-ups rather than on crane shots to convey the scope of the conflict. With our bare-bones budget, my DP, the talented Israeli cameraman Adam Greenberg, was a blessing. Greenberg could overcome every hurdle. Adam now lives in Hollywood and shoots big studio pictures, like *The Terminator* (1984), *Ghost* (1990), and *Sister Act* (1992). Arne Schmidt, my assistant director, was terrific. He's a prominent producer today. His sweet wife, Laurel, came along as our set photographer.

Everyone recognized this was my beloved project and worked their asses off for me. Since they understood the high aspirations of the film, I didn't want to let them down. For everyone who'd put their trust in me, I was intent on making *The Big Red One* a film they'd be proud of. Most of all, it had to honor the soldiers from the First Division, especially the ones who didn't survive.

The irony of shooting the century's biggest yarn in the little country of Israel was constantly apparent. I had Israelis costumed as soldiers of the Reich, wearing their yarmulkes under Nazi helmets. For the part of Schroeder, the SS commander, I'd cast the German actor Siegfried Rauch. His getup brought back terrible memories, and the Israeli crew treated him coldly. Rauch had been born after the war and felt lousy about his country's legacy. Still, as long as he wore that SS uniform, people had a knee-jerk reaction and scorned him. The greatest irony of it all was that I, a nonpracticing Jew, skeptical of all religions, had wound up directing my most cherished picture in the land of Abraham, Isaac, and Jacob.

Feeding the crew was problematic because many kept kosher. Our caterers did the best they could. Slipups were inevitable. Somebody once sent us a box of delicious American doughnuts. We wanted to share the goodies, so we offered them around. With disapproving looks, the kosher eaters refused to even taste them. The doughnuts were *traife*, or unclean.

Every day of *The Big Red One* shoot, I was thankful for my independent production. Cast and crew slowly got caught up in my story and worked around every obstacle. Holy smoke, to think that at one time I'd been close to signing with Warner Brothers to do a big studio picture with John Wayne! When you're making small-budget films, you've got to be constantly on your toes, shooting at an incredible pace. On top of that, the heat in the Mideast is phenomenal, like being in a permanent sauna. Despite my slight sixty-six-year-old body, I felt like a spring chicken on the set of *The Big Red One,* solving problems right and left. Even then, I'd get sideswiped unexpectedly. My crew revolted one day because a costume designer from California who'd been doing excellent work made an unthinking anti-Semitic remark. Narrowly averting total mutiny, I fired the man on the spot and sent him back to the States. We finished the picture with Israeli costumers.

One of the big disasters was Gene Corman's hiring of an inexperienced film editor. I found out later the guy had never cut a feature film before. No wonder he'd overlooked numbering the cans of exposed film coming off the set each day. When I found out, I blamed myself. I should've insisted on having my own editor with me, a real pro like Gene Fowler Jr. I thought Corman knew what he was doing, but he was trying to save money in the wrong place.

During most of the production, Christa, Samantha, and I were staying at the Sharon Hotel in Herzliyya. Samantha was three and a half by then, picking up Hebrew easily. She called us *Ima* and *Aba,* the Hebrew words for "Mother" and "Father." To this day, my daughter is comfortable around people of different languages and ethnic backgrounds because of all the countries we lived in when she was a little girl. Many evenings, after the day's shooting was finished, I took the family to nearby Netanya in a horse carriage, where we'd have supper in a modest restaurant on the beach. One evening, we met another couple with a small boy at that place. The man bore a striking resemblance to François Truffaut. He was Elie Wiesel, who'd win the 1985 Nobel Prize for Peace for his writings on the Holocaust. There and then, we struck up a friendship with Elie, his wife, Marion, and their little boy, Elijah. Marion wanted to bring Elijah to the set because the boy was dying to meet "Luke Skywalker" in person. A visit with Mark Hamill was arranged.

The Wiesels were warmhearted, intelligent people. As the world knew, Elie's whole family of fourteen had been wiped out in the Nazi camps. He gave me one of his books that evening. Since then, I've read all his stuff. I have only admiration for the way Elie Wiesel has used the terrible legacy from the Holocaust to search for spirituality and purpose, to remind us not only of the pain that we can inflict on each other but also of the damage we can absorb. Weisel has never seen his prominence as anything but a platform to raise a red flag against injustice and to warn against apathy.

I've heard critics chide Wiesel for making a career out of the Holocaust. What bullshit! Those are the same insensitive idiots who called me a warmonger. Why are they jealous of a writer using tragic experiences to come to grips with the incomprehensible? Somehow, I'd survived those horror-filled years of total war. The only way to live with those goddamned memories and keep my sanity was to talk about them, write about them, and, finally, three and a half decades later, make a motion picture about them.

"The opposite of love is not hate, it's indifference," wrote Wiesel. "The opposite of art is not ugliness, it's indifference. The opposite of faith is not heresy, it's indifference. And the opposite of life is not death, it's indifference."[2]

Whether it's Wiesel's writing and lectures, or Claude Lanzmann's eloquent nine-and-a-half-hour documentary, *Shoah* (1985), or Steven Spielberg's brilliant *Schindler's List* (1993), the world must be reminded of mankind's insanity. Murder has been going on since man invented weapons. The Nazis thought they could get away with genocide. Stark images of both the oppressed and the oppressors wouldn't let them. Some of the first scenes I'd ever shoot with a movie camera were recorded in 1945 at the liberation of the Falkenau camp. What I saw and recorded was unthinkable yet undeniable. It must never—never!—happen again.

After Israel, we went to Ireland to finish the picture. A forest is a symbol of life and renewal, but not for me. During our advance through Belgium, I remembered the American GIs we found hanging from the branches, executed summarily by the retreating Germans. It was a terrible sight, with rays of sunlight filtering through the treetops, the bodies of those dogfaces swinging back and forth like macabre pendulums.

My friend the director John Boorman was of great assistance with his local contacts in Ireland. He invited us over to his farm and named one of his new colts "Big Red One" in our honor. Over a wonderful meal, John told me about the World War II movie he wanted to make, based on his own childhood experiences. For a little boy growing up in London, he explained, it was a time of total upheaval. With the men at war, the women left behind took charge, and discipline was sacrificed to survival. Boorman's memories were the backbone of his wonderful film *Hope and Glory* (1987).

Once in California, I discovered the mix-up in the labeling of our film cans. It took weeks of maddening work just to organize all the footage. My first cut produced a six-hour movie. Paring down everything I felt was justified, I delivered a four-and-a-half-hour final cut of *The Big Red One* to Lorimar.

They said it was too long to be commercially viable and, over my objections, took over the reediting process. A film editor named David Bretherton cut *The Big Red One* down to one hour and fifty-three minutes. Bretherton was very competent, but the result was a painful experience. To

Another scene cut from
The Big Red One *was one*
that involved soldiers on
horseback attacking a tank
in a Roman amphitheater.

this day, I'm still mourning all the wonderful scenes that were eliminated, such as the one in which Lee Marvin's sergeant shoots a double-crossing German countess, played wonderfully by Christa.

The Big Red One was an official entry at the 1980 Cannes Film Festival. Even in its incomplete length, critics called it one of the best war movies ever made, comparing it to classics like Lewis Milestone's *All Quiet on the Western Front* (1930). *Time, Newsweek,* and the *Wall Street Journal* all published wonderful articles. The French writers lauded it. For Chrissakes, one compared my work to that of Apollinaire's poetry!

Sure, I was thrilled by the almost universal esteem. Yet I can't stop thinking about my four-and-a-half-hour version of the movie, which is somewhere in the vaults at Warner Brothers, who bought the rights several years ago. Someday soon I hope that an intelligent studio executive will authorize the restoration of *The Big Red One* and let people see the "director's cut." It could be broadcast on television in three segments, those miniseries that have become so common. That format was unheard of when I was fighting for an unabridged version of the picture. Neither the studio nor the television network would regret bringing out the original. I am confident that my full-length version of *The Big Red One* will hold an audience with its honesty and dry lyricism.

Hell, I know you've got to accept compromise if you want to make motion pictures. I'd swallowed my share, believe me. Nevertheless, my longtime dream had finally come true. That *The Big Red One* now existed, even in an abridged version, was miraculous and, without any doubt, my most important achievement. Future audiences and film historians will judge it for themselves. All I ask is that they be given the opportunity to see the movie I lived, wrote, directed, and edited with my heart and soul— the entire four-and-a-half-hour movie—before they render their final judgment.

50

Four-Legged
Time Bomb

In 1982, Wim Wenders cast me in *The State of Things,* this time playing the role of a veteran cameraman patterned after my colleague and friend Joe Biroc. The movie was shooting in Portugal. I joined Wim and his crew in Sintra, a jewel of a place with an exquisite macroclimate, ornate villas, and gorgeous gardens. I told Wim that Biroc didn't like to talk much but he loved to improvise. So Wim let me make up lines for my character as we went along, based on each emotional situation. Wenders shot scenes in one take or kept the camera rolling until something interesting happened.

In one scene, my character is supposed to find out about his wife's death by telephone. I picked up the phone very hesitantly, reacting to the bad news, so wrapped up in the moment that I blurted out my real phone number. Then I hung up and started pacing back and forth. I fully expected Wim to yell "Cut!" However, he kept the camera on me and ended up using my worried walk in the picture.

It has always been a joy to work with Wim Wenders. In 1983, I'd do a cameo role for him in a pool hall scene in *Hammett.* And, fittingly enough, my last appearance in front of a movie camera would be for him in *The End of Violence* (1997). I'm grateful for Wim's friendship and esteem all these years.

With *The Big Red One* finally under my belt, I needed to move on. The picture did reasonable business but was by no means a box-office smash. I was obviously burnt up by the way they'd cut it down to half of its intended length, yet there was no way in hell I was going to see myself as a victim. My way of coping with disappointments was to keep banging out stories.

Jotting down ideas constantly in a little notebook I kept with me day and night, I continued writing new stories, researching current events, reading history books, coming up with ideas almost every day. At the end of the seventies, I had over one hundred titles registered with the Writer's

Guild, some with entire scripts already written, some based on stories or treatments, and some just titles for future development.[1]

Unexpectedly, high-paying offers started to come my way again. The capriciousness of the movie business made me laugh. One day, you couldn't get *Gone with the Wind* made. The next, you had producers vying for your attention, waving money at you like a checkered flag at the finishing line of Daytona Speedway.

First, producers Dan Blatt and Michael Singer brought me *Let's Get Harry*, a one-page treatment for an adventure movie about the kidnapping of an American businessman that's supposed to take place in Japan. They offered me two hundred grand to write a script and four hundred grand to direct it. I hadn't seen that kind of dough in a while. With Samantha now five, I knew I needed to sock away some wherewithal for her future. I accepted the project, banging out a thriller about some American ex-GIs who rescue their kidnapped buddy from a gang of Japanese fanatics. The idea of going back to Japan with my family to direct the film was exciting, because I'd had such a great experience shooting *House of Bamboo* over there in 1955. Besides, I yearned for an opportunity to revisit a culture that had always intrigued me. The country must have changed so drastically since then. Among the bedtime tales I'd been reading Samantha were those of Lafcadio Hearn.[2] Thanks to him, Japanese folklore had become accessible in the West.

Out of the blue, producer Jon Davison telephoned Christa, saying he was a big Fuller fan. He'd just had a big hit with *Airplane!* (1980). Davison wanted me to write and direct a movie before the impending writers' strike. I was flying home that day from Buenos Aires after the Argentinian premiere of *The Big Red One*. Christa explained to them that I'd made a commitment to do *Let's Get Harry* in Japan. Davison wouldn't take no for an answer, insisting on a meeting with me as soon as I'd landed. That same afternoon, with the rain falling like cats and dogs, Davison showed up at the Shack with one of Paramount's top executives, Don Simpson. Simpson would later go on to produce blockbusters like *Flashdance* (1983), *Beverly Hills Cop* (1984), and *Top Gun* (1986), then burning out at age fifty-two, dying of a supposed overdose in 1996.

To me, Simpson looked more like a hippie than a studio exec, or maybe a matador, a real Don Juan in tight pants. Davison had a sweet, cherubic face and a broad knowledge of movies. As soon as we'd settled down in our living room, they announced they had a project for me called *White Dog*. At the very mention of the title, my eyes started twinkling. Hell, I knew the Romain Gary tale about goddamned dogs being trained to attack black people. *Life* magazine had done a famous cover with a snarling white dog when the story was published. The yarn had the makings of a helluva movie. Paramount had bought the rights and already sunk a million bucks into the project, first turning to Roman Polanski, then Arthur Penn. Still there wasn't a script that the studio was willing to green-light.

"Mr. Fuller, we want you to write and direct *White Dog*," said Simpson.

I explained that, first, I had to direct *Let's Get Harry* in Japan. They asked me to push that movie back and do *White Dog* first. They kept talking to me like I was an exotic bird they wanted to put in a cage. A cage! Yeah, suddenly I saw a big circus cage with an animal trainer inside—a *black* animal trainer—trying to deprogram a racist canine bent on tearing the trainer to pieces.

Despite my jet lag from the flight from Argentina, I got very excited, jumping up and acting out scenes that I was already dreaming up. Davison was amused. Simpson was a little startled by my carryings-on. As I talked about characters and scenes, I grabbed Simpson's wrist and almost twisted his arm out of the socket. Every time I became a little too aggressive, Christa broke in, sending me over to the bar for more drinks or sweet-talking them. She was afraid I was going to grab the studio executive by the balls to punctuate one of my ideas!

We made a handshake deal. I'd postpone *Let's Get Harry* and write a script for *White Dog* that they'd approve. Time was short. We had about six weeks before the threatened writers' strike would shut down all production.

I asked the producers of *Let's Get Harry* to push back their start date. They said they couldn't, so I told them they'd have to find another director. *Let's Get Harry* ended up being made five years later in Mexico with my original script totally rewritten, transferring the action to South America and butchering the yarn with an unbelievable plot about an American engineer and ambassador kidnapped by drug dealers. The only thing tolerable about the movie was Robert Duvall's performance. The director, Stuart Rosenberg, wisely had his name removed from the credits. I was never given the choice. Mine remains for "story," even though they never asked my permission, nor told me what they were up to. This was a violation of Writers' Guild rules, and the guild eventually upheld my formal complaint.

All my attention now was focused on *White Dog*. Jon Davison proved to be a dream producer, a guy who sincerely loved films and devoted enough resources to a project to get it right. Jon not only respected my work but gave me complete support on *White Dog*. His first decision was to allow me to bring in my young friend Curtis Hanson as co-screenwriter to help pull the script together fast. Curtis and I went to work, talking out each scene excitedly, then banging out pages of action and dialogue, hardly

On the set of White Dog *with Paul Winfield. Paul is an imposing actor who'd never fallen into the black exploitation quagmire. He'd received an Oscar nomination for his portrayal of a dignified sharecropper in* Sounder *(1972).*

stopping to sleep. We had ten days to deliver a finished script. Curtis is even-tempered, easy to talk to, perceptive. Despite, or maybe because of, the thirty-five-year difference in our ages, Curtis and I had a productive, effervescent collaboration. Christa left us to our mad rhythm, cooking steaks and broccoli for us in the middle of the night when we were hungry.

First, we had to get a handle on the yarn of a normal-looking dog who'd been conditioned by sick people to be a racist monster. Our story began with Julie, a young actress who adopts a big white German shepherd that she has accidentally hit with her car. The dog recovers and saves her from an intruder in her apartment. Julie discovers that her new pet is violently aggressive, especially toward black people. She takes the dog to an animal-training center, where she meets Keys, an anthropologist who accepts the animal as a scientific challenge. He's tried to cure "white dogs" before, but he's always failed. How can Keys reverse what someone has done to this animal? How can he get inside a racist dog's brain without using a knife? He cages the dog and starts his experimental regime, but the animal manages to escape. The white dog spots a well-dressed black man and chases him down the street and into a church, knocking him down between the pews and killing him.

In that disturbing church scene, I wanted to pan the camera away from the bloody victim and up to the stained-glass window of St. Francis of Assisi, the only witness to the savagery below. Curtis thought it was too much of a cliché to have the black man attacked by the dog in a church with the image of St. Francis above. I explained to my young partner that, cliché or not, it would underscore the spiritual as well as the physical violation in the sequence. The attack happens in a very sacred place, a place of peace and regeneration. Having the image of St. Francis in the background would be a reminder of our two intertwining themes, that of tolerance and torment. I won Curtis over. Later, he told me the scene really worked in the completed film.[3]

The church killing sets up the big confrontation between Keys and Julie about the fate of her monstrous pet:

> KEYS
> . . . There's still a chance to cure him!

> JULIE
> Cure him? He just killed a man! There is no way you can cure that dog! I want you to shoot him now before he kills more blacks!

> KEYS
> So you finally joined the club! A club of horrified people who raise holy hell about that disease, that racist hate! But do absolutely nothing to stamp it out! That dog is the only weapon we have to at least remove a part of it! *If* I cure him!

> JULIE
> *If*? "If" is not going to stop him from killing people!

> KEYS
> Yes, Julie, I can't guarantee the result. But if I fail, I'll get another white dog. And another! Or another! Or another! And another! And keep on working until I lick it! Because that's

>the only way to stop sick people from breed-
>ing sick dogs! And goddamnit, *I can't experi-
>ment on a dead dog!*

After we'd polished the script for *White Dog,* honing it down to under a hundred pages, with a ballsy finish, we delivered it to Paramount on schedule. Don Simpson and Jon Davison both loved it. They gave us a green light to get into production immediately. I started casting. Jodie Foster was everyone's first choice as Julie. Jodie really wanted to do the picture but unfortunately wouldn't be free in time. Other prominent young actresses tested. The one I liked best was Kristy McNichol, a nineteen-year-old who'd been doing television since the age of twelve. Kristy was unpretentious and had a helluva lot of charm. Her enthusiasm, her authenticity, her easygoing smile won me over.

Paul Winfield, an accomplished actor, got the role of Keys. Paul was a real trooper. The only problem was that he kept pestering me to give him one of my cigars. It was my custom to never offer a cigar to anybody on a shoot, because, before you knew it, everybody on the crew wanted one. Paul was such a good guy, though, I made an exception and gave him one of my Camacho No. 1s. As Carruthers, the head of the animal-training center, the old pro Burl Ives did a solid job. A cigar smoker himself, Burl brought along his own smokes to the set.

We hired an experienced cameraman, Bruce Surtees, who worked with the newly devised Steadicam. Our shoot went smoothly despite all the hazards of working with the four different dogs that were needed to portray our lead canine. The dog trainer, Karl Miller, was a master with animals large and small. Our main location was called Wildlife Station, located on the outskirts of Los Angeles and run by Martine, a terrific lady and committed animal lover. She'd rescued every kind of animal you could imagine and boarded them all at her place. Martine gave Paramount permission to let our crew build a huge animal cage on her property. The cage alone was supposed to have cost 750,000 bucks. Martine got to keep it after the shoot as part of our arrangement.

A special scene for me to direct was the one with the kind-looking old bigot who shows up along with his two granddaughters to reclaim his white dog. The old guy looks like such a sweet gentleman, but he's actually the racist sonofabitch who's turned the dog into a freak. The old guy, unaware that Julie knows about his treatment of the white dog, offers her a box of chocolates, which she throws back in his face. One of the little girls in the scene was our own Samantha, making her debut as an actress. I made sure Samantha got a line to say on camera with her lovable baby lisp:

With Kristy McNichol in the animal cage on White Dog

Samantha Fuller, as the old racist's granddaughter

"Where is my dog?" Christa played a small role in the picture, too, as the veterinarian's nurse. With my two favorite women on set, an $8 million budget, and a strong cast and crew, everything seemed to be looking rosy.

Then something strange and ugly happened. An NAACP spokesperson named Willis Edwards showed up on our set one day. He'd cleared his visit with the studio to see if our film was "distorting the image of black people." I was flabbergasted. Why hadn't an organization as prestigious as the NAACP done their homework and checked out my record before sending a man to spy on my work? If they had, they would've found out that I was one of the first directors in Hollywood to use actors of color in intelligent, complex roles: the black medic in *The Steel Helmet;* Nat King Cole's sensitive soldier, in *China Gate;* Harry Rhodes's twisted college dropout, in *Shock Corridor;* James Shigeta's detective who gets the gal, in *The Crimson Kimono.* Our world was multiracial. I'd been depicting it that way since my first picture. And why the hell hadn't they checked out my military record? For Chrissakes, I'd put my life on the line to stand up for democracy, fighting fascism because it was antagonistic to the Jeffersonian principle that all men are created equal, endowed by their Creator with certain unalienable rights, among these life, liberty, and the goddamned pursuit of happiness!

After depicting the little guy and his right to be different in movie after movie, no matter what economic status or race, I thought I'd made my position on integration and equality crystal clear. What right did this man have to snoop around, making a nuisance of himself, no matter the honorable objectives of his organization? The NAACP should have, at the very least, had the courtesy and respect to wait and see the finished movie. I was deeply offended by this intrusion, and I told Jon Davison in no uncertain terms that I didn't want this Mr. Edwards on my set. Davison agreed with me completely and asked the NAACP man to leave.

We delivered our final cut of *White Dog* on time, thanks to terrific work from our veteran editor, Bernie Gribble. Christa had the idea of asking Ennio Morricone to do the film score. Morricone had earned a worldwide reputation because of his music for Sergio Leone's movies. Paramount was resistant but finally allowed me to use him. His visceral, haunting music added just the right touch to the picture. Since then, Ennio has written many memorable scores, among them Roland Joffé's *The Mission* (1986), Brian De Palma's *The Untouchables* (1987), and Giuseppe Tornatore's *Nuovo Cinema Paradiso* (1988).

To my amazement and consternation, rumors began to circulate that *White Dog* was a "racist" movie even before the picture had even been previewed in public. Paramount hadn't set a release date yet. Where the

We used several white dogs on the production and an experienced trainer to make the violence feel real. To some, it was too real. White Dog *changed the course of my career and my life.*

rumors came from was vague, but it was not unreasonable to suspect that Mr. Edwards, the NAACP spokesperson who'd never seen one frame of my picture, had something to do with it. A meeting was called at Paramount with studio heads Michael Eisner and Jeffrey Katzenberg. As soon as I sat down in their conference room, they dropped the bomb. They were going to shelve my film. Releasing *White Dog* would risk an ugly controversy that wasn't worth the film's profit potential. In the most absurd twist of events I'd ever heard of, the studio was backing down from opening my picture because of rumors from people who'd never seen it. What's more, the rumors were ludicrous, pure horseshit. One comment that came back to us was that *White Dog* would incite race violence, inspiring madmen to train their own white dogs to attack black people.

It was 1982, Reagan was president, and the Republicans had the country's morality by the balls. Shelve the film without letting anyone see it? I was dumbfounded. It's difficult to express the hurt of having a finished film locked away in a vault, never to be screened for an audience. It's like someone putting your newborn baby in a goddamned maximum-security prison forever.

It was little consolation that the movie was released later in Europe to rave reviews. A prominent Swedish critic wrote that "no one has used the color white in such a dramatically symbolic way since Herman Melville's *Moby-Dick*." It would be ten years before *White Dog* was shown in the States, but in art houses only.

Holy shit, if the chopping up of *The Big Red One* had put a few dents in my resolve to pursue moviemaking in Hollywood, then the lockup of *White Dog* had totally wrecked it! I was deeply hurt. The studio had used me as a scapegoat for their lack of determination and courage. *White Dog* was a thought-provoking movie exposing the stupidity and irrationality of racism in our society. Nothing more, nothing less.

I'd been offered a film in Paris and decided to take it. Moving to France for a while would alleviate some of the pain and doubt that I had to live with because of *White Dog*. It would be a relief to get away from the perversity and backbiting of Hollywood. Europeans seemed to respect their filmmakers as artists. You never had to fight for the final cut on your films. It was your prerogative.

We packed some clothes, Samantha's favorite toys, and my old Royal, leaving the Shack and all our furnishings in the care of some dependable tenants. When we flew to Paris in 1982, I never dreamed it would be the debut of a thirteen-year, self-imposed exile.

PART VI

Still trying to capture emotion on film after all these years.

51

A Third Face

For me, coming back to Paris was full of good feelings. Seventeen years earlier, Christa and I had first met and fallen in love in the City of Light. For our daughter, Samantha, it would be an opportunity to expand cultural horizons. In the past, while working on movie projects in Europe, I had considered settling over there for good. Other American directors— Joseph Losey, Stanley Kubrick, Fred Zinnemann, Nicholas Ray—had made terrific pictures in Europe. John Huston had lived for a while in Ireland. Why couldn't I live out my days in France? There were still plenty of movies in me, weren't there? But holy shit, who was I bullshitting? Wasn't Paris really the beginning of the end? Deep down, the truth was inescapable. You can't hide anything from your third face.

See, you've got three faces. Your first face is the one you're born with, the one in the mirror every morning, a touch of your mama in those blue eyes, Papa's ruddy cheeks and thin lips, or maybe, like me, a set of crooked chops from an ancestor only some fake genealogist could identify. Your second face is the one you develop thanks to ego, ingenuity, and sensitivity, the one people identify as "you," laughing at punch lines, downcast when things aren't going well, exhilarated by passion and success, cold when confusion and fear set in, charming when seduction is part of the battle plan.

Then there's your third face. No one ever gets to see that one. It'll never show up in any mirror nor be visible to the eyes of parents, lovers, or friends. It's the face that no one knows but you. It's the *real* you. Always privy to your deepest fears, hopes, and desires, your third face can't lie or be lied to. I call it my mind mistress, guardian of my secret utopias, bitter disappointments, and noble visions.

Being back in Paris should have been an antidote for any residual bitterness about Hollywood. But I couldn't escape myself. I took my early-morning walks, had my coffee, and read the *Herald Tribune.* I ended up

Above: With director Wim Wenders, cameraman Joe Birco, and actor Frederick Forrest on one of my quick acting gigs in the eighties, Hammet. *Below: On the set of* Slapstick *with Jerry Lewis and Madeline Kahn*

strolling for long stretches along the banks of the Seine, my newspaper sticking out of the pocket of my trench coat, reflecting on my past and future. As I watched the murky waters of the river, I couldn't help thinking about *White Dog,* wishing I'd never set foot in Hollywood. I should've pursued my dream of becoming editor in chief of my own newspaper in some small town, writing articles, composing headlines, concocting crusading editorials. It seemed that I was shrinking into nothingness, unable to fulfill any of the dreams still bouncing around my mind. I was over seventy already. Would I have enough time to achieve anything significant?

By taking refuge in my third face, I faced my anxiety straight on and got over the numbness. My third face was my own holy sanctuary. There, my crown was buried. It was a storage room that nobody but me could enter. I'd cultivated it like a secret shrine. There, I was my own spiritual and creative master. There, I put all my noble yearnings, all my naïve dreams for a utopian world, all the yarns that weren't for sale.

Not finding a catchy name in psychology for the private me, I came up with "third face." It wasn't just a concept for me but a very real locale, captivating and whimsical, cozy and seductive, the geisha girl of my brain. I welcomed solitude because I wasn't really ever alone. Maybe I was an old fart, yet a helluva lot of dreams and desires were still knocking around deep down there. My third face always reinvigorated me. There was no chance of me drying up, no way I'd be running on empty.

Your third face remains a secret to even your dearest loved ones. It's what makes every person unique and unfathomable. One of life's inscrutable mysteries is why our innermost personality remains unknowable. Many people are sad to realize they'll never completely know anybody else, never "see" their third face. For me, the perpetuation of our secret selves is what makes life both survivable and glorious.

The offer to write and direct *Thieves After Dark* (1984) came about because of a deal with French producer Jo Siritzky, who'd made a bundle distributing *Shock Corridor* in the sixties through his company, Parafrance. The project began with an ambitious young writer named Olivier Beer, who had wrangled an interview out of me in California then dropped off his book called *Le Chant des Enfants Morts.*[1] Olivier then convinced Siritzky to back a movie based on his book if I were attached as director. Olivier and I were to cowrite the screenplay. The yarn was about a young French couple who are out of work and dysfunctional, their lives turned upside down by the harsh realities of modern-day life.

My experiences cowriting with people like Hank Wales and Curtis Hanson were very positive. Those guys were professionals. It was soon obvious that Olivier, though an accomplished journalist and novelist, didn't know a damn thing about writing screenplays. With professionals, I never have a problem. There are compromises to make, story twists to hammer out, characters to interpret. There's only one goal that counts whatever the shortcuts you take, the arguments you have, or the rewrites you end up doing, and that's to make a damn good finished movie. Olivier would get credit as cowriter, but I got little help from him. Our relationship turned sour.

Christa, Samantha, and I were staying in a hotel in Montmartre on a little square called Place Charles Dullin. The Atelier Theatre, an illustrious place once run by the great French actor-director Louis Jouvet, was around the corner. Everything in the quarter—the old facades, uneven sidewalks, water trickling down the gutters, streetlamps, bakery aromas—was inspiring. It reminded me of the city I'd first discovered in 1945 after the end of the war, and the one I'd gotten to know pretty well in 1965 during the *Flowers of Evil* project. I put the *White Dog* fiasco out of my mind and got back to moviemaking.

For my female lead, I sought out Isabelle Huppert, one of the most interesting actresses in France. Jo Siritzky was pushing for Véronique Jannot. She had just appeared on the cover of *Paris Match* because of her role in a popular French soap opera. I was okay with Véronique, as she was a strong actress, enthusiastic and lovely. For my male lead, I insisted on Bobby Di Cicco, who'd been with me on *The Big Red One.* We hired Victor Lanoux as a police inspector. Claude Chabrol did a walk-on as a personal favor. Siritzky hired Antoine Gannage to put together a great crew, notably the cameraman Philippe Rousselot and set decorator Dominique André. I insisted on Ennio Morricone for the musical score.

The shoot went quite well, except for the behind-the-scenes struggle between Jo, his nephew, Serge, and his sister, Nadja, for control of their family company. I stayed out of it. Jo Siritzky had been completely on the up-and-up with me, honoring our contract to the letter. Serge finally took over Parafrance, but it floundered and was eventually acquired by foreign investors. The movie business is damned chaotic.

Thieves After Dark was an official selection at the 1984 Berlin Film Festival. John Cassavetes and Gena Rowlands were also in Germany that year to present *Love Streams.* Their beautiful movie won the Golden Bear, the festival's top prize. For my screening, Gena and John insisted on sitting next to Christa and me. There was a big crowd in the hall. Midway through the movie, some spectators started booing. I didn't give a damn, but John, sensitive to the situation, grabbed my arm, whispering that he loved my film. The night ended in a bar on some backstreet of Berlin eating herring, drinking beer, and telling hilarious stories about our humiliating, exhilarating business. Gena, John, Christa, and I laughed so hard our ribs hurt. I discussed making a picture about Dorothy Thompson with Gena, the one actress whom I thought had the balls to play the lady journalist. Gena loved the character, but it never came together.

Painful memories of the *White Dog* affair wouldn't go away. While I'd been cutting *Thieves After Dark* in Paris, we got word that NBC had refused to broadcast *White Dog* on prime-time television, calling the film "inappropriate." My yarn, inappropriate? Here's what's inappropriate: the goddamned way American racists have treated blacks, Hispanics, Asians, and everybody who wasn't as white as Shirley Temple. The NBC refusal came about the same time as the film was being released in Europe to good reviews. I took the nonsensical situation in my stride. What really mattered to me was my family's well-being. I focused on making a living for us in Paris.

We settled into a spacious, high-ceilinged apartment on rue de la Baume in the Eighth Arrondissement, a place that had belonged to the Duchess of Marlborough. The duchess had left the duke and married Jacques Balsan. His son, Humbert, a young actor who had become a formidable producer, sublet the apartment out to people in the movie business. Andrzej Wajda and his wife had lived there. So had Ismail Merchant and James Ivory. It was like residing in some bygone era, every room sporting a hilarious array of ostentatious divans, armoirs, statues, and four-poster beds. The place was drafty and hard to heat and the plumbing was lousy, but we felt right at home. The cobblestone courtyard, built for horses and carriages, was now jammed with Mercedes-Benzes and BMWs. I had a quiet study all to myself where I set up my Royal and happily started cooking up my yarns.

Only a short walk from our front door was Monceau Park, with its golden gates and beautiful flowers. Every morning, I took Samantha by the hand, walked her through the park, and delivered her to the front door of her new school, L'École Bilingue. She assimilated just fine with the other children, picking up French quickly. Her schoolmates made a crack about her "grandfather" one day, the old guy who always walked her to school. Samantha told them proudly that the old guy was her daddy, and that was that.

My adventure novel, *Quint's World*, retitled *La Grande Mêlée*, had come out in France, Germany, Portugal, and Spain, published by Christian Bourgois. Christian was respected, having done books by William Burroughs and Susan Sontag, too. Reviews of *Thieves After Dark* were mixed. To the French, I represented the quintessential American director. Making a French movie about a domestic problem like unemployment had thrown them off balance.

Good or bad, I was getting a helluva lot of attention in Paris, with invi-

With Alain Robbe-Grillet,
novelist, screenwriter, and
director, who won a Golden
Lion in Venice (with Alain
Resnais) for Last Year
at Marienbad *(*L'année
Dernière à Marienbad,
1961). French intellectuals
were a conflicted group,
but affable toward me.
I have no idea why.

tations arriving regularly, the telephone ringing at all hours of the day and night with somebody asking us to attend their gallery opening, dinner party, or film festival. Thank God Christa shielded me from all that stuff so that I could concentrate on my writing. The one person I wished I could've seen more of was François Truffaut. I even dreamed of collaborating with François on a picture. I'd cherished the few times he'd visited with us in Los Angeles. Full of respect and camaraderie, Truffaut was a delightful guy, yet there was always a little melancholy in his eyes and in his voice. Once we were talking about fame and the strange tricks it plays.

"Most people in America," said Truffaut, "know about me because of that crazy scientist I played in Spielberg's *Close Encounters,* not because of my own films."

The sad reality was that few Americans recognized the remarkable films the French had been producing all along, from Renoir to Pagnol, from René Clair to Jean-Pierre Melville, from Marcel Carné to Truffaut. At the same time, French filmgoers were familiar with every genre of American film. It was out of kilter. Living in Paris, I could feel the undercurrent of animosity toward Americans, especially those in the film business, whetted by admiration, jealousy, and box-office competition. I didn't like the inequity of the situation either, but hell if I was going to let myself be a scapegoat in some transatlantic movie-business rivalry.

Not long after we'd settled in Paris, we got the shocking news that Truffaut had a fatal brain tumor. He died in 1984, only fifty-two years old. For me, the saddest part was that, for a man who loved children so much, François would never see his new daughter, Josephine, grow up. I actually felt guilty being twenty years older, still kicking, living in his hometown, able to share in the joy of watching my Samantha bloom.

Christa and I went to Truffaut's funeral. Jack Lang, minister of culture at the time, gave a stirring eulogy. After the service, we walked quietly through the Père-Lachaise cemetery looking at all the tombstones of the great artists who were buried there. I hadn't known François that well, but I felt a deep sense of loss about his untimely death. He left me a warm souvenir of friendship, and he left all of us a wonderful legacy of films.

In June 1984, the fortieth anniversary of D day, the popular left-wing paper *Libération* wanted to do an article about my memories of landing on Omaha Beach with the Big Red One. About thirty thousand American veterans had come over for the commemorative ceremonies. We saw President Mitterrand and President Reagan along with other heads of state and royalty, from Queen Elizabeth and Maggie Thatcher of England to Pierre Elliott Trudeau of Canada. Along with the multitude of tourists were an army of salesmen hawking war memorabilia.

The person I most wanted to visit in Normandy was Monsieur Brobant, in Colleville-sur-Mer, the first civilian our squad had encountered after surviving the amphibious assault. Still ebullient, Monsieur Brobant was then in his eighties. He lived in the same little house above the beach, the first sign of civilization we'd seen that terrible day in 1944. I was thrilled to introduce Monsieur Brobant to my family. When we gave him the cognac and flowers we'd brought along, there were tears in his eyes. He was the high point for me of a memory-laden visit.

The *Libération* article filled two entire pages under the headline "FULLER DÉBARQUE SES SOUVENIRS ("Fuller Unloads His Memories"). A good freelance writer named Laurent Joffrin wrote the piece, mentioning little Samantha running among the tombstones in the cemetery where I'd been looking for the names of dead comrades from the First Division. They ran a picture of me wearing a steel helmet with the Big Red One on it. The photo had been taken in my office back at the Shack. It made me feel homesick for our little house up in Laurel Canyon, for my old rolltop desk surrounded by all my books, for America.

On Omaha Beach, I held Samantha's and Christa's hands as we walked along the sand down where the sea rolled in so peacefully. Forty years before, I'd struggled through those bloody waters, shells exploding overhead, dead soldiers strewn across the beach, Nazi mines and machine guns popping all around me. I was so grateful to be standing there once again, now with my young wife and my beautiful nine-year-old daughter. Samantha tossed stones into the ocean, playing where so many had fought and died. It was cleansing to see it through her innocent blue eyes, still unaware of the burden of memory or history. I thanked God that she still didn't have the faintest idea of the violence man could wreak on his fellow human beings.

By then, Samantha was speaking perfect French. She turned to her mother and asked: *"Quand est-ce que nous allons revenir en Amérique?"*— "When are we going back to America?"

Neither of us knew the answer.

52

Breadwinner
in France

In over eight decades of very active life, I've rarely been ill enough to be confined to a bed, even for one day. Directing pictures on tight schedules requires vigor and durability. My stamina developed from running around the streets of New York as a crime reporter in my teens, bumming across the country in my twenties, and fighting with the infantry in my thirties. Not to mention smoking cigars, which keeps the lungs clean and the mind tranquil. In my seventies, I still ran circles around all the young people working with me on a movie set. While we were editing *Thieves After Dark,* in 1984, a minor incident showed me my limits.

Early on a cold winter morning, I'd left our apartment to go out to the Boulogne-Billancourt Studio. As if I were in California, I wore a summer shirt and a light jacket. There was just too much on my mind. Christa ran after me outside our apartment and made me put on a wool sweater and a jacket. That evening, she joined me along with Samantha for a big party to celebrate the centennial of the studio. I'd worked hard all day long in an editing room and forgotten about eating. We all met on a big soundstage where hundreds of guests munched hors d'oeuvres and sipped champagne. There was loud music, and young people were dancing. The last thing I remember were the clips from old French movies being projected on specially erected screens. I fainted dead away. Horrified, Christa and Samantha got down on the floor, trying to revive me. People crowded around.

"It's Samuel Fuller," somebody said calmly. "He's had a heart attack."

"Fuller's dead," said another person.

I came around. Claude Chabrol and his wife, Aurore, took us home. Claude and Aurore even helped get me into bed. I thanked everyone and said I was okay, but I still felt weak. The next day our French doctor told me that I'd passed out because of abnormally low blood sugar, or hypoglycemia. It wasn't anything serious, but it made me realize I'd better take care of myself.

For months after that, the rumor went around that I'd died of a heart attack in France. Incredibly, the "news" traveled to the four corners of the globe and back. F. Scott Fitzgerald said there were no second acts in American life. Here I was starting my third, and I was already dead. I got calls from kind people on every continent. I thanked everyone for their concern, laughed, and reassured everyone that I was just fine, stealing Mark Twain's line that "reports of my death have been greatly exaggerated."

All the fuss about my dying was funny but disquieting. Having already stared death in the face a few times, dying really didn't bother me. I regretted it more for my wife and daughter than for myself. The only thing about kicking the bucket that worried me was how it would put a crimp in my ability to tell any more stories. Hell, not being able to spin any more yarns would have really killed me!

A little while after the hypoglycemia incident, we got a call from producer David Brown, who was in town making *Target* (1985), directed by Arthur Penn and starring Gene Hackman and Matt Dillon. We invited David over to our place for a home-cooked meal. He was missing his wife, Helen, who had to stay in New York in her capacity as editor in chief of *Cosmopolitan*. David loved Christa's cooking, kidding around that her delicious *poulet aux morilles*—chicken with special wild mushrooms—was "chicken with morals." David ended up spending a couple more evenings with us. He'd been a story executive at Fox under Zanuck, then rose to production chief and went on to start his own company, partnering with Darryl's son, Richard.

Witty and worldly, David was a great raconteur. He laughed just as heartily about his flops, like *Steelyard Blues* (1973), as he did about hits like *The Sting* (1973) and *Jaws* (1975). David would go on to produce *Driving Miss Daisy* (1989) and *The Player* (1992), among many other quality pictures. We talked about our days at Fox and the atmosphere at the studio under Zanuck's reign, making me miss old Darryl more than words can describe.

It was David Brown who'd offered me the directing job on *The Young Lions* (1958). I'd turned him down because I thought it was ridiculous having Marlon Brando play a Nazi soldier in that picture, though I don't think David held any grudges about it. Then again, David never bought one of my scripts or hired me to make another picture after I passed on that one. For Chrissakes, when I thought about all the movies I'd turned down, I felt like kicking myself in the ass. But what about all those directing jobs on major films for which I'd been passed over? As long as a good director got the gig, it was okay by me. Many good directors needed somebody else's story to make a movie. I took pride in being an original, a direc-

With David Brown, a first-class guy and highly successful independent producer. Both of us were tickled to still be alive and in the movie business.

tor who creates characters, dialogue, and action out of his own experience and imagination. From a blank piece of paper, I made motion pictures.

One evening after dinner, David and I smoked cigars until late into the night, comparing the Hollywood of the eighties with that of the fifties. Holy shit, it was like night and day! For me the biggest difference was that we used to have handshake deals back then. A man's word still meant something. Not to mention that those deals were struck by colorful characters, every one of them a story lover and gambler at heart. We reminisced about that dying breed of risk takers—men like Zanuck—who'd launched this crazy business, then made it grow into an international gold mine. David and I remembered some of the unsung heros, guys like Buddy Adler, my producer on *House of Bamboo,* a helluva moviemaker who'd gone on to do *Bus Stop* (1956), *A Hatful of Rain* (1957), and *South Pacific* (1958) before lung cancer cut him down at age fifty-one. Buddy was responsible for getting Ingrid Bergman back to Hollywood, to star in *Anastasia* (1956). All said and done, David and I agreed that we were lucky old farts to still be working, getting invitations to lunch, and most importantly, blessed with loving wives at our sides.

Christa and I decided to prolong our stay in France, paying another year's rent up front to our landlord on rue de la Baume. We were assisted by the dollar's strong exchange rate at the time. I was tremendously homesick, but Samantha was doing beautifully at the *école bilingue*. It seemed right to let her continue her French education uninterrupted. Besides, jobs were coming my way—not well-paid gigs by Hollywood standards, but steady breadwinning projects. Some wheeler-dealer producers in San Francisco paid me to write a script on the Iran hostage situation. I delivered it, but they never produced it. Two Hollywood gals, Anne Kimmel and Cathy Rabin, took an option on *The Charge at San Juan Hill*, then couldn't get the financing together. A young director named Bertrand Fevre asked me to play a part in *Bleeding Star*, his debut short film. *Télérama*, a widely read TV magazine, hired me to write a children's book entitled *Pecos Bill and the Soho Kid*, a Western based on an idea I'd had for a TV show. Like the treatment for the show, the book featured an adult who'd never grown up and a kid with a Cockney accent and mature beyond his years, who took imaginary trips together, catching clouds with lassos. Illustrated by Belgian artist Frank le Gall, my little book was dedicated to John Ford. I was thrilled when my publisher received hundreds of enthusiastic letters from young French readers.

Next door to us in Paris lived the Cerrato family. They had twin daughters, Claudia and Sabina, Samantha's playmates. I vividly remember those three little girls getting dressed up and presenting numbers from American musicals for the adults. I can still hear them belting out "Tomorrow," from *Annie*. Mr. Cerrato worked at the American embassy as a "commercial attaché," whatever the hell that was. I veered away from talking politics, as it would have surely soured our neighborly relations. Those were the Reagan years, and I was fundamentally against old Ronnie's politics. On our yearly trips back to the States, we saw how Reaganomics had created a widening gap, with more wealthy people controlling a greater share of the resources and more and more poor people undernourished and badly educated. I was shocked to see so many homeless people on American streets. Our country was supposed to be the richest country in the world. How could we still have so many people without roofs over their heads? How could we still have one of the highest rates of illiteracy? Living in France under their special brand of socialism had been eye-opening for me about what a government can do when it's committed to decent education and health care for all its citizens.

No matter how good life was in Paris, serious offers for making films were in short supply. But that didn't stop the unending flow of invitations from film festivals in France, Europe, and around the world that came in at an astounding rate. There was no way we could attend more than a tiny fraction of all those enticing events. Edinburgh, run by the wonderful Murray and Barbara Grigor, and Locarno, programmed by our good friend Marco Mueller, were delightful. We had a great time at San Sebastian, its festival managed by the industrious Diego Galán, a critic from Spain's leading left-wing paper, *El País*. In the years to come, I'd also attend Sundance and Telluride, both great events.

Deauville, on the coast of Normandy, became a regular autumn weekend outing for the entire family. The American Festival there, run by Lionel Chouchan and André Halimi, invited us each year. We'd take the train to Deauville and check into one of those grand hotels built at the beginning of the century. Samantha enjoyed the beach, and Christa, all the schmoozing and seafood. Since the war, Normandy would always occupy a special place in my soul. One year at the festival, I was delighted to run into two guys from the old days who had my complete respect: Richard Brooks and Joseph Mankiewicz. Richard came to France to show his last picture, *Fever Pitch* (1985). It was great getting back together with him, one of my closest buddies in Hollywood in the fifties. Mankiewicz was unique, a great director and one helluva writer. Yet Joe hadn't made a movie since *Sleuth* (1972). Hollywood had a horrible habit of putting its most talented and experienced artists into mothballs before their passion and their creativity had dried up. Directors over sixty were judged "too old" to work. It was goddamned age discrimination! If I'd hung around Hollywood waiting for some thirty-year-old studio exec to green-light one of my scripts, I'd have seen myself as part of that group, too.

My only regret about the movie business, if I had to name one, was not having become my own producer along the way. I could have financed my own pictures and backed great filmmakers like Mankiewicz, allowing masters like him to get behind a camera again to make their dream movies. My big problem in Hollywood was that power and money never gave me a hard-on.

At Deauville, we also ran into members of Hollywood's new generation, guys like Walter Hill and Jonathan Demme. I enjoyed Hill's hard-hitting, entertaining pictures, like *Red Heat* (1988), which he brought to the festival that year. Walter was a no-bullshit kind of director with whom I got along right away. Demme was presenting *Married to the Mob* (1988). I'd been friends with Jonathan since the seventies, when he'd directed *Caged Heat* (1974). His films would get better over the years, and, just as importantly, he'd always remain a down-to-earth, unpretentious man with strong democratic ideals.

Another festival the entire family enjoyed attending year after year was Avignon. In that beautiful Provençal town on the banks of the Rhône, Jerome Rudes had concocted his unique crossroads of French and American independent cinema in the shadow of Avignon's medieval Palace of the

Popes. Writer and teacher, Jerry was crazy about movies. I'd first met him at a dinner in Deauville where we'd sat with the veteran director Robert Wise, cracking jokes and exchanging stories all night long. Jerry was a warm, genuine guy, and we immediately struck up a friendship that would deepen over the years. Every June, Christa, Samantha, and I would go down to Avignon for a week to enjoy the Provençal sun and the hospitality that Jerry and his team showered on us.

In Avignon, I met up with a helluva lot more fine filmmakers, whether veterans, like Louis Malle, or youngsters breaking into the business, like Quentin Tarantino. Malle was a great director and a gracious human being who told me he was fed up with shooting films in America. At that time, he was developing one of his greatest yarns, *Au Revoir les Enfants,* which he'd shoot in France. Tarantino had a passionate and voracious mind for movies. Holy cow, he'd memorized entire dialogues, word for word, from my films! I hit it off right away with Quentin and thought he did a damn good job on his debut picture, *Reservoir Dogs* (1992), a heist movie about a bunch of dumb crooks. I hung out with Quentin, Alexandre Rockwell, and other young directors during late-night parleys on a terrace overlooking Avignon's red-tiled rooftops, drinking vodka and telling stories. I admired the cordial atmosphere of the Avignon Film Festival and supported Jerry's inexhaustible efforts to give young directors a break, so I accepted his offer to become the organization's honorary president.

Meanwhile, something ugly was happening in the eighties to French politics. The National Front, an extreme right-wing party, was rising in popularity and winning large percentages in local elections. Their leader was a hatemonger named Jean-Marie Le Pen. Arab people from North Africa were Le Pen's primary political scapegoat, but his tirades against immigrants were loosely aimed at anyone not white and Catholic. If that wasn't enough, Le Pen and his followers had the audacity to proclaim that the Holocaust wasn't really that bad, that the German concentration camps were "a minor historical episode." I decided to take a stand against the sonofabitch's ranting by helping a committed filmmaker named Emil Weiss make a cherished documentary about the Holocaust.

As his documentary's centerpiece, Weiss asked my permission to use those twenty minutes of 16-mm film that I'd shot in May 1945 in the Falkenau death camp. I said yes. I'd stored that footage away for all those years because it was so appalling. Now it was time to let people see those terrible images. Christa brought my forty-year-old reels back to Paris on one of her trips to California and entrusted them to Emil Weiss. As part of the story Emil wanted to tell, he took me back to the town of Falkenau in Czechoslovakia, today renamed Sokolow. Emil interviewed me on camera with the site of the old Nazi camp in the background. It was painful to relive those terrible times, so many decades old yet so fresh in my mind, but I felt we were honoring the memory of the camp's prisoners. In my own way, I was also paying tribute to my squad's decent-minded commander, Captain Richmond, who had made sure some of the camp's victims got proper burials that day.

Emil's film, entitled *Falkenau, Vision of the Impossible* (1988), was invited to the Cannes Film Festival and praised for its straightforwardness and soul. I was proud to have participated, finally getting an opportunity to show my own proof of man's inhumanity to man. After all, I'd been an eyewitness to the crime of the century. There will always be fundamentalist bastards trying to minimize the Holocaust's significance. The truth won't let them. People can see the horrible reality for themselves in grisly images like those I recorded at Falkenau with my old Bell & Howell. Fanatics can never—never!—revise history to suit their political agenda. Film doesn't lie.

53

Half Full,
Not Half Empty

It was a joy to live in Paris, but after five years it seemed time to go home. Samantha was nine already, and we wanted our daughter to spend some of her formative years in the States. She came back from her *école* nibbling on a baguette, like a real little Parisian. She spoke perfect French, though she retained her American candor.

Once we attended a prestigious human rights colloquium at the Sorbonne. We brought Samantha to the reception at the Elysées Palace afterward. There was a gorgeous buffet, but, as is the custom in France, nobody could eat until the president had formally greeted his guests. François Mitterrand finally showed up. As soon as we got through with all the handshaking, our hungry daughter said in a loud voice: *"J'ai serré la main du Président, maintenant en peut tous manger!"*—"I shook hands with the president, now we can all eat!" Everybody in earshot laughed at our little girl's sincerity, then hurried over to enjoy the delicious chow.

In 1986, like a lightning bolt striking, we got the shattering news that Samantha had Hodgkin's disease, a form of cancer that attacks the lymphatic tissues. Distraught is hardly a powerful enough word to describe Christa's state. I tried to stay calm, but everything turned inescapably dark for me, too. We put aside all our plans until they figured out the appropriate remedy for Samantha at the Marie Curie Hospital in the Latin Quarter, one of the best cancer clinics in Europe. Samantha was put under the supervision of the wonderful Doctors Zucker and Quintana, who told us that Hodgkin's was curable when detected at that early stage. My daughter's treatments were successful, thank God. For the next year, without missing much school, Samantha was admitted to Marie Curie every six weeks for checkups. To make sure the Hodgkin's was eradicated, the doctors advised us that Samantha needed regular checkups over the next ten years. Any hope of returning home evaporated in the twinkle of a little girl's eye. We'd have to hang on in Paris as best we could until our daughter was completely healed. What a relief that Samantha had pulled through the crisis!

With real projects so few and far between, I'd have to learn to live with my professional frustration. Sure, anger about the scarcity of directing gigs boiled to the surface sometimes. However, I'd keep writing and take whatever acting work came my way. I didn't give a damn as long as my daughter was out of danger. I'd always see my cup as half full, not half empty.

One day, the writer-director Larry Cohen called from Los Angeles to say he'd created a leading role especially for me in a picture he was shooting in Vermont. It was called *A Return to Salem's Lot* (1987), based on the Stephen King novel.

"Sam, I want you to play a Nazi-hunter," said Cohen.

"How many weeks?" I asked.

"About three."

"What's the loot?"

"Thirty-eight grand."

"It's a deal. Send me the script."

"Will do."

Larry Cohen was a real pro, honest and warmhearted. He'd earned a lot of dough in the sixties on a successful TV series called *Branded,* then gone on to write and direct some ballsy pictures like *Bone* (1972) and *The Private Files of J. Edgar Hoover* (1977) as well as the money-making gore trilogy *It's Alive!* I'd first met Cohen in the late seventies, at a reception in a swank Los Angeles hotel. He surprised me by explaining that he was living in my old house in Coldwater Canyon. I'd lost track of the big Spanish-style mansion I'd bought in the fifties when I was flush. It'd been sold by my ex-wife, passing through the hands of a succession of owners. Cohen had acquired it from the actor Clint Walker.

One weekend, Christa and I went over to Coldwater Canyon for lunch with Larry and his wife, Janelle. I wanted to show Christa how I used to live, despite the risk that she might get depressed about the big difference between the Shack and my luxurious villa from the fifties. However, Christa was a good sport and thoroughly enjoyed seeing the big mansion. We also cemented a great friendship with Larry and Janelle.

It was damned cold in Vermont on Cohen's location for *Salem's Lot,* with several all-night shoots. Many of the younger actors complained about the weather, the food, the accommodations, or whatever. Not me. Being on an American movie set again was simply delightful. Larry and his crew were amazed by my seventy-five-year-old energy. Halfway through the movie, my character gets his foot caught in a bear trap. As I moved quickly around the set puffing on my cigar, I kept forgetting that I was

With my wooden stake and hammer, I tracked down Nazis-turned-vampires as Van Meer in Larry Cohen's A Return to Salem's Lot.

supposed to have a bum foot. The crew had to keep reminding me to limp. As an actor, I tried giving Larry exactly what he wanted. As a fellow director, I tried cheering him up when he needed it, staying out of his hair as much as possible.

Another young friend, Finnish director Mika Kaurismäki, asked me to play an American gangster in his movie *Helsinki Napoli All Night Long,* shooting in Germany in 1987. The pay was okay, the prospect of spending a few weeks in Berlin, appealing. About the same time, Christa got cast as Hemingway's mother in a European TV series entitled *The White Whale,* shooting near Trieste. Afterward, Christa met me in Berlin. Our pal Barbara Grigor came down from Edinburgh to Paris to look after Samantha while we were away.

A big, likable man, Kaurismäki, like most Finns, drank lots of very cold vodka and never seemed to be affected by it. We'd gotten to know the Finns during our visit to Sodankylä, where Mika and his filmmaker brother, Aki, had launched their Midnight Sun Film Festival, in 1986. Contrary to what people think, the Finns aren't native Scandinavians, but descendants of nomadic tribes of Hungarians who migrated up from the Baltic region. At various times, they've been ruled by Sweden and Russia. Finland gained its independence in the turmoil of the 1917 Russian Revolution. The Finns are a proud and decent people, who, as I informed Mika, were the only Europeans to ever pay back their war debt to the States.

Sodankylä is within the Arctic Circle. Six months out of the year the people there live in darkness, which may explain why they're such ardent movie buffs. For the summer solstice in June, however, the sun never sets. So the Midnight Sun festivalgoers stay up all night, drinking vodka and watching movies. We really enjoyed the atmosphere that inaugural year, as well as the company of the other directors, like Jonathan Demme and Bertrand Tavernier. I was honored to discover that a street in Sodankylä was later renamed for me. Unfortunately, I probably won't ever make it back to Finland and see the sign that says "Samuel Fullerin Katu."

Helsinki Napoli was a delight to make. Mika cast veteran Eddy Constantine as the male lead. Discovered by Edith Piaf, Constantine had been a big star in France in the fifties and sixties. Eddy was a good guy, even if he had a hard time holding his liquor. He'd worked with Christa on Godard's *Alphaville* (1965). In Berlin, Eddy enjoyed grabbing us at any time day or night to recount tales from his glory days. That got old fast.

Mika's female lead, newcomer Margi Clark, was a lot of fun to be with. Margi looked like a younger version of Janet Leigh. Her boyfriend had been a member of the Sex Pistols. Margi would regale us with hilarious stories about growing up in a poor Catholic family in the suburbs of Liverpool. I loved people who could laugh at misfortune and hardship.

Berlin was both inspiring and disturbing to me. So many accomplished people had worked in the great city, yet Hitler plotted his conquest of Europe there, laying plans for the Final Solution. Every time I saw the wall that cut through the heart of Berlin, I got a pang in my heart. Built in 1961, the wall was a harsh reminder of the cold war, a terrible waste of energy and resources. Both systems that had sustained the wall, capitalism and communism, were terribly flawed. Neither had made the world a peaceful, democratic place. The Soviet Union wasn't the "evil empire" that Reagan called it, but their gulags, censorship, and oppression were horrible. In America, racism, homelessness, illiteracy, violence, and poverty still flourished, making a mockery of our motto "home of the free and the brave." After dinner one night, Christa and I wrote our names on the big, ugly monolithic wall, not imagining that it would come down a few years later, ending years of harsh division.

When we had a break in the shoot, I'd end up in the Café Einstein on the Lindengasse, where I'd read the *Herald Tribune* and jot down ideas for future scenes and dialogue in a small notebook I always kept with me. One weekend, Kaurismäki's people got us a car and a driver so we could visit East Berlin to see the Max Reinhardt Theatre, where great talents like Marlene Dietrich had emerged. When the car drove us to Checkpoint Charley, Christa and I had to separate for passport control. Christa, a German citizen, had to stand in a long line to get through the border check. I was whisked through because they thought I was a well-to-do American businessman. Exasperated, Christa decided then and there to request U.S. citizenship, something she'd put off for too long.

We talked about Ernest Hemingway that day in the car in East Berlin. Christa had been rereading his books in order to play his mother in that TV series. I'd never liked Hemingway, neither the man nor his incessant macho persona. Sure, some of his writing was damn good. However, I'd never forgiven him for badmouthing my outfit, commenting once that the Big Red One acted "as if they'd won the war all by themselves." Nothing could've been further from the truth. What the hell did Hemingway know about fighting on front lines anyway?

The Parisian leftist newspaper *Libération* had published an article calling me "the Jewish Hemingway," which hadn't pleased me at all. Pigeonholing an artist with a tag line, especially a religious one, was ludicrous. Would a Catholic author known for fantasy writing enjoy being called "the gentile Kafka"? Another French reporter had once referred to me as "a Jewish John Ford." As much as I loved Ford, that was just as ridiculous an allusion, appealing to simple minds with simplistic notions. The Parisian intelligentsia just didn't know how to get a handle on me, a bang-for-the-buck moviemaker on a self-imposed exile in their country, minding my own business and taking care of my family, far from soulless, guileful Hollywood. French intellectuals were ready to analyze everything into the ground. One writer called me a "prophet without honor." Bullshit! For Chrissakes, what was all the fuss about? The articles and comments, even the complimentary ones, didn't put any butter on your spinach. The movie business in France, like the one in America, was full of intrigues, cliques, and power games that needed to be avoided at all costs. What it all boiled down to was this: Who was working and who wasn't? Fortunately, I was, even though the gigs were for acting, not directing.

My next job was for Jacques Perrin in a show called *Doctors of Mankind*, part of a twelve-part TV series about a humanitarian organization of French physicians who donate their services in trouble spots around the world.[1] Perrin was a wonderful man, one of the finest Frenchmen I'd ever meet, a filmmaker with a genuine democratic spirit and unshakable code of ethics. Perrin had begun his career as an actor and moved into producing, with such accomplished, thought-provoking pictures as *Z* (1969), *State of Siege* (1973), *The Children of Lumière* (1995), and *Microcosmos* (1996) to his credit. Perrin's understanding and tolerance were evident. I loved the guy because he put his ideals into action, staying clear of heavy-handed political contrivances and nationalistic generalizations.

Jacques's segment of *Doctors of Mankind* was set among the boat people of the Philippines. He cast me as a callous ship captain who eventually shows some concern for the miserable conditions of the boat people who live in the harbor where his ship is anchored. The lead was played by Jane Birkin, with whom I got along beautifully in our rehearsals in Paris. Jane had been married to the French singer and cult figure Serge Gainsbourg, who looked to me like the spitting image of the tormented painter Chaim Soutine.[2] I'd written an outline for a movie about Soutine, but Gainsbourg wouldn't live long enough for me to get it made.

Returning to the Philippines was always in the back of my mind after I had discovered that island country while making *Merrill's Marauders* in the early sixties. Christa and I took a long flight from Paris, via Bangkok, to Manila. Cast and crew were then moved to the island of Palawan, where the boat people lived in primitive shelters. It was like a refugee camp in a war zone, living conditions at their worst. The sickly people and undernourished children were pitiful to see. We shot most of the story aboard a freighter anchored in the harbor, but some scenes took place in the boat people's village too. Seeing old ladies and children scavenging for food from garbage dumps in order to survive was revolting. Such hunger left you feeling speechless. The gap between rich and poor in the Philippines was so appallingly wide. It was hard not to get emotional after seeing those abysmal living conditions. I kept thinking of Jean Valjean in *Les Misérables,* begging for a morsel of bread. A century later, a continent away, human beings were clawing and scratching for food like starving animals.

I wondered how in the hell President Corazon Aquino was going to reduce her people's suffering. When I remembered Imelda Marcos and her thousands of pairs of shoes, purchased with some of the millions that the Marcoses had plundered from the Philippine people, those scenes of poverty really made me angry. Jacques Perrin's film tried to show the outside world the distressful truth.

The main reason Perrin's shoot went smoothly was Bernard Lorrain, one of the best production managers I'd ever encountered on a movie set. Lorrain handled actors and extras with respect and kindness, attending to details with expertise while juggling a small budget. I knew I wanted to hire Lorrain on the next picture I'd direct. But then, who knew if I'd ever get the opportunity to direct another movie?

54

Sons and
Sonsofbitches

In 1988, the bad news reached me in Paris that John Cassavetes was very sick. Alexandre Rockwell, a young filmmaker whom John had mentored, came to see me about playing a role in his independent movie, *Sons*. Alex had written the part especially for John, that of a paralyzed father whose three sons decide to take him for a final, sentimental visit to France. When Alex had finally pieced together the dough to make the picture, John was too ill with cirrhosis of the liver. He told Alex to come see me. I said I'd do it. We dedicated the entire project to John.

Cassavetes and I had first crossed paths in the fifties when I was at Fox. For John, being a terrific actor making good money wasn't enough. He was intent on becoming a director, too, though no one wanted to back his first film, *Shadows*. In 1961, John bankrolled it himself, making a drama about interracial romance with a cast of unknowns, partially improvised, shot on a 16-mm camera on weekends when his crew got off their regular jobs, edited by John at home over many months of sleepless nights. Talk about balls! After *Park Row*, I knew how consuming it was to write, direct, and produce a picture *and* pay for it yourself. Cassavetes couldn't find any other way to tell his yarn. I loved this guy!

Cassavetes's daring and defiance of studio filmmaking got him plenty of attention from critics and from—who else?—the studios. They solicited him to direct a couple of conventional pictures in the early sixties, *Too Late Blues* (1962), and *A Child Is Waiting* (1963). Cassavetes was thoroughly dissatisfied with the experience.

"How the hell did you ever tolerate working in the factories, Sammy?" Cassavetes once asked me.

"Zanuck!" I replied.

John understood. I was lucky enough to have stumbled upon producers who loved good stories, mensches whose word was better than a contract, decisionmakers who green-lighted a picture with nothing more than "Okay, let's make it!"

With John Cassavetes and Gena Rowlands at the Shack. Cassavetes was an original all the way. Gena was a ballsy lady.

Cassavetes went on doing pictures on shoe-string budgets that he could control. He'd learned the first law of independence: Keep your budget small so you don't need the studio's goddamned big bucks to make your movie. Cassavetes juggled everything—scripts, technicians, actors, money men—to get those movies done. And what movies! *Faces* (1968), *A Woman Under the Influence* (1974), *The Killing of a Chinese Bookie* (1976), *Opening Night* (1977), *Gloria* (1980), *Love Streams* (1984). It was beautiful, what John had accomplished by dint of his relentless work, fierce talent, and roguish charm.

John and Gena had been our neighbors in Laurel Canyon for a helluva long time. I didn't spend that much time with Cassavetes, but when I did, there was a lot of kidding around and bawdy jokes. Underneath the high-spiritedness, an unspoken complicity kicked in, something raw and solemn that we identified in each other. What we shared, I think, was the same agony that a helluva lot of writer-directors live with, which is having a goddamned shelf chock-full of movie projects that, for whatever reason, just didn't get produced.

Cassavetes died on February 3, 1989. All young filmmakers today who call themselves "independent" owe a tremendous debt to him. I hope they pay it down by tapping into their heart of hearts, taking risks, making the kinds of personal films that John had the talent and courage to do.

No doubt about it, Alexandre Rockwell was one of Cassavetes's cine-matic heirs. Tall and charming, as handsome as a young Peter O'Toole, Alex had a gift for storytelling. I came aboard *Sons* because I was so fond of Alex, even if the money was less than minimal. The shoot kicked off in a New Jersey veteran's hospital where my character is vegetating, unable to walk or speak. My three sons, each sired with a different wife, decide to schlep me to France in a wheelchair for one last family adventure. We went to Paris and ended up shooting in Normandy, where the sons take their old man to revisit his D-day memories.

Hell, that was an independent picture! Talk about shooting a movie on a wing and a prayer; Alex was constantly struggling with money, crew, loca-tions, and actors. The three young men who played my sons begrudged working for a pittance. Though Rockwell's producer promised us all more money when the picture went into profit, we'd never see a penny of those deferments. For me, because of the great chemistry I had with Alex, the shoot was bearable. I remember how the poor guy, beset with so many obstacles, tried to keep us all smiling. Sometimes at the end of the long days, Rockwell needed a little cheering up himself. So I made a point of telling him funny stories about my own calamities directing dirt-cheap pictures. My tales cracked him up, allowing him some blessed relief. After all, the crap that always happens behind the scenes on a movie set becomes a joke in years to come. Only the movie remains.

Sons turned out to be a damn good picture, as if Cassavetes's spirit had been watching over us during the entire production. The film was invited to festivals all over the world, including Venice and Rio de Janeiro. The Brazilians awarded me the Best Actor Award, even though my character sits almost motionless in a wheelchair throughout the picture, a stroke vic-tim who manages just one line of dialogue. I never dreamed that only a few years later I'd end up a stroke victim myself, playing that character from *Sons* for real.

Like so many small-budget movies, *Sons* never got distributed cor-rectly. Alex has gone on to make other lovely movies, like *In the Soup* (1992), with Steve Buscemi, and *Somebody to Love* (1994), with Rosie Perez. In the latter, Alex flew me over to LA for one well-paid scene with Perez, playing a feisty, veteran movie producer à la Sam Spiegel who crashes a Rolls on a winding Hollywood street, says a few wise words, and kicks the bucket.

It wasn't until the late eighties that I finally got the chance to direct another picture, this one a TV movie called *The Madonna and the Dragon*. It was based on a story about a couple of news photographers covering the "People's Revolution" in the Philippines. Written by Reza Degathi and

In the Philippines working on The Madonna and the Dragon

Selim Nassib, the yarn was pretty good, but I still insisted on writing my own adaptation. The picture was financed by Jean-François Lepetit, the French producer behind the original *Three Men and a Baby*. He got me the cast I wanted, which included Jennifer Beals, who played photographer Patty Meredith, and Patrick Bauchau, as the arms dealer, Pavel. For Christa, I wrote the juicy little role of Mama, the madam of a local bordello, which she had fun doing. For myself, I created a cameo role as bureau chief of a big international news magazine.

The prospect of shooting another movie in the Philippines was exhilarating but also daunting. The country was now fraught with political unrest as well as tremendous poverty. I was able to hire the wonderful production coordinator Bernard Lorrain, who knew the Philippines and understood how to treat people respectfully. I knew he'd avoid the many pitfalls that awaited us and set the right tone for the entire crew. He did. The film opened with a map of the world, focusing on hot spots of political unrest, panning across the South China Sea to a close up of the Philippines, as Jennifer Beals's character says, "Everyone here is booby-trapped, double-crossing, or double-crossed."

We shot in Super 16 mm, my first experience with one of those smaller, hi-tech cameras. I enjoyed all the opportunities for unusual angles and original camera movements based on the new technology. Even so, I resorted to my old ways, firing a pistol to get scenes started, then shouting

"Forget it!" to stop the action. Conditions were tough in Manila, but our cast was wonderful, always cooperative. I remember a long sequence we filmed of Jenny Beals as she climbed a hill of stinking garbage, cameras slung around her neck. The place was horrible, an enormous dump surrounded by shanties. A trooper all the way, Beals plodded through the muck and fuming mess as if it were nothing, while the crew held handkerchiefs over their noses to stifle the stench.

On that shoot, I was pushing eighty but just as energetic as ever. Being in production always got my adrenaline pumping. After the day's scenes were in the can, I'd go to production meetings or watch dailies until late at night. When I finally returned to our hotel, high above Manila Bay, it was like landing on another planet, far from the squalor and poverty below. The view from our room's balcony was splendid, but I couldn't get the abominable sights of hungry people out of my head.

One night when I walked in, four beautiful ladies—Jenny Beals, makeup artist Diane Duchene, my Christa, and Assumpta Serna, Patrick Bauchau's girlfriend—were gossiping frivolously over cocktails on the hotel terrace. I was tempted to join them, basking in their sensuous voices and laughter. But I couldn't. I was haunted by the nightmarish visions of hungry people. I sat down and made extensive notes for my editor back in Paris. My idea was to show footage of Imelda Marcos's enormous collection of designer shoes juxtaposed with those Filipinos scavenging through garbage for something to eat.

For Chrissakes, people didn't have to live in garbage! Hell, when a crooked leader plunders a nation's resources, citizens always end up with the short end of the stick. Whatever "ism" was leveraged to their private advantage, all those sonsofbitches had the cheek to call themselves "patriots" while fleecing their countries. I hated the Marcoses and all the rest of the horrible demagogues in this world.

Once *The Madonna and the Dragon* was finished, I started work on an interview book called *Il Était une Fois Samuel Fuller* (*Once Upon a Time There Was Samuel Fuller*) for the *Cahiers du Cinéma* people. Publishers had often approached me about doing an autobiography. I'd refused all offers, too busy dreaming up my own tales, creating characters much more interesting than me. The idea of a series of taped conversations with film critics Noel Simsolo and Jean Narboni was less cumbersome, more easygoing. Telling stories is what I like to do the best. Simsolo and Narboni did a good job shaping all the material into an oral portrait, warts and all.

In honor of the publication of *Il Était une Fois*, a launch party and luncheon was organized at Fouquet's, the world-famous brasserie where French movie people hang out. I'd had my share of encounters with wheeler-dealers and bullshitters there. Discussing movie projects that never happened at Fouquet's seemed as French as fois gras. That day, a lot of good people stopped in to say hello. Some, like Agnès Varda and Roman Polanski, I knew well. Others, like Yves Montand and Fanny Ardant, were casual acquaintances. The French press had given my interview book terrific reviews, calling me a "visionary" or "lyrical poet." Still, Paris critics were politicized. Many remembered and still clung to Georges Sadoul's flawed, prehistoric judgment of me as a hard-line, anticommunist right-winger.

Montand was seated next to me at the luncheon. As a young man, he'd been fully committed to leftist causes, drawn to communism like many artists and intellectuals around the world. At one point during the meal, Yves leaned over toward me.

"Sam, you were right," he said confidentially.

"Right about what?" I said.

"Stalin," said Montand, shaking his head wistfully, almost whispering the Russian tyrant's name. I didn't respond. Evidently, my reputation as an anticommunist, seeded in the fifties by the French critical establishment trying to overanalyze *Pickup on South Street* and *China Gate,* was still embedded in French minds. It was useless to explain to the great star that my disdain for Joseph Stalin was not because of his ideology. I just didn't like dictators.

At least, Montand (born Ivo Livi) had woken up, coming out publicly against the Soviet Union's deplorable violations of human rights. Other die-hard leftists would continue to hold on to a thread of hope for the future of communism even as the Berlin Wall was being toppled. I'd never had any hope for communism. Decades before, Will Rogers used to say that communism was "like Prohibition, a good idea that just won't work." One of my heroes, Adlai E. Stevenson, put it more succinctly back in 1951 when he said, "Communism is the corruption of a dream of justice." Let me set the record straight for all time: I'm antitotalitarian, not anticommunist.

I remember a Russian filmmaker named Andrei Smirnov I met in the eighties at the Tours Film Festival, in the Loire Valley, the French heartland. Smirnov was an accomplished filmmaker and an animated kibbitzer. We shared too many Bloody Marys one evening at the festival.[1] Smirnov's movie, *Byelorussia Station* (1970), had been an official smash in the Soviet Union, with over twenty-eight million tickets sold at the box office. Yet Smirnov never got an extra kopeck. All profits went to the state. Worse, Smirnov told me, he got no respect, having to scramble to get each subsequent movie off the ground. Apparently cameramen had more clout than directors in Russia. Since Gorbachev had legitimized *glasnost,* Smirnov could complain openly. But there wasn't a thing he could do about the situation.

I'm proud to be an *American* filmmaker. We complain about our system, but at least profits go back into making movies, not into propping up a Politburo. Believe me, I'm not condoning bloated studios or dishonest producers who rip off screenwriters by underpaying them residuals. Some even refuse to pay anything until audits force them to cough up a little of their profits. Look at guys like Julius Epstein, who fought for forty years for a piece of the royalties from *Casablanca* (1942) after the millions the picture generated. It's disgusting. Nevertheless, in this country we have guilds that mediate in our behalf and civil courts that can be called upon to force dishonest producers to pay up.

After that evening with Smirnov, I had a terrible nightmare. Maybe it was a reaction to the Russian director's tales of woe, or to the thought-provoking Amos Gitai movie, *Berlin-Jerusalem* (1989), about the poetess Else Lasker-Schüler, which we watched that night at the festival. In my dream, I was sitting atop the Berlin Wall. A gigantic hand picked me up. A voice was singing "Humpty Dumpty sat on a wall, Humpty Dumpty had a great fall." Then a giant hand dropped me into the emptiness. I fell and fell and fell, finally landing on Jerusalem's Wailing Wall. I woke up in a sweaty flush. I couldn't figure out what the hell the dream's message was, except to stay far away from Bloody Marys.

At the end of the eighties, a grand celebration of international news photography held in Paris stands out in my mind. Thousands of stills had been submitted as part of a competition, and I was asked to be president of a jury of artists, writers, and photographers. We were driven from gallery to gallery across Paris to look at all those incredible photos from around the world. Many were devoted to life in Latin America, powerful portraits of soldiers, street urchins, shopkeepers, artisans, and peasants, so many noble and mysterious faces.

Ever since my journalism days, images of real people in real-life situations had always had an intense effect on me. One moment's emotion, frozen in time, was very inspiring. I've tried to construct my movies around those kinds of simple compositions that bring up complicated feelings. They speak in a way that people everywhere understand. I thought of that world-famous photo from the sixties of peasant children in Vietnam running in terror from a napalm bomb. That shot did more to end the Vietnam War than all the peace conferences and protest marches that were ever organized.

As part of that big photo show, there were exhibitions by the masters—

Edward Steichen, Henri Cartier-Bresson, Ernst Haas, Robert Capa—which I loved revisiting. Seeing the work of Capa again touched me deeply, and not only because I'd known the man, loved his fervor, and mourned his death. As corny as it sounds, Robert's stuff made me realize that, for better or worse, my past was always part of my today.

55

Being Serious
Without Taking
It Seriously

When producer Jacques Bral approached me about writing and directing a film based on the David Goodis novel *Street of No Return*, I got a hard-on right away. The book was the story of a crooner who's in love with a gangster's girlfriend. The crooner gets his throat cut by the gangster's goons, narrowly escaping death. With his vocal cords out of commission, the singer's career is finished. He becomes an alcoholic bum, obsessed with getting his gal back and getting even with the heavies. My script changed the crooner into a modern pop singer. The race riot from the book became my opening, guaranteed to jolt any audience to attention. See, the book's title referred to Market Street in San Francisco, where, for Chinese immigrants forced to work under horrible conditions, there was "no going home." The situation exploded frequently.[1] As a reporter, I'd covered a horrifying race riot in the streets of Harlem in the early thirties. Nothing on a movie screen could come close to the chaos and destruction I'd seen with my own eyes between people who attacked others just because of the color of their skin.

When I'd met David Goodis in 1946, he and I were both knocking out scripts and trying to sell them to the studios "in between novels," like a lot of aspiring writers. Neither of us were doing that well at the time. David and I would chow down together at Musso & Frank's, drink vodka, and commiserate. He was a sensitive soul, deeply affected when one of the studio goons, upon rejecting somebody's original script, would say something discouraging like, "You should go back to driving trucks." I didn't give a damn about what those meatheads said about my work, but David took it hard. He was a brilliant, shy loner searching for utopias who never quite made it as screenwriter.

David's novels brought him a measure of respect in Hollywood, beginning with *Dark Passage* (1947), the Delmer Daves Bogart-Bacall vehicle. David gave me a first edition of the book, which I still have and cherish.[2]

Bogart played a man convicted of murdering his wife who escapes from prison in order to prove his innocence. He finds that his features are too well known, so he's forced to seek some illicit backroom plastic surgery. The postoperation part of the film is shot from Bogart's bandaged point of view. The audience doesn't see his face until the Bacall character takes off his bandages. Holy cow, that was great moviemaking!

Jacques Bral's fascination with *Street of No Return* followed a long line of French filmmakers who'd turned David's books into films, starting with François Truffaut's *Shoot the Piano Player* (1960), adapted from *Down There*.[3] General recognition came too late for David Goodis. Booze killed him in 1967, at age fifty.

I told Bral that I'd been pals with Goodis. In my mind, by doing that film, it was my chance to do right by an old friend and a helluva writer. I had a great time adapting David's book, almost as if he were looking over my shoulder all the while. I think he'd have been happy with my script.

The production got off on the right track. I got the cast I wanted, with the brilliant Keith Carradine as my lead, Michael, transforming himself from a slick rock 'n' roll star into a long-haired vagrant roaming the streets in search of another shot of whiskey. His love interest, Celia, was played by the sensual Valentina Vargas. The imposing Bill Duke took the role of my tough cop, Lieutenant Borel. I'd met Bill in 1984 at the Antwerp Film Festival, where he was presenting his film *The Killing Floor* (1984). It was a moving story about a poor black southerner who travels to Chicago to find work in the slaughterhouses, then gets embroiled in the organized-labor movement. Duke was a gracious, talented man.

Since a lot of my movie's financing came from Portugal, we shot *Street of No Return* near Lisbon, in the magical town of Sintra. The place had a dreamlike atmosphere, making everything look irrational, almost utopic. That suited my yarn perfectly. Sintra's town square was perfect for my "video clip" scene, which we shot late one night, with Vargas riding naked through the streets on a white stallion while Carradine's character sings a love song to her. Night lighting is always tricky. Keeping the nervous horse with the nude actress in our viewfinder was even more difficult. The scene was handled expertly by my cameraman, Pierre-William Glen, one of the top cameramen in France—and certainly the tallest, at well over six feet. I affectionately called him "Willy Boy," even though he towered over me. Glen and I worked great together, first planning out how each scene would look, then nailing it every time. A real pro, Glen had already shot movies for François Truffaut, Costa-Gavras, Joseph Losey, Bertrand Tavernier, and John Berry, among others. It was a pleasure to work with a cameraman who was that experienced.

*Keith Carradine and Bill
Duke in* Street of No Return.
*By adapting David Goodis's
yarn, I was trying to create
a ballsy kind of pulp poetry.
The extraordinary urban
cityscape of Portugal gave the
movie a universal look.*

We finished *Street of No Return* on time and under budget. I supervised the editing, then turned my cut over to Jacques Bral. Instead of releasing the picture, Bral spent an entire year recutting it. Throughout that period, I asked him what the hell was going on and got only obscure answers. At one point, I was so fed up with the situation that I told him that he should've written and directed the goddamned movie himself and left me out of it. On top of the delay, members of the crew were calling me to complain about Bral. They contended they hadn't been paid. The situation was terribly embarrassing, especially since I was powerless to help. The fact was that I hadn't been paid my entire goddamned fee either.

Throughout my life, I've always paid people their money on time. Back in California, when Anita Uphoff was my hardworking, full-time assistant, she got her paycheck on schedule for eighteen years, no matter how I had to scramble to cover it. Living extravagantly but not paying people what he owed them, Jacques Bral had a very different notion of ethics. The long hiatus between the end of principal photography and the eventual release of *Street of No Return* drove me crazy. I didn't hold any grudges against Bral, who was basically a sweet man, but when he asked me to do another picture with him, I had three words for him: "No thanks, handsome."

Street of No Return was finally released in Paris on a hot weekend in August 1990, around the time of my birthday. The posters were unappealing, the marketing campaign, nil. What difference did it make anyway? For cryin' out loud, most Parisian moviegoers were on summer vacation! I knew the box-office results were sabotaged from the get-go, but I didn't lose my temper about it. After all, a seventy-eight-year-old still directing feature films with a loving wife and a healthy daughter had much to be grateful for and little time or energy for anger.

The movie's premiere was organized in a Left Bank theater somewhere on Boulevard St. Germain. Christa, Samantha, and I attended. Afterward, Jacques Bral threw a surprise birthday party for me. A huge cake came floating down from the ceiling with the Big Red One insignia on it while the entire audience sang "Joyeux Anniversaire." It was very sweet. I chuckled at the razzle-dazzle, feeling like the Zero Mostel character in Mel Brooks's *The Producers,* celebrating a preordained flop.

The words of the great cinematographer Henri Alekan were ringing in my brain: "Be serious about the movie business without taking it too seriously." Brooding was never in my nature anyway. I'd take the box-office disaster of *Street of No Return* in my stride. There were still plenty more yarns in me.

56

Still Burning
Inside

Working has always been synonymous with living for me. What difference that I was pushing eighty? Inside, the fires were still burning. Not once did the thought of "retiring" cross my mind. No matter your age, filmmaking means taking chances, so you'd better enjoy living on the edge. Each movie project propels you into a strange new orbit, taking you to a unique place with distinct dilemmas. Maybe you do a picture to exorcise old demons. Then your yarn makes you start grinding your teeth all over again, tormented by images that you've concocted—say, of pitiful chickens cooped up in dark cages under deathly red lights.

Who the hell could have predicted that I'd cast thousands of French chickens as extras in my next movie project? It was a British-French TV coproduction that was part of a series based on a Patricia Highsmith short story. The producers had asked me to pick out a Highsmith tale from over a dozen that dealt with mankind tampering with ecology then suffering nature's revenge. Highsmith's "The Day of Reckoning" seemed the most fun and challenging to turn into a movie. It was about a couple involved in industrial chicken farming. The animals are kept in rows and rows of cages, then systematically slaughtered for processing into packaged meat or animal food. The husband is greedy, his wife, restless, and their disturbed teenage daughter drowns herself in a silo filled with chicken feed.

Christa cowrote a damn good script with me. For inspiration, we reread some of those formulaic detective tales from the forties like "The Case of the Lame Canary," by Erle Stanley Gardner, and "Bats Fly at Dusk," by A. A. Fair. I knew Highsmith's work from the many screen adaptations of her writings. My favorites were Alfred Hitchcock's *Strangers on a Train* (1951), with Farley Granger, and René Clément's *Plein Soleil* (*Purple Sun*, 1960), with Alain Delon. Not to mention Wim Wenders's *American Friend* (1977), which I'd appeared in, based on *Ripley's Game*.

The Day of Reckoning wouldn't be green-lighted until Highsmith herself had approved our script. She did. When we met the grand dame in Paris during a stopover on her way home to Switzerland, she told us she loved our adaptation. The film was to be a twelve-day shoot on a strict budget with everything tightly synchronized. We cast French actor Philippe Léotard to play the greedy husband and Spanish-born Assumpta Serna as his sensual wife. Cris Campion, who'd played opposite Walter Matthau in Roman Polanski's *Pirates* (1986), got cast as the handsome nephew who destabilizes the wife and flirts with her teenage daughter. For that role, our own Samantha was perfect. She'd watched us working on the script and wanted to be part of it. I could hardly believe Samantha was already an adolescent. She was a natural in front of the camera and enjoyed being on set, most recently in Portugal as an extra on *Street of No Return*. Wasn't it only yesterday that I was making up bedtime stories for her with our own characters, Nuki and Mush? She was no longer that sweet little girl, but a testy adolescent playing loud music and talking back to her parents. Samantha's teenage hormones were on full throttle. Though she was in her rebel phase, Samantha made her papa proud when it came time to do her job on *The Day of Reckoning*.

While we were in preproduction, the unit manager was scouting for just the right chicken farm as our principal location. They chose a place not far from Paris. The first time I went inside the coop where they raised the birds, the odor and the cackling were overwhelming. The crew had to wear masks. Though we spent many intense hours inside that horrible place, we never really got used to it. I swore I'd never eat another goddamned piece of chicken.

At the end of our movie, the wife locks the husband in the coop and releases the chickens. The animals go mad and peck the poor sonofabitch to death. To film that scene, hundreds of chickens were to be set loose in a closed courtyard. What we didn't know was that the poor animals would be driven mad by their first contact with direct sunlight. The farm owner did. Since the animals were soon going to be slaughtered anyway, he was only too willing to have them die and charge the producers for damaged poultry, making double money on the deal. It was one of the saddest, most agonizing spectacles I'd ever witnessed. Blinded and terrified, the maniacal chickens scurried around until they finally dropped dead on the ground right in front of our crew. We hurriedly shot the scene before the chickens were nothing more than a sea of quivering feathers.

With Anthony Perkins introducing our episode, *The Day of Reckoning* turned out to be one of the most popular programs in the Highsmith series. We managed to get the chicken feathers out of our hair and clothes, but it would be a long time before I could put the terrible sight of all those crazed

*Sharing a good
cigar with
Australian director
George Miller
(of* Mad Max
fame*) at the
Avoriaz Film
Festival in France*

animals out of my mind. I was so agitated, I couldn't sleep for many nights. I'd get up, go in my office, and put on a Beethoven concert or symphony. That helped a helluva lot. Then I leafed through my frayed poetry anthology, rereading one of the poems that always soothed my spirits. It was "The Day Is Done," by Henry Wadsworth Longfellow, which concluded:

> *. . . And the night shall be filled with music*
> *And the cares that infest the day,*
> *Shall fold their tents, like the Arabs,*
> *And as silently steal away.*

The good thing about all those insane chickens was that they got my creative juices really stirred up. I'd been dabbling with a novel called *Brainquake* for quite a while. Now I decided to finish it. Writing without distractions was getting hard at our place on rue de la Baume. The telephone was constantly ringing with an invitation to something or other, a wheeler-dealer pitching his movie project, or an earnest film student writing a doctoral thesis about my films. Good friends were always stopping by, ending up at our table for long meals. Samantha and her teenage pals made quite a racket, too. I decided I needed to get the hell out of Paris so that I could concentrate on the book. Our good friend in Provence, Jerry Rudes, had invited me to stay with him at his place outside Avignon. I took him up on the offer in the summer of '91, hopping on a train with my manuscript and a couple boxes of cigars.

Jerry set me up in a quiet room on the second floor of his cozy house overlooking the Rhône. I didn't need much more than a good table and chair, an ashtray, and a small bed in one corner next to a nightstand. Christa had shipped down my Royal. Besides the birds chirping and the

Mistral blowing, there was hardly any noise to distract me. It was a writer's paradise. I got into a terrific groove in Provence, and in about five weeks, I'd finished *Brainquake*. It opened with a bang:

> Sixty seconds before the baby shot its father, leaves fell lazily in Central Park. Sparrow-weight with bulging jugular, the balloon peddler's face appeared coated in white ashes of cow dung used against flies, but the pallor was really from his anemia.

Brainquake was about a bagman named Paul who delivers cash for the mob day and night in an old black leather bag. Paul drops off thousands of dollars with judges, police commissioners, CEOs, lawyers, assemblymen. Everyone's on the take. Paul never opens the bag or utters a word. Bagmen are a special breed of colorless guys who strictly obey the mob's rules. No girlfriends or wives. No friends. No hobbies. No alcohol or dope. No gambling. No talking. No quitting. Break a rule, and they eliminate you immediately.

Paul secretly suffers from seizures. I coined the term "brainquake" for the attacks that send tidal waves of pain through his head. The novel had a bunch of colorful characters: Michelle, the ivory-faced young woman whom Paul falls for; Zara, the black homicide detective who nails killers with a sexy flair all her own; Father Flanagan, a professional hit man who crucifies his victims; Cornelius Hampshire, czar of the civilized and uncivilized worlds of crime; and Captain Lafitte, a colorful war veteran and now skipper of a barge navigating the rivers and canals of France.

Down in Provence, I remember one interruption to my writing, a middleweight title fight that took place one August night in what was left of the Roman coliseum in the nearby town of Arles. One of Jerry's journalist pals invited us. We had swell ringside seats. Before the fight began, the announcer introduced me to the big crowd, and I took a bow. I hadn't been to a prizefight since the thirties. Back then, sportswriters like Ring Lardner and William Farnsworth would let me tag along with them to see Jack Dempsey, Jack Sharkey, Max Baer, and Primo Carnera in fights at Madison Square Garden. Arles was a million years and a million miles from Manhattan.

The manuscript for *Brainquake* knocked around some major publishers in New York without any bites. I had a meeting in Paris about the book with a top literary agent, Swifty Lazar, the man who'd sold Nixon's autobiography. Lazar returned my manuscript several weeks later from Beverly Hills with a note that the book was "too European." A French publisher, Les Belles Lettres, published it in French in 1993 as *Cerebro-Choc*. It has since come out in several other languages, but ironically never in the language in which it was written.

Most of the young editors in the States who passed on *Brainquake* didn't know much about my movies or my other books. I was like a foreigner in my own country, nothing more than a flicker in the history of American cinema. In France, by contrast, I was always treated with esteem. I couldn't take a subway or a bus without people recognizing me and coming up to talk to me. President François Mitterrand and his culture minister, Jack Lang, had always made quite a fuss, annointing me "Commander of the Arts and Letters," whatever the hell that was. The French had been good to me, and I'd never forget it.

Christa and I were fed up with living in the chic and expensive Eighth Arrondissement. What we wanted was a more working-class quarter with its markets, bakeries, bistros, and corner cafés. We found a little apartment we could afford on the other side of town, not far from the Lyon train station, and bought it. Our new neighbors on rue de Reuilly were everything except bourgeois. They went off to regular jobs early in the morning, hung out their wet laundry in the interior courtyard, and fed their cats on windowsills. People from other apartments in the building sometimes gathered in the courtyard to gossip or share picnics. We loved the authentic atmosphere of our new home in Paris, even if it was quite small. Rue de Reuilly simplified our lives and put us in touch with hardworking French people, a tough, vigorous lot. But it also squeezed Christa, Samantha, and me into a sharply reduced space, making us sometimes feel like we were living in a sardine can.

We developed a special fondness for one of our new neighbors, a solitary old lady named Madame Simone who lived with a few cats. Born in Brittany, she'd never married, working at a menial job in a nearby hospital. Neighbors would drop off food at Madame Simone's front door to help her out, because she evidently had trouble paying her bills. One time, the bags of fruit and vegetables on her threshold remained untouched for a couple of days. That's how we discovered that she'd died. We learned later it was a lung embolism and that Madame Simone was only in her fifties, though she looked twenty years older. There was a collection among the neighbors so that she could get a simple funeral in her native village in Brittany. The cats were adopted by everybody, and we went on watering the rose bush in front of the apartment. A couple of distant relatives showed up from Brittany and gave away all the crucifixes and Virgin Marys that Madame Simone had been collecting for years. They must have brought her contentment and peace. Samantha was sad about the loss of our neighbor but surprised me with her sharp comment that

Madame Simone belonged more to the nineteenth than to the twentieth century. For school, Samantha was reading Flaubert's *Un Coeur Simple* (*A Simple Heart*), and we'd been discussing the story. In her naïve good faith, our deceased neighbor reminded us of Felicity in Flaubert's tale. We'd miss her.

That fall I was invited to Japan for the presentation of the Japanese translation of *Il Était une Fois Samuel Fuller.* Our hosts would also be screening a number of my movies as part of a retrospective. It would be great to revisit Tokyo with my wife and daughter. I hadn't been there since I'd shot *House of Bamboo,* thirty-five years before, and I was anxious to see how it had changed. The trip would also be a welcome respite to our crammed existence in Paris.

We were put up in a modern hotel in Tokyo, too modern for cantankerous Samantha, who had illusions of sleeping on a bamboo mat. I could hardly recognize the city, so drastic were the changes from the fifties. Gone were the little houseboats on the river. Everything was now covered with asphalt. Aluminum and glass buildings soared up into the sky. Japan was a world power again, economically vibrant. Western-style music was being played everywhere. T-shirts, blue jeans, and American-style hairdos were standard fare. The theater in Tokyo's Shibaku district where they showed my pictures was packed with avid fans. Their love of movies was unchanged. Men and women came up to me afterward with bouquets of flowers, the Japanese custom of showing satisfaction and respect. At a press conference and in one-on-one interviews, journalists wanted to know why *White Dog,* which was so well received in Japan, had never been released in the States. I retold the story, but it was still tough talking about that debacle.

A reunion was organized with Shirley Yamaguchi, my leading lady from *House of Bamboo.* Shirley had gone into politics and was by then a senator. She came to visit with us at the hotel with a slew of bodyguards. I was so happy to see her again. She was still as warm and beautiful as ever, with those high cheekbones and twinkling almond-shaped eyes. Shirley and I reminisced about the delightful Robert Ryan, who'd since passed away. One of the bodyguards signaled it was time to go. The senator was on a tight schedule. Shirley stood to bid us farewell, first kissing Christa and Samantha good-bye. I put my arms around her and held her for a moment. It was beautiful but hard to swallow that this was probably the last time we'd meet up, at least on earth.

A Tokyo magazine had organized a trip for me to the Lafcadio Hearn Museum, in the coastal town of Matsue, on the Sea of Japan. I'd often spoken to the press about my love of Lafcadio Hearn, the first Westerner to penetrate Japanese culture and write extensively about it. First, we took a train to Kyoto, visiting the Buddhist monasteries there with their lush, peaceful landscaping. Samantha got her wish to sleep on a mat on the floor and eat her fill of sushi. From Kyoto, we boarded a small plane to Matsue, arriving exactly one hundred years after Hearn went there.

Hearn had come to Matsue in 1890 on a magazine assignment and stayed on to teach in the local school. He'd ended up marrying his house-keeper, Setzu, who was in disgrace because her samurai husband had left her penniless. Hearn became a Japanese citizen in 1895 under the name of Yakumo Koizumi. Nowadays, the townspeople of Matsue were only too happy to commercialize his legacy, having learned a few American tricks about attaching Hearn's name to souvenirs—coffee, tea, noodles, any-thing—in order to turn a few yen with the tourists.

Hearn's grandson, Bon Koizumi, and his lovely wife, Shoho, invited us to share a meal with them at their home. They didn't speak any English, so a translator tried to keep up with me as I told them how I'd always been intrigued by Hearn.

"And your grandmother, what a woman she must have been!" I told Bon enthusiastically.

Before I knew it, I was describing scenes to them from a movie about Hearn that I'd have loved to make, a love story between Hearn and Setzu overlaid with Japanese folklore. Intercut into my picture, I explained, would be animated sequences from Hearn's wonderful fairy tales.

I promised the Koizumis that I'd try to find a producer for the film, keeping them abreast of our progress. Back in Paris, I'd do more research on Hearn, rereading some of his wonderful books and fairy tales, then knocking out a treatment. Through friends, a Japanese producer living in Germany contacted me about backing the picture, but then never came up with the dough. I wished I could've gotten on the phone with a big-time producer like Darryl Zanuck and jumped right into making that pic-ture. I considered approaching Steven Spielberg about the project because it seemed to be up his alley. By then, he was not only directing but pro-ducing movies, too. But even if Steven had always been respectful of me, we didn't have that kind of relationship. It would've looked like begging, and my pride wouldn't allow that.

The Koizumis regularly wrote to us from Japan. In one letter, they announced the birth of a baby son, assuring the perpetuation of the Hearn clan. Someone will make a pisscutter of a film about that boy's great-grandfather someday. But it won't be me.

Metamorphosis of a Melody

During my years in Paris, I remained an outsider. I paid no attention to anti-American slurs, especially in French filmmaker circles. Jealousies and national rivalries were going to be felt by any American living abroad. That stuff didn't mean a damn thing to me. I felt fortunate to be in our new working-class digs on rue de Reuilly, set back from the busy street, the aromas of fresh-baked bread, mint tea, and beef stew wafting through the courtyard. I was as comfortable as Albert Einstein must have been, living the end of his life in a modest neighborhood in Princeton.

Don't get me wrong, I was only putting my lifestyle on a par with Albert's, not my accomplishments. I've never been the least tempted to evaluate my place in movie history. I'll leave that to the specialists. Hunkered down in a corner of our bedroom where I'd set up a makeshift office, all I was thinking about were the yarns I was spinning. My old Royal was still banging away, thanks to my friend Curtis Hanson, who would send over my favorite silk ribbons from a Santa Monica stationery store. I was so proud to see cool, sensible Curtis fulfilling his potential as a top-class director.

Every morning, before I started writing, I'd go out for my typical walk, stopping at a nearby café to have a coffee and croissant and read the *Herald Tribune*. On my way home, I'd buy a couple of baguettes for the family, sometimes strolling back along boulevard Diderot. Diderot, what balls on that guy, secretly printing his groundbreaking, seventeen-volume encyclopedia even after the King's Council formally forbade it![1] Other mornings, I'd walk along rue Faubourg-Saint Antoine, past where the hated Bastille prison fortress used to stand, where so many political prisoners of every class were locked up. The Bastille was one of the first buildings destroyed in 1789 at the outbreak of the bloody French Revolution. I loved strolling in Paris, where every corner, square, and quarter was steeped in history. And what a violent history it was.

The French had always tagged me as a "violent" director. My movies are frank. But violent? Maybe, but it's relative. You switch on a TV anywhere in the world, and all you get is violence—news, video clips, ads, TV movies, nonstop, day and night. I'm not condoning it. But for cryin' out loud, violence is an inescapable part of our heritage, like greed, sex, religion, or politics, a constant theme in human history, no matter the continent or culture. To deny its existence is to be a goddamned hypocrite. How much violence can a filmmaker legitimately show audiences in his or her story? Does violence on the screen encourage people, especially youngsters, to be destructive? These are valid questions. I don't have the answers.

I remember the premiere of Sam Peckinpah's *The Wild Bunch* (1969), at the DGA theater in Los Angeles, with its beautiful cinematography and bloody battles. The first twenty minutes of *The Wild Bunch,* with the children watching red ants devouring scorpions, was just great. DGA members got very upset with the film's brutal images. Critics railed. Hell, I didn't care how many critics took Peckinpah to task. I agreed with him about wanting people to be aware of the danger of desensitizing violence by making audiences feel the horror and the pain.

Back in 1978, when I was in preproduction for *The Big Red One,* Peckinpah phoned me and offered to be my second-unit director on the picture without salary. It wasn't a joke. I was touched by the gesture. Sam and I were living a similar paradox. We both were known as tough guys making tough films. The yarns we chose to tell weren't comedies. There was action, drawn from real life, and many times disturbed, flawed, or tyrannical characters who, based on their nature, resorted to violence. What Peckinpah and I feared most was people becoming indifferent to violence. He'd served in the Marine Corps and detested war. I'd been an infantryman and was tortured the rest of my life by the atrocities I'd witnessed on the front lines. We knew the truth about violence, that it was visceral, merciless, and unnecessary. We also knew it wasn't glamorous.

I talked to Peckinpah about my novel *The Rifle,* set in the Vietnam War. The yarn began as a script, but when no producer was willing to back it, I wrote it as a book, following a rifle as it moved through the hands of combatants and civilians caught up in the strife. Peckinpah loved my slant. He was one of a dying breed in Hollywood, a straight shooter who told you what he thought whether you liked it or not. How could I not empathize with a guy who'd fought tooth and nail for his vision of a movie, tangling with any studio trying to tamper with his final cut? I missed Sam.

My old body started playing tricks on me. At my yearly checkup, Doctor Weinberger discovered a lump that turned out to be an aneurysm. A top French surgeon, Professor Lagneau, operated a few days later at the

Thank God for Beethoven's music. Ludwig got me through a lot of rough times. He said, "Music is a higher revelation than all wisdom and philosophy." Holy cow, was he right!

American Hospital, inserting a prosthesis to save my life. All the doctors and nurses were simply terrific. In no time I was back on my feet, gradually able to resume my morning walks around the neighborhood, only at a slower pace than before.

While recovering from that operation, I got a call from Israeli filmmaker Amos Gitai. He wanted to cast me in a film that he was about to shoot in Paris called *Golem, The Spirit of the Exile* (1992), the last part of his trilogy that began with *Esther* (1986) and *Berlin-Jerusalem* (1989). Anxious to get back to work but still not up to full speed, I got Amos's assurance that my role was passive. I was to play the venerable Elimelech, who was dead. Hell, you can't get more passive than a corpse! The cast Amos assembled was impressive: filmmakers Bernardo Bertolucci and Philippe Garrel; actresses Marisa Paredes from Spain, Hanna Schygulla from Germany, and Ophrah Shemesh from Israel; and the critic Bernard Eisenschitz. To top it off, Amos's DP was the legendary cameraman Henri Alekan, who was a few years older than me.[2] Damn it, if Alekan was doing *Golem,* so was I.

Amos's script was based on the Old Testament and the sixteenth-century cabalistic legend about wise men who could instill life in effigies, or "golems." My scenes took place in a courtyard at the Gare du Nord train station. Amos, a talented storyteller, loved mixing the contemporary and the ancient, juxtaposing shots of Paris with scenes from the Middle East, supposedly ancient Moab. According to the Book of Ruth, Naomi, her husband, Elimelech, and their family, including their daughter-in-law, Ruth, took refuge in Moab from a famine in Bethlehem. Played by the beautiful Ophrah Shemesh, Naomi is bereaved by the loss of her old husband. She tries to breathe life back into Elimelech's corpse, but it's hopeless. It was good being on a movie set again, lying there under the hot lights and busy crew with my eyes closed and Ophrah's mouth close to mine, her exotic perfume filling my nostrils. So what if I didn't have any lines and was half asleep? It beat the crap out of being cooped up in a hospital room that smelled of ammonia.

Amos Gitai's film turned out beautifully. Working on it was hypnotic. I was hooked on the guy's worldly vision. Gitai was well read and thoughtful, with a smart, attractive wife and two beautiful children. At a young age, he'd lost his father, a respected architect and one of the founders of the Bauhaus school of design in Berlin. I loved the way Amos had sent for his mother, then in her eighties, to be with her son and grandchildren on location.

By the time we'd finished *Golem,* Amos and I had become friends. He asked me to take part in another of his pet projects, a live spectacle—part theater, part opera—called *Metamorphosis of a Melody.* Amos was going to produce and direct this grand event in a Roman amphitheater at Gibbelina, on the island of Sicily, near Palermo, in the summer of 1992. His script was based on the writings of Flavius Josephus, the Jewish historian whose seven-volume *History of the Jewish War* described the revolt by the Jewish Zealots against Roman rule.[3] Begun in A.D. 66, the uprising was finally squelched in A.D. 73 after a two-year siege of the mountain fortress at Masada. As the world now knows, a thousand men, women, and children killed themselves rather than surrender to the Roman Tenth Legion in Masada, today an Israeli shrine.

I was to play Flavius, narrating the Roman armies' destruction of Jerusalem, while an international cast acted out scenes across Gibbelina's amphitheater, its massive white stones in chaos since an earthquake had struck it a few decades earlier. My fellow cast members were from many countries, all speaking or singing in their native tongues, be it Hebrew, Italian, French, German, or English. Many were nonactors like Jerome Koenig, who played Titus, the general in command of the Roman armies. Koenig was a newspaperman from New York. Eating and working together, we were like a big family that wonderful summer in Sicily.

My narrative was lifted directly from Flavius's writings. For the other actors, Amos weaved together artful passages borrowed from Oscar Wilde and Rainer Maria Rilke. To make the show contemporary and ballsy, Amos took some flights of fancy, like having Roman soldiers ride in on Harley-Davidson motorcycles as their chariots. The show was an amazing gamble, mixing fact with poetry and fantasy to create an emotional, haunting evening, revisiting that terrible, two-thousand-year-old conflict.

Amos and I shared a passion for unearthing historical events to get a better perspective on our own times. He was amazed that I knew a helluva lot about Flavius Josephus. I told him I owned my own copy of *Jewish War,* which once belonged to President Andrew Jackson. My guess was that Flavius had tried to be as impartial as he could, but his writings also had to glorify Roman power and military prowess. After all, he was on their payroll. Any modern reader of Flavius's account is impressed by the Jews' strength and tenacity. A helluva war correspondent, Flavius's descriptions of atrocities were still moving two millennia later:

> All human feelings, alas, yield to hunger, of which decency is always the first victim; for when hunger reigns, restraint is abandoned. Wives snatched food out of husbands' mouths, children out of fathers' mouths, and the most sorrowful sight of all: mothers snatching food out of their babies' mouths. Everywhere the partisans were ready to swoop on such pickings. Wherever they saw a locked door, they rushed in, and hardly stopped short at squeezing throats to force out the morsels of food! No one was spared or pitied.

For the premiere of *Metamorphosis of a Melody,* the amphitheater at Gibbelina was packed. Electricity was in the air. The lights came down. Then a small spot came up on me, sitting on a podium just above the audience, the battlefield behind. No silly toga and sandals for me, I wore jeans, a sweater, and a jacket.

"Ruins," I said, beginning the performance, "that is all that is left of the city." Playing Flavius with conviction was a natural. I empathized with the man's passion for recounting war experiences, his exactitude as a reporter, his good fortune to have survived those violent times. "A bitter war between two factions. And in the midst of all of this was the people, like one great body writhing in agony, yet still breathing."

Metamorphosis of a Melody was an unabashed success. My participation was exciting for me because it was a journey back to my roots as a crime reporter. I was thrilled that Amos Gitai had taken me with him to Sicily. I'd last seen the island's turquoise skies and deep blue Mediterranean waters in July 1943. Back then, the star-studded nights were distressful and restless, as I lay thinking of the next day's battles. Now in the twilight of my life, the same crystal-clear night skies filled me with a sense of peace and contentment. I smelled the scent of jasmine and lemon blossoms, put aside thoughts of wars and movies, and relished the marvelous gift of life.

Amos Gitai announced he was putting on *Metamorphosis* the following summer in Italy as part of the renowned *Biennale* of Venice. He was enthusiastic about wanting me in it again. Though I wasn't used to being a member of another director's family of actors, the satisfaction of playing Flavius was matched by my delight at being able to contribute to a work of such force and harmony. "Next summer in Venice" sounded damned good to my ears. I told Amos I'd do it, but only if I were still alive.

58

Long, Long
Thoughts

Y ou gotta be kidding!"

Wim Wenders was calling to tell me Japanese designer Yohji Yamamoto wanted me to model some of his new clothes in a Paris fashion show. Me, a model in a fashion show? I trusted Wenders completely, but, for Chrissakes, this had to be a joke. My everyday wardrobe looked like it had come from the local thrift shop, peppered with cigar burns and coffee stains. Yamamoto's offer was for real. I hesitated until I saw Samantha get all excited about her daddy being in a fashion show. I said I'd do it.

The walkway was lined with fashion critics, bright lights, and photographers. I came out three times in three different outfits. A flock of Yamamoto's assistants backstage helped me change. As I strolled onstage, there was a helluva ovation, pop music pounding and photographers' cameras clicking. For a guy who'd never given a good goddamn about his outward appearance, there I was strutting up and down the runway, my long white hair brushed back like a lion's mane, as I cockily looked left and right at the noisy onlookers and flashing cameras. At the end of the show, Yamamoto joined all the models onstage and the audience went wild. The biggest thrill for me was the look in my daughter's eyes. She was so proud of her father.

Afterward, Yamamoto organized a dinner for his crew and models. Late that night, Christa, Samantha, and I walked back home along the banks of the Seine. We were in a great mood after the memorable evening, singing silly songs like drunken sailors as we strolled together. With the two women of my life on either arm, I considered myself damned lucky.

Harvard University hosted the Avignon Film Festival in the spring of 1993, calling the American version of the event "Avignon/Cambridge." Screenings of my films were set up along with a parallel series of discussions and panels with students and teachers. We flew over to Boston with Jerry Rudes to participate. The Harvard Film Archive decided to give me

Why a top designer like Yohji Yamamoto would want me in his fashion show was a mystery, but there I was, strolling down the runway and feeling proud to be there.

some kind of achievement award. I was touched more deeply than they could imagine. After all, here I was being recognized by one of the world's greatest institutions of higher learning, and I'd never even finished high school.

From Boston, we took a delightful train ride down to New York City. Christa had never been to Manhattan before, and I wanted to show it to her myself. Like the multitudes of tourists, we visited some of Manhattan's most famous landmarks. Christa loved it all, the towering skyscrapers, the noise, the energy, the light. Among the must-sees, we went down to Park Row, the street that used to be the epicenter of American journalism, and up to Washington Heights, where Rebecca Fuller had moved our family in 1923 to give her fatherless children new opportunities.

One evening we had a delightful meal with a group of young filmmaker friends, including Mika Kaurismäki, Jim Jarmusch, and Sara Driver. The conversation somehow turned to my old Bell & Howell 16-mm camera and the footage of my 1954 visit to Brazil that was stored away at the Shack. I told them how Zanuck sent me into the jungles of South America to scout locations for a movie called *Tigrero* that I was supposed to do for Fox. Over dinner, Christa suggested we all take a journey back into the same jungles today and make a movie about the adventure. Mika and Jim loved the idea of returning with me to Brazil's Mato Grosso forty years later. By the third bottle of wine, Mika had promised to write a treatment, put together financing, and get a crew. Christa would recover my old footage in California so that it could be incorporated into the new movie. Jim would be my sidekick on this escapade, and Sara would shoot stills.

Knowing how few movie projects actually get any further than animated dinner-table conversations, I played it cool. Sure, it was thrilling to fantasize about a journey back into the Mato Grosso. Would we even be able to locate the Karajá tribe, the joyful, generous Indians who'd welcomed me into their village in the fifties? The prospect made my heart beat wildly. Outwardly, I gave the young, upbeat filmmakers a paternal smile, grateful for their support and love. I said I'd do the picture, half-expecting them to fail to put together the project.

During our stay in New York, Jonathan Demme invited us for lunch at his country home up in Nyack. An assistant picked up Christa and me and drove us north along the Hudson. As I puffed on my cigar and gazed out the car window, I thought about my old health-crazed boss, Bernarr Macfadden of the *New York Evening Graphic,* who'd lived in Nyack and actually walked into Manhattan barefoot. Thinking about the *Graphic* and the twenties made me remember my friend and mentor Gene Fowler. Then my mind wandered to all those other remarkable characters I'd crossed paths with in the twenties. My reverie was interrupted when the car pulled up at Jonathan's tasteful New England–style cottage. Jonathan and his wife, Joanne, couldn't have been sweeter or more gracious. Their two beautiful kids, Ramona and Brooklyn, were delightful.

While the hamburgers were cooking on the outdoor grill, we drank

Walking with Jerry Rudes to a seminar at Harvard University as special guest of Avignon/Cambridge. Behind us are (left) cinematographer John Bailey and (right) Columbia Studio vice president Michael Schlesinger. Christa is directly behind me, unseen, gabbing to the boys.

wine, chatted, and laughed at each other's anecdotes. Despite having just made two of the outstanding movies of the nineties, *The Silence of the Lambs* (1991) and *Philadelphia* (1993), Jonathan was still the same unpretentious, congenial guy we'd known for the last twenty years. Out of the blue, he turned to me and said the goddamnedest thing: "Sam, Marty Scorsese and I want to produce a Fuller movie."

My cigar almost fell out of my mouth. Holy mackerel, two of the world's most respected filmmakers wanted to back my next picture!

"For real?"

"We're serious," said Demme. "What've you got for us?"

Suddenly all the juices started to flow, my brain was afire, and my heart was pounding like a youngster. My daydreaming during the ride up from Manhattan suddenly made perfect sense.

"Ruth Snyder!" I said excitedly, grabbing Jonathan's arm tightly. "Ruth Snyder, for Chrissakes, that's what!"

Ruth Snyder, the first woman executed in the United States in the electric chair. The date was frozen in my memory—Friday, January 12, 1928—as was the tabloid shot of Ruth at Sing Sing. It was one of the biggest stories Gene Fowler had ever covered, probably the biggest of the decade, knocking everything—Sacco and Vanzetti, even President Coolidge—off the front page.

I explained to Jonathan that Ruth Snyder had been damned, applauded, shunned, envied, and devoured by newspaper readers across America. Her love affair with Judd Gray and their complicity in the murder of her husband, Albert, had inspired James M. Cain's novel *The Postman Always Rings Twice.* Cain's book had been turned into a play in 1936, and adapted twice for the movies, first in 1946, with Lana Turner, then in 1981, with Jessica Lange. I'd always wanted to do the yarn my own way, not like those pictures or Lawrence Kasdan's *Body Heat* (1981), coined from the lustful aspects of the story.

"You're going to be Ruth Snyder for fourteen years, my boy!" I told Jonathan. "From 1914 to 1928, you'll live inside Ruth's passionate, complex head. And on that Friday morning in January of 1928, you'll burn with her as thousands of volts surge through your body!"

Excited with my Ruth Snyder yarn, I forgot how hard I was squeezing Jonathan's arm. He was thoroughly enjoying my impassioned pitch, relishing the heady atmosphere of the freewheeling twenties. Back then, I was still a copyboy dreaming of becoming a crime reporter. Ruth Snyder had fascinated me ever since her case exploded across every front page in the country. I described for Jonathan the national media circus that swelled around the pro- and anti-Ruth camps, those bellowing for Ruth to get the chair and those clamoring for Ruth to be spared, bolstered by a national outcry of injustice that rose out of the Sacco and Vanzetti electrocutions in August 1927. I'd weave some of that era's remarkable characters into my yarn, reporters Gene Fowler, Damon Runyon, and Rhea Gore, *Chicago Tribune* news photographer Tom Howard, *New York Evening World* editor Charles Chapin, boxer Jess Willard, poet Carl Sandburg, evangelist Billy Sunday, New York governor Alfred E. Smith, Sing Sing prison warden Lewis E. Lawes, and pioneer moviemaker D. W. Griffith. I already had a title for the movie: *The Chair vs. Ruth Snyder.*

After the picnic with Jonathan Demme, I could hardly sleep. I kept waking up in the middle of the night to jot down notes for my Ruth Snyder yarn. Before we returned to Paris, Marty Scorsese invited us over to dinner at his place, a narrow, black, ultramodern skyscraper next to Carnegie Hall. We ate in an elegant private dining room about forty floors up. Along with Marty, there was his longtime editor, Thelma Schoonmaker, and actress Illeana Douglas. Marty loved my stories about the old studio days, working with Zanuck, so I tried not to disappoint him. We finally got around to discussing the Ruth Snyder project. Marty reconfirmed that he and Jonathan were committed to coproducing *The Chair vs. Ruth Snyder,* though he was especially aware of the difficulties of making period movies after adapting *The Age of Innocence* (1993). Their plan was to get one of the studios to put up the dough, then guide the project, shielding me from all the pitfalls.

As Christa and I flew back to France, I stared out the window of the jet at the passing clouds, feeling as if I'd sprouted wings myself. Like the mythical fire bird, the phoenix consumed by flames yet reborn from his own ashes, this old fart was getting new opportunities. I had reason to rejoice. Not only had I survived the risky aorta operation, but I'd weathered all the years of pitching yarns to wheeler-dealers who didn't really have the power to get movies made. I'd been able to scratch out a living for my family while holding my head high. Best of all, Samantha's cancer was in remission. My daughter was developing into a well-rounded young woman, preparing her *baccalauréat* diploma at a private French *lycée*. The Ruth Snyder picture, endorsed by Scorsese and Demme, was the icing on the cake.

Back in Paris, nobody could take my wings away from me. I plunged back into the twenties. I was only sixteen when Ruth went to the chair, so I needed to open up my memory full throttle and be as scrupulously accurate as possible about the facts. Gene Fowler, Damon Runyon, and H. L. Mencken were high on my reading list. Fowler's great *A Solo in Tom Toms* opens with a quote I loved, from a poem by Longfellow:

> *A boy's will is the wind's will,*
> *And the thoughts of youth are long, long thoughts.*

My brain was humming. Images, scenes, and even smells, Proust-like, came back to me. I was greatly assisted by Runyon's wit—"The race is not always to the swift, nor the battle to the strong but that's the way to bet"— and the sagacity of Mencken—"A celebrity is one who is known to many persons he is glad he doesn't know." I also reread Flaubert's *Emma Bovary* to remind myself of how he'd given a newspaper story passion and soul.

Still remarkably agile, my old hands started to bang away on my Royal. Neighbors passing underneath our windows heard the tap, tap, tapping, and went quietly on their way, knowing I was too absorbed to gibble-gabble. I didn't shave, and I rarely changed my clothes. Christa had to coax me out of my little office for meals. Unsociable and uncouth, I ate hastily and hurried back to work. It was a great time, my mind bubbling with ideas. I let it loose to gallop at full speed down the racetrack to the finish line. Maybe I was just coming full circle, back to a precious time in my life when everything seemed possible.

Developing a pisscutter of a movie from scratch was what I loved doing most. I went to work on a treatment recreating the sensational atmosphere surrounding the first-degree murder trial of *State of New York vs. Ruth Snyder*. Ruth was a daunting character. Millions of words had been written about her. She was the "granite woman" who killed in cold blood, a saint, a sex maniac, a drunk, a whore, an egomaniac, a Joan of Arc. One of the first lightning rods of female liberation, Ruth received over twenty-five hundred letters from women approving of her homicidal revolt against marital bondage. Men found her irresistible, too. Waiting in her cell, only a short walk to the horrible room where the electric chair would fry her to death, Ruth received 164 separate offers of marriage. Most important to her were the poignant notes from her nine-year-old daughter, praying for her to come home soon. But Ruth wasn't ever going anywhere, except to the electric chair, guilty as charged.

Jonathan Demme called me regularly to see how I was progressing. He informed us that actress Laura Dern wanted to play Ruth. Dern seemed perfect for the role. An important factor in getting the picture off the ground would be the fact that she'd starred in Steven Spielberg's *Jurassic Park* (1993), a box-office smash. Everything seemed to be coming together. I wasn't going to let my natural skepticism put any salt on my wings. Still flying high, I finished the 112-page treatment and sent it off to Demme and Scorsese. With all my heart and soul, I trusted that the Ruth Snyder picture was going to happen.

Meanwhile, Christa shipped Mika Kaurismäki all my footage from my 1954 trip to Brazil. Happily, Mika had raised enough money to produce our documentary/road movie that was to be called *Tigrero: A Film That Was Never Made*. Going back to the Amazon to revisit the Karajá was something I'd been dreaming about for a long time, and I was finally getting my chance, accompanied by my young filmmaker friends. While Demme and Scorsese were talking to major studios about *The Chair vs. Ruth Snyder*, Christa and I boarded a plane for Brazil. Samantha was happy to have our apartment to herself and her boyfriend-of-the-month.

Throughout the long flight to Rio de Janeiro, memories of my first pilgrimage into the Mato Grosso flashed through my brain. I was nervous about what I'd find down there nowadays. How had four decades changed the Karajá? Would they remember me, with my movie camera and my boxes of cigars? Were they still as kindhearted and content, or had civilization, with its power, greed, and egotism, encroached on their idyllic existence?

59

State of Peace

Kaurismäki's big house in the Santa Theresa quarter of Rio de Janeiro was built during the heyday of Portuguese colonialism. He lived there with his lovely lady, Pia. We all moved into the place to prepare for the shoot. Nowadays, Santa Theresa was afflicted with poverty. I was warned against taking my early-morning walks on those mean streets, but I didn't pay any attention. After soaking up the local sights and sounds, I'd return to Mika's place and sit down under the palm trees in the garden. There I'd light up a cigar, one of the few I permitted myself after the aorta operation. A twelve-year-old girl with big, brown eyes brought me a bowl of caffe latte. She waited at my side until I took a sip.

"*Boa?*" she asked me in Portuguese. "Good?"

"*Boa,*" I repeated.

The little girl was pleased. She was one of several youngsters who helped with the cleaning and cooking in the big, tiled kitchen. Happy to be off the streets, they ate their fill of rice, beans, and breaded fish and made a little dough for their families. They were great kids.

Mika, Jim, and I got down to planning the tricky shoot ahead of us. Along with the DP, Jacques Cheuiche, we talked for hours about my memories of the 1954 trip into the Mato Grosso. Over and over, we watched a video of the footage I'd shot back then. Mika had cooked up a loose shooting script, having Jarmusch and me gibble-gabble as we went along. The dialogue would have to be spontaneous, because no one had any idea of exactly what we'd find on our journey.

Jim and I were an odd couple—he, the tall, irreverent young skeptic, and I, the short, quixotic old curmudgeon. On a beach in front of a fancy Rio hotel, Mika and his crew started shooting our contentious twosome. Hell, a film needs some goddamned conflict, so we found some right away, disagreeing about my chances of ever finding the Karajá Indians and making friends with them again.

With Jim Jarmusch on the beach in Rio before heading inland for the Mato Grosso. Thanks to my young filmmaker friends, my dream of revisiting the Karajà Indians was fulfilled.

"You know, damn it, Jim, my hunch is right, and yours is wrong!" I said, puffing on a cigar. "My hunch is they're going to buy it!"

"It'll never work, Sam," said Jarmusch.

"It's gotta work!"

"Come on, that was forty years ago. They don't even remember who the hell you are."

"We've got to take a crack at it!"

"Sam, I think you're ON crack, man."

I could see the grinning face of Jacques Cheuiche behind the viewfinder, and I knew we were on the right track. Being in the dark about what lay ahead, I realized that that movie was the only one that I'd ever done without knowing the ending before I began. Still, I was game. My only worry was that the Karajá had vanished, leaving nothing more than the images on my old footage. Or worse, that civilization had reached far into the jungle and changed their Xanadu into paradise lost.

The journey wasn't going to be easy, but it would certainly be better than my first one back in the fifties, when riding horses was the fastest means of penetrating into the jungle with mules lugging our equipment. Nowadays, there was a landing strip for our chartered plane at São Felix, a village on the Araguaia River. A short boat trip from there along the "river of the dead," as the Karajá called the Araguaia, would take us near the jungle where the tribe had lived. After seeing all the crocodiles popping out of the river in my old footage, my young friends were uneasy about boating on the Araguaia. I laughed and told them there was nothing to worry about. All they had to do was keep counting their fingers along the way.

The five-hour flight to São Felix was without a hitch. The best motel in town was a dilapidated place with frayed mosquito nets over the beds. Jim and I took a walk down to the banks of the river while Mika and his crew followed us with their equipment.

"Sam, do you remember any of this?"

"The river is the same," I replied, seeing the women washing clothes on the banks. "But the rest is different, so much concrete everywhere."

I saw the worried look on Jim's face.

"Rip van Winkle fell asleep for only twenty years," I told him. "It's been twice as long since I was here!"

A couple days later, we set off down the Araguaia. Jim and I paddled in a dugout canoe while Mika's crew shot the scene from a riverboat at our side. Scouts kept us on course. We finally came to a rise on the bank where natives were watching us from up above. I did a double take. The Indians wore some familiar feather ornaments. Holy cow, they looked like Karajá! We maneuvered the canoe to the shore, got out, and walked up to greet them, with Mika and his crew following.

Their village was so much more developed than the primitive place I'd visited in the fifties. The brush and trees had been cleared away, and there were telephone poles everywhere. Instead of going naked with body paint, now the Karajá wore T-shirts. Curious faces stared at me. Many of the Karajá spoke a little Portuguese. Mika explained the point of our visit. They were just as friendly as I remembered, guiding us back to their village to find rooms for us. Instead of the hand-tied huts that I remembered, they lived in tin-roofed shacks with electricity. Chief Atau and the other elders greeted us warmly, but no one remembered me. I was disappointed. Their faces didn't look familiar to me either.

The next night, Mika's crew set up a movie projector and, for a screen, stretched out a bedsheet between two trees. We were going to show my footage to the Karajá and capture their reactions on film. Everyone was excited about seeing my reels, but no one more than me. I felt more nervous than ever before at a premiere, be it in Hollywood, New York, Paris, or London. That footage was very dear to me, because it was completely authentic. How would the Karajá react to seeing their relatives again on a screen? What would they think of the crazy white man who'd filmed their grandmothers and grandfathers?

Wordlessly, the Karajá watched the opening shots of my arriving in the Mato Grosso forty years before. They were mesmerized. Their faces became even more intense when my scenes of the tribal fertility dance flashed on the screen, women rubbing their bellies, men wearing masks as they pranced around. The only sounds came from giggling youngsters. It was exactly how our kids would react to seeing their grandparents dancing, say, the fox trot. The elders stared silently, then they began to moan or talk to each other, enthralled when a young man's legs were scratched bloody with a piranha's teeth and when newborns were painted with images of fish and jaguars. As people recognized family members, waves of joy washed over the audience. If there was still any doubt, now I knew for sure these people were descendants of the gentle Indians I'd stumbled upon four decades before. I shivered when I thought about what could've happened to me if I'd landed across the Araguaia with the Jervantes or Jivaros, both reputed to be headhunters.

After the screening, Chief Atau made us understand that he did remember me and my cigars. I was thrilled. We smiled at each other, glad to still be alive, bemused at having crossed paths twice. His face was wise and compassionate. We had a chat that Mika filmed for the documentary. Confined to simple sentences, we talked basics. We couldn't tell each other where life had taken us over the last forty years. We didn't have to. Warm smiles and twinkling eyes did most of the talking. Chief Atau saw my deep admiration for his people's graciousness. He showed me his respect and appreciation for my film, something I valued more than any award or critical praise.

Jim, Mika, Pia, and Sara came to realize that everything I'd told them about the Karajá was true. A state of peace still reined over their land. They shared the abundance of nature in a wonderful communal spirit. Harmony and contentment manifested in many ways. The Karajá took care of one another; they were generous and playful with each other; they were kind to strangers. Passions that had pushed our civilization to the brink of destruction, and beyond—greed, hubris, and lust for power—just weren't in their hearts.

To thank us for the screening, two of the elders put on a special dance for us. They wore traditional costumes with feather headdresses, chanting what sounded to us like "Hollywood! Hollywood!" Everyone found it very entertaining and chuckled. I was deeply touched by the gesture. A proud people, the Karajá would never ask for anything. As a present for them, we'd brought along a modern electric stove. After trying it out, they continued cooking over wood fires. It was easier, and food tasted better.

Above the riverbank, there was a majestic tree on a hill. We quickly realized that it was the same tree that had appeared in my fifties footage. I'd framed a couple of Karajá boys shooting arrows by that tree. We sat down there, and some Karajá started to come over and tell me about relatives and friends they'd recognized in my film. An old man remembered the two boys with the bows and arrows. Their names were Kubereue and Iroa. The man explained that the Karajá originally migrated from the Andes in Peru. They'd always lived on the rivers, their most important asset, their bank account. From it, they withdrew all the fish they needed to feed their families. The Karajá considered themselves independent of Brazil. Despite efforts to "civilize" them, the Brazilian government had accorded the tribe special status, letting them remain autonomous but printing the portrait of an old Karajá woman, a storyteller, on a thousand-cruzeiro bill to show they were still part of the nation.

Another man told me he was so happy to see his father as a youngster. His father had been killed while fishing when a crocodile attacked his canoe.

"In your movie, I felt he was alive again."

An old woman, now a widow, spotted her deceased husband as a young man in the footage.

"I miss the safety he gave me," she told me shyly. "He came into my hut one night, and the next morning we were husband and wife."

"Lonely?" I asked.

"Yes, yes," she said. "He was a very good person, very kind and hard-working."

The day came when we had to say good-bye to the Karajá. I had only love and respect for these people. It was a great gift to find them again, still thriving, the women still humming songs as they washed their clothes in the river, the children still munching on mangoes. No need to make any sweeping statements comparing our society to theirs. Except how could the Karajá's simple well-being not make you think about the excesses of our world, our governments' wrongheaded, aggressive policies, not to mention the general decline in decency and good will as Judeo-Christian-Muslim civilizations have accrued military might and economic power?

Making *Tigrero: A Film That Was Never Made* was a powerful experience for me and my young filmmaker friends. We'd expanded our vision of the world by leaping froglike into a strange world. As much as I've been obsessed with my own country's history and development, I better understand America from having seen how other people live in faraway lands, feasting on their charms and plunging into their cultures. I had to go back to the Amazon for a second dose of the Karajá's laughter and harmony to come full circle in my own life.

You young people sitting around watching the goddamned television! Get off your asses and go see the world! Throw yourselves into different cultures! You will be always be wealthy if you count your riches, as I do, in adventures, full of life-changing experiences.

The day before we had to leave the Karajá, they painted Jarmusch with their traditional symbols of peace and friendship.

"One marks the sun," Jim explained, showing me proudly the two circles under his eyes. "The other, the moon."

Giggling little boys and girls surrounded us.

"Sam, I'm not going," he said. "Come back and pick me up in forty years."

"Okay," I said, only half joking. "For now, I have to go back to our uncivilized world."

To my dying day in this flawed world that I proudly call home, I'll cherish the gentle memory of the Karajá and their joy for living.

Kiss Me, Baby

Even with Marty Scorsese and Jonathan Demme behind *The Chair vs. Ruth Snyder,* Universal Studios wouldn't green-light the picture. Studio chief Tom Pollock said a period movie was just too expensive an enterprise at that time. Hell if I know what the real reason was. No doubt my age worked against me. Maybe it was my reputation as an "independent." I took the setback in stride. No one but my inscrutable third face would see the hurt of yet another unproduced movie.

To get over the disappointment, I revisited Rodin's great statue of a defiant Balzac in a bathrobe, now located in Montparnasse. I don't know why, but that imposing bronze statue always lifted my spirits with its indefatigable spirit, reminding me of my beloved British friend Alex Jacobs and the movie about Balzac we dreamed of doing together.[1] I'd wanted Alex not only to cowrite the screenplay but also to play the chubby, rosy-cheeked writer. Set in the 1830s, the picture would have our hero embroiled in daring episodes, pursuing the Polish countess Eveline Hanska, staying one step ahead of his many creditors, struggling with his arch rival, author Alexandre Dumas. That was going to be one helluva picture, too, if I ever got the chance to make it. Except I wouldn't. Time was running out.

Still, Tom Pollock at Universal came back to me with an offer to write and direct a remake of the 1948 noir *Night Has a Thousand Eyes,* with Marty and Jonathan executive producing. The original, starring Edward G. Robinson, had been directed by John Farrow, whom I'd known back in the fifties. Farrow was a helluva writer. He'd married actress Maureen O'Sullivan, Tarzan's Jane, and had seven children, including the actress Mia Farrow. Adapted from the novel by Cornell Woolrich, *Night Has a Thousand Eyes* was a tale about precognition. The book had all the elements for a good picture. There'd be a million ways to make a "Fuller" film out of it, first writing a "grab 'em by the balls" script, then getting a powerful cast, inventing exciting shots and setups. "Hell yes, let's do it!" I said to Pollock, and I got down to banging out yet another script.

See, I had to keep making movies. It was in my blood after all these years. Sure, I had serious misgivings about my physical condition, but I didn't tell anyone, not even Christa. I felt depleted, increasingly out of breath. My hands trembled without reason. And since our return from Brazil, nightmares made sleeping hellish. In my bad dreams, I became characters in my movies, sometimes the old Indian in *Run of the Arrow* who is scorned by the young braves, sometimes the commanding general in *Merrill's Marauders* trekking through the jungle with his soldiers, sometimes Johnny Barrett trapped in an asylum in *Shock Corridor*. I woke up before dawn, soaked from my own sweat, as if I'd been running from a vicious white dog.

Pushing aside doubts about my health, I decided to move forward as best I could on upcoming projects. Maybe it was pride or stubbornness, but even at eighty-two, I still wanted to think of myself as productive.

While working on a new adaptation for *Night Has a Thousand Eyes,* I also wrote an original script with Christa called *Girls in Prison* (1994) for director John McNaughton, whose *Mad Dog and Glory* (1993) had really impressed us. Made for TV and starring novice actress Anne Heche, *Girls in Prison* was a pastiche of prison movies, even poking fun at my nymphomaniac scene in *Shock Corridor.*

Inspired by our trip to Brazil, Christa and I also did a children's book together, *Sarikina and the Crocodiles.* She wrote the tale about a young Karajá Indian whose father is killed by crocodiles, and I did the drawings that illustrated the story.

In addition, two documentaries with me were going into production. I was too busy and too tired to participate, but I'd given my word to the filmmakers and I wouldn't let them down. First, there was *An American in Normandy,* produced for a French/German cable channel, Arte.[2] A crew under director Jean-Louis Comolli filmed me in Normandy reminiscing about the Big Red One's landing at Omaha and our battles through the hedgerows behind the coast. *An American in Normandy* followed the route of my division via all those little towns with unforgettable names that I'd jotted down hurriedly in my journal and engraved in my brain, names like Colleville-sur-Mer, Colombieres, Marigny, Cametours, Carantilly, Dangy, Gavray, and Mortain.

For a war veteran, revisiting the rolling fields of white crosses in Normandy is overwhelming. I made a point of stopping by a more recent grave, that of Monsieur Brobant, the first civilian we'd come across after the assault on Colleville. He was the only man who had seemed normal to

me in the frenzy of June 6, 1944. Now he was
gone. I laid a bouquet of flowers and a small bottle
of cognac on his gravestone.

Then came *The Typewriter, the Rifle & the
Movie Camera,* brainchild of actor Tim Robbins,
backed by the Independent Film Channel and British Film Institute. We'd
met Robbins at the Deauville Festival, where he was presenting *Bobby
Roberts* (1992), a smart political film. He'd always wanted to branch out
into directing. Like Cassavetes, Tim had the vision and tenacity to do it.
Along with director Adam Simon and a full crew, Tim arrived in Paris that
winter to shoot a series of interviews with me. Robbins was bright, respectful, and fun to be with. Besides, he asked smart questions. I loved his spirit
and tried to give him good stuff for his documentary without being
boring.

Tim came up with a word-association game we played on camera, the
lens right in my face. He'd throw out an idea and I'd respond, like mental
Ping-Pong.

"Hero," Robbins said.

"Don't believe in it," I said.

"Coward."

"Don't believe in it."

"Fascist."

"Enemy of mankind."

"Communist."

"Enemy of mankind."

"Democrat."

"Mankind."

We were in the middle of shooting *The Typewriter, the Rifle & the Movie Camera* when we heard that a big earthquake had hit California. With many telephone lines down, it was hard to place a call to our tenants to find out about damage to the Shack. We finally got through. Other than falling books and a broken globe, our home had survived unscathed. Leaving Paris for other commitments, Tim Robbins made a date with me to return to shoot the final interviews for his film.

I continued plugging away on the screenplay of *Night Has a Thousand Eyes*, working late into the night. To get me out of the house, Christa urged me to accept a few of the scores of invitations from festivals. A few of them brought a warm smile to my old face: Locarno, where Marco Mueller gave me a lifetime achievement award and screened *Forty Guns* on the gigantic screen in the town's central piazza to thunderous applause; Berlin, where Mika Kaurismäki presented *Tigrero: A Film That Was Never Made* to a packed house that came to their feet and clapped wildly at the end; Cattolica, where I met novelist James Ellroy, a tall, lean guy wearing a colorful shirt and spectacles.[3] A fan of my movies, Ellroy had an acerbic wit I enjoyed. He anointed me with the Rabelaisian moniker "crusty old cocksucker." I loved it and started referring to myself as "this crusty old cocksucker."

One night that remains vague to me, I fainted dead away in front of my Royal. Christa found me and called *les pompiers,* the great French firemen, who whisked me to the emergency room of the American Hospital, in Neuilly. I had an abscess on my lungs and an irregular heartbeat. The doctors inserted a pacemaker in my chest to keep my ticker beating on time. My lungs cleared up beautifully, but my cigar-smoking days were over.

I returned to rue de Reuilly in a horribly weakened state. The summer of 1994 came and went as I gradually recovered my mobility. Tim Robbins called, but Christa regretfully told him that I was too frail to work. She gave him our blessing to shoot footage in my office along with Quentin Tarantino back at the Shack. They were able to finish *The Typewriter, the Rifle & the Movie Camera* with that footage, clips from my films, and interviews with Marty Scorsese and Jim Jarmusch.

America had been calling me home for a long time. Plans for returning always seemed to be pushed back. My poor health put off the move yet again. The closest I could get to my beloved office in Laurel Canyon was to

Playing the sick, old papa of Gabriel Byrne in Wim Wenders's End of Violence, 1997

shut my eyes tight and picture the crammed bookshelves, the stacks of newspaper clippings, the film cans, the World War II artifacts, the humidors, and the framed posters from all my movies. How I yearned to go home once and for all!

Then I fell into the black hole of my stroke. That fall, it clobbered me in the courtyard of our apartment. How I survived is still bewildering to me. I wondrously pulled through, thanks to my fabulous French doctors and the loving care of my wife and my daughter. For the last couple months of my convalescence, I was moved to St. Maurice Hospital, built inside a Napoleonic château outside of Paris. I gradually regained my strength and capacities, but my speech was blurred. I'd launch into a story, then find myself in a verbal dead end, saying unintelligible words, or calling things by new names. "Telephone" became "blue bell blue," which made my girls laugh hilariously. Laughing turned out to be one of the only things I could still do effortlessly. Good friends like Peter Bogdanovich, Curtis Hanson, and Jerry Rudes came to visit. Jonathan Demme sent his producing partner, Ed Saxon, to see me. Saxon, a lovely man, made me feel great by wishing me a speedy recovery so I could get back to work on *Night Has a Thousand Eyes*. I appreciated

With their love and support, Christa and Samantha kept me going through thick and thin.

the gesture. But we all knew that it was a thousand-to-one long shot that I'd ever be vigorous enough to direct a motion picture again. It was sweet to dream about it, though.

By the fall of 1995, my doctors gave me their blessing for the trip back to California. We were finally going home. Samantha postponed her studies at the Sorbonne to come with us. My poor health had been very stressful for my daughter. Through it all, she was a real trooper, making me feel like the luckiest father in the world. She's going to be a helluva lady.

It felt so damn good to get back to the Shack. The place needed some repair, but nothing too serious. Christa and Samantha took charge. I've been the best-cared-for outpatient in the world. It was no piece of cake, believe me, because I was as cantankerous as ever, and hated like hell not being independent. No matter, their affection and good spirits always brought a smile to the wrinkled face on this crusty old cocksucker. Like in the old days, good friends dropped in, and once again, the Shack was host to long lunches out by the pool and boisterous dinners around our "Mark Twain" dining-room table.

I was in no shape to go out. When I did, it was for special occasions.

One was to shoot a scene for Wim Wenders in his film *The End of Violence* (1997), playing Gabriel Byrne's father, who—what else?—is a recovering stroke victim. It was hardly acting, but it was good to smell the lights and cameras on a movie set again. Another memorable outing was to a big Hollywood shindig to receive something called the "Independent Spirit Award," presented by my old pal Peter Bogdanovich. Peter brought the prize over to where I was sitting because there was no way in hell I could walk up to the podium to accept it. I stood up and put my arms around him. The audience applauded.

"Kiss me!" I said. An actor by training, Bogdanovich took direction perfectly. He kissed me.

Since the stroke, all my attention has been focused on these memoirs. Progress was slow indeed. Remembering is hard work, even when your brain is in perfect shape. Christa has helped me through the tough task of getting it all down on paper, her love and care allowing me to survive. As surely as this book must end, my life must soon come to a close.

So here's my last word, dear reader.

Love.

That's right. Love.

I don't give a damn if it sounds like some corny ending to a B movie. Everybody's got troubles, setbacks, frustrations, tragedies. Love gets us through them. Love inspires generosity, patience, and compassion. Love keeps us healthy and whole. If I've learned anything at all from writing all those stories, from fighting a world war, from making all those films, from being way up and being way down, I've learned that everything—*everything!*—can be expressed in just four god-blessed words: *Love is the answer.*

Okay, now all you new voices, let yourselves be heard!

Thirty.

Notes

CHAPTER 2: PLUNGING IN HEAD FIRST

1. Sarah Margaret Fuller (1810–50), an American social reformer and author who espoused transcendentalism and fought for equal rights for women and, with the aid of Ralph Waldo Emerson, founded *The Dial,* a periodical dedicated to publishing verse and philosophical writings; Melville Weston Fuller (1833–1910), the American politician and jurist, and eighth chief justice of the United States; and Loie Fuller (1862–1928), the American dancer, actor, producer, and playwright who achieved sensational fame for her improvisatory dances and was the subject of portraits by Henri de Toulouse-Lautrec and Auguste Rodin.

CHAPTER 3: MAMA'S BOY

1. The exact line was, "Get out o' Mr. Fletcher's road, ye idle lounging little vagabond."

CHAPTER 4: MANHATTAN EXPLORER

1. Hoppy was no relation to another mentor, Gene Fowler. To honor him and that era, I had a character named Hoppy in one of my early novels, *The Dark Page.*

CHAPTER 5: RUN SAMMY RUN

1. Carl Chapman was a well-known convicted killer, waiting to be executed on death row.

2. The Fabian Society was a British socialist educational organization affiliated with the Labour Party. The Fabian Society was founded in London in 1884 by a group of middle-class intellectuals who rejected the Marxist theory of class struggle but wished to promote equality for all through collective ownership and democratic control of the nation's resources. Believers in peaceful and gradual change, they named their group for the ancient Roman general Fabius Cunctator, who wore down a powerful enemy by using delaying tactics and avoiding decisive battles. In time, local Fabian societies affiliated with the parent body were founded all over Britain.

3. Fourier's *Theory of the Four Movements and of General Destinies* (1808) expounded his social system and his plans for the cooperative organization of society. The system, known as Fourierism, is based on his belief in a universal principle of harmony, displayed in four departments: the material universe, organic life, animal life, and human society. This harmony can flourish only when the restraints that conventional social behavior places upon the full gratification of desire have been abolished, allowing people to live free and complete lives.

   Brook Farm was a cooperative community established in 1841 in West Roxbury (now part of Boston) by leaders of the philosophical movement known as transcendentalism. Among the American literary and religious leaders associated with Brook

Farm were Amos Bronson Alcott, William Ellery Channing, Charles Anderson Dana, Ralph Waldo Emerson, Margaret Fuller, Nathaniel Hawthorne, Theodore Parker, and Orestes Augustus Brownson. In 1843 the community came under the influence of Albert Brisbane (1809–90), father of Arthur. For two years the community was known as the Brook Farm Phalanx and was one of the headquarters of the Fourierist movement in the United States. From 1845 to 1849 the Brook Farm community published a weekly newspaper, *The Harbinger.* In 1846 the central building, or phalanstery, burned, and the community was subsequently abandoned in 1847. Brook Farm was the setting of a novel by Hawthorne, *The Blithedale Romance* (1852).

4. George Stoneman (1822–94) was a brigadier general under General McClellan (1861); served in Peninsular campaign (1861–62); major general of volunteers (1862); engaged at Fredericksburg; under orders from General Hooker, led raid (April 13–May 2, 1863) toward Richmond; chief of cavalry bureau, Washington, D.C. (1863); engaged in Atlanta campaign under Sherman (1864); led raids in southwestern Virginia, eastern Tennessee, and the Carolinas (1864–65); retired (1871); and was governor of California (1883–87).

5. Villa was a cattle rustler, but turned revolutionary when President Díaz put a price on his head. Francisco Madero was the leader of the revolt against Díaz, though he was quickly overthrown by General Victoriano Huerta.

CHAPTER 6: FLASH LIKE A NEW COMET

1. *The Four Horsemen of the Apocalypse* (1921), *The Sheik* (1921), *Blood and Sand* (1922), *Monsieur Beaucaire* (1923), *The Eagle* (1925), and *The Son of the Sheik* (1926).

CHAPTER 7: WORLD OF NEVERTHELESS

1. He began an article about a Colorado gal of ill repute who had murdered her boyfriend: "She laid her wanton red head on her lover's breast, then plugged him through the heart."

2. Son of Whitelaw Reid, the one-time Civil War correspondent and late ambassador to the Court of St. James.

3. From Gene Fowler's *Skyline,* his great reminiscence of being a journalist in the twenties.

CHAPTER 13: HUSKY

1. Before the producers released the movie, they chopped more than two hours, including some of my best scenes.

CHAPTER 15: IMPOSSIBLE TO FEEL BLESSED

1. Terry Allen was reassigned after Sicily to the 104th "Timberwolf" Division. We wouldn't see Terry again until his troops and ours teamed up fighting side by side in the final assault on Germany, first in Aachen, then during the breakthrough at the Remagen bridgehead.

CHAPTER 26: PURSUIT OF HAPPINESS

1. Paul Jarrico wrote this 1948 picture about a silent nine-year-old Czech boy, a survivor of Auschwitz, who flees a refugee center in postwar Germany and is found by an American GI.

CHAPTER 27: A LITTLE BLACK-AND-WHITE PICTURE

1. Among his many credits, Russell shot Hitchcock's *Psycho* (1960).
2. The date of Gutenberg's first bible is generally recognized to be 1456.

3. Used by reporters since the time of Bennett and Greeley, this was the traditional closure for a reporter's copy, i.e., "The End."

CHAPTER 28: DON'T WAVE THE FLAG AT ME

1. This line, already absurd when I wrote it in the fifties, makes audiences nowadays roar with laughter at the paranoid patriotism of those times.

CHAPTER 30: CHERRY BLOSSOMS AND WHIRLIGIGS

1. Born to Japanese parents in Manchuria in 1920, Shirley used the Chinese name Li Xianglan (Ri Koran, in Japanese) and made pro-Japanese films in Japanese-occupied areas in China. Shirley was nicknamed "the Judy Garland of Japan," with many hit recordings. She married sculptor Isamu Noguchi and became a political personality in Japan, elected to several terms in the House of Councillors, the upper body of Japan's parliament. Her life story was made into a musical that appeared on Tokyo stages.

CHAPTER 32: WHERE'S YOUR PRIDE, MA?

1. O'Meara's mother is played by Olive Carey, who appeared in a lot of John Ford pictures.
2. Cooper (1789–1851) was the author of, among many popular classics, *The Spy* (1821), *The Pioneers* (1823), *The Last of the Mohicans* (1826), *The Pathfinder* (1840), and *The Deerslayer* (1841).
3. This song was part of Young's score for *Around the World in 80 Days* (1956).

CHAPTER 37: BREATHING REVENGE

1. Anslinger was head of a federal crime commission at that time in Washington, in charge of a number of criminal investigations across the country.
2. *Paradise Lost,* Book I, by John Milton (1608–74).

CHAPTER 40: LOVE YOUR COUNTRY DESPITE THE ULCERS

1. Born in Russia, Lourie had a big career in France before the war designing sets and costumes for ballet companies. He had worked on Renoir's *La Grande Illusion* (1937) as well as Max Ophüls's *Sans Lendemain* (1939). Eugene came to America in 1941 and was art director on scores of pictures, among them Charlie Chaplin's *Limelight* (1952).

CHAPTER 41: WANT TO BE A LINDY?

1. I shot those home movies myself with my 16-mm Bell & Howell.

CHAPTER 42: TWO TO TANGO

1. Darryl had produced his final picture, *The Longest Day,* in 1962.
2. Written in 411 B.C., the play is a satire on war, in which women strike for peace by practicing celibacy. Aristophanes (448–385 B.C.), an Athenian playwright, is considered one of the greatest writers of comedy in literary history.

CHAPTER 46: TURMOIL AND WASTE

1. *Riata* means "lariat" in Spanish.
2. *Fearless Vampire Killers* was released in the States with the subtitle *Pardon Me, But Your Teeth Are in My Neck.*

CHAPTER 47: MAKING IT ALL WORTHWHILE

1. Pirandello wrote, "Life is full of infinite absurdities, which, strangely enough, do not even need to appear plausible, since they are true."

2. *Der Amerikanische Freund* is a thriller about a picture framer in Hamburg, Zimmermann, played by Bruno Ganz, who is diagnosed as having leukemia. Ripley, an American art dealer dealing in forgeries, played by Dennis Hopper, uses this fact to recruit Zimmermann as a hit man.

3. *Our American Cousin*, at Ford's Theatre in Washington, D.C., on April 14, 1865, ended with President Abraham Lincoln's assassination.

CHAPTER 48: THE UNMAKING OF A KLANSMAN

1. Terence had made his reputation with the early James Bond films *Dr. No* (1962), *From Russia with Love* (1963), and *Thunderball* (1965).

CHAPTER 49: LET THEM JUDGE FOR THEMSELVES

1. Jack was Francis Ford Coppola's brother-in-law by way of his marriage to Francis's sister, Talia Shire.

2. From a quote in *U.S. News & World Report*.

CHAPTER 50: FOUR-LEGGED TIME BOMB

1. A few of the titles registered with the Writer's Guild were: Powderkeg (love story); Charge at San Juan Hill (script, war melodrama); Yank in West Berlin (three love stories, today); Hold for Release (newspaper comedy); The Blue Pagoda of Fuji (ex-GI returns to Japan); Corporal Tex (fantasy of GI in old days of the West); The Lady Who Raised Cain (comedy); The Bell (Sicilian family story); Wise Is the Child (father's search for POW son); Island of the True Cross (Mato Grosso suspense adventure); The Jumping River (Young Lee licks Mississippi River as engineer); War Is Hell (story of General Sherman); Pickup in Paris (U.S. students in Paris); Once Upon a Prayer (fantasy, child picks parents in heaven); Sarung Banggi (love story, one night in Philippines); Quake at Noon (love, suspense story in Utah); Old Glory (three stories about the same flag); Ben Franklin, the Tex Rickard Story (sports in the twenties); The Lusty Years (script, romantic melodrama); High and Dry (chase romance in Venice); Dutch Treat (foreign correspondent yarn); and Quincannon (Confederate raiders in Mexican border town).

2. Patricio Lafcadio Tessima Carlos Hearn (1850–1904) was from an Irish-Greek family, raised in Ireland, England, and France. He immigrated to the United States at the age of nineteen, working as a journalist. To supplement his income, Hearn translated exotic, unusual stories.

3. The stained-glass window we created for that set had St. Francis surrounded by loving animals. I liked the prop so much that I saved it and had it installed permanently in the Shack.

CHAPTER 51: A THIRD FACE

1. *The Song of Dead Children*, based on the Gustav Mahler composition.

CHAPTER 53: HALF FULL, NOT HALF EMPTY

1. This nonprofit, nonpolitical group, based in Paris, is called Médicins du Monde, Doctors of the World, helping out from war-torn Afghanistan to drought-stricken Africa.

2. Chaim Soutine was a Russian-born French expressionist painter (1894–1943), born near Minsk, Belarus. He immigrated to Paris in 1913 and soon developed his highly personal vision and technique. Soutine sacrificed careful composition and good drawing to feverish intensity, employing thick pigment in vivid, often deliberately ugly, colors. His works include pitiless psychological portraits of bakers, valets, and choirboys,

still lifes of sides of meat in various stages of putrefaction, and anguished landscapes with scudding clouds and bending trees. He often reworked or destroyed his earlier paintings, and produced little new work after 1930.

CHAPTER 54: SONS AND SONSOFBITCHES

1. Smirnov confessed his family had nothing to do with the vodka we were drinking.

CHAPTER 55: BEING SERIOUS WITHOUT TAKING IT SERIOUSLY

1. The first measure enacted by Congress restricting immigration was a law in 1862 forbidding American vessels to transport Chinese immigrants to the United States; twenty years later, Congress passed the Chinese Exclusion Act, which excluded Chinese immigrants.

2. Inside the jacket cover, there are some little drawings he doodled for me, along with the following inscription: "December 1946. To Sammy, I agree that the outlook is emphatically DARK, so why not put our heads together and try this gimmick: the lighted cellar, the white nose, the blazing sound stage, the glaring exit, the beige dawn, the bright future, the illuminating truss . . . David."

3. Other French films from Goodis novels include Francis Girod's *Descente aux Enfers* (1986), from *Descent into Hell;* Gilles Béhat's *Rue Barbare* (1984), from *Epaves;* Jean-Jacques Beineix's *La Lune Dans le Caniveau* (1983), from *The Moon in the Gutter;* René Clément's *La Course du Lièvre à Travers les Champs* (1972), from *Black Friday;* and Henri Verneuil's *Le Casse* (1972), from *The Burglar.*

CHAPTER 57: METAMORPHOSIS OF A MELODY

1. Denis Diderot (1713–84) was a French encyclopedist and philosopher; he also wrote novels, essays, plays, and art and literary criticism.

2. From Jean Cocteau's *La Belle et la Bête* (1946) through Wim Wenders's *Wings of Desire* (1987), Alekan had shot over sixty features for some of the world's top directors.

3. His birth name was Joseph Ben Matthias, born in Jerusalem in A.D. 37 of both royal and priestly lineage. Learned and worldly, he was a member of the Pharisees, and also a public figure who, before the Jewish revolt against Rome, had made friends at the court of Emperor Nero. He enjoyed the imperial patronage of Vespasian, adopting the family name of Flavius. He accompanied Vespasian's son, Titus, on the Roman siege of Jerusalem in A.D. 70. He devoted himself to writing until his death in 100. Besides *History of the Jewish War,* his books include a twenty-volume history of the Jews (*The Antiquities of the Jews*), an autobiography (*Life*), and a refutation of anti-Semitism (*Against Apion*).

CHAPTER 60: KISS ME, BABY

1. Alex was a witty, talented screenwriter with one of the best noir films of the sixties to his credit, *Point Blank,* directed by John Boorman and starring Lee Marvin. Jacobs died at the all-too-early age of fifty-one.

2. This project had been a labor of love of French journalist Jean-Pierre Catherine and American producer Michael Seiler.

3. Author of *Blue Dahlia,* Ellroy also wrote *L.A. Confidential,* which Curtis Hanson adapted for his 1997 movie.

The Works of Samuel Fuller

SAMUEL FULLER: THE DIRECTOR

I Shot Jesse James (1949)
The Baron of Arizona (1950)
The Steel Helmet (1951)
Fixed Bayonets (1951)
Park Row (1952)
Pickup on South Street (1953)
Hell and High Water (1954)
House of Bamboo (1955)
Run of the Arrow (1957)
Forty Guns (1957)
China Gate (1957)
Verboten! (1958)
The Crimson Kimono (1959)
Underworld, U.S.A. (1961)
Merrill's Marauders (1962)
The Dick Powell Show,
    "330 Independence S.W." (1962) (TV)
Shock Corridor (1963)
The Naked Kiss (1964)
Shark! (1970)
Dead Pigeon on Beethoven Street (1972)
The Big Red One (1980)
White Dog (1982)
Thieves After Dark (1983)
Street of No Return (1989)

SAMUEL FULLER: THE ACTOR

Pierrot le Fou (1965), as Himself
    Directed by Jean-Luc Godard

Brigitte et Brigitte (1966), as Himself
    Directed by Luc Moullet
The Last Movie (1971), as Director
    Directed by Dennis Hopper
The Young Nurses (1973), as Doc Haskell
    Directed by Clinton Kimbrough
The American Friend (1977), as Mobster
    Directed by Wim Wenders
1941 (1979), as Interceptor Commander
    Directed by Steven Spielberg
White Dog (1982), as Charlie Felton
    Directed by Samuel Fuller
The State of Things (1982), as Joe
    Directed by Wim Wenders
Thieves After Dark (1983), as Zoltan
    Directed by Samuel Fuller
Hammett (1983), as Old Man
    Directed by Wim Wenders
Slapstick (1984), as Colonel Sharp
    Directed by Steven Paul
A Return to Salem's Lot (1987), as Van Meer
    Directed by Larry Cohen
Helsinki Napoli All Night Long (1987), as Boss
    Directed by Mika Kaurismäki
Falkenau, Vision of the Impossible (1988), as Himself
    Directed by Emil Weiss
Sons (1989), as Father
    Directed by Alexandre Rockwell
David Lansky (L'Enfant Américain) (1990), as Capodagli
    Directed by Hervé Palud (TV)
Golem, l'esprit de l'exil (1992), as Elimelech
    Directed by Amos Gitai
La Vie de Bohème (1992), as Gassot
    Directed by Aki Kaurismäki
Tigrero: A Film That Was Never Made (1994), as Himself
    Directed by Mika Kaurismäki
An American in Normandy (1994), as Himself
    Directed by Jean-Louis Comolli
The Typewriter, the Rifle & the Movie Camera (1996), as Himself
    Directed by Adam Simon
Somebody to Love (1996), as Sam Silverman
    Directed by Alexandre Rockwell
The End of Violence (1997), as Louis Bering
    Directed by Wim Wenders

SAMUEL FULLER: THE WRITER

Produced Screenplays
(written & directed by Mr. Fuller, unless otherwise credited)

Hats Off (1936)
  Directed by Boris Petroff
It Happened in Hollywood (1937)
  Directed by Harry Lachman
The Gangs of New York (1938)
  Directed by James Cruze
Adventure in Sahara (1938)
  Directed by D. Ross Lederman
Confirm or Deny (1941)
  Directed by Archie Mayo
Bowery Boy (1941)
  Directed by William Morgan
Power of the Press (1943)
  Directed by Lew Landers
Gangs of the Waterfront (1945)
  Directed by George Blair
Shockproof (1949)
  Directed by Douglas Sirk
I Shot Jesse James (1949)
The Baron of Arizona (1950)
The Tanks Are Coming (1951)
  Directed by D. Ross Lederman & Lewis Seiler, from original Fuller
  story
The Steel Helmet (1951)
Fixed Bayonets (1951)
Scandal Sheet (1952)
  From the Fuller novel *The Dark Page,* directed by Phil Karlson
The Command (1954)
  With Russell Hughes, from the James Warner Bellah novel *Rear
  Guard,* directed by David Butler
Park Row (1952)
Pickup on South Street (1953)
Hell and High Water (1954)
House of Bamboo (1955)
Run of the Arrow (1957)
Forty Guns (1957)
China Gate (1957)
Verboten! (1958)
The Crimson Kimono (1959)
Underworld, U.S.A. (1961)

Merrill's Marauders (1962)

The Virginian (1962) (TV)
   TV series, one episode written and directed by Fuller, "It Tolls for Thee"

Shock Corridor (1963)

The Naked Kiss (1964)

The Iron Horse (1966) (TV)
   TV series, five episodes written and directed by Fuller, "Banner with a Strange Device," "Hellcat," "High Devil," "The Man from New Chicago," and "Volcano Wagon"

The Meanest Men in the West (1967) (TV)
   With Ed Waters

Shark! (1970)
   Based on the Victor Canning novel *His Bones Are Coral*

Dead Pigeon on Beethoven Street (1972)

The Deadly Trackers (1973)
   By Luka Heller, from original Fuller script, *Riata,* directed by Barry Shear

The Klansman (1974)
   By Millard Kaufman, from original Fuller script, book by William Bradford Huie, directed by Terence Young

The Big Red One (1980)

Thieves After Dark (1983)

Let's Get Harry (1986)
   By Charles Robert Carner, from original Fuller script, directed by Alan Smithee

Street of No Return (1989)

The Day of Reckoning (1990) (TV)
   With Christa Lang, from a Patricia Highsmith novel

Girls in Prison (1994) (TV)
   With Christa Lang, directed by John McNaughton

Published Books

Burn, Baby, Burn (1935)
   Published by Phoenix Press, New York

Test Tube Baby (1936)
   Published by William Godwin, New York

Make Up and Kiss (1938)
   Published by William Godwin, New York

The Dark Page (1944)
   Published by Duell, Sloan & Pearce, New York

Crown of India (1966)
   Published by Award, New York

144 Piccadilly (1971)
  Published by Baron, New York, and New English Library, London
Dead Pigeon on Beethoven Street (1974)
  Published by Pyramid, New York
The Big Red One (1980)
  Published by Bantam, New York
Quint's World (1984)
  Published by Don Mills, Ontario, and as *La Grande Mêlée* in French
  by Christian Bourgois, Paris
Pecos Bill and the Soho Kid (1986)
  Published as *Pecos Bill et le Kid Cavale* in French by Les Editions
  Bayard, Paris
Brainquake (1993)
  Published as *Cérébro-Choc* in French by Les Belles Lettres, Paris

Unproduced Screenplays, Plays, Stories, and Treatments

Angelo
  Story, Italian boy who is son of black GI left behind in Sicily, is
  reunited with father.
Au Revoir Madeleine
  Story, French girl in Normandy during the occupation, falls in love
  with Nazi, invaders kill her boyfriend, and she is obsessed with
  finding the GI "murderer."
Balzac
  Original screenplay based on the great writer's life.
Cain and Abel
  Original screenplay, the birth of emotions, the first murder,
  volcanoes erupt, civilization is born.
Charge of San Juan Hill
  Original screenplay, Teddy Roosevelt's public relations campaign to
  get elected president by capitalizing on his military exploits.
Custer
  Story, famous "last stand" from four viewpoints of participating
  Indians.
The Eye of Paris
  Treatment, detective tale set in City of Light.
Flowers of Evil
  Original screenplay, modern version of the Greek tragedy *Lysistrata*,
  by Aristophanes, set in Paris.
Generalissimo
  Story, the long march for the liberation of China, two men, Chiang
  Kai-Shek and Mao Zedong, together but going different directions.

The Lusty Days
> Original screenplay, a mercenary in the Civil War who goes out on battlefield to collect the soldier's absentee ballots to get Lincoln elected.

Mazeppa
> Story, based on life of Adah Menken, beautiful actress who was Confederate spy during Civil War.

Pearl Harbor
> Treatment, life of kamikaze as he prepares for suicide run on U.S. Navy.

Pecos Bill and the Soho Kid
> Original screenplay, the Kid from Soho, a tough fourteen-year-old Cockney, finds himself riding with a legend, Pecos Bill.

Pigalle
> Story, a bunch of GIs return to "Pig Alley" after the war.

Riata
> An implacable lawman tracks a killer from Texas halfway across Mexico to avenge his son's death.

The Rifle
> Novel and original screenplay, drama during Vietnamese War about an M1 rifle and the people who fire it.

Ring Around the Roses
> Original two-act, fourteen-scene play, with music, depicts events at Château Coburg in Belgium during the winter German counteroffensive, the "Battle of the Bulge."

Ruth Snyder vs. the Chair
> Treatment for drama about the first woman executed in the electric chair.

Tigrero
> Original screenplay, ex-con has life-changing adventures in the jungles of Brazil.

Bibliography

Ambrose, Stephen E. 1997. *New History of World War II*. New York: Viking.

Baumgartner, Lt. John W. 1946. *The 16th Infantry*. By Al de Poto, Sgt. William Fraccio, and Cpl. Samuel Fuller, private edition.

Duranty, Walter. 1937. *One Life, One Kopeck*. New York: Literary Guild of America.

Fowler, Gene. 1961. *Skyline*. New York: Viking Press.

Fuller, Samuel. 1980. *The Big Red One*. New York: Bantam.

1910. *Life and Adventures of A-No. 1*. Erie, Pa.

Mallen, Frank. 1954. *Sauce for the Gander*. New York: Baldwin Publishing.

1996. *Marseille et les Américains, 1940–1946*. Marseille: Museum of Marseille History.

Naboni, Jean, and Noël Simsolo. 1986. *Il Était une Fois . . . Samuel Fuller*. Paris: Cahiers du Cinéma.

Rothberg, Abraham. 1962. *Eyewitness History of World War II*. New York: Bantam Books.

Server, Lee. 1994. *Sam Fuller: Film Is a Battleground*. New York: McFarland & Company.

Whiting, Charles. 1982. *The Home Front: Germany*. New York: Time-Life Books.

Acknowledgments

We would like to extend the warmest thanks to the following individuals for their help, support, and inspiration on this book:

Adam Olech
Alex Rockwell
Anna Lee Nathan
Anne Douglas
Angie Dickinson
Anjelica Huston
Annie Nocenti
Claudine Pacquot
Constance Towers
Curtis Hanson
Cynthia Cohen
David Brown
Dominique Villain
Donata Wenders
Ed Saxon
Fraucke Hanke
Gena Rowlands

Howard Rodman
Jean Narboni
Jennifer Beals
Larry Cohen
Lloyd Kaufman
Marjorie Johnson-Fowler
Martin Scorsese
Michael Schlesinger
Noel Simsolo
Peter Bogdanovich
Phil Parmet
Polly Platt
Robert Stack
Thys Ockerson
Terri R. Davis
Wim Wenders

And finally, to two good ladies without whom this book could not have happened: our agent, Fifi Oscard, and our editor, Victoria Wilson.

Index

Note: Page numbers in *italics* refer to illustrative material.

PERMISSIONS ACKNOWLEDGMENTS

Grateful acknowledgment is made to the following:

Ben Barry Associates: Exerpts from the motion pictures *Shock Corridor* and *Naked Kiss.* Reprinted by permission of Ben Barry Associates.

Columbia Pictures: Excerpt from the screenplay *Crimson Kimono* and an excerpt from the screenplay *Underworld U.S.A.* Reprinted by permission of Columbia Pictures.

MGM: Excerpts from the screenplay *Park Row.*

Paramount: Excerpts from the screenplay *White Dog.*

Twentieth Century Fox: Excerpts from the screenplays *Pickup on South Street, China Gate* and *House of Bamboo.*

Warner Bros.: Excerpts from the screenplays *Merrill's Marauders* and *Verboten!*

Warner Bros. Publications U.S. Inc.: Excerpt from the song lyric "China Gate" by Harold Adamson and Victor Young. Copyright © 1956, 1957 (Copyrights Renewed) Chappell & Co. All rights reserved. Reprinted by permission of Warner Bros. Publications U.S. Inc., Miami, FL 33014.

Weiss Global Enterprises: Excerpts from the motion pictures *Steel Helmet, I Shot Jesse James,* and *Baron of Arizona.* Reprinted by permission of Weiss Global Enterprises.

A NOTE ON THE TYPE

This book was set in Adobe Garamond. Designed for the
Adobe Corporation by Robert Slimbach, the fonts are based on
types first cut by Claude Garamond (c. 1480–1561). Garamond
was a pupil of Geoffroy Tory and is believed to have followed
the Venetian models, although he introduced a number of
important differences, and it is to him that we owe the letter we
now know as "old style." He gave to his letters a certain ele-
gance and feeling of movement that won their creator an
immediate reputation and the patronage of Francis I of France.

Composed by North Market Street Graphics,
Lancaster, Pennsylvania
Printed and bound by Sheridan Books,
Ann Arbor, Michigan
Designed by Anthea Lingeman